Microeconomics
fifth edition

David C. COLANDER
Middlebury College

Customized for

 Custom Publishing

Boston Burr Ridge, IL Dubuque, IA Madison, WI New York San Francisco St. Louis
Bangkok Bogotá Caracas Lisbon London Madrid
Mexico City Milan New Delhi Seoul Singapore Sydney Taipei Toronto

Microeconomics, Fifth Edition
Customized for National American University

1 2 3 4 5 6 7 8 9 0 QSR QSR 0 9 8 7 6 5

ISBN 0-07-320863-9

Editor: Shawn Allen
Production Editor: Nicole Baumgartner
Printer/Binder: Quebecor World

BRIEF CONTENTS

TRADE, TRADE-OFFS, AND GOVERNMENT POLICY

Economics is a science of thinking in terms of models, joined
to the art of choosing models which are relevant to
the contemporary world.

—*J. M. Keynes*

E very economy must solve three main coordination problems:

1. What, and how much, to produce.
2. How to produce it.
3. For whom to produce it.

In Chapter 1, I suggested that you can boil down all economic knowledge into the single phrase "There ain't no such thing as a free lunch." There's obviously more to economics than that, but it's not a bad summary of the core of economic reasoning—it's relevant for an individual, for nonprofit organizations, for governments, and for nations. Oh, it's true that once in a while you can snitch a sandwich, but what economics tells you is that if you're offered something that approaches free-lunch status, you should also be on the lookout for some hidden cost.

A key element in getting people to recognize that lunches aren't free is the concept of opportunity cost—every decision has a cost in forgone opportunities—which I introduced you to in Chapter 1. Economists have a model, the production possibility model, that conveys the concept of opportunity costs both numerically and graphically. This model is important for understanding not only opportunity cost but also why people specialize in what they do and trade for the goods they need. Through specialization and trade, individuals, firms, and countries can achieve greater levels of production than they could otherwise achieve.

THE PRODUCTION POSSIBILITIES MODEL

The production possibilities model shows trade-offs and can be presented both in a table and in a graph. I'll start with the table and then move from that to the graph. Opportunity cost can be seen numerically with a **production possibility table**—*a table that lists a choice's opportunity costs by summarizing what alternative outputs you can achieve with your inputs.* An **output** is simply *a result of an activity,*

After reading this chapter, you should be able to:

- Demonstrate opportunity cost with a production possibility curve.

- Relate the concept of comparative advantage to the production possibility curve.

- State the principle of increasing marginal opportunity cost.

- State how through comparative advantage and trade, production possibilities increase.

- State six roles of government.

- Compare the regulation of international markets to the regulation of domestic markets.

Figure 2-1 (a and b)   A Production Possibility Table and Curve for Grades in Economics and History
The production possibility table (a) shows the highest combination of grades you can get with only 20 hours available for studying economics and history. The information in the production possibility table in (a) can be plotted on a graph, as is done in (b). The grade received in economics is on the vertical axis, and the grade received in history is on the horizontal axis.

Hours of Study in History	Grade in History	Hours of Study in Economics	Grade in Economics
20	98	0	40
19	96	1	43
18	94	2	46
17	92	3	49
16	90	4	52
15	88	5	55
14	86	6	58
13	84	7	61
12	82	8	64
11	80	9	67
10	78	10	70
9	76	11	73
8	74	12	76
7	72	13	79
6	70	14	82
5	68	15	85
4	66	16	88
3	64	17	91
2	62	18	94
1	60	19	97
0	58	20	100

(a) Production possibility table

(b) Production possibility curve

and an **input** is *what you put into a production process to achieve an output.* For example, your grade in a course is an output and your study time is an input.

A PRODUCTION POSSIBILITY CURVE FOR AN INDIVIDUAL

Q-1 What is the opportunity cost of producing an extra unit of good X in terms of good Y?

Let's consider the study-time/grades example. Say you have exactly 20 hours a week to devote to two courses: economics and history. (So maybe I'm a bit optimistic.) Grades are given numerically and you know that the following relationships exist: If you study 20 hours in economics, you'll get a grade of 100; 18 hours, 94; and so forth.[1]

Let's say that the best you can do in history is a 98 with 20 hours of study a week; 19 hours of study guarantees a 96, and so on. The production possibility table in Figure 2-1(a) shows the highest combination of grades you can get with various allocations of the 20 hours available for studying the two subjects. One possibility is getting 70 in economics and 78 in history.

Notice that the opportunity cost of studying one subject rather than the other is embodied in the production possibility table. The information in the table comes from

[1]Throughout the book I'll be presenting numerical examples to help you understand the concepts. The numbers I choose are often arbitrary. After all, you have to choose something. As an exercise, you might choose different numbers than I did, numbers that apply to your own life, and work out the argument using those numbers.

Knowing my own students, I can see the red flags rising, the legs tensing up, the fear flooding over many of you. Here it comes—the math and the graphs.

I wish I could change things by saying to you, "Don't worry—the mathematics and graphical analysis are easy." But I can't. That doesn't mean math and graphical analysis aren't wonderful tools that convey ideas neatly and efficiently. They are. But I've had enough teaching experience to know that somewhere back in elementary school some teacher blew it and put about 40 percent of you off mathematics for life. A tool that scares you to death is not useful; it can be a hindrance, not a help, to learning. Nothing your current teacher or I now can say, write, or do is going to completely reassure you, but I'll do my best to relieve your anxiety.

Try to follow the numerical and graphical examples carefully, because they not only cement the knowledge into your minds; they also present in a rigorous manner the ideas I'm discussing. The ideas conveyed in the numerical and graphical examples will be explained in words—and the graphical analysis (the type of mathematical explanation most used in introductory economics) generally will simply be a more precise presentation of the accompanying discussion in words. In most economics courses the exams pose the questions in graphical terms, so there's no getting around the need to understand the ideas graphically. And it is easier than you think. (Appendix A at the end of this chapter discusses the basics of graphical analysis.)

---

experience: We are assuming that you've discovered that if you transfer an hour of study from economics to history, you'll lose 3 points on your grade in economics and gain 2 points in history. Thus, the opportunity cost of a 2-point rise in your history grade is a 3-point decrease in your economics grade.

The information in the production possibility table can also be presented graphically in a diagram called a production possibility curve. A **production possibility curve** is *a curve measuring the maximum combination of outputs that can be obtained from a given number of inputs.* It is a graphical presentation of the opportunity cost concept.

A production possibility curve is created from a production possibility table by mapping the table in a two-dimensional graph. I've taken the information from the table in Figure 2-1(a) and mapped it into Figure 2-1(b). The history grade is mapped, or plotted, on the horizontal axis; the economics grade is on the vertical axis.

As you can see from the bottom row of Figure 2-1(a), if you study economics for all 20 hours and study history for 0 hours, you'll get grades of 100 in economics and 58 in history. Point A in Figure 2-1(b) represents that choice. If you study history for all 20 hours and study economics for 0 hours, you'll get a 98 in history and a 40 in economics. Point *E* represents that choice. Points *B*, *C*, and *D* represent three possible choices between these two extremes.

Notice that the production possibility curve slopes downward from left to right. That means that there is an inverse relationship (a trade-off) between grades in economics and grades in history. The better the grade in economics, the worse the grade in history, and vice versa. That downward slope represents the opportunity cost concept—you get more of one benefit only if you get less of another benefit.

The production possibility curve not only represents the opportunity cost concept but also measures the opportunity cost. For example, in Figure 2-1(b), say you want to raise your grade in history from a 94 to a 98 (move from point *D* to point *E*). The opportunity cost of that 4-point increase would be a 6-point decrease in your economics grade, from 46 to 40.

To summarize, the production possibility curve demonstrates that:

The production possibility curve is a curve measuring the maximum combination of outputs that can be obtained from a given number of inputs.

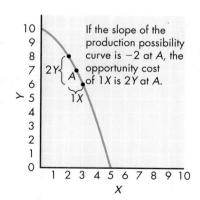

If the slope of the production possibility curve is −2 at A, the opportunity cost of 1X is 2Y at A.

The slope of the production possibility curve tells you the opportunity cost of good X in terms of good Y. You have to give up 2Y to get 1X when you're around point A.

**Figure 2-2 (a and b)   A Production Possibility Table
                          and Curve**

The table in (a) contains information on the trade-off between the
production of guns and butter. This information has been plotted on
the graph in (b). Notice in (b) that as we move along the production
possibility curve from A to F, trading butter for guns, we get fewer
and fewer guns for each pound of butter given up. That is, the
opportunity cost of choosing guns over butter increases as we
increase the production of guns. This concept is called the principle
of increasing marginal opportunity cost. The phenomenon occurs
because some resources are better suited for the production of butter
than for the production of guns, and we use the better ones first.

% of Resources Devoted to Production of Guns	Number of Guns	% of Resources Devoted to Production of Butter	Pounds of Butter	Row
0	0	100	15	A
20	4	80	14	B
40	7	60	12	C
60	9	40	9	D
80	11	20	5	E
100	12	0	0	F

(a) Production possibility table

(b) Production possibility curve

1. There is a limit to what you can achieve, given the existing institutions,
   resources, and technology.

2. Every choice you make has an opportunity cost. You can get more of something
   only by giving up something else.

A PRODUCTION POSSIBILITY CURVE FOR A SOCIETY

The grade example shows a production possibility curve representing the choices facing
an individual. The production possibility curve can also be used to model how societies
must consider opportunity costs in their decisions, so let's now move on to an example
of such a societal production possibility curve. In this example I also discuss how opportunity costs typically change over a range of decisions and how that change in
opportunity cost influences the shape of the curve.

   I chose an unchanging trade-off in the study-time/grade example because it made
the initial presentation of the production possibility curve easier. Since, by assumption,
you could always trade two points on your history grade for three points on your economics grade, the production possibility curve was a straight line. But is that the way
we'd expect reality to be? Probably not. So let's use a more realistic, outward-bowed production possibility curve, as in Figure 2-2(b).

   Why are production possibility curves typically bowed outward? Because some resources are better suited for the production of certain kinds of goods than they are for
the production of other kinds of goods. To make the answer more concrete, let's talk
specifically about society's choice between defense spending (guns) and spending on

PRODUCTION POSSIBILITY CURVES

Definition	Shape	Shifts	Points In, Out, and On
The production possibility curve is a curve that measures the maximum combination of outputs that can be obtained with a given number of inputs.	Most are outward bowed because of increasing marginal opportunity cost; if opportunity cost doesn't change, the production possibility curve is a straight line.	Increases in inputs or increases in the productivity of inputs shift the production possibility curve out; decreases have the opposite effect; the production possibility curve shifts along the axis whose input is changing.	Points inside the production possibility curve are points of inefficiency; points on the production possibility curve are points of efficiency; points outside the production possibility curve are not obtainable.

domestic needs (butter). The graph in Figure 2-2(b) is derived from the table in Figure 2-2(a).

Let's see what the shape of the curve means in terms of numbers. Let's start with society producing only butter (point A). Giving up a little butter (1 pound) initially gain us a lot of guns (4), moving us to point B. The next 2 pounds of butter we give up gain us slightly fewer guns (point C). If we continue to trade butter for guns, we find that at point D we gain very few guns from giving up a pound of butter. The opportunity cost of choosing guns over butter increases as we increase the production of guns.

The reason the opportunity cost of guns increases as we produce more guns is that some resources are relatively better suited to producing guns, while others are relatively better suited to producing butter. Put in economists' terminology, some resources have a **comparative advantage** over other resources—*the ability to be better suited to the production of one good than to the production of another good.* In this example, some resources have a comparative advantage over other resources in the production of butter, while other resources have a comparative advantage in the production of guns.

When making small amounts of guns and large amounts of butter, in the production of those guns we use the resources whose comparative advantage is in the production of guns. All other resources are devoted to producing butter. Because the resources used in producing guns aren't good at producing butter, we're not giving up much butter to get those guns. As we produce more and more of a good, we must use resources whose comparative advantage is in the production of the other good—in this case, more suitable for producing butter than for producing guns. As we remove resources from the production of butter to get the same additional amount of guns, we must give up increasing amounts of butter. An alternative way of saying this is that the opportunity cost of producing guns becomes greater as the production of guns increases. As we continue to increase the production of guns, the opportunity cost of more guns becomes very high because we're using resources to produce guns that have a strong comparative advantage for producing butter.

Let's consider two more examples. Say the United States suddenly decides it needs more wheat. To get additional wheat, we must devote additional land to growing it. This land is less fertile than the land we're already using, so our additional output of wheat per acre of land devoted to wheat will be less. Alternatively, consider the use of relief pitchers in a baseball game. If only one relief pitcher is needed, the manager sends in the best; if he must send in a second one, then a third, and even a fourth, the likelihood of winning the game decreases.

Q-2 If no resource had a comparative advantage in the production of any good, what would the shape of the production possibility curve be? Why?

Slope is flat at A. Low opportunity cost of guns.

Slope is steep at B. High opportunity cost of guns.

Butter

Guns

The production possibility curve presents choices in a timeless fashion and therefore makes opportunity costs clear-cut; there are two choices, one with a higher cost and one with a lower cost. The reality is that most choices are dependent on other choices; they are made sequentially. With sequential choices you cannot simply reverse your decision. Once you have started on a path, to take another path you have to return to the beginning. Thus, following one path often lowers the costs of options along that path, but it raises the costs of options along another path.

Such sequential decisions can best be seen within the framework of a decision tree—a visual description of sequential choices. A decision tree is shown in the accompanying figure.

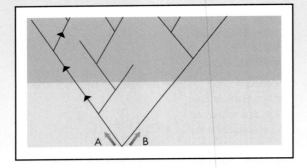

Once you make the initial decision to go on path A, the costs of path B options become higher; they include the costs of reversing your path and starting over. The decision trees of life have thousands of branches; each decision you make rules out other paths, or at least increases your costs highly. (Remember that day you decided to blow off your homework? That decision may have changed your future life.)

Another way of putting this same point is that *all decisions are made in context:* What makes sense in one context may not make sense in another. For example, say you're answering the question "Would society be better off if students were taught literature or if they were taught agriculture?" The answer depends on the institutional context. In a developing country whose goal is large increases in material output, teaching agriculture may make sense. In a developed country, where growth in material output is less important, teaching literature may make sense.

Recognizing the contextual nature of decisions is important when interpreting the production possibility curve. Because decisions are contextual, what the production possibility curve for a particular decision looks like depends on the existing institutions, and the analysis can be applied only in institutional and historical context. The production possibility curve is not a purely technical phenomenon. The curve is an engine of analysis to make contextual choices, not a definitive tool to decide what one should do in all cases.

INCREASING MARGINAL OPPORTUNITY COST

For many of the choices society must make, opportunity costs tend to increase as we choose more and more of an item. The reason is that the resources we devote to its production will be less and less good at producing it. (Remember, we use those resources with the greatest comparative advantage first.). Such a phenomenon about choice is so common, in fact, that it has acquired a name: the **principle of increasing marginal opportunity cost.** That principle states:

> *In order to get more of something, one must give up ever-increasing quantities of something else.*

The principle of increasing marginal opportunity cost states that opportunity costs increase the more you concentrate on the activity. In order to get more of something, one must give up ever-increasing quantities of something else.

In other words, initially the opportunity costs of an activity are low, but they increase the more we concentrate on that activity. Sometimes this law is called the flowerpot law because, if it didn't hold, all the world's food could be grown in a flowerpot. But it can't be. As we add more seeds to a fixed amount of soil, there won't be enough nutrients or room for the roots, so output per seed decreases.

Figure 2-3 (a, b, and c)   Efficiency, Inefficiency, and Technological Change
The production possibility curve helps us see what is meant by efficiency. At point A, in (a), all inputs are used to make 4 pounds of butter and 6 guns. This is inefficient since there is a way to obtain more of one without giving up any of the other, that is, to obtain 6 pounds of butter and 6 guns (point C) or 8 guns and 4 pounds of butter (point B). All points inside the production possibility curve are inefficient. With fixed inputs and given technology, we cannot go beyond the production possibility curve. For example, point D is unattainable.

A technological change that improves production techniques will shift the production possibility curve outward, as shown in both (b) and (c). How the curve shifts outward depends on how technology improves. For example, if we become more efficient in the production of both guns and butter, the curve will shift out as in (b). If we become more efficient in producing butter, but not in producing guns, then the curve will shift as in (c).

(a) Efficiency and inefficiency   **(b) Neutral technological change**   **(c) Biased technological change**

EFFICIENCY

We would like, if possible, to get as much output as possible from a given amount of inputs or resources. That's **productive efficiency**—*achieving as much output as possible from a given amount of inputs or resources.* We would like to be efficient. The production possibility curve helps us see what is meant by productive efficiency. Consider point A in Figure 2-3(a), which is inside the production possibility curve. If we are producing at point A, we are using all our resources to produce 6 guns and 4 pounds of butter. Point A represents **inefficiency**—*getting less output from inputs which, if devoted to some other activity, would produce more output.* That's because with the same inputs we could be getting either 8 guns and 4 pounds of butter (point B) or 6 pounds of butter and 6 guns (point C). As long as we prefer more to less, both points B and C represent **efficiency**—*achieving a goal using as few inputs as possible.* We always want to move our production out to a point on the production possibility curve.

Why not move out farther, to point D? If we could, we would, but by definition the production possibility curve represents the most output we can get from a certain combination of inputs. So point D is unattainable, given our resources and technology.

When technology improves, when more resources are discovered, or when the economic institutions get better at fulfilling our wants, we can get more output with the same inputs. What this means is that when technology or an economic institution improves, the entire production possibility curve shifts outward from AB to CD in Figure 2-3(b). How the production possibility curve shifts outward depends on how the technology improves. For example, say we become more efficient in producing butter, but not more efficient in producing guns. Then the production possibility curve shifts outward to AC in Figure 2-3(c).

Q.3 Identify the point(s) of inefficiency and efficiency. What point(s) are unattainable?

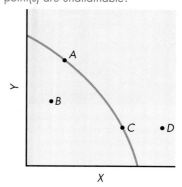

Efficiency involves achieving a goal as cheaply as possible. Efficiency has meaning only in relation to a specified goal.

Figure 2-4   Examples of Shifts in Production Possibility Curves
Each of these curves reflects a different type of shift. Your assignment is to match these shifts with the situations given in the text.

(a)

(b)

(c)

(d)

Q.4   Your firm is establishing a trucking business in Saudi Arabia. The managers have noticed that women are generally paid much less than men in Saudi Arabia, and they suggest that hiring women would be more efficient than hiring men. What should you respond?

Innovations such as the automation of production shown here shifts the production possibility curve out.
Photodisc

DISTRIBUTION AND PRODUCTIVE EFFICIENCY

In discussing the production possibility curve for a society, I avoided questions of distribution: Who gets what? But such questions cannot be ignored in real-world situations. Specifically, if the method of production is tied to a particular income distribution and choosing one method will help some people but hurt others, we can't say that one method of production is efficient and the other inefficient, even if one method produces more total output than the other. As I stated above, the term *efficiency* involves achieving a goal as cheaply as possible. The term has meaning only in regard to a specified goal. Say, for example, that we have a society of ascetics who believe that consumption above some minimum is immoral. For such a society, producing more for less (productive efficiency) would not be efficient since consumption is not its goal. Or say that we have a society that cares that what is produced is fairly distributed. An increase in output that goes to only one person and not to anyone else would not necessarily be efficient.

In our society, however, most people prefer more to less, and many policies have relatively small distributional consequences. On the basis of the assumption that more is better than less, economists use their own kind of shorthand for such policies and talk about efficiency as identical to productive efficiency—increasing total output. But it's important to remember the assumption under which that shorthand is used: that the distributional effects that accompany the policy aren't undesirable and that we, as a society, prefer more output.

EXAMPLES OF SHIFTS IN THE PRODUCTION POSSIBILITY CURVE

To see whether you understand the production possibility curve, let us now consider some situations that can be shown with it. In Figure 2-4 I demonstrate four situations with production possibility curves. Below, I list four situations. To test your understanding of the curve, match each situation to one of the curves in Figure 2-4.

1. A meteor hits the world and destroys half the earth's natural resources.
2. Nanotechnology is perfected that lowers the cost of manufactured goods.
3. A new technology is discovered that doubles the speed at which all goods can be produced.
4. Global warming increases the cost of producing agricultural goods.

Q.5   When a natural disaster hits the midwestern United States, where most of the U.S. butter is produced, what happens to the U.S. production possibility curve for guns and butter?

The correct answers are: 1–d; 2–a; 3–b; 4–c.

If you got them all right, you are well on your way to understanding the production possibility curve.

TRADE AND COMPARATIVE ADVANTAGE

Now that we have gone through the basics of the production possibility curve, let's dig a little deeper. From the above discussion, you know that production possibility curves are generally bowed outward and that the reason for this is comparative advantage. To remind you of the argument, consider Figure 2-5, which is the guns and butter production possibility example I presented earlier.

At point A, all resources are being used to produce butter. As more guns are produced, we take resources away from producing butter that had a comparative advantage in producing guns, so we gain a lot of guns for little butter (the opportunity cost of additional guns is low). As we continue down the curve, the comparative advantage of the resources we use changes, and as we approach B, we use almost all resources to produce guns, so we are using resources that aren't very good at producing guns. Thus, around point B we gain few guns for a lot of butter (the opportunity cost of additional guns is high).

A society wants to be on the frontier of its production possibility curve. This requires that individuals produce those goods for which they have a comparative advantage. The question for society, then, is how to direct individuals toward those activities. For a firm, the answer is easy. A manager can allocate the firm's resources to their best use. For example, he or she can assign an employee with good people skills to the human resources department and another with good research skills to research and development. But our economy has millions of individuals, and no manager directing everyone what to do. How do we know that these individuals will be directed to do those things for which they have a comparative advantage? It was this question that was central to a British moral philosopher named Adam Smith when he wrote his most famous book, *The Wealth of Nations* (1776). In it he argued that it was humankind's proclivity to trade that leads to individuals using their comparative advantage. He writes:

> This division of labour, from which so many advantages are derived, is not originally the effect of any human wisdom, which foresees and intends that general opulence to which it gives occasion. It is the necessary, though very slow and gradual consequence of a certain propensity in human nature which has in view no such extensive utility; the propensity to truck, barter, and exchange one thing for another. . . . [This propensity] is common to all men, and to be found in no other race of animals, which seem to know neither this nor any other species of contracts. . . . Nobody ever saw a dog make a fair and deliberate exchange of one bone for another with another dog. Nobody ever saw one animal by its gestures and natural cries signify to another, this is mine, that yours; I am willing to give this for that.

As long as people trade, Smith argues, the market will guide people, like an invisible hand, to gravitate toward those activities for which they have a comparative advantage. By specializing in the production of goods in which they have a comparative advantage, they will produce the most goods they can. They can then trade with other people who specialize in the production of other goods. For Smith, what was especially neat about this process was that it could take place without enormous amounts of government intervention. Smith writes:

Figure 2-5 Comparative Advantage and the Production Possibility Curve

A — Opportunity cost of additional guns is low.

Butter

Opportunity cost of additional guns is high.

B

Guns

Adam Smith argued that it was humankind's proclivity to trade that leads to individuals using their comparative advantage.

Figure 2-6   Growth in the Past Two Millennia
For 1,700 years the world economy grew very slowly. Then at the end of the 18th century with the introduction of markets and the spread of democracy, the world economy has grown at increasing rates.

Source: Angus Maddison, *Monitoring the World Economy*, OECD, 1995; Angus Maddison, "Poor Until 1820," *The Wall Street Journal,* January 11, 1999.

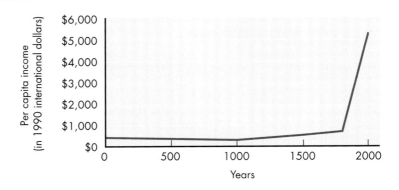

Man has almost constant occasion for the help of his brethren, and it is in vain for him to expect it from their benevolence only. He will be more likely to prevail, if he can interest their self-love in his favour, and show them that it is for their own advantage to do for him what he requires of them. Whoever offers to another a bargain of any kind proposes to do this. Give me that which I want, and you shall have that which you want, is the meaning of every such offer; and it is in this manner that we obtain from one another the far greater part of those good offices which we stand in need of. It is not from the benevolence of the butcher, the brewer, or the baker, that we expect our dinner, but from their regard to their own interest. We address ourselves, not to their humanity but to their self-love, and never talk to them of our own necessities but of their advantages.

MARKETS, SPECIALIZATION, AND GROWTH

We can see the effect of trade on our well-being empirically by considering the growth of economies. As you can see from Figure 2-6, for 1,700 years the world economy grew very slowly. Then, at the end of the 18th century, the world economy started to grow, and it has grown at an increasing rate since then.

What changed? The introduction of markets that facilitate trade and the spread of democracy. There's something about markets that leads to economic growth. Markets allow specialization and encourage trade. The bowing out of the production possibilities from trade is part of the story, but a minor part. As individuals compete and specialize they learn by doing, becoming even better at what they do. Markets also foster competition, which pushes individuals to find better ways of doing things. They devise new technologies that further the growth process.

The new millennium is offering new ways for individuals to specialize and compete. More and more businesses are trading on the Internet. For example, colleges, such as the University of Phoenix, are providing online competition for traditional colleges. Similarly, online bookstores and drugstores are proliferating. As Internet technology becomes built into our economy, we can expect more specialization, more division of labor, and the economic growth that follows.

Markets can be very simple or very complicated.
Jon Riley/Stone/Getty Images

THE BENEFITS OF TRADE

The reasons why markets can direct people to use their comparative advantages follows from a very simple argument: When people freely enter into a trade, both parties can be expected to benefit from the trade; otherwise, why would they have traded in the first place? So when the butcher sells you meat, he's better off with the money you give him, and you're better off with the meat he gives you.

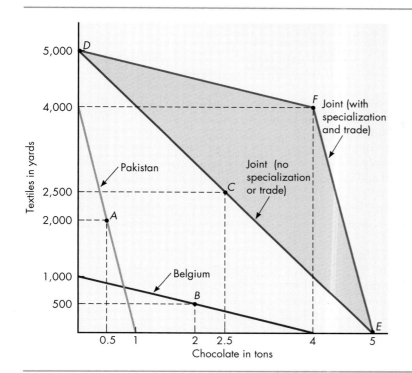

Figure 2-7   The Gains from Trade

Trade makes those involved in the trade better off. When the countries produce goods in equal proportions and don't specialize or trade, their combined production possibilities curve is shown by the red line. If each country specializes and takes advantage of its comparative advantage, the combined production possibilities curve becomes bowed outward. The blue shaded region represents the gains from specialization and trade.

When there is competition in trading, such that individuals are able to pick the best trades available to them, each individual drives the best bargain he or she can. The end result is that both individuals in the trade benefit as much as they possibly can, given what others are willing to trade. This argument for the benefits from trade underlies the general policy of **laissez-faire**—*an economic policy of leaving coordination of individuals' actions to the market.* (*Laissez-faire*, a French term, means "Let events take their course; leave things alone.")

Let's consider a numerical example of the gains that accrue to two countries when they trade, and show how that trade increases the production possibilities, creating the bowed shape of the production possibility curve. I use an international trade example so that you can see that the argument holds for international trade as well as domestic trade.

Let's say that the two countries are Pakistan and Belgium, and that Pakistan has a comparative advantage in producing textiles, while Belgium has a comparative advantage in producing chocolate. Specifically, Pakistan can produce 4,000 yards of textiles a day, or 1 ton of chocolate a day, or any proportional combination in between. (Pakistan's opportunity cost of 1 ton of chocolate is 4,000 yards of textiles.) Pakistan's production possibility curve is shown by the orange line in Figure 2-7. In a given day Belgium can produce either 1,000 yards of textiles, 4 tons of chocolate, or any proportion in between. (Belgium's opportunity cost of 1 ton of chocolate is 250 yards of textiles.) Its production possibility curve is shown by the purple line in Figure 2-7.

The most each country can produce is some combination along its production possibility curve. Say Pakistan has chosen to produce 2,000 yards of textiles and 0.5 tons of chocolate (point A), while Belgium has chosen to produce 500 yards of textiles and 2 tons of chocolate (point B). Together the countries produce 2.5 tons of chocolate and 2,500 thousand yards of textiles, as shown in the following table:

Web Note 2.1
Wine and Cloth

Laissez-faire is an economic policy of leaving coordination of individuals' actions to the market.

What argument underlies the general laissez-faire policy argument?

Pakistan	2,000 yards textiles	0.5 ton chocolate
Belgium	500 yards textiles	2 tons chocolate
Total	2,500 yards textiles	2.5 tons chocolate

This combination is also shown as point C in Figure 2.7. Point C is just one possible combination. The two countries could select other production combinations. Let's assume each country has the same consumption pattern and devotes the same proportion of resources to the consumption of each good. Two extreme combinations are both countries producing only chocolate and both producing only textiles. These cases are 5,000 yards of textiles and no chocolate (point D) and 5 tons of chocolate and no textiles (point E). Generally, however, countries want to consume a mix of goods such as combination C. The red line connecting points D and E represents all possible combinations (including C) of chocolate and textiles where the countries produce goods in the same proportions.

What if each specialized, doing what it does best, and then traded with the other for the goods it wants? This separates the production and consumption decisions. It makes sense for Pakistan to specialize in textiles, producing 4,000 yards. Similarly, it makes sense for Belgium to specialize in chocolate, producing 4 tons. By specializing, the countries together produce 4 tons of chocolate and 4,000 yards of textiles—point F in Figure 2-7. By specializing and trading, they can each have the same amount of chocolate and textiles as before (point C), *plus an additional 1,500 yards of textiles and 1.5 tons of chocolate to split up between them.* The following table summarizes these gains:

Specialization and trade create gains that make all better off.

| | Combined Production Possibilities | | |
	(I) No Specialization or Trade	(II) Specialization and Trade	(III) Gains to Trade
Fabric	2,500 yards	4,000 yards	1,500 yards
Chocolate	2.5 tons	4 tons	1.5 tons

Column I shows the combination with no specialization or trade. Column II represents the amount the countries can produce if each specializes in what it does best and then trades. Column III is the difference between Column II and Column I. How these gains are distributed is up to negotiation, but the total combination of goods has risen. It is these gains from trade that lead to economists' support of free trade and their opposition to barriers to trade.

The numbers in the table represent one possibility of the gains from specialization and trade. Other combinations are possible. Connecting points D, E, and F in Figure 2-7 tells us all potential combinations of output with trade. The extremes (points D and E) are where both countries are using all their resources in the production of one or the other goods. Point F represents the combined total output when each specializes in the good for which it has a comparative advantage. Connecting points D, E, and F (the blue line) gives us the combined production possibility curve with specialization and trade. The shaded area graphically represents the gains from specialization and trade.

Notice that the combined production possibility curve has the same slope as Belgium's from D to F, and the same slope as Pakistan's from F to E. That is because, when trade is allowed, the slope of the combined production possibility curve is determined by the country with the lowest opportunity cost. It is by producing where costs are lowest that countries can achieve gains from trade. This principle—*lowest cost rules*—gives us a sense of what happens when we expand the production possibility curve analysis to

Q-7 Steve can bake either 4 loaves of bread or 8 dozen cookies a day. Sarah can bake either 4 loaves of bread or 4 dozen cookies a day. Show, using production possibility curves, that Steve and Sarah would be better off specializing in their baking activities and then trading, rather than baking only for themselves.

Q-8 True or false? Two countries can achieve the greatest gains from trade by each producing the goods for which the opportunity costs are greatest and then trading those goods.

include many countries rather than just two: The production possibility curve becomes smoother as each country's comparative advantage governs a smaller portion of the shape. Eventually, as the number of countries that trade gets large, it becomes the smooth bowed curve we drew above for guns and butter.

U.S. TEXTILE PRODUCTION AND TRADE

When each country follows its comparative advantage, production becomes more efficient and the production possibilities curve increases the amount of goods that can be produced. Because of these benefits, most economists support free markets and free trade. The market system gives individual firms an incentive to search for comparative advantages, and to produce with lowest-cost methods at lowest-cost locations. This pressures other producers to lower their costs or get out of the business.

The pressure to find comparative advantages is never ending, in part because comparative advantage can change. Two hundred years ago the United States had a comparative advantage in producing textiles. It was rich in natural resources and labor, and it had a low-cost source of power (water). As the cost of U.S. labor went up, and as trade opportunities widened, that comparative advantage disappeared. As it did, the United States moved out of the textile industry. Countries with cheaper labor, such as Bangladesh, today have the comparative advantage in textiles. As firms have relocated textile production to Bangladesh, total costs have fallen. The gains from trade show up as higher pay for Bangladeshi workers and lower-priced cloth for U.S. consumers. Of course, trade is a two-way street. In return for Bangladesh's textiles, the United States sends computer software and airplanes, products that would be highly expensive, indeed almost impossible, for Bangladesh to produce on its own. So Bangladeshi consumers, on average, are also made better off by the trade.

> The pressure to find comparative advantages is never ending.

Web Note 2.2
Wage Comparison

REGULATING TRADE: INSTITUTIONS, GOVERNMENT, AND TRADE

We've spent a lot of time going through the production possibility curve model, and the underlying comparative advantage argument. Now let's turn to the implications of the model for policy. Clearly, one of the lessons of the model and its analysis is that *trade is good*—if that conclusion didn't hit you over the head, you probably were daydreaming as you read the preceding sections. But does the model mean that we should fully support free trade and a laissez-faire policy? What policy should society have regarding trade? The answers to these questions are more subtle than the general conclusion. To find the answers, you have to know not only what the model is telling us about policy but also what assumptions—both implicit and explicit—are included in the model, because it is those assumptions that lead us to that conclusion. (Here is an example of the proposition I presented in Chapter 1: To truly know a model you have to know both the model and its assumptions.)

Let's start with the easy part: What is the model, given its assumptions, telling us about policy? Trade expands the production possibilities one faces and, by encouraging individuals to take advantage of their comparative advantage, it allows individuals to achieve gains they couldn't otherwise achieve. This argument is quite robust and can be applied in many different instances. Now let's turn to the harder part—the assumptions of the model upon which that argument is based. The important assumption of the model that we're going to concentrate on here is that trade is costless, or, put another way, that there are no transactions costs to trade. This assumption is not true in the real world. Trade can be extraordinarily costly. For markets to develop, trading partners need to cooperate, which requires a complex institutional environment. Rules and methods

> To apply the model one must know its assumptions; thus, while the model tells us that trade is generally good, it may not be good in particular instances.

Q.9   True or false? If a country doesn't have an effective government, then the market will be more efficient because the government will have to follow a laissez-faire policy.

of trading need to become codified. To have ongoing trade you have to have enforce-able contracts, a commercial code (laws about what is allowable in trade and what isn't), rules about what happens when someone does not fulfill an obligation they incur in trade, methods to make trade easier, and a whole lot more. Somebody has to supply all that, and in the United States (and, more generally, in domestic economies) that somebody is the government of the country. In countries where an effective govern-ment does not exist, as in Somalia, you don't have these institutions and you don't have effective markets.

One way domestic governments make trading easier is to limit private restrictions on trade. U.S. states, for example, are not allowed to place taxes on goods as they cross their borders. (In countries where there is not an effective government, such as Afghanistan, that is not the case; warlords charge for any goods passing through their territory, making trade difficult and costly.) Another way is to provide a common cur-rency for traders to use. In the United States you can spend a dollar in any state. Cross the border into Canada or Mexico, and you have to switch currencies. Common cur-rencies provided by government make trades much easier, which is why the European Union, for example, has organized to establish a common currency—the euro. I could go on, but the examples given so far should make my point: Domestic governments are part and parcel of modern functioning markets. An important reason why international trade is much more difficult than domestic trade is that no world government exists to assist in that trade. Instead, voluntary organizations, such as the World Bank, the World Court, the International Monetary Fund, and the World Trade Organization fill some of the roles internationally that a national government fills domestically.

I raise these issues here to point out to you that while we rely on government to reg-ulate markets, government is also part of the institutional structure of markets (because it provides the institutional environment in which markets exist). So when you think about policy, don't think of government and markets as totally separate. Think of them as intertwined entities, both of whose continued existence depends on the existence of the other. (We'll talk more about such issues in later chapters.)

You must use the insight that institutions and government are central to trade when interpreting the implications of the production possibilities model for policy. It tells us that while markets work like an invisible hand—guiding individuals to make choices that work for the good of society, even as those individuals pursue their own welfare—we can't think of markets as operating alone. Instead we must think of them as operat-ing in conjunction with social and political forces. The invisible hand works as well as it does only because it is part of a broader institutional structure. Society appropriately regulates markets, preventing trades that are harmful to its members and encouraging trades that are helpful. Who decides what hurts and what helps? Within the United States, the government decides. Government stands as the arbiter of whether the trade is actually helping society or not.

When you think about policy, don't think about government and markets as totally separate.

ROLES OF GOVERNMENT IN A MARKET

Economists have thought a lot about why government should not allow some trades and should limit or highly regulate others. This thinking goes back to Adam Smith, who in *The Wealth of Nations* explored a number of roles for government in a market economy. Later economists have expanded thinking about those roles. So let us now take a look at the roles of government in restricting trade. These roles include (1) providing a stable set of institutions and rules, (2) promoting effective and workable competition, (3) cor-recting for externalities, (4) ensuring economic stability and growth, (5) providing pub-lic goods, and (6) adjusting for undesired market results.

Roles of government in a market economy are:

1. providing a stable set of institutions and rules,
2. promoting effective and workable competition,
3. correcting for externalities,
4. ensuring economic stability and growth,
5. providing public goods, and
6. adjusting for undesired market results.

Most reasons for government intervention discussed in this chapter are debatable.

There is, however, one governmental role that even the strongest laissez-faire advocates generally accept. That role is for government to set up an appropriate institutional and legal structure within which markets can operate.

The reason there's little debate about this role is that all economists recognize that markets do not operate when there is anarchy. They require institutional structures that determine the rules of ownership, what types of trade are allowable, how contracts will be enforced, and what productive institutions are most desirable.

Before anyone conducts business, he or she needs to know the rules of the game and must have a reasonable expectation that those rules will not be changed. The operation of the modern economy requires that contractual arrangements be made among individuals. These contractual arrangements must be enforced if the economy is to operate effectively.

Economists differ significantly on what the rules for such a system should be and whether any rules that already exist should be modified. Even if the rules are currently perceived as unfair, it can be argued that they should be kept in place. Individuals have already made decisions based on those rules, and it's unfair to them to change the rules in the middle of the game.

Stability of rules is a benefit to society. When the rules are perceived as unfair, and changing them is also perceived as unfair, the government must find a balance between the two degrees of unfairness. Government often finds itself in that difficult position. Thus, while there's little debate about government's role in providing some institutional framework, there's heated debate about which framework is most appropriate.

Provide a Stable Set of Institutions and Rules   A basic role of government is to provide a stable institutional framework that includes the set of laws specifying what can and cannot be done as well as a mechanism to enforce those laws. For example, if someone doesn't pay you, you can't go take what you are owed; you have to go through the government court system. The government restricts individuals from enforcing contracts; it retains that role for itself. Before people conduct business, they need to know the rules of the game and have a reasonable belief about what those rules will be in the future. These rules can initially develop spontaneously, but as society becomes more complex, the rules must be codified; enforcement mechanisms must be established. The modern market economy requires enforceable complex contractual arrangements among individuals. Where governments don't provide a stable institutional framework, as often happens in developing and transitional countries, economic activity is difficult; usually such economies are stagnant. Zimbabwe in the early 2000s is an example. As various groups fought for political control, the Zimbabwe economy stagnated.

Promote Effective and Workable Competition   In a market economy the forces of monopoly—the control of a market by one firm—and competition are always in conflict, and the government must decide what role it is to play in protecting or promoting competition. Thus, when Microsoft gained a monopolistic control of the computer operating system market with Windows, the U.S. government took the company to court and challenged that monopoly.

Historically, U.S. sentiment runs against **monopoly power**—*the ability of individuals or firms currently in business to prevent other individuals or firms from entering the same kind of business.* Monopoly power gives existing firms and individuals the ability to raise their prices. Similarly, individuals' or firms' ability to enter freely into business activities is generally seen as good. Government's job is to promote competition and prevent excess monopoly power from limiting competition.

What makes this a difficult function for government is that most individuals and firms believe that competition is far better for the other guy than it is for themselves, that their own monopolies are necessary monopolies, and that competition facing them is unfair competition. For example, most farmers support competition, but these same farmers also support government farm subsidies (payments by government to producers based on production levels) and import restrictions. Likewise, most firms support competition, but these same firms also support tariffs, which protect them from foreign competition. Most professionals, such as architects and engineers, support competition, but they also support professional licensing, which limits the number of competitors who can enter their field. Now, as you will see in reading the newspapers, there are always arguments for limiting entry into fields. The job of the government is to determine whether these arguments are strong enough to overcome the negative effects those limitations have on competition.

Correct for Externalities   When two people freely enter into a trade or agreement, they both believe that they will benefit from the trade. But unless they're required to do so, traders are unlikely to take into account any effect that an action may have on a third party. Economists call *the effect of a decision on a third party not taken into account by the decision maker* an **externality.** An externality can be positive (in which case society as a whole benefits from the trade between the two parties) or negative (in which case society as a whole is harmed by the trade between the two parties).

An example of a positive externality is education. When someone educates herself or himself, all society benefits, since better-educated people usually make better citizens and are better equipped to figure out new approaches to solving problems—approaches that benefit society as a whole. An example of a negative externality is pollution. Air conditioners emit a small amount of chlorofluorocarbons into the earth's atmosphere and contribute to the destruction of the ozone layer. Since the ozone layer protects all living things by filtering some of the sun's harmful ultraviolet light rays, a thinner layer of ozone can contribute to cancer and other harmful or fatal conditions. Neither the firms that produce the air conditioners nor the consumers who buy them take those effects into account. This means that the destruction of the ozone layer is an externality—the result of an effect that is not taken into account by market participants.

When there are externalities, there is a potential role for government.
Charles O'Rear/Corbis

When there are externalities, there is a potential role for government to adjust the market result. If one's goal is to benefit society as much as possible, actions with positive externalities should be encouraged and actions with negative externalities should be restricted. Governments can step in and change the rules so that the actors must take into account the effect of their actions on society as a whole. I emphasize that the role is a potential one for two reasons. The first is that government often has difficulty dealing with externalities in such a way that society gains. For example, even if the U.S. government totally banned products that emit chlorofluorocarbons, other countries might not do the same and the ozone layer would continue to be destroyed. The second reason is that government is an institution that reflects, and is often guided by, politics and vested interests. It's not clear that, given the political realities, government intervention to correct externalities would improve the situation. In later chapters I'll have a lot more to say about government's role in correcting for externalities.

Ensure Economic Stability and Growth   In addition to providing general stability, government has the potential role of providing economic stability. If it's possible, most people would agree that government should prevent large fluctuations in the level of economic activity, maintain a relatively constant price level, and provide an economic environment conducive to economic growth. These aims, which became the goals of the U.S. government in 1946 when the Employment Act was passed, are generally considered macroeconomic goals. They're justified as appropriate aims for government to pursue because they involve **macroeconomic externalities** (*externalities that affect the levels of unemployment, inflation, or growth in the economy as a whole*).

Here's how a macro externality could occur. When individuals decide how much to spend, they don't take into account the effects of their decision on others; thus, there may be too much or too little spending. Too little spending often leads to unemployment. But in making their spending decision, people don't take into account the fact that spending less might create unemployment. So their spending decisions can involve a macro externality. Similarly, when people raise their price and don't consider the effect on inflation, they too might be creating a macro externality.

Provide for Public Goods   Another role for government is to supply public goods. A **public good** is *a good that if supplied to one person must be supplied to all and whose consumption by one individual does not prevent its consumption by another individual.* In contrast, a **private good** is *a good that, when consumed by one individual, cannot be consumed by another individual.* An example of a private good is an apple; once I eat that apple, no one else can consume it. An example of a public good is national defense. In order to supply defense, governments must force people to pay for it with taxes, rather than leaving it to the market to supply it.

There are very few pure public goods, but many goods have public good aspects to them, and in general economists use the term *public good* to describe goods that are most efficiently provided collectively rather than privately. Parks, playgrounds, roads, and (as noted above) national defense are examples. Let's consider national defense more closely. For technological reasons national defense must protect all individuals in an area; a missile system cannot protect some houses in an area without protecting others nearby.

Everyone agrees that national defense is needed, but not everyone takes part in it. If someone else defends the country, you're defended for free; you can be a **free rider**—*a person who participates in something for free because others have paid for it.* Because self-interested people would like to enjoy the benefits of national defense while letting someone else pay for it, everyone has an incentive to be a free rider. But if everyone tries to be a free rider, there won't be any national defense. In such cases government can step in and require that everyone pay part of the cost of national defense, reducing the free rider problem.

Adjust for Undesired Market Results   A controversial role for government is to adjust the results of the market when those market results are seen as socially undesirable. Government redistributes income, taking it away from some individuals and giving it to others whom it sees as more deserving or more in need. In doing so, it attempts to see that the outcomes of trades are fair. Determining what's fair is a difficult philosophical question. Let's consider two of the many manifestations of the fairness problem. Should the government use a **progressive tax** (*a tax whose rates increase as a person's income increases*) to redistribute money from the rich to the poor? (A progressive income tax schedule might tax individuals at a rate of 15 percent for income up to $20,000; at 25 percent for income between $20,000 and $40,000; and at 35 percent for every dollar earned over $40,000.) Or should government impose a **regressive tax** (*a tax whose rates decrease as income rises*) to redistribute money from the poor to the rich? Or should government impose a flat or **proportional tax** (*a tax whose rates are constant at all income levels, no matter what a taxpayer's total annual income is*)? Such a tax might be, say, 25 percent of every dollar of income. The United States has chosen a somewhat progressive income tax, while the Social Security tax is a proportional tax up to a specified earned income. Economists can tell government the effects of various types of taxes and

A macroeconomic externality is the effect of an individual decision that affects the levels of unemployment, inflation, or growth in an economy as a whole but is not taken into account by the individual decision maker.

Web Note 2.3
Minimum Wage

forms of taxation, but we can't tell government what's fair. That is for the people, through the government, to decide.

Another example of this role involves having government decide what's best for people, independently of their desires. The market allows individuals to decide. But what if people don't know what's best for themselves? Or what if they do know but don't act on that knowledge? For example, people might know that addictive drugs are bad for them, but because of peer pressure, or because they just don't care, they may take drugs anyway. Government action prohibiting such activities through laws or high taxes may then be warranted. *Goods or activities that government believes are bad for people even though they choose to use the goods or engage in the activities* are called **demerit goods or activities.** Illegal drugs are a demerit good and using addictive drugs is a demerit activity.

Alternatively, there are some activities that government believes are good for people, even if people may not choose to engage in them. For example, government may believe that going to the opera or contributing to charity is a good activity. But in the United States only a small percentage of people go to the opera, and not everyone in the United States contributes to charity. Similarly, government may believe that whole-wheat bread is more nutritious than white bread. But many consumers prefer white bread. Goods like whole-wheat bread and activities like contributing to charity are known as **merit goods or activities**—*goods and activities that government believes are good for you even though you may not choose to engage in the activities or consume the goods*. Government sometimes provides support for them through subsidies or tax benefits.

MARKET FAILURES AND GOVERNMENT FAILURES

The reasons for government intervention are often summed up in the phrase *market failure*. **Market failures** are *situations in which the market does not lead to a desired result*. In the real world, market failures are pervasive—the market is always failing in one way or another. But the fact that there are market failures does not mean that government intervention will improve the situation. There are also **government failures**—*situations in which the government intervenes and makes things worse*. Government failures are pervasive in the government—the government is always failing in one way or another. So real-world policymakers usually end up choosing which failure—market failure or government failure—will be least problematic.

REGULATING MARKETS INTERNATIONALLY

When thinking about the various roles of government, it is useful to contrast what happens domestically with what happens internationally, where there is no central world government. As I stated above, internationally, some of the roles of a government are not performed and others are performed by voluntary organizations or statelike institutions. For example, some countries have entered into free trade agreements and trade organizations that limit their ability to restrict trade. Similarly, other countries have entered into agreements to have a common currency. So these roles of government seem to carry over to situations where there is no government, and voluntary institutions are created to provide those roles.

While governments enter into voluntary agreements to fulfill some of the roles of government in the international market, for other roles we see far fewer agreements. For example, we see far less attempted redistribution of income at the international level than at the domestic level (foreign aid accounts for about 0.1 percent of U.S. income) and far less provision of public goods. Because there is no way to force countries to

With merit and demerit goods, individuals are assumed not to be doing what is in their self-interest.

Q-10 If there is an externality, does that mean that the government should intervene in the market to adjust for that externality?

There are strong pressures to secure and institutionalize the benefits of free international trade, and numerous international institutions have developed, or are developing, to achieve that end. Let's consider some of them.

EU

In 1957, several governments of Europe formed the European Economic Community (EEC). This organization has undergone many changes since its founding, changes that have strengthened the economic and political ties among the countries. The EEC eventually came to be called the European Union (EU) as it evolved into both an economic free trade area and a loose political organization. In the EU, as in any economic union, members allow free trade among themselves to help their economies by providing a larger marketplace and more competition for their own companies. Economic union also increases the market power of the combined countries. In 2002 the EU currently had 15 members, 12 of which shared a common currency, the euro. Thirteen other countries from southern and eastern Europe plan to join the EU in the next few years. (For more information, you can go to www.europa.eu.int.)

NAFTA

Partly in response to the growing strength of the EU, in 1994 the United States entered into a free trade agreement with Canada and Mexico called the North American Free Trade Agreement (NAFTA). Under NAFTA, trade barriers between the United States, Canada, and Mexico will be eliminated over a 15-year period. U.S. firms will be able to produce in Mexico and Canada—and vice versa—subject to Mexican or Canadian regulations and at each country's wage rates, and ship directly to the United States without international legal hurdles or barriers to trade. (To read the agreement go to www.nafta-sec-alena.org.)

MERCOSUR

In 1991, a group of four South American countries (Argentina, Paraguay, Uruguay, Brazil) launched Mercosur (Mercado Comun del Sur, meaning "common market of the south") to develop a common market without trade barriers and coordinated economic policies. Since 1991, Bolivia and Chile have joined. (Go to www.mercosur.org to find out more.) In 1994 an effort began to develop an even larger free trade area that encompasses both NAFTA and Mercosur, called the Free Trade Area of the Americas (FTAA). While negotiations regarding the structure of the trade agreement among 34 proposed members are due to be completed in 2005, it is unclear whether such an agreement will ever be accepted. (Go to www.ftaa-alca.org to check the progress.)

AFTA

Asia does not have a free trade association, but it is working toward one, and the Association of Southeast Asian Nations (ASEAN) has been discussing the creation of what would be called the Asian Free Trade Association (AFTA). Even though its work toward a free trade association is not complete, ASEAN includes many agreements to limit tariffs and to facilitate trade among its member countries. (Go to www.aseansec.org.)

WTO

Economists are of two minds about the regional free trade associations described above. While such associations promote trade among themselves, they often also establish strong barriers with outside countries and thereby limit free trade. Thus, many economists argue that the policy focus should be on the World Trade Organization (WTO), whose purpose is to promote free trade among all member countries.

---

comply with international agreements, governments have been unable to come up with an effective means of dealing with various environmental issues, such as global warming, and disputes among countries can lead to war and terrorism rather than being solved by a system of world courts. The point I am making is that, internationally, we don't have world government failure because we don't have a world government. But we also don't get the benefits that a world government would provide.

The push for globalization that has characterized the last decades of international relations is also a push for stronger international organizations that can make

International policymaking differs from domestic policymaking because there is no international government.

trading easier. Whether establishing those stronger organizations makes sense is an open question, but its existence shows the interconnection between markets and governments.

THE PRODUCTION POSSIBILITIES MODEL AND GOVERNMENT POLICY

As you can see, there are many roles for government that are consistent with the production possibilities model, once we modify the model to fit the real world. The model says that trade is good and that it therefore makes sense for us to rely on the market to solve our problems. The model applied to the real world (which means we take its assumptions into account) says that trade can be good, although at times it can cause problems and government regulation may be needed to adjust for those problems. This latter lesson is far less precise than the former, but it is more accurate. Debate often exists among economists about whether government should intervene.

If the real-world policy implications of the model are ambiguous, why learn the model in the first place? The answer is: because the model structures the discourse of debate about regulating the market. Economists will say, "Oh, that's an externality problem," "That's a public good problem," or "That's a government failure problem"—and policymakers will know what they mean. Then the policymakers go back and study similar events in history to determine how those events worked out in the real world, and to see if this instance is any different. They then come up with a policy position in relation to the model, to history, and to politics. That's what we mean by the art of economics.

Models are important because they structure the discourse of debate about regulating the market.

CONCLUSION

While the production possibility curve model does not give unambiguous answers as to what government's role should be in regulating trade, it does serve a very important purpose. It is a geometric tool that summarizes a number of ideas in economics—opportunity cost, comparative advantage, efficiency, and how trade leads to efficiency. These ideas are all essential to economists' conversations. They provide the framework within which those conversations take place. Thinking of the production possibility curve (and picturing the economy as being on it) directs you to think of the trade-offs involved in every decision.

The production possibility curve represents the tough choices society must make.

Look at questions such as: Should we save the spotted owl or should we allow logging in the western forests? Should we expand the government health care system or should we strengthen our national defense system? Should we emphasize policies that allow more consumption now or should we emphasize policies that allow more consumption in the future? Such choices involve difficult trade-offs that can be pictured by the production possibility curve.

Not everyone recognizes these trade-offs. For example, politicians often talk as if the production possibility curve were nonexistent. They promise voters the world, telling them, "If you elect me, you can have more of everything." When they say that, they obscure the hard choices and increase their probability of getting elected.

Economists continually point out that seemingly free lunches often involve significant hidden costs.

Economists do the opposite. They promise little except that life is tough, and they continually point out that seemingly free lunches often involve significant hidden costs. Alas, political candidates who exhibit such reasonableness seldom get elected. Economists' reasonableness has earned economics the nickname *the dismal science*.

SUMMARY

- The production possibility curve measures the maximum combination of outputs that can be obtained from a given number of inputs. It embodies the opportunity cost concept.

- In general, in order to get more and more of something, we must give up ever-increasing quantities of something else. This is the principle of increasing marginal opportunity cost.

- Trade allows people to use their comparative advantage and shift out society's production possibility curve.

- The rise of markets coincided with significant increases in output. Specialization, trade, and competition have all contributed to the increase.

- Points inside the production possibility curve are inefficient, points along the production possibility curve are efficient, and points outside are unattainable.

- By specializing in producing those goods for which one has a comparative advantage (lowest opportunity cost), one can produce the greatest amount of goods with which to trade. Doing so shifts the production possibility curve out.

- The typical outward bow of the production possibility curve is the result of comparative advantage and trade.

- There is no central world government. Governments enter voluntary agreements that perform the role of regulating international markets.

- Six roles of government are (1) to provide a stable set of institutions and rules, (2) to promote effective and workable competition, (3) to correct for externalities, (4) to ensure economic stability and growth, (5) to provide public goods, and (6) to adjust for undesired market results.

KEY TERMS

comparative advantage (25)
demerit good or activity (38)
efficiency (27)
externality (36)
free rider (37)
government failure (38)

inefficiency (27)
input (22)
laissez-faire (31)
macroeconomic externality (37)
market failure (38)
merit good or activity (38)

monopoly power (35)
output (21)
principle of increasing marginal opportunity cost (26)
private good (37)
production possibility curve (23)

production possibility table (21)
productive efficiency (27)
progressive tax (37)
proportional tax (37)
public good (37)
regressive tax (37)

QUESTIONS FOR THOUGHT AND REVIEW

1. Design a grade production possibility table and curve that embody the principle of increasing marginal opportunity cost.

2. What would the production possibility curve look like if there were decreasing marginal opportunity costs? Explain. What is an example of decreasing marginal opportunity costs?

3. Show how a production possibility curve would shift if a society became more productive in its output of widgets but less productive in its output of wadgets.

4. Show how a production possibility curve would shift if a society became more productive in the output of both widgets and wadgets.

5. How does the theory of comparative advantage relate to production possibility curves?

6. When all people use economic reasoning, inefficiency is impossible, because if the benefit of reducing that inefficiency were greater than the cost, the inefficiency would be eliminated. Thus, if people use economic reasoning, it's impossible to be on the interior of a production possibility curve. Is this statement true or false? Why?

7. How does the democratic political system lead politicians to emphasize points outside the production possibility curve?

8. If neither of two countries has a comparative advantage in either of two goods, what will their combined production possibility curve look like?

9. If neither of two countries has a comparative advantage in either of two goods, what are the gains from trade?

10. If income distribution is tied to a particular production technique, how might that change one's view of alternative production techniques?

11. Does the fact that the production possibilities model tells us that trade is good mean that in the real world free trade is necessarily the best policy? Explain.

12. What are the six roles of government listed in the text? Which do you believe is the most controversial? Why?

13. You've set up the rules for a game and started the game, but now realize that the rules are unfair. Should you change the rule?

14. Say the government establishes rights to pollute so that without a pollution permit you aren't allowed to emit pollutants into the air, water, or soil. Firms are allowed to buy and sell these rights. In what way will this correct for an externality?

PROBLEMS AND EXERCISES

1. A country has the following production possibility table:

Resources Devoted to Clothing	Output of Clothing	Resources Devoted to Food	Output of Food
100%	20	0%	0
80	16	20	5
60	12	40	9
40	8	60	12
20	4	80	14
0	0	100	15

   a. Draw the country's production possibility curve.
   b. What's happening to marginal opportunity costs as output of food increases?
   c. Say the country gets better at the production of food. What will happen to the production possibility curve?
   d. Say the country gets equally better at producing both food and clothing. What will happen to the production possibility curve?

2. Suppose the United States and Japan have the following production possibility tables:

Japan		United States	
Bolts of Cloth	Tons of Wheat	Bolts of Cloth	Tons of Wheat
1,000	0	500	0
800	100	400	200
600	200	300	400
400	300	200	600
200	400	100	800
0	500	0	1,000

   a. Draw each country's production possibility curve.
   b. In what good does the United States have a comparative advantage? Japan?
   c. Draw the joint possibility curve if the United States and Japan devote the same proportion of resources to the production of both goods and do not trade.

   d. Draw their joint production possibility curve if the countries take advantage of their comparative advantages and trade.

3. Assume the United States can produce Toyotas at the cost of $8,000 per car and Chevrolets at $6,000 per car. In Japan, Toyotas can be produced at 1,000,000 yen and Chevrolets at 500,000 yen.
   a. In terms of Chevrolets, what is the opportunity cost of producing Toyotas in each country?
   b. Who has the comparative advantage in producing Chevrolets?
   c. Assume Americans purchase 500,000 Chevrolets and 300,000 Toyotas each year. The Japanese purchase far fewer of each. Using productive efficiency as the guide, which country should most likely produce Chevrolets and which should produce Toyotas, assuming Chevrolets are going to be produced in one country and Toyotas in the other?

4. Lawns produce no crops but occupy more land (25 million acres) in the United States than any single crop, such as corn. This means that the United States is operating inefficiently and hence is at a point inside the production possibility curve. Right? If not, what does it mean?

5. Groucho Marx is reported to have said, "The secret of success is honesty and fair dealing. If you can fake those, you've got it made." What would likely happen to society's production possibility curve if everyone could fake honesty? Why? (Hint: Remember that society's production possibility curve reflects more than just technical relationships.)

6. Go to a store in your community.
   a. Ask what limitations the owners faced in starting their business.
   b. Were these limitations necessary?
   c. Should there have been more or fewer limitations?
   d. Under what heading of reasons for government intervention would you put each of the limitations?
   e. Ask what kinds of taxes the business pays and what benefits it believes it gets for those taxes.
   f. Is it satisfied with the existing situation? Why? What would it change?

7. Give an example of a merit good, a demerit good, a public good, and a good that involves an externality.
   a. How might individuals disagree about the government's role in intervening in the market for each of the goods you listed?
   b. Discuss the concepts of market failure and government failure in relation to the goods you listed.

WEB QUESTIONS

1. Select a foreign country and, using the CIA World Factbook (www.cia.gov/cia/publications/factbook), answer the following questions:
   a. What goods does the country produce? Purchase from another country?
   b. In what goods does it have a comparative advantage? Explain your answer.
   c. Name one of its trading partners. Why do you think that country is a trading partner?

2. Go to www.libertarian.org to read about libertarians and to answer the following questions:
   a. Click "Intro." What is a libertarian's defining belief?
   b. Click "Policy." Take the world's smallest quiz and report your score. Do you agree with the result?
   c. Continue with "Policy." What are libertarians' main objections to government regulation?

ANSWERS TO MARGIN QUESTIONS

1. You must give up 2 units of good Y to produce 4 units of good X, so the opportunity cost of X is ½ Y. (22)

2. If no resource had a comparative advantage, the production possibility curve would be a straight line connecting the points of maximum production of each product as in the graph below.

At all points along this curve, the opportunity cost of producing guns and butter is equal. (25)

3. Points A and C are along the production possibility curve, so they are points of efficiency. Point B is inside the production possibility curve, so it is a point of inefficiency. Point D is to the right of the production possibility curve, so it is unattainable. (27)

4. I remind them of the importance of cultural forces. In Saudi Arabia women are not allowed to drive. (28)

5. The production possibility curve shifts in along the butter axis as in the graph below. (28)

6. The argument that underlies the general laissez-faire policy argument is that when there is competition in trade, individuals are able to pick the best trades available to them and the end result is that both parties to the trade benefit as much as they possibly can. (31)

7. If Steve and Sarah devote the same resources to baking each good and do not trade, the combined production possibility is the orange line in the graph on the following page. Their combined production possibility curve is shown in blue. The production possibility curve with specialization and trade is farther to the right than the one without trade. Steve and Sarah can each end up with more bread and cookies if they take advantage of their

comparative advantages and trade than if they work on their own. *(32)*

8. False. By producing the good for which it has a comparative advantage (lowest opportunity cost) a country will have the greatest amount of goods with which to trade and will reap the greatest gains from trade. *(32)*

9. False. Governments are needed for effective markets to function. At a minimum, they must provide the rules and the institutional structure within which the market operates. *(34)*

10. Not necessarily. The existence of an externality creates the possibility that government intervention might help. But there are also government failures in which the government intervenes and makes things worse. *(38)*

APPENDIX A

Graphish: The Language of Graphs

A picture is worth 1,000 words. Economists, being efficient, like to present ideas in **graphs,** *pictures of points in a coordinate system in which points denote relationships between numbers.* But a graph is worth 1,000 words only if the person looking at the graph knows the graphical language: *Graphish,* we'll call it. (It's a bit like English.) Graphish is usually written on graph paper. If the person doesn't know Graphish, the picture isn't worth any words and Graphish can be babble.

I have enormous sympathy for students who don't understand Graphish. A number of my students get thrown for a loop by graphs. They understand the idea, but Graphish confuses them. This appendix is for them, and for those of you like them. It's a primer in Graphish.

TWO WAYS TO USE GRAPHS

In this book I use graphs in two ways:

1. To present an economic model or theory visually, to show how two variables interrelate.
2. To present real-world data visually. To do this, I use primarily bar charts, line charts, and pie charts.

Actually, these two ways of using graphs are related. They are both ways of presenting visually the *relationship* between two things.

Graphs are built around a number line, or axis, like the one in Figure A2-1(a). The numbers are generally placed in order, equal distances from one another. That number line allows us to represent a number at an appropriate point on the line. For example, point A represents the number 4.

The number line in Figure A2-1(a) is drawn horizontally, but it doesn't have to be; it can also be drawn vertically, as in Figure A2-1(b).

How we divide our axes, or number lines, into intervals is up to us. In Figure A2-1(a), I called each interval 1; in Figure A2-1(b), I called each interval 10. Point A appears after 4 intervals of 1 (starting at 0 and reading from left to right), so it represents 4. In Figure A2-1(b), where each interval represents 10, to represent 5, I place point B halfway in the interval between 0 and 10.

So far, so good. Graphish developed when a vertical and a horizontal number line were combined, as in Figure A2-1(c). When the horizontal and vertical number lines are put together, they're called *axes*. (Each line is an axis. *Axes* is the plural of *axis*.) I now have a **coordinate system**—*a two-dimensional space in which one point represents two numbers.* For example, point A in Figure A2-1(c) represents the numbers (4, 5)—4 on the horizontal number line and 5 on the vertical number line. Point B represents the numbers (1, 20). (By convention, the horizontal numbers are written first.)

Being able to represent two numbers with one point is neat because it allows the relationships between two numbers to be presented visually instead of having to be expressed verbally, which is often cumbersome. For example, say the cost of producing 6 units of something is $4 per unit and the cost of producing 10 units is $3 per unit. By

Figure A2-1 (a, b, and c)   Horizontal and Vertical Number Lines and a Coordinate System

(a) Horizontal number line   **(b) Vertical number line**   **(c) Coordinate system**

putting both these points on a graph, we can visually see that producing 10 costs less per unit than does producing 6.

Another way to use graphs to present real-world data visually is to use the horizontal line to represent time. Say that we let each horizontal interval equal a year, and each vertical interval equal $100 in income. By graphing your income each year, you can obtain a visual representation of how your income has changed over time.

USING GRAPHS IN ECONOMIC MODELING

I use graphs throughout the book as I present economic models, or simplifications of reality. A few terms are often used in describing these graphs, and we'll now go over them. Consider Figure A2-2(a), which lists the number of pens bought per day (column 2) at various prices (column 1).

We can present the table's information in a graph by combining the pairs of numbers in the two columns of the table and representing, or plotting, them on two axes. I do that in Figure A2-2(b).

By convention, when graphing a relationship between price and quantity, economists place price on the vertical axis and quantity on the horizontal axis.

I can now connect the points, producing a line like the one in Figure A2-2(c). With this line, I interpolate the numbers between the points (which makes for a nice visual presentation). That is, I make the **interpolation assumption**—*the assumption that the relationship between variables is the same between points as it is at the points.* The interpolation assumption allows us to think of a line as a collection of points and therefore to connect the points into a line.

Even though the line in Figure A2-2(c) is straight, economists call any such line drawn on a graph a *curve.*

Because it's straight the curve in A2-2(c) is called a **linear curve**—*a curve that is drawn as a straight line.* Notice that this curve starts high on the left-hand side and goes down to the right. Economists say that any curve that looks like that is *downward-sloping.* They also say that a downward-sloping curve represents an **inverse relationship**—*a relationship between two variables in which when one goes up, the other goes down.* In this example, the line demonstrates an inverse relationship between price and quantity—that is, when the price of pens goes up, the quantity bought goes down.

Figure A2-2(d) presents a **nonlinear curve**—*a curve that is drawn as a curved line.* This curve, which really is curved, starts low on the left-hand side and goes up to the right. Economists say any curve that goes up to the right is *upward-sloping.* An upward-sloping curve represents a **direct relationship**—*a relationship in which when one variable goes up, the other goes up too.* The direct relationship I'm talking about here is the one between the two variables (what's measured on the horizontal and vertical lines). *Downward-sloping* and *upward-sloping* are terms you need to memorize if you want to read, write, and speak Graphish, keeping graphically in your mind the image of the relationships they represent.

SLOPE

One can, of course, be far more explicit about how much the curve is sloping upward or downward by defining it in terms of **slope**—*the change in the value on the vertical axis divided by the change in the value on the horizontal axis.* Sometimes the slope is presented as "rise over run":

$$\text{Slope} = \frac{\text{Rise}}{\text{Run}} = \frac{\text{Change in value on vertical axis}}{\text{Change in value on horizontal axis}}$$

Figure A2-2 (a, b, c, and d) A Table and Graphs Showing the Relationships between Price and Quantity

	Price per Pen	Quantity of Pens Bought per Day
A	$3.00	4
B	2.50	5
C	2.00	6
D	1.50	7
E	1.00	8

(a) Price quantity table

(b) From a table to a graph (1)

(c) From a table to a graph (2)

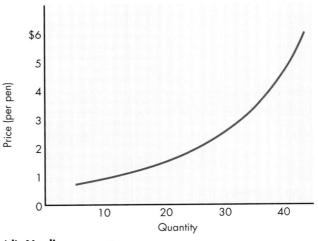

(d) Nonlinear curve

SLOPES OF LINEAR CURVES

In Figure A2-3, I present five linear curves and measure their slope. Let's go through an example to show how we can measure slope. To do so, we must pick two points. Let's use points A (6, 8) and B (7, 4) on curve a. Looking at these points, we see that as we move from 6 to 7 on the horizontal axis, we move from 8 to 4 on the vertical axis. So when the number on the vertical axis falls by 4, the number on the horizontal axis increases by 1. That means the slope is −4 divided by 1, or −4.

Notice that the inverse relationships represented by the two downward-sloping curves, a and b, have negative slopes, and that the direct relationships represented by the two upward-sloping curves, c and d, have positive slopes. Notice also that the flatter the curve, the smaller the

numerical value of the slope; and the more vertical, or steeper, the curve, the larger the numerical value of the slope. There are two extreme cases:

1. When the curve is horizontal (flat), the slope is zero.

2. When the curve is vertical (straight up and down), the slope is infinite (larger than large).

Knowing the term *slope* and how it's measured lets us describe verbally the pictures we see visually. For example, if I say a curve has a slope of zero, you should picture in your mind a flat line; if I say "a curve with a slope of minus one," you should picture a falling line that makes a 45° angle with the horizontal and vertical axes. (It's the hypotenuse of an isosceles right triangle with the axes as the other two sides.)

Figure A2-3 Slopes of Curves
The slope of a curve is determined by rise over run. The slope of curve *a* is shown in the graph. The rest are shown below:

	Rise	÷	Run	=	Slope
b	−1		+2		−.5
c	1		1		1
d	4		1		4
e	1		1		1

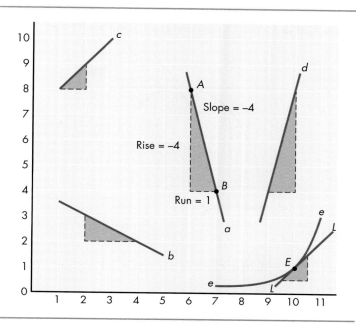

INVERSE AND DIRECT RELATIONSHIPS

Knowing the Tools

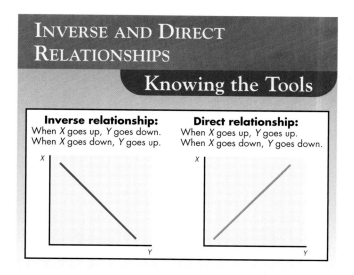

Inverse relationship:
When X goes up, Y goes down.
When X goes down, Y goes up.

Direct relationship:
When X goes up, Y goes up.
When X goes down, Y goes down.

SLOPES OF NONLINEAR CURVES

The preceding examples were of *linear (straight) curves.* With *nonlinear curves*—the ones that really do curve—the slope of the curve is constantly changing. As a result, we must talk about the slope of the curve at a particular point, rather than the slope of the whole curve. How can a point have a slope? Well, it can't really, but it can almost, and if

that's good enough for mathematicians, it's good enough for us.

Defining the slope of a nonlinear curve is a bit more difficult. The slope at a given point on a nonlinear curve is determined by the slope of a linear (or straight) line that's tangent to that curve. (A line that's tangent to a curve is a line that just touches the curve, and touches it only at one point in the immediate vicinity of the given point.) In Figure A2-3, the line *LL* is tangent to the curve *ee* at point *E*. The slope of that line, and hence the slope of the curve at the one point where the line touches the curve, is +1.

MAXIMUM AND MINIMUM POINTS

Two points on a nonlinear curve deserve special mention. These points are the ones for which the slope of the curve is zero. I demonstrate those in Figure A2-4(a) and (b). At point A we're at the top of the curve, so it's at a maximum point; at point B we're at the bottom of the curve, so it's at a minimum point. These maximum and minimum points are often referred to by economists, and it's important to realize that the value of the slope of the curve at each of these points is zero.

There are, of course, many other types of curves, and much more can be said about the curves I've talked about. I won't do so because, for purposes of this course, we won't need to get into those refinements. I've presented as much Graphish as you need to know for this book.

Figure A2-4 (a and b)   A Maximum and a Minimum Point

(a) Maximum point

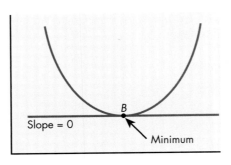

(b) Minimum point

Figure A2-5   A Shifting Curve versus a Movement along a Curve

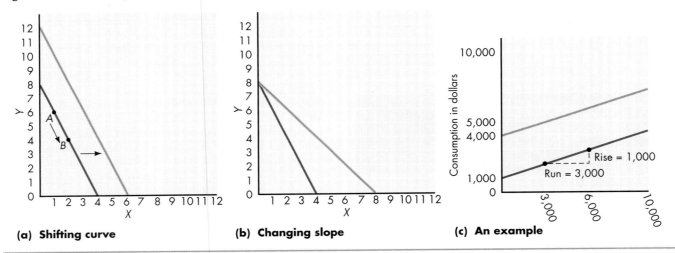

(a) Shifting curve

(b) Changing slope

(c) An example

EQUATIONS AND GRAPHS

Sometimes economists depict the relationships shown in graphs using equations. Since I present material algebraically in the appendixes to a few chapters, let me briefly discuss how to translate a linear curve into an equation. Linear curves are relatively easy to translate because all linear curves follow a particular mathematical form: $y = mx + b$, where y is the variable on the vertical axis, x is the variable on the horizontal axis, m is the slope of the line, and b is the vertical-axis intercept. To write the equation of a curve, look at that curve, plug in the values for the slope and vertical-axis intercept, and you've got the equation.

For example, consider the blue curve in Figure A2-5(a). The slope (rise over run) is -2 and the number where the curve intercepts the vertical axis is 8, so the equation that depicts this curve is $y = -2x + 8$. It's best to choose variables that correspond to what you're measuring on each axis, so if price is on the vertical axis and quantity is on the horizontal axis, the equation would be $p = -2q + 8$. This equation is true for any point along this line. Take point A $(1, 6)$, for example. Substituting 1 for x and 6 for y into the equation, you see that $6 = -2(1) + 8$, or $6 = 6$. At point B, the equation is still true: $4 = -2(2) + 8$. A move from point A to point B is called a *movement along a curve*. A movement along a curve does not change the relationship of the variables; rather, it shows how a change in one variable affects the other.

Sometimes the relationship between variables will change. The curve will either shift, change slope, or both shift and change slope. These changes are reflected in changes to the m and b variables in the equation. Suppose the vertical-axis intercept rises from 8 to 12, while the

Figure A2-6 (a, b, and c)   Presenting Information Visually

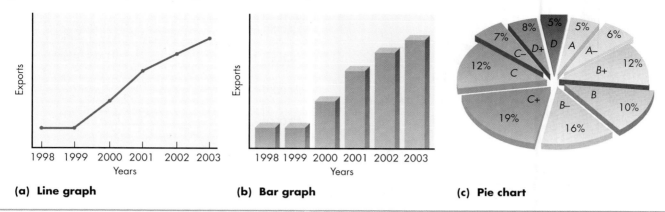

(a) Line graph   **(b) Bar graph**   **(c) Pie chart**

slope remains the same. The equation becomes $y = -2x + 12$; for every value of y, x has increased by 4. Plotting the new equation, we can see that the curve has *shifted* to the right, as shown by the orange line in Figure A2-5(a). If instead the slope changes from -2 to -1, while the vertical-axis intercept remains at 8, the equation becomes $y = -x + 8$. Figure A2-5(b) shows this change graphically. The original blue line stays anchored at 8 and rotates out along the horizontal axis to the new orange line.

Here's an example for you to try. The lines in Figure A2-5(c) show two relationships between consumption and income. Write the equation for the blue line.

The answer is $C = \frac{1}{3}Y + \$1,000$. Remember to write the equation you need to know two things: the vertical-axis intercept ($1,000) and the slope (⅓). If the intercept changes to $4,000, the curve will shift up to the orange line as shown.

PRESENTING REAL-WORLD DATA IN GRAPHS

The previous discussion treated the Graphish terms that economists use in presenting models which focus on hypothetical relationships. Economists also use graphs in presenting actual economic data. Say, for example, that you want to show how exports have changed over time. Then you would place years on the horizontal axis (by convention) and exports on the vertical axis, as in Figure A2-6(a) and (b). Having done so, you have a couple of choices: you can draw a **line graph**—*a graph where the data are connected by a continuous line*; or you can make a **bar graph**—*a graph where the area under each point is filled in to look like a bar*. Figure A2-6(a) shows a line graph and Figure A2-6(b) shows a bar graph.

Another type of graph is a **pie chart**—*a circle divided into "pie pieces," where the undivided pie represents the total amount and the pie pieces reflect the percentage of the whole pie that the various components make up*. This type of graph is useful in visually presenting how a total amount is divided. Figure A2-6(c) shows a pie chart, which happens to represent the division of grades on a test I gave. Notice that 5 percent of the students got As.

There are other types of graphs, but they're all variations on line and bar graphs and pie charts. Once you understand these three basic types of graphs, you shouldn't have any trouble understanding the other types.

INTERPRETING GRAPHS ABOUT THE REAL WORLD

Understanding Graphish is important because, if you don't, you can easily misinterpret the meaning of graphs. For example, consider the two graphs in Figure A2-7(a) and (b). Which graph demonstrates the larger rise in income? If you said (a), you're wrong. The intervals in the vertical axes differ, and if you look carefully you'll see that the curves in both graphs represent the same combination of points. So when considering graphs, always make sure you understand the markings on the axes. Only then can you interpret the graph.

QUANTITATIVE LITERACY: AVOIDING STUPID MATH MISTAKES

The data of economics are often presented in graphs and tables. Numerical data are compared by the use of percentages, visual comparisons, and simple relationships based on quantitative differences. Economists who have

Figure A2-7 (a and b)   The Importance of Scales

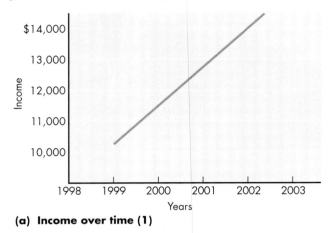

(a) Income over time (1)

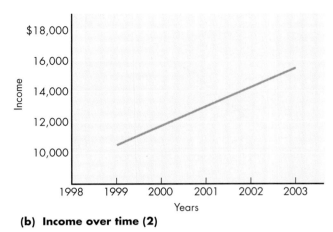

(b) Income over time (2)

studied the learning process of their students have found that some very bright students have some trouble with these presentations. Students sometimes mix up percentage changes with level changes, draw incorrect implications from visual comparisons, and calculate quantitative differences incorrectly. This is not necessarily a math problem—at least in the sense that most economists think of math. The mistakes are in relatively simple stuff—the kind of stuff learned in fifth, sixth, and seventh grades. Specifically, as reported in "Student Quantitative Literacy: Is the Glass Half-full or Half-empty?" (Robert Burns, Kim Marie McGoldrick, Jerry L. Petr, and Peter Schuhmann, 2002 University of North Carolina at Wilmington Working Paper) when the professors gave a test to students at a variety of schools, they found that a majority of students missed the following questions.

1. What is 25 percent of 400?
   a. 25   b. 50   c. 100
   d. 400   e. none of the above

2. Consider Figure A2-8 where U.S oil consumption and U.S. oil imports are plotted for 1990–2000. Fill in the blanks to construct a true statement: U.S. domestic oil consumption has been steady while imports have been _____; therefore U.S. domestic oil production has been _____.
   a. rising; rising   b. falling; falling
   c. rising; falling   d. falling; rising

3. Refer to the following table to select the true statement.

Figure A2-8

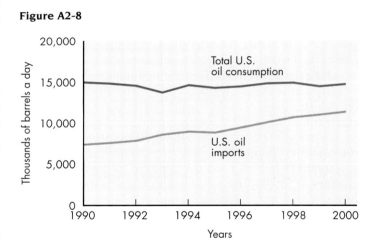

Economic Growth in Poland

Percent Increase in GDP, 1990–1994				
1990	1991	1992	1993	1994
−11.7	−7.8	−1.5	4.0	3.5

a. GDP in Poland was larger in 1992 than in 1991.
b. GDP in Poland was larger in 1994 than in 1993.
c. GDP in Poland was larger in 1991 than in 1992.
d. GDP in Poland was larger in 1993 than in 1994.
e. Both b and c are true.

4. If U.S. production of corn was 60 million bushels in 2002 and 100 million bushels in 2003, what was the percentage change in corn production from 2002 to 2003?
a. 40   b. 60   c. 66.67
d. 100   e. 200

The reason students got these questions wrong is unknown. Many of them had had higher-level math courses, including calculus, so it is not that they weren't trained in math. I suspect that many students missed the questions because of carelessness: the students didn't think about the question carefully before they wrote down the answer.

Throughout this book we will be discussing issues assuming a quantitative literacy sufficient to answer these questions. Moreover, questions using similar reasoning will be on exams. So it is useful for you to see whether or not you fall in the majority. So please answer the four questions given above now if you haven't done so already.

Now that you've answered them, I give you the correct answers upside-down in the footnote at the bottom of the page.[1]

If you got all four questions right, great! You can stop reading this appendix now. If you missed one or more, read the explanations of the correct answers carefully.

1. The correct answer is c. To calculate a percentage, you multiply the percentage times the number. Thus 25 percent of 400 is 100.

2. The correct answer is c. To answer it you had to recognize that U.S. consumption of oil comes from U.S. imports and U.S. production. Thus, the distance between the two lines represents U.S. production, which is clearly getting smaller from 1990 to 2000.

3. The correct answer is e. The numbers given to you are percentage changes, and the question is about levels. If the percentage change is positive, as it is in 1993 and 1994, the level is increasing. If the percentage change is negative, as it is in 1992, the level is falling. Thus 1994 is greater (by 3.5 percent) than 1993, even though the percentage change is smaller than in 1993. Because income fell in 1992, the level of income in 1991 is greater than the level of income in 1992.

4. The correct answer is c. To calculate percentage change, you first need to calculate the change, which in this case is 100− 60 or 40. So corn production started at a base of 60 and rose by 40.

To calculate the percentage change that this represents you divide the amount of the rise, 40, by the base, 60. Doing so gives us 40/60 = 2/3 = .6667, which is 66.67 percent.

Now that I've given you the answers I suspect that most of you will recognize that they are the right answers. If, after reading the explanations, you still don't follow the reasoning, you should look into getting some extra help in the course either from your teacher, your TA, or from some program the college has. If, after reading the explanations, you follow them and believe that if you had really thought about them you would have gotten them right, then the next time you see a chart or a table of numbers being compared *really think about them*. Be a bit slower in drawing inferences since they are the building blocks of economics discussions. If you want to do well on exams it probably makes sense to practice some similar questions to make sure that you have concepts down.

A REVIEW

Let's now review what we've covered.

- A graph is a picture of points on a coordinate system in which the points denote relationships between numbers.
- A downward-sloping line represents an inverse relationship or a negative slope.
- An upward-sloping line represents a direct relationship or a positive slope.
- Slope is measured by rise over run, or a change of y (the number measured on the vertical axis) over a change in x (the number measured on the horizontal axis).
- The slope of a point on a nonlinear curve is measured by the rise over run of a line tangent to that point.
- At the maximum and minimum points of a nonlinear curve, the value of the slope is zero.
- A linear curve has the form $y = mx + b$.
- A shift in a linear curve is reflected by a change in the b variable in the equation $y = mx + b$.
- A change in the slope of a linear curve is reflected by a change in the m variable in the equation $y = mx + b$.
- In reading graphs, one must be careful to understand what's being measured on the vertical and horizontal axes.

KEY TERMS

bar graph *(49)*   graphs *(44)*   inverse relationship *(45)*   nonlinear curve *(45)*
coordinate system *(44)*   interpolation   line graph *(49)*   pie chart *(49)*
direct relationship *(45)*   assumption *(45)*   linear curve *(45)*   slope *(45)*

QUESTIONS FOR THOUGHT AND REVIEW

1. Create a coordinate space on graph paper and label the following points:
   a. $(0, 5)$ c. $(2, -3)$
   b. $(-5, -5)$ d. $(-1, 1)$

2. Graph the following costs per unit, and answer the questions that follow.

Horizontal Axis: Output	Vertical Axis: Cost per Unit
1	$30
2	20
3	12
4	6
5	2
6	6
7	12
8	20
9	30

   a. Is the relationship between cost per unit and output linear or nonlinear? Why?
   b. In what range in output is the relationship inverse? In what range in output is the relationship direct?
   c. In what range in output is the slope negative? In what range in output is the slope positive?
   d. What is the slope between 1 and 2 units?

3. Within a coordinate space, draw a line with:
   a. Zero slope.   c. Positive slope.
   b. Infinite slope.   d. Negative slope.

4. Calculate the slope of lines *a* to *e* in the following coordinate system.

   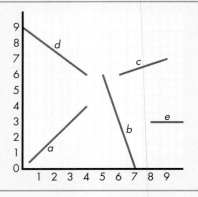

5. Given the following nonlinear curve, answer the following questions:

   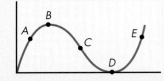

   a. At what point(s) is the slope negative?
   b. At what point(s) is the slope positive?
   c. At what point(s) is the slope zero?
   d. What point is the maximum? What point is the minimum?

6. Draw the graphs that correspond to the following equations:
   a. $y = 3x - 8$
   b. $y = 12 - x$
   c. $y = 4x + 2$

7. Using the equation $y = 3x + 1,000$, demonstrate the following:
   a. The slope of the curve changes to 5.
   b. The curve shifts up by 500.

8. State what type of graph or chart you might use to show the following real-world data:
   a. Interest rates from 1929 to 2003.
   b. Median income levels of various ethnic groups in the United States.
   c. Total federal expenditures by selected categories.
   d. Total costs of producing between 100 and 800 shoes.

SUPPLY AND DEMAND

4

Teach a parrot the terms *supply* and *demand*
and you've got an economist.

—*Thomas Carlyle*

Supply and demand. Supply and demand. Roll the phrase around in your mouth, savor it like a good wine. *Supply* and *demand* are the most-used words in economics. And for good reason. They provide a good off-the-cuff answer for any economic question. Try it.

Why are bacon and oranges so expensive this winter? *Supply and demand.*

Why are interest rates falling? *Supply and demand.*

Why can't I find decent wool socks anymore? *Supply and demand.*

The importance of the interplay of supply and demand makes it only natural that, early in any economics course, you must learn about supply and demand. Let's start with demand.

DEMAND

People want lots of things; they "demand" much less than they want because demand means a willingness and ability to pay. Unless you are willing and able to pay for it you may *want* it, but you don't *demand* it. For example, I want to own a Maserati. But, I must admit, I'm not willing to do what's necessary to own one. If I really wanted one, I'd mortgage everything I own, increase my income by doubling the number of hours I work, not buy anything else, and get that car. But I don't do any of those things, so at the going price, $240,000, I do not demand a Maserati. Sure, I'd buy one if it cost $10,000, but from my actions it's clear that, at $240,000, I don't demand it. This points to an important aspect of demand: The quantity you demand at a low price differs from the quantity you demand at a high price. Specifically, the quantity you demand varies inversely—in the opposite direction—with price.

Prices are the tool by which the market coordinates individuals' desires and limits how much people are willing to buy—how much they demand. When goods become scarce, the market reduces the quantity of those scarce goods people demand; as their prices go up, people buy fewer goods. As goods become abundant, their prices go down, and people want more of them. The invisible hand—the price mechanism—sees to it that what people demand (do what's

After reading this chapter, you should be able to:

- State the law of demand and draw a demand curve from a demand table.

- Explain the importance of substitution to the laws of supply and demand.

- Distinguish a shift in demand from a movement along the demand curve.

- State the law of supply and draw a supply curve from a supply table.

- Distinguish a shift in supply from a movement along the supply curve.

- Explain how the law of demand and the law of supply interact to bring about equilibrium.

- Show the effect of a shift in demand and supply on equilibrium price and quantity.

- State the limitations of demand and supply analysis.

necessary to get) matches what's available. In doing so, the invisible hand coordinates individuals' demands.

THE LAW OF DEMAND

The law of demand states that the quantity of a good demanded is inversely related to the good's price.

When price goes up, quantity demanded goes down. When price goes down, quantity demanded goes up.

The ideas expressed above are the foundation of the **law of demand:**

> *Quantity demanded rises as price falls, other things constant.*

Or alternatively:

> *Quantity demanded falls as price rises, other things constant.*

This law is fundamental to the invisible hand's ability to coordinate individuals' desires: as prices change, people change how much of a particular good they're willing to buy.

What accounts for the law of demand? Individuals' tendency to substitute other goods for goods whose relative price has gone up. If the price of music downloads from the Internet rises but the price of CDs stays the same, you're more likely to buy that new Sheryl Crow recording on CD than to download it from the Internet.

To see that the law of demand makes intuitive sense, just think of something you'd really like but can't afford. If the price is cut in half, you—and other consumers—become more likely to buy it. Quantity demanded goes up as price goes down.

Just to be sure you've got it, let's consider a real-world example: demand for vanity—specifically, vanity license plates. When the North Carolina state legislature increased the vanity plates' price from $30 to $40, the quantity demanded fell from 60,334 at $30 a year to 31,122 at $40 a year. Assuming other things remained constant, that is the law of demand in action.

Web Note 4.1
Markets without Money

THE DEMAND CURVE

A **demand curve** is *the graphic representation of the relationship between price and quantity demanded.* Figure 4-1 shows a demand curve.

As you can see, in graphical terms, the law of demand states that as the price goes up, the quantity demanded goes down, other things constant. An alternative way of saying the same thing is that price and quantity demanded are inversely related, so the demand curve slopes downward to the right.

Q-1 Why does the demand curve slope downward?

Notice that in stating the law of demand, I put in the qualification "other things constant." That's three extra words, and unless they were important I wouldn't have put them in. But what does "other things constant" mean? Say that over a period of two years, both the price of cars and the number of cars purchased rise. That seems to

"Other things constant" places a limitation on the application of the law of demand.

Figure 4-1   A Sample Demand Curve
The law of demand states that the quantity demanded of a good is inversely related to the price of that good, other things constant. As the price of a good goes up, the quantity demanded goes down, so the demand curve is downward-sloping.

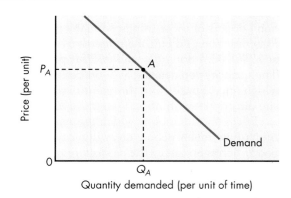

violate the law of demand, since the number of cars purchased should have fallen in response to the rise in price. Looking at the data more closely, however, we see that a third factor has also changed: Individuals' income has increased. As income increases, people buy more cars, increasing the demand for cars.

The increase in price works as the law of demand states—it decreases the number of cars bought. But in this case, income doesn't remain constant; it increases. That rise in income increases the demand for cars. That increase in demand outweighs the decrease in quantity demanded that results from a rise in price, so ultimately more cars are sold. If you want to study the effect of price alone—which is what the law of demand refers to—you must make adjustments to hold income constant. That's why the qualifying phrase "other things constant" is an important part of the law of demand.

The other things that are held constant include individuals' tastes, prices of other goods, and even the weather. Those other factors must remain constant if you're to make a valid study of the effect of an increase in the price of a good on the quantity demanded. In practice, it's impossible to keep all other things constant, so you have to be careful when you say that when price goes up, quantity demanded goes down. It's likely to go down, but it's always possible that something besides price has changed.

SHIFTS IN DEMAND VERSUS MOVEMENTS ALONG A DEMAND CURVE

To distinguish between the effects of price and the effects of other factors on how much of a good is demanded, economists have developed the following precise terminology—terminology that inevitably shows up on exams. The first distinction to make is between demand and quantity demanded.

- **Demand** refers to *a schedule of quantities of a good that will be bought per unit of time at various prices, other things constant.*
- **Quantity demanded** refers to *a specific amount that will be demanded per unit of time at a specific price, other things constant.*

In graphical terms, the term *demand* refers to the entire demand curve. Demand tells how much of a good will be bought *at various prices. Quantity demanded* tells how much of a good will be bought at a specific price; it refers to a point on a demand curve, such as point A in Figure 4-1. This terminology allows us to distinguish between *changes in quantity demanded* and *shifts in demand.* A change in the quantity demanded refers to the effect of a price change on the quantity demanded. It refers to a **movement along a demand curve**—*the graphical representation of the effect of a change in price on the quantity demanded.* A **shift in demand** refers to *the effect of anything other than price on demand.*

SHIFT FACTORS OF DEMAND

Shift factors of demand are factors that cause shifts in the demand curve. A change in anything that affects demand besides price causes a shift of the entire demand curve.

Important shift factors of demand include:

1. Society's income.
2. The prices of other goods.
3. Tastes.
4. Expectations.
5. Taxes on and subsidies to consumers.

Income From our example above of "the other things constant" qualification, we saw that a rise in income increases the demand for goods. For most goods this is true. As

Q-2 The uncertainty caused by the terrorist attacks of September 11, 2001, made consumers reluctant to spend on luxury items. This reduced _____. Should the missing words be *demand for luxury goods* or *quantity of luxury goods demanded?*

individuals' income rises, they can afford more of the goods they want, such as steaks, computers, or clothing. These are normal goods. For other goods, called inferior goods, an increase in income reduces demand. An example is urban mass transit. A person whose income has risen tends to stop riding the bus to work because she can afford to buy a car and rent a parking space.

Price of Other Goods   Because people make their buying decisions based on the price of related goods, demand will be affected by the prices of other goods. Suppose the price of jeans rose from $25 to $35, but the price of khakis remained at $25. Next time you need pants, you're apt to try khakis instead of jeans. They are substitutes. When the price of a substitute declines, demand for the good whose price has remained the same will fall. Or consider another example. Suppose the price of movie tickets falls. What will happen to the demand for popcorn? You're likely to increase the number of times you go to the movies, so you'll also likely increase the amount of popcorn you purchase. The lower cost of a movie ticket increases the demand for popcorn because popcorn and movies are complements. When the price of a good declines, the demand for its complement rises.

Tastes   An old saying goes: "There's no accounting for taste." Of course, many advertisers believe otherwise. Changes in taste can affect the demand for a good without a change in price. As you become older, you may find that your taste for rock concerts has changed to a taste for an evening at the opera or local philharmonic.

Expectations   Finally, expectations will also affect demand. Expectations can cover a lot. If you expect your income to rise in the future, you're bound to start spending some of it today. If you expect the price of computers to fall soon, you may put off buying one until later.

Taxes and Subsidies   Taxes levied on consumers increase the cost of goods to consumers and therefore reduce demand for those goods. Subsidies to consumers have the opposite effect. When states host tax-free weeks during August's back-to-school shopping season, consumers load up on products to avoid sales taxes. Demand for retail goods rises during the tax holiday.

These aren't the only shift factors. In fact anything—except the price of the good itself—that affects demand (and many things do) is a shift factor. While economists agree these shift factors are important, they believe that no shift factor influences how much is demanded as consistently as does price of the specific item. That's what makes economists focus first on price as they try to understand the world. That's why economists make the law of demand central to their analysis.

To make sure you understand the difference between a movement along a demand curve and a shift in demand, let's consider an example. Singapore has one of the world's highest number of cars per mile of road. This means that congestion is considerable. Singapore adopted two policies to reduce road use: It increased the fee charged to use roads, and it provided an expanded public transportation system. Both policies reduced congestion. Figure 4-2(a) shows that increasing the toll charged to use roads from $1 to $2 per 50 miles of road reduces quantity demanded from 200 to 100 cars per mile every hour (a movement along the demand curve). Figure 4-2(b) shows that providing alternative methods of transportation such as buses and subways shifts the demand curve for roads. Demand for road use shifts in to the left so that at every price, demand drops by 100 cars per mile every hour (the demand curve shifts to the left).

Q-3   Explain the effect of each of the following on the demand for new computers:

1. The price of computers falls by 30 percent.

2. Total income in the economy rises.

Change in price causes a movement along a demand curve; a change in a shift factor causes a shift in demand.

Figure 4-2   Shift in Demand versus a Change in Quantity Demanded

A rise in a good's price results in a reduction in quantity demanded and is shown by a movement up along a demand curve from point A to point B in (**a**). A change in any other factor besides price that affects demand leads to a shift in the entire demand curve, as shown in (**b**).

(a) Movement along a demand curve   **(b) Shift in demand**

A REVIEW

Let's test your understanding by having you specify what happens to your demand curve for videocassettes in the following examples: First, let's say you buy a DVD player. Next, let's say that the price of videocassettes falls; and finally, say that you won $1 million in a lottery. What happens to the demand for videocassettes in each case? If you answered: It shifts in to the left; it remains unchanged; and it shifts out to the right—you've got it.

THE DEMAND TABLE

As I emphasized in Chapter 2, introductory economics depends heavily on graphs and graphical analysis—translating ideas into graphs and back into words. So let's graph the demand curve.

Figure 4-3(a), a demand table, describes Alice's demand for renting DVDs. For example, at a price of $2 Alice will rent (buy the use of) 6 DVDs per week, and at a price of 50 cents she will rent 9.

There are four points about the relationship between the number of DVDs Alice rents and the price of renting them that are worth mentioning. First, the relationship follows the law of demand: As the rental price rises, quantity demanded decreases. Second, quantity demanded has a specific *time dimension* to it. In this example demand refers to the number of DVD rentals per week. Without the time dimension, the table wouldn't provide us with any useful information. Nine DVD rentals per year is quite a different concept from 9 DVD rentals per week. Third, Alice's DVD rentals are interchangeable—the 9th DVD rental doesn't significantly differ from the 1st, 3rd, or any other DVD rental. The fourth point is already familiar to you: The schedule assumes that everything else is held constant.

**Figure 4-3 (a and b)   From a Demand Table to a
                          Demand Curve**

The demand table in (a) is translated into a demand curve in
(b). Each combination of price and quantity in the table
corresponds to a point on the curve. For example, point A on
the graph represents row A in the table: Alice demands 9 DVD
rentals at a price of 50 cents. A demand curve is constructed by
plotting all points from the demand table and connecting the
points by a line.

	Price per DVD	DVD rentals demanded per week
A	$0.50	9
B	1.00	8
C	2.00	6
D	3.00	4
E	4.00	2

(a) A demand table

(b) A demand curve

FROM A DEMAND TABLE TO A DEMAND CURVE

Figure 4-3(b) translates the demand table in Figure 4-3(a) into a graph. Point A (quantity = 9, price = $.50) is graphed first at the (9, $.50) coordinates. Next we plot points B, C, D, and E in the same manner and connect the resulting dots with a solid line. The result is the demand curve, which graphically conveys the same information that's in the demand table. Notice that the demand curve is downward sloping (from left to right), indicating that the law of demand holds in the example.

> The demand curve represents the maximum price that an individual will pay.

The demand curve represents the *maximum price* that an individual will pay for various quantities of a good; the individual will happily pay less. For example, say someone offers Alice 6 DVD rentals at a price of $1 each (point F of Figure 4-3(b)). Will she accept? Sure; she'll pay any price within the shaded area to the left of the demand curve. But if someone offers her 6 rentals at $3.50 each (point G), she won't accept. At a rental price of $3.50 apiece, she's willing to rent only 3 DVDs.

INDIVIDUAL AND MARKET DEMAND CURVES

Normally, economists talk about market demand curves rather than individual demand curves. A **market demand curve** is *the horizontal sum of all individual demand curves*. Market demand curves are what most firms are interested in. Firms don't care whether individual A or individual B buys their goods; they only care that *someone* buys their goods.

It's a good graphical exercise to add individual demand curves together to create a market demand curve. I do that in Figure 4-4. In it I assume that the market consists of three buyers, Alice, Bruce, and Carmen, whose demand tables are given in Figure 4-4(a). Alice and Bruce have demand tables similar to the demand tables discussed previously. At a price of $3 each, Alice rents 4 DVDs; at a price of $2, she rents 6. Carmen is an all or nothing individual. She rents 1 DVD as long as the price is equal to or below $1; otherwise she rents nothing. If you plot Carmen's demand curve, it's a vertical line. However, the law of demand still holds: As price increases, quantity demanded decreases.

Q-4 Derive a market demand curve from the following two individual demand curves:

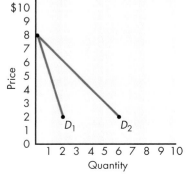

Figure 4-4 (a and b)   From Individual Demands to a Market Demand Curve

The table **(a)** shows the demand schedules for Alice, Bruce, and Carmen. Together they make up the market for DVD rentals. Their total quantity demanded (market demand) for DVD rentals at each price is given in column 5. As you can see in **(b)**, Alice's, Bruce's, and Carmen's demand curves can be added together to get the total market demand curve. For example, at a price of $2, Carmen demands 0, Bruce demands 3, and Alice demands 6, for a market demand of 9 (point *D*).

	(1) Price (per DVD)	(2) Alice's demand	(3) Bruce's demand	(4) Carmen's demand	(5) Market demand
A	$0.50	9	6	1	16
B	1.00	8	5	1	14
C	1.50	7	4	0	11
D	2.00	6	3	0	9
E	2.50	5	2	0	7
F	3.00	4	1	0	5
G	3.50	3	0	0	3
H	4.00	2	0	0	2

(a) A demand table   **(b) Adding demand curves**

The quantity demanded by each consumer is listed in columns 2, 3, and 4 of Figure 4-4(a). Column 5 shows total market demand; each entry is the horizontal sum of the entries in columns 2, 3, and 4. For example, at a price of $3 apiece (row *F*), Alice demands 4 DVD rentals, Bruce demands 1, and Carmen demands 0, for a total market demand of 5 DVD rentals.

Figure 4-4(b) shows three demand curves: one each for Alice, Bruce, and Carmen. The market, or total, demand curve is the horizontal sum of the individual demand curves. To see that this is the case, notice that if we take the quantity demanded at $1 by Alice (8), Bruce (5), and Carmen (1), they sum to 14, which is point *B* (14, $1) on the market demand curve. We can do that for each price. Alternatively, we can simply add the individual quantities demanded, given in the demand tables, prior to graphing (which we do in column 5 of Figure 4-4(a)), and graph that total in relation to price. Not surprisingly, we get the same total market demand curve.

In practice, of course, firms don't measure individual demand curves, so they don't sum them up in this fashion. Instead, they estimate total demand. Still, summing up individual demand curves is a useful exercise because it shows you how the market demand curve is the sum (the horizontal sum, graphically speaking) of the individual demand curves, and it gives you a good sense of where market demand curves come from. It also shows you that, even if individuals don't respond to small changes in price, the market demand curve can still be smooth and downward sloping. That's because, for the market, the law of demand is based on two phenomena:

1. At lower prices, existing demanders buy more.

2. At lower prices, new demanders (some all or nothing demanders like Carmen) enter the market.

For the market, the law of demand is based on two phenomena:

1. At lower prices, existing demanders buy more.

2. At lower prices, new demanders enter the market.

- A demand curve follows the law of demand: When price rises, quantity demanded falls; and vice versa.
- The horizontal axis—quantity—has a time dimension.
- The quality of each unit is the same.
- The vertical axis—price—assumes all other prices remain the same.

- The curve assumes everything else is held constant.
- Effects of price changes are shown by movements along the demand curve. Effects of anything else on demand (shift factors) are shown by shifts of the entire demand curve.

SUPPLY

In one sense, supply is the mirror image of demand. Individuals control the factors of production—inputs, or resources, necessary to produce goods. Individuals' supply of these factors to the market mirrors other individuals' demand for those factors. For example, say you decide you want to rest rather than weed your garden. You hire someone to do the weeding; you demand labor. Someone else decides she would prefer more income instead of more rest; she supplies labor to you. You trade money for labor; she trades labor for money. Her supply is the mirror image of your demand.

For a large number of goods and services, however, the supply process is more complicated than demand. For many goods there's an intermediate step in supply: individuals supply factors of production to firms.

Let's consider a simple example. Say you're a taco technician. You supply your labor to the factor market. The taco company demands your labor (hires you). The taco company combines your labor with other inputs like meat, cheese, beans, and tables, and produces tacos (production), which it supplies to customers in the goods market. For produced goods, supply depends not only on individuals' decisions to supply factors of production but also on firms' ability to produce—to transform those factors of production into usable goods.

The supply process of produced goods is generally complicated. Often there are many layers of firms—production firms, wholesale firms, distribution firms, and retailing firms—each of which passes on in-process goods to the next layer of firms. Real-world production and supply of produced goods is a multistage process.

The supply of nonproduced goods is more direct. Individuals supply their labor in the form of services directly to the goods market. For example, an independent contractor may repair your washing machine. That contractor supplies his labor directly to you.

Thus, the analysis of the supply of produced goods has two parts: an analysis of the supply of factors of production to households and to firms, and an analysis of the process by which firms transform those factors of production into usable goods and services.

Supply of produced goods involves a much more complicated process than demand and is divided into analysis of factors of production and the transformation of those factors into goods.

THE LAW OF SUPPLY

There's a law of supply that corresponds to the law of demand. The **law of supply** states:

Quantity supplied rises as price rises, other things constant.

Figure 4-5   A Sample Supply Curve
The supply curve demonstrates graphically the law of supply, which states that the quantity supplied of a good is directly related to that good's price, other things constant. As the price of a good goes up, the quantity supplied also goes up, so the supply curve is upward sloping.

Or alternatively:

Quantity supplied falls as price falls, other things constant.

Price regulates quantity supplied just as it regulates quantity demanded. Like the law of demand, the law of supply is fundamental to the invisible hand's (the market's) ability to coordinate individuals' actions.

What accounts for the law of supply? When the price of a good rises, individuals and firms can rearrange their activities in order to supply more of that good to the market. They want to supply more because the opportunity cost of *not* producing the goods rises as its price rises. Thus, the law of supply is based on a firm's ability to substitute production of one good for another, or vice versa. If the price of corn rises and the price of wheat has not changed, farmers will grow less wheat and more corn, other things constant.

With firms, there's a second explanation of the law of supply. Assuming firms' costs are constant, a higher price means higher profits (the difference between a firm's revenues and its costs). The expectation of those higher profits leads it to increase output as price rises, which is what the law of supply states.

The law of supply is based on substitution and the expectation of profits.

THE SUPPLY CURVE

A **supply curve** is *the graphical representation of the relationship between price and quantity supplied.* A supply curve is shown graphically in Figure 4-5.

Notice how the supply curve slopes upward to the right. That upward slope captures the law of supply. It tells us that the quantity supplied varies *directly*—in the same direction—with the price.

As with the law of demand, the law of supply assumes other things are held constant. Thus, if the price of wheat rises and quantity supplied falls, you'll look for something else that changed—for example, a drought might have caused a drop in supply. Your explanation would go as follows: Had there been no drought, the quantity supplied would have increased in response to the rise in price, but because there was a drought, the supply decreased, which caused prices to rise.

As with the law of demand, the law of supply represents economists' off-the-cuff response to the question "What happens to quantity supplied if price rises?" If the law seems to be violated, economists search for some other variable that has changed. As was the case with demand, these other variables that might change are called shift factors.

SHIFTS IN SUPPLY VERSUS MOVEMENTS ALONG A SUPPLY CURVE

The same distinctions in terms made for demand apply to supply.

> **Supply** refers to *a schedule of quantities a seller is willing to sell per unit of time at various prices, other things constant.*

> **Quantity supplied** refers to *a specific amount that will be supplied at a specific price.*

In graphical terms, supply refers to the entire supply curve because a supply curve tells us how much will be offered for sale at various prices. "Quantity supplied" refers to a point on a supply curve, such as point A in Figure 4-5.

The second distinction that is important to make is between the effects of a change in price and the effects of shift factors on how much of a good is supplied. Changes in price cause changes in quantity supplied; such changes are represented by a **movement along a supply curve**—*the graphic representation of the effect of a change in price on the quantity supplied.* If the amount supplied is affected by anything other than price, that is, by a shift factor of supply, there will be a **shift in supply**—*the graphic representation of the effect of a change in a factor other than price on supply.*

SHIFT FACTORS OF SUPPLY

Other factors besides price that affect how much will be supplied include the price of inputs used in production, technology, expectations, and taxes and subsidies. Let's see how.

Price of Inputs   Firms produce to earn a profit. Since their profit is tied to costs, it's no surprise that costs will affect how much a firm is willing to supply. If costs rise, profits will decline, and a firm has less incentive to supply. Supply falls when the price of inputs rises. If costs rise substantially, a firm might even shut down.

Technology   Advances in technology change the production process, reducing the number of inputs needed to produce a given supply of goods. Thus, a technological advance that reduces the number of workers will reduce costs of production. A reduction in the costs of production increases profits and leads suppliers to increase production. Advances in technology increase supply.

Expectations   Supplier expectations are an important factor in the production decision. If a supplier expects the price of her good to rise at some time in the future, she may store some of today's supply in order to sell it later and reap higher profits, decreasing supply now and increasing it later.

Taxes and Subsidies   Taxes on suppliers increase the cost of production by requiring a firm to pay the government a portion of the income from products or services sold. Because taxes increase the cost of production, profit declines and suppliers will reduce supply. The opposite is true for subsidies. Subsidies to suppliers are payments by the government to produce goods; thus, they reduce the cost of production. Subsidies increase supply. Taxes on suppliers reduce supply.

These aren't the only shift factors. As was the case with demand, a shift factor of supply is anything that affects supply, other than its price.

A SHIFT IN SUPPLY VERSUS A MOVEMENT ALONG A SUPPLY CURVE

The same "movement along" and "shift of" distinction that we developed for demand exists for supply. To make that distinction clear, let's consider an example: the supply of

Q-5   In the 1980s and 1990s, as animal activists caused a decrease in the demand for fur coats, the prices of furs fell. This made _____ decline. Should the missing words be *the supply* or *the quantity supplied?*

Q-6   Explain the effect of each of the following on the supply of romance novels:

1. The price of paper rises by 20 percent.
2. Government increases the sales tax on producers on all books by 5 percentage points.

Figure 4-6   Shift in Supply versus Change in Quantity Supplied
A change in quantity supplied results from a change in price and is shown by a movement along a supply curve like the movement from point A to point B in (**a**). A shift in supply—a shift in the entire supply curve—brought about by a change in a nonprice factor is shown in (**b**).

(a) Movement along a supply curve

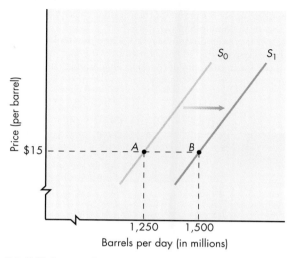

(b) Shift in supply

oil. In 1990 and 1991, world oil prices rose from $15 to $36 a barrel when oil production in the Persian Gulf was disrupted by the Iraqi invasion of Kuwait. U.S. oil producers, seeing that they could sell their oil at a higher price, increased oil production. As the price of oil rose, domestic producers increased the quantity of oil supplied. The change in domestic quantity supplied in response to the rise in world oil prices is illustrated in Figure 4-6(a) as a movement up along the U.S. supply curve from point A to point B. At $15 a barrel, producers supplied 1,500 million barrels of oil a day, and at $36 a barrel they supplied 1,750 million barrels per day.

Earlier, in the 1980s, technological advances in horizontal drilling more than doubled the amount of oil that could be extracted from some oil fields. Technological innovations such as this reduced the cost of supplying oil and shifted the supply of oil to the right, as shown in Figure 4-6(b). Before the innovation, suppliers were willing to provide 1,250 million barrels of oil per day at $15 a barrel. After the innovation, suppliers were willing to supply 1,500 million barrels of oil per day at $15 a barrel.

Photodisc

A REVIEW

To be sure you understand shifts in supply, explain what is likely to happen to your supply curve for labor in the following cases: (1) You suddenly decide that you absolutely need a new car. (2) You win a million dollars in the lottery. And finally, (3) the wage you earn doubles. If you came up with the answers: shift out to the right, shift in to the left, and no change—you've got it down. If not, it's time for a review.

Do we see such shifts in the supply curve often? Yes. A good example is computers. For the past 30 years, technological changes have continually shifted the supply curve for computers out to the right.

Figure 4-7 (a and b)   From Individual Supplies to a Market Supply

As with market demand, market supply is determined by adding all quantities supplied at a given price. Three suppliers—Ann, Barry, and Charlie—make up the market of DVD suppliers. The total market supply is the sum of their individual supplies at each price, shown in column 5 of (a).

Each of the individual supply curves and the market supply curve have been plotted in (b). Notice how the market supply curve is the horizontal sum of the individual supply curves.

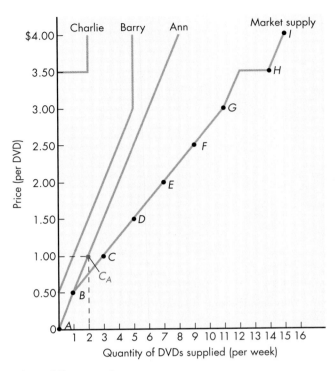

(1) Quantities supplied	(2) Price (per DVD)	(3) Ann's supply	(4) Barry's supply	(5) Charlie's supply	Market supply
A	$0.00	0	0	0	0
B	0.50	1	0	0	1
C	1.00	2	1	0	3
D	1.50	3	2	0	5
E	2.00	4	3	0	7
F	2.50	5	4	0	9
G	3.00	6	5	0	11
H	3.50	7	5	2	14
I	4.00	8	5	2	15

Note: column headers (3)–(5) reading Ann's supply, Barry's supply, Charlie's supply, and (5) Market supply.

(a) A supply table

(b) Adding supply curves

THE SUPPLY TABLE

Remember Figure 4-4(a)'s demand table for DVD rentals? In Figure 4-7(a), columns 2 (Ann), 3 (Barry), and 4 (Charlie), we follow the same reasoning to construct a supply table for three hypothetical DVD suppliers. Each supplier follows the law of supply: When price rises, each supplies more, or at least as much as each did at a lower price.

FROM A SUPPLY TABLE TO A SUPPLY CURVE

Figure 4-7(b) takes the information in Figure 4-7(a)'s supply table and translates it into a graph of each supplier's supply curve. For instance, point C_A on Ann's supply curve corresponds to the information in columns 1 and 2, row C. Point C_A is at a price of $1 per DVD and a quantity of 2 DVDs per week. Notice that Ann's supply curve is upward sloping, meaning that price is positively related to quantity. Charlie's and Barry's supply curves are similarly derived.

The supply curve represents the set of *minimum* prices an individual seller will accept for various quantities of a good. The market's invisible hand stops suppliers from charging more than the market price. If suppliers could escape the market's invisible hand and charge a higher price, they would gladly do so. Unfortunately for them, and fortunately for consumers, a higher price encourages other suppliers to begin selling DVDs. Competing suppliers' entry into the market sets a limit on the price any supplier can charge.

- A supply curve follows the law of supply. When price rises, quantity supplied increases, and vice versa.
- The horizontal axis—quantity—has a time dimension.
- The quality of each unit is the same.
- The vertical axis—price—assumes all other prices remain constant.

- The curve assumes everything else is constant.
- Effects of price changes are shown by movements along the supply curve. Effects of nonprice determinants of supply are shown by shifts of the entire supply curve.

INDIVIDUAL AND MARKET SUPPLY CURVES

The market supply curve is derived from individual supply curves in precisely the same way that the market demand curve was. To emphasize the symmetry, I've made the three suppliers quite similar to the three demanders. Ann (column 2) will supply 2 at $1; if price goes up to $2, she increases her supply to 4. Barry (column 3) begins supplying at $1, and at $3 supplies 5, the most he'll supply regardless of how high price rises. Charlie (column 4) has only two units to supply. At a price of $3.50 he'll supply that quantity, but higher prices won't get him to supply any more.

The **market supply curve** is *the horizontal sum of all individual supply curves.* In Figure 4-7(a) (column 5), we add together Ann's, Barry's, and Charlie's supplies to arrive at the market supply curve, which is graphed in Figure 4-7(b). Notice that each point on it corresponds to the information in columns 1 and 5 for each row. For example, point H corresponds to a price of $3.50 and a quantity of 14.

The market supply curve's upward slope is determined by two different sources: by existing suppliers supplying more and by new suppliers entering the market. Sometimes existing suppliers may not be willing to increase their quantity supplied in response to an increase in prices, but a rise in price often brings brand-new suppliers into the market. For example, a rise in teachers' salaries will have little effect on the amount of teaching current teachers do, but it will increase the number of people choosing to be teachers.

The law of supply is based on two phenomena:

1. At higher prices, existing suppliers supply more.
2. At higher prices, new suppliers enter the market.

THE INTERACTION OF SUPPLY AND DEMAND

Thomas Carlyle, the English historian who dubbed economics "the dismal science," also wrote this chapter's introductory tidbit. "Teach a parrot the terms *supply* and *demand* and you've got an economist." In earlier chapters, I tried to convince you that economics is *not* dismal. In the rest of this chapter, I hope to convince you that, while supply and demand are important to economics, parrots don't make good economists. If students think that when they've learned the terms *supply* and *demand* they've learned economics, they're mistaken. Those terms are just labels for the ideas behind supply and demand, and it's the ideas that are important. What matters about supply and demand isn't the labels but how the concepts interact. For instance, what happens if a freeze kills the blossoms on the orange trees? The quantity of oranges supplied isn't expected to equal the quantity demanded. It's in understanding the interaction of supply and demand that economics becomes interesting and relevant.

Web Note 4.2
Online Markets

EQUILIBRIUM

When you have a market in which neither suppliers nor consumers collude and in which prices are free to adjust, the forces of supply and demand interact to arrive at an equilibrium. The concept of equilibrium comes from physics—classical mechanics. **Equilibrium** is *a concept in which opposing dynamic forces cancel each other out*. For example, a hot-air balloon is in equilibrium when the upward force exerted by the hot air in the balloon equals the downward pressure exerted on the balloon by gravity. In supply/demand analysis, equilibrium means that the upward pressure on price is exactly offset by the downward pressure on price. **Equilibrium price** is *the price toward which the invisible hand drives the market*. At the equilibrium price, quantity demanded equals quantity supplied. **Equilibrium quantity** is *the amount bought and sold at the equilibrium price*.

So much for what equilibrium is. Now let's consider what it isn't.

WHAT EQUILIBRIUM ISN'T

First, equilibrium isn't a state of the world. It's a characteristic of the model—the framework you use to look at the world. The same situation could be seen as an equilibrium in one framework and as a disequilibrium in another. Say you're describing a car that's speeding along at 100 miles an hour. That car is changing position relative to objects on the ground. Its movement could be, and generally is, described as if it were in disequilibrium. However, if you consider this car relative to another car going 100 miles an hour, the cars could be modeled as being in equilibrium because their positions relative to each other aren't changing.

Equilibrium is not inherently good or bad.

Second, equilibrium isn't inherently good or bad. It's simply a state in which dynamic pressures offset each other. Some equilibria are awful. Say two countries are engaged in a nuclear war against each other and both sides are blown away. An equilibrium will have been reached, but there's nothing good about it.

What happens if the market is not in equilibrium—if quantity supplied doesn't equal quantity demanded? You get either excess supply or excess demand, and a tendency for prices to change.

EXCESS SUPPLY

If there is **excess supply** (a surplus), *quantity supplied is greater than quantity demanded*, and some suppliers won't be able to sell all their goods. Each supplier will think: "Gee, if I offer to sell it for a bit less, I'll be the lucky one who sells my goods; someone else will be stuck with not selling their goods." But because all suppliers with excess goods will be thinking the same thing, the price in the market will fall. As that happens, consumers will increase their quantity demanded. So the movement toward equilibrium caused by excess supply is on both the supply and demand sides.

Bargain hunters can get a deal when there is excess supply.
Elena Rooraid/Photoedit

EXCESS DEMAND

The reverse is also true. Say that instead of excess supply, there's **excess demand** (a shortage)—*quantity demanded is greater than quantity supplied*. There are more consumers who want the good than there are suppliers selling the good. Let's consider what's likely to go through demanders' minds. They'll likely call long-lost friends who just happen to be sellers of that good and tell them it's good to talk to them and, by the way, don't they want to sell that . . . ? Suppliers will be rather pleased that so many of their old friends have remembered them, but they'll also likely see the connection between excess demand and their friends' thoughtfulness. To stop their phones from ringing all the time, they'll likely raise their price. The reverse is true for excess supply. It's amazing how friendly suppliers become to potential consumers when there's excess supply.

PRICE ADJUSTS

This tendency for prices to rise when the quantity demanded exceeds the quantity supplied and for prices to fall when the quantity supplied exceeds the quantity demanded is a central element to understanding supply and demand. So remember:

When quantity demanded is greater than quantity supplied, prices tend to rise.
When quantity supplied is greater than quantity demanded, prices tend to fall.

Two other things to note about supply and demand are (1) the greater the difference between quantity supplied and quantity demanded, the more pressure there is for prices to rise or fall, and (2) when quantity demanded equals quantity supplied, the market is in equilibrium.

People's tendencies to change prices exist as long as there's some difference between quantity supplied and quantity demanded. But the change in price brings the laws of supply and demand into play. As price falls, quantity supplied decreases as some suppliers leave the business (the law of supply). And as some people who originally weren't really interested in buying the good think, "Well, at this low price, maybe I do want to buy," quantity demanded increases (the law of demand). Similarly, when price rises, quantity supplied will increase (the law of supply) and quantity demanded will decrease (the law of demand).

Whenever quantity supplied and quantity demanded are unequal, price tends to change. If, however, quantity supplied and quantity demanded are equal, price will stay the same because no one will have an incentive to change.

THE GRAPHICAL INTERACTION OF SUPPLY AND DEMAND

Figure 4-8 shows supply and demand curves for DVD rentals and demonstrates the force of the invisible hand. Let's consider what will happen to the price of DVD in three cases:

1. When the price is $3.50 each;
2. When the price is $1.50 each; and
3. When the price is $2.50 each.

1. When price is $3.50, quantity supplied is 7 and quantity demanded is only 3. Excess supply is 4. Individual consumers can get all they want, but most suppliers can't sell all they wish; they'll be stuck with DVDs that they'd like to rent. Suppliers will tend to offer their goods at a lower price and demanders, who see plenty of suppliers out there, will bargain harder for an even lower price. Both these forces will push the price as indicated by the A arrows in Figure 4-8.

Now let's start from the other side.

2. Say price is $1.50. The situation is now reversed. Quantity supplied is 3 and quantity demanded is 7. Excess demand is 4. Now it's consumers who can't get what they want and suppliers who are in the strong bargaining position. The pressures will be on price to rise in the direction of the B arrows in Figure 4-8.

3. At $2.50, price is at its equilibrium: quantity supplied equals quantity demanded. Suppliers offer to sell 5 and consumers want to buy 5, so there's no pressure on price to rise or fall. Price will tend to remain where it is (point E in Figure 4-8). Notice that the equilibrium price is where the supply and demand curves intersect.

Prices tend to rise when there is excess demand and fall when there is excess supply.

Figure 4-8   The Interaction of Supply and Demand
Combining Ann's supply from Figure 4-7 and Alice's demand from
Figure 4-4, let's see the force of the invisible hand. When there is
excess demand there is upward pressure on price. When there is
excess supply there is downward pressure on price. Understanding
these pressures is essential to understanding how to apply economics
to reality.

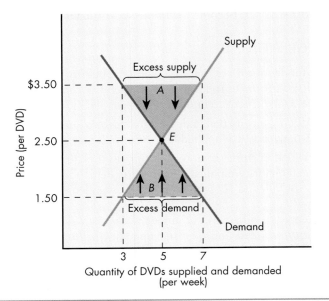

Price (per DVD)	Quantity supplied	Quantity demanded	Surplus (+)/ shortage (−)
$3.50	7	3	+4
$2.50	5	5	0
$1.50	3	7	−4

POLITICAL AND SOCIAL FORCES AND EQUILIBRIUM

When I discussed equilibrium, I emphasized that equilibrium is a characteristic of the
framework of analysis, not of the real world. Understanding that idea is important in applying economic models to reality. For example, in the preceding description I said equilibrium occurs where quantity supplied equals quantity demanded. In a model where the
invisible hand is the only force operating, that's true. In the real world, however, other
forces—political and social forces—are operating. These will likely push price away
from that supply/demand equilibrium. Were we to consider a model that included all
these forces—political, social, and economic—equilibrium would be likely to exist
where quantity supplied isn't equal to quantity demanded. For example:

- Farmers use political pressure to obtain prices that are higher than supply/
  demand equilibrium prices.
- Social pressures often offset economic pressures and prevent unemployed
  individuals from accepting work at lower wages than currently employed
  workers receive.
- Existing firms conspire to limit new competition by lobbying Congress to
  pass restrictive regulations and by devising pricing strategies to scare off new
  entrants.
- Renters often organize to pressure local government to set caps on the rental
  price of apartments.

If social and political forces were included in the analysis, they'd provide a counter-
pressure to the dynamic forces of supply and demand. The result would be an equilibrium with continual excess supply or excess demand if the market were considered only
in reference to economic forces. The invisible hand pushing toward a supply/demand
equilibrium would be thwarted by social and political forces pushing in the other
direction.

Figure 4-9 (a and b)   Shifts in Supply and Demand

When there is an increase in demand (the demand curve shifts outward), there is upward pressure on the price, as shown in (a). If demand increases from D_0 to D_1, the quantity of DVD rentals that was demanded at a price of $2.25, 8, increases to 10, but the quantity supplied remains at 8. This excess demand tends to cause prices to rise. Eventually, a new equilibrium is reached at the price of $2.50, where the quantity supplied and the quantity demanded is 9 (point B).

   If supply of DVD rentals decreases, then the entire supply curve shifts inward to the left, as shown in (b), from S_0 to S_1. At the price of $2.25, the quantity supplied has now decreased to 6 DVDs, but the quantity demanded has remained at 8 DVDs. The excess demand tends to force the price upward. Eventually, an equilibrium is reached at the price of $2.50 and quantity 7 (point C).

(a) **A shift in demand**   (b) **A shift in supply**

SHIFTS IN SUPPLY AND DEMAND

Supply and demand are most useful when trying to figure out what will happen to equilibrium price and quantity if either supply or demand shifts. Figure 4-9(a) deals with an increase in demand. Figure 4-9(b) deals with a decrease in supply.

   Let's consider again the supply and demand for DVD rentals. In Figure 4-9(a), the supply is S_0 and initial demand is D_0. They meet at an equilibrium price of $2.25 per DVD and an equilibrium quantity of 8 DVDs per week (point A). Now say that the demand for DVD rentals increases from D_0 to D_1. At a price of $2.25, the quantity of DVD rentals supplied will be 8 and the quantity demanded will be 10; excess demand of 2 exists.

   The excess demand pushes prices upward in the direction of the small arrows, decreasing the quantity demanded and increasing the quantity supplied. As it does so, movement takes place along both the supply curve and the demand curve.

   The upward push on price decreases the gap between the quantity supplied and the quantity demanded. As the gap decreases, the upward pressure decreases, but as long as that gap exists at all, price will be pushed upward until the new equilibrium price ($2.50) and new quantity (9) are reached (point B). At point B, quantity supplied equals quantity demanded. So the market is in equilibrium. Notice that the adjustment is twofold: The higher price brings about equilibrium by both increasing the quantity supplied (from 8 to 9) and decreasing the quantity demanded (from 10 to 9).

   Figure 4-9(b) begins with the same situation that we started with in Figure 4-9(a); the initial equilibrium quantity and price are 8 DVDs per week and $2.25 per DVD

Q-7   Demonstrate graphically the effect of a heavy frost in Florida on the equilibrium quantity and price of oranges.

In Chapter 1, I distinguished between an economic force and a market force. Economic forces are operative in all aspects of our lives; market forces are economic forces that are allowed to be expressed through a market. My examples in this chapter are of market forces—of goods sold in a market—but supply and demand can also be used to analyze situations in which economic, but not market, forces operate. An economist who is adept at this is Gary Becker of the University of Chicago. He has applied supply and demand analysis to a wide range of issues, even the supply and demand for children.

Becker doesn't argue that children should be bought and sold. But he does argue that economic considerations play a large role in people's decisions on how many chil-

dren to have. In farming communities, children can be productive early in life; by age six or seven, they can work on a farm. In an advanced industrial community, children provide pleasure but generally don't contribute productively to family income. Even getting them to help around the house can be difficult.

Becker argues that since the price of having children is lower for a farming society than for an industrial society, farming societies will have more children per family. Quantity of children demanded will be larger. And that's what we find. Developing countries that rely primarily on farming often have three, four, or more children per family. Industrial societies average fewer than two children per family.

(point A). In this example, however, instead of demand increasing, let's assume supply decreases—say because some suppliers change what they like to do, and decide they will no longer supply DVDs. That means that the entire supply curve shifts inward to the left (from S_0 to S_1). At the initial equilibrium price of \$2.25, the quantity demanded is greater than the quantity supplied. Two more DVDs are demanded than are supplied. (Excess demand = 2.)

This excess demand exerts upward pressure on price. Price is pushed in the direction of the small arrows. As the price rises, the upward pressure on price is reduced but will still exist until the new equilibrium price, \$2.50, and new quantity, 7, are reached. At \$2.50, the quantity supplied equals the quantity demanded. The adjustment has involved a movement along the demand curve and the new supply curve. As price rises, quantity supplied is adjusted upward and quantity demanded is adjusted downward until quantity supplied equals quantity demanded where the new supply curve intersects the demand curve at point C, an equilibrium of 7 and \$2.50.

Here is an exercise for you to try. Demonstrate graphically how the price of computers could have fallen dramatically in the past 10 years, even as demand increased. (Hint: Supply has shifted even more, so even at lower prices, far more computers have been supplied than were being supplied 10 years ago.)

THE LIMITATIONS OF SUPPLY/DEMAND ANALYSIS

Supply and demand are tools, and, like most tools, they help us enormously when used appropriately. Used inappropriately, however, they can be misleading. Throughout the book I'll introduce you to the limitations of the tools, but let me discuss an important one here.

In supply/demand analysis other things are assumed constant. If other things change, then one cannot directly apply supply/demand analysis. Sometimes supply and demand are interconnected, making it impossible to hold other things constant. Let's take an example. Say we are considering the effect of a fall in the wage rate. In

Q-8 Demonstrate graphically the likely effect of an increase in the price of gas on the equilibrium quantity and price of compact cars.

supply/demand analysis, you would look at the effect that fall would have on workers' decisions to supply labor, and on business's decision to hire workers. But there are also other effects. All actions have a multitude of ripple and possible feedback effects—they create waves, like those that spread out from a stone thrown into a pool. For instance, the fall in the wage lowers people's income and thereby reduces demand. That reduction may feed back to firms and reduce the demand for their goods and that reduction might reduce the firms' demand for workers. If these effects do occur, and are important enough to affect the result, those effects have to be added to the analysis in order for you to have a complete analysis.

There is no single answer to the question of which ripples must be included, and much debate among economists involves which ripple effects to include. But there are some general rules. Supply/demand analysis, used without adjustment, is most appropriate for questions where the goods are a small percentage of the entire economy. That is when the other-things-constant assumption will most likely hold. As soon as one starts analyzing goods that are a large percentage of the entire economy, the other-things-constant assumption is likely not to hold true. The reason is found in the **fallacy of composition**—*the false assumption that what is true for a part will also be true for the whole*.

Consider the example of one supplier lowering the price of his or her good. People will substitute that good for other goods, and the quantity of the good demanded will increase. But what if all suppliers lower their prices? Since all prices have gone down, why should consumers switch? The substitution story can't be used in the aggregate. There are many such examples.

An understanding of the fallacy of composition is of central relevance to macroeconomics. In the aggregate, whenever firms produce (whenever they supply), they create income (demand for their goods). So in macro, when supply changes, demand changes. This interdependence is one of the primary reasons we have a separate macroeconomics. In macroeconomics, the other-things-constant assumption central to microeconomic supply/demand analysis cannot hold.

It is to account for these interdependencies that we separate macro analysis from micro analysis. In macro we use curves whose underlying foundations are much more complicated than the supply and demand curves we use in micro.

One final comment: The fact that there may be an interdependence between supply and demand does not mean that you can't use supply/demand analysis; it simply means that you must modify its results with the interdependency that, if you've done the analysis correctly, you've kept in the back of your head. Thus, using supply and demand analysis is generally a step in any good economic analysis, but you must remember that it may be only a step.

CONCLUSION

Throughout the book I'll be presenting examples of supply and demand. So I'll end this chapter here because its intended purposes have been served. What were those intended purposes? First, I exposed you to enough economic terminology and economic thinking to allow you to proceed to my more complicated examples. Second, I have set your mind to work putting the events around you into a supply/demand framework. Doing that will give you new insights into the events that shape all our lives. Once you incorporate the supply/demand framework into your way of looking at the world, you will have made an important step toward thinking like an economist.

Q.9 When determining the effect of a shift factor on price and quantity, in which of the following markets could you likely assume that other things will remain constant?

1. Market for eggs.
2. Labor market.
3. World oil market.
4. Market for luxury boats.

The fallacy of composition is the false assumption that what is true for a part will also be true for the whole.

Q.10 Why is the fallacy of composition relevant for macroeconomic issues?

It is to account for interdependency between aggregate supply decisions and aggregate demand decisions that we have a separate micro analysis and a separate macro analysis.

SUMMARY

- The law of demand states that quantity demanded rises as price falls, other things constant.

- The law of supply states that quantity supplied rises as price rises, other things constant.

- Factors that affect supply and demand other than price are called shift factors. Shift factors of demand include income, prices of other goods, tastes, expectations, and taxes on and subsidies to consumers. Shift factors of supply include the price of inputs, technology, expectations, and taxes on and subsidies to producers.

- A change in quantity demanded (supplied) is a movement along the demand (supply) curve. A change in demand (supply) is a shift of the entire demand (supply) curve.

- The laws of supply and demand hold true because individuals can substitute.

- A market demand (supply) curve is the horizontal sum of all individual demand (supply) curves.

- When quantity supplied equals quantity demanded, prices have no tendency to change. This is equilibrium.

- When quantity demanded is greater than quantity supplied, prices tend to rise. When quantity supplied is greater than quantity demanded, prices tend to fall.

- When the demand curve shifts to the right (left), equilibrium price rises (declines) and equilibrium quantity rises (falls).

- When the supply curve shifts to the right (left), equilibrium price declines (rises) and equilibrium quantity rises (falls).

- In the real world, one must add political and social forces to the supply/demand model. When you do, equilibrium is likely not going to be where quantity demanded equals quantity supplied.

- In macro, small side effects that can be assumed away in micro are multiplied enormously. Thus, they can significantly change the results and cannot be ignored. To ignore them is to fall into the fallacy of composition.

KEY TERMS

demand (85)
demand curve (84)
equilibrium (96)
equilibrium price (96)
equilibrium quantity (96)
excess demand (96)
excess supply (96)

fallacy of composition (101)
law of demand (84)
law of supply (90)
market demand curve (88)
market supply curve (95)

movement along a demand curve (85)
movement along a supply curve (92)
quantity demanded (85)
quantity supplied (92)
shift in demand (85)

shift in supply (92)
supply (92)
supply curve (91)

QUESTIONS FOR THOUGHT AND REVIEW

1. State the law of demand. Why is price inversely related to quantity demanded?

2. State the law of supply. Why is price directly related to quantity supplied?

3. List four shift factors of demand and explain how each affects demand.

4. Distinguish the effect of a shift factor of demand on the demand curve from the effect of a change in price on the demand curve.

5. Mary has just stated that normally, as price rises, supply will increase. Her teacher grimaces. Why?

6. List four shift factors of supply and explain how each affects supply.

7. Derive the market supply curve from the following two individual supply curves.

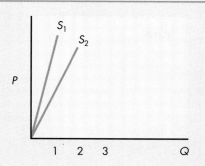

8. It has just been reported that eating red meat is bad for your health. Using supply and demand curves, demonstrate the report's likely effect on the equilibrium price and quantity of steak sold in the market.

9. Why does the price of airline tickets rise during the summer months? Demonstrate your answer graphically.

10. Why does sales volume rise during weeks when states suspend taxes on sales by retailers? Demonstrate your answer graphically.

11. What is the expected impact of increased security measures imposed by the federal government on airlines on fares and volume of travel? Demonstrate your answer graphically.

12. Explain what a sudden popularity of "Economics Professor" brand casual wear would likely do to prices of that brand.

13. In a flood, usable water supplies ironically tend to decline because the pumps and water lines are damaged. What will a flood likely do to prices of bottled water?

14. Oftentimes, to be considered for a job, you have to know someone in the firm. What does this observation tell you about the wage paid for that job?

15. In most developing countries, there are long lines of taxis at airports, and these taxis often wait two or three hours. What does this tell you about the price in that market? Demonstrate with supply and demand analysis.

16. Define the fallacy of composition. How does it affect the supply/demand model?

17. Why is a supply/demand analysis that includes only economic forces likely to be incomplete?

18. In which of the following three markets is there likely to be the greatest feedback effects: market for housing, market for wheat, market for manufactured goods?

PROBLEMS AND EXERCISES

1. You're given the following individual demand tables for comic books.

Price	John	Liz	Alex
$ 2	4	36	24
4	4	32	20
6	0	28	16
8	0	24	12
10	0	20	8
12	0	16	4
14	0	12	0
16	0	8	0

a. Determine the market demand table.
b. Graph the individual and market demand curves.
c. If the current market price is $4, what's total market demand? What happens to total market demand if price rises to $8?
d. Say that an advertising campaign increases demand by 50 percent. Illustrate graphically what will happen to the individual and market demand curves.

2. You're given the following demand and supply tables:

	Demand		
P	D_1	D_2	D_3
$37	20	4	8
47	15	2	7
57	10	0	6
67	5	0	5

	Supply		
P	S_1	S_2	S_3
$37	0	4	14
47	0	8	16
57	10	12	18
67	10	16	20

a. Draw the market demand and market supply curves.
b. What is excess supply/demand at price $37? Price $67?
c. Label equilibrium price and quantity.

3. Draw hypothetical supply and demand curves for tea. Show how the equilibrium price and quantity will be affected by each of the following occurrences:
   a. Bad weather wreaks havoc with the tea crop.
   b. A medical report implying tea is bad for your health is published.
   c. A technological innovation lowers the cost of producing tea.
   d. Consumers' income falls. (Assume tea is a normal good.)

4. You're a commodity trader and you've just heard a report that the winter wheat harvest will be 2.09 billion bushels, a 44 percent jump, rather than an expected 35 percent jump to 1.96 billion bushels.
   a. What would you expect would happen to wheat prices?
   b. Demonstrate graphically the effect you suggested in *a*.

5. In the United States, gasoline costs consumers about $1.50 per gallon. In Italy it costs consumers about $5 per gallon. What effect does this price differential likely have on:
   a. The size of cars in the United States and in Italy?
   b. The use of public transportation in the United States and in Italy?
   c. The fuel efficiency of cars in the United States and in Italy? What would be the effect of raising the price of gasoline in the United States to $4 per gallon?

6. State whether supply/demand analysis used without significant modification is suitable to assess the following:
   a. The impact of an increase in the demand for pencils on the price of pencils.
   b. The impact of an increase in the supply of labor on the quantity of labor demanded.
   c. The impact of an increase in aggregate savings on aggregate expenditures.
   d. The impact of a new method of producing CDs on the price of CDs.

WEB QUESTIONS

1. Go to the U.S. Census Bureau's home page (www.census.gov) and navigate to the population pyramids for 2000, for 2025, and for 2050. What is projected to happen to the age distribution in the United States? Other things constant, what do you expect will happen in the next 50 years to the relative demand and supply for each of the following, being careful to distinguish between shifts of and a movement along a curve:
   a. Nursing homes.
   b. Prescription medication.
   c. Baby high chairs.
   d. College education.

2. Go to the Energy Information Administration's home page (www.eia.doe.gov) and look up its most recent "Short-Term Energy Outlook" and answer the following questions:
   a. List the factors that are expected to affect demand and supply for energy in the near term. How will each affect demand? Supply?
   b. What is the EIA's forecast for world oil prices? Show graphically how the factors listed in your answer to *a* are consistent with the EIA's forecast. Label all shifts in demand and supply.
   c. Describe and explain EIA's forecast for the price of gasoline, heating oil, and natural gas. Be sure to mention the factors that are affecting the forecast.

3. Go to the Tax Administration home page (www.taxadmin.org) and look up sales tax rates for the 50 U.S. states.
   a. Which states have no sales tax? Which state has the highest sales tax?
   b. Show graphically the effect of sales tax on supply, demand, equilibrium quantity, and equilibrium price.
   c. Name two neighboring states that have significantly different sales tax rates. How does that affect the supply or demand for goods in those states?

ANSWERS TO MARGIN QUESTIONS

1. The demand curve slopes downward because price and quantity demanded are inversely related. As the price of a good rises, people switch to purchasing other goods whose prices have not risen by as much. (84)

2. *Demand for luxury goods.* The other possibility, *quantity of luxury goods demanded,* is used to refer to movements along (not shifts of) the demand curve. (85)

3. (1) The decline in price will increase the quantity of computers demanded (movement down along the demand curve); (2) With more income, demand for computers will rise (shift of the demand curve out to the right). (86)

4. When adding two demand curves, you sum them horizontally, as in the accompanying diagram. (88)

5. *The quantity supplied* declined because there was a movement along the supply curve. The supply curve itself remained unchanged. (92)

6. (1) The supply of romance novels declines since paper is an input to production (supply shifts in to the left); (2) the supply of romance novels declines since the tax increases the cost to the producer (supply shifts in to the left). (92)

7. A heavy frost in Florida will decrease the supply of oranges, increasing the price and decreasing the quantity demanded, as in the accompanying graph. (99)

8. An increase in the price of gas will likely increase the demand for compact cars, increasing their price and increasing the quantity supplied, as in the accompanying graph. (100)

9. Other things are most likely to remain constant in the egg and luxury boat markets because each is a small percentage of the whole economy. Factors that affect the world oil market and the labor market will have ripple effects that must be taken into account in any analysis. (101)

10. The fallacy of composition is relevant for macroeconomic issues because it reminds us that, in the aggregate, small effects that are immaterial for micro issues can add up and be material. (101)

USING SUPPLY AND DEMAND

> It is by invisible hands that we are bent
> and tortured worst.
>
> —*Nietzsche*

Supply and demand give you a lens through which to view the economy. That lens brings into focus issues that would otherwise seem like a muddle. In this chapter we use the supply/demand lens to consider real-world events.

REAL-WORLD SUPPLY AND DEMAND APPLICATIONS

I begin this section by presenting various applications of supply/demand analysis to show you how the supply/demand model works. These applications show you the power of supply and demand and also how the invisible hand interacts with social and political forces.

THE MARKET FOR ADVERTISING

From the supply/demand analysis in Chapter 4, you might get the idea that prices are constantly fluctuating in response to changes in supply and demand. This is true for commodities such as gold and agricultural products, but for 90 percent of final goods sold, prices are often slow to adjust. That doesn't mean that supply and demand forces aren't working and that prices won't eventually adjust. It just means that the process of adjustment takes time, often because other forces are influencing events. In our example, we consider a market in which supply and demand are operating but are affecting actions in a way that does not show up directly in reported prices.

Companies spend a lot of resources to influence your buying habits, so the market for television advertising is a big market. Companies in the United States spend in excess of $100 billion each year on advertising. Advertising creates brand-name recognition and that "gotta-have" feeling among consumers. The supply in this market is relatively constant—there are only so many minutes on shows that they can fill up with advertising (although the amount has been creeping up so that now the typical half-hour show is really only 19 minutes; the remainder is advertising).

PART II

MICROECONOMICS

In my vacations, I visited the poorest quarters of several cities and walked through one street after another, looking at the faces of the poorest people. Next I resolved to make as thorough a study as I could of Political Economy.

You may remember having already seen this quotation from Alfred Marshall. It began the first chapter. I chose this beginning for two reasons. First, it gives what I believe to be the best reason to study economics. Second, the quotation is from a hero of mine, one of the economic giants of all times. His *Principles of Economics* was the economists' bible in the late 1800s and early 1900s. How important was Marshall? It was Marshall who first used the supply and demand curves as an engine of analysis.

I repeat this quotation here in the introduction to the microeconomics section because for Marshall economics was microeconomics, and it is his vision of economics that underlies this book's approach to microeconomics. For Marshall, economics was an art that was meant to be applied—used to explain why things were the way they were, and what we could do about them. He had little use for esoteric theory that didn't lead to a direct application to a real-world problem. Reflecting on the state of economics in 1906, Marshall wrote to a friend:

> I had a growing feeling in the later years of my work at the subject that a good mathematical theorem dealing with economic hypotheses was very unlikely to be good economics: and I went more and more on the rules—(1) Use mathematics as a shorthand language, rather than as an engine of inquiry. (2) Keep to them until you have done. (3) Translate into English. (4) Then illustrate by examples that are important in real life. (5) Burn the mathematics. (6) If you can't succeed in (4), burn (3). This last I did often. (From a letter from Marshall to A. L. Bowley, reprinted in A. C. Pigou, *Memorials of Alfred Marshall*, p. 427.)

Marshall didn't feel this way about mathematical economics because he couldn't do mathematics. He was trained as a formal mathematician, and he was a good one. But, for him, mathematics wasn't economics, and the real world was too messy to have applied to it much of the fancy mathematical economic work that some of his fellow economists were doing. Marshall recognized the influence of market, political, and social forces and believed that all three had to be taken into account in applying economic reasoning to reality.

Since 1906, when Marshall wrote this letter, the economics profession has moved away from its Marshallian roots. The profession has found other heroes who have created a mathematical foundation for economics that's both impressive and stultifying. Mathematical economics that has only the slightest connection to the real world has overwhelmed much of the real-world economics that Marshall followed. That's sad.

Not to worry. You won't see such highfalutin mathematical economics in these microeconomic chapters. The chapters follow the Marshallian methodology and present the minimum of formal theory necessary to apply the concepts of economics to the real world, and then they do just that: start talking about real-world issues.

Section I, Microeconomics: The Basics (Chapters 6 and 7), and Section II, Foundations of Supply and Demand (Chapters 8–10), present the background theory necessary to understand the economic way of thinking. These sections introduce you to the foundations of economic reasoning and to some central terms and ideas of microeconomics. But even in these theoretical chapters the focus is on intuition, policy, and on putting the economic approach to problems into perspective, rather than on presenting technique for the sake of technique.

Section III, Market Structure and Policy (Chapters 11–15), introduces you to various market structures, providing you with a way of approaching real-world markets. Chapter 15 provides an overview of government's policy on market structure—antitrust policy.

Section IV, Factor Markets (Chapters 16–17), looks at a particular set of markets—factor markets. These markets play a central role in determining the distribution of income. These chapters won't tell you how to get rich (you'll have to wait for the sequel for that), but they will give you new insights into how labor markets work.

Section V, Applying Economic Reasoning to Policy (Chapters 18–21), provides an overview of the implications of microeconomics for policy. It includes both general overviews and analyses of specific issues.

Describing Supply and Demand: Elasticities

After reading this chapter, you should be able to:

- Use the terms *price elasticity of supply* and *price elasticity of demand* to describe the responsiveness of quantity supplied and quantity demanded to changes in price.

- Calculate elasticity graphically and numerically.

- Distinguish five elasticity terms that are used to differentiate varying degrees of responsiveness.

- Explain the importance of substitution in determining elasticity of supply and demand.

- Relate price elasticity of demand to total revenue.

- State how other elasticity concepts are useful in describing the effect of shift factors on demand.

- Explain how the concept of *elasticity* makes supply and demand analysis more useful.

The master economist must understand symbols and speak in words. He must contemplate the particular in terms of the general, and touch abstract and concrete in the same flight of thought.

—J. M. Keynes

Chapters 4 and 5 gave you a good sense of supply and demand. In this chapter I introduce you to the concept of elasticity, a term economists use to describe supply and demand. Elasticity refers to responsiveness; for example, elasticity can be used to describe the responsiveness of quantity supplied or quantity demanded to price.

In economics the term elasticity comes up continually. For example, policymakers use it to describe by how much quantity demanded will fall in response to an increase in taxes. Firms use elasticity to describe the responsiveness of consumers to an increase in price. In general, the greater the elasticity, the more responsive quantity is to a change in price.

Information about elasticity is extremely important to firms in making their pricing decisions, and to economists in their study of the economy. Consider the decision by America West Airlines to cut airfares for business travelers by 50 percent. That decision was based on the prediction that lowering price would entice a large number of business travelers to switch carriers and book travel with America West. That is, the airline was hoping that quantity demanded was very responsive to a change in price, or, in other words, that demand for business travel was elastic. Alternatively, consider some school boards' decisions to raise teachers' salaries by 10 percent because of a shortage of teachers in their districts. The boards were hoping that the number of individuals choosing jobs as teachers would increase significantly with a rise in salaries; that is, they were hoping that the supply of teachers was highly elastic.

PRICE ELASTICITY

The most commonly used elasticity concept is price elasticity of demand and supply. **Price elasticity of demand** is *the percentage change in quantity demanded divided by the percentage change in price:*

$$E_D = \frac{\text{Percentage change in quantity demanded}}{\text{Percentage change in price}}$$

Price elasticity of supply is *the percentage change in quantity supplied divided by the percentage change in price*:

$$E_S = \frac{\text{Percentage change in quantity supplied}}{\text{Percentage change in price}}$$

Let's consider some numerical examples. Say the price of a good rises by 10 percent and, in response, quantity demanded falls by 20 percent. The price elasticity of demand is 2 (−20 percent/10 percent). Notice that I said 2, not −2. Because quantity demanded is inversely related to price, the calculation for the price elasticity of demand comes out negative. Despite this fact, economists talk about price elasticity of demand as a positive number. (Those of you who remember some math can think of elasticity as an *absolute value* of a number, rather than a simple number.) Using this convention makes it easier to remember that a *larger* number for price elasticity of demand means quantity demanded is *more responsive* to price.

To make sure you have the idea down, let's consider two more examples. Say that when price falls by 5 percent, quantity supplied falls by 2 percent. In this case, the price elasticity of supply is 0.4 (2 percent/5 percent). And, finally, say the price goes up by 10 percent and in response the quantity demanded falls by 15 percent. Price elasticity of demand is 1.5 (15 percent/10 percent).

WHAT INFORMATION PRICE ELASTICITY PROVIDES

Price elasticity of demand and supply gives us information about the exact quantity response to a change in price. A price elasticity of demand of 0.3 tells us that a 10 percent rise in price will lead to a 3 percent decline in quantity demanded. If the elasticity of demand were a larger number, say 5, the same 10 percent rise in price will lead to a 50 percent decline in quantity demanded. As elasticity increases, responsiveness of quantity to price increases.

CLASSIFYING DEMAND AND SUPPLY AS ELASTIC OR INELASTIC

It is helpful to classify elasticities by relative responsiveness. Economists usually describe supply and demand by the terms *elastic* and *inelastic*. Formally, demand or supply is **elastic** if *the percentage change in quantity is greater than the percentage change in price* ($E > 1$). Conversely, demand or supply is **inelastic** if *the percentage change in quantity is less than the percentage change in price* ($E < 1$). In the last two examples, an elasticity of supply of 0.3 means supply is inelastic ($E_S < 1$), and an elasticity of supply of 5 means supply is elastic ($E_S > 1$).

The commonsense interpretation of these terms is the following: An *inelastic* supply means that the quantity supplied doesn't change much with a change in price. For example, say the price of land rises. The amount of land supplied won't change much, so the supply of land is inelastic. An *elastic* supply means that quantity supplied changes by a larger percentage than the percentage change in price. For example, say the price of pencils doubles. What do you think will happen to the quantity of pencils supplied? I suspect it will more than double, which means that the supply of pencils is elastic.

The same terminology holds with demand. Consider a good such as a brand A ballpoint pen that has a close substitute, a brand B ballpoint pen. If brand A's price rises, the quantity demanded will fall a lot as people shift to the substitute (a brand B ballpoint pen). So the demand for brand A ballpoint pens would be highly elastic. Alternatively, consider table salt, which has no close substitute at current prices. Demand for table salt

Price elasticity is the percentage change in quantity divided by the percentage change in price.

Q.1 If when price rises by 4 percent, quantity supplied rises by 8 percent, what is the price elasticity of supply?

Elastic: $E > 1$
Inelastic: $E < 1$

Q.2 If price elasticity of demand is greater than 1, what would we call demand: elastic or inelastic?

is highly inelastic. That is, a rise in the price of table salt does not result in a large decline in quantity demanded.

ELASTICITY IS INDEPENDENT OF UNITS

Before continuing, notice that elasticity measures the percentage, not the absolute, change in variables. Using percentages allows us to have a measure of responsiveness that is independent of units, making comparisons of responsiveness among different goods easier. Say a $1 increase in the price of a $2,000 computer decreases the quantity demanded by 1, from 10 to 9. Say also that a $1 increase in the price of a pen, from $1 to $2, decreases quantity demanded by 1—from 10,000 to 9,999. Using absolute numbers, the $1 price increase reduced the quantities demanded for both pens and computers by 1. But such a comparison of absolute numbers is not very helpful. To see that, ask yourself if you were planning on raising your price, which good you'd rather be selling.

The computer price increased by 1/2,000 of its original price, a relatively small percentage increase, and quantity demanded declined by 1/10 of original sales, a large percentage decline. The percentage decline in quantity demanded exceeded the percentage rise in price, so your total revenue (Price × Quantity) would decrease. The percentage increase in price of pens was relatively large—100 percent—and the percentage decline in quantity demanded was relatively small—1/10 of 1 percent. So if you raise the price of pens, total revenue increases. Clearly, if you're raising your price in these examples, you'd rather be selling pens than computers.

By using percentages, this is made clear: With computers, a 0.05 percent increase in price decreases quantity demanded by 10 percent, so the elasticity is 200. With pens, a 100 percent increase in price decreases quantity demanded by 0.01 percent—an elasticity of 0.0001.

CALCULATING ELASTICITIES

To see that you've got the analysis down, calculate price elasticity of demand or supply in the following three real-world examples:

> *Case 1:* In 2000, the Metropolitan Atlanta Rapid Transit Authority (MARTA) proposed raising one-way bus fare by 12.5 percent and estimated that ridership would decline by 5 percent.

> *Case 2:* In the 1980s, when gasoline prices rose by 9 percent in Washington, D.C., the quantity of gasoline demanded there fell by 40 percent.

> *Case 3:* In the mid-1990s, when the minimum wage in Vermont rose by 10 percent, the quantity of labor supplied for relevant jobs increased by about 1.8 percent.

In the first case price elasticity of demand is 0.4. The quantity of rides demanded in the MARTA system was not expected to respond much to the increase in price. Elasticity was less than 1, so demand was inelastic. In the second case, price elasticity of demand is 4.4. The quantity of gas demanded in Washington, D.C., responded by a lot to a relatively small change in gas prices. Elasticity was greater than 1, so demand was elastic. The price elasticity of supply in the third case is 0.18. The quantity of labor supplied did not respond much to the change in wage. Elasticity was less than 1, so supply was inelastic.

Let's now calculate some elasticities graphically. Let's begin by determining the price elasticity of demand between points A and B in Figure 6-1(a).

The demand curve in the figure is a hypothetical demand for WolfPack Simulation Software. You can see that as the price of the software rises from $20 to $26, the quantity demanded falls from 14,000 to 10,000 units a year. To determine the price elasticity

Figure 6-1 (a, b, and c)   Graphs of Elasticities
In **(a)** we are calculating the elasticity of the demand curve between *A* and *B*. We essentially calculate the midpoint and use that midpoint to calculate percentage changes. This gives us a percentage change in price of 26 percent and a percentage change in quantity of 33 percent, for an elasticity of 1.27. In **(b)** the percentage change in price is 10.53 percent and the percentage change in quantity is 1.87 percent, giving an elasticity of 0.18. In **(c)**, the calculations are left for you to do.

(a)   Elasticity of demand   **(b)   Elasticity of supply**   **(c)   Some examples**

Answers to (c): $a = 4$; $b = 0.54$, $c = 0.67$

of demand, we need to determine the percentage change in quantity and the percentage change in price. In doing so, there is a small problem that is sometimes called the *end-point problem*: The percentage change differs depending on whether you view the change as a rise or a decline. For example, say you calculate the rise in price from $20 to $26, starting from $20. That gives you a percentage increase in price of $[(20 - 26)/20] \times 100 = 30$ percent. If, however, you calculate that same change in price, $6, as a fall in price from $26 to $20, the percentage decrease in price is $[(26 - 20)/26] \times 100 = 23$ percent. The easiest way to solve this problem is to use the average of the two end values to calculate percentage change. In our example, instead of using 20 or 26 as a starting point, you use $(20 + 26)/2$, or 23. So the percentage change in price is

Economists use the average of the two end values to get around the end-point problem.

$$\frac{P_2 - P_1}{\frac{1}{2}(P_1 + P_2)} = \frac{(26 - 20)}{23} \times 100 = 26 \text{ percent}$$

Similarly the percentage change in quantity is

$$\frac{Q_2 - Q_1}{\frac{1}{2}(Q_1 + Q_2)} = \frac{(10 - 14)}{12} \times 100 = -33 \text{ percent}$$

Having done this, we can calculate elasticity as usual by dividing the percentage change in quantity by the percentage change in price:

$$\text{Elasticity} = \frac{\text{Percentage change in quantity}}{\text{Percentage change in price}} = \frac{-33}{26} = 1.27[1]$$

[1] I dropped the negative sign because, as discussed earlier, economists talk about price elasticity of demand as a positive number.

Knowing the Tools

The text explained how to calculate elasticity of a range along a demand and supply curve. But what if you're asked to calculate elasticity at a specific point and you don't know the percentage change in price and quantity? In that case, you can use the following procedure.

Say you want to determine the elasticity at point A in Figure (a). First create a line segment, with the point as the segment's midpoint. The segment can be of any length. In Figure (a) I have selected a segment that begins 4 units on the quantity axis before the quantity at A and extends 4 units beyond the quantity at A. Thus, the quantity extends from 20 to 28. Next, determine the price relevant for the quantities chosen. In the example, the price corresponding to the quantity 28 is $3, and the price corresponding to the quantity 20 is $5.

I've now got my line segment, so I am ready to calculate the relevant percent changes. Percentage change in quan-

tity = [(28 − 20)/24] × 100 = 33 percent. Percentage change in price = [(5 − 3)/4] × 100 = 50 percent. Elasticity at point A is 33/50 = 0.66.

To see that you've got the calculation down, in Figure (b) I present four points—two on the demand curve and two on a supply curve. Your assignment is to determine the elasticity of the four points on your own.

Now that you've done the calculations—you have, right?—you can look at the bottom of Figure (b), where I give you the correct answers. If you got all four right, you're in good shape. If not, it's time for a review. (And if you're taking the easy road and not calculating them on your own, it's time to get yourself in gear and start studying—remember, this stuff doesn't get into your head through osmosis.)

(a) **Elasticity of demand**

(b) **Some examples**

Answers to (b): A = 2.33; B = 0.11; C = 0.75; D = 0.86.

The elasticity of demand between points A and B is approximately 1.3. This means that a 10 percent increase in price will cause a 13 percent fall in quantity demanded. Thus, demand between A and B is elastic.

OTHER EXAMPLES

In Figure 6-1(b) I go through another example, this time using the supply elasticity from case 3 on p. 134. Initially, the Vermont minimum wage was $4.50 an hour; it was then raised to $5 an hour. The average of the two end points is $4.75 and so the percentage change in price is $(0.50/4.75) \times 100 = 10.53$ percent. The initial quantity of labor supplied I estimated for my area in Vermont was 476; the rise in the minimum wage increased that number to 485, which gives us a percentage change in quantity of $(9/480.5) \times 100 = 1.87$ percent. To calculate the elasticity of supply, divide the percentage change in quantity by the percentage change in price to get $1.87/10.53 = 0.18$. A 10 percent rise in the minimum wage will bring about a 1.8 percent increase in quantity of labor supplied. The minimum-wage labor supply in Vermont is inelastic.

Learning the mechanics of calculating elasticities takes some practice, so in Figure 6-1(c) I give you three additional examples, leaving the calculations for you.

a. Move from A to B on the demand curve.

b. Move from C to D on the demand curve.

c. Move from E to F on the supply curve.

Now that you've calculated them (you have, haven't you?), I'll let you know that the answers can be found upside down at the bottom of the figure.

ELASTICITY AND SUPPLY AND DEMAND CURVES

There are two important points to remember about elasticity and supply and demand curves. The first is that elasticity is related to (but is not the same as) slope, and the second is that elasticity changes along straight-line demand and supply curves.

ELASTICITY IS NOT THE SAME AS SLOPE

Let's begin with the first point. The relationship between elasticity and slope is the following: The steeper the curve becomes at a given point, the less elastic is supply or demand. The limiting examples of this are a vertical curve (most steep), shown in Figure 6-2(a), and a horizontal (least steep) curve, shown in Figure 6-2(b).

The vertical demand curve shown in Figure 6-2(a) demonstrates how a change in price leads to no change in quantity demanded. Economists describe this curve as **perfectly inelastic**—*quantity does not respond at all to changes in price* $(E = 0)$. Curves that are vertical are perfectly inelastic. The demand curve shown in Figure 6-2(b), in contrast, is horizontal. A change in price from above or below P_0 results in an infinitely large increase in quantity demanded. This curve is **perfectly elastic**, reflecting the fact that *quantity responds enormously to changes in price* $(E = \infty)$. Horizontal curves are perfectly elastic. From these extreme cases, you can see that steeper (more vertical) curves at a given point are more *in*elastic and less steep (more horizontal) curves at a given point are more elastic. Elasticity, however, is not the same as slope. The second point illustrates this well.

ELASTICITY CHANGES ALONG STRAIGHT-LINE CURVES

On straight-line supply and demand curves, slope does not change, but elasticity does. Figure 6-2(c and d) shows how elasticity changes along demand and supply curves. At the price intercept of the demand curve in Figure 6-2(c), demand is perfectly elastic $(E_D = \infty)$; elasticity becomes smaller as price declines until it becomes perfectly inelastic $(E_D = 0)$ at the quantity intercept. At one point along the demand curve, between an elasticity of infinity and zero, demand is **unit elastic**—*the percentage change in quantity equals the percentage change in price* $(E = 1)$. In Figure 6-2(c) demand is unit elastic at a price of $5. To confirm this, calculate elasticity of demand between $4 and $6. The percentage change in price is $(2/5) \times 100 = 40$ percent, and the percentage change in quantity is $(2/5) \times 100 = 40$ percent. The point at which demand is unit elastic divides

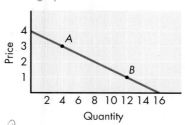

Q-3 What is the approximate elasticity between points A and B on the graph below?

Q-4 Your study partner, Nicole, has just stated that a straight-line demand curve is inelastic. How do you respond?

Figure 6-2 (a–d) Elasticities and Supply and Demand Curves

In (a) and (b), two special elasticity cases are shown. A perfectly inelastic curve is vertical; a perfectly elastic curve is horizontal. In (c) and (d), I show how elasticity generally varies along both supply and demand curves. Along demand curves it always goes from infinity at the vertical axis intercept to zero at the horizontal axis intercept. How elasticity of supply varies depends on which axis the supply curve intersects. If it intersects the vertical axis, elasticity starts at infinity and declines, and eventually approaches 1. If it intersects the horizontal axis, it starts at zero and increases, and eventually approaches 1. The one exception is when the supply curve intersects the origin. A good exercise is to determine what happens to elasticity in that case. (Hint: See Knowing the Tools box on page 139.)

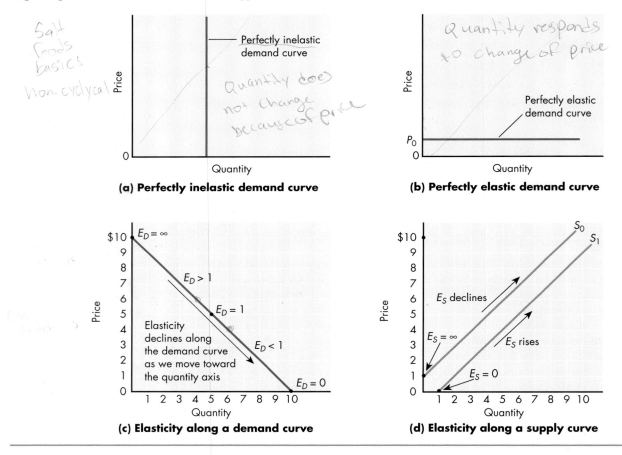

(a) Perfectly inelastic demand curve

(b) Perfectly elastic demand curve

(c) Elasticity along a demand curve

(d) Elasticity along a supply curve

the demand curve into two sections—an elastic portion ($E_D > 1$) above the point at which demand is unit elastic and an inelastic portion ($E_D < 1$) below the point at which demand is unit elastic.

The change in elasticity along a supply curve is less dramatic. At the point on a straight-line supply curve that intercepts the price axis, supply is perfectly elastic ($E_S = \infty$). Points become less elastic as you move out along the supply curve. At the point on a straight-line supply curve that intercepts the quantity axis, supply is perfectly inelastic ($E_S = 0$); it becomes more elastic as you move out along the supply curve. These changes are labeled in Figure 6-2(d). I leave it to you to determine what happens to the elasticity of the supply curve if the supply curve intercepts the origin. (Hint: See the Knowing the Tools box "Geometric Tricks for Estimating Price Elasticity.")

As a review, the five terms to describe elasticity along a curve are listed here from most to least elastic:

Knowing the Tools

There are a couple of tricks that are useful in determining whether a point on a straight-line supply or demand curve is elastic or inelastic. The trick with demand is the following: (1) Determine where the demand curve intersects the price and quantity axes. (2) At a point midway between the origin and the quantity line intersection, draw a vertical line back up to the demand curve. The point where it intersects the demand curve will have an elasticity of 1; it will be unit elastic; all points to the left of that line will be elastic, and all points to the right of that will be inelastic.

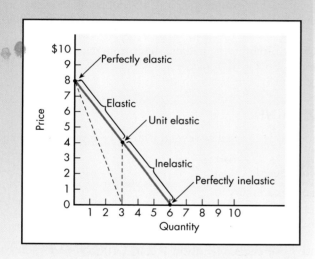

To determine whether a straight-line supply curve is elastic or inelastic you simply extend it to one of the axes, as in the following graph. The point at which this extension intersects the axes indicates the elasticity of the supply curve:

- If the extension intersects the vertical (price) axis, as does S_1, all points on the supply curve have an elasticity greater than 1; the supply curve is elastic.
- If the extension intersects the horizontal (quantity) axis, as does S_2, all points on the supply curve have an elasticity less than 1; the supply curve is inelastic.
- If the extension intersects the two axes at the origin, the supply curve has an elasticity of 1; the supply curve has unit elasticity.

If you combine these tricks with a knowledge that a perfectly elastic supply or demand curve is horizontal and crosses the price axis, and a perfectly inelastic supply or demand curve is vertical and crosses the quantity axis, you can even remember which is which. If a straight-line supply curve crosses the quantity axis, all points on it are inelastic; if it crosses the price axis, all points on it are elastic. Similarly, the top half of the demand curve (the part that crosses the price axis) is elastic; the bottom half (the part that crosses the quantity axis) is inelastic.

1. *Perfectly elastic:* Quantity responds enormously to changes in price ($E = \infty$).
2. *Elastic:* The percentage change in quantity exceeds the percentage change in price ($E > 1$).
3. *Unit elastic:* The percentage change in quantity is the same as the percentage change in price ($E = 1$).
4. *Inelastic:* The percentage change in quantity is less than the percentage change in price ($E < 1$).
5. *Perfectly inelastic:* Quantity does not respond at all to changes in price ($E = 0$).

Five elastic terms are: perfectly elastic ($E = \infty$); elastic ($E > 1$); unit elastic ($E = 1$); inelastic ($E < 1$); and perfectly inelastic ($E = 0$).

Now that you have seen that elasticity changes along straight-line supply and demand curves, the first point—that elasticity is related to but not the same as slope—should be clear. Whereas elasticity changes along a straight-line curve, slope does not.

SUBSTITUTION AND ELASTICITY

Now that you know how to measure elasticity, let's consider some of the factors that are likely to make supply and demand more or less elastic.

How responsive quantity demanded and quantity supplied will be to changes in price can be summed up in one word: substitution. As a general rule, the more substitutes a good has, the more elastic is its supply or demand.

The reasoning is as follows: If a good has substitutes, a rise in the price of that good will cause the consumer to shift consumption to those substitute goods. Put another way, when a satisfactory substitute is available, a rise in that good's price will have a large effect on the quantity demanded. For example, I think a Whopper is a satisfactory substitute for a Big Mac. If most people agree with me, the demand for Big Macs would be very elastic.

Factors that affect a good's substitutability of demand differ from factors that affect a good's substitutability of supply. So I will consider each separately. I begin with demand.

SUBSTITUTION AND DEMAND

The number of substitutes a good has is affected by several factors. Four of the most important are:

1. The time period being considered.
2. The degree to which a good is a luxury.
3. The market definition.
4. The importance of the good in one's budget.

These four reasons are derivatives of the substitution factor. Let's consider each to see why.

1. *The period being considered.*   The larger the time interval considered, or the longer the run, the more elastic is the good's demand curve. There are more substitutes in the long run than in the short run. That's because the long run provides more alternatives. For example, let's consider the World War II period, when the price of rubber went up considerably. In the short run, there were few substitutes; the demand for rubber was inelastic. In the long run, however, the rise in the price of rubber stimulated research for alternatives. Many alternatives were found. Today automobile tires, which were all made of rubber at the time World War II broke out, are almost entirely made from synthetic materials. In the long run, the demand curve was very elastic.

2. *The degree to which a good is a luxury.*   The less a good is a necessity, the more elastic is its demand curve. Because by definition one cannot do without necessities, they tend to have fewer substitutes than do luxuries. Insulin for a diabetic is a necessity; the demand is highly inelastic. Chocolate Ecstasy cake, however, is a luxury. A variety of other luxuries can be substituted for it (for example, cheesecake or a ball game).

3. *The market definition.*   As the definition of a good becomes more specific, demand becomes more elastic. If the good we're talking about is broadly defined (say, transportation), there aren't many substitutes and demand will be inelastic. If you want to get from A to B, you need transportation. If the definition of the good is narrowed—say, to "transportation by bus"—there are more substitutes. Instead of taking a bus you

The most important determinant of price elasticity of demand is the number of substitutes for the good.

The more substitutes, the more elastic the demand and the more elastic the supply.

Q-5   What are four important factors affecting the number of substitutes a good has?

can walk, ride your bicycle, or drive your car. In that case the demand curve is more elastic.

4. *The importance of the good in one's budget.*   Demand for goods that represent a large proportion of one's budget are more elastic than demand for goods that represent a small proportion of one's budget. Goods that cost very little relative to your total expenditures aren't worth spending a lot of time figuring out whether there's a good substitute. An example is pencils. Their low price means most people would buy just as many even if their price doubled. Their demand is inelastic. It is, however, worth spending lots of time looking for substitutes for goods that take a large portion of one's income. The demand for such goods tends to be more elastic. Many colleges have discovered this as they tried to raise tuition when other colleges did not. The demand curve they faced was elastic.

SUBSTITUTION AND SUPPLY

The same general issues involving substitution are relevant when considering determinants of the elasticity of supply. But when it comes to supply, economists focus on time rather than on other factors because time plays such a central role in determining supply elasticity. The general rule is: The longer the time period considered, the more elastic is the supply curve. The reasoning is the same as with demand; in the long run there are more alternatives, so it is easier (less costly) for suppliers to change and produce other goods.

To emphasize the importance of time, economists distinguish three time periods relevant to supply:

1. In the instantaneous period, quantity supplied is fixed, so supply is perfectly inelastic. This supply is sometimes called the momentary supply.

2. In the short run, some substitution is possible, so the short-run supply curve is somewhat elastic.

3. In the long run, significant substitution is possible; the supply curve becomes very elastic.

In determining the elasticity of supply, one must, however, remember an additional factor: Many supplied goods are produced, so we must take into account how easy it is to increase production of those same goods. For example, if the cost per unit of producing a good is constant, its supply is likely highly elastic. Before we can discuss such issues in detail, we need to talk about the production process in detail. And that will take two entire chapters, so I will put off the discussion for now.

HOW SUBSTITUTION FACTORS AFFECT SPECIFIC DECISIONS

Let's consider how some of the substitution factors affect a specific decision. Let's say you've been hired by two governments (the city of Washington, D.C., and the U.S. government) to advise them about the effect that raising the gas tax by 10 percent will have on tax revenues. You look at the three factors that affect elasticity of demand.

In your report to the two governments, you would point out that in the short run the demand curve is less elastic than in the long run, since people aren't going to trade in their gas-guzzling cars for fuel-efficient cars immediately in response to a 10 percent rise in gas taxes—partly because they can't afford to, partly because they don't want to, and partly because not that many fuel-efficient cars are available to buy at the moment. When the time comes, however, that they would ordinarily purchase a new car, they're likely to switch to cars that are more fuel-efficient than their old cars, and to switch as much as they can to forms of transportation that are more fuel-efficient than cars. In the long run the demand will be far more elastic.

The longer the time period considered, the more elastic the supply.

Q.6 Is supply generally more elastic in the short run or in the long run?

In the long run, demand generally becomes more elastic.

The second point you'd note is that gasoline is generally considered a necessity, although not all driving is necessary. However, since gasoline is only a small part of what it costs to drive a car, demand will probably tend to be inelastic.

As for the third factor (how specifically the good is defined) you have to be careful. It makes your recommendations for the government of the city of Washington, D.C., and the U.S. government quite different from each other. For the U.S. government, which is interested in the demand for gasoline in the entire United States, gasoline has a relatively inelastic demand. The general rule of thumb is that a 1-cent rise in tax will raise tax revenues by $1 billion. That inelasticity can't be carried over to the demand for gasoline in a city such as Washington, D.C. Because of the city's size and location, people in Washington have a choice. A large proportion of the people who buy gas in Washington could as easily buy gas in the adjacent states of Maryland or Virginia. Gasoline in Washington is a narrowly defined good and therefore has a quite elastic demand. A rise in price will mean a large fall in the quantity of gas demanded.

I mention this point because someone forgot about it when the city of Washington, D.C., raised the tax on a gallon of gasoline by 8 cents, a rise at that time of about 9 percent (this was case 2 in our discussion of calculating elasticities on p. 134). In response, monthly gasoline sales in Washington fell from 16 million gallons to less than 11 million gallons, a 40 percent decrease! The demand for gas in Washington was not inelastic, as it was for the United States as a whole; it was very elastic ($E_D = 4.4$). Washingtonians went elsewhere to buy gas.

The fact that smaller geographic areas have more elastic demands limits how highly state and local governments can tax goods relative to their neighboring localities or states. Where there are tax differences, new stores open all along the border and existing stores expand to entice people to come over that border and save on taxes. For example, the liquor tax is higher in Vermont than in New Hampshire, so it isn't surprising that right across the border from Vermont, New Hampshire has a large number of liquor stores. Here's one final example: If you look at license plates in Janzen Beach, Oregon (right across the Washington state border), you'll see a whole lot of Washington license plates. Why? If you answered that it likely has something to do with differential sales taxes in Washington and Oregon, you've got the idea.

EMPIRICAL ESTIMATES OF ELASTICITIES OF DEMAND AND SUPPLY

Table 6-1 presents empirical estimates of elasticity of demand. Notice that, as expected, different estimates are provided for the short- and long-run elasticities of each good. Also notice that the estimates are for the entire United States; estimates for a specific region in the United States could be expected to show more elasticity.

Taking an example from Table 6-1, notice that the long-run demand for movies is elastic. If movie theaters raise their prices, it's relatively easy for individuals simply to stay home and watch television. Movies have close substitutes, so we would expect the demand to be relatively elastic.

As a second example, in the short run the demand for electricity is highly inelastic. Either people have electrical appliances or they don't. In the long run, however, it becomes elastic since people can shift to gas for cooking and oil for heating, and can buy more energy-efficient appliances. As an exercise, you might see if you can explain why each of the other goods listed in the table has the elasticity of demand reported.

There are many fewer empirical measurements of supply than there are of demand. The reason concerns the structure of markets of produced goods, and the complicated nature of production. Most retail markets have seller-set or posted prices—you go to the

Table 6-1 Short-Run and Long-Run Elasticities of Demand

Product	Price Elasticity	
	Short-Run	Long-Run
Tobacco products	0.46	1.89
Electricity (for household consumption)	0.13	1.89
Health services	0.20	0.92
Toys (nondurable)	0.30	1.02
Movies/motion pictures	0.87	3.67
Foreign travel by U.S. residents	0.14	1.77
Beer	.56	1.39
Wine	.68	.84
University tuition	.52	—
Rail transit	.62	1.59

Sources: Hendrik S. Houthakker and Lester D. Taylor, *Consumer Demand in the United States: Analyses and Projections*, 2nd ed. (Cambridge, Mass.: Harvard University Press, 1970); W. S. Comanor and T. A. Wilson, *Advertising and Market Power* (Cambridge, Mass.: Harvard University Press, 1974); Shermon Folland, Allen C. Goodman, and Miron Stano, *The Economics of Health Care* (New York: Macmillan, 1993); Yu Hsing and Hui S. Chang, "Testing Increasing Sensitivity of Enrollment at Private Institutions to Tuition and Other Costs," *The American Economist* 41, no. 1 (Spring 1996); Richard Voith, "The Long-Run Elasticity of Demand for Commuter Rail Transportation," *Journal of Urban Economics* 30 (1991).

store and pay the listed price of toothpaste. You can buy as much as you want at that price, so in a sense the supply of toothpaste (and most retail goods) is perfectly elastic until the store runs out, whereupon the supply becomes perfectly inelastic. But in another sense there is no supply curve since the selling price is determined by the seller's pricing strategy, not by the market. I will hold off discussion of such issues until after we discuss costs, production, and various market structures.

We do find empirical measurements of supply in factor markets, such as the market for labor services. For example, economist David Blau has estimated that the supply of child care labor is elastic—it may be as high as 1.9—which means that a 10 percent rise in the wages paid to child care workers will lead to a 19 percent increase in the quantity of child care workers. More generally, economists have estimated that the labor supply elasticity of heads of households is about 0.1, and for secondary workers is about 1.1. A good test of whether you intuitively understand elasticities is whether you can explain why the latter is more elastic.

Other areas in which elasticities of supply are estimated are agricultural and raw materials markets. Estimating supply elasticities here is possible because these goods are often sold in auction markets where price is directly determined by supply and demand, rather than in posted-price markets. In these markets, economists have generally found that the short-run supplies are highly inelastic and that the long-run supplies are highly elastic.

ELASTICITY, TOTAL REVENUE, AND DEMAND

For sellers, knowing elasticity of demand is useful because from it they can tell whether the total revenue will go up or down when they raise or lower their prices. The total revenue a supplier receives is the price he or she charges times the quantity he or she sells. (Total revenue equals total quantity sold multiplied by the price of the good.) Elasticity tells sellers what will happen to total revenue if their price changes. Specifically:

● If demand is elastic ($E_D > 1$), a rise in price lowers total revenue. (Price and total revenue move in opposite directions.)

Figure 6-3 (a, b, and c)   Elasticity and Total Revenue

Total revenue is measured by the rectangle produced by extending lines from the demand curve to the price and quantity axes. The change in total revenue resulting from a change in price can be estimated by comparing the sizes of the before and after rectangles. If price is being raised, total revenue increases by rectangle C and decreases by rectangle B. As you can see, the effect of a price rise on total revenue differs significantly at different points on a demand curve; (a) shows an almost unitary elastic range, (b) shows an inelastic range, and (c) shows an elastic range.

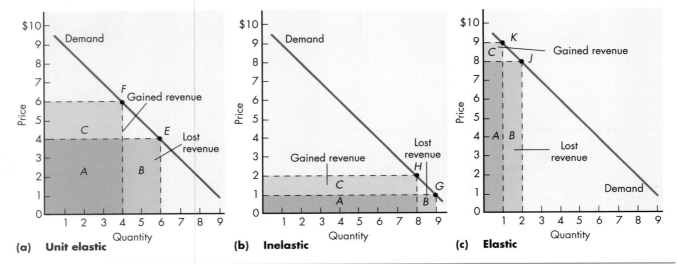

(a)   Unit elastic   **(b)   Inelastic**   **(c)   Elastic**

Q.7
If demand is inelastic and a firm raises price, what happens to total revenue?

● If demand is unit elastic ($E_D = 1$), a rise in price leaves total revenue unchanged.

● If demand is inelastic ($E_D < 1$), a rise in price increases total revenue. (Price and total revenue move in the same direction.)

The relationship between elasticity and total revenue is no mystery. There's a very logical reason why they are related, which can be seen most neatly by recognizing that total revenue ($P \times Q$) is represented by the area under the demand curve at that price and quantity. For example, at point E on the demand curve in Figure 6-3(a), the total revenue at price $4 and quantity 6 is the area designated by the A and B rectangles, $24.

If we increase price to $6, quantity demanded decreases to 4, so total revenue is still $24. Total revenue has remained constant, so the demand curve from point E to point F is unit elastic. The new total revenue is represented by the A and C rectangles. The difference between the old total revenue (A and B) and the new total revenue (A and C) is the difference between the rectangles B and C. Comparing these rectangles provides us with a visual method of estimating elasticities.

Figure 6-3(b) shows an inelastic range; Figure 6-3(c) shows a highly elastic range. While in Figure 6-3(b) the slope of the demand curve is the same as in Figure 6-3(a), we begin at a different point on the demand curve (point G). If we raise our price from $1 to $2, quantity demanded falls from 9 to 8. The gained area (rectangle C) is much greater than the lost area (rectangle B). In other words, total revenue increases significantly, so the demand curve between points H and G is highly inelastic.

In Figure 6-3(c) the demand curve is again the same, but we begin at still another point, J. If we raise our price from $8 to $9, quantity demanded falls from 2 to 1. The gained area (rectangle C) is much smaller than the lost area (rectangle B). In other words, total revenue decreases significantly, so the demand curve from points J to K is highly elastic.

Figure 6-4 (a and b)   How Total Revenue Changes

Total revenue is at a maximum when elasticity equals 1, as you can see in (**a**) and (**b**). When demand is elastic, total revenue decreases with an increase in price. When demand is inelastic, total revenue increases with an increase in price.

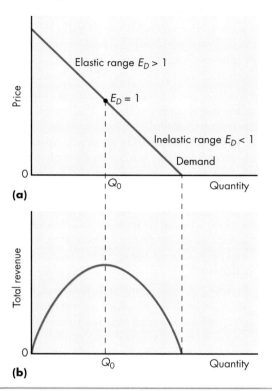

(a)

(b)

Relationship between Elasticity (E) and Total Revenue (TR)		
	Price Rise	Price Decline
Elastic ($E_D > 1$)	$TR \downarrow$	$TR \uparrow$
Unit Elastic ($E_D = 1$)	TR constant	TR constant
Inelastic ($E_D < 1$)	$TR \uparrow$	$TR \downarrow$

TOTAL REVENUE ALONG A DEMAND CURVE

The way in which elasticity changes along a demand curve and its relationship to total revenue can be seen in Figure 6-4. When output is zero, total revenue is zero; similarly, when price is zero, total revenue is zero. That accounts for the two end points of the total revenue curve in Figure 6-4(b). Let's say we start at a price of zero, where demand is perfectly inelastic. As we increase price (decrease quantity demanded), total revenue increases significantly. As we continue to do so, the increases in total revenue become smaller until finally, after output of Q_0, total revenue actually starts decreasing. It continues decreasing at a faster and faster rate until finally, at zero output, total revenue is zero.

As an example of where such calculations might come in handy, recall the vanity license plates that we used to illustrate the law of demand in Chapter 4. A rise in the price of vanity plates of about 29 percent, from $30 to $40, decreased the quantity demanded about 64 percent, from 60,334 to 31,122, so the price elasticity of demand was about 0.64/0.29 = 2.2. Since demand was elastic, total revenue fell. Specifically, total revenue fell from $1,810,020 ($30 × 60,334) to $1,244,880 ($40 × 31,122).

With elastic demands, a rise in price decreases total revenue. With inelastic demands, a rise in price increases total revenue.

Web Note 6.1
Elasticity and Cartels

ELASTICITY OF INDIVIDUAL AND MARKET DEMAND

In thinking about elasticity of demand, keep in mind the point made in Chapter 4: The market demand curve is the horizontal summation of individual demand curves; some individuals have highly inelastic demands and others have highly elastic demands. A slight rise in the price of a good will cause some people to stop buying the good; the slight increase won't affect other people's quantity demanded for the good at all. Market demand elasticity is influenced both by how many people drop out totally and by how much an existing consumer marginally changes his or her quantity demanded.

If a firm can somehow separate the people with less elastic demand from those with more elastic demand, it can charge more to the individuals with inelastic demands and less to individuals with elastic demands. Economists call this *price discrimination*. We see firms throughout the economy trying to use price discrimination. Let's consider three examples:

1. Airlines' Saturday stay-over specials. If you stay over a Saturday night, usually you can get a much lower airline fare than if you don't. The reason is that businesspeople have inelastic demands and don't like to stay over Saturday nights, while pleasure travelers have more elastic demands. By requiring individuals to stay over Saturday night, airlines can separate out businesspeople and charge them more.

2. The phenomenon of selling new cars. Most new cars don't sell at the listed price. They sell at a discount. Salespeople are trained to separate out comparison shoppers (who have more elastic demands) from impulse buyers (who have inelastic demands). By not listing the selling price of cars so that the discount can be worked out in individual negotiations, salespeople can charge more to customers who have inelastic demands.

3. The almost-continual-sale phenomenon. Some items, such as washing machines, go on sale rather often. Why don't suppliers sell them at a low price all the time? Because some buyers whose washing machines break down have inelastic demand. They can't wait, so they'll pay the "unreduced" price. Others have elastic demands; they can wait for the sale. By running sales (even though they're frequent sales), sellers can separate consumers with inelastic demand curves from consumers with elastic demand curves.

OTHER ELASTICITY CONCEPTS

There are many other elasticity concepts besides the price elasticity of demand and the price elasticity of supply. Since these other elasticities can be useful in specifying the effects of shift factors on the demand for a good, I will introduce you to two of them: income elasticity of demand and cross-price elasticity of demand.

The definition of these concepts is straightforward. **Income elasticity of demand** is defined as *the percentage change in demand divided by the percentage change in income*. Put another way,

$$\text{Income elasticity of demand} = \frac{\text{Percentage change in demand}}{\text{Percentage change in income}}$$

It tells us the responsiveness of demand to changes in income. (Notice I used *demand*, not *quantity demanded*, to emphasize that in response to a change in anything but the price of that good, the entire demand curve shifts; there's no movement along the demand curve.) **Cross-price elasticity of demand** is defined as *the percentage change in demand divided by the percentage change in the price of a related good*. Put another way,

$$\text{Cross-price elasticity of demand} = \frac{\text{Percentage change in demand}}{\text{Percentage change in price of a related good}}$$

In the text, the discussion of determining elasticity concentrates on the technical aspects of the calculation. It assumes we know at what point on the supply and demand curve we are. In the real world, economists don't have the luxury of that knowledge. The data points they use involve interactions of supply and demand, and they must use statistical tools to ensure that they are holding "other things constant." Specifically, to determine points on a demand curve we must vary supply (and nothing else); to determine points on a supply curve we must vary demand (and nothing else).

In practice, holding everything else constant is difficult to do, which means real-world estimates of elasticity are often less than perfect. The tables presented in the text are some economists' estimates, but there are often disputes and technical issues that could lead to different estimates.

Where do firms get the information they need to calculate elasticities? Think of the grocery store where you can get a special buyer's card; you show it to the checkout clerk and you get all the discounts. And the card is free! Those grocery stores are not just being nice. When the clerk scans your purchases, the store gets information that is forwarded to a central processing unit that can see how people react to different prices. This information is valuable; it allows firms to fine-tune their pricing—raising prices on goods for which the demand is inelastic, and lowering prices on goods for which the demand is elastic.

Alternatively, think of the warranty cards that you send in when you buy a new computer or a new TV. The information goes into the firms' information bases and is used by their economists in future price-setting decisions.

These other elasticity concepts tell you how much the demand curve will shift when there is a change in a shift factor. Let's consider each separately.

INCOME ELASTICITY OF DEMAND

The most commonly used of the elasticity terms introduced above is *income elasticity of demand*. Income elasticity of demand tells us how much demand will change with a change in income. An increase in income generally increases one's consumption of almost all goods, although the increase may be greater for some goods than for others. **Normal goods**—*goods whose consumption increases with an increase in income*—have income elasticities greater than zero.

Normal goods are sometimes divided into luxuries and necessities. **Luxuries** are *goods that have an income elasticity greater than 1*—their percentage increase in demand is greater than the percentage increase in income. For example, say your income goes up 10 percent and your consumption of DVDs goes up 20 percent. The income elasticity of DVDs is 2; thus, DVDs are a luxury good. Alternatively, say your income goes up by 100 percent and your demand for shoes goes up by 50 percent. Your income elasticity for shoes would be 0.5. Shoes are a **necessity**—*a good that has an income elasticity less than 1*. The consumption of a necessity rises by a smaller proportion than the rise in income.

It is even possible that an increase in income can affect relative preferences so much that an increase in income can cause a *decrease* in the consumption of a particular good. These goods have a negative income elasticity of demand. The term applied to such goods is **inferior goods**—*goods whose consumption decreases when income increases*. In some circumstances, potatoes could be an example of an inferior good. As income goes up, people might so significantly shift their consumption toward meat and away from potatoes that their total consumption of potatoes decreases. A study by a Stanford economist also found tortillas to be an inferior good in Mexico.

Table 6-2 presents income elasticities measured for some groups of goods. Notice a few things about this table. In the short run, people often save high proportions of their

Q-8 If a good's consumption increases with an increase in income, what type of good would you call it?

Web Note 6.2
Inferior Goods

Table 6-2 Income Elasticities for Selected Goods

| | Income Elasticity | |
Commodity	Short-Run	Long-Run
Motion pictures	0.81	3.41
Foreign travel	0.24	3.09
Tobacco products	0.21	0.86
Food produced and consumed on farms	−0.61	—
Furniture	2.60	0.53
Jewelry and watches	1.00	1.64
Beer	—	0.84
Hard liquor	—	2.5
Dental services	—	1.6
Private university tuition	—	1.1

Sources: Hendrik S. Houthakker and Lester D. Taylor, *Consumer Demand in the United States: Analyses and Projections,* 2nd ed. (Cambridge, Mass.: Harvard University Press, 1970); E. A. Selvanthan, "Cross-Country Alcohol Consumption: An Application of the Rotterdam Demand System," *Applied Economics* 23 (1991); Shermon Folland, Allen C. Goodman, and Miron Stano, *The Economics of Health Care* (New York: Macmillan, 1993); Yu Hsing and Hui S. Chang, "Testing Increasing Sensitivity of Enrollment at Private Institutions to Tuition and Other Costs," *The American Economist* 41, no. 1 (Spring 1996).

increases in income, so most goods, other than impulse goods, such as furniture, have low short-run income elasticities. To avoid this problem, economists generally focus on long-run income elasticities. Notice which goods are necessities (the ones with long-run income elasticities less than 1). Notice also which goods are luxuries (the ones with elasticities greater than 1).

Finally, notice the one good with a negative income elasticity—food produced and consumed on farms. As mentioned above, such goods are called inferior goods. As income rises, people buy proportionately less of such goods.

CROSS-PRICE ELASTICITY OF DEMAND

Cross-price elasticity of demand is another frequently used elasticity concept. Let's consider an example. Say the price of Toyotas rises. What is likely to happen to the demand for Fords? It is likely to rise, so the cross-price elasticity between the two is positive. Positive cross-price elasticities of demand mean the goods are **substitutes**—*goods that can be used in place of one another.* When the price of a good goes up, the demand for the substitute goes up.

Most goods have substitutes, so most cross-price elasticities are positive. But not all. To see that, let's consider another example: Say the price of hot dogs rises; what is likely to happen to the demand for ketchup? If you're like me and use lots of ketchup on your hot dogs, as I cut my consumption of hot dogs I will also cut my consumption of ketchup. Ketchup and hot dogs are not substitutes but rather complements. **Complements** are *goods that are used in conjunction with other goods.* A fall in the price of a good will increase the demand for its complement. The cross-price elasticity of complements is negative.

Some estimates of cross-price elasticities of demand are shown in Table 6-3. You can see that the strongest substitutes are European autos for U.S. and Asian autos. A 10 percent fall in the price of U.S. and Asian autos leads to a 6 percent fall in the demand for European autos. Hard liquor and beer are complements. If the price of beer falls by 10 percent, the demand for hard liquor increases by 1.1 percent.

Substitutes have positive cross-price elasticities; complements have negative cross-price elasticities.

Table 6-3 Cross-Price Elasticities

Commodities	Cross-Price Elasticity
Beef in response to price changes in pork	0.11
Beef in response to price changes in chicken	0.02
U.S. automobiles in response to price changes in European and Asian automobiles	0.28
European automobiles in response to price changes in U.S. and Asian automobiles	0.61
Beer in response to price changes in wine	0.23
Hard liquor in response to price changes in beer	−0.11

Sources: J. A. Johnson and E. H. Oksanen, "Socioeconomic Determinants of the Consumption of Alcoholic Beverages," *Applied Economics* (1974); Patrick S. McCarthy, "Market Price and Income Elasticities of New Vehicle Demand," *Review of Economics and Statistics* (August 1996); Kuo S. Huang, "Nutrient Elasticities in a Complete Food Demand System," *American Journal of Agricultural Economics* (February 1996).

SOME EXAMPLES

To make sure you've got these concepts down, see Figure 6-5, which demonstrates two examples. In Figure 6-5(a), income has risen by 20 percent, increasing demand at price P_0 from 20 to 26. To determine the income elasticity we must first determine the percentage change in demand. We calculate the percentage demand to be $6/[(20 + 26)/2]$ $= (6/23) \times 100 = 26$ percent. The percentage change in income is 20, so the income elasticity is 26/20, or 1.3.

In Figure 6-5(b), a 33 percent fall in the price of pork has caused the demand for beef to fall by 3.8 percent—from 108 to 104 at a price of P_0. The cross-price elasticity of demand is 3.8/33 = 0.12.

THE POWER OF SUPPLY/DEMAND ANALYSIS

Now that you've got the elasticity terms down, let's consider some examples that demonstrate the power of supply/demand analysis when it is combined with the concept of elasticity. Let's start with some easy cases.

Figure 6-5 (a and b)   Calculating Elasticities
Shift factors, such as income or price of another good, shift the entire demand curve. To calculate these elasticities, we see how much demand will shift at a constant price and then calculate the relevant elasticities.

(a)   Calculating income elasticity

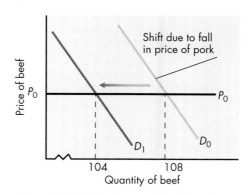

(b)   Calculating cross-price elasticity

Income elasticity of demand is defined as *the percentage change in demand divided by the percentage change in income.*

$$\text{Income elasticity of demand} = \frac{\text{Percentage change in demand}}{\text{Percentage change in income}}$$

Cross-price elasticity of demand is defined as *the percentage change in demand divided by the percentage change in the price of a related good.*

$$\text{Cross-price elasticity of demand} = \frac{\text{Percentage change in demand}}{\text{Percentage change in price of a related good}}$$

Complement: Cross-price elasticity of demand is negative.

Substitute: Cross-price elasticity of demand is positive.

Normal good: Income elasticity of demand is positive.

Luxury: Income elasticity is greater than 1.

Necessity: Income elasticity is less than 1.

Inferior good: Income elasticity of demand is negative.

WHEN SHOULD A SUPPLIER NOT RAISE PRICE?

Q-9 A firm faces an elastic demand for its product. It has come to an economist to advise it on whether to lower its price. The answer she gives is: Maybe. Why is this the right answer?

First, let's say a firm is trying to increase its profits and hires you to tell it whether it should raise or lower its price. The firm knows that it faces an inelastic demand. Should it raise its price?

I hope your answer was: Definitely yes. How can I be so sure the correct answer is yes? Because I remembered the discussion of the relationship between price elasticity of demand with total revenue. With an inelastic demand the percentage change in quantity is less than the percentage change in price, so total revenue must increase with an increase in price. Total costs will also decrease, so profits—total revenues minus total costs—must also increase.

Along those same lines, consider a university president thinking of raising tuition. Say that raising tuition by 10 percent will decrease the number of students by 1 percent. What's the price elasticity? The percentage change in quantity is 1 percent; the percentage change in price is 10. Dividing the percentage change in quantity by the percentage change in price, we have an elasticity of 0.1. That's an inelastic demand ($E_D < 1$), so raising tuition will increase the university's total revenue.

But if a 10 percent rise in tuition will decrease the enrollment by 25 percent, the elasticity will be large (2.5). In response to an increase in tuition, the university's total revenue will decrease significantly. When you have an elastic demand, you should hesitate to increase price. To make sure you're following the argument, explain the likely effect an elastic demand will have on lowering tuition. (Your argument should involve the *possibility* of increasing profit.) If you're not following the argument, go back to the section on elasticity and total revenue, especially Figure 6-3.

When the long-run and short-run elasticities differ, the analysis becomes somewhat more complicated. Consider the case of a local transit authority that, faced with a budget crisis, increased its fares from $1.50 to $1.75. The rise in revenue during the first

Figure 6-6 (a and b)   Effects of Shifts in Supply on Price and Quantity

In both (**a**) and (**b**) the supply shifts out from S_0 to S_1. Initial price is P_0 and quantity is Q_0. The new equilibrium is P_1 and Q_1. In (**a**), supply intersects demand where demand is inelastic and the quantity effects are relatively small. In (**b**), the demand is more elastic and the quantity effects are much larger. In general the effects of shifts in supply on equilibrium quantity and price are determined by the elasticity of demand. When demand is inelastic, price changes are large and quantity changes are small. A useful exercise is to go through the same two cases for demand shifts, showing how the quantity effect is determined by the elasticity of supply.

(a) Inelastic supply and inelastic demand

(b) Inelastic supply and elastic demand

year helped the authority balance its books. But in the two years following, ridership de-clined so much that total revenue fell. What happened? In the short-run, commuters had few substitutes to taking the bus—demand was relatively inelastic so that total revenue rose when fares were increased. But, as time went on, commuters found alter-native ways to get to work. Long-run demand was more elastic in this case, so much so that total revenue declined.

ELASTICITY AND SHIFTING SUPPLY AND DEMAND

Let's now turn to shifts in supply and demand. Knowing the elasticity of the supply and demand curves allows us to be more specific about the effects of shifts in supply and demand.

Figure 6-6 demonstrates the relative effects of supply shifts on equilibrium price and quantity under different assumptions about elasticity. As you can see, the more elastic the demand, the greater the effect of a supply shift on quantity, and the smaller the effect on price. Going through a similar exercise for demand shifts with various supply elasticities is also a useful exercise. If you do so, you will see that the more elastic the supply, the greater the effect of a demand shift on quantity, and the smaller the effect on price.

We can be even more precise with regard to the percentage change in price. Specif-ically, when demand shifts,

$$\text{Percentage change in price} = \frac{\text{Percentage change in demand}}{E_D + E_S}$$

When supply shifts,

$$\text{Percentage change in price} = \frac{\text{Percentage change in supply}}{E_D + E_S}$$

Let's consider two examples. Suppose demand shifts out to the right by 5 percent, the elasticity of demand is 0.8, and the elasticity of supply is 2. Price will rise by 5%/2.8, or 1.8 percent. Alternatively, if supply shifts out to the right by 33 percent and the

$\frac{.05}{.8 + 2} = \frac{.05}{2.8} = 1.8$

$\frac{33}{2} = .165$

Q-10 The elasticity of supply is 1 and the elasticity of demand is 2. If demand increases by 10 percent, by what percent will price change?

elasticity of demand and supply are both 1, price will fall by 33%/2, or 16.5 percent. In general, the more elastic supply and demand, the less price will change for a given percentage change in either demand or supply.

To be sure that you have understood elasticity, consider the following three observations about price and quantity and match them with the three descriptions of supply and demand:

a. Price rises significantly; quantity hardly changes at all.

b. Price remains almost constant; quantity increases enormously.

c. Price falls significantly; quantity hardly changes at all.

1. Demand highly elastic; supply shifts out.

2. Supply highly inelastic; demand shifts out.

3. Demand is highly inelastic; supply shifts out.

The answers are a–2; b–1; c–3.

CONCLUSION

I'll stop the exercises here. As you can see, the elasticity concept is important. Economists use it all the time when discussing supply and demand.

However, the elasticity concept is not easy to remember, or to calculate, so working with it takes some practice. It becomes a bit less forbidding if you remember that elasticity is what your shorts lose when they've been through the washer and drier too many times. If a relationship is elastic, price (for price elasticity) exerts a strong pull on quantity. If it's inelastic, there's little pull on quantity.

SUMMARY

- Elasticity is defined as percentage change in quantity divided by percentage change in some variable that affects demand (or supply) or quantity demanded (or supplied). The most common elasticity concept used is price elasticity.

- Elasticity is a better descriptor than is slope because it is independent of units of measurement.

- To calculate percentage changes in prices and quantities use the average of the end values:

$$E_D = \frac{\text{Percentage change in quantity demanded}}{\text{Percentage change in price}}$$

$$E_S = \frac{\text{Percentage change in quantity supplied}}{\text{Percentage change in price}}$$

- Five elasticity terms are: *elastic* ($E > 1$); *inelastic* ($E < 1$); *unit elastic* ($E = 1$); *perfectly inelastic* ($E = 0$); and *perfectly elastic* ($E = \infty$).

- The more substitutes a good has, the greater its elasticity.

- Factors affecting the number of substitutes in demand are (1) time period considered, (2) the degree to which the good is a luxury, (3) the market definition, and (4) the importance of the good in one's budget.

- The most important factor affecting the number of substitutes in supply is time. As the time interval lengthens, supply becomes more elastic.

- Elasticity changes along straight-line demand and supply curves. Demand becomes less elastic as we move down along a demand curve.

- When a supplier raises price, if demand is inelastic total revenue increases; if demand is elastic, total revenue decreases; if demand is unit elastic total revenue remains constant.

- Other important elasticity concepts are income elasticity and cross-price elasticity of demand.

- $$\text{Income elasticity of demand} = \frac{\text{Percentage change in demand}}{\text{Percentage change in income}}$$

- $$\text{Cross-price elasticity of demand} = \frac{\text{Percentage change in demand}}{\text{Percentage change in price of a related good}}$$

- Knowing elasticities allows us to be more precise about the qualitative effects that shifts in demand and supply have on prices and quantities.

- When demand shifts, percentage change in price
$$= \frac{\text{percentage change in demand}}{E_D + E_S}$$

- When supply shifts, percentage change in price
$$= \frac{\text{percentage change in supply}}{E_D + E_S}$$

KEY TERMS

complement (148)
cross-price elasticity of
  demand (146)
elastic (133)
income elasticity of
  demand (146)

inelastic (133)
inferior good (147)
luxury (147)
necessity (147)
normal good (147)
perfectly elastic (137)

perfectly inelastic (137)
price elasticity of
  demand (132)
price elasticity of
  supply (133)
substitute (148)

unit elastic (137)

QUESTIONS FOR THOUGHT AND REVIEW

1. Determine the price elasticity of demand if, in response to an increase in price of 10 percent, quantity demanded decreases by 20 percent. Is demand elastic or inelastic?

2. A firm has just increased its price by 5 percent over last year's price, and it found that quantity sold remained the same. The firm comes to you and wants to know its price elasticity of demand. How would you calculate it? What additional information would you search for before you did your calculation?

3. When tolls on the Dulles Airport Greenway were reduced from $1.75 to $1.00, traffic increased from 10,000 to 26,000 trips a day. Assuming all changes in quantity were due to the change in price, what is the price elasticity of demand for the Dulles Airport Greenway?

4. In 1999 Domino's Pizza, a corporate sponsor of the Washington Redskins (a football team) offered to reduce the price of its medium-size pizza by $1 for every touchdown scored by the Redskins during the previous week. Until that year, the Redskins weren't scoring many touchdowns. Much to the surprise of Domino's, in one week in 1999, the Redskins scored six touchdowns. (Maybe they like pizza.) Domino's pizzas were selling for $2 a pie! The quantity of pizzas demanded soared the following week from 1 pie an hour to 100 pies an hour. What was price elasticity of demand for Domino's pizza?

5. Which of the pairs of goods would you expect to have a greater price elasticity of demand?
   a. Cars, transportation.
   b. Housing, leisure travel.
   c. Rubber during World War II, rubber during the 20th century.

6. Which has greater elasticity: a supply curve that goes through the origin with slope of 1 or a supply curve that goes through the origin with slope of 4?

7. Why would an economist be more hesitant about making an elastic estimate of the effect of an increase in price of 1 percent rather than an increase in price of 50 percent?

8. Demand for "prestige" college education is generally considered to be highly inelastic. What does this suggest about tuition increases at prestige schools in the future? Why don't colleges raise tuition by amounts even greater than they already do?

9. Once a book has been written, would an author facing an inelastic demand curve for the book prefer to raise or lower the book's price? Why?

10. Colleges have increasingly used price sensitivity to formulate financial aid. The more eager the student, the less aid he or she can expect to get. Use elasticity to explain this phenomenon. Is this practice justified?

11. In the discussion of elasticity and raising and lowering prices, the text states that if you have an elastic demand you should hesitate to raise your price, and that lowering price can *possibly* increase profits (total revenue minus total cost). Why is the word *possibly* used?

12. For each of the following goods, state whether it is a normal good, a luxury, a necessity, or an inferior good. Explain your answers.
    a. Vodka.
    b. Table salt.
    c. Furniture.
    d. Perfume.
    e. Beer.
    f. Sugar.

13. For each of the following pairs of goods, state whether the cross-price elasticity is likely positive, negative, or zero. Explain your answers.
    a. Lettuce, carrots.
    b. Housing, furniture.
    c. Nike sneakers, LA Gear sneakers.
    d. Jeans, formal suits.

14. If there were only two goods in the world, can you say whether they would be complements or substitutes? Explain your answer.

15. How is elasticity related to the revenue from a sales tax?

PROBLEMS AND EXERCISES

1. A major cereal producer decides to lower price from $3.60 to $3 per 15-ounce box.
   a. If quantity demanded increases by 18 percent, what is the price elasticity of demand?
   b. What if, instead of lowering its price, the cereal producer had increased the size of the box from 15 to 17.8 ounces? What would you expect that the response would have been? Why?

2. In the 1960s coffee came in 1-pound cans. Today, most coffee comes in 11-ounce cans.
   a. Can you think of an explanation why?
   b. Can you think of other products besides coffee whose standard size has shrunk? (Often the standard size is supplemented by a "super-size" alternative.)

3. The president of a liberal arts college in Pennsylvania asked economist Paul Heise about the effect of a particular proposal on net income, enrollment, and student GPA. The proposal was the following: "For the incoming class: (1) cut tuition for students in the top 10 percent of their high school class by 50 percent; (2) cut tuition for students in the 10th to 20th percentiles of their high school class by 33 percent; (3) cut tuition for students in the 20th to 30th percentiles of their high school class by 25 percent; (4) leave tuition the same for all others." He believed the demand was highly elastic.
   a. What was Professor Heise's response?
   b. What would his response have been if the demand had been highly inelastic?

4. Economists William Hunter and Mary Rosenbaum wrote an article in which they estimated the demand elasticity for motor fuel to be between 0.4 and 0.85.
   a. If the price rises 10 percent and the initial quantity sold is 10 million gallons, what is the range of estimates of the new quantity demanded?

   b. In carrying out their estimates they came up with different elasticity estimates for rises in price than for falls in price, with an increase in price having a larger elasticity than a decrease in price. What hypothesis might you propose for their findings?

5. In the box "Geometric Tricks for Estimating Price Elasticity," there are three statements about the elasticities of straight-line supply curves. One of those statements is that supply curves intersecting the quantity axis are inelastic. Can you prove that that is true by algebraic manipulation of the elasticity formula?

6. Calculate the price elasticities of the designated points on the following graph. (Reread the box "Calculating Elasticity at a Point.")

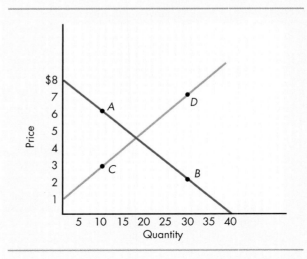

7. Calculate the elasticity of the designated ranges of supply and demand curves on the following graph.

8. Calculate the income elasticities of demand for the following:
   a. Income rises by 20 percent; demand rises by 10 percent.
   b. Income rises from $30,000 to $40,000; demand increases (at a constant price) from 16 to 19.

9. When the price of ketchup rises by 15 percent, the demand for hot dogs falls by 1 percent.
   a. Calculate the cross-price elasticity of demand.
   b. Are the goods complements or substitutes?

c. By how much would the demand have to rise for the goods to switch from complements to substitutes, or vice versa?

10. According to *The Wall Street Journal*, in the 1990s the going price for live worms was $1.17 a dozen. Then a drought hit.
   a. Demonstrate graphically what happened to the price and quantity of worms sold.
   b. If the price rose to $1.75 and the quantity sold fell from 90,000 to 60,000, what would your estimate of the elasticity of demand be?

11. What will be the percentage change in price in the following instances?
   a. Demand shifts to the right by 10 percent, elasticity of demand is 1, elasticity of supply is 2.
   b. Demand shifts to the right by 10 percent, elasticity of demand is 0.2, elasticity of supply is 0.5.
   c. Supply shifts to the right by 25 percent, elasticity of demand is 3, elasticity of supply is 2.

12. Economists have estimated the following transportation elasticities. For each pair, explain possible reasons why the elasticities differ.
   a. Elasticity of demand for buses is 0.23 during peak hours and 0.42 during off-peak hours.
   b. Elasticity of demand for buses is 0.7 in the short run and 1.5 in the long run.
   c. Elasticity of demand for toll roads is 4.7 for low-income commuters and 0.63 for high-income commuters.

WEB QUESTIONS

1. Cigarette smoking is widely recognized as the number one cause of cancer in the United States. One method the government can use to reduce cigarette smoking is to tax cigarettes. Read "The Impact of Proposed Cigarette Price Increases" by Frank J. Chaloupka at www.advocacy.org/publications/mtc/priceincreases.htm to answer the following questions about the effect of taxation on cigarette smoking.
   a. Who is likely to be more affected by tax increases on cigarettes—all adults or young adults? Cite specific elasticity of demand estimates from the article to support your answer.
   b. To have the greatest effect on reducing cancer from tobacco use, what other products should government tax?
   c. What is the long-run elasticity of demand for cigarette smoking? What does this mean for the likely impact of taxes on long-run cigarette use?

2. The effect of the minimum wage on employers and employees depends on the elasticity of demand and

supply for labor. Go to the Employment Policies Institute at www.epionline.org/study_MacphersonFlo_6-2002.pdf to read an article by David A. McPherson, "The Employment Impact of a Comprehensive Minimum Wage Law," and answer the following questions:
   a. What was the percentage increase in the minimum wage in Oregon from 1998 to 1999?
   b. What is the elasticity of demand for labor used in the study? Is demand elastic or inelastic?
   c. What is the effect of the increase in the minimum wage on labor costs for Oregon firms? Is this consistent with the elasticity of demand for labor? How would the effect on labor costs change if elasticity of demand for labor were greater than 1?
   d. In the long run what will happen to the change in labor costs compared to the change in labor costs in the short run? What accounts for the difference?

ANSWERS TO MARGIN QUESTIONS

1. Price elasticity of supply = Percentage change in quantity supplied divided by percentage change in price = 8/4 = 2. *(133)*

2. If price elasticity of demand is greater than 1, by definition demand is elastic. *(133)*

3. The percentage change in quantity is 100 (8/8 × 100) and the percentage change in price is 100 (2/2 × 100). Elasticity, therefore, is approximately 1 (100/100). *(137)*

4. I tell her that she is partially right (for the bottom part of the curve), but that elasticity on a straight-line demand curve changes from perfectly elastic at the vertical axis intersection to perfectly inelastic at the horizontal axis intersection. *(137)*

5. Four factors affecting the number of substitutes in demand are (1) time period considered, (2) the degree to which the good is a luxury, (3) the market definition, and (4) importance of the good in one's budget. *(140)*

6. Supply is generally more elastic in the long run because there are more alternative goods and services for producers to produce. *(141)*

7. If demand is inelastic, total revenue increases with an increase in price. *(144)*

8. If consumption increases with an increase in income, the good is a normal good. *(147)*

9. With an elastic demand, lowering price will increase total revenue because it will increase sales. But producing more will increase costs, so information about total revenue is not enough to answer the question. *(150)*

10. Price increases 3⅓ percent. Percentage change in price is the percentage change in demand (10) divided by the sum of the elasticities of supply and demand (1 + 2). *(151)*

TAXATION AND GOVERNMENT INTERVENTION

Collecting more taxes than is absolutely
necessary is legalized robbery.

—*Calvin Coolidge*

**After reading this
chapter, you should
be able to:**

- Show how equilibrium
  maximizes producer and
  consumer surplus.

- Demonstrate the cost of
  taxation to consumers and
  producers.

- Distinguish between the
  benefit principle and the
  ability-to-pay principle.

- Explain why the person who
  physically pays the tax is
  not necessarily the person
  who bears the burden of
  the tax.

- Demonstrate how an
  effective price ceiling is
  the equivalent of a tax on
  producers and a subsidy
  to consumers.

- Define rent seeking and
  show how it is related to
  elasticity.

Chapter 6 introduced you to the term *elasticity*. In this chapter we will have a chance to apply what you learned. As we do that you'll see that when combined with the concept of elasticity, the supply and demand tools become even more useful. We'll see why by considering two policy issues: taxation and government intervention into markets.

PRODUCER AND CONSUMER SURPLUS

We begin our discussion of the effects of taxation and government intervention by showing how economists measure the benefits of the market to consumers and producers. That benefit can be seen by considering what the supply and demand curves are telling us. Each of these curves tells us how much individuals will be willing to pay (in the case of demand) or accept (in the case of supply) for a good. Thus, in Figure 7-1(a) a consumer would be willing to pay $8 each for 2 units of the good. The supplier is willing to sell 2 units for $2 apiece.

If the consumer pays less than what he's willing to pay, he walks away better off. Thus, the distance between the demand curve and the price he pays is a net gain for the consumer. Economists call this net benefit **consumer surplus**—*the value the consumer gets from buying a product less its price*. It is represented by the area underneath the demand curve and above the price that an individual pays. Thus, with the price at equilibrium ($5), consumer surplus is represented by the blue area.

Similarly, if a producer receives more than the price she would be willing to sell it for, she too receives a net benefit. Economists call this gain **producer surplus**—*the price the producer sells a product for less the cost of producing it*. It is represented by the area above the supply curve but below the price the producer receives. Thus, with the price at equilibrium ($5), producer surplus is represented by the red area.

What's good about market equilibrium is that it makes the combination of consumer and producer surpluses as large as it can be. To see this, say that for some reason the equilibrium price is held at $6. Consumers will demand only 4 units of

Figure 7-1 (a and b)   Consumer and Producer Surplus
Market equilibrium price and quantity maximizes the combination of consumer surplus (shown in blue) and producer surplus (shown in red) as demonstrated in (**a**). When price deviates from its equilibrium, as in (**b**), combined consumer and producer surplus falls. The gray shaded region shows the loss of total surplus when price is $1 higher than equilibrium price.

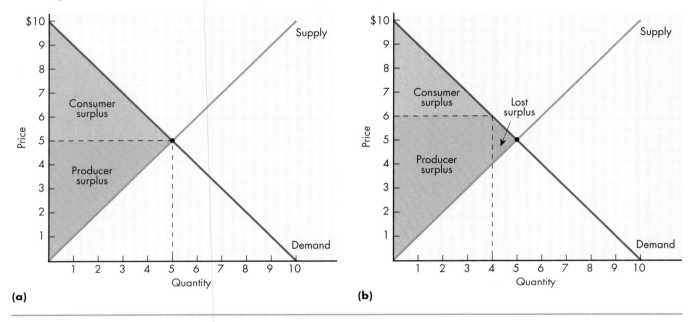

(a)   (b)

Q-1   If price moves from disequilibrium to equilibrium, what happens to the combination of producer and consumer surplus in the market?

the good, and some suppliers are not able to sell all the goods they would like. The combined producer and consumer surplus will decrease, as shown in Figure 7-1(b). The gray triangle represents lost consumer and producer surplus. In general, a deviation of price from equilibrium lowers the combination of producer and consumer surplus. This is one of the reasons economists support markets and why we teach the supply/demand model. It gives us a visual sense of what is good about markets: By allowing trade, markets maximize the combination of consumer and producer surplus.

To fix the ideas of consumer and producer surplus in your mind, let's consider a couple of real-world examples. Think about the water you drink. What does it cost? Almost nothing. Given that water is readily available, it has a low price. But since you'd die from thirst if you had no water, you are getting an enormous amount of consumer surplus from that water. Next, consider a ballet dancer who loves the ballet so much he'd dance for free. But he finds that people are willing to pay to see him and that he can receive $4,000 a performance. He is receiving producer surplus.

TAXATION AND GOVERNMENT

Now that we've seen how market equilibrium maximizes consumer and producer surplus, we're in a position to explore the costs and benefits of government intervention and taxation. An old saying goes, "The only things in life that are certain are death and taxes." And if you ask individuals what they dislike most about government, many would say taxes. Unfortunately, the government needs taxes to function, and the market likewise needs government. When governments do not have a well-functioning tax system, as is the case in some developing and transitional economies such as Russia's, the government is unable to provide the institutional structure markets need to work

Taxes are a pain, but some taxes are necessary.

To talk about consumer and producer surplus we must figure out a way of taking into account people's valuation of surplus. The market does that—it allows each person to vote with their income in the buying of goods. This means that whoever has the income plays a role in determining how we measure total surplus. This presents a circular reasoning problem in moving from total surplus to social welfare, and in talking about efficiency as if it involves maximizing total surplus. If the distribution of income is one of society's goals, then efficiency cannot unambiguously be defined without also specifying distributional goals.

Let's consider an extreme example to show the problems this can present. Say we start with two individuals, Jules and Jim, and two goods, apples and oranges. Jules likes only oranges and Jim likes only apples. If Jim has all the income, only apples count for determining total output because Jim likes only apples. Since no oranges are traded, oranges are given no weight because Jules has no income. Now, say that Jules has all the income. In that case only oranges contribute to total output. More generally, when two individuals have different tastes, the way in which income is distributed can change the contribution of goods to the valuation of total output.

Economists get around part of the problem theoretically either by assuming individuals have the same tastes or by assuming that income can be costlessly redistributed. This separates the issue of equity from the issue of efficiency. In practice, economists recognize that these conditions do not hold. They know that in the real world it is extraordinarily difficult to redistribute income. You can't go up to Bill Gates and tell him, "Hey, you need to give $10 billion to some poor people." For this reason economists are careful to apply the producer and consumer surplus analysis only to those cases where the conditions are "reasonable" approximations of reality—where distributional and taste issues do not play a big role in a policy recommendation. Of course, economists may disagree on what are "reasonable" approximations of reality. That is why economic policy is an art, not a science.

effectively. The connection between taxes and the roles of government led American jurist Oliver Wendell Holmes, Jr., to state that taxes are the price we pay for civilization.

Tax rates depend on what goods and services government provides. Having more government-provided goods and services means having higher taxes. The taxes can be low if government plays a minor role in the market—simply providing an institutional framework—or they can be high if government plays a major role such as providing free education and free health care to all citizens. Figure 7-2 gives you a sense of tax rates

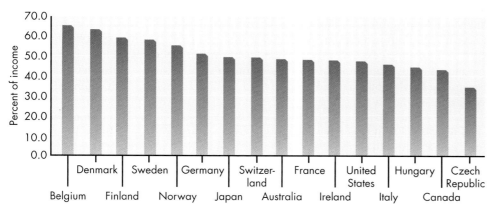

Figure 7-2   Highest Tax Rates on Wage Income (2001)

As you can see from this figure that shows the highest tax rates on wage income for various countries, the United States is one of the lower tax-rate countries.

Source: OECD.

Figure 7-3   The Costs of Taxation
A per unit tax t paid by the supplier shifts the supply curve up from S_0 to S_1.
Equilibrium price rises from P_0 to P_1, and equilibrium quantity falls from Q_0 to
Q_1. Consumer surplus is represented by areas A, B, and C before the tax and
area A after the tax. Producer surplus is represented by areas D, E, and F
before the tax and area F after the tax. Government collects tax shown by
areas B and D. The tax imposes a deadweight loss, represented by the welfare
loss triangle of areas C and E.

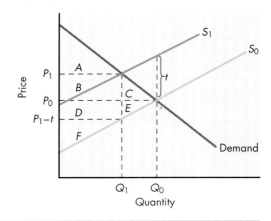

in various countries. As you can see, the United States is one of the lower tax-rate
countries.

HOW MUCH SHOULD GOVERNMENT TAX?

How should a country decide how much to tax? An economist would answer that question by asking another question: What are the costs and the benefits of taxation?

The Costs of Taxation[1]   The costs of taxation to society include the direct cost of
the revenue paid to government, the loss of consumer and producer surplus caused by
the tax, and the cost of administering the tax codes. Figure 7-3 provides the basic framework for understanding the costs of taxation. For a given good, a per unit tax t paid by
the supplier increases the price at which suppliers are willing to sell that good. The increase in price is shown by a shift upward of the supply curve from S_0 to S_1. The equilibrium price of the good rises and the quantity sold declines.

Before the tax, consumers pay P_0 and producers keep P_0. Consumer surplus is represented by areas $A + B + C$, and producer surplus is represented by areas $D + E + F$.
With the tax t, equilibrium price rises to P_1 and equilibrium quantity falls to Q_1. Consumers now pay P_1, but producers keep only $P_1 - t$. Tax revenue paid equals the tax t
times equilibrium quantity Q_1, or areas B and D.

The total cost to consumers and producers is more than tax revenue. Consumers pay
area B in tax revenue and also lose area C in consumer surplus. Producers pay area D in
tax revenue and lose area E in producer surplus. The triangular area $C + E$ represents a
cost of taxation in excess of the revenue paid to government. It is lost consumer and
producer surplus that is not gained by government. *The loss of consumer and producer surplus from a tax* is known as **deadweight loss.** Deadweight loss is shown graphically by the
welfare loss triangle—*a geometric representation of the welfare cost in terms of misallocated
resources caused by a deviation from a supply/demand equilibrium*. Keep in mind that with
the tax, quantity sold declines. The loss of welfare therefore represents a loss for those
consumers and producers who would have traded without the tax but do not trade with
the tax.

A tax paid by the supplier shifts the
supply curve up by the amount of
the tax.

Q-2   Demonstrate the welfare loss
of a tax when the supply is highly
elastic and the demand is highly
inelastic.

---

[1]The analysis presented here is highly simplified. Numerous points can be added to the analysis, some of
which will be discussed in later chapters. Despite its limitations, the visual sense of the costs and benefits
that the producer and consumer surplus concepts convey is a fundamental building block of the economic way of thinking.

The costs of taxation don't end there. Resources must be devoted by government to administer the tax code and by individuals to comply with it. Firms and individuals either spend hours filling out income tax forms or pay others to do so. Firms hire accountants and lawyers to take full advantage of any tax-code allowances. Administration costs can be as much as 5 percent of the total tax revenue paid to government. Like the tax itself, these costs increase the price at which producers are willing to sell their goods, reducing quantity sold and further increasing welfare loss.

The cost of taxation includes the direct cost of revenue paid, lost surplus, and administrative cost.

The Benefits of Taxation   The benefits of taxes are the gains to society that result from the goods and services government provides when fulfilling the six roles in a market economy discussed in Chapter 2:

Web Note 7.1
What Taxes Buy

1. Provide a stable set of institutions and rules.
2. Promote effective and workable competition.
3. Correct for externalities.
4. Ensure economic stability and growth.
5. Provide public goods.
6. Adjust for undesired market results.

Some government-provided goods are part of the basic institutional structure of a market economy and must be supplied if the market is to function effectively. The basic legal system is an example. Other goods are provided by government because they have the qualities of a public good; national defense is an example.

Still other goods are provided by government for reasons of equity or because they create positive externalities. Private markets will provide these goods but perhaps not distribute them equitably or in sufficient quantities. Education up through high school is an example; it is publicly supplied even though it could be privately supplied. A number of governments supply health care publicly. In the United States most health care is supplied privately, although portions of it are paid for by government through Medicare and Medicaid.

The policy debate about the benefits of taxation generally focuses on goods that could be supplied by the market or by government. The various elements of health care, such as prescription drug insurance, are examples that have recently been much in the news. Some people want the government to provide greater amounts of health care free to individuals. Others oppose such plans because they would require higher taxes.

Another policy debate that has been much in the news is the use of voucher systems to fund education. In a voucher system each student would be given a certain amount of money, in the form of a voucher, to be used to attend the school of his or her choice. Although a voucher system would likely decrease the amount of education government supplies, it would not reduce taxes, since taxes would still have to be collected to fund the vouchers. Private supply of education would have each family paying for their education without any vouchers.

Measuring the benefits of government-supplied goods is difficult, mainly because they are not provided in a market setting. Because of this difficulty, along with the problem of deciding whether certain goods should be provided by government at all, the task of choosing which goods and services to provide and how to finance them is always surrounded by debate.

TWO PRINCIPLES OF TAXATION

I'll discuss the problems government faces in choosing what goods to provide in Chapter 18. In this chapter I will focus on the taxes needed to pay for the goods that government does provide. In making decisions about taxes, government follows two general principles: the *benefit principle*, and the *ability-to-pay principle*.

The Benefit Principle   The **benefit principle** of taxation follows the same principle as the market: *The individuals who receive the benefit of a good or service should pay the tax necessary to supply that good.* An example of a tax based on the benefit principle is the gasoline tax levied to finance road construction in the United States. Since those who buy gasoline are using the roads, there is a connection between use and payment; however, unlike a toll, the tax is not direct—people do not pay each time they use the road. Another example is airport use taxes, which provide funding for the building of airports.

The difference between paying for goods through taxes and paying for them in a market is that, with government-supplied goods, consumers aren't directly paying for the goods and consequently do not reveal their preference for the good. The connection between benefit and cost in the decision to buy a publicly provided good is looser than it is with a privately supplied good.

With government-supplied goods individuals do not reveal their preference for the good.

The Ability-to-Pay Principle   The **ability-to-pay principle** of taxation does not make any connection between use and payment but simply states: *The individuals who are most able to bear the burden of the tax should pay the tax.* Generally this principle is interpreted as supporting a progressive tax—one whose rate increases with increases in income. With a progressive tax, the tax on the first $10,000 a person earns might be 14 percent and the tax on the next $10,000 might be 20 percent. (A person earning $20,000 would pay an average rate of 17 percent.) During World War II the United States had a highly progressive tax, with the top rate reaching 95 percent; it has declined since then, and the top federal income tax rate is now 38.6 percent. (State income taxes can add another 10 percent.)

The reasoning behind the ability-to-pay principle is that similar tax rates represent a smaller sacrifice for those with higher incomes compared to those with lower incomes. The wealthy should pay more because they can. Since the ability-to-pay principle of taxation makes no attempt to relate the benefit to the tax, the income tax revenue is used to finance a wide variety of government activities such as welfare and defense.

Q-3   If the tax on the first $20,000 is zero and thereafter the tax is 20 percent, what average tax rate would a person earning $30,000 pay?

Difficulty of Applying the Principles of Taxation   The two principles of taxation discussed above are the ones that economists and policymakers use most often to assess tax structures. Unfortunately, they are not easy to apply and often conflict. For example, the benefits of the goods that government supplies are often difficult to assign, making the benefit principle ambiguous. Consider education; it benefits not only the recipient but also the general public. How much does each benefit? (If you asked many high school students whether they would be willing to pay the $8,000 a year it costs to educate them in public school, I suspect many would say no.) Or consider funding health insurance for poor individuals. Under the benefit principle the poor would pay the majority of the costs. Under the ability-to-pay principle the rich would pay.

When taxes are based on the ability-to-pay principle, many high-income individuals ask why they should pay disproportionately more for goods such as income-support programs that are benefiting others, not them. The conflict between these two principles, combined with people's general desire to have "the other person" pay the taxes while they receive the benefits, often leads to significant debates about what to tax. Thus, we see debates about whether education should be financed by a *property tax*—a tax on houses and land—or by a *sales tax*—a tax on goods and services sold to consumers. Should income be taxed, or should only specific goods, like gasoline, be taxed? Should we use a corporate income tax or the general income tax?

The two principles of taxation, the benefit principle and the ability-to-pay principle, are often in conflict with each other.

What goods should be taxed depends on the goal of government. If the goal is to fund a program with as little loss as possible in consumer and producer surplus, then the government should tax a good whose supply or demand is inelastic. If the goal is to change behavior, taxes will be most effective if demand or supply is elastic. As a quick review, use the following table:

Goal of Government	Most Effective When
Raise revenue, limit deadweight loss	Demand or supply is inelastic
Change behavior	Demand or supply is elastic

Distributional issues must also be considered when determining what goods are to be taxed. In general, the group with the relatively more inelastic supply or demand will bear a greater portion of the tax. The following table reviews these conclusions:

Elasticity	Who Bears the Burden?
Demand inelastic and supply elastic	Consumers
Supply inelastic and demand elastic	Producers
Both supply and demand elastic	Shared; but the group whose supply or demand is more inelastic

The elasticity concept helps provide insight into the above debates. One of the facts you learned about elasticity is that the more broadly the good is defined, the more inelastic is the demand. Thus, the demand for all goods is much more inelastic than the demand for a particular good, since individuals cannot switch their consumption out of all goods but can switch from one specific good to another. This means that if government, given its targeted revenue, wants to have as little effect on individual actions as possible—or, in the language of consumer and producer surplus, if government wants to minimize the welfare loss—then it should tax goods with inelastic supplies or demands. Broad-based taxes such as income and sales taxes—which represent over 50 percent of state, local, and federal tax revenue—do just that. Most countries use a broad-based income tax, value-added tax, or general sales tax as their primary source of tax revenue.

If the government wants to minimize the welfare loss it should tax goods with inelastic supplies and demands.

WHO BEARS THE BURDEN OF A TAX?

Taxes are like hot potatoes: Everyone wants to pass them on to someone else. Nobody wants to pay taxes, and there are usually large political fights about whom government should tax. For example, should the Social Security tax (mandated by the Federal Insurance Contributions Act, or FICA) be placed on workers or on the company that hires them? Or does it matter? The supply/demand framework gives an unexpected answer to this question.

Burden Depends on Relative Elasticity Let's consider the issue of who bears the burden of a tax by looking at the example involving excise taxes introduced in Chapter 5. There I defined an **excise tax** as *a tax levied on a specific good* and gave the example of a luxury tax on expensive boats that the United States imposed in 1990. An excise tax can be levied (who will physically pay the tax) on the consumer or on the seller.

The person who *physically pays* the tax, however, is not necessarily the person who *bears the burden* of the tax. Who bears the burden of the tax (also known as tax

Figure 7-4 (a, b, and c)   Who Bears the Burden of a Tax?
In the general case the burden of a tax is determined by the relative elasticities of supply and demand. The blue shaded area shows the burden on the consumer; the red shaded area shows the burden on the supplier. This split occurs regardless of who actually pays the tax, as can be seen by noticing that the burden of the tax is equal in (**a**), where the supplier pays the tax, and in (**c**), where the consumer pays the tax. In (**b**) you can see how consumers with an inelastic demand bear a greater burden of the tax. The blue shaded area represents the burden paid by consumers; the red area shows the burden on suppliers.

(**a**)   **Supplier pays tax**   (**b**)   **Demand is inelastic**   (**c**)   **Consumer pays tax**

incidence) depends on who is best able to change his or her behavior in response to the tax, or who has the greater elasticity. Elasticity and supply/demand analysis lets us answer the question "Who will end up bearing the burden of the tax?" (More technically: "What is the incidence of the tax?")

Figure 7-4(a) shows the case I considered in Chapter 5. A $10,000 per unit tax levied on the supplier shifts the supply curve up from S_0 to S_1. That reduces quantity supplied and quantity demanded by 90—from 600 to 510. The equilibrium price rises from $60,000 to $65,000. Suppliers are able to shift $5,000 of the total $10,000 per unit tax onto consumers, leaving the suppliers the burden of the remaining $5,000.

Had we known elasticities at the market equilibrium, we could have stated, without additional calculations, that the tax burden would be shared equally. Specifically, suppliers sold and consumers purchased 90 fewer boats, an approximate 15 percent reduction. The suppliers' price fell by about 8 percent while the consumers' price rose by about 8 percent, meaning the elasticity of both supply and demand was approximately 1.9.[2] With equal elasticities, the tax burden will be divided equally.

In reality the tax burden is rarely shared equally because elasticities are rarely equal. The relative burden of the tax follows this general rule: *The more inelastic one's relative supply and demand, the larger the burden of the tax one will bear.* If demand were more inelastic, sellers would have been able to sell the boats at a higher price and could have passed more of the tax along to the buyers.

Figure 7-4(b) shows what the divisions would have been had the demand curve been highly inelastic. In this case the price would rise more, the supplier would pay a lower proportion of the tax (the red area), and the consumer would pay a much larger

---

[2]There will be slight variations in the measured elasticities depending on how they are calculated. The precise equality holds only for point elasticities. (See Chapter 6.)

proportion (the blue area). The general rule about elasticities and the tax burden is this: If demand is more inelastic than supply, consumers will pay a higher percentage of the tax; if supply is more inelastic than demand, suppliers will pay a higher share. This rule makes sense—*elasticity is a measure of how easy it is for the supplier and consumer to change behavior and substitute another good.*

More specifically, we can calculate the percentage of the tax actually borne by the demander by dividing the price elasticity of supply by the sum of the price elasticities of supply and demand and multiplying by 100. Similarly, we can calculate the percentage of the tax borne by the supplier by dividing the price elasticity of demand by the sum of the price elasticities of supply and demand and multiplying by 100. For example, say the price elasticity of supply is 1 and the price elasticity of demand is 3. In that case the consumer will pay one-fourth [1/(1 + 3)] of the tax and the supplier will pay three-fourths [3/(1 + 3)] of the tax.

The rule about the elasticities and the tax burden can lead to some unexpected consequences of taxation. For example, the U.S. luxury tax on boats was initially implemented as a way to tax the wealthy. It turned out, however, that the wealthy found substitutes for American-made boats; their demand was relatively elastic. They either purchased other luxury items or purchased their boats from foreign firms. U.S. boat manufacturers, however, couldn't easily switch to producing other products. Their supply was inelastic. As a result, they tried to pass on the cost increase to consumers, but they saw their sales plummet. They had to lower their price by almost as much as the tax, which meant that they were bearing most of the burden of the tax. As noted in Chapter 5, pressured by boat manufacturers, the government repealed the luxury tax on boats three years after it was instituted.

Who Pays a Tax Is Not Necessarily Who Bears the Burden　　The allocation of tax burden by relative elasticity means that it doesn't matter who actually pays the tax and that, as I said earlier, the person who bears the burden can differ from the person who pays. To assure yourself that it doesn't matter who pays the tax, ask yourself how your answer would have differed if the tax of $10,000 had been paid by the consumer. Figure 7-4(c) shows this case. Because the tax is paid by the consumer, the demand curve shifts down by the amount of the tax. As you can see, the results of the tax are identical. The percentage of the tax paid by the supplier and the consumer, after adjusting for the changes in supply and demand price, is independent of who actually makes the physical payment of the tax.

TAX INCIDENCE AND CURRENT POLICY DEBATES

Now let's consider two policy questions in relation to what we have learned about tax incidence.

Social Security Taxes　　The first policy question concerns the Social Security (or payroll) tax, which accounts for 36 percent of federal government revenue. In 2003, the Social Security tax rate was 12.4 percent on wages up to an annual maximum wage of $87,000, and another 2.9 percent on all wages, no matter how high, designed to finance Medicare. As a political compromise, half of Social Security taxes are placed on the employee and half on the employer. But the fact that the law places the tax equally on both does not mean that the burden of the tax is shared equally between employees and employers. On average, labor supply tends to be less elastic than labor demand. This means that the Social Security tax burden is primarily on the employees, even though employees see only their own statutory portion of the Social Security tax on their pay stub.

Tax burden is allocated by relative elasticities.

Q-4　How much of a $100 tax would a consumer pay if elasticity of demand is .2 and price elasticity of supply is 1.8?

The burden is independent of who physically pays the tax.

Q-5　If Social Security taxes were paid only by employees, what would likely happen to workers' pretax pay?

Web Note 7.2
Pensions

What makes sense politically is
not always what makes sense
economically.

Now, let's say that you are advising a person running for Congress who has come up with the idea to place the entire tax on the employer and eliminate the tax on the employee. What will the effect of that be? Our tax incidence analysis tells us that, ultimately, it will have no effect. Wages paid to employees will fall to compensate employers for the cost of the tax. This example shows that who is assessed the tax can be quite different than who actually bears the burden, or incidence, of the tax. The burden will be borne by those with the most inelastic supply or demand, because they have no way of getting out of paying the tax by substitution.

So what do you tell the candidate? Is the idea a good one or not? Although economically it will not make a difference who pays the tax, politically it may be a popular proposal because individuals generally look at statutory assessment, not incidence. The candidate may gain significant support from workers, since they would no longer see a Social Security tax on their pay stub. The moral, then, is this: Politics often focuses on surface appearance; economics tries to get under the surface, and what is good economics is not always good politics.

Sales Taxes   Our second policy question concerns sales taxes paid by retailers on the basis of their sales revenue. In my state the general sales tax is 5 cents on the dollar. Since sales taxes are broadly defined, consumers have little ability to substitute. Demand is inelastic and consumers bear the greater burden of the tax. Although stores could simply incorporate the tax into the price of their goods, most stores add the tax onto the bill after the initial sale is calculated, to make you aware of the tax. Again, it doesn't matter whether the tax is assessed on the store or on you.

Recently, however, the Internet has given consumers a substitute to shopping at actual retail stores. Retail sales over the Internet are over $36 billion annually and are continuing to grow. States have found it very difficult to tax Internet sales because the supplier has no retail address. The point of sale is in cyberspace. Technically in these cases, the buyer is required to pay the tax to the state where he or she lives, but in practice that seldom happens. How to tax Internet sales will be heavily debated over the next few years. The federal government has placed a moratorium on new Internet sales taxes until 2003. As Internet sales grow, states will lose more and more sales tax revenue and retail shops will bear a larger portion of the tax levied on their sales, which together will invite strong pressure to end the moratorium.

GOVERNMENT INTERVENTION

Taxes are not the only way government affects our lives. For example, government establishes laws that dictate what we can do, what prices we can charge for goods, and what working conditions are and are not acceptable. This second part of the chapter continues the discussion of such issues, which began in Chapter 5. I show how the elasticity concept can help us talk about such interventions and how, using the producer and consumer surplus framework, such interventions can be seen as a combination of tax and subsidy that does not show up on government books.

GOVERNMENT INTERVENTION AS IMPLICIT TAXATION

To see how government intervention in the market can be seen as a combination tax and subsidy, let's first consider the two types of price controls mentioned in Chapter 5: price ceilings and price floors.

Price Ceilings and Floors   As I discussed in Chapter 5, a **price ceiling** is a government-set price below the market equilibrium price. It is in essence an implicit tax

Figure 7-5 (a and b)   Effect of Price Controls on Consumer and Producer Surplus
Price floors and price ceilings create deadweight loss just as taxes do. In (a) we see how a price ceiling, P_1, transfers surplus D from producers to consumers. Price ceilings are equivalent to a tax on producers and a subsidy to consumers. In (b) we see how a price floor, P_2, transfers surplus B from consumers to producers. With both a price floor and a price ceiling, areas C and E represent the welfare loss triangle.

(a)   Price ceiling   **(b)   Price floor**

on producers and an implicit subsidy to consumers. Consider the effect of a price ceiling on producer and consumer surplus, shown in Figure 7-5(a).

If the price were at the market equilibrium price, the total surplus would be the combination of the areas A through F. But with an effective price ceiling P_1, the quantity supplied falls from Q_0 to Q_1. The combined producer and consumer surplus is reduced by triangles C and E. The loss of surplus represents those individuals who would like to make trades—the individuals represented by the demand and supply curves between Q_1 and Q_0—but cannot do so because of the price ceiling.

This loss of consumer and producer surplus is identical to the welfare loss from taxation.[3] That is not a coincidence. The price ceiling is a combination implicit tax on suppliers, shown by area D, and implicit subsidy to consumers of that same area. It is as if government places a tax on suppliers when they buy the good, and then gives that tax revenue to consumers when they consume the good.

Price floors have the opposite effect on the distribution of consumer and producer surplus. **Price floors**—*government-set prices above equilibrium price*—transfer consumer surplus to producers. They can be seen as a tax on consumers of area B and a subsidy to producers of that same area, as shown in Figure 7-5(b). Price floors also impose a deadweight loss, shown by the welfare loss triangle, areas C and E.

The Difference between Taxes and Price Controls   While the effects of taxation and controls are similar, there is an important difference: *Price ceilings create shortages; taxes do not.* The reason is that taxes leave people free to choose how much they want to supply and consume as long as they pay the tax. Thus, taxes create a wedge between the price the consumers pay and the price the suppliers receive. That difference is just enough to equate quantity demanded with quantity supplied.

Q-6   Demonstrate the effect of an effective price ceiling on producer and consumer surplus when both supply and demand are highly inelastic.

A price ceiling is a combination implicit tax on suppliers and implicit subsidy to consumers.

Price ceilings create shortages; taxes do not.

---

[3]As I will discuss below, for price controls the welfare triangle provides a minimum amount of loss in consumer and producer surplus; the actual loss may be greater.

Since with price ceilings the price consumers pay is the same as the price suppliers receive, as long as the price ceiling is below equilibrium price the desired quantity demanded will not be equal to the desired quantity supplied. Some method of rationing—limiting the demand or increasing the supply in the case of price ceilings, and limiting the supply and increasing the demand in the case of price floors—must be found. In the examples of price ceilings so far, we have assumed that suppliers can choose to supply how much or how little they want. Thus, there are shortages. Such shortages create black markets—markets in which individuals buy or sell illegally. (Black markets may also be created by taxes if buyers and sellers attempt to evade the tax.)

A Price Ceiling with Forced Supply: The Draft   There are other ways of dealing with shortages. For example, there could be "forced supply"—that is, suppliers could be required by law to supply all the goods demanded at the ceiling price. The military draft is an example. A draft is a law that requires some people to serve a set period in the armed forces at whatever pay the government chooses. It has often been used as a way of meeting the military's need for soldiers. The draft is a price ceiling combined with forced supply. (This case study may become highly relevant because, in recent years, the military has been falling short of the number of recruits it needs and some members of Congress have been suggesting that the United States reinstitute the draft. The legislative authority to do so already exists, and currently all men are legally required to register for the draft when they turn 18.)[4]

> The draft is a price ceiling combined with forced supply.

The effects of a draft are shown in Figure 7-6. A draft must be imposed when the wage offered by the army is below equilibrium because the quantity of soldiers demanded exceeds the quantity supplied. In Figure 7-6 the offered wage W_0 is below the equilibrium wage W_e. The market answer to the shortage would be to increase the wage to W_e, which would both reduce the quantity of soldiers demanded by government and increase the quantity of men willing to become soldiers. How much the wage would need to be increased to bring about equilibrium depends on the elasticity of supply and demand. If both supply and demand are inelastic, then the pay will need to be increased enormously; if both are elastic, the pay will need to be increased only slightly.

The people who are proposing the draft suspect that both supply and demand are inelastic, in which case the market solution would be very expensive to the government, requiring large increases in taxes. They argue that a draft is much cheaper, and requires lower taxes.

Our supply/demand analysis reveals the fallacy in that reasoning. Government interventions, such as the draft, transfer surplus from one set of individuals to another. Any intervention is the equivalent of a tax on the one from whom the surplus is taken and a subsidy to the one to whom the surplus is given. So the draft imposes a tax, but it is a tax that doesn't show up on the government books. Rather, the tax is on all individuals drafted (young men), and the subsidy is given to those who demand defense services. So, yes, with a draft the government does not have to collect as much revenue as it would if it raised the wage to a market-clearing wage, but the draft places the equivalent of an explicit tax on young men. Instead of being able to do what they want, they must serve in the armed forces.

By paying a lower-than-equilibrium wage, the government is transferring surplus from those drafted to itself. To get around the shortage, the draft requires men to serve whether they want to or not. The effective supply curve becomes the horizontal line W_0. The quantity supplied is forced to meet the quantity demanded at the price ceiling.

> **Q-7**   Does a draft allow the government to have lower taxes?

Courtesy Selective Service System

---

[4]Women are not, which raises some questions that will likely be much discussed if the draft is reinstituted.

Figure 7-6 Effect of a Draft on Surplus
The military draft is one solution to the shortage that occurs when wages are below the equilibrium wage. The market solution to the shortage of soldiers is for the army to offer soldiers a higher wage. This, however, would require government to raise taxes on the general public. The draft solution would not require an increase in explicit taxes. Instead, it forces young men to supply the quantity demanded by the army. Those who are drafted will accept a lower wage than they could get in the market, which is a transfer of surplus to government. The amount of the transferred surplus is shown by the red shaded region. The gray shaded region shows the deadweight loss associated with the draft.

In this case of forced supply even more surplus is transferred than in the previous cases we considered. Specifically, in Figure 7-6 the red shaded area is transferred from suppliers to consumers of national defense. In this case the welfare loss triangle is the shaded triangle to the right of the market equilibrium. It is the opportunities that the suppliers lose but that the demanders do not receive.

The above analysis of welfare loss due to the price ceiling is the minimum loss that the ceiling will create. The analysis assumes that the individuals drafted will be those whose opportunity cost of being drafted is lowest. In fact, that is not the case. The actual amount of loss depends on how the draft selects individuals. If it selects individuals totally randomly (which in principle is how drafts are structured), it will draft some into the armed forces who would not consider serving even at the equilibrium wage. (For example, Elvis Presley was drafted; when he entered the army he gave up millions of dollars of income, so his opportunity cost was extremely high.) Thus, the welfare loss is larger for interferences in the market such as the draft than it is for an equivalent tax, although it is difficult to specify how much larger it is.

Generally, the welfare loss is larger for controls than for an equivalent tax.

RENT SEEKING, POLITICS, AND ELASTICITIES

If price controls reduce total producer and consumer surplus, why do governments institute them? The answer is that *people care more about their own surplus than they do about total surplus*. As we have seen, price ceilings redistribute surplus from producers to consumers, so if the consumers have the political power there will be strong pressures to create price ceilings. Alternatively, if the suppliers have the political power, there will be strong pressures to create price floors.

The possibility of transferring surplus from one set of individuals to another causes people to spend time and resources on doing so. For example, if criminals know that $1 million ransoms are commonly paid for executives, it will be worthwhile for them to figure out ways to kidnap executives—which happens in some developing and transitional economies. (That's why all countries state that they will never pay ransoms; however, not all countries follow their stated policies.)

The possibility of kidnapping, in turn, causes executives to hire bodyguards, which in turn causes kidnappers to think of ingenious ways to kidnap (which in turn . . .). The result is that, as one group attempts to appropriate surplus from another group, enormous amounts of resources are spent on activities that benefit no one.

The same reasoning holds for lobbying government. Individuals have an incentive to spend resources to lobby government to institute policies that increase their own surplus. Others have an incentive to spend money to counteract those lobbying efforts.

Figure 7-7   Inelastic Demand and the Incentive to Restrict Supply
When demand is inelastic, increases in productivity that shift the supply curve
to the right result in lower revenue for suppliers. Although suppliers gain area B,
they lose the much larger area A. Suppliers have an incentive to restrict supply
when demand is inelastic because, by doing so, they will increase their revenues.

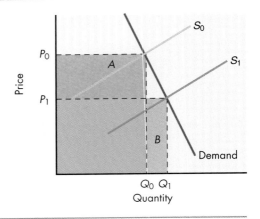

Activities designed to transfer surplus from one group to another are called **rent-seeking activities.** Rent-seeking activities require resources, and the net result is unproductive. **Public choice economists**—*economists who integrate an economic analysis of politics with their analysis of the economy*—argue that rent seeking through government is significant, and that much of the transfer of surplus that occurs through government intervention creates an enormous waste of resources. They argue that the taxes and the benefits of government programs offset each other and do not help society significantly, but they do cost resources. These economists point out that much of the redistribution through government is from one group of the middle class to another group of the middle class.

Inelastic Demand and Incentives to Restrict Supply   To understand the rent-seeking process a bit better, let's look more carefully at the incentives that consumers and producers have to lobby government to intervene in the market. We'll begin with suppliers. A classic example of the political pressures to limit supply is found in agricultural markets. Within the past century new machinery, new methods of farming, and hybrid seeds have increased the productivity of farmers tremendously. You might think that because farmers can now produce more at a lower cost, they'd be better off. But if you think that, you're ignoring the interaction of supply and demand. As advances in productivity increase supply they do increase the quantity sold, but they also result in lower prices. Farmers sell more but they get less for each unit they sell. Because food is a necessity and has few substitutes, the demand for many agricultural goods is inelastic. Since demand is inelastic the price declines by a greater proportion than the rise in quantity sold, meaning that total revenue declines and the farmers are actually worse off. The situation is shown in Figure 7-7.

Because of the increase in supply, price declines from P_0 to P_1 and quantity sold increases from Q_0 to Q_1. The farmer's revenue rises by area B but also falls by larger area A. To counteract this trend, farmers have an incentive to get government to restrict supply or create a price floor, thereby raising their revenue. In fact, that's what they did in the 1930s. Farmers then were instrumental in getting the government to establish the Farm Board, a federal agency whose job was to manage productivity of agricultural goods. The benefits of limiting competition are greatest for suppliers when demand is inelastic because price will rise proportionately more than quantity will fall.

This simple example provides us with an important insight about how markets work and how the politics of government intervention work. Inelastic demand creates an enormous incentive for suppliers either to pressure government to limit the quantity

Q.8 Would a firm's research and development expenditures be classified as rent seeking?

Q.9 How can an increase in productivity harm suppliers?

Web Note 7.4
Professional Licensing

When talking about price increases in the text, I mean percentage price increases, which is what the elasticity concept relates to the percentage changes in quantity. A $20 price increase on a $20,000 car is insignificant, because it is such a small percentage of the total price (0.1 percent). So remember, when deciding whether a price increase is significant or not, think of the price increase in percentage, not absolute, terms.

The difference between percentage change and absolute change is a source of constant confusion. Consider the discussions of fluctuations in the Dow Jones Industrial Average. On March 16, 2000, the Dow Jones Industrial Average rose 499 points—its biggest point gain in a single day and 118 points more than the next-largest single-day

gain. In percentage terms, however, the Dow had risen 4.93 percent—a less-than-historical gain. It was not even large enough to make the top 35 list of largest single-day percentage gains. The day that holds the record for the largest percentage gain the Dow is October 6, 1931, when it rose by 99.34 points. But, because the day's beginning the Dow was 668, the 99-point rise represented a whopping 14.87 percent single-day gain.

Another way to look at it is this: A movement of 100 when the Dow was 600 is a 16.7 percent change in the value of the stocks. A movement of 100 when the Dow is 10,000 is a 1 percent change. So remember to think percentages when deciding whether a change in price (or in anything) is large or small.

---

supplied or to get together and look for other ways to limit the quantity supplied. The more inelastic demand is, the more farmers have to gain by restricting supply. By limiting quantity supplied they can raise the price, increasing total revenue.

Sometimes sellers can get government to limit quantity supplied through licensing; other times the existing suppliers can limit supply by force. A well-placed threat ("If you enter this market, I will blow up your store") is often effective. In some transitional economies, such threats are common. What stops existing suppliers from making good on such threats? Government. But the government also creates opportunities for individuals to prevent others from entering the market. Therein lies a central problem of political economy. You need government to see that competition works—to ensure that existing suppliers don't prevent others from entering the market—but government can also be used to prevent competition and protect existing suppliers. Hence, the point that we will return to throughout this book: Government is part of both the problem and the solution.

The central problem of political economy is that you need government to ensure that competition works, but government can also be used to prevent competition.

Inelastic Supplies and Incentives to Restrict Prices   Firms aren't the only ones who can lobby government to intervene. Consider consumers. When supply is inelastic, consumers can face significant price increases if their demand increases. Thus, when the supply of a good is inelastic and the demand for that good rises, prices will rise significantly and consumers will scream for price controls.

This is what happened in the New York City rent-control example (price ceilings imposed on apartments) in Chapter 5. During World War II an influx of short-term workers into New York City increased demand for apartments. Because supply was inelastic, rents rose tremendously. To keep apartments affordable, the city capped rents.

Such controls are not costless. One of the results of rent control was to create an ongoing shortage of apartments. As we noted earlier, effective price ceilings will cause a shortage unless suppliers are forced to supply a market-clearing quantity. With the knowledge of elasticities you also know whether a large or small shortage will develop with a price ceiling and whether a large or small surplus will develop with a price floor.

Figure 7-8 (a, b, and c)   Price Floors and Elasticity of Demand and Supply

A price floor above equilibrium market price will always create a surplus. The extent of the surplus created depends on the elasticity of the curves. With elastic curves, a large surplus is created by price controls; with inelastic curves, a small surplus is created. Thus, in **(a)** the intersection of supply and demand occurs where the curves are most elastic and the result is the largest surplus. In **(b)** demand and supply intersect where the demand curve is less elastic and the surplus declines. In **(c)** demand and supply intersect where supply and demand are most inelastic and the result is the smallest surplus.

**(a) Price floor with elastic
   supply and demand**

**(b) Price floor with elastic supply
   and inelastic demand**

**(c) Price floor with inelastic supply
   and demand**

> The more elastic supply and demand, the larger the surplus or shortage created by price controls.

To make sure you understand how elasticity can tell you the relative size of a surplus or shortage when there are price controls, look at Figure 7-8, which shows three cases of price floors, each with different elasticities of supply and demand.

As you can see, all three cases create excess supply—surpluses—but the proportional amount of excess supply depends on the elasticity. In Figure 7-8(a), supply and demand intersect at P_E, where they are relatively elastic. There, the price floor, P_F, leads to a relatively large surplus. Figure 7-8(b) represents an intermediate case: The intersection is where supply is elastic and demand is highly inelastic, and a relatively smaller surplus is created by the price floor. In Figure 7-8(c), where the demand and supply curves intersect at relatively inelastic portions, the surplus created by the price floor is relatively small. A good exercise is to go through the same analysis for price ceilings.

The Long-Run/Short-Run Problem of Price Controls   Now let's combine our analysis of price controls with another insight from the elasticity chapter—that in the long run, supply and demand tend to be much more elastic than in the short run. This means that price controls will cause only relatively small shortages or surpluses in the short run, but large ones in the long run. Let's consider how this would play out in our rent-control example—see Figure 7-9. In the short run, both supply and demand are inelastic; thus, if the government allows landlords to charge the price they want and demand shifts from D_0 to D_1, they will raise their price significantly, from P_0 to P_1.

In the long run, however, additional apartments will be built and other existing buildings will be converted into apartments. Supply becomes more elastic, rotating from S_0 to S_1. Faced with additional competition, landlords will lower their price to P_2. In the long run price will fall and the number of apartments rented will increase.

Herein lies another political policy problem. In large part, it is the rise in price that brings in new competitors and increases in output. But if the government imposes price controls, the long-run incentives for competitors to enter the market will be eliminated. The political problems arise because politics generally responds to short-run pressures. In the short run demand and supply are generally inelastic, making it look like the price

Q-10   Why do price controls tend to create ongoing shortages or surpluses in the long run?

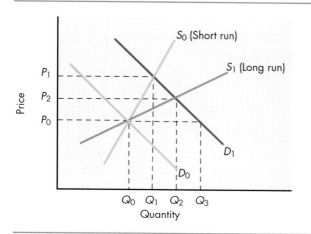

Figure 7-9   Long-Run and Short-Run Effects of Price Controls
This exhibit shows how an increase in demand from D_0 to D_1 raises equilibrium price from P_0 to P_1. As time progresses, the supply curve becomes flatter, which is shown as a rotation of the supply curve from S_0 to S_1. Equilibrium price falls to P_2. If a price ceiling of P_0 had been imposed, the incentive for suppliers to build more apartments would be eliminated. Instead, landlords would convert their apartments to different uses and potential landlords would choose to build fewer apartments, and the shortage resulting from the price control $(Q_3 - Q_0)$ would remain.

ceiling will not create significant problems. But in the long run, supply is usually elastic. Landlords will convert their rent-controlled apartments to different uses, fewer resources will be spent keeping up existing apartments, and fewer new apartments will be built. In the long run, the shortage becomes even more severe. As we noted in Chapter 5, the rent-control laws in New York City were initially written to be effective whenever the vacancy rate was below 5 percent, which was the vacancy rate at the time. But the rent controls stopped new apartments from being built and old ones from being maintained. Today, the vacancy rate is less than 4 percent and many rent-controlled apartments have deteriorated. The government's imposition of a price ceiling prevents the market from achieving a more desirable long-run equilibrium, at which output has expanded and price has fallen from its initially high level.

CONCLUSION

Government is a part of our life and, therefore, so too are taxes. Economic theory doesn't say government should or shouldn't play any particular role in the economy or what the taxes should be. Those decisions depend on normative judgments and the relevant costs and benefits. What economic theory does is to help point out the costs and benefits. For example, in the case of taxes economists can show that the cost of taxation in terms of lost surplus is independent of who physically pays the tax.

In thinking about taxes and government involvement the public often perceives economic theory and economists as suggesting the best policy is one of laissez-faire, or government noninvolvement in the economy. Many economists do suggest a laissez-faire policy, but that suggestion is based on empirical observations of government's role in the past, not on economic theory.

Still, economists as a group generally favor less government involvement than does the general public. I suspect this is because economists are taught to look below the surface at the long-run effect of government actions. They've discovered that the effects often aren't the intended effects, and that programs frequently have long-run consequences that make the problems worse, not better. Economists, both liberal and conservative, speak in the voice of reason: "Look at all the costs; look at all the benefits. Then decide whether government should or should not intervene." The supply/demand framework and the elasticity concept are extremely useful tools in making those assessments.

Economists as a group favor less government than does the general public.

SUMMARY

- Equilibrium maximizes the combination of consumer surplus and producer surplus. Consumer surplus is the net benefit a consumer gets from purchasing a good, while producer surplus is the net benefit a producer gets from selling a good.

- Government taxes firms and individuals in order to carry out its six roles in a market economy. A government will maximize benefits to society only if it chooses to tax when the marginal benefit of the goods and services provided with the revenue of the tax exceeds the cost of the tax.

- Taxes create a loss of consumer and producer surplus known as deadweight loss, which graphically is represented by the welfare loss triangle.

- The cost of taxation to consumers and producers includes the actual tax paid, the deadweight loss, and the costs of administering the tax.

- Government follows both the benefit principle (individuals who receive the benefit should pay the tax) and the ability-to-pay principle (individuals who are most able to pay should pay the tax) when deciding on whom to levy taxes.

- Who bears the burden of the tax depends on the relative elasticities of demand and supply. The more inelastic one's relative supply and demand, the larger the burden of the tax one will bear.

- Although Social Security taxes are levied equally on employers and employees, the supply of labor tends to be more inelastic than the demand for labor, so workers bear the greater burden of these taxes.

- Price ceilings and price floors, like taxes, result in loss of consumer and producer surplus.

- Price ceilings transfer producer surplus to consumers and therefore are equivalent to a tax on producers and a subsidy to consumers. Price floors have the opposite effect; they are a tax on consumers and a subsidy to producers.

- Rent-seeking activities are designed to transfer surplus from one group to another. Producers facing inelastic demand for their product will benefit more from rent-seeking activities than producers facing elastic demand. Consumers facing inelastic supply for a product benefit more from rent-seeking activities such as lobbying for price ceilings than consumers facing an elastic supply.

- The more elastic supply and/or demand is, the greater the surplus is with an effective price floor and the greater the shortage is with an effective price ceiling.

- Price controls worsen as the length of time considered rises because elasticity rises as time progresses.

KEY TERMS

ability-to-pay
   principle (162)
benefit principle (162)
consumer surplus (157)

deadweight loss (160)
excise tax (163)
price ceiling (166)
price floor (167)

producer surplus (157)
public choice
   economist (170)

rent-seeking
   activity (170)
welfare loss triangle (160)

QUESTIONS FOR THOUGHT AND REVIEW

1. Explain why the combination of consumer and producer surplus is not maximized if there is either excess demand or supply.

2. Use economic reasoning to explain why nearly every purchase you make provides you with consumer surplus.

3. Name one local tax that is based on the ability-to-pay principle and one local tax that is based on the benefit principle. State your reason for categorizing the taxes as you did.

4. How is elasticity related to the revenue from a sales tax?

5. If the federal government wanted to tax a good and suppliers were strong lobbyists, but consumers were not, would government prefer supply or demand to be more inelastic? Why?

6. What types of goods would you recommend government tax if it wants the tax to result in no welfare loss? Name a few examples.

7. Suppose demand for cigarettes is inelastic and the supply of cigarettes is elastic. Who would bear the larger burden of a tax placed on cigarettes?

8. If the demand for a good is perfectly elastic and the supply is elastic, who will bear the burden of a tax on the good paid by consumers?

9. What percent of a tax will the demander pay if price elasticity of supply is .3 and price elasticity of demand is .7? What percent will the supplier pay?

10. Which good would an economist normally recommend taxing if government wanted to minimize welfare loss and maximize revenue: a good with an elastic or inelastic supply? Why?

11. Should tenants who rent apartments worry that increases in property taxes will increase their rent? Does your answer change when considering the long run?

12. Can you explain the tax system that led to this building style, which was common in old Eastern European cities?

13. In which case would the shortage resulting from a price ceiling be greater—when supply is inelastic or elastic? Explain your answer.

14. Define rent seeking. Do firms have a greater incentive to engage in rent-seeking behavior when demand is elastic or when it is inelastic?

PROBLEMS AND EXERCISES

1. A political leader comes to you and wonders from whom she will get the most complaints if she institutes a price ceiling when demand is inelastic and supply is elastic.
   a. How do you respond?
   b. Demonstrate why your answer is correct.

2. Suppose the government established a requirement that everyone consume 10 percent more beets than he or she is currently consuming.
   a. Show graphically the welfare loss that would occur.
   b. If someone shows you that the welfare loss is small, say 0.5 percent of the cost of beets, and that eating beets improves people's health, would you support a beet-eating requirement? Why or why not?

3. Demonstrate the welfare loss of:
   a. A restriction on output when supply is perfectly elastic.
   b. A tax *t* placed on suppliers that shifts up a supply curve.
   c. A subsidy *s* given to suppliers that shifts down a supply curve.
   d. A restriction on output when demand is perfectly elastic.

4. Because of the negative incentive effect that taxes have on goods with elastic supply, in the late 1980s Margaret Thatcher (then prime minister of Great Britain) changed the property tax to a poll tax (a tax at a set rate that every individual must pay).
   a. Show why the poll tax is preferable to a property tax in terms of consumer and producer surplus.
   b. What do you think the real-life consequences of the poll tax were?

5. Demonstrate how a price floor is like a tax on consumers and a subsidy to suppliers.
   a. Who gets the revenue in the case of a tax? Label the area that illustrates the tax.
   b. Who gets the revenue in the case of a price floor? Label the transfer of surplus from consumers to suppliers.
   c. Label welfare loss of the tax and the price floor.

6. Suppose government imposed a minimum wage above equilibrium wage.
   a. What do you expect to happen to the resulting shortage of jobs as time progresses? (Assume that inflation and economic growth are both zero.)
   b. What do you expect to happen to the producer surplus transferred to minimum wage earners as time progresses?

7. Use the graph below to answer the following questions:

a. What is equilibrium price and quantity?

b. What is producer surplus when the market is in equilibrium?

c. What is consumer surplus when the market is in equilibrium?

d. If price were held at $10 a unit, what is consumer and producer surplus?

8. Use the graph below that shows the effect of a $4 per unit tax on suppliers to answer the following questions:

a. What is equilibrium price and quantity before the tax? After the tax?

b. What is producer surplus when the market is in equilibrium before the tax? After the tax?

c. What is consumer surplus when the market is in equilibrium before the tax? After the tax?

d. What is total tax revenue collected after the tax is implemented?

9. Calculate the percent of the tax borne by the demander and supplier in each of the following cases:

a. $E_D = .3, E_S = 1.2$

b. $E_D = 3, E_S = 2$

c. $E_D = .5, E_S = 1$

d. $E_D = .5, E_S = .5$

e. Summarize your findings regarding relative elasticity and tax burden.

WEB QUESTIONS

1. Gasoline taxes are commonly used to fund transportation-related expenditures. Cal-Tax is an advocacy group in California whose mission is to protect taxpayers from unnecessary taxes and to promote efficient, quality government services. Read their analysis of gasoline taxes in California at www.caltax.org/research/gastax.htm to answer the following questions:

a. How does California rank relative to other states in terms of taxes per gallon?

b. How does California rank in transportation expenditures relative to other states?

c. Is the gas tax in California based on the benefit principle, the ability-to-pay principle, or some other principle?

d. What has happened to revenue from gas taxes on a revenue-per-mile basis over the past few years? What accounts for this change?

e. Is the gas tax in California a progressive or a regressive tax? (*Regressive* means that the tax rate falls with income.)

2. Henry George, an American economist living in the 1800s, had very specific views on taxation. Read about

these by clicking on *Taxation* on the Henry George Institute's home page at www.henrygeorge.org and answer the following questions:

a. What are the four criteria of a good tax according to Classical economists?

b. In what way do broad-based taxes fulfill those criteria? In what way do they fail to fulfill those criteria?

c. What good in our economy, according to Henry George, best fits the four criteria?

d. Demonstrate the welfare loss associated with the taxation of the good Henry George believes should be taxed. Who will bear the burden of the tax?

3. Go to www.ecommercetimes.com. Using its search engine, find recent articles about taxes on Internet sales to answer the following:

a. What is the current status of the Federal government moratorium on new Internet taxes?

b. What do analysts say will be the impact of new taxes on Internet sales? What does this imply about their estimates of the elasticity of demand for online purchases?

c. What argument can you give to support taxing Internet sales?

ANSWERS TO MARGIN QUESTIONS

1. The combination of consumer and producer surplus will increase since there will be no lost surplus at the equilibrium price. *(158)*

2. Welfare loss when supply is highly elastic and demand is highly inelastic is shown by the shaded triangle in the graph below. The supply curve shifts up by the amount of the tax. Since equilibrium quantity changes very little, from Q_0 to Q_1, welfare loss is very small. *(160)*

3. The average tax would be total tax divided by total income, or $2,000 (20% of $10,000) divided by $30,000 = 6.7%. *(162)*

4. The percentage of the tax borne by the consumer equals price elasticity of supply divided by the sum of the price elasticities of demand and supply, or

$$\frac{1.8}{(0.2 + 1.8)} = 0.9.$$

The consumer pays $90 of the tax. *(165)*

5. If the entire amount of the tax were levied on employees, their before-tax income would rise because employers would have to compensate their employees for the increased taxes they would have to physically pay. The burden of the taxation does not depend on who pays the tax. It depends on relative elasticities. *(165)*

6. The effect of a price ceiling below equilibrium price when demand and supply are inelastic is shown in the following graph. Quantity demanded exceeds quantity supplied, but because demand and supply are both inelastic, the short-age is not big. Likewise, the welfare loss triangle, shown by the shaded area in the graph, is not large. *(167)*

7. Yes and no. A draft, by reducing the taxes needed to pay wages to soldiers, lowers taxes that show up in government coffers, but does place an implicit tax on young men. Those who are drafted must accept the below-equilibrium wage, and give up the wage they could have made in the marketplace. The difference can be considered a tax paid to government. *(168)*

8. No. Research and development expenditures are an effort to increase technology to either lower production costs or discover a new product that can be marketed. If the firm can get a patent on that new product, the firm will have a monopoly and be able to restrict supply, transferring surplus from consumers to themselves, but this is not rent seeking. Rent-seeking activities are designed to transfer surplus from one group to another given current technology. They are unproductive. *(170)*

9. If suppliers are selling a product for which demand is inelastic, increases in productivity would result in a drop in price that would be proportionately greater than the rise in equilibrium quantity. Total revenue would decline for suppliers. *(170)*

10. Price controls tend to create ongoing shortages and surpluses in the long run because they prevent market forces from working. *(172)*

THE LOGIC OF INDIVIDUAL CHOICE: THE FOUNDATION OF SUPPLY AND DEMAND

> The theory of economics must begin with a correct theory of consumption.
>
> —*Stanley Jevons*

The analysis of how individuals make choices is central to microeconomics. It is the foundation of economic reasoning and it gives economics much of its power. The first part of this chapter shows you that foundation and leads you through some exercises to make sure you understand the reasoning. The second part of the chapter relates that analysis to the real world, giving you a sense of when the model is useful and when it's not.

As you go through this chapter, think back to Chapter 1, which set out the goals for this book. One goal was to get you to think like an economist. This chapter, which formally develops the reasoning process behind economists' cost/benefit approach to problems, examines the underpinnings of how to think like an economist.

UTILITY THEORY AND INDIVIDUAL CHOICE

Different sciences have various explanations for why people do what they do. For example, Freudian psychology tells us we do what we do because of an internal fight between the id, ego, and superego plus some hangups we have about our bodies. Other psychologists tell us it's a search for approval by our peers; we want to be OK. Economists agree that these are important reasons but argue that if we want an analysis that's simple enough to apply to problems, these heavy psychological explanations are likely to get us all mixed up. At least to start with, we need an easier underlying psychological foundation. And economists have one—self-interest. People do what they do because it's in their self-interest.

Economists' analysis of individual choice doesn't deny that most of us have our quirks. That's obvious in what we buy. On certain items we're penny-pinchers; on others we're big spenders. For example, how many of you or your parents clip coupons to save 40 cents on cereal but then spend $40 on a haircut? How many save 50 cents a pound by buying a low grade of meat but then spend $20 on a bottle of wine, $75 on dinner at a restaurant, or $60 for a concert ticket?

But through it all comes a certain rationality. Much of what people do reflects their rational self-interest. That's why economists start their analysis of individual choice with a relatively simple, but powerful, underlying psychological foundation.

Using that simple theory, two things determine what people do: the pleasure people get from doing or consuming something, and the price of doing or consuming that something. Price is the tool the market uses to bring the quantity supplied equal to the quantity demanded. Changes in price provide incentives for people to change what they're doing. Through those incentives the invisible hand guides us all. To understand economics you must understand how price affects our choices. That's why we focus on the effect of price on the quantity demanded. We want to understand the way in which a change in price will affect what we do.

In summary, economists' theory of rational choice is a simple, but powerful, theory that shows how these two things—pleasure and price—are related.

MEASURING PLEASURE

Let's start with an analysis of what we buy. Why do we buy what we buy? Economists' analysis of individual choice starts with the proposition that individuals try to get as much pleasure as possible out of life. To analyze the choice formally we must measure pleasure.

How does one measure pleasure? I don't know the answer to that, but back in the 1800s economists such as Jeremy Bentham thought that eventually they would be able to measure pleasure by measuring brain waves. In the expectation of this discovery they even developed a measure of pleasure they called a *util*. They predicted that someday a machine that could measure utils would be developed. Not surprisingly they called this machine a *utilometer*. This utilometer was to be connected to people's heads and an economist would read it as people went through their daily activities. Eating broccoli might give 10 utils; eating a hot fudge sundae might give 10,000 utils.

Eventually these 19th-century economists gave up hope of developing a utilometer, but economists still use a quaint shorthand term, **utility,** for *the pleasure or satisfaction that one expects to get from consuming a good or service.* (And you thought that economists didn't have a sense of humor.) Utility serves as the basis of economists' analysis of individual choice.

Economists initially used actual numbers to represent utility. But no economist today believes that the actual numbers given to utility have meaning. Economists have gone to great lengths to show that all you need is a relative ranking of goods that people reveal when they choose one good over another.

It's important to keep in the back of your mind that economists don't need actual numbers to discuss utility, especially if you're going on in economics. In introductory economics there's nothing quite as useful as a unit of utility. It gives us real numbers to work with rather than all kinds of fancy measure theories. So here's the deal: I'll use real numbers in discussing utility and you promise that you'll remember they're not really needed. (If you don't accept this deal, see Appendix A, where I go through the same analysis without using actual numbers.)

TOTAL UTILITY AND MARGINAL UTILITY

In thinking about utility, it's important to distinguish between *total utility* and *marginal utility.* **Total utility** refers to *the total satisfaction one gets from consuming a product.* **Marginal utility** refers to *the satisfaction one gets from consuming one additional unit of a product above and beyond what one has consumed up to that point.* For example, eating a whole pound of Beluga caviar might give you 4,700 units of utility.[1] Consuming the first 15

Web Note 8.1
Pleasure and Pain

Utility refers to the satisfaction one gets from consuming a good or service.

Q.1 One of the assumptions of economists' theory of choice is that utility must be measured. True or false? Why?

It is important to distinguish between marginal and total utility.

---

[1]Throughout the book I choose specific numbers to make the examples more understandable and to make the points I want to make. A useful exercise is for you to choose different numbers and reason your way through the same analysis.

ounces may have given you 4,697 units of utility. Consuming the last ounce of caviar might give you an additional 3 units of utility. The 4,700 is total utility; the 3 is the marginal utility of eating that last ounce of caviar.

An example of the relationship between total utility and marginal utility is given in Figure 8-1. Let's say that the marginal utility of the 1st slice of pizza is 14, and since you've eaten only 1 slice, the total utility is also 14. Let's also say that the marginal utility of the 2nd slice of pizza is 12, which means that the total utility of 2 slices of pizza is 26 (14 + 12). Similarly for the 3rd, 4th, and 5th slices of pizza, whose marginal utilities are 10, 8, and 6, respectively. The total utility of your eating those 5 pieces of pizza is the sum of the marginal utilities you get from eating each of the 5 slices. The fifth row of column 2 of Figure 8-1(a) shows that sum.

Notice that marginal utility shows up between the lines. It is the utility of changing consumption levels. For example, the marginal utility of changing from 1 to 2 slices of pizza is 12. The relationship between total and marginal utility can also be seen graphically. In Figure 8-1(b) we graph total utility (column 2 of the utility table) on the vertical axis, and the number of slices of pizza (column 1 of the utility table) on the horizontal axis. As you can see, total utility increases up to 7 slices of pizza; after 8 slices it starts decreasing—after 8 pieces of pizza you're so stuffed that you can't stand to look at another slice.

In Figure 8-1(c) we graph marginal utility (column 3 of the utility table) on the vertical axis and slices of pizza (column 1) on the horizontal axis. Notice how marginal utility decreases while total utility increases. When total utility stops increasing (between 7 and 8 slices), marginal utility is zero. Beyond this point total utility decreases and marginal utility is negative. An additional slice of pizza will actually make you worse off.

DIMINISHING MARGINAL UTILITY

Now let's consider the shapes of these curves a bit more carefully: What are they telling us about people's choices? As we've drawn the curves, the marginal utility that a person gets from each additional slice of pizza decreases with each slice of pizza eaten. Economists believe that the shapes of these curves is generally a reasonable description of the pattern of people's enjoyment. They call that pattern the **principle of diminishing marginal utility:**

As you consume more of a good, after some point the marginal utility received from each additional unit of a good decreases with each additional unit consumed, other things equal.

As individuals increase their consumption of a good, at some point consuming another unit of the product will simply not yield as much additional pleasure as did consuming the preceding unit.

Consider, for example, that late-night craving for a double-cheese-and-pepperoni pizza. You order one and bite into it. Ah, pleasure! But if you've ordered a large pizza and you're eating it all by yourself, eventually you'll get less additional enjoyment from eating additional slices. In other words, the marginal utility you get is going to decrease with each additional slice of pizza you consume. That's the principle of diminishing marginal utility.

Notice that the principle of diminishing marginal utility does not say that you don't enjoy consuming more of a good; it simply states that as you consume more of the good, you enjoy the additional units less than you did the initial units. A fourth slice of pizza still tastes good, but it doesn't match the taste of the third slice. At some point, however, marginal utility can become negative. Say you had two large pizzas and only two hours in which to eat them. Eating the last slice could be pure torture. But in most

Q-2 If the total utility curve is a straight line—that is, does not exhibit diminishing marginal utility—what will the marginal utility curve look like?

The principle of diminishing marginal utility states that, after some point, the marginal utility received from each additional unit of a good decreases with each additional unit consumed, other things equal.

Q-3 Consuming more of a good generally increases its marginal utility. True or false? Why?

Figure 8-1 (a, b, and c)   Marginal and Total Utility

Marginal utility tends to decrease as consumption of a good increases. Notice how the information in the table (**a**) can be presented graphically in two different ways. The two different ways are, however, related. The downward slope of the marginal utility curve (**c**) is reflected in the total utility curve bowed downward in (**b**). Notice that marginal utility relates to changes in quantity so the marginal utility line is graphed at the halfway point. For example, in (**c**), between 7 and 8, marginal utility becomes zero.

Number of pizza slices	Total utility	Marginal utility
1	14	14
2	26	12
3	36	10
4	44	8
5	50	6
6	54	4
7	56	2
8	56	0
9	54	-2

(a) Utility table   **(b) Total utility**   **(c) Marginal utility**

situations you have the option *not* to consume any more of a good. When consuming a good becomes torture (meaning its utility is negative), you simply don't consume any more of it. If you eat a slice of pizza (or consume an additional unit of a good), that's a good indication that its marginal utility is still positive.

RATIONAL CHOICE AND MARGINAL UTILITY

The analysis of rational choice is the analysis of how individuals choose goods within their budget in order to maximize total utility, and how maximizing total utility can be accomplished by considering marginal utility. That analysis begins with the premise that rational individuals want as much satisfaction as they can get from their available resources. The term *rational* in economics means, specifically, that people prefer more to less and will make choices that give them as much satisfaction as possible. The problem is that people face a budget constraint. They must choose among the alternatives. How do they do that?

> Because people face a budget constraint, they must choose among alternatives.

SOME CHOICES

Let's start by considering three choices. (Answer each choice as you read it.)[2]

> Web Note 8.2
> Tastes and Choices

   Choice 1:   Between spending another dollar on a slice of pizza that gives you an additional 41 units of utility or spending another dollar on a hero sandwich that gives you an additional 30 units of utility.

   Choice 2:   Between reading an additional chapter in this book that gives you an additional 200 units of utility at a cost of one hour of your time, or reading an

---

[2]To keep the analysis simple in this example, I consider either/or decisions. Below, I show how to extend the analysis to marginal choices.

More and more psychology is being integrated into economics and economic reasoning. Instead of just assuming that individuals act rationally, modern economists are conducting experiments to determine how individuals act. In 2002 the Nobel Prize Committee recognized this change when it awarded the Nobel Prize in Economics to a professor of psychology, Danny Kahneman, and to an economist, Vernon Smith.

Smith was given the award for being a leader in experimental economics. He has played a central role in getting economists to test their theories with laboratory experiments, in which one can observe, rather than assume, how people behave. In these experiments economists have found that individuals have a sense of fairness along with economic rationality that guides their decisions.

Kahneman, together with Amos Tversky (who died in 1996), developed the theory of behavioral economics and argued that people aren't as calculating as economists often assume and that they repeatedly make errors in judgment that can be predicted and categorized. For example, a principle of economic rationality is that a sunk cost is a sunk cost, and should not be taken into account in decisions. But consistently individuals take sunk costs into account. He found that people are far less likely to sell a share of stock that they bought for $90 for $70 than they are to sell a share of stock for $70 that they bought for $50, even though economic rationality says that a rational person will not take into account the purchase price of a stock when deciding whether to sell it; they will only take into account future stock prices. Such insights are changing the face of modern economics, but they should be seen as complements to, rather than substitutes for, standard economic reasoning.

---

additional chapter in psychology that gives you an additional 100 units of utility at a cost of 40 minutes of your time.

Choice 3: Between having your next date with that awesome guy Jerry, which gives you an additional 2,000 units of utility and costs you $70, or taking out plain Jeff on your next date, which gives you an additional 200 units of utility and costs you $10.

The correct choices, in terms of marginal utility, are (1) the pizza, (2) a chapter of this book, and (3) Jerry.

If you answered all three correctly, either you're lucky or you have a good intuitive understanding of the principle of rational choice. Now let's explore the principle of rational choice more thoroughly by considering each of the three examples.

Choice 1 Since the slice of pizza and the hero sandwich both cost $1, and the pizza gives you more units of utility than the hero, the pizza is the rational choice. If you spend $1 on the hero rather than the pizza, you're losing 11 units of utility and not making yourself as happy as you could be. You're being irrational. Any choice (for the same amount of money) that doesn't give you as much utility as possible is an irrational choice.

But now let's say that the price of heroes falls to 50 cents so that you can buy two heroes for the same price you previously had to pay for only one. Let's also say that two heroes would give you 56 units of utility (not 2 × 30 = 60—remember the principle of diminishing marginal utility). Which would now be the more rational choice? The two heroes, because their 56 units of utility are 15 more than you would get from that dollar spent on one slice of pizza.

Another way of thinking about your choice is to recognize that essentially what you're doing is buying units of utility. Obviously you want to get the most for your money, so you choose goods that have the highest units of utility per unit of cost. Let's see how this way of thinking about a decision works by considering our second choice.

Choice 2   Here the two alternatives have a cost in time, not money. The analysis, however, is the same. You calculate the marginal utility (additional units of utility) of the choice facing you, and divide that by the costs of the activity; that gives you the marginal utility per unit of cost. Then choose the activity that has the highest marginal utility per unit of cost or lowest cost per unit of utility. When you do that, you see that this chapter gives you 3⅓ units of utility per minute (200/60 = 3⅓), while the psychology chapter gives you 2½ units of utility per minute. So you choose to read another chapter in this book.[3]

Choice 3   Taking out Jerry gives you 28½ units of utility per dollar (2,000/$70), while taking out Jeff gives you 20 units of utility per dollar (200/$10). So you choose to take out Jerry.[4]

THE PRINCIPLE OF RATIONAL CHOICE

The **principle of rational choice** is as follows: *Spend your money on those goods that give you the most marginal utility (MU) per dollar.* The principle of rational choice is important enough for us to restate.

If $\dfrac{MU_x}{P_x} > \dfrac{MU_y}{P_y}$, choose to consume an additional unit of good *x*.

If $\dfrac{MU_x}{P_x} < \dfrac{MU_y}{P_y}$, choose to consume an additional unit of good *y*.

By substituting the marginal utilities and prices of goods into these formulas, you can always decide which good it makes more sense to consume. Consume the one with the highest marginal utility per dollar.

SIMULTANEOUS DECISIONS

So far in discussing our examples, we've considered the choices separately. But in real life, choices aren't so neatly separated. Say you were presented with all three choices simultaneously. If you make all three of the decisions given in the examples, are you being rational? The answer is no. Why? The pizza gives you 41 units of utility per dollar; taking out Jerry gives you 28½ units of utility per dollar. You aren't being rational; you aren't maximizing your utility. It would clearly make sense to eat more pizza, paying for it by cutting the date with Jerry short. (Skip the coffee at the end of the meal.)

But what about the other choice: studying psychology or economics? We can't compare the costs of studying to the costs of the other goods because, as I noted earlier, the costs of both studying alternatives are expressed in terms of time, not money. If we can assign a money value to the time, however, we can make the comparison. Let's say you can earn $6 per hour, so the value of your time is 10 cents per minute. This allows us to think about both alternatives in terms of dollars and cents. Since a chapter in economics takes an hour to read, the cost in money of reading a chapter is

Q-4 Which is the rational choice—watching one hour of MTV that gives you 20 units of utility or watching a two-hour movie that gives you 30 units of utility?

The principle of rational choice tells us to spend our money on those goods that give us the most marginal utility per dollar.

---

[3]As I've pointed out before, I choose the numbers to make the points I want to make. A good exercise for you is to choose different numbers that reflect your estimate of the marginal utility you get from choice, and see what your rational choices are. And remember our deal.

[4]In these examples I am implicitly assuming that the "goods" are divisible. Technically, this assumption is needed for marginal utilities to be fully specified.

Q-5 True or false? You are maximizing total utility only when the marginal utility of all goods is zero. Explain your answer.

60 minutes × 10 cents = $6. Similarly, the cost of the 40 minutes you'd take to read the psychology chapter is $4.

With these values we can compare our studying decisions with our other decisions. The value in units of utility per dollar of reading a chapter of this book is:

$$\frac{200}{\$6} = 33\tfrac{1}{3} \text{ units of utility per dollar}$$

So forget about dating Jerry with its 28½ units of utility per dollar. Your rational choice is to study this chapter while stuffing yourself with pizza.

But wait. Remember that, according to the principle of diminishing marginal utility, as you consume more of something, the marginal utility you get from it falls. So as you consume more pizza and spend more time reading this book, the marginal utilities of these activities will fall. Thus, as you vary your consumption, the marginal utilities you get from the goods are changing.

MAXIMIZING UTILITY AND EQUILIBRIUM

When do you stop changing your consumption? The principle of rational choice says you should keep adjusting your spending within your budget if the marginal utility per dollar (MU/P) of two goods differs. The only time you don't adjust your spending is when there is no clear winner. *When the ratios of the marginal utility to price of the two goods are equal*, you're maximizing utility; this is the **utility-maximizing rule:**

The utility maximizing rule:
$$\frac{MU_x}{P_x} = \frac{MU_y}{P_y}$$

$$If \frac{MU_x}{P_x} = \frac{MU_y}{P_y}, \text{ you're maximizing utility}.$$

When you're maximizing utility, you're in equilibrium. To understand how, by adjusting your spending, you can achieve equilibrium, it's important to remember the principle of diminishing marginal utility. As we consume more of an item, the marginal utility we get from the last unit consumed decreases. Conversely, as we consume *less* of an item, the marginal utility we get from the last unit consumed *increases*. (The principle of diminishing marginal utility operates in reverse.)

Achieving equilibrium by maximizing utility (juggling your choices, adding a bit more of one and choosing a bit less of another) requires more information than I've so far presented. We need to know the marginal utility of alternative amounts of consumption for each choice and how much we have to spend on all those items. With that information we can choose among alternatives, given our available resources.

AN EXAMPLE OF MAXIMIZING UTILITY

Table 8-1 offers an example in which we have the necessary information to make simultaneous decisions and maximize utility. In this example, we have $7 to spend on ice cream cones and Big Macs. The choice is between ice cream at $1 a cone and Big Macs at $2 apiece. In the table you can see the principle of diminishing marginal utility in action. The marginal utility (MU) we get from either good decreases as we consume more of it. Marginal utility (MU) becomes negative after 5 Big Macs or 6 ice cream cones.

The key columns for your decision are the *MU/P* columns. They tell you the *MU* per dollar spent on each of the items. By following the rule that we choose the good with the higher marginal utility per dollar, we can quickly determine the optimal choice.

Let's start by considering what we'd do with our first $2. Clearly we'd only eat ice cream. Doing so would give us 29 + 17 = 46 units of utility, compared to 20 units of utility if we spent the $2 on a Big Mac. How about our next $2? Again the choice is

Table 8-1 Maximizing Utility

This table provides the information needed to make simultaneous decisions. Notice that the marginal utility we get from another good declines as we consume more of it. To maximize utility, adjust your choices until the marginal utility of all goods is equal.

Big Macs (P = $2)					Ice Cream (P = $1)			
Q	TU	MU	MU/P		Q	TU	MU	MU/P
0	0				0	0		
		20	10				29	29
1	20				1	29		
		14	7				17	17
2	34				2	46		
		10	5				7	7
3	44				3	53		
		3	1.5				2	2
4	47				4	55		
		0	0				1	1
5	47				5	56		
		−5	−2.5				0	0
6	42				6	56		
		−10	−5				−4	−4
7	32				7	52		

clear; the 10 units of utility per dollar from the Big Mac are plainly better than the 7 units of utility per dollar we can get from ice cream cones. So we buy 1 Big Mac and 2 ice cream cones with our first $4.

Now let's consider our fifth and sixth dollars. The MU/P for a second Big Mac is 7. The MU/P for a third ice cream cone is also 7, so we could spend the fifth dollar on either—if McDonald's will sell us half a Big Mac. We ask them if they will, and they tell us no, so we must make a choice between either two additional ice cream cones or another Big Mac for our fifth and sixth dollars. Since the marginal utility per dollar of the fourth ice cream cone is only 2, it makes sense to spend our fifth and sixth dollars on another Big Mac. So now we're up to 2 Big Macs and 2 ice cream cones and we have one more dollar to spend.

Now how about our last dollar? If we spend it on a third ice cream cone we get 7 additional units of utility. If McDonald's maintains its position and only sells whole Big Macs, this is our sole choice since we only have a dollar and Big Macs sell for $2. But let's say that McDonald's wants the sale and this time offers to sell us half a Big Mac for $1. Would we take it? The answer is no. One-half of the next Big Mac gives us only 5 units of utility per dollar whereas the third ice cream cone gives us 7 units of utility per dollar. So we spend the seventh dollar on a third ice cream cone.

With these choices and $7 to spend we've arrived at equilibrium—the marginal utilities per dollar are the same for both goods and we're maximizing total utility. Our total utility is 34 from 2 Big Macs and 53 units of utility from the 3 ice cream cones, making a total utility of 87.

Why do these two choices make sense? Because they give us the most total utility for the $7 we have to spend. We've followed the utility-maximizing rule: Maximize utility by adjusting your choices until the marginal utilities per dollar are the same. These choices make the marginal utility per dollar between the last Big Mac and the last ice cream cone equal. The marginal utility per dollar we get from our last Big Mac is:

$$\frac{MU}{P} = \frac{14}{\$2} = 7$$

The marginal utility per dollar we get from our last ice cream cone is:

$$\frac{MU}{P} = \frac{7}{\$1} = 7$$

The marginal utility per dollar of each choice is equal, so we know we can't do any better. For any other choice we would get less total utility, so we could increase our total utility by switching to one of these two choices.

EXTENDING THE PRINCIPLE OF RATIONAL CHOICE

Our example involved only two goods, but the reasoning can be extended to the choice among many goods. Our analysis has shown us that the principle of rational choice among many goods is simply an extension of the principle of rational choice applied to two goods. That general principle of rational choice is to consume more of the good that provides a higher marginal utility per dollar.

When $\dfrac{MU_x}{P_x} > \dfrac{MU_z}{P_z}$, consume more of good x.

When $\dfrac{MU_y}{P_y} > \dfrac{MU_z}{P_z}$, consume more of good y.

Stop adjusting your consumption when the marginal utilities per dollar are equal.

So the general utility-maximizing rule is that you are maximizing utility when the marginal utilities per dollar of the goods consumed are equal.

When $\dfrac{MU_x}{P_x} = \dfrac{MU_y}{P_y} = \dfrac{MU_z}{P_z}$ you are maximizing utility.

When this rule is met, the consumer is in equilibrium; the cost per additional unit of utility is equal for all goods and the consumer is as well off as it is possible to be.

Notice that the rule does not say that the rational consumer should consume a good until its marginal utility reaches zero. The reason is that consumers don't have enough money to buy all they want. They face a budget constraint and do the best they can under that constraint—that is, they maximize utility. To buy more goods a person has to work more, so she should work until the marginal utility of another dollar earned just equals the marginal utility of goods purchased with another dollar. According to economists' analysis of rational choice, a person's choice of how much to work is made simultaneously with the person's decision of how much to consume. So when you say you want a Porsche but can't afford one, economists ask whether you're working two jobs and saving all your money to buy a Porsche. If you aren't, you're demonstrating that you don't really want a Porsche, given what you would have to do to get it.

Q-6 If you are initially in equilibrium and the price of one good rises, how would you adjust your consumption to return to equilibrium?

RATIONAL CHOICE AND THE LAWS OF DEMAND AND SUPPLY

Now that you know the rule for maximizing utility, let's see how it relates to the laws of demand and supply. We begin with demand. The law of demand says that the quantity demanded of a good is inversely related to its price. That is, when the price of a good goes up, the quantity we consume of it goes down.

In the discussion of the law of demand I didn't say precisely how much the quantity demanded would decrease with an increase in the price of an ice cream cone from $1 to $2. I didn't because of a certain ambiguity that arises when one talks about changes in nominal prices. To understand the cause of this ambiguity, notice that if the price of an ice cream cone has risen to $2, with $7 we can no longer consume 2 Big Macs and 3 ice cream cones. We've got to cut back for two reasons: First, we're poorer due to the rise in price. The reduction in quantity demanded because we're poorer is called the *income effect*. Second, the *relative* prices have changed. The price of ice cream has risen relative to the price of Big Macs. The reduction in quantity demanded because relative price has risen is called a *substitution effect*. Technically the law of demand is based only on the substitution effect.

To separate the two effects, let's assume that somebody compensates us for the rise in price of ice cream cones. Since it would cost $10 [(2 × $2 = $4) + (3 × $2 = $6)] to buy what $7 bought previously, we'll assume that someone gives us an extra $3 to compensate us for the rise in price. Since we are not any poorer because of the price change, this eliminates the income effect. We now have $10, so we can buy 2 Big Macs and the 3 ice cream cones as we did before. If we do so, our total utility is once again 87 (34 units of utility from 2 Big Macs and 53 units of utility from 3 ice cream cones.) But will we do so? We can answer that with the table.

We see that Big Macs give us more *MU* per dollar. What happens if we exchange an ice cream cone for an

Big Macs (P = $2)				Ice Cream (P = $2)			
Q	TU	MU	MU/P	Q	TU	MU	MU/P
0	0			0	0		
		20	10			29	14.5
1	20			1	29		
		14	7			17	8.5
2	34			2	46		
		10	5			7	3.5
3	44			3	53		

additional Big Mac, so instead of buying 3 ice cream cones and 2 Big Macs, we buy 3 Big Macs and 2 ice cream cones? The *MU* per dollar of Big Macs falls from 7 to 5 and the *MU* per dollar of the ice cream cone (whose price is now $2) rises from 3.5 to 8.5. Our total utility rises to 44 from 3 Big Macs and 46 from 2 ice cream cones, for a total of 90 units of utility rather than the previous 87. We've increased our total utility by shifting our consumption out of ice cream, the good whose price has risen. The price of ice cream went up and, even though we were given more money so we could buy the same amount as before, we did not; we bought fewer ice cream cones. That's the substitution effect in action: It tells us that when the relative price of a good goes up, the quantity purchased of that good decreases, *even if you're given money to compensate you for the rise.*

Now let's consider the law of demand in relation to our principle of rational choice. When the price of a good goes up, the marginal utility *per dollar* we get from that good goes down. So when the price of a good goes up, if we were initially in equilibrium, we no longer are. Therefore, we choose to consume less of that good. The principle of rational choice shows us formally that following the law of demand is the rational thing to do.

Let's see how. If:

$$\frac{MU_x}{P_x} = \frac{MU_y}{P_y}$$

and the price of good y goes up, then:

$$\frac{MU_x}{P_x} > \frac{MU_y}{P_y}$$

According to the principle of rational choice, if there is diminishing marginal utility and the price of a good goes up, we consume less of that good. Hence, the principle of rational choice leads to the law of demand.

Our utility-maximizing rule is no longer satisfied. Consider the preceding example, in which we were in equilibrium with 87 units of utility (34 from 2 Big Macs and 53 from 3 ice cream cones) with the utility-maximizing rule fulfilled:

$$\underset{\text{Big Mac}}{\frac{14 \text{ units of utility}}{\$2}} = \underset{\text{Ice cream}}{\frac{7 \text{ units of utility}}{\$1}} = 7$$

If the price of an ice cream cone rises from $1 to $2, the marginal utility per dollar for Big Macs (whose price hasn't changed) exceeds the marginal utility per dollar of ice cream cones:

$$\underset{\text{Big Mac}}{\frac{14}{\$2}} > \underset{\text{Ice cream}}{\frac{7}{\$2}}$$

To satisfy our utility-maximizing rule so that our choice will be rational, we must some-how raise the marginal utility we get from the good whose price has risen. Following the principle of diminishing marginal utility, we can increase marginal utility only by *decreasing* our consumption of the good whose price has risen. As we consume fewer ice cream cones and more Big Macs, the marginal utility of ice cream rises and the marginal utility of a Big Mac falls.

This example can be extended to a general rule: If the price of a good rises, you'll in-crease your total utility by consuming less of it. When the price of a good goes up, con-sumption of that good will go down. Our principle of rational choice underlies the law of demand:

Quantity demanded rises as price falls, other things constant.

Or alternatively:

Quantity demanded falls as price rises, other things constant.

This discussion of marginal utility and rational choice shows the relationship be-tween marginal utility and the price we're willing to pay. When marginal utility is high, as it is with diamonds, the price we're willing to pay is high. When marginal utility is low, as it is with tap water, the price we're willing to pay is low. Since our demand for a good is an expression of our willingness to pay for it, quantity demanded is related to marginal utility.

THE LAW OF SUPPLY

According to the principle of ra-tional choice, if there is diminishing marginal utility and the price of supplying a good goes up, you supply more of that good.

The above discussion focused on demand and goods we consume, but this analysis of choice holds for the law of supply of factors of production, such as labor, that individu-als supply to the market, as well as for demand. In supply decisions you are giving up something—your time, land, or some other factor of production—and getting money in return. To show you how this works, let's consider one final example—how much labor you should supply to the market.

Say that working another hour at your part-time job pays you another $5 and that you currently work 20 hours per week. That additional income from the final hour of work gives you an additional 24 units of utility. Also assume that your best alternative use of that hour—studying economics—gives you another 24 units of utility. (You didn't know economics gave you so much pleasure, did you?) So what should you do when your boss asks you to work an extra hour? Tell her no, you are already satisfying the utility-maximum rule $MU_w/W = MU_s/W$.

$$\frac{\overset{\text{Studying}}{24 \text{ units of utility}}}{\$5} = \frac{\overset{\text{Working}}{24 \text{ units of utility}}}{\$5}$$

The price of studying an additional hour is also your wage per hour because that wage is the opportunity cost of studying.

But now say that your boss offers to raise your wage to $5.50 per hour for work you do over 20 hours. That means that both your wage at work and the price of studying have increased. But now you can get more goods for working that additional hour. Let's say that those additional goods raise the marginal utility you get from an additional hour of work to 32 additional units of utility. Now the marginal utility of working an additional hour exceeds the marginal utility of studying an additional hour:

$$\frac{\overset{\text{Studying}}{24 \text{ units of utility}}}{\$5.50} < \frac{\overset{\text{Working}}{32 \text{ units of utility}}}{\$5.50}$$

So you work the extra hour.

Now say your boss comes to you and asks what it would take to get you to work five hours more per week. After running the numbers through your computer-mind, you solve the utility-maximizing rule and tell her, "$8.00 an hour for overtime work and you've got your worker." Combining these hours and wages gives you the supply curve shown in Figure 8-2, which demonstrates the law of supply.

To see that you have the reasoning down, say that an exam is coming, and you haven't studied. This will likely raise the marginal utility of studying sufficiently, so you will choose to work less, if you have a choice. What will that change do to the supply curve?

If you answered that it will shift it to the left, you're in good shape.

Q-7 Use the principle of rational choice to explain how you would change your quantity of work supplied if your employer raised your wage by $1 per hour.

OPPORTUNITY COST

Before we leave the principle of rational choice, let's consider how it relates to the opportunity cost concept that I presented in earlier chapters. *Opportunity cost* was the benefit forgone of the next-best alternative. Now that you've been through the principle of rational choice, you have a better sense of what is meant by opportunity cost of a forgone opportunity—it is essentially the marginal utility per dollar you forgo from the consumption of the next-best alternative.

To say $MU_x/P_x > MU_y/P_y$ is to say that the opportunity cost of not consuming good x is greater than the opportunity cost of not consuming good y. So you consume x.

The principle of rational choice states that, to maximize utility, choose goods until the opportunity costs of all alternatives are equal.

Figure 8-2   Deriving Labor Supply from Marginal Utility
Factor supply curves can be derived from a comparison of marginal utilities for various activities in relation to work. In this example the higher the wage, the higher the marginal utility of the goods you can get for the wage relative to the next-best alternative, giving you an upward-sloping labor supply curve.

Q.8 If the opportunity cost of consuming good *x* is greater than the opportunity cost of consuming good *y*, which good has the higher marginal utility per dollar?

When the marginal utilities per dollar spent are equal, the opportunity cost of the alternatives are equal. In reality people don't use the utility terminology, and, indeed, a specific measure of utility doesn't exist. But the choice based on the price of goods relative to the benefit they provide is used all the time. Instead of utility terminology, people use the "really need" terminology. They say they will work the extra hour rather than study because they *really need* the money. To say you are working because you "really need" the money is the equivalent of saying the marginal utility of working is higher than the opportunity cost of other choices. So the general rule fits decisions about supply, even if most people don't use the word *utility*. The more you "really, really need" something, the higher its marginal utility.

APPLYING ECONOMISTS' THEORY OF CHOICE TO THE REAL WORLD

Understanding a theory involves more than understanding how a theory works; it also involves understanding the limits the assumptions underlying the theory place on the use of the theory. So let's consider some of the assumptions on which economists' analysis of choice is based. The first assumption we'll consider is the implicit assumption that decisions can be made costlessly.

implicit – not clear
explicit – clear

THE COST OF DECISION MAKING

The principle of rational choice makes reasonably good intuitive sense when we limit our examples to two or three choices, as I did in this chapter. But in reality, we make hundreds of thousands of choices simultaneously. It simply doesn't make intuitive sense that we're going to apply rational choice to all those choices at once—that would exceed our decision-making abilities. This cost of decision making means that it is only rational to be somewhat irrational—to do things without applying the principle of rational choice. Thinking about decisions is one of the things we all economize on.

How real-world people make decisions in real-world situations is an open question that modern economists are spending a lot of time researching. Following the work of Nobel Prize winner Herbert Simon, a number of economists have come to believe that, to make real-world decisions, most people use *bounded rationality*—rationality based on rules of thumb—rather than using the principle of rational choice. They argue that many of our decisions are made with our minds on automatic pilot. This view of rationality has significant implications for interpreting and predicting economic events. For example, one rule of thumb is "You get what you pay for," which means that something with a high price is better than something with a low price. Put technically, we rely on price to convey information about quality. This reliance on price for information changes the inferences one can draw from the analysis, and can lead to upward-sloping demand curves.

Q.9 Bounded rationality violates the principle of rational choice. True or false?

A second rule of thumb that people sometimes use is "Follow the leader." If you don't know what to do, do what you think smart people are doing. Consider the clothes you're wearing. I suspect many of your choices of what to wear reflect this and the previous rules of thumb. Suppliers of clothing certainly think so and spend enormous amounts of money to exploit these rules of thumb. They try to steer your automatic pilot toward their goods. The suppliers emphasize these two rules ("You get what you pay for" and "Follow the leader") to convince people their product is the "in" thing to buy. If they succeed, they've got a gold mine; if they fail, they've got a flop. Advertising is designed to mine these rules of thumb.

Advertising is designed to mine rules of thumb.

In technical terms, the "Follow the leader" rule leads to *focal point equilibria*, in which a set of goods is consumed, not because the goods are objectively preferred to all other goods, but simply because, through luck, or advertising, they have become focal points to which people have gravitated. Once some people started consuming a good, others followed.

GIVEN TASTES

A second assumption implicit in economists' theory of rational choice is that our preferences are given, and are not shaped by society. In reality our preferences are determined not only by nature but also by our experiences—by nurture. Let's consider an example: Forty percent of major league baseball players chew tobacco, but close to zero percent of college professors chew tobacco. Why? Are major league baseball players somehow born with a tobacco-chewing gene while college professors are not? I doubt it. Tastes often are significantly influenced by society.

CONSPICUOUS CONSUMPTION

Another aspect of taste that has been described by economists is **conspicuous consumption**—*the consumption of goods not for one's direct pleasure, but simply to show off to others.* The term was created approximately 100 years ago by Thornstein Veblen. Veblen argued that, just as some animals strut around to show their abilities, humans consume to show that they can "afford it." For Veblen, mansions, designer clothing, and $300 appetizers were all examples of conspicuous consumption. He further argued that male industrialists (which were all industrialists at the time) were so busy with business that they didn't have time to show off enough, so they married a trophy spouse whose purpose was to show off for them in the most ostentatious manner possible.

TASTES AND INDIVIDUAL CHOICE

One way in which economists integrate the above insights into economics is by emphasizing that the analysis is conducted on the assumption of "given tastes." As discussed above, in reality, economists agree that often forces besides price and marginal utility play a role in determining what people demand. They fully recognize that a whole other analysis is necessary to supplement theirs—an analysis of what determines taste.

Web Note 8.3
Veblen Goods

Ask yourself what you ate today. Was it health food? Pizza? Candy? Whatever it was, it was probably not the most efficient way to satisfy your nutritional needs. The most efficient way to do that would be to eat only soybean mush and vitamin supplements at a cost of about $300 per year. That's less than one-tenth of what the average individual today spends on food per year. Most of us turn up our noses at soybean mush. Why? Because tastes are important.

I emphasize this point because some economists have been guilty of forgetting their simplifying assumption. Some economists in the 1800s thought that society's economic needs eventually would be fully met and that we would enter a golden age of affluence where all our material wants would be satisfied. They thought there would be surpluses of everything. Clearly that hasn't happened. Somehow it seems that whenever a need is met, it's replaced by a want, which soon becomes another need.

There are, of course, examples of wants being temporarily satisfied, as a U.S. company on a small island in the Caribbean is reported to have discovered. Employees weren't showing up for work. The company sent in a team of efficiency experts who discovered the cause of their problem: The firm had recently raised wages, and workers had decided they could get all they wanted (warm weather, a gorgeous beach, plenty of food, and a little bit of spending money) by showing up for work once, maybe twice, a week. Such a situation was clearly not good for business, but the firm found a solution. It sent

Somehow, whenever a need is met, it's replaced by a want, which soon becomes another need.

It is hard to make good decisions. You need lots of training—in math, in economics, in logic. Think of kids—do five-year-olds make rational decisions? Some dyed-in-the-wool utilitarians might argue that whatever decision one makes must, by definition, be rational, but such usage makes the concept tautological—true by definition.

When applying the theory of rational choice, most economists agree that some decisions people make can be irrational. For example, they will concede that five-year-olds make a lot of what most parents would call stupid (or irrational) decisions. By a stupid decision they mean a decision with expected consequences that, if the child had logically thought about them, would have caused the child not to make that particular decision. But five-year-olds often haven't learned how to think logically about expected consequences, so economists don't assume decisions made by five-year-olds reflect the rational choice model.

In the real world, parents and teachers spend enormous effort to teach children what is rational, reasonable, and "appropriate." Children's decision-making process reflects that teaching. But parents and teachers teach more than a decision-making process; they also teach children a moral code that often includes the value of honor and the value of selflessness. These teachings shape their children's decision-making process (although not always in the way that parents or teachers think or hope) and modify their preferences. So our decision-making process and our preferences are, to some degree, taught to us.

Recognizing that preferences and decision-making processes are, to some degree, taught, not inherent, eliminates the fixed point by which to judge people's decisions: Are they making decisions that reflect their true needs, or are they simply reflecting what they have been taught? Eliminating that fixed point makes it difficult to draw unambiguous policy implications from economists' model of rational choice.

---

in thousands of Sears catalogs (back when Sears sent catalogs), and suddenly the workers were no longer satisfied with what they already had. They wanted more and went back to work to get it. When they were presented with new possibilities, their wants increased. Companies know that tastes aren't constant, and they spend significant amounts of money on advertising to make consumers have a taste for their goods. It works, too.

Tastes are also important in explaining differences in consumption between countries. For example, a Japanese person wouldn't consider having a meal without rice. Rice has a ceremonial, almost mystical value in Japan. In many parts of the United States supper means meat and potatoes. In Germany, carp (a large goldfish) is a delicacy; in the United States many people consider carp inedible. In the United States corn is a desirable vegetable; in parts of Europe, until recently, it was considered pig food.

To say we don't analyze tastes in the core of economic theory doesn't mean that we don't take them into account. Think back to Chapter 4, when we distinguished shifts in demand (the entire demand schedule shifts) from movements along the demand curve. Those movements along the demand curve were the effect of price. Tastes were one of the shift factors of demand. So economists do include tastes in their analysis; a change in tastes makes the demand curve shift.

Q-10 Using the principle of rational choice, explain why a change in tastes will shift a demand curve.

Economists take into account changes in tastes as shift factors of demand.

CONCLUSION

We began this chapter with a discussion of the simplifying nature of the economists' analysis of rational choice. Now that you've been through it, you may be wondering if it's all that simple. In any case, I'm sure most of you would agree that it's complicated enough. When we're talking about formal analysis, I'm in total agreement.

But if you're talking about informal analysis and applying the analysis to the real world, most economists would also agree that this theory of choice is in no way acceptable. Economists believe that there's more to life than maximizing utility. We believe in love, anger, and doing crazy things just for the sake of doing crazy things. We're real people.

But, we argue, simplicity has its virtue, and often people hide their selfish motivations. Few people like to go around and say, "I did this because I'm a self-interested, calculating person who cares primarily about myself." Instead they usually emphasize other motives. "Society conditioned me to do it"; "I'm doing this to achieve fairness"; "It's my upbringing." And they're probably partially right, but often they hide and obscure their self-interested motives in their psychological explanations. The beauty of economists' simple psychological assumption is that it cuts through many obfuscations (that's an obfuscating word meaning "smokescreens") and, in doing so, often captures a part of reality that others miss. Let's consider a couple of examples.

Why does government have restrictions on who's allowed to practice law? The typical layperson's answer is that these restrictions exist to protect the public. The economists' answer is that many of the restrictions do little to protect the public. Instead their primary function is to restrict the number of lawyers and thereby increase the marginal utility of existing lawyers and the price they can charge.

Why do museum directors almost always want to increase the size of their collections? The layperson's (and museum directors') answer is that they're out to preserve our artistic heritage. The economists' answer is that it often has more to do with maximizing the utility of the museum staff. (Economist William Grampp made this argument in a book about the economics of art. He supported his argument by pointing out that more than half of museums' art is in storage and not accessible to the public. Acquiring more art will simply lead to more art going into storage.)

Now in no way am I claiming that the economic answer based on pure self-interest is always the correct one. But I am arguing that approaching problems by asking the question "What's in it for the people making the decisions?" is a useful approach that will give you more insight into what's going on than many other approaches. It gets people to ask tough, rather than easy, questions. After you've asked the tough questions, then you can see how to modify the conclusions by looking deeply into the real-world institutions.

All too often students think of economics and economic reasoning as establishment reasoning. That's not true. Economic reasoning can be extremely subversive to existing establishments. But whatever it is, it is not subversive in order to be subversive, or proestablishment to be proestablishment. It's simply a logical application of a simple idea—individual choice theory—to a variety of problems.

> Economists use their simple self-interest theory of choice because it cuts through many obfuscations, and in doing so, often captures a part of reality that others miss.

> Approaching problems by asking the question "What's in it for the people making the decision?" is a useful approach that will give you more insight than many other approaches.

Subversive = against civil authority or government

SUMMARY

- Total utility is the satisfaction obtained from consuming a product; marginal utility is the satisfaction obtained from consuming one additional unit of a product.

- The principle of diminishing marginal utility states that after some point, the marginal utility of consuming more of the good will fall.

- The principle of rational choice is:

  If $\dfrac{MU_x}{P_x} > \dfrac{MU_y}{P_y}$, choose to consume more of good x.

  If $\dfrac{MU_x}{P_x} < \dfrac{MU_y}{P_y}$, choose to consume more of good y.

- The utility-maximizing rule says:

  If $\dfrac{MU_x}{P_x} = \dfrac{MU_y}{P_y}$, you're maximizing utility; you're indifferent between good x and good y.

- Unless $MU_x/P_x = MU_y/P_y$, an individual can rearrange his or her consumption to increase total utility.

- Opportunity cost is essentially the marginal utility per dollar one forgoes from the consumption of the next-best alternative.

- The law of demand can be derived from the principle of rational choice.

- If you're in equilibrium and the price of a good rises, you'll reduce your consumption of that good to reestablish equilibrium.

- The law of supply can be derived from the principle of rational choice.

- If your wage rises, the marginal utility of the goods you can buy with that wage will rise and you will work more to satisfy the utility-maximizing rule.

- To apply economists' analysis of choice to the real world, we must carefully consider, and adjust for, the underlying assumptions, such as costlessness of decision making and given tastes.

KEY TERMS

conspicuous
   consumption (191)
marginal utility (179)

principle of diminishing
   marginal utility (180)

principle of rational
   choice (183)
total utility (179)

utility (179)
utility-maximizing
   rule (184)

QUESTIONS FOR THOUGHT AND REVIEW

1. Explain how marginal utility differs from total utility.

2. According to the principle of diminishing marginal utility, how does marginal utility change as more of a good is consumed? As less of a good is consumed?

3. How would the world be different than it is if the principle of diminishing marginal utility seldom held true?

4. It is sometimes said that an economist is a person who knows the price of everything but the value of nothing. Is this statement true or false? Why?

5. Assign a measure of utility to your studying for various courses. Do your study habits follow the principle of rational choice?

6. What key psychological assumptions do economists make in their theory of individual choice?

7. Explain your motivation for four personal decisions you have made in the past year, using economists' model of individual choice.

8. State the law of demand and explain how it relates to the principle of rational choice.

9. State the law of supply and explain how it relates to opportunity cost.

10. If the supply curve is perfectly inelastic, what is the opportunity cost of the supplier?

11. There is a small but growing movement known as "voluntary simplicity," which is founded on the belief in a simple life of working less and spending less. Do Americans who belong to this movement follow the principle of rational choice?

12. Although the share of Americans who say they are "very happy" hasn't changed much in the last five decades, the number of products produced and consumed per person has risen tremendously. How can this be?

13. Early Classical economists found the following "diamond/water" paradox perplexing: "Why is water, which is so useful and necessary, so cheap, when diamonds, which are so useless and unnecessary, so expensive?" Using the utility concept, explain why it is not really a paradox.

14. Give an example of a recent purchase for which you used a rule of thumb in your decision-making process. Did your decision follow the principle of rational choice? Explain.

15. According to Thorstein Veblen what is the purpose of conspicuous consumption? Does the utility derived from the consumption of these goods come from their price or functionality? Give an example of such a good.

PROBLEMS AND EXERCISES

1. Complete the following table of Scout's utility from drinking cans of soda and answer the questions below.

Cans of Soda	Total Utility	Marginal Utility
0	___	
		10
1	___	
		12
2	22	
3	32	___
		8
4	___	
		4
5	___	
6	44	___
7	42	___

a. At what point does marginal utility begin to fall?
b. Will Scout consume the 7th can of soda? Explain your answer.
c. True or false? Scout will be following the utility-maximizing rule by consuming 2 cans of soda. Explain your answer.

2. The following table gives the price and total units of three goods: A, B, and C.

Good	Price	Total Utility							
		1	2	3	4	5	6	7	8
A	$10	200	380	530	630	680	700	630	430
B	2	20	34	46	56	64	72	78	82
C	6	50	60	70	80	90	100	90	80

As closely as possible, determine how much of the three goods you would buy with $20. Explain why you chose what you did.

3. The following table gives the marginal utility of John's consumption of three goods: A, B, and C.

Units of Consumption	MU of A	MU of B	MU of C
1		25	45
	20		
2		20	30
	18		
3		15	24
	16		
4		10	18
	14		
5		8	15
	12		
6		6	12
	10		

a. Good A costs $2 per unit, good B costs $1, and good C costs $3. How many units of each should a consumer with $12 buy to maximize his or her utility?
b. How will the answer change if the price of B rises to $2?
c. How about if the price of C is 50 cents but the other prices are as in a?

4. The total utility of your consumption of widgets is 40; it changes by 2 with each change in widgets consumed. The total utility of your consumption of wadgets is also 40 but changes by 3 with each change in wadgets consumed. The price of widgets is $2 and the price of wadgets is $3. How many widgets and wadgets should you consume?

5. Nobel Prize–winning economist George Stigler explains how the famous British economist Phillip Wicksteed decided where to live. His two loves were fresh farm eggs, which were more easily obtained the farther from London he was, and visits from friends, which decreased the farther he moved away from London. Given these two loves, describe the decision rule that you would have expected Wicksteed to follow.

6. You are buying your spouse, significant other, or close friend a ring. You decide to show your reasonableness, and buy a cubic zirconium ring that sells at ⅟₅₀ the cost of a mined diamond and that any normal person could not tell from a mined diamond just by looking at it. In fact, the zirconium will have more brilliance and fewer occlusions (imperfections) than a mined diamond.

a. How will your spouse (significant other, close friend) likely react?

b. Why?

c. Is this reaction justified?

7. Suppose Charlie Parker CDs cost $10 apiece and Lester Young CDs cost $5 apiece. You have $40 to spend on CDs. The marginal utility that you derive from additional CDs is as follows:

Number of CDs	Charlie Parker	Lester Young
0		30
	60	
1		28
	40	
2		24
	30	
3		20
	20	
4		10
	10	
5		

How many of each CD would you buy? Suppose the price of a Lester Young CD rises to $10. How many of each CDs would you buy? Use this to show how the principle of rational choice leads to the law of demand.

WEB QUESTIONS

1. Go to www.travelocity.com.
   a. Find a selection of prices of airline fares between two cities for a period of one month ahead of time and staying over a Saturday night. If there are differences in the prices explain why they likely differ.
   b. Now shorten your stay, and do not include a Saturday-night stay. What happens to the prices? Explain why.
   c. Now find the price of the same flight you had in *a*, only this time booking only three days ahead. What happens to prices? Explain why.

2. Go to www.iwon.com.
   a. What does this site do?
   b. Why do they give out a $10,000 daily prize and a $25 million yearly prize for using the site?
   c. What advertisements were shown there?
   d. What does the existence of these advertisements suggest about economists' assumption that tastes are fixed?

ANSWERS TO MARGIN QUESTIONS

1. False. Economists' theory of choice does not require them to measure utility. It only requires that the marginal utility of one good be compared to the marginal utility of another. *(179)*

2. If the total utility curve is a straight line, the marginal utility curve will be flat with a slope of zero since marginal utility would not change with additional units. *(180)*

3. False. The principle of diminishing marginal utility is that as one increases consumption of a good, the good's marginal utility decreases. *(180)*

4. Given a choice between the two, the rational choice is to watch MTV for one hour since it provides the highest marginal utility per hour. *(183)*

5. False. You are maximizing total utility when the marginal utilities per dollar are the same for all goods. This does not have to be where marginal utility is zero. *(184)*

6. If I am currently in equilibrium, then $MU_x/P_x = MU_y/P_y = MU_z/P_z$ for all goods I consume. If the price of one good goes up, I will decrease my consumption of that good and increase the consumption of other goods until the equilibrium is met again where $MU_x/P_x = MU_y/P_y = MU_z/P_z$. *(186)*

7. If offered one more dollar per hour, I would choose to substitute labor for leisure since the price of leisure (pay per hour of work) has increased. Following the principle of rational choice, I would work more to lower the marginal utility of work so that $MU_w/P_w = MU_l/P_l$. *(189)*

8. Good y has the higher marginal utility per dollar since the opportunity cost of consuming good x is the marginal utility per dollar of consuming good y. *(190)*

9. This could be true or false. It depends on how you interpret bounded rationality. If it is interpreted within a costless decision-making environment, it does violate the principle of rational choice since there is no reason to be less than rational. If, however, it is interpreted within a costly decision-making environment, then you can be making decisions within a range because the marginal

cost of increasing the range of choices exceeds the marginal benefit of doing so, and in that case bounded rationality is consistent with the principle of rational choice. Information is not costless. *(190)*

10. If a person is in equilibrium and a change in tastes leads to an increase in the marginal utility for one good, he will increase consumption of that good to reestablish equilibrium. A change in tastes will shift a demand curve because it will cause a change in quantity consumed without a change in the good's price. *(192)*

APPENDIX A

Indifference Curve Analysis

As I stated in the chapter, analyzing individual choice using actual numbers is unnecessary. In the chapter, I asked you to make a deal with me: You'd remember that actual numbers are unnecessary and I'd use them anyway. This appendix is for those who didn't accept my deal (and for those whose professors want them to get some practice in Graphish). It presents an example of a more formal analysis of individual choice.

SOPHIE'S CHOICE

Sophie is a junk food devotee. She lives on two goods: chocolate bars, which cost $1 each, and cans of soda, which sell for 50 cents apiece. Sophie is trying to get as much pleasure as possible, given her resources. Alternatively expressed, Sophie is trying to maximize her utility, given a budget constraint.

By translating this statement of Sophie's choice into graphs, I can demonstrate the principle of rational choice without ever mentioning any specific amount of utility.

The graph we'll use will have chocolate bars on the vertical axis and cans of soda on the horizontal axis, as in Figure A8-1.

GRAPHING THE
BUDGET CONSTRAINT

Let's begin by asking: How can we translate her budget constraint (the $10 maximum she has to spend) into Graphish? The easiest way to do that is to ask what would happen if she spends her $10 all on chocolate bars or all on cans of soda. Since a chocolate bar costs $1, if she

Figure A8-1   Graphing the Budget Constraint

spends it all on chocolate bars she can get 10 bars (point A in Figure A8-1). If she spends it all on cans of soda, she can get 20 cans of soda (point B). This gives us two points.

But what if she wants some combination of soda and chocolate bars? If we draw a line between points A and B, we'll have a graphical picture of her budget constraint and can answer that question because a **budget constraint** is *a curve that shows us the various combinations of goods an individual can buy with a given amount of money.* The line is her budget constraint in Graphish.

To see that it is, say Sophie is spending all her money on chocolate bars. She then decides to buy one fewer chocolate bar. That gives her $1 to spend on soda, which, since those cans cost 50 cents each, allows her to buy 2 cans. Point C (9 chocolate bars and 2 cans of soda) represents that decision. Notice how point C is on the budget constraint. Repeat this exercise from various starting points until you're comfortable with the fact that the line does indeed represent the various combinations of soda and chocolate bars Sophie can buy with the $10. It's a line with a slope of −½ and intersects the chocolate-bars-axis at 10 and the cans-of-soda axis at 20.

To be sure that you've got it, ask yourself what would happen to the budget constraint if Sophie got another $4 to spend on the two goods. Going through the same reasoning should lead you to the conclusion that the budget constraint will shift to the right so that it will intersect the cans-of-soda axis at 28 (point D), but its slope won't change. (I started the new line for you.) Make sure you can explain why.

Now what if the price of a can of soda goes up to $1? What happens to the budget line? (This is a question many people miss.) If you said the budget line becomes steeper, shifting in along the cans-of-soda axis to point E while remaining anchored along the chocolate-bars-axis until the slope equals −1, you've got it. If you didn't say that, go through the same reasoning we went through at first (if Sophie buys only cans of soda . . .) and then draw the new line. You'll see it becomes steeper. Put another way, the absolute value of the slope of the curve is the ratio of the price of cans of soda to the price of chocolate bars; the absolute value of the slope becomes greater with a rise in the price of cans of soda.

GRAPHING THE INDIFFERENCE CURVE

Now let's consider the second part of Sophie's choice: the pleasure part. Sophie is trying to get as much pleasure as she can from her $10. How do we deal with this in Graphish?

To see, let's go through a thought experiment. Say Sophie had 14 chocolate bars and 4 cans of soda (point A in Figure A8-2). Let's ask her, "Say you didn't know the price of either good and we took away 4 of those chocolate bars (so you had 10). How many cans of soda would we have to give you so that you would be just as happy as before we took away the 4 chocolate bars?"

Since she's got lots of chocolate bars and few cans of soda, her answer is probably "Not too many; say, 1 can of soda." This means that she would be just as happy to have 10 chocolate bars and 5 cans of soda (point B) as she would to have 14 chocolate bars and 4 cans of soda (point A). Connect those points and you have the beginning of a "just-as-happy" curve. But that doesn't sound impressive enough, so, following economists' terminology, we'll call it an **indifference curve**—*a curve that shows combinations of goods among which an individual is indifferent.* She's indifferent between points A and B.

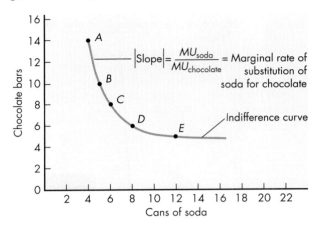

Figure A8-2 Sophie's Indifference Curve

Chocolate bars	Cans of soda	
14	4	A
10	5	B
8	6	C
6	8	D
5	12	E

If you continue our thought experiment, you'll get a set of combinations of chocolate bars and cans of soda like that shown in the table in Figure A8-2.

If you plot each of these combinations of points on the graph in Figure A8-2 and connect all these points, you have one of Sophie's indifference curves: a curve representing combinations of cans of soda and chocolate bars among which Sophie is indifferent.

Let's consider the shape of this curve. First, it's downward-sloping. That's reasonable; it simply says that if you take something away from Sophie, you've got to give her something in return if you want to keep her indifferent between what she had before and what she has now. The absolute value of the slope of an indifference curve is the **marginal rate of substitution**—*the rate at which one good must be added when the other is taken away in order to keep the individual indifferent between the two combinations.*

Second, it's bowed inward. That's because as Sophie gets more and more of one good, it takes fewer and fewer of another good to compensate for the loss of the good she incurred in order to get more of the other good. The underlying reasoning is similar to that in our discussion of the law of diminishing marginal utility, but notice we haven't even mentioned utility. Technically the reasoning for the indifference curve being bowed inward is called the

Figure A8-3   A Group of Indifference Curves

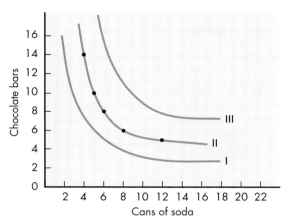

Figure A8-4   Why Indifference Curves Cannot Cross

law of diminishing marginal rate of substitution—which tells us that *as you get more and more of a good, if some of that good is taken away, then the marginal addition of another good you need to keep you on your indifference curve gets less and less.*

Even more technically we can say that the absolute value of the slope of the indifference curve equals the ratio of the marginal utility of cans of soda to the marginal utility of chocolate bars:

$$\left| \text{Slope} \right| = \frac{MU_{soda}}{MU_{chocolate}} = \text{Marginal rate of substitution}$$

That ratio equals the marginal rate of substitution of cans of soda for chocolate bars. Let's consider an example. Say that in Figure A8-2 Sophie is at point A and that the marginal utility she gets from an increase from 4 to 5 cans of soda is 10. Since we know that she was willing to give up 4 chocolate bars to get that 1 can of soda (and thereby move from point A to point B), that 10 must equal the loss of utility she gets from the loss of 4 chocolate bars out of the 14 she originally had. So the marginal rate of substitution of cans of soda for chocolate bars between points A and B must be 4. That's the absolute value of the slope of that curve. Therefore, her *MU* of a chocolate bar must be about 2.5 (10 for 4 chocolate bars).

You can continue this same reasoning, starting with various combinations of goods. If you do so, you can get a whole group of indifference curves like that in Figure A8-3. Each curve represents a different level of happiness. Assuming she prefers more to less, Sophie is better off if she's on Curve II than if she's on Curve I, and even better off if she's on Curve III. Her goal in life is to get out to the furthest indifference curve she can.

To see whether you've followed the reasoning, ask yourself the following question: "Assuming Sophie prefers more of a good to less (which seems reasonable), can any two of Sophie's indifference curves cross each other as the ones in Figure A8-4 do?"

The answer is no, no, no! Why? Because they're indifference curves. If the curves were to cross, the "prefer-more-to-less" principle would be violated. Say we start at point A: Sophie has 8 chocolate bars and 6 cans of soda. We know that since A (8 chocolate bars and 6 sodas) and B (6 chocolate bars and 8 cans of soda) are on the same indifference curve, Sophie is indifferent between A and B. Similarly with points B and C: Sophie would just as soon have 9 chocolate bars and 7 cans of soda as she would 6 chocolate bars and 8 cans of soda.

It follows by logical deduction that point A must be indifferent to C. But consider points A and C carefully. At point C, Sophie has 7 cans of soda and 9 chocolate bars. At point A she has 6 cans of soda and 8 chocolate bars. At point C she has more of both goods than she has at point A, so to say she's indifferent between these two points violates the "prefer-more-to-less" criterion. Ergo (that's Latin, meaning "therefore"), two indifference curves cannot intersect. That's why we drew the group of indifference curves in Figure A8-3 so that they do not intersect.

COMBINING INDIFFERENCE CURVES AND BUDGET CONSTRAINTS

Now let's put the budget constraint and the indifference curves together and ask how many chocolate bars and cans of soda Sophie will buy if she has $10, given the

Figure A8-5   Combining Indifference Curves and Budget Constraint

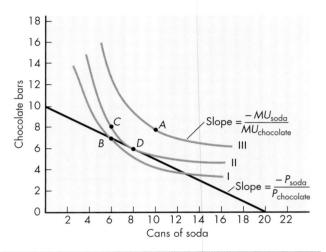

budget line $(-P_s/P_c)$ equals the slope of the indifference curve $(-MU_s/MU_c)$. Equating those slopes gives $P_s/P_c = (MU_s/MU_c)$, or:

$$MU_c/P_c = MU_s/P_s$$

This equation, you may remember from the chapter, is the equilibrium condition of our principle of rational choice. So by our Graphish analysis we arrived at the same conclusion we arrived at in the chapter, only this time we did it without using actual numbers. This means that even without a utilometer, economists' principle of rational choice is internally logical.

DERIVING A DEMAND CURVE FROM THE INDIFFERENCE CURVE

Not only can we derive the principle of rational choice with indifference curve/budget line analysis, we can also derive a demand curve. To do so, ask yourself what a demand curve is. It's the quantity of a good that a person will buy at various prices. Since the budget line gives us the relative price of a good, and the point of tangency of the indifference curve gives us the quantity that a person would buy at that price, we can derive a demand curve from the indifference curves and budget lines. To derive a demand curve we go through a set of thought experiments asking how many cans of soda Sophie would buy at various prices. We'll go through one of those experiments.

We start with the analysis we used before when Sophie started with $10 and chose to buy 8 cans of soda when the price of a can of soda was 50 cents (point A in Figure A8-6(a)). That analysis provides us with one point on the demand curve. I represent that by point A in Figure A8-6(b). At a price of 50 cents, Sophie buys 8 cans of soda.

Now say the price of a can of soda rises to $1. That rotates the budget line in, from budget line 1 to budget line 2 as in Figure A8-6(a). She can't buy as much as she could before. But we can determine how much she'll buy by the same reasoning we used previously. She'll choose a point at which her lower indifference curve is tangent to her new budget line. As you can see, she'll choose point B, which means that she buys 6 cans of soda when the price of a can of soda is $1. Graphing that point (6 cans of soda at $1 each) on our price/quantity axis in Figure A8-6(b), we have another point on our demand curve, point B. Connect these two together and you can see we're getting a downward-sloping demand curve, just as the law of

psychological makeup described by the indifference curves in Figure A8-3.

To answer that question, we must put the budget line of Figure A8-1 and the indifference curves of Figure A8-3 together, as we do in Figure A8-5.

As we discussed, Sophie's problem is to get to as high an indifference curve as possible, given her budget constraint. Let's first ask if she should move to point A (8 chocolate bars and 10 cans of soda). That looks like a good point. But you should quickly recognize that she can't get to point A; her budget line won't let her. (She doesn't have enough money.) Well then, how about point B (7 chocolate bars and 6 cans of soda)? She can afford that combination; it's on her budget constraint. The problem with point B is the following: She'd rather be at point C since point C has more chocolate bars and the same amount of soda (8 chocolate bars and 6 cans of soda). But, you say, she can't reach point C. Yes, that's true, but she can reach point D. And, by the definition of indifference curve, she's indifferent between point C and point D, so point D (6 chocolate bars and 8 cans of soda), which she can reach given her budget constraint, is preferred to point B.

The same reasoning holds for all other points. The reason is that the combination of chocolate bars and cans of soda represented by point D is the best she can do. It is the point where the indifference curve and the budget line are tangent—the point at which the slope of the

Figure A8-6 (a and b)   From Indifference Curves to Demand Curves

(a)

(b)

demand said we would. To make sure you understand, continue the analysis for a couple of additional price changes. You'll see that the demand curve you derive will be downward-sloping.

There's much more we can do with indifference curves. We can distinguish income effects and substitution effects. (Remember, when the price of a can of soda rose, Sophie was worse off. So to be as well off as before, as is required by the substitution effect, she'd have to be compensated for that rise in price by an offsetting fall in the price of chocolate bars.) But let's make a deal. You tentatively believe me when I say that all kinds of stuff can be done with indifference curves and budget constraints, and I'll leave the further demonstration and the proofs for you to experience in the intermediate microeconomics courses.

Key Terms

budget constraint (197)
indifference curve (198)

law of diminishing marginal rate of substitution (199)

marginal rate of substitution (198)

Questions for Thought and Review

1. Zachary has $5 to spend on two goods: video games and hot dogs. Hot dogs cost $1 apiece while video games cost 50 cents apiece.
   a. Draw a graph of Zachary's budget constraint, placing videos on the Y axis.
   b. Suppose the price of hot dogs falls to 50 cents apiece. Draw the new budget constraint.

   c. Suppose Zachary now has $8 to spend. Draw the new budget constraint using the prices from b.

2. Zachary's indifference curves are shown in the following graph. Determine on which indifference curve Zachary will be, given the budget constraints and prices in a, b, and c from problem 1.

a. Given a choice, which budget constraint would Zachary prefer most? Least?

b. What is the marginal rate of substitution of hot dogs for videos at each of the combinations chosen with budget constraints *a*, *b*, and *c* in problem 1?

3. What would an indifference curve look like if the marginal rate of substitution were zero? If it were constant?

4. What might an indifference curve look like if the law of diminishing marginal utility did not hold?

PRODUCTION AND COST ANALYSIS I

> Production is not the application of tools
> to materials, but logic to work.
>
> —*Peter Drucker*

The ability of market economies to supply material goods and services to members of their societies makes them the envy of many other societies and is one of the strongest arguments for using the market as a means of organizing society. Somehow markets are able to channel individuals' imagination, creativity, and drive into the production of material goods and services that other people want. They do this by giving people incentives to supply goods and services to the market.

Ultimately all supply comes from individuals. Individuals control the factors of production such as land, labor, and capital. Why do individuals supply these factors to the market? Because they want something in return. This means that industry's ability to supply goods is dependent on individuals' willingness to supply the factors of production they control. This connection became obvious in the formerly socialist countries in the late 1980s and early 1990s when consumer goods were often unavailable. People in those countries stopped working (supplying their labor). They reasoned: Why supply our labor if there's nothing to get in return?

The analysis of supply is more complicated than the analysis of demand. In the supply process, people first offer their factors of production to the market. Then the factors are transformed by firms, such as GM or IBM, into goods that consumers want. **Production** is the name given to that *transformation of factors into goods and services*.

To make it simple for you, I separate out the analysis of the supply of factors of production (considered in detail in later chapters) from the supply of produced goods. This allows us to assume that the prices of factors of production are constant, which simplifies the analysis of the supply of produced goods enormously. There's no problem with doing this as long as you remember that behind any produced good are individuals' factor supplies. Ultimately people, not firms, are responsible for supply.

Even with the analysis so simplified, there's still a lot to cover—so much, in fact, that we devote two chapters (this chapter and the next) to considering production, costs, and supply. In this chapter I introduce you to the production

After reading this chapter, you should be able to:

- Differentiate economic profit from accounting profit.

- Distinguish between long-run and short-run production.

- State the law of diminishing marginal productivity.

- Calculate fixed costs, variable costs, marginal costs, total costs, average fixed costs, average variable costs, and average total costs, given the appropriate information.

- Distinguish the various kinds of cost curves and describe the relationships among them.

- Explain why the marginal and average cost curves are U-shaped.

- Explain why the marginal cost curve always goes through the minimum point of an average cost curve.

process and short-run cost analysis. Then, in the next chapter, I focus on long-run costs and how cost analysis is used in the real world.

THE ROLE OF THE FIRM

Web Note 9.1
Virtual Firms

Firms:

1. Organize factors of production,

2. produce goods and services, and/or

3. sell produced goods and services.

With goods that already exist, like housing and labor, the law of supply is rather intuitive. Their supply to the market depends on people's opportunity costs of keeping them for themselves and of supplying them to the market. But many of the things we buy (such as VCRs, cars, and jackets) don't automatically exist; they must be produced. The supply of such goods depends on production.

A key concept in production is the firm. A **firm** is *an economic institution that transforms factors of production into goods and services.* A firm (1) organizes factors of production; and/or (2) produces goods; and/or (3) sells produced goods to individuals, businesses, or government.

Which combination of activities a firm will undertake depends on the cost of undertaking each activity relative to the cost of subcontracting the work out to another firm. When the firm only organizes production, it is called a *virtual firm.* Virtual firms organize the factors of production and subcontract out all production. Let's consider an example—a "psychic superline" that provides super psychic advice to individuals. If it is a virtual firm, it hires individuals to act as psychics, an advertising company to convince gullible people to call in, a phone routing company to route incoming calls, and a billing company to bill callers (the telephone company does this for them). The firm's sole role is organization. While most firms are not totally virtual, more and more of the organizational structure of businesses is being separated from the production process. As cost structures change because of technological advances such as the Internet, an increasing number of well-known firms will likely concentrate on organizational instead of production activities.

More and more of the organizational structure of business is being separated from the production process.

THE FIRM AND THE MARKET

Firms replace the market with command and control.

The firm operates within a market, but, simultaneously, it is a negation of the market in the sense that it replaces the market with command and control. How an economy operates—which activities are organized through markets, and which activities are organized through firms—depends on *transactions costs* (costs of undertaking trades through the market) and the rent or command over resources that organizers can appropriate to themselves by organizing production in a certain way. Ronald Coase won a Nobel Prize in 1991 for pathbreaking work on the nature of the firm and transactions costs.

In Chapter 3 we discussed the types of firms that exist in real life. They include sole proprietorships, partnerships, corporations, for-profit firms, nonprofit firms, and cooperatives. These various firms are the production organizations that translate factors of production into consumer goods.

FIRMS MAXIMIZE PROFIT

The firm plays the same role in the theory of supply that the individual does in the theory of demand. The difference is that whereas individuals maximize utility, firms maximize profit. Profit is defined as follows:

Profit = *Total revenue − Total cost*

In accounting, total revenue equals total sales times price; if a firm sells 1,000 pairs of earrings at $5 each, its total revenue is $5,000. For an accountant, total costs are the

This book (like all economics textbooks) treats production as if it were a one-stage process—as if a single firm transformed a factor of production into a consumer good. Economists write like that to keep the analysis manageable. (Believe me, it's complicated enough.) But you should keep in mind that reality is more complicated. Most goods go through a variety of stages of production.

For example, consider the production of desks. One firm transforms raw materials into usable raw materials (iron ore into steel); another firm transforms usable raw materials into more usable inputs (steel into steel rods, bolts, and nuts); another firm transforms those inputs into desks, which it sells wholesale to a general distributor, which then sells them to a retailer, which sells them to consumers. Many goods go through five or six stages of production and distribution. As a result, if you added up all the sales of all the firms you would overstate how much total production was taking place.

To figure out how much total production is actually taking place, economists use the concept *value added*. Value added is the contribution that each stage of production makes to the final value of a good. A firm's value added is determined by subtracting from the firm's total output the cost of the inputs bought from other firms. For example, if a desk assembly firm spends $4,000 of its revenue on component parts and sells its output for $6,000, its value added is $2,000, or 33⅓ percent of its revenue.

When you add up all the stages of production, the value added of all the firms involved must equal 100 percent, and no more, of the total output. When I discuss "a firm's" production of a good in this book, to relate that discussion to reality, you should think of that firm as a composite firm consisting of all the firms contributing to the production and distribution of that product.

Why is it important to remember that there are various stages of production? Because it brings home to you how complicated producing a good is. If any one stage gets messed up, the good doesn't get to the consumer. Producing a better mousetrap isn't enough. The firm must also be able to get it out to consumers and let them know that it's a better mousetrap. The standard economic model doesn't bring home this point. But if you're ever planning to go into business for yourself, you'd better remember it. Many people's dreams of supplying a better product to the market have been squashed by this reality.

---

wages paid to labor, rent paid to owners of capital, interest paid to lenders, and actual payments to other factors of production. If the firm paid $2,000 to employees to make the earrings and $1,000 for the materials, total cost is $3,000.

In determining what to include in total revenue and total costs, accountants focus on such explicit revenues and explicit costs. That's because they must have quantifiable measures that go into a firm's income statement. For this reason, you can think of *accounting profit* as explicit revenue less explicit cost. The accounting profit for the earring firm is $2,000.

Economists have different measures of revenues and costs and hence have a different measure of profit. Economists include in revenue and costs both explicit and implicit costs and revenues. Their measure of profit is both explicit and implicit revenue less both explicit and implicit costs.

What are implicit costs and implicit revenue? Implicit costs include the opportunity costs of the factors of production provided by the owners of the business. Say that the owner of our earring firm could have earned $1,500 working elsewhere if he did not own the earring firm. The opportunity cost of working in his own business is $1,500. It is an implicit cost of doing business and would be included as a cost. For economists, **total cost** is *explicit payments to the factors of production plus the opportunity cost of the factors provided by the owners of the firm*. Total cost of the earring firm is $3,000 in explicit cost and $1,500 in implicit cost, or $4,500. Generally implicit costs must be estimated and are not directly measurable, which is why accountants do not include them.

Accounting focuses on explicit costs and revenues; economics focuses on both explicit and implicit costs and revenues.

205

Issues of accounting were much in the news in 2002 when Enron Corporation went into bankruptcy and its accounting practices were questioned. What Enron did was to use accounting gimmicks to record implicit revenue on its books while keeping implicit costs off its books, thereby inflating profits. (Its accounting firm, Arthur Andersen, should have disallowed the practice, but did not and was convicted for failing to do so.) To understand why Enron wanted to overstate profits requires us to go beyond the standard theory of the firm. Standard theory assumes that the owner of the firm is the person making the decisions, so he gets the profit he maximizes. It is economic profit that he wants to maximize; accounting, for him, is simply a way of figuring out what he is earning.

As discussed in Chapter 3, corporations do the great majority of business in the real world. In corporations owners of the business (whose interest is in economic profits) do not make decisions; instead corporate managers, whose compensation is often tied to accounting profits, not economic profits, do. This can give managers an incentive to overstate accounting profits, which is what Enron did. The result, in this case, was bankruptcy.

Implicit revenues include the increase in the value of assets. Say the earring firm owns a kiosk whose market value rises from $10,000 to $11,000. The economic concept of revenue would include the $1,000 increase in the value of the kiosk as part of total revenue. For economists, **total revenue** is *the amount a firm receives for selling its product or service plus any increase in the value of the assets owned by the firm.* Total revenue of the earring firm is $5,000 in explicit revenue plus $1,000 in implicit revenue, or $6,000. For economists,

Economic profit = *(Explicit and implicit revenue)* − *(Explicit and implicit cost)*

So in this case, economic profit is ($5,000 + $1,000) − ($3,000 + $1,500) = $1,500. The difference really has to do with measurability. Implicit costs must be estimated, and the estimations can sometimes be inexact. General accounting rules do not permit such inexactness because it might allow firms to misstate their profit, something accounting rules are designed to avoid.

THE PRODUCTION PROCESS

As I stated at the beginning of the chapter, supply is the key to the market's ability to provide the goods people want. Underlying supply is production; firms are important because they control the production process.

THE LONG RUN AND THE SHORT RUN

The production process is generally divided into a *long-run* planning decision, in which a firm chooses the least expensive method of producing from among all possible methods, and a *short-run* adjustment decision, in which a firm adjusts its long-run planning decision to reflect new information.

In a **long-run decision** *a firm chooses among all possible production techniques.* This means that it can choose the size of the plant it wants, the type of machines it wants, and the location it wants. The firm has fewer options in a **short-run decision,** in which *the firm is constrained in regard to what production decisions it can make.*

The terms *long run* and *short run* do not necessarily refer to specific periods of time independent of the nature of the production process. They refer to the degree of flexibility the firm has in changing the level of output. In the long run, by definition, the

A long-run decision is a decision in which the firm can choose among all possible production techniques.

A short-run decision is a decision in which the firm is constrained in regard to what production decisions it can make.

firm can vary the inputs as much as it wants. In the short run some of the flexibility that existed in the long run no longer exists. In the short run some inputs are so costly to adjust that they are treated as fixed. *So in the long run all inputs are variable; in the short run some inputs are fixed.*

PRODUCTION TABLES AND PRODUCTION FUNCTIONS

How a firm combines factors of production to produce goods and services can be presented in a **production table** *(a table showing the output resulting from various combinations of factors of production or inputs).*

Real-world production tables are complicated. They often involve hundreds of inputs, hundreds of outputs, and millions of possible combinations of inputs and outputs. Studying these various combinations and determining which is best requires expertise and experience. Business schools devote entire courses to it (operations research and production analysis); engineering schools devote entire specialties to it (industrial engineering).

Studying the problems and answering the questions that surround production make up much of what a firm does: What combination of outputs should it produce? What combination of inputs should it use? What combination of techniques should it use? What new techniques should it explore? To answer these questions, the managers of a firm look at a production table.

Production tables are so complicated that in introductory economics we concentrate on short-run production analysis in which one of the factors is fixed. Doing so allows us to capture some important technical relationships of production without getting too tied up in numbers. The relevant part of a production table of earrings appears in Figure 9-1(c). In it the number of the assumed fixed inputs (machines) has already been determined. Columns 1 and 2 of the table tell us how output of earrings varies as the variable input (the number of workers) changes. For example, you can see that with 3 workers the firm can produce 17 pairs of earrings. Column 3 tells us workers' **marginal product** *(the additional output that will be forthcoming from an additional worker, other inputs constant).* Column 4 tells us workers' **average product** *(output per worker).*

It is important to distinguish marginal product from average product. Workers' average product is the total output divided by the number of workers. For example, let's consider the case of 5 workers. Total output is 28, so average product is 5.6 (28 divided by 5). To find the marginal product we must ask how much additional output will be forthcoming if we change the number of workers. For example, if we change from 4 to 5 workers, the additional worker's marginal product will be 5; if we change from 5 to 6, the additional worker's marginal product will be 3. That's why the marginal products are written between each level of output.

The information in a production table is often summarized in a production function. A **production function** is *the relationship between the inputs (factors of production) and outputs.* Specifically, the production function tells the maximum amount of output that can be derived from a given number of inputs. Figure 9-1(a) is the production function that displays the information in the production table in Figure 9-1(c). The number of workers is on the horizontal axis and the output of earrings is on the vertical axis.

THE LAW OF DIMINISHING MARGINAL PRODUCTIVITY

Figure 9-1(b) graphs the workers' average and marginal productivities from the production function in Figure 9-1(a). (Alternatively you can determine those graphs by plotting columns 3 and 4 from the table in Figure 9-1(c).) Notice that both marginal and average productivities are initially increasing, but that eventually they both

The marginal product is the additional output forthcoming from an additional input, other inputs constant; the average product is the total output divided by the quantity of the input.

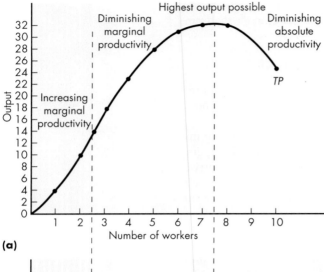

(a)

(b)

Figure 9-1 (a, b, and c)   A Production Table and Production Function

The production function in (a) is a graph of the production table in (c). Its shape reflects the underlying production technology. The graph in (b) shows the marginal and average product. Notice that when marginal product is increasing, the production function is bowed upward; when marginal product is decreasing, the production function is bowed downward, and when marginal product is zero, the production function is at its highest point. Firms are interested in producing where both average product and marginal product are positive and falling, which starts at 4 workers and ends at 7.5 workers.

Number of workers	Total output	Marginal product (change in total output)	Average product (total product/ number of workers)	
1	4	4	4	Increasing
2	10	6	5	marginal productivity
3	17	7	5.7	
4	23	6	5.8	Diminishing
5	28	5	5.6	marginal
6	31	3	5.2	productivity
7	32	1	4.6	
8	32	0	4.0	Diminishing
9	30	−2	3.3	absolute
10	25	−5	2.5	productivity

(c)

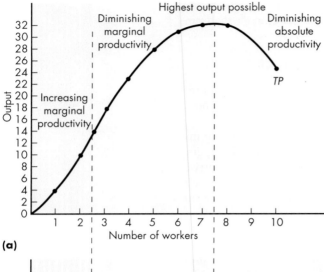

Q-1 What are the normal shapes of marginal productivity and average productivity curves?

decrease. Between 7 and 8 workers, the marginal productivity of workers actually becomes negative.

This means that initially this production function exhibits increasing marginal productivity and then it exhibits *diminishing marginal productivity*. Eventually it exhibits negative marginal productivity.

The same information can be gathered from Figure 9-1(a), but it's a bit harder to interpret.[1] Notice that initially the production function is bowed upward. Where it's bowed upward there is increasing marginal productivity, as you can see if you extend a line down to Figure 9-1(b). Then, between 2.5 and 7.5 workers, the production function is bowed downward but is still rising. In this range there's diminishing marginal productivity, as you can see by extending a line down to Figure 9-1(b). Finally marginal productivity is negative.

---

[1]Technically the marginal productivity curve is a graph of the slope of the total product curve.

The most important area of these relationships is the area of diminishing marginal productivity and falling average product (between 4 and 7.5 workers). Why? Because that's the most likely area for a firm to operate in. For example, if it's in the first range and marginal productivity is increasing, a firm can increase its existing workers' output by hiring more workers; it will have a strong incentive to do so and get out of that range. Similarly, if hiring an additional worker actually cuts total output (as it does when marginal productivity is negative), the firm would be crazy to hire that worker. So it stays out of that range.

This range of the relationship between fixed and variable inputs is so important that economists have formulated a law that describes what happens in production processes when firms reach this range—when more and more of one input is added to a fixed amount of another input. The **law of diminishing marginal productivity** states that *as more and more of a variable input is added to an existing fixed input, eventually the additional output one gets from that additional input is going to fall.*

As I stated in Chapter 2, the law of diminishing marginal productivity is sometimes called the *flowerpot law* because if it didn't hold true, the world's entire food supply could be grown in one flowerpot. In the absence of diminishing marginal productivity, we could take a flowerpot and keep adding seeds to it, getting more and more food per seed until we had enough to feed the world. In reality, however, a given flowerpot is capable of producing only so much food no matter how many seeds we add to it. At some point, as we add more and more seeds, each additional seed will produce less food than did the seed before it. Eventually the pot reaches a stage of diminishing absolute productivity, in which the total output, not simply the output per unit of input, decreases as inputs are increased.

Q.2 Firms are likely to operate on what portion of the marginal productivity curve?

The law of diminishing marginal productivity states that as more and more of a variable input is added to an existing fixed input, after some point the additional output one gets from the additional input will fall.

THE COSTS OF PRODUCTION

In any given firm, owners and managers probably discuss costs far more than anything else. Invariably costs are too high and the firm is trying to figure out ways to lower them. But the concept *costs* is ambiguous; there are many different types of costs and it's important to know what they are. Let's consider some of the most important categories of costs in reference to Table 9-1, which shows costs associated with making between 3 and 32 pairs of earrings.

FIXED COSTS, VARIABLE COSTS, AND TOTAL COSTS

Fixed costs are *costs that are spent and cannot be changed in the period of time under consideration.* There are no fixed costs in the long run since all inputs are variable and hence their costs are variable. In the short run, however, a number of costs will be fixed. For example, say you make earrings. You buy a machine for working with silver, but suddenly there's no demand for silver earrings. Assuming that machine can't be modified and used for other purposes, the money you spent on it is a fixed cost. So within the model, all fixed costs are assumed to be sunk costs.

Fixed costs are shown in column 2 of Table 9-1. Notice that fixed costs remain the same ($50) regardless of the level of production. As you can see, it doesn't matter whether output is 15 or 20; fixed costs are always $50.

Besides buying the machine, the silversmith must also hire workers. These workers are the earring firm's **variable costs**—*costs that change as output changes.* The earring firm's variable costs are shown in column 3. Notice that as output increases, variable costs increase. For example, when the firm produces 10 pairs of earrings, variable costs are $108; when it produces 16, variable costs rise to $150.

Web Note 9.2
What's Fixed? What's Variable?

Table 9-1 The Cost of Producing Earrings

1	2	3	4	5	6	7	8
Output	Fixed Costs (FC)	Variable Costs (VC)	Total Costs (TC) (FC + VC)	Marginal Costs (MC) (Change in total costs/ Change in output)	Average Fixed Costs (AFC) (FC/Output)	Average Variable Costs (AVC) (VC/Output)	Average Total Costs (ATC) (AFC + AVC)
3	$50	$ 38	$ 88	$12	$16.67	$12.66	$29.33
4	50	50	100		12.50	12.50	25.00
9	50	100	150	8	5.56	11.11	16.67
10	50	108	158		5.00	10.80	15.80
16	50	150	200	7	3.13	9.38	12.50
17	50	157	207		2.94	9.24	12.18
22	50	200	250	10	2.27	9.09	11.36
23	50	210	260		2.17	9.13	11.30
27	50	255	305	15	1.85	9.44	11.30
28	50	270	320		1.79	9.64	11.43
32	50	400	450		1.56	12.50	14.06

All costs are either fixed or variable in the standard model, so the *total cost* is the sum of the fixed and variable costs:

TC = FC + VC

The earring firm's total costs are presented in column 4. Each entry in column 4 is the sum of the entries in columns 2 and 3 in the same row. For example, to produce 16 pairs of earrings, fixed costs are $50 and variable costs are $150, so total cost is $200.

AVERAGE TOTAL COST, AVERAGE FIXED COST, AND AVERAGE VARIABLE COST

Total cost, fixed cost, and variable cost are important, but much of a firm's discussion is about average cost. So the next distinction we want to make is between total cost and average cost. To arrive at the earring firm's average cost, we simply divide the total amount of whatever cost we're talking about by the quantity produced. Each of the three costs we've discussed has a corresponding average cost.

For example, **average total cost** (often called average cost) equals *total cost divided by the quantity produced*. Thus:

ATC = TC/Q

Average fixed cost equals *fixed cost divided by quantity produced*:

AFC = FC/Q

Average variable cost equals *variable cost divided by quantity produced*:

AVC = VC/Q

Average fixed cost and average variable cost are shown in columns 6 and 7 of Table 9-1. The most important average cost concept, average total cost, is shown in column 8. Average total cost can also be thought of as the sum of average fixed cost and average variable cost:

ATC = AFC + AVC

Margin notes:

TC = FC + VC

Average cost equals total cost divided by quantity.

Q-3 If total costs are 400, fixed costs are 0, and output is 10, what are average variable costs?

As you can see, the average total cost of producing 16 pairs of earrings is $12.50. It can be calculated by dividing total cost ($200) by output (16).

MARGINAL COST

All these costs are important to our earring firm, but they are not the most important cost it considers when deciding how many pairs of earrings to produce. That distinction goes to marginal cost, which appears in column 5.[2] **Marginal cost** is *the increase (decrease) in total cost from increasing (or decreasing) the level of output by one unit*. Let's find marginal cost by considering what happens if our earring firm increases production by one unit—from 9 to 10. Looking again at Table 9-1, we see that the total cost rises from $150 to $158. In this case the marginal cost of producing the 10th unit is $8.

GRAPHING COST CURVES

Let's say that the owner of the earring firm is a visually oriented person who asks you (an economic consultant) to show her what all those numbers in Table 9-1 mean. To do so, you first draw a graph, putting quantity on the horizontal axis and a dollar measure of various costs on the vertical axis.

TOTAL COST CURVES

Figure 9-2(a) graphs the total cost, total fixed cost, and total variable costs of all the levels of output given in Table 9-1.[3] The total cost curve is determined by plotting the entries in column 1 and the corresponding entries in column 4. For example, point *L* corresponds to a quantity of 10 and a total cost of $158. Notice that the curve is upward-sloping: Increasing output increases total cost.

The total fixed cost curve is determined by plotting column 1 and column 2 on the graph. The total variable cost curve is determined by plotting column 1 and column 3.

As you can see, the total variable cost curve has the same shape as the total cost curve: Increasing output increases variable cost. This isn't surprising, since the total cost curve is the vertical summation of total fixed cost and total variable cost. For example, at output 10, total fixed cost equals $50 (point M); total variable cost equals $108 (point O); and total cost equals $158 (point L).

AVERAGE AND MARGINAL COST CURVES

Figure 9-2(b) presents the average fixed cost curve, average total cost curve (or average cost curve, as it's generally called), average variable cost curve, and marginal cost curve associated with the cost figures in Table 9-1. Each point on the four curves represents a combination of two corresponding entries in Table 9-1. Points on the average variable cost curve are determined by plotting the entries in column 1 and the corresponding entries in column 7. Points on the average fixed cost curve are determined by entries in column 1 and the corresponding entries in column 6. Points on the average total cost curve are determined by entries in column 1 and the corresponding entries in column 8. Finally, the marginal cost curve is determined by plotting the entries in column 1 and the corresponding entries in column 5. As was the case with the total cost curves, all

The marginal cost curve goes through the minimum point of the average total cost curve and average variable cost curve; each of these curves is U-shaped. The average fixed cost curve slopes down continuously.

---

[2]Since only selected output levels are shown, not all entries have marginal costs. For a marginal cost to exist, there must be a marginal change, a change by only one unit.
[3]To keep the presentation simple, we focus only on the most important part of the total cost curve, that part that follows the simplest rules. Other areas of the total cost curve can be bowed downward rather than bowed upward.

Figure 9-2 (a and b)   Total and per Unit Output Cost Curves

Total fixed costs, shown in (a), are always constant; they don't change with output. All other total costs increase with output. As output gets high, the rate of increase has a tendency to increase. The average fixed cost curve shown in (b), is downward-sloping; the average variable cost curve and average total cost curve are U-shaped. The U-shaped MC curve goes through the minimum points of the AVC and ATC curves. (The AFC curve is often not drawn since AFC is also represented by the distance between the AVC and ATC.)

(a) Total cost curves   **(b) Per unit output cost curves**

the firm's owner need do is look at this graph to find the various costs associated with different levels of output.

One reason the graphical visualization of cost curves is important is that the graphs of the curves give us a good sense of what happens to costs as we change output.

DOWNWARD-SLOPING SHAPE OF THE AVERAGE FIXED COST CURVE

Let's start our consideration with average fixed cost. Average fixed cost is decreasing throughout. The average fixed cost curve looks like a child's slide: It starts out with a steep decline; then it becomes flatter and flatter. What this tells us about production is straightforward: As output increases, the same fixed cost can be spread over a wider range of output, so average fixed cost falls. Average fixed cost initially falls quickly but then falls more and more slowly. As the denominator gets bigger while the numerator stays the same, the increase has a smaller and smaller effect.

THE U SHAPE OF THE AVERAGE AND MARGINAL COST CURVES

Q-4 Draw a graph of both the marginal cost curve and the average cost curve.

Let's now move on to the average and marginal cost curves. Why do they have the shapes they do? Or, expressed another way, how does our analysis of production relate to our analysis of costs? You may have already gotten an idea of how production and costs relate if you remembered Figure 9-1 and recognized the output numbers that we presented there were similar output numbers to those that we used in the cost analysis. Cost analysis is simply another way of considering production analysis. The laws governing costs are the same laws governing productivity that we just saw in our consideration of production.

In the short run, output can be raised only by increasing the variable input. But as more and more of a variable input is added to a fixed input, the law of diminishing marginal productivity enters in. Marginal and average productivities fall. The key insight here is that when marginal productivity falls, marginal cost must rise, and when average productivity of the variable input falls, average variable cost must rise. So to say that productivity falls is equivalent to saying that cost rises.

It follows that if eventually the law of diminishing marginal productivity holds true, then eventually both the marginal cost curve and the average cost curve must be upward-sloping. And, indeed, in our examples they are. It's also generally held that at low levels of production, marginal and average productivities are increasing. This means that marginal cost and average variable cost are initially falling. If they're falling initially and rising eventually, at some point they must be neither rising nor falling. This means that both the marginal cost curve and the average variable cost curve are U-shaped.

As you can see in Figure 9-2(b), the average total cost curve has the same general U shape as the average variable cost curve. It has the same U shape because it is the vertical summation of the average fixed cost curve and the average variable cost curve. Its minimum, however, is to the right of the minimum of the average variable cost curve. We'll discuss why after we cover the shape of the average variable cost curve.

Average total cost initially falls faster and then rises more slowly than average variable cost. If we increased output enormously, the average variable cost curve and the average total cost curve would almost meet. Average total cost is of key importance to the firm's owner. She wants to keep it low.

THE RELATIONSHIP BETWEEN THE MARGINAL PRODUCTIVITY AND MARGINAL COST CURVES

Let's now consider the relationship between marginal product and marginal cost. In Figure 9-3(a), I draw a marginal cost curve and average variable cost curve. Notice their U shape. Initially costs are falling. Then there's some minimum point. After that, costs are rising.

In Figure 9-3(b), I graph the average and marginal productivity curves similar to those that I presented in Figure 9-1(b), although this time I relate average and marginal productivities to output, rather than to the number of workers. This allows us to relate output per worker and output. Say, for example that we know that the average product of 2 workers is 5, and that 2 workers can produce an output of 10. This means that when output is 10, the workers' average productivity is 5. By continuing this reasoning we can construct the curves. Point A corresponds to an output of 10 and average productivity of 5.

Now let's compare the graphs in Figure 9-3 (a and b). If you look at the two graphs carefully, you'll see that one is simply the mirror image of the other. The minimum point of the average variable cost curve (output = 21) is the same level of output as the maximum point of the average productivity curve; the minimum point of the marginal cost curve (output = 12) is at the same level of output as the maximum point on the marginal productivity curve. When the productivity curves are falling, the corresponding cost curves are rising. Why is that the case? Because as productivity falls, costs per unit increase; and as productivity increases, costs per unit decrease.

THE RELATIONSHIP BETWEEN THE MARGINAL COST AND AVERAGE COST CURVES

Now that we've considered the shapes of each cost curve, let's consider some of the important relationships among them—specifically the relationships between the marginal

As more and more of a variable input is added to a fixed input, the law of diminishing marginal productivity causes marginal and average productivities to fall. As these fall, marginal and average costs rise.

Q-5 What determines the distance between the average total cost and the average variable cost?

Q-6 If you increase output enormously, what two cost curves would almost meet?

If $MP > AP$, then AP is rising.
If $MP < AP$, then AP is falling.

Q-7 When the marginal cost equals the minimum point of the average variable cost, what is true about the average productivity and marginal productivity of workers?

When the productivity curves are falling, the corresponding cost curves are rising.

Web Note 9.3
Marginal Costs in the
Information Economy

Figure 9-3 (a and b)   The Relationship between Productivity and Costs

The shapes of the cost curves are mirror-image reflections of the shapes of the corresponding productivity curves. (The corresponding productivity curve is an implicit function in which marginal productivity is related to output rather than inputs. At each output there is an implicit number of workers who would supply that output.) When one is increasing, the other is decreasing; when one is at a minimum, the other is at a maximum.

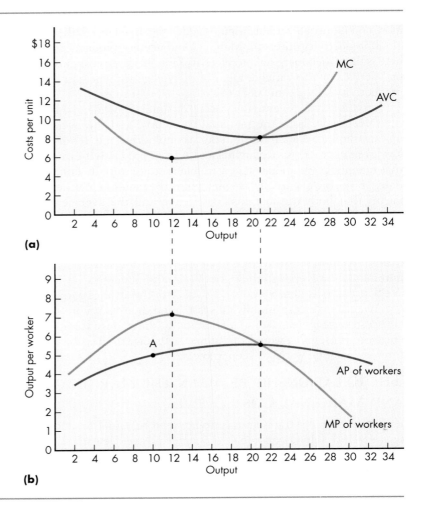

cost curve on the one hand and the average variable cost and average total cost curves on the other. These relationships are shown graphically for a different production process in Figure 9-4.

Let's first look at the relationship between marginal cost and average total cost. In areas A and B at output below 5, even though marginal cost is rising, average total cost is falling. Why? Because in areas A and B the marginal cost curve is below the average total cost curve. At point B, where average total cost is at its lowest, the marginal cost curve intersects the average total cost curve. In area C, above output 5, where average total cost is rising, the marginal cost curve is above the ATC curve.

The positioning of the marginal cost curve is not happenstance. The position of marginal cost relative to average total cost tells us whether average total cost is rising or falling.

If MC > ATC, then ATC is rising.

If MC = ATC, then ATC is at its low point.

If MC < ATC, then ATC is falling.

To understand why this is, think of it in terms of your grade point average. If you have a B average and you get a C on the next test (that is, your marginal grade is a C),

When marginal cost exceeds average cost, average cost must be rising. When marginal cost is less than average cost, average cost must be falling. This relationship explains why marginal cost curves always intersect the average cost curve at the minimum of the average cost curve.

We've covered a lot of costs and cost curves quickly, so a review is in order. First, let's list the cost concepts and their definitions.

1. Marginal cost: the additional cost resulting from a one-unit increase in output.

2. Total cost: the sum of all costs.

3. Average total cost: total cost divided by total output (TC/Q).

4. Fixed cost: cost that is already spent and cannot be recovered. (It exists only in the short run.)

5. Average fixed cost: fixed cost divided by total output (FC/Q).

6. Variable cost: cost of variable inputs. Variable cost does not include fixed cost.

7. Average variable cost: variable cost divided by total output (VC/Q).

Each of these costs can be represented by a curve. A number of these curves have specific relationships to the other cost curves.

1. MC: MC intersects AVC and ATC at their minimum points.

2. If $MC > AVC$, then AVC is rising. If $MC < AVC$, then AVC is falling.

3. If $MC > ATC$, then ATC is rising. If $MC < ATC$, then ATC is falling.

4. ATC: a U-shaped curve higher than the AVC.

5. AVC: a U-shaped curve lower than the ATC, with the minimum point slightly to the left.

6. AFC: a downward-sloping curve that starts high, initially decreases rapidly, and then decreases slowly.

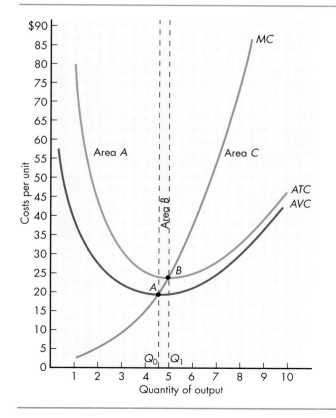

Figure 9-4   The Relationship of Marginal Cost Curve to Average Variable Cost and Average Total Cost Curves

The marginal cost curve goes through the minimum point of both the average variable cost curve and the average total cost curve. Thus, there is a small range where average total costs are falling and average variable costs are rising.

Q-8 If marginal costs are increasing, what is happening to average total costs?

Q-9 If marginal costs are decreasing, what must be happening to average variable costs?

Q-10 Why does the marginal cost curve intersect the average total cost curve at the minimum point?

Dr. Seuss books are often more interesting than economics books. From HORTON HATCHES THE EGG by Dr. Seuss, TM & Copyright © by Dr. Seuss Enterprises, L. P. 1940. Renewed 1968. Used by permission of Random House Children's Books, a Division of Random House, Inc.

your grade point average will fall below a B. Your marginal grade is below your average grade, so your average grade is falling. If you get a C+ on the next exam (that is, your marginal grade is a C+), *even though your marginal grade has risen from a C to a C+,* your grade point average will fall. Why? Because your marginal grade is still below your average grade. To make sure you understand the concept, explain the next two cases:

1. If your marginal grade is above your average grade, your average grade will rise.
2. If your marginal grade and average grade are equal, the average grade will remain unchanged.

Marginal and average reflect a general relationship that also holds for marginal cost and average variable cost.

If MC > AVC, then AVC is rising.

If MC = AVC, then AVC is at its low point.

If MC < AVC, then AVC is falling.

This relationship is best seen in area B of Figure 9-4, when output is between Q_0 and Q_1. In this area the marginal cost curve is above the average variable cost curve, so average variable cost is rising; but the MC curve is below the average total cost curve, so average total cost is falling.

The intuitive explanation for what is represented in this area is that average total cost includes average variable cost, but it also includes average fixed cost, which is falling. As long as short-run marginal cost is only slightly above average variable cost, the average total cost will continue to fall. Put another way: Once marginal cost is above average variable cost, as long as average variable cost doesn't rise by more than average fixed cost falls, average total cost will still fall.

INTERMISSION

At this point I'm going to cut off the chapter, not because we're finished with the subject, but because there's only so much that anyone can absorb in one chapter. It's time for a break.

Those of you with significant others, go out and do something significant. Those of you with parents bearing the cost of this education, give them a call and tell them that you appreciate their expenditure on your education. Think of the opportunity cost of that education to them; it's not peanuts. Those of you who are married should go out and give your spouse a big kiss; tell him or her that the opportunity cost of being away for another minute was so high that you couldn't control yourself. Those of you with kids, go out and read them a Dr. Seuss book. (My favorite is about Horton.) Let's face it—Seuss is a better writer than I, and if you've been conscientious about this course, you may not have paid your kids enough attention. We'll return to the grind in the next chapter.

SUMMARY

- Accounting profit is explicit revenue less explicit cost. Economists include implicit revenue and cost in their determination of profit.

- Implicit revenue includes the increases in the value of assets owned by the firm. Implicit costs include opportunity cost of time and capital provided by the owners of the firm.

- In the long run a firm can choose among all possible production techniques; in the short run it is constrained in its choices.

- The law of diminishing marginal productivity states that as more and more of a variable input is added to a fixed input, the additional output the firm gets will eventually be decreasing.

- Costs are generally divided into fixed costs, variable costs, and total costs.

- $TC = FC + VC$; $MC =$ change in TC; $AFC = FC/Q$; $AVC = VC/Q$; $ATC = AFC + AVC$.

- The average variable cost curve and marginal cost curve are mirror images of the average product curve and the marginal product curve, respectively.

- The law of diminishing marginal productivity causes marginal and average costs to rise.

- If $MC > ATC$, then ATC is rising.
  If $MC = ATC$, then ATC is constant.
  If $MC < ATC$, then ATC is falling.

- The marginal cost curve goes through the minimum points of the average variable cost curve and average total cost curve.

KEY TERMS

average fixed cost *(210)*
average product *(207)*
average total cost *(210)*
average variable
  cost *(210)*
economic profit *(206)*

firm *(204)*
fixed costs *(209)*
law of diminishing
  marginal
  productivity *(209)*
long-run decision *(206)*

marginal cost *(211)*
marginal product *(207)*
production *(203)*
production
  function *(207)*
production table *(207)*

profit *(204)*
short-run decision *(206)*
total cost *(205)*
total revenue *(206)*
variable costs *(209)*

QUESTIONS FOR THOUGHT AND REVIEW

1. What costs and revenues do economists include when calculating profit that accountants don't include? Give an example of each.

2. "There is no long run; there are only short and shorter runs." Evaluate that statement.

3. What is the difference between marginal product and average product?

4. If average product is falling, what is happening to short-run average variable cost?

5. If marginal cost is increasing, what do we know about average cost?

6. If average productivity falls, will marginal cost necessarily rise? How about average cost?

7. Say that neither labor nor machines are fixed but that there is a 50 percent quick-order premium paid to both workers and machines for delivery of them in the short run. Once you buy them, they cannot be returned, however. What do your short-run marginal cost and short-run average total cost curves look like?

8. If machines are variable and labor fixed, how will the general shapes of the short-run average cost curve and marginal cost curve change?

9. If you increase production to an infinitely large level, the average variable cost and the average total cost will merge. Why?

10. Explain whether the following statements are true or false: Supplying labor depends on opportunity costs because labor already exists. Supplying goods that need to be produced does not depend on opportunity costs since they do not already exist.

11. Explain how studying for an exam is subject to the law of diminishing marginal productivity.

12. Labor costs are 17.5 percent of revenue per vehicle for General Motors. In union negotiations in the late 1990s, GM attempted to cut its workforce to increase productivity. Together with the reductions they expected in jobs, GM officials hoped to make its North American operations fully competitive with its U.S. and Japanese rivals on total costs. Why are productivity gains so important to GM?

13. It is obvious that all for-profit businesses in the United States will maximize profit. True or false? Why? (Requires reading "Applying the Tools: Enron, Accounting Gimmicks, and the Theory of the Firm")

PROBLEMS AND EXERCISES

1. Peggy-Sue's cookies are the best in the world, or so I hear. She has been offered a job by Cookie Monster, Inc., to come to work for them at $125,000 per year. Currently, she is producing her own cookies, and she has revenues of $260,000 per year. Her costs are $40,000 for labor, $10,000 for rent, $35,000 for ingredients, and $5,000 for utilities. She has $100,000 of her own money invested in the operation, which, if she leaves, can be sold for $40,000 that she can invest at 10 percent per year.
   a. Calculate her accounting and economic profits.
   b. Advise her as to what she should do.

2. Economan has been infected by the free enterprise bug. He sets up a firm on extraterrestrial affairs. The rent of the building is $4,000, the cost of the two secretaries is $40,000, and the cost of electricity and gas comes to $5,000. There's a great demand for his information, and his total revenue amounts to $100,000. By working in the firm, though, Economan forfeits the $50,000 he could earn by working for the Friendly Space Agency and the $4,000 he could have earned as interest had he saved his funds instead of putting them in this business. Is he making a profit or loss by an accountant's definitions of profit and loss? How about by an economist's definition?

3. Find and graph the TC, AFC, AVC, AC, and MC from the following table.

Units	FC	VC
0	$100	$ 0
1	100	40
2	100	60
3	100	70
4	100	85
5	100	130

4. An economic consultant is presented with the following total product table and asked to derive a table for average variable costs. The price of labor is $15 per hour.

Labor	TP
1	5
2	15
3	30
4	36
5	40

   a. Help him do so.
   b. Show that the graph of the average productivity curve and average variable cost curve are mirror images of each other.
   c. Show the marginal productivity curve for labor inputs between 1 and 5.
   d. Show that the marginal productivity curve and marginal cost curve are mirror images of each other.

5. A firm has fixed costs of $100 and variable costs of the following:

Output	1	2	3	4	5	6	7	8	9
Variable costs	$35	75	110	140	175	215	260	315	390

   a. Graph the AFC, ATC, AVC, and MC curves.
   b. Explain the relationship between the MC curve and the two average cost curves.
   c. Say fixed costs dropped to $50. Graph the new AFC, ATC, AVC, and MC curves.
   d. Which curves shifted in c? Why?

6. Say that a firm has fixed costs of $100 and constant average variable costs of $25.
   a. Graph the AFC, ATC, AVC, and MC curves.
   b. Explain why the curves have the shapes they do.
   c. What law is not operative for this firm?
   d. Say that instead of remaining a constant $25, average variable costs increase by $5 for each unit, so that the cost of 1 is $25, the cost of 2 is $30, the cost of 3 is $35, and so on. Graph the AFC, ATC, AVC, and MC curves associated with these costs.
   e. Explain how costs would have to increase in d in order for the curves to have the "normal" shapes of the curves presented in the text.

7. Explain how each of the following will affect the average fixed cost, average variable cost, average total cost, and marginal cost curves faced by a steel manufacturer:
   a. New union agreement increases hourly pay.
   b. Local government imposes an annual lump-sum tax per plant.
   c. Federal government imposes a "stack tax" on emission of air pollutants by steel mills.
   d. New steel-making technology increases productivity of every worker.

WEB QUESTIONS

1. Go to the Avis Rent A Car, Inc., home page at
   www.avis.com, and find out how much it costs to rent a
   car for a week, driving from your city to a city in another
   state.
   a. Fill in the following cost table:

Miles	Total Cost	Marginal Cost	Average Fixed Cost	Average Variable Cost
0	_____	_____	_____	_____
500	_____	_____	_____	_____
1,000	_____	_____	_____	_____
1,500	_____	_____	_____	_____
2,500	_____	_____	_____	_____

   b. How does average fixed cost change as total number
      of miles driven increases?
   c. How does marginal cost change as total number of
      miles driven increases?

2. Go to www.ers.usda.gov. Click on the "data" button, look
   for cost data on corn, and answer the following questions:
   a. What is the cost of producing an acre of corn?
   b. State two major components of the variable (operat-
      ing) costs of corn production.
   c. State two major components of fixed (allocated over-
      head) costs of corn production.
   d. What price of corn was needed to cover operating
      costs?
   e. What price of corn was needed to cover corn's total
      operating costs?

ANSWERS TO MARGIN QUESTIONS

1. Normally the marginal productivity curve and average
   productivity curve are both inverted U shapes. (*208*)

2. Firms are likely to operate on the downward-sloping
   portion of the marginal productivity curve because on the
   upward-sloping portion, firms could increase workers'
   output by hiring more workers. It will continue to hire
   more workers at least to the point where diminishing
   marginal productivity sets in. (*209*)

3. Average variable costs would be 40. (*210*)

4. As you can see in the graph, both these curves are
   U-shaped and the marginal cost curve goes through the
   average cost curve at the minimum point of the average
   cost curve. (*212*)

5. The distance between the average total cost and the
   average variable cost is determined by the average fixed
   cost at that quantity. As quantity increases, the average
   fixed cost decreases, so the two curves get closer and
   closer together. (*213*)

6. As output increases, the average total costs and average
   variable costs come closer and closer together. (*213*)

7. Since the average productivity and marginal productivity
   of workers are the mirror images of average costs and
   marginal costs, and when the marginal costs and average
   costs intersect the two are equal, it follows that the
   average productivity and marginal productivity of
   workers must be equal at that point. (*213*)

8. It is impossible to say what is happening to average total
   costs on the basis of what is happening to marginal costs.
   It is the magnitude of marginal costs relative to average
   total costs that is important. (*216*)

9. It is impossible to say because it is the magnitude of marginal cost relative to average variable cost that determines what is happening to average variable cost. (*216*)

10. The marginal cost curve intersects the average total cost
    curve at the minimum point because once the marginal
    cost exceeds average total costs, the average total costs
    must necessarily begin to rise, and vice versa. (*216*)

PRODUCTION AND COST ANALYSIS II

> Economic efficiency consists of making things
> that are worth more than they cost.
>
> —J. M. Clark

Welcome back. I hope you've reestablished your relationship with the real world and are ready to return, with renewed vigor, to the world of economics. When we took our intermission last chapter, we had worked our way through the various short-run costs. That short run is a time period in which some inputs are fixed. In the first part of this chapter we consider firms' long-run decisions and the determinants of the long-run cost curves. Then in the second part we'll talk about applying cost analysis to the real world.

MAKING LONG-RUN PRODUCTION DECISIONS

Firms have many more options in the long run than they do in the short run. They can change any input they want. Plant size is not given; neither is the technology available given.

To make their long-run decisions, firms look at the costs of the various inputs and the technologies available for combining those inputs, and then decide which combination offers the lowest cost.

Say you're opening a hamburger stand. One decision you'll have to make is what type of stove to buy. You'll quickly discover that many different types are available. Some use more gas than others but cost less to buy; some are electric; some are self-cleaning and hence use less labor; some are big; some are little; some use microwaves; some use convection. Some have long-term guarantees; some have no guarantees. Each has a colorful brochure telling you how wonderful it is. After studying the various detailed specifications and aspects of the production technology, you choose the stove that has the combination of characteristics that you believe best fits your needs.

Next you decide on workers. Do you want bilingual workers, college-educated workers, part-time workers, experienced workers . . . ? You get the idea: Even simple production decisions involve complicated questions. These decisions are made on the basis of the expected costs, and expected usefulness, of inputs.

TECHNICAL EFFICIENCY AND ECONOMIC EFFICIENCY

When choosing among existing technologies in the long run, firms are interested in the lowest cost, or most economically efficient, methods of production. They consider all technically efficient methods and compare their costs. The terms *economically efficient* and *technically efficient* differ in meaning. Here's how: **Technical efficiency** in production means that *as few inputs as possible are used to produce a given output.*

Many different production processes can be technically efficient. For example, say you know that to produce 100 tons of wheat you can use 10 workers and 1 acre or use 1 worker and 100 acres. Which of these two production techniques is more efficient? Both can be technically efficient since neither involves the use of more of both inputs than the other technique. But that doesn't mean that both are equally economically efficient. That question can't be answered unless you know the relative costs of the two inputs. If an acre of land rents for $1 million and each worker costs $10 a day, our answer likely will be different than if land rents for $40 an acre and each worker costs $100 a day. The **economically efficient** method of production is *the method that produces a given level of output at the lowest possible cost.*

In long-run production decisions, firms will look at all available production technologies and choose the technology that, given the available inputs and their prices, is the economically efficient way to produce. These choices will reflect the prices of the various factors of production. Those prices, in turn, will reflect the factors' relative scarcities.

Consider the use of land by firms in the United States and in Japan. The United States has large amounts of land (8 acres) per person, so the price of land is lower than in Japan, which has only 0.74 acre per person. An acre of rural land in the United States might cost about $700; in Japan it costs over $10,000. Because of this difference in the price of inputs, production techniques use land much more intensively in Japan than in the United States. Similarly with China: Labor is more abundant and capital is scarcer, so production techniques in China use capital much more intensively than it is used in the United States. Whereas China would use hundreds of workers, and very little machinery, to build a road, the United States would use three or four people along with three machines. Both countries are being economically efficient, but because costs of inputs differ, the economically efficient method of production differs. Thus, the economically efficient method of production is the technically efficient method of production that has the lowest cost. (For a further, graphical analysis of economic efficiency, see Appendix A.)

DETERMINANTS OF THE SHAPE OF THE LONG-RUN COST CURVE

In Chapter 9 we saw that the law of diminishing marginal productivity accounted for the shape of the short-run average cost curve. The firm was adding more of a variable input to a fixed input. The law of diminishing marginal productivity doesn't apply to the long run since in the long run all inputs are variable. The most important determinants of what is economically efficient in the long run are economies and diseconomies of scale. Let's consider each of these in turn and see what effect they will have on the shape of the long-run average cost curve.

ECONOMIES OF SCALE

We say that production exhibits **economies of scale** *when long-run average total costs decrease as output increases.* For example, if producing 40,000 VCRs costs a firm

Web Note 10.1
Cheap Labor

Q-1 True or false? If a process is economically efficient it is also technically efficient. Explain your answer.

Q-2 Why does China use production techniques that require more workers per acre of land than does the United States?

The shape of the long-run cost curve is due to the existence of economies and diseconomies of scale.

In the late 1980s the normal production run of a U.S. automobile was 200,000 units per year. Why was it so high? Because of indivisible setup costs of the then-current production technology. In order to reduce those indivisible setup costs to an acceptable level, the production level per year had to equal at least 200,000 or the car was considered an economic failure. The Pontiac Fiero, a sporty two-seater, was dropped in 1988 because it didn't sell well enough to sustain that production level.

But what is an indivisible setup cost depends on the structure of production. Japanese companies structured production differently from U.S. companies and had a much lower level of indivisible setup costs. For example, at just about the same time as Pontiac dropped the Fiero, a Japanese company, Mazda, entered the market with the Miata, another sporty two-seater. Because Mazda's assembly line was designed to handle different sizes and shapes of vehicles (which permits economies of scope, discussed later in the chapter), its minimum profitable production level for the Miata was about 30,000, not 200,000. This alternative structure of production made it possible for the Miata to do well in a market that buys a total of about 40,000 two-seater sports coupes annually. In response to this competition, U.S. companies followed suit and in the early 2000s they changed production methods. Now, indivisible setup costs make up a smaller portion of the total costs, thereby lowering their minimum efficient level of production. That's why you have seen an increase in the number of sporty two-seaters you can buy.

$16 million ($400 each), but producing 200,000 VCRs costs the firm $40 million ($200 each), between 40,000 and 200,000 units, the production of VCRs exhibits significant economies of scale. One can also say that there are increasing returns to scale.

In real-world production processes, at low levels of production economies of scale are extremely important because many production techniques require a certain minimum level of output to be useful. For example, say you want to produce a pound of steel. You can't just build a mini blast furnace, stick in some coke and iron ore, and come out with a single pound of steel. The smallest technically efficient blast furnaces have a production capacity measured in tons per hour, not pounds per year. The cost of the blast furnace is said to be an **indivisible setup cost** (*the cost of an indivisible input for which a certain minimum amount of production must be undertaken before the input becomes economically feasible to use*).

Indivisible setup costs are important because they create many real-world economies of scale: As output increases, the costs per unit of output decrease. As an example, consider this book. Setting the type for it is an indivisible setup cost; it is a cost that must be incurred if any production is to take place, but it is not a cost that increases with the number of books produced. That means that the more copies of the book that are produced, the lower the typesetting cost per book. That's why it costs more per book to produce a textbook for an upper-level, low-enrollment course than it does for a lower-level, high-enrollment course. The same amount of work goes into both (both need to be written, edited, and set into type), and the printing costs differ only slightly. The actual print-run costs of printing a book are only about $3 to $8 per book. The other costs are indivisible setup costs. Prices of produced goods, including books, reflect their costs of production. As you move to upper-level academic courses, where print runs are smaller, you'll likely discover that the books are smaller and less colorful but are priced the same as, or more than, this introductory text.

In the long-run planning decisions about the cost of producing this book, the expected number of copies to be sold was an important element. That figure influenced the number of books produced, which in turn affected the expected cost per unit. This

In the production of steel, the cost of a blast furnace is an indivisible setup cost that requires a minimum level of production to be economically feasible.

Q-3 Why are larger production runs often cheaper per unit than smaller production runs?

Figure 10-1 (a and b)   A Typical Long-Run Average Total Cost Table and Curve

In the long run, average costs initially fall because of economies of scale; then they are constant for a while, and finally they tend to rise due to diseconomies of scale.

Quantity	Total Costs of Labor	Total Costs of Machines	Total Costs = $TC_L + TC_M$	Average Total Costs = TC/Q
11	$381	$254	$ 635	$58
12	390	260	650	54
13	402	268	670	52
14	420	280	700	50
15	450	300	750	50
16	480	320	800	50
17	510	340	850	50
18	549	366	915	51
19	600	400	1,000	53
20	666	444	1,110	56

(a) Long-run production table

(b) Long-run average cost curve

will be the case anytime there are economies of scale. With economies of scale, cost per unit of a small production run is higher than cost per unit of a large production run.

Figure 10-1(a) demonstrates a normal long-run production table; Figure 10-1(b) shows the related typical shape of a long-run average cost curve. (Notice that there are no fixed costs. Because we're in the long run, all costs are variable.) Economies of scale account for the downward-sloping part. Cost per unit of output is decreasing.

Because of the importance of economies of scale, businesspeople often talk of a minimum efficient level of production. What they mean by minimum efficient level of production is that, given the price at which they expect to be able to sell a good, the indivisible setup costs are so high that production runs of less than a certain size don't make economic sense. Thus, the **minimum efficient level of production** is *the amount of production that spreads setup costs out sufficiently for a firm to undertake production profitably.* At this point, the market has expanded to a size large enough for firms to take advantage of all economies of scale. The minimum efficient level of production is where the average total costs are at a minimum.

> In the longer run all inputs are variable, so only economies of scale can influence the shape of the long-run cost curve.

DISECONOMIES OF SCALE

Notice that on the right side of Figure 10-1(b) the long-run average cost curve is upward-sloping. Average cost is increasing. We say that production exhibits **diseconomies of scale** *when long-run average total costs increase as output increases.* For example, if producing 200,000 VCRs costs the firm $40 million ($200 each) and producing 400,000 VCRs costs the firm $100 million ($250 each), there are diseconomies of scale associated with choosing to produce 400,000 rather than 200,000. One can also say there are decreasing returns to scale. Diseconomies of scale usually, but not always, start occurring as firms get large.

Diseconomies of scale could not occur if production relationships were only technical relationships. If that were the case, the same technical process could be used over and over again at the same cost. In reality, however, production relationships have social dimensions, which introduce the potential for important diseconomies of scale into the production process in two ways:

> Diminishing marginal productivity refers to the decline in productivity caused by increasing units of a variable input being added to a fixed input. Diseconomies of scale refer to the decreases in productivity that occur when there are equal increases of all inputs (no input is fixed).

Q-4   If production involved only technical relationships and had no social dimension, what would the long-run average total cost curve look like?

As firms become larger, monitoring costs increase and achieving team spirit is more difficult.

1. As the size of the firm increases, monitoring costs generally increase.
2. As the size of the firm increases, team spirit or morale generally decreases.

Monitoring costs are *the costs incurred by the organizer of production in seeing to it that the employees do what they're supposed to do.* If you're producing something yourself, the job gets done the way you want it done; monitoring costs are zero. However, as the scale of production increases, you have to hire people to help you produce. This means that if the job is to be done the way you want it done, you have to monitor (supervise) your employees' performance. The cost of monitoring can increase significantly as output increases; it's a major contributor to diseconomies of scale. Most big firms have several layers of bureaucracy devoted simply to monitoring employees. The job of middle managers is, to a large extent, monitoring.

The other social dimension that can contribute to diseconomies of scale is the loss of **team spirit** (*the feelings of friendship and being part of a team that bring out people's best efforts*). Most types of production are highly dependent on team spirit. When the team spirit or morale is lost, production slows considerably. The larger the firm is, the more difficult it is to maintain team spirit.

An important reason diseconomies of scale can come about is that the bigger things get, the more checks and balances are needed to ensure that the right hand and the left hand are coordinated. The larger the organization, the more checks and balances and the more paperwork.

Some large firms manage to solve these problems and avoid diseconomies of scale. But problems of monitoring and loss of team spirit often limit the size of firms. They underlie diseconomies of scale in which relatively less output is produced for a given increase in inputs, so that per-unit costs of output increase.

CONSTANT RETURNS TO SCALE

Sometimes in a range of output a firm does not experience either economies of scale or diseconomies of scale. In this range there are **constant returns to scale** *where long-run average total costs do not change with an increase in output.* Constant returns to scale are shown by the flat portion of the average total cost curve in Figure 10-1(b). Constant returns to scale occur when production techniques can be replicated again and again to increase output. This occurs before monitoring costs rise and team spirit is lost.

THE IMPORTANCE OF ECONOMIES AND DISECONOMIES OF SCALE

Economies and diseconomies of scale play important roles in real-world long-run production decisions.

Economies and diseconomies of scale play important roles in real-world long-run production decisions. Economies of scale underlie firms' attempts to expand their markets either at home or abroad. If they can make and sell more at lower per-unit costs, they will make more profits. Diseconomies of scale prevent a firm from expanding and can lead corporate raiders to buy the firm and break it up in the hope that the smaller production units will be more efficient, thus eliminating some of the diseconomies of scale.

The long-run and the short-run average cost curves have the same U shape. But it's important to remember that the reasons why they have this U shape are quite different. The assumption of initially increasing and then eventually diminishing marginal productivity (as a variable input is added to a fixed input) accounts for the shape of the short-run average cost curve. Economies and diseconomies of scale account for the shape of the long-run average total cost curve. (See the box "Distinguishing Diseconomies of Scale from Diminishing Marginal Productivity" for a review of why.)

Q-5   Why is the short-run average cost curve a U-shaped curve?

Q-6   Why is the long-run average total cost curve generally considered to be a U-shaped curve?

DISTINGUISHING DISECONOMIES OF SCALE FROM DIMINISHING MARGINAL PRODUCTIVITY

As pointed out in the text, the shapes of the short-run average cost curve and the long-run average cost curve are similar. But the reasons underlying those shapes are quite different. It is important to reemphasize that difference. In the short run, some inputs are fixed; in the long run, all inputs vary.

Let's first review why the short-run average cost curve is U-shaped. What accounts for its shape is what's happening to marginal productivity of each additional unit of input *keeping all other inputs fixed*. Since costs are based on inputs, how much an input contributes to output directly affects the costs of production. Average total costs in the short run fall initially because of the assumption of increasing marginal productivity: Additional inputs are able to produce increasing increments of output. An example of increasing marginal productivity is a 5 percent increase in the quantity of labor, holding capital constant, leading to a 5 percent increase in output, and the next 5 percent increase leading to a 10 percent increase in output.

Eventually, marginal productivity falls and the short-run average cost curve slopes upward. Adding more of *one* factor of production, holding the others constant, contributes less and less to output, causing marginal costs, and eventually average costs, to rise. An example of diminishing marginal productivity is a 5 percent increase in the quantity of labor, holding capital constant, leading to a 2 percent increase in output and the next 5 percent increase, holding capital constant, leading to a 1 percent increase in output. The assumption of initially increasing marginal productivity and eventually diminishing marginal productivity leads to the U shape of the short-run average cost curve.

Now consider the long-run average cost curve. Its shape is determined by what's happening to returns to scale. Returns to scale are not about how changes in one input affect output. Instead, they involve changing *all inputs equally*. If there are economies of scale, increasing all factors of production equally, say by 5 percent, leads to a greater increase in output, say by 8 percent.

The assumption economists make in the long run is that initially economies of scale cause the long-run average total cost curve to slope downward. Eventually, however, there are diseconomies of scale. That is, increasing all inputs equally, say by 5 percent, leads to a smaller increase in output, say by 3 percent. Diseconomies of scale cause average total costs to rise and the long-run average total cost curve to slope upward. If there are neither economies of scale nor diseconomies of scale, the average total cost curve is flat because inputs and output both are changing by equal proportions. An example of constant returns to scale is a 5 percent increase in all inputs leading to a 5 percent increase in output. With constant returns to scale, average costs do not change.

The assumption we make about production in the long run is that there are first increasing, then constant, and finally decreasing returns to scale. That assumption about returns to scale accounts for the U shape of the long-run average cost curve.

ENVELOPE RELATIONSHIP

Since in the long run all inputs are flexible, while in the short run some inputs are not flexible, long-run cost will always be less than or equal to short-run cost at the same level of output. To see this, let's consider a firm that had planned to produce 100 but now adjusts its plan to produce more than 100. We know that in the long run the firm chooses the lowest-cost method of production. In the short run it faces an additional constraint: All expansion must be done by increasing only the variable input. That constraint must increase average cost (or at least not decrease it) compared to what average cost would have been had the firm planned to produce that level to begin with. If it didn't, the firm would have chosen that new combination of inputs in the long run. Additional constraints increase cost. The *envelope relationship* is the relationship between long-run and short-run average total costs. It is shown in Figure 10-2.

Why it's called an envelope relationship should be clear from the figure. Each short-run average total cost curve touches (is tangent to) the long-run average total cost

The envelope relationship is the relationship explaining that, at the planned output level, short-run average total cost equals long-run average total cost, but at all other levels of output, short-run average total cost is higher than long-run average total cost.

Figure 10-2   Envelope of Short-Run Average Total Cost Curves

The long-run average total cost curve is an envelope of the short-run average total cost curves. Each short-run average total cost curve touches the long-run average total cost curve at only one point. (SR stands for short run; LR stands for long run.)

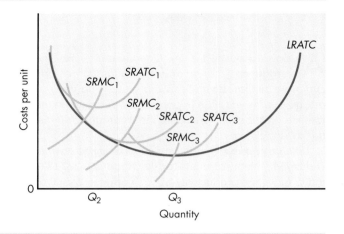

curve at one, and only one, output level; at all other output levels, short-run average cost exceeds long-run average cost. The long-run average total cost curve is an envelope of short-run average total cost curves.

The intuitive reason why the short-run average total cost curves always lie above the long-run average cost curve is simple. In the short run, you have chosen a plant; that plant is fixed, and its costs for that period are part of your average fixed costs. Changes must be made within the confines of that plant. In the long run you can change everything, choosing the combination of inputs in the most efficient manner. The more options you have to choose from, the lower the costs of production. Put another way: Constraints always raise costs (or at least won't lower them). So in the long run, costs must be the same or lower.

Another insight to note about this envelope relationship is the following: When there are economies of scale and you have chosen a plant size that is efficient, given output, your short-run average costs will fall as you increase production. Technically, this must be the case because the short-run marginal cost ($SRMC$) curve goes through the minimum point of the short-run average total cost ($SRATC$) curve, and the minimum point of the $SRATC$ curve is to the right of the efficient level of production in the long run. That means that at output Q_2, $SRMC_2$ has to be below $SRATC_2$ and short-run average total cost is falling. Intuitively, what's happening is that at output Q_2, your fixed costs are high. Now demand increases and you increase production. Your average fixed costs are high; your marginal costs are low; and initially the fall in average fixed costs more than offsets the increased marginal cost. Once marginal cost exceeds $SRATC$, that no longer is the case.[1]

Only when the firm is at the minimum point of the long-run average total cost ($LRATC$) curve (at output Q_3) is the $SRATC_3$ curve tangent to the $LRATC$ curve at a

---

[1]The above reasoning is dependent on the curves being smooth (i.e., having no kinks). This smoothness is a standard assumption of the model. If we give up the smoothness assumption, the $SRATC$ curve could be kinked and the $SRMC$ curve could be discontinuous. In that case, the $SRATC$ curve might be tangent to the $LRATC$ curve from the left, but not from the right, and it might not decrease. This would make movement from the long to the short run a discrete jump, whereas the existing model and smoothness assumption make it a smooth continuous movement. So if your intuition doesn't lead you to understand the model, you are probably thinking of a model with different assumptions. You'll be in good company, too. When an economist by the name of Jacob Viner first created this model, his intuition led him to a different result because his intuition was basing the analysis on different assumptions than he was using in his formal model.

Understanding costs and their structure will help you understand why intro economics textbooks are so long—and why their length is to your advantage.

The majority of the costs of a book are fixed costs in relation to the length of the book. The initial costs in terms of length are about 20 percent of the total price of the book. So increasing the length of the book increases costs slightly. But the longer length allows the writer to include more issues that some professors want, and many professors will not consider using the book unless it does include these issues. That means that greater length can allow publishers to sell more books, allowing the fixed costs to be divided over more output. This decrease in fixed cost per unit can lower average total cost more than increasing the length of the book increases average total costs per unit. So if the added length increases the number of users, the additional length can lower the average cost of the book.

It does lower the costs of the book—up to a point. Textbook publishers are continually looking for that point. They direct authors to shorten their books but also to include almost all issues that various groups want. The latter direction—in favor of inclusion—often takes precedence, which is why textbooks are so long. This doesn't mean that textbooks will always be longer. Recently, economics textbooks have become smaller because students began to complain that the texts were getting too heavy to carry.

---

point where the *SRMC* curve intersects both the curves. For large markets, this point is the least-cost production level of a firm.

ENTREPRENEURIAL ACTIVITY AND THE SUPPLY DECISION

In this chapter and the preceding one we have discussed the technical nature of costs and production. In the next chapter we will formally relate costs of production to the supply of goods. As a bridge between the two chapters, let's consider the entrepreneur, who establishes the relationship between costs and the supply decision, and discuss some of the problems of using cost analysis in the real world.

In thinking about the connection between cost and supply, one fundamental insight is that the revenue received for a good must be greater than the planned cost of producing it. Otherwise why would anyone supply it? The difference between the expected price of a good and the expected average total cost of producing it is the supplier's expected economic profit per unit. It's profit that underlies the dynamics of production in a market economy.

The expected price must exceed the opportunity cost of supplying the good for a good to be supplied.

Cost curves do not become supply curves through some magic process. To move from cost to supply, entrepreneurial initiative is needed. An **entrepreneur** is *an individual who sees an opportunity to sell an item at a price higher than the average cost of producing it.* The entrepreneur is the organizer of production and the one who visualizes the demand and convinces the individuals who own the factors of production that they want to produce that good. Businesses work hard at maintaining the entrepreneurial spirit in their employees. The greater the difference between price and average total cost, the greater the entrepreneur's incentive to tackle the organizational problems and supply the good.

Q-7 Why is the role of the entrepreneur central to the production process in the economy?

USING COST ANALYSIS IN THE REAL WORLD

All too often students walk away from an introductory economics course thinking that cost analysis is a relatively easy topic. Memorize the names, shapes, and relationships of the curves, and you're home free. In the textbook model, that's right. In real life, it's not, because actual production processes are marked by economies of scope, learning by doing and technological change, many dimensions, unmeasured costs, joint costs, indivisible costs, uncertainty, asymmetries, and multiple planning and adjustment periods with many different short runs. And this is a short list!

ECONOMIES OF SCOPE

Web Note 10.2
Increasing the Scope

Q-8   What is the difference between an economy of scope and an economy of scale?

The cost of production of one product often depends on what other products a firm is producing. Economists say that in the production of two goods there are **economies of scope** *when the costs of producing products are interdependent so that it's less costly for a firm to produce one good when it's already producing another.* For example, once a firm has set up a large marketing department to sell cereal, the department might be able to use its expertise in marketing a different product—say, dog food. A firm that sells gasoline can simultaneously use its gas station attendants to sell soda, milk, and incidentals. The minimarts so common along our highways and neighborhood streets developed because gasoline companies became aware of economies of scope.

Economies of scope play an important role in firms' decisions about what combination of goods to produce. They look for both economies of scope and economies of scale. When you read about firms' mergers, think about whether the combination of their products will generate economies of scope. Many otherwise unexplainable mergers between seemingly incompatible firms can be explained by economies of scope.

By allowing firms to segment the production process, globalization has made economies of scope even more important to firms in their production decisions. Low-cost labor in other countries has led U.S. firms to locate their manufacturing processes in those countries and to concentrate domestic activities on other aspects of production. As I have stressed throughout this book, production is more than simply manufacturing; the costs of marketing, advertising, and distribution are often larger

Production then: The nature of production has changed considerably in the last 70 years. This picture shows a 1933 production line in which people did the work as the goods moved along the line.
Bettmann/CORBIS.

components of the cost of a good than are manufacturing costs. Each of these involves special knowledge and expertise, and the U.S. companies are specializing in the marketing, advertising, and distribution aspects of the production process. By concentrating on those aspects, and by making themselves highly competitive by taking advantage of low-cost manufacturing elsewhere, U.S. firms become more competitive and expand, increasing demand for U.S. labor. Often they expand into new areas, taking advantage of economies of scope in distribution and marketing.

Consider Nike—it produces shoes, right? Wrong. It is a U.S. marketing and distribution company; it outsources all its production to affiliate companies. Nike is expanding, but not in the production of shoes. It is expanding into leisure clothing, where it hopes economies of scope in its marketing and distribution specialties will bring it success.

Nike is only one of many examples. The large wage differentials in the global economy are causing firms to continually reinvent themselves—to shed aspects of their business where they do not have a comparative advantage, and to add new businesses where their abilities can achieve synergies and economies of scope.

LEARNING BY DOING AND TECHNOLOGICAL CHANGE

The production terminology that we've been discussing is central to the standard economic models. In the real world, however, other terms and concepts are also important. The production techniques available to real-world firms are constantly changing because of *learning by doing* and *technological change*. These changes occur over time and cannot be accurately predicted.

Unlike events in the standard economic model, all events in the real world are influenced by the past. That's why learning by doing is important in the real world, but isn't a part of the standard economic model. **Learning by doing** simply means that *as we do something, we learn what works and what doesn't, and over time we become more proficient at it*. Practice may not make perfect, but it certainly makes better and more efficient.

Q.9 Does learning by doing cause the cost curve to be downward-sloping?

Production now: The nature of production has changed considerably in the last 70 years. This picture shows a modern production line. Robots do much of the work.
© Keystone/The Image Works.

Many firms estimate worker productivity to grow 1 to 2 percent a year because of learning by doing.

Many firms estimate that output per unit input will increase by 1 or 2 percent a year, even if no changes in inputs or technologies occur, as employees learn by doing.

The concept of learning by doing emphasizes the importance of the past in trying to predict performance. Let's say a firm is deciding between two applicants for the job of managing its restaurant. One was a highly successful student but has never run a restaurant; the other was an OK student who has run a restaurant that failed. Which one does the firm hire? The answer is unclear. The first applicant may be brighter, but the lack of experience will likely mean that the person won't be hired. Businesses give enormous weight to experience. So this firm may reason that in failing, the second applicant will have learned lessons that make her the better candidate. U.S. firms faced such a choice when they were invited to expand into the new market economies of Eastern Europe in the early 1990s. Should they hire the former communist managers who had failed to produce efficiently, or should they hire the reformers? (Generally they decided on the former communist managers, hoping they had learned by failing.)

Technological change is *an increase in the range of production techniques that leads to more efficient ways of producing goods as well as the production of new and better goods.* That is, technological change offers an increase in the known range of production. For example, at one point automobile tires were made from rubber, clothing was made from cotton and wool, and buildings were made of wood. As a result of technological change, many tires are now made from petroleum distillates, much clothing is made from synthetic fibers (which in turn are made from petroleum distillates), and many buildings are constructed from steel.

Technological change can fundamentally alter the nature of production costs.

The standard long-run model takes technology as a given. From our experience, we know that technological change affects firms' decisions and production. Technological change can fundamentally alter the nature of production costs.

In some industries technological change is occurring so fast that it overwhelms all other cost issues. The computer industry is a good example. The expectation of technological change has been built into the plans of firms in that industry. The industry has followed Moore's law, which states that the cost of computing will fall by half every 18 months. Indeed, that has happened since the 1980s. With costs falling that fast because of learning by doing and technological change, all other cost components are overwhelmed, and, instead of costs increasing as output rises significantly, as might be predicted because of diseconomies of scale, costs keep going down.

Web Note 10.3
Moore's Law

The fall in the cost of computer chips has affected other industries as well. All types of household goods that use computer technology—including telephones, refrigerators, automobiles, TVs and VCRs, and compact disc players—are undergoing enormous change. For instance, in Asia, VCRs are now almost extinct; they have been replaced by digital video disc (DVD) players—where all images are transmitted digitally. The same is happening in the United States. Another change is that mass-stamped CDs will soon be replaced by individual CDs created by downloading files from the Internet using MP3 technology. In a few years, CDs may not be used at all—music will be stored in music memory banks that will be modified computer hard drives. Computer technology has also revolutionized automobiles, making them more reliable and cheaper. In the 1960s, I could work on my own car, changing the points or modifying the carburetor. Modern cars have no such parts; they have been replaced by electronic parts. When a car isn't running right its owner must now take it to a garage. My point, however, is that automobiles have fundamentally changed; they are much more efficient and reliable and their price has fallen because of the introduction of computer technology. Technological change drives costs down, and can overwhelm diseconomies of scale, causing prices to fall more and more.

Technological change occurs in all industries, not only high-tech industries.

Don't think of technological change as occurring only in high-tech industries. Consider chicken production. The price of chickens has fallen enormously over the past

50 years. Why? Because of technological change. At one time chickens were raised in farmyards. They walked around, ate scraps and feed, and generally led a chicken's life. Walking around had definite drawbacks—it took space (which cost money); it made standardization (a requirement of taking advantage of economies of scale) difficult, which prevented lowering costs; it used energy, which meant more feed per pound of chicken; and sometimes it led to disease, since chickens walked in their own manure.

The technological change was to put the chickens in wire cages so that the manure falls through to a conveyor belt and is transferred outside. Another conveyor belt feeds the chickens food laced with antibiotics to prevent disease. Soft music is played to keep them calm (they burn fewer calories). Once they reach the proper weight, they are slaughtered in a similar automated process. Perdue Farms Inc., which led the way in developing this new technology, does not grow any chickens itself. It outsources this approach to chicken farms. Farmers bid for the right to grow the chickens for Perdue. Perdue then puts its label on the chickens, ships them to the supermarkets, and advertises the plump chickens with its name on them. How the chickens feel about this technological change is not clear. (When I asked them, all they had to say was *cluck*.)

This method of raising chickens will likely be replaced in the next couple of decades by another technological change—genetic engineering that will allow chicken parts to be produced directly from single cells. Only the breasts and drumsticks will be produced (and wings if you live in Buffalo). All low-efficiency, low-profit-margin parts such as necks, feet, and heads will be eliminated.

In many businesses the effect of learning by doing and technological change on prices is built into the firm's pricing structure. If they expect their costs to fall with more experience, or if they expect technological advances to lower costs in the future, they might bid low for a big order to give themselves the chance to lower their costs through learning by doing or technological change.

Technological change and learning by doing are intricately related. The efficient chicken production we now have did not come about overnight. It occurred over a 20-year period as firms learned how to do it. Chickens respond to Mozart better than to hip-hop. That had to be learned. Similarly, genetic reproduction of chicken parts will evolve as scientists and firms learn more about cloning and DNA.

Technological change and learning by doing are intricately related.

MANY DIMENSIONS

The only dimension of output in the standard model is how much to produce. Many, if not most, decisions that firms make are not the one-dimensional decisions of the standard model, such as "Should we produce more or less?" They're multidimensional questions like "Should we change the quality? Should we change the wrapper? Should we improve our shipping speed? Should we increase our inventory?" Each of these questions relates to a different dimension of the production decision and each has its own marginal costs. Thus, there isn't just one marginal cost; there are 10 or 20 of them. Good economic decisions take all relevant margins into account.

Good economic decisions take all relevant margins into account.

The reason that the standard model is important is that each of these questions can be analyzed by applying the same reasoning used in the standard model. But you must remember, *in applying the analysis, it's the reasoning, not the specific model, that's important.*

UNMEASURED COSTS

If asked, "In what area of decision making do businesses most often fail to use economic insights?" most economists would say costs. The relevant costs are generally not the costs you'll find in a firm's accounts.

Why the difference? Economists operate conceptually; they include in costs exactly what their theory says they should. They include all opportunity costs. Accountants who have to measure firms' costs in practice and provide the actual dollar figures take a much more pragmatic approach; their concepts of costs must reflect only explicit costs—those costs that are reasonably precisely measurable.

Here I review the difference between explicit and implicit costs (discussed in Chapter 9) and introduce another difference—how economists and accountants measure depreciation of capital.

Economists Include Opportunity Cost   First, say that a business produces 1,000 widgets[2] that sell at $3 each for a total revenue of $3,000. To produce these widgets the business had to buy $1,000 worth of widgetgoo, which the owner has hand-shaped into widgets. An accountant would say that the total cost of producing 1,000 widgets was $1,000 and that the firm's profit was $2,000. That's because an accountant uses explicit costs that can be measured.

Economic profit is different. An economist, looking at that same example, would point out that the accountant's calculation doesn't take into account the time and effort that the owner put into making the widgets. While a person's time involves no explicit cost in money, it does involve an opportunity cost, the forgone income that the owner could have made by spending that time working in another job. If the business takes 400 hours of the person's time and the person could have earned $6 an hour working for someone else, then the person is forgoing $2,400 in income. Economists include that implicit cost in their concept of cost. When that implicit cost is included, what looks like a $2,000 profit becomes a $400 economic loss.

Economic Depreciation versus Accounting Depreciation   Now let's take depreciation. Say a firm buys a machine for $10,000 that's meant to last 10 years. After 1 year, machines like that become in short supply, so instead of falling, its value rises to $12,000. An accountant, looking at the firm's costs that year, would use historical cost (what the machine cost in terms of money actually spent) depreciated at, say, 10 percent per year, so the machine's cost for each of its 10 years of existence would be $1,000. An economist would say that since the value of the machine is rising, the machine has no cost; in fact, it provides a revenue of $2,000 to the firm. The standard model avoids such messy, real-world issues of measuring costs and instead assumes that all costs are measurable in a single time period.

THE STANDARD MODEL AS A FRAMEWORK

The standard model can be expanded to include these real-world complications. I don't do so because I suspect that even with its simplifications, the standard model has been more than enough to learn in an introductory course. Learning the standard model, however, provides you with only the rudiments of cost analysis, in the same way that learning the rules of mechanics provides you with only the basics of mechanical engineering. In addition to a knowledge of the laws of mechanics, building a machine requires years of experience. Similarly for economics and cost analysis. Introductory economics provides you with a superb framework for starting to think about real-world cost measurement, but it can't make you an expert cost analyst.

Q-10 As the owner of the firm, Jim pays himself $1,000. All other expenses of the firm add up to $2,000. What would an economist say are the total costs for Jim's firm?

Despite its limitations the standard model provides a good framework for cost analysis.

---

[2]What's a widget? It's a wonderful little gadget that's the opposite of a wadget. (No one knows what they look like or what they are used for.) Why discuss widgets? For the same reason that scientists discuss fruit flies—their production process is simple, unlike most real-world production processes.

Factories run by numbers. Numbers to calculate profit and losses; to analyze the costs of new products; and to chart corporate strategy. But a lot of managers are relying on the wrong numbers.

As they adopt new manufacturing techniques like computer-aided design, just-in-time stock management, and total quality control, many firms are discovering that their existing account systems also need dragging into the 1990s. Unless the bean-counters join the manufacturing revolution, traditional cost accounting will have little place in the factory of the future.

The above quote introduced an article in *The Economist* (March 3, 1990, p. 61) describing a conference on strategic manufacturing. This conference focused on managerial or cost accounting (the application of cost analysis to managerial decisions). Unlike *financial accounting* (which involves keeping track of income, assets, and liabilities), managerial accounting is used to help managers determine the cost of producing products and plan future investment. It's the direct application of microeconomics to production.

In the 1980s and 1990s cost accounting changed enormously. The leaders of this change—such as Robert Kaplan of the Harvard Business School—argue that cost accounting systems based on traditional concepts of fixed and variable costs lead firms consistently to make the wrong decisions. They argue that in today's manufacturing, direct labor costs have fallen substantially—in many industries to only 2 or 3 percent of the total cost—and overhead costs have risen substantially. This change in costs facing firms requires a much more careful division among types of overhead costs, and a recognition that what should and should not be assigned as a cost to a particular product differs with each decision.

These developments in managerial accounting require an even deeper understanding of costs than accountants have previously needed. As one firm's director of manufacturing was quoted in *The Economist* article, "Unless management accountants move fast [to incorporate these new concepts], they will be almost without use to the manufacturing manager."

CONCLUSION AND A LOOK AHEAD

We've come to the end of our discussion of production, cost, and supply. The two chapters we spent on them weren't easy; there's tons of material here, and, quite frankly, it will likely require at least two or three reads and careful attention to your professor's lecture before your mind can absorb it. So if you're planning to sleep through a lecture, the ones on these chapters aren't the ones for that.

These chapters, in combination with our discussion of individual choice, will provide the framework for most of the later chapters, which really do get into interesting real-world issues. But you've got to know the basics to truly understand those issues. So, now that you've come to the end of these two chapters, unless you really feel comfortable with the analysis, it's probably time to review them from the beginning. (Sorry, but remember, there ain't no such thing as a free lunch.)

SUMMARY

- An economically efficient production process must be technically efficient, but a technically efficient process need not be economically efficient.

- The long-run average total cost curve is U-shaped. Economies of scale initially cause average total cost to decrease; diseconomies eventually cause average total cost to increase.

233

- Production is a social, as well as a technical, phenomenon; that's why concepts like team spirit are important—and that's why diseconomies of scale occur.

- The marginal cost and short-run average cost curves slope upward because of diminishing marginal productivity. The long-run average cost curve slopes upward because of diseconomies of scale.

- There is an envelope relationship between short-run average cost curves and long-run average cost curves. The short-run average cost curves are always above the long-run average cost curve.

- An entrepreneur is an individual who sees an opportunity to sell an item at a price higher than the average cost of producing it.

- Once we start applying cost analysis to the real world, we must include a variety of other dimensions of costs that the standard model does not cover.

- Costs in the real world are affected by economies of scope, learning by doing and technological change, the many dimensions to output, and unmeasured costs such as opportunity costs.

KEY TERMS

constant returns to
   scale (*224*)
diseconomies of
   scale (*223*)

economically
   efficient (*221*)
economies of scale (*221*)
economies of scope (*228*)
entrepreneur (*227*)

indivisible setup
   cost (*222*)
learning by doing (*229*)
minimum efficient level
   of production (*223*)

monitoring costs (*224*)
team spirit (*224*)
technical efficiency (*221*)
technological
   change (*230*)

QUESTIONS FOR THOUGHT AND REVIEW

1. Distinguish technical efficiency from economic efficiency.

2. A student has just written on an exam that in the long run fixed cost will make the average total cost curve slope downward. Why will the professor mark it incorrect?

3. What inputs do you use in studying this book? What would the long-run average total cost and marginal cost curves for studying look like? Why?

4. Why could diseconomies of scale never occur if production relationships were only technical relationships?

5. When economist Jacob Viner first developed the envelope relationship, he told his draftsman to make sure that all the marginal cost curves went through both (1) the minimum point of the short-run average cost curve and (2) the point where the short-run average total cost curve was tangent to the long-run average total cost curve. The draftsman told him it couldn't be done. Viner told him to do it anyhow. Why was the draftsman right?

6. What is the role of the entrepreneur in translating cost of production into supply?

7. Your average total cost is $40; the price you receive for the good is $12. Should you keep on producing the good? Why?

8. A student has just written on an exam that technological change will mean that the cost curve is downward-sloping. Why did the teacher mark it wrong?

9. If you were describing the marginal cost of an additional car driving on a road, what costs would you look at? What is the likely shape of the marginal cost curve?

10. The cost of setting up a steel mill is enormous. For example, a Gary, Indiana, hot-strip mill would cost an estimated $1.5 billion to build. Using this information and the cost concepts from the chapter, explain the following quotation: "To make operations even marginally profitable, big steelmakers must run full-out. It's like a car that is more efficient at 55 miles an hour than in stop-and-go traffic at 25."

11. One farmer can grow 1,000 bushels of corn on 1 acre of land with 200 hours of labor and 20 pounds of seed. Another farmer can grow 1,000 bushels of corn on 1 acre of land with 100 hours of labor and 20 pounds of seed. Could both methods be technically efficient? Is it possible that both of these production processes are economically efficient?

PROBLEMS AND EXERCISES

1. Visit a nearby company and ask it what would happen to its per-unit costs if sales increased by 10 percent. Try to figure out how its answer relates to the concepts in this and the preceding chapter, remembering especially the discussion about using cost analysis in the real world.

2. A pair of shoes that wholesale for $28.79 has approximately the following costs:

Manufacturing labor	$ 2.25
Materials	4.95
Factory overhead, operating expenses, and profit	8.50
Sales costs	4.50
Advertising	2.93
Research and development	2.00
Interest	.33
Net income	3.33
Total	$28.79

   a. Which of these costs would likely be a variable cost?
   b. Which would likely be a fixed cost?
   c. If output were to rise, what would likely happen to average total costs? Why?

3. Find out the total budget of your college or university. (It often takes a bit of sleuthing, but almost all college and university budgets are in the public record.) Find out the number of students. What is the total cost per student? What is the relevant marginal cost of an additional student?

   Now say you're on a planning committee charged with eliminating an expected 2 percent budget deficit next year. Using the budget figures, make some suggestions. Have a college administrator (preferably the treasurer or comptroller) visit your class and react to those sugges-

tions. Explain why presidents of universities and colleges don't last long.

4. Draw a long-run cost curve.
   a. Why does it slope downward initially?
   b. Why does it eventually slope upward?
   c. How would your answers to a and b differ if you had drawn a short-run cost curve?
   d. How large is the fixed-cost component of the long-run cost curve?
   e. If there were constant returns to scale everywhere, what would the long-run cost curve look like?

5. A major issue of contention at many colleges concerns the cost of meals that is rebated when a student does not sign up for the meal plan. The administration usually says that it should rebate only the marginal cost of the food alone, which it calculates at, say, $1.25 per meal. Students say that the marginal cost should include more costs, such as the saved space from fewer students using the facilities and the reduced labor expenses on food preparation. This can raise the marginal cost to $6.00.
   a. Who is correct, the administration or the students?
   b. How might your answer to a differ if this argument were being conducted in the planning stage, before the dining hall is built?
   c. If you accept the $1.25 figure of a person not eating, how could you justify using a higher figure of about $6.00 for the cost of feeding a guest at the dining hall, as many schools do?

6. A dressmaker can sew 800 garments with 160 bolts of fabric and 3,000 hours of labor. Another dressmaker can sew 800 garments with 200 bolts of fabric and 2,000 hours of identical labor. Fabric costs $100 a bolt and labor costs $10 an hour.
   a. Is it possible that both methods are technically efficient? Why or why not?
   b. Is it possible that both methods are economically efficient?

WEB QUESTIONS

1. Go to the Internet site About.com (www.about.com) and answer the following questions:
   a. What services does About.com provide? What does it charge for those services?
   b. What are the fixed costs associated with running About.com? What is the marginal cost of providing About.com to one additional person?
   c. List the advertising you saw while visiting About.com.
   d. Under what circumstances will an entrepreneur supply a good to the market? What incentives do the owners of About.com have to supply this product on the Internet? (Hint: Look at your answer to c).

2. Go to the business section of The Guardian Unlimited at www.guardian.co.uk/business, the website of a British newspaper, and search for the article, "Drug Cocktail Is a Downer" to answer the following questions:
   a. What are possible reasons Glaxo and SmithKline merged?
   b. What problems is the combined company facing?
   c. How do the problems you mentioned in b relate to diseconomies of scale?

ANSWERS TO MARGIN QUESTIONS

1. True. Since an economically efficient method of production is that method that produces a given level of output at the lowest possible cost, it must also use as few inputs as possible. It is also technically efficient. *(221)*

2. China uses more labor-intensive techniques than does the United States because the price of labor is much lower in China relative to the United States. Both countries are producing economically efficiently. *(221)*

3. Larger production runs are generally cheaper per unit than smaller production runs because of indivisible setup costs, which do not vary with the size of the run. *(222)*

4. Because the same technical process could be used over and over again at the same cost, the long-run average cost curve would never become upward-sloping. *(224)*

5. The short-run average total cost curve initially slopes downward because of increasing marginal productivity and large average fixed costs, then begins sloping upward because of diminishing marginal productivity, giving it a U shape. *(224)*

6. The long-run average total cost curve is generally considered to be U-shaped because initially there are economies of scale and, for large amounts of production, there are diseconomies of scale. *(224)*

7. Economic activity does not just happen. Some dynamic, driven individual must instigate production. That dynamic individual is called an entrepreneur. *(227)*

8. Economies of scale are economies that occur because of increases in the amount of one good a firm is producing. Economies of scope occur when producing different types of goods lowers the cost of each of those goods. *(228)*

9. Learning by doing causes a shift in the cost curve because it is a change in the technical characteristics of production. It does not cause the cost curve to be downward-sloping—it causes it to shift downward. *(229)*

10. An economist would say that he doesn't know what total cost is without knowing what Jim could have earned if he had undertaken another activity besides running his business. Just because he paid himself $1,000 doesn't mean that $1,000 is his opportunity cost. *(232)*

APPENDIX A

Isocost/Isoquant Analysis

In the long run, a firm can vary more than one factor of production. One of the decisions firms face in this long run is which combination of factors of production to use. Economic efficiency involves choosing those factors so that the cost of production is at a minimum.

In analyzing this choice of which combination of factors to use, economists have developed a graphical technique called *isocost/isoquant analysis*. In this technique the analyst creates a graph placing one factor of production, say labor, on one axis and another factor, say machines, on the other axis, as I have done in Figure A10-1. Any point on that graph represents a combination of machines and labor that can produce a certain amount of output, say pairs of earrings. For example, point A represents 3 machines and 4 units of labor being used to produce 8 pairs of earrings. Any point in the blue shaded area represents more of one or both factors and any point in the red shaded area represents less of one or both factors.

Figure A10-1   The Isocost/Isoquant Graph

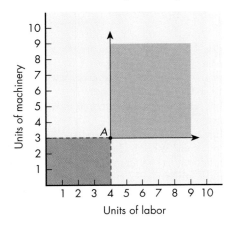

THE ISOQUANT CURVE

The firm's problem is to figure out how to produce its output—let's say it has chosen an output of 60 pairs of earrings—at as low a cost as possible. That means somehow we must show graphically the combinations of machines and labor that can produce 60 pairs of earrings as cheaply as possible. We do so with what is called an isoquant curve. An **isoquant curve** is *a curve that represents combinations of factors of production that result in equal amounts of output.* (*Isoquant* is a big name for an "equal quantity.") At all points on an isoquant curve the firm can produce the same amount of output. So, given a level of output, a firm can find out what combinations of the factors of production will produce that output. Suppose a firm can produce 60 pairs of earrings with the following combination of labor and machines:

	Labor	Machines	Pairs of Earrings
A	3	20	60
B	4	15	60
C	6	10	60
D	10	6	60
E	15	4	60
F	20	3	60

This table shows the technical limits of production. It shows that the firm can use, for example, 3 units of labor and 20 machines or 20 units of labor and 3 machines to produce 60 pairs of earrings. The isoquant curve is a graphical representation of the table. I show the isoquant curve for producing 60 pairs in Figure A10-2. Points A to F represent rows A to F in the table.

To be sure you understand it, let's consider some points on the curve. Let's start at point A. At point A the firm is producing 60 pairs of earrings using 20 machines and 3 workers. If the firm wants to reduce the number of machines by 5, it must increase the number of units of labor by 1 to keep output constant. Doing so moves the firm to point B. At point B the firm is also producing 60 pairs of earrings, but is doing it with 15 machines and 4 workers. Alternatively, if the firm were at point D, and it wants to reduce the number of machines from 6 to 4, it must increase the number of units of labor from 10 to 15 to keep output constant at 60. At any point on this isoquant curve the firm is being technically efficient—it is using as few resources as possible to produce 60 pairs of earrings. Thus, it would never want to produce 60 at a point like G, because that point uses more inputs. It is a technically inefficient method of production.

Figure A10-2   Isoquant Curve for 60 Earrings

The numbers in the production table and the shape of the curve were not chosen randomly. They were chosen to be consistent with the law of diminishing marginal productivity, which means the curve is bowed inward. That is because as the firm increases the use of one factor more and more, it must use fewer and fewer units of the other factor to keep output constant. This reflects the technical considerations embodied in the law of diminishing marginal productivity. Thus, the chosen numbers tell us that if a firm wants to keep output constant, as it adds more and more of one factor (and less of the other factor), it has to use relatively more of that factor. For example, initially it might add 1 machine to replace 1 worker, holding output constant. If it continues it will have to use 1.5 machines, then 2 machines, and so on.

The rate at which one factor must be added to compensate for the loss of another factor, to keep output constant, is called the **marginal rate of substitution.** To say that there is diminishing marginal productivity is to say that there is a diminishing marginal rate of substitution. It is because the table assumes a diminishing marginal rate of substitution that the isoquant curve is bowed inward.

Graphically, the slope of the isoquant curve is the marginal rate of substitution. To be exact, the absolute value of the slope at a point on the isoquant curve equals the ratio of the marginal productivity of labor to the marginal productivity of machines:

$$|\,Slope\,| = MP_{labor}/MP_{machines}$$
$$= \text{Marginal rate of substitution}$$

With this equation, you can really see why the isoquant is downward sloping. As the firm moves from point A to point F it is using more labor and fewer machines. Because of the law of diminishing marginal productivity, as the

Figure A10-3   An Isoquant Map

Figure A10-4   Isocost Curves

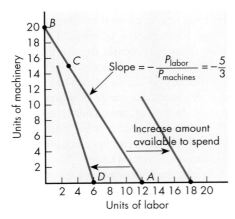

firm moves from A to F, the marginal productivity of labor decreases and the marginal productivity of machines increases. The slope of the isoquant falls since the marginal rate of substitution is decreasing.

Let's consider a specific example. Say in Figure A10-2 the firm is producing at point B. If it cuts its input by 5 machines but also wants to keep output constant, it must increase labor by 2 (move from point B to point C). So the marginal rate of substitution of labor for machines between points B and C must be 5/2 or 2.5.

The firm can complete this exercise for many different levels of output. Doing so will result in an **isoquant map,** *a set of isoquant curves that show technically efficient combinations of inputs that can produce different levels of output.* Such a map for output levels of 40, 60, and 100 is shown in Figure A10-3.

Each curve represents a different level of output. Isoquant I is the lower level of output, 40, and the isoquant III is the highest level of output. When a firm chooses an output level it is choosing one of those isoquants. The chosen isoquant represents the technically efficient combinations of resources that can produce the desired output.

THE ISOCOST LINE

So far I have only talked about technical efficiency. To move to economic efficiency, we have to bring in the costs of production. We do so with the **isocost line**—*a line that represents alternative combinations of factors of production that have the same costs.* (Isocost is a fancy name for "equal cost.") Each point on the isocost line represents a combination of factors of production which, in total, cost the firm an equal amount.

To draw the isocost line you must know the cost per unit of each input as well as the amount the firm has chosen to spend on production. Say labor costs $5 a unit and machinery costs $3 a unit and that the firm has chosen to

spend $60. What is the greatest number of earrings it can produce with that $60? To answer that question, we need to create a curve representing the various amounts of inputs a firm can get with that $60. We do so in the following manner. Say the firm decides to spend the entire $60 on labor. Since labor costs $5 a unit, if the firm spends all of the $60 on labor it can buy 12 units of labor. This alternative is represented by point A in Figure A10-4.

Alternatively, since machines cost $3 a unit, if the firm chooses to spend all of the $60 on machines it can buy 20 machines (point B in Figure A10-4). This gives us two points on the isocost curve. Of course, the assumption of diminishing marginal rates of substitutions makes it highly unlikely that firm would want to produce at either of these points. Instead, it would likely use some combination of inputs. But these extreme points are useful nonetheless, because by connecting them (the line that goes from A to B in Figure A10-4), we can see the various combinations of inputs that also cost $60.

To see that this is indeed the case, say the firm starts with 20 machines and no labor. If the firm wants to use some combination of labor and machinery, it can give up some machines and use the money it saves by using fewer machines to purchase units of labor. Let's say it gives up 5 machines, leaving it with 15. That means it has $15 to spend on labor, for which it can buy 3 units of labor. That means 15 machines and 3 units of labor is another combination of labor and machines that cost the firm $60. This means that point C is also a point on the isocost line. You can continue with this exercise to prove to yourself that the line connecting points A and B does represent various combinations of labor and machinery the firm can buy with $60. Thus, the line connecting A and B is the $60 isocost line.

To see that you understand the isocost line, it is useful to go through a couple of examples that would make it shift. For example, what would happen to the isocost line if the firm chooses to increase its spending on production to $90? To see the effect we go through the same exercise as before: If it spent it all on labor, it could buy 18 units of labor. If it spent it all on machines, it could buy 30 units of machinery. Connecting these points will give us a curve to the right of and parallel to the original curve. It has the same slope because the relative prices of the factors of production, which determines the slope, have not changed.

Now ask yourself, What happens to the isocost line if the price of labor rises to $10 a unit? If you said the isocost curve becomes steeper, shifting along the labor axis to point *D* while remaining anchored along the machinery axis until the slope is −10/3, you've got it. In general, the absolute value of the slope of the isocost curve is the ratio of the price of the factor of production on the *x*-axis to the price of the factor of production on the *y*-axis. That means that as the price of a factor rises, the end point of the isocost curve shifts in on the axis on which that factor is measured.

CHOOSING THE ECONOMICALLY EFFICIENT POINT OF PRODUCTION

Now let's move on to a consideration of the economically efficient combination of resources to produce 60 pairs of earrings with $60. To do that we must put the isoquant cost curve from Figure A10-2 and the isocost curve from Figure A10-4 together. We do so in Figure A10-5.

The problem for the firm is to produce as many pairs of earrings as possible with the $60 it has to spend. Or, put another way, given a level of production it has chosen, it wants to produce at the least-cost combination of the factors of production.

Let's now find the least-cost combination of inputs to produce 60 pairs of earrings. Let's say that, initially, the firm chooses point A on its isoquant curve—that's at 15 machines and 4 workers. That produces 60 pairs of earrings, but has a cost of $45 + $20 = $65. The firm can't produce 60 pairs of earrings unless it is willing to spend more than $60. If it fires a worker to bring its cost in line, moving it to point B, it moves down to a lower isoquant—it is producing only 40 pairs.

If the firm has a less-than-competent manager, that manager will conclude that you can't produce 60 for $60. But say the firm has an efficient manager—one who has taken introductory economics. As opposed to *reducing* the number of workers as the other manager did, she *increases* the number of workers to 6 and reduces the number of

Figure A10-5   Combining Isoquant and Isocost Curves

machines to 10. Doing so still produces 60 pairs of earrings, since C is a point on the isoquant curve, but the strategy reduces the cost from $65 at point A to $60 (10 machines at $3 = $30, and 6 workers at $5 = $30). So she is producing 60 pairs of earrings at a cost of $60. She is operating at the economic efficient point—point C.

Let's talk about the characteristics of Point C. Point C is the point where the isoquant curve is tangent to the isocost curve—the point at which the slope of the isoquant curve ($-MP_L/MP_M$) equals the slope of the isocost curve ($-P_L/P_M$). That is, $-MP_L/MP_M = -P_L/P_M$. This can be rewritten as:

$$MP_L/P_L = MP_M/P_M$$

What this equation says is that when the additional output per dollar spent on labor equals the additional output per dollar spent on machines, the firm is operating efficiently. It makes sense. If the additional output per dollar spent on labor exceeded the additional output per dollar spent on machines, the firm would do better by increasing its use of labor and decreasing its use of machines.

Point C represents the combination of labor and machines that will result in the highest output given the isocost curve facing the firm. To put it in technical terms, the firm is operating at an economically efficient point where marginal rate of substitution equals the ratio of the factor prices. Any point other than C on the isocost curve will cost $60 but produce fewer than 60 pairs of earrings. Any other point than C on the isoquant curve will produce 60 pairs of earrings but cost more than $60. Only C is the economically efficient point given the factor costs.

To see that you understand the analysis, say that the price of labor falls to $3 and you still want to produce 60. What will happen to the amount of labor and machines you hire? Alternatively, say that the price of machines rises to $5 and you want to spend only $60. What will happen to the amount of labor and machines you hire?

If your answers are (1) you hire more workers and fewer machines, and (2) you reduce production using fewer machines and, maybe, less labor, you've got the analyses down. If you didn't give those answers, I suggest rereading this appendix, if it is to be on the exam, and working through the questions for thought and review.

KEY TERMS

isocost line (238)
isoquant curve (237)

isoquant map (238)

marginal rate of substitution (237)

QUESTIONS FOR THOUGHT AND REVIEW

1. What happens to the marginal rate of substitution as a firm increases the use of one input, keeping output constant? What accounts for this?

2. Draw an isocost curve for a firm that has $100 to spend on producing jeans. Input includes labor and materials. Labor costs $8 and materials cost $4 a unit. How does each of the following affect the isocost curve? Show your answer graphically.
   a. Production budget doubles.
   b. Cost of materials rises to $10 a unit.
   c. Costs of labor and materials each rise by 25 percent.

3. Show, using isocost/isoquant analysis, how firms in the United States use relatively less labor and relatively more land than Japan for the production of similar goods, yet both are behaving economically efficiently.

4. Demonstrate the difference between economic efficiency and technical efficiency, using the isocost/isoquant analysis.

5. Draw a hypothetical isocost curve and an isoquant curve tangent to the isocost curve. Label the combination of inputs that represents an efficient use of resources.
   a. How does a technological innovation affect your analysis?
   b. How does the increase in the price of the input on the x-axis affect your analysis?

6. Show graphically the analysis of the example in Figure A10-5 if the price of labor falls to $3. Demonstrate that the firm can increase production given the same budget.

7. Show graphically the analysis of the example in Figure A10-5 if the price of machines rises to $5. Demonstrate that the firm must reduce production if it keeps the same budget.

PERFECT COMPETITION

> There's no resting place for an enterprise
> in a competitive economy.
>
> —*Alfred P. Sloan*

The concept *competition* is used in two ways in economics. One way is as a process. *Competition as a process* is a rivalry among firms and is prevalent throughout our economy. It involves one firm trying to figure out how to take away market share from another firm. An example is my publishing firm giving me a contract to write a great book like this in order for the firm to take market share away from other publishing firms that are also selling economics textbooks. The other use of *competition* is as a *perfectly competitive market structure*. It is this use that is the subject of this chapter. Although perfect competition has highly restrictive assumptions, it provides us with a reference point we can use to think about various market structures and competitive processes. Why is such a reference point important? Think of the following analogy.

In physics when you study the laws of gravity, you initially study what would happen in a vacuum. Perfect vacuums don't exist, but talking about what would happen if you dropped an object in a perfect vacuum makes the analysis easier. So too with economics. Our equivalent of a perfect vacuum is perfect competition. In perfect competition the invisible hand of the market operates unimpeded. In this chapter we'll consider how perfectly competitive markets work and see how to apply the cost analysis developed in Chapters 9 and 10.

A PERFECTLY COMPETITIVE MARKET

A **perfectly competitive market** is *a market in which economic forces operate unimpeded*. For a market to be called *perfectly competitive*, it must meet some stringent conditions:

1. Both buyers and sellers are price takers.
2. The number of firms is large.
3. There are no barriers to entry.
4. Firms' products are identical.
5. There is complete information.
6. Selling firms are profit-maximizing entrepreneurial firms.

After reading this chapter, you should be able to:

- List the six conditions for a perfectly competitive market.

- Explain why producing an output at which marginal cost equals price maximizes total profit for a perfect competitor.

- Demonstrate why the marginal cost curve is the supply curve for a perfectly competitive firm.

- Determine the output and profit of a perfect competitor graphically and numerically.

- Construct a market supply curve by adding together individual firms' marginal cost curves.

- Explain why perfectly competitive firms make zero economic profit in the long run.

- Explain the adjustment process from short-run equilibrium to long-run equilibrium.

These conditions are needed to ensure that economic forces operate instantaneously and are unimpeded by political and social forces. For example, if there weren't a large number of firms, the few firms in the industry would have an incentive to get together and limit output so they could get a higher price. They would stop the invisible hand from working. Similarly for the other conditions, although the reasoning why they're necessary can get rather complicated.

THE NECESSARY CONDITIONS FOR PERFECT COMPETITION

To give you a sense of these conditions, let's consider each a bit more carefully.

1. *Both buyers and sellers are price takers.* A **price taker** is *a firm or individual who takes the price determined by market supply and demand as given.* When you buy, say, toothpaste, you go to the store and find that the price of toothpaste is, say, $2.33 for the medium-size tube; you're a price taker. The firm, however, is a price maker since it set the price at $2.33. So even though the toothpaste industry is highly competitive, it's not a perfectly competitive market. In a perfectly competitive market, market supply and demand determine the price; both firms and consumers take the market price as given.

2. *The number of firms is large.* This is almost self-explanatory. *Large* means sufficiently large so that any one firm's output compared to the market output is imperceptible, and what one firm does has no influence on what other firms do.

Q.1 Why is the assumption of no barriers to entry necessary for the existence of perfect competition?

3. *There are no barriers to entry.* **Barriers to entry** are *social, political, or economic impediments that prevent firms from entering a market.* They might be legal barriers such as exist when firms acquire a patent to produce a certain product. Barriers might be technological, such as when the minimum efficient scale of production allows only one firm to produce at the lowest average total cost. Or barriers might be created by social forces, such as when bankers will lend only to individuals with specific racial characteristics. Perfect competition can have no barriers to entry.

4. *Firms' products are identical.* This requirement means that each firm's output is indistinguishable from any other firm's output. Corn bought by the bushel is relatively homogeneous. One kernel is indistinguishable from any other kernel. In contrast, you can buy 30 different brands of many goods—soft drinks, for instance: Pepsi, Coke, 7UP, and so on. They are all slightly different from one another and thus not identical.

5. *There is complete information.* In a perfectly competitive market, firms and consumers know all there is to know about the market—prices, products, and available technology, to name a few aspects. If any firm experiences a technological breakthrough, all firms know about it and are able to use the same technology instantaneously. No firm or consumer has a competitive edge over another.

6. *Selling firms are profit-maximizing entrepreneurial firms.* Firms can have many goals and be organized in a variety of ways. For perfect competition to exist, firms must seek maximum profit and only profit, and the people who make the decisions must receive only profits and no other form of income from the firms.

THE DEFINITION OF SUPPLY AND PERFECT COMPETITION

These are enormously strong conditions and are seldom met simultaneously. But they are necessary for a perfectly competitive market to exist. Combined, they create an

Recent technological developments are making the perfectly competitive model more directly relevant to our economy. Specifically, the Internet has eliminated the spatial dimension of competition (except for shipping), allowing individuals to compete globally rather than locally. When you see a bid on the Internet, you don't care where the supplier is (as long as you do not have to pay shipping fees). Because it allows access to so many buyers and sellers, the Internet reduces the number of seller-set posted price markets (such as found in retail stores), and replaces them with auction markets.

The Internet has had its biggest impact in firms' buying practices. Today, when firms want to buy standardized products, they will often post their technical requirements for desired components on the Net and allow suppliers from all over the world to bid to fill their orders. Firms have found that buying in this fashion over the Internet has on average lowered the prices they pay by over 10 percent.

Similar changes are occurring in consumer markets. With sites like Priceline.com, individuals can set the price they are willing to pay for goods and services (such as hotel rooms and airline tickets) and see if anyone wants to supply them. (Recently, I successfully bid $120 for a $460 retail price hotel room in New York City.) With sites such as eBay you can buy and sell almost anything. The Internet is even developing its own payment systems, such as PayPal.

In short, with the Internet, entry and exit are much easier than in traditional brick-and-mortar business, and that makes the market more like a perfectly competitive market. As Internet search engines become better designed for commerce, and as more people become Internet savvy, the economy will more and more closely resemble the perfectly competitive model.

---

environment in which each firm, following its own self-interest, will offer goods to the market in a predictable way. If these conditions hold, we can talk formally about the supply of a produced good and how it relates to costs. This follows from the definition of supply we gave in Chapter 4:

> *Supply* is a schedule of quantities of goods that will be offered to the market at various prices.

This definition requires the supplier to be a price taker (our first condition). In almost all other market structures (frameworks within which firms interact economically), firms are not price takers; they are price makers. They don't ask, "How much should I supply, given the market price?" Instead they ask, "Given a demand curve, how much should I produce and what price should I charge?" In other market structures, the supplier sets the quantity and price, based on costs, at whatever level is best for it.[1]

The second condition—that the number of firms is large—is necessary so that firms have no ability to *collude* (to operate in concert so that they can get more for themselves). Conditions 3 through 5 are closely related to the first two; they make it impossible for any firm to forget about the hundreds of other firms out there just waiting to replace their supply. Condition 6 tells us a firm's goals. If we didn't know the goals, we wouldn't know how firms would react when faced with the given price.

What's nice about these conditions is that they allow us to formally relate supply to the cost concept we developed in Chapters 9 and 10: marginal cost. If the conditions

---

[1] A firm's ability to set price doesn't mean that it can choose just any price it pleases. Other market structures can be highly competitive, so the range of prices a firm can charge and still stay in business is often limited. Such highly competitive firms are not perfectly competitive—they still set price rather than supply a certain quantity and accept whatever price they get.

Figure 11-1 (a and b)   Market Demand Curve versus Individual Firm Demand Curve
Even though the demand curve for the market is downward-sloping, the perceived demand curve of an individual firm is perfectly elastic because each firm is so small relative to the market.

(a)   Market

(b)   Firm

Web Note 11.1
Barriers to Entry

Even if we can't technically specify a supply curve, supply forces are still strong and many of the insights of the competitive model carry over.

 Q-2   How can the demand curve for the market be downward-sloping but the demand curve for a competitive firm be perfectly elastic?

hold, a firm's supply curve will be that portion of the firm's short-run marginal cost curve above the average variable cost curve, as we'll see shortly.

If the conditions for perfect competition aren't met, then we can't use our formal concept of supply and how it relates to cost; we can still talk informally about the supply of produced goods and cost conditions. We generally talk informally about perfect competition, keeping in the back of our minds which conditions aren't met and modifying the analysis accordingly. Even if the conditions for perfect competition don't fully exist, supply forces are still strong and many of the insights of the competitive model can be applied to firm behavior in other market structures.

DEMAND CURVES FOR THE FIRM AND THE INDUSTRY

Now that we've considered the competitive supply curve for the firm, let's turn our attention to the competitive demand curve for the firm. Here we must recognize that the demand curve for the industry is downward-sloping as in Figure 11-1(a), but the perceived demand curve for the firm is horizontal (perfectly elastic), as in Figure 11-1(b).

Why the difference? It's a difference in perception. Each firm in a competitive industry is so small that it perceives that its actions will not affect the price it can get for its product. Price is the same no matter how much the firm produces. Think of an individual firm's actions as removing one piece of sand from a beach. Does that lower the level of the beach? For all practical, and even most impractical, purposes, we can assume it doesn't. Similarly for a perfectly competitive firm. That is why we consider the demand curve facing the firm to be horizontal.

The price the firm can get is determined by the market supply and demand curves shown in Figure 11-1(a). Market price is $7, and the firm represented in Figure 11-1(b) will get $7 for each unit of its product whether it produces 10 units (point A), 20 units (point B), or 30 units (point C). Its demand curve is perfectly elastic even though the demand curve for the market is downward sloping.

This difference in perception is extremely important. It means that firms will increase their output in response to an increase in market demand even though that

Figure 11-2 (a and b)   Marginal Cost, Marginal Revenue, and Price

The profit-maximizing output for a firm occurs where marginal cost equals marginal revenue. Since for a competitive firm $P = MR$, its profit-maximizing output is where $MC = P$. At any other output it is forgoing profit.

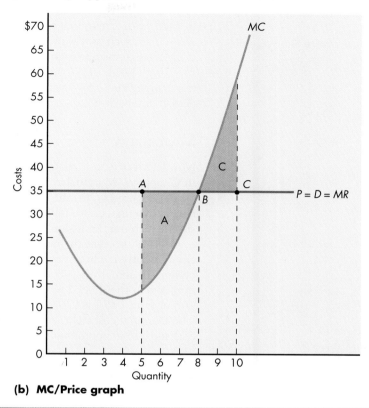

Price = MR	Quantity Produced	Marginal Cost
$35.00	0	
		$28.00
35.00	1	
		20.00
35.00	2	
		16.00
35.00	3	
		14.00
35.00	4	
		12.00
35.00	5	
		17.00
35.00	6	
		22.00
35.00	7	
		30.00
35.00	8	
		40.00
35.00	9	
		54.00
35.00	10	

(a) MC/Price table

(b) MC/Price graph

increase in output will cause price to fall and can make all firms collectively worse off. But since, by the assumptions of perfect competition, they don't act collectively, each firm follows its self-interest. Let's now consider that self-interest in more detail.

THE PROFIT-MAXIMIZING LEVEL OF OUTPUT

The goal of a firm is to maximize profits—to get as much for itself as possible. So when it decides what quantity to produce, it will continually ask the question "What will changes in how much I produce do to profit?" Since profit is the difference between total revenue and total cost, what happens to profit in response to a change in output is determined by **marginal revenue (MR)**, *the change in total revenue associated with a change in quantity*, and **marginal cost (MC)**, *the change in total cost associated with a change in quantity*. That's why marginal revenue and marginal cost are key concepts in determining the profit-maximizing or loss-minimizing level of output of any firm.

To emphasize the importance of *MR* and *MC*, those are the only cost and revenue figures shown in Figure 11-2. Notice that we don't illustrate profit at all. We'll calculate profit later. All we want to determine now is the profit-maximizing level of output. To do this you need only know MC and *MR*. Specifically, a firm maximizes profit when $MC = MR$. To see why, let's first look at MC and *MR* more closely.

To determine the profit-maximizing output, all you need to know is MC and MR.

MARGINAL REVENUE

For a competitive firm, MR = P.

Let's first consider marginal revenue. Since a perfect competitor accepts the market price as given, marginal revenue is simply the market price. In the example shown in Figure 11-2, if the firm increases output from 2 to 3, its revenue rises by $35 (from $70 to $105). So its marginal revenue is $35, the price of the good. Since at a price of $35 it can sell as much as it wants, for a competitive firm, $MR = P$.

Marginal revenue is given in column 1 of Figure 11-2(a). As you can see, MR equals $35 for all levels of output. But that's what we saw in Figure 11-1, which showed that the demand curve for a perfect competitor is perfectly elastic at the market price. For a perfect competitor, the marginal revenue curve and demand curve it faces are the same.

MARGINAL COST

Now let's move on to marginal cost. I'll be brief since I discussed marginal cost in detail in Chapter 9. Marginal cost is that change in total cost that accompanies a change in output. Figure 11-2(a) shows marginal cost in column 3. Notice that initially in this example, marginal cost is falling, but by the fifth unit of output, it's increasing. This is consistent with our discussion in earlier chapters.

Notice also that the marginal cost figures are given for movements from one quantity to another. That's because marginal concepts tell us what happens when there's a change in something, so marginal concepts are best defined between numbers. The numbers in the shaded rows are the marginal costs. So the marginal cost of increasing output from 1 to 2 is $20, and the marginal cost of increasing output from 2 to 3 is $16. The marginal cost right at 2 (which the marginal cost graph shows) would be between $20 and $16 at approximately $18.

PROFIT MAXIMIZATION: MC = MR

As I noted above, to maximize profit, a firm should produce where marginal cost equals marginal revenue. Looking at Figure 11-2(b), we see that a firm following that rule should produce at an output of 8, where $MC = MR = \$35$. Now let me try to convince you that 8 is indeed the profit-maximizing output. To do so, let's consider three different possible quantities the firm might look at.

Q.3 What are the two things you must know to determine the profit-maximizing output?

Let's say that initially the firm decides to produce 5 widgets, placing it at point A in Figure 11-2(b). At output A, the firm gets $35 for each widget but its marginal cost of increasing output is $17. We don't yet know the firm's total profit, but we do know how changing output will affect profit. For example, say the firm increases production from 5 to 6. Its revenue will rise by $35. (In other words, its marginal revenue is $35.) Its marginal cost of increasing output is $17. Since profit increases by $18 (the difference between MR, $35, and MC, $17), it makes sense (meaning the firm can increase its profit) to increase output from 5 to 6 units. It makes sense to increase output as long as the marginal cost is below the marginal revenue. The blue shaded area (A) represents the entire increase in profit the firm can get by increasing output.

Now let's say that the firm decides to produce 10 widgets, placing it at point C. Here the firm gets $35 for each widget. The marginal cost of producing that 10th unit is $54. So, $MC > MR$. If the firm decreases production by one unit, its cost decreases by $54 and its revenue decreases by $35. Profit increases by $19 ($54 − $35 = $19), so at point C, it makes sense to decrease output. This reasoning holds true as long as the marginal cost is above the marginal revenue. The red shaded area (C) represents the increase in profits the firm can get by decreasing output.

At point B (output = 8) the firm gets $35 for each widget, and its marginal cost is $35, as you can see in Figure 11-2(b). The marginal cost of increasing output by one unit is $40 and the marginal revenue of selling one more unit is $35, so its profit falls by $5. If the firm decreases output by one unit, its MC is $30 and its MR is $35, so its profit falls by $5. Either increasing or decreasing production will decrease profit, so at point B, an output of 8, the firm is maximizing profit.

Since MR is just market price, we can state the **profit-maximizing condition** of a competitive firm as MC = MR = P.

You should commit this profit-maximizing condition to memory. You should also be sure that you understand the intuition behind it. If marginal revenue isn't equal to marginal cost, a firm obviously can increase profit by changing output. If that isn't obvious, the marginal benefit of an additional hour of thinking about this condition will exceed the marginal cost (whatever it is), meaning that you should . . . right, you guessed it . . . study some more.

Profit-maximizing condition for a competitive firm: MC = MR = P.

If marginal revenue does not equal marginal cost, a firm can increase profit by changing output.

THE MARGINAL COST CURVE IS THE SUPPLY CURVE

Now let's consider again the definition of the supply curve as a schedule of quantities of goods that will be offered to the market at various prices. Notice that the marginal cost curve fits that definition. It tells how much the firm will supply at a given price. Figure 11-3 shows the various quantities the firm will supply at different market prices. If the price is $35, we showed that the firm would supply 8 (point A). If the price had been $19.50, the firm would have supplied 6 (point B); if the price had been $61, the firm would have supplied 10 (point C). Because the marginal cost curve tells us how much of a produced good a firm will supply at a given price, *the marginal cost curve is the firm's supply curve*. The MC curve tells the competitive firm how much it should produce at a given price. (As you'll see later, there's an addendum to this statement. Specifically, the marginal cost curve is the firm's supply curve only if price exceeds average variable cost.)

Because the marginal cost curve tells us how much of a produced good a firm will supply at a given price, the marginal cost curve is the firm's supply curve.

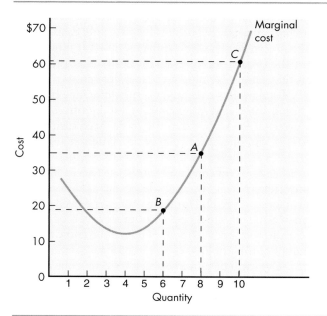

Figure 11-3   The Marginal Cost Curve Is a Firm's Supply Curve

Since the marginal cost curve tells the firm how much to produce, the marginal cost curve is the perfectly competitive firm's supply curve. This exhibit shows three points on a firm's supply curve; as you can see the quantity the firm chooses to supply depends on the price. For example, if market price is $19.50 the firm produces 6 units.

This Marginal revenue = Marginal cost equilibrium condition is simple, but it's enormously powerful. As we'll see, it carries over to other market structures. If you replace revenue with benefits, it also forms the basis of economic reasoning. With whom should you go out? What's the marginal benefit? What's the marginal cost? Should you marry Pat? What's the marginal benefit? What's the marginal cost? As we discussed in Chapter 1, thinking like an economist requires thinking in these marginal terms and applying this marginal reasoning to a wide variety of activities. Understanding this condition is to economics what understanding gravity is to physics. It gives you a sense of if, how, and why prices and quantities will move.

Q-4 Why do firms maximize total profit rather than profit per unit?

FIRMS MAXIMIZE TOTAL PROFIT

Notice that when you talk about maximizing profit, you're talking about maximizing *total profit*, not profit per unit. Profit per unit would be maximized at a much lower output level than is total profit. Firms don't care about profit per unit; as long as an increase in output will increase total profits, a profit-maximizing firm should increase output. That's difficult to grasp, so let's consider a concrete example.

Say two people are selling T-shirts that cost $4 each. One sells 2 T-shirts at a price of $6 each and makes a profit per shirt of $2. His total profit is $4. The second person sells 8 T-shirts at $5 each, making a profit per unit of only $1 but selling 8. Her total profit is $8, twice as much as the fellow who had the $2 profit per unit. In this case, $5 (the price with the lower profit per unit), not $6, yields more total profit.

PROFIT MAXIMIZATION USING TOTAL REVENUE AND TOTAL COST

An alternative method of determining the profit-maximizing level of output is to look at the total revenue and total cost curves directly. Figure 11-4 shows total cost and total revenue for the firm we're considering so far. The table in Figure 11-4(a) shows total revenue in column 2, which is just the number of units sold times market price. Total cost is in column 3. Total cost is the cumulative sum of the marginal costs from Figure 11-2(a) plus a fixed cost of $40. Total profit (column 4) is the difference between total revenue and total cost. The firm is interested in maximizing total profit. Looking down column 4 of Figure 11-4(a), you can quickly see that the profit-maximizing level of output is 8, as it was using the MR = MC rule, since total profit is highest at an output of 8.

In Figure 11-4(b) we plot the firm's total revenue and total cost curves from the table in Figure 11-4(a). The total revenue curve is a straight line; each additional unit sold increases revenue by the same amount, $35. The total cost curve is bowed upward at most quantities, reflecting the increasing marginal cost at different levels of output. The firm's profit is represented by the distance between the total revenue curve and the total cost curve. For example, at output 5, the firm makes $45 in profit.

Total profit is maximized where the vertical distance between total revenue and total cost is greatest. In this example total profit is maximized at output 8, just as in the alternative approach. At that output, marginal revenue (the slope of the total revenue curve) and marginal cost (the slope of the total cost curve) are equal.

Figure 11-4 (a and b)   Determination of Profits by Total Cost and Total Revenue Curves

The profit-maximizing output level can also be seen by considering the total cost curve and the total revenue curve. Profit is maximized at the output where total revenue exceeds total cost by the largest amount. This occurs at an output of 8.

Quantity	Total Revenue	Total Cost	Total Profit
0	$ 0	$ 40	$−40
1	35	68	−33
2	70	88	−18
3	105	104	1
4	140	118	22
5	175	130	45
6	210	147	63
7	245	169	76
8	280	199	81
9	315	239	76
10	350	293	57

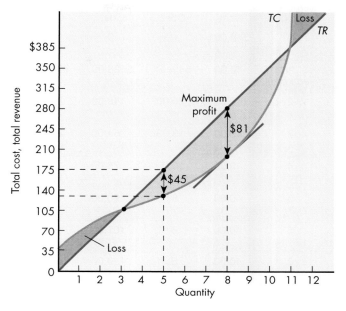

(a) Total revenue and total cost table   **(b) Total revenue and total cost curves**

TOTAL PROFIT AT THE PROFIT-MAXIMIZING LEVEL OF OUTPUT

In the initial discussion of the firm's choice of output, given price, I carefully presented only marginal cost and price. We talked about maximizing profit, but nowhere did I mention what profit, average total cost, average variable cost, or average fixed cost is. I mentioned only marginal cost and price to emphasize that marginal cost is all that's needed to determine a competitive firm's supply curve (and a competitive firm is the only firm that has a supply curve) and the output that will maximize profit. Now that you know that, let's turn our attention more closely to profit.

Marginal cost is all that is needed to determine a competitive firm's supply curve.

DETERMINING PROFIT FROM A TABLE OF COSTS AND REVENUE

The $P = MR = MC$ condition tells us how much output a competitive firm should produce to maximize profit. It does not tell us the profit the firm makes. Profit is determined by total revenue minus total cost. Table 11-1 expands Figure 11-2(a) and presents a table of all the costs relevant to the firm. Going through the columns and reminding yourself of the definition of each is a good review of Chapters 9 and 10. If the definitions don't come to mind immediately, you need a review. If you don't know the definitions of MC, AVC, ATC, FC, and AFC, go back and reread Chapters 9 and 10.

The firm is interested in maximizing profit. Looking at Table 11-1, you can quickly see that the profit-maximizing position is 8, as it was before, since at an output of 8, total profit is highest.

Table 11-1 Costs Relevant to a Firm

Price = Marginal Revenue	1 Quantity Produced	2 Total Fixed Cost	3 Average Fixed Cost	4 Total Variable Cost	5 Average Variable Cost	6 Total Cost	7 Marginal Cost	8 Average Total Cost	9 Total Revenue	10 Total Profit
$35.00	0	$40.00	—	0	—	$ 40.00		—	0	$−40.00
							$28.00			
35.00	1	40.00	$40.00	$ 28.00	$28.00	68.00		$68.00	$ 35.00	−33.00
							20.00			
35.00	2	40.00	20.00	48.00	24.00	88.00		44.00	70.00	−18.00
							16.00			
35.00	3	40.00	13.33	64.00	21.33	104.00		34.67	105.00	1.00
							14.00			
35.00	4	40.00	10.00	78.00	19.50	118.00		29.50	140.00	22.00
							12.00			
35.00	5	40.00	8.00	90.00	18.00	130.00		26.00	175.00	45.00
							17.00			
35.00	6	40.00	6.67	107.00	17.83	147.00		24.50	210.00	63.00
							22.00			
35.00	7	40.00	5.71	129.00	18.43	169.00		24.14	245.00	76.00
							30.00			
35.00	8	40.00	5.00	159.00	19.88	199.00		24.88	280.00	81.00
							40.00			
35.00	9	40.00	4.44	199.00	22.11	239.00		26.56	315.00	76.00
							54.00			
35.00	10	40.00	4.00	253.00	25.30	293.00		29.30	350.00	57.00

Using the $MC = MR = P$ rule, you can also see that the profit-maximizing level of output is 8. Increasing output from 7 to 8 has a marginal cost of $30, which is less than $35, so it makes sense to do so. Increasing output from 8 to 9 has a marginal cost of $40, which is more than $35, so it does not make sense to do so. The output 8 is the profit-maximizing output. At that profit-maximizing level of output, the profit the firm earns is $81, which is calculated by subtracting total cost of $199 from total revenue of $280. Notice also that average total cost is lowest at an output of about 7, and the average variable cost is lowest at an output of about 6.[2] Thus, the profit-maximizing position (which is 8) is *not* necessarily a position that minimizes either average variable cost or average total cost. It is only the position that maximizes total profit.

DETERMINING PROFIT FROM A GRAPH

These relationships can be seen in a graph. In Figure 11-5(a) I add the average total cost and average variable cost curves to the graph of marginal cost and price first presented in Figure 11-2. Notice that the marginal cost curve goes through the lowest points of both average cost curves. (If you don't know why, it would be a good idea to go back and review Chapter 9.)

The profit-maximizing output can be determined in a table (as in Table 11-1) or in a graph (as in Figure 11-5).

---

[2] I say "about 6" and "about 7" because the table gives only whole numbers. The actual minimum point occurs at 5.55 for average variable cost and 6.55 for average total cost. The nearest whole numbers to these are 6 and 7.

Figure 11-5 (a, b, and c)   Determining Profits Graphically

The profit-maximizing output depends *only* on where the MC and MR curves intersect. The total amount of profit or loss that a firm makes depends on the price it receives and its average total cost of producing the profit-maximizing output. This exhibit shows the case of (a) a profit, (b) zero profit, and (c) a loss.

(a) **Profit case**   (b) **Zero profit case**   (c) **Loss case**

Find Output Where MC = MR   The way you find profit graphically is first to find the point where MC = MR (point A). That intersection determines the quantity the firm will produce if it wants to maximize profit. Why? Because the vertical distance between a point on the marginal cost curve and a point on the marginal revenue curve represents the additional profit the firm can make by changing output. For example, if it increases production from 6 to 7, its marginal cost is $22 and its marginal revenue is $35. By increasing output it can increase profit by $13 (from $63 to $76). The same reasoning holds true for any output less than 8. For outputs higher than 8, the opposite reasoning holds true. Marginal cost exceeds marginal revenue, so it pays to decrease output. So, to maximize profit, the firm must see that there is no distance between the two curves—it must see where they intersect.

Find Profit per Unit Where MC = MR   After having determined the profit-maximizing quantity, drop a vertical line down to the horizontal axis and see what average total cost is at that output level (point B). Doing so determines the profit per unit at the profit-maximizing output because it's the difference between the price the firm receives (its average revenue) and its average cost. Since the firm will earn that profit on each unit sold, you next extend a line back to the vertical axis (point C). That tells us that the average total costs per unit are $25. Next go up the price axis to the price that the firm receives (point D). For a competitive firm, that price is the marginal revenue. Connecting these points gives us the shaded rectangle, ABCD, which is the total profit earned by the firm (the total quantity times the profit per unit).

Notice that at the profit-maximizing position, the profit per unit isn't at its highest because average total cost is *not* at its minimum point. Profit per unit of output would be highest at point E. A common mistake that students make is to draw a line up from point E when they are finding profits. That is wrong. It is important to remember: *To*

Q-5 If the firm described in Figure 11-5 is producing 4 units, what would you advise it to do, and why?

When the *ATC* curve is below the marginal revenue curve, the firm makes a profit. When the *ATC* curve is above the marginal revenue curve, the firm incurs a loss.

Applying the Tools

Most real-world firms do not have profit as their only goal. The reason is that, in the real world, the decision maker's income is part of the cost of production. For example, a paid manager has an incentive to hold down costs, but has little incentive to hold down his income which, for the firm, is a cost. Alternatively, say that a firm is a worker-managed firm. If workers receive a share of the profits, they'll push for higher profits, but they'll also see to it that in the process of maximizing profits they don't hurt their own interest—maximizing their wages.

A manager-managed firm will push for high profits but will see to it that it doesn't achieve those profits by hurting the manager's interests. Managers' pay will be high. In short, real-world firms will hold down the costs of factors of production *except* the cost of the decision maker.

In real life, this problem of the lack of incentives to hold down costs is important. For example, firms' managerial expenses often balloon even as firms are cutting "costs." Similarly, CEOs and other high-ranking officers of the firm often have enormously high salaries. How and why the lack of incentives to hold down costs affects the economy is best seen by first considering the nature of an economy with incentives to hold down all costs. That's why we use as our standard model the profit-maximizing firm. (*Standard model* means the model that economists use as our basis of reasoning; from it, we branch out.)

To determine maximum profit, you must first determine what output the firm will choose to produce by seeing where *MC* equals *MR*, and then dropping a line down to the *ATC* curve.

determine maximum profit you must first determine what output the firm will choose to produce by seeing where MC equals MR and then determine the average total cost at that quantity by dropping a line down to the ATC *curve*. Only then can you determine what maximum profit will be.

Zero Profit or Loss Where MC = MR   Notice also that as the curves in Figure 11-5(a) are drawn, *ATC* at the profit-maximizing position is below the price, and the firm makes a profit per unit of a little over $10. The choice of short-run average total cost curves was arbitrary and doesn't affect the firm's profit-maximizing condition: MC = MR. It could have been assumed that fixed cost was higher, which would have shifted the *ATC* curve up. In Figure 11-5(b) it's assumed that fixed cost is $81 higher than in Figure 11-5(a). Instead of $40, it's $121. The appropriate average total cost curve for a fixed cost of $121 is drawn in Figure 11-5(b). Notice that in this case economic profit is zero and the marginal cost curve intersects the minimum point of the average total cost curve at an output of 8 and a price of $35. In this case, the firm is making zero economic profit. (Remember from Chapter 10 that even though economic profit is zero, all resources, including entrepreneurs, are being paid their opportunity cost.)

In Figure 11-5(c), fixed cost is much higher—$169. Profit-maximizing output is still 8, but now at an output of 8, the firm is making an economic loss of $6 on each unit sold, since its average total cost is $41. The loss is given by the shaded rectangle. In this case, the profit-maximizing condition is actually a loss-minimizing condition. So MC = MR = P is both a *profit-maximizing condition* and a *loss-minimizing condition*.

I draw these three cases to emphasize to you that determining the profit-maximizing output level doesn't depend on fixed cost or average total cost. It depends only on where marginal cost equals price.

THE SHUTDOWN POINT

Earlier I stated the supply curve of a competitive firm is its marginal cost curve. More specifically, the supply curve is the part of the marginal cost curve that is above the

Q-6   What is wrong with the following diagram?

(a) The shutdown decision

(b) Long-run equilibrium

Figure 11-6   The Shutdown Decision and Long-Run Equilibrium

A firm should continue to produce as long as price exceeds average variable cost. Once price falls below that, it will do better by temporarily shutting down and saving the variable costs. This occurs at point A in (a). In (b), the long-run equilibrium position for a marginal firm in an industry is shown. In that long-run equilibrium, only normal profits are made.

average variable cost curve. Considering why this is the case should help the analysis stick in your mind.

Let's consider Figure 11-6(a)—a reproduction of Figure 11-5(c)—and the firm's decision at various prices. At a price of $35, it's incurring a loss of $6 per unit. If it's making a loss, why doesn't it shut down? The answer lies in the fixed costs. There's no use crying over spilt milk. In the short run a firm knows these fixed costs are sunk costs; it must pay them regardless of whether or not it produces. The firm considers only the costs it can save by stopping production, and those costs are its variable costs. As long as a firm is covering its variable costs, it pays to keep on producing. By producing, its loss is $48; if it stopped producing, its loss would be all the fixed costs ($169). So it makes a smaller loss by producing.

However, once the price falls below average variable costs (below $17.80), it will pay to shut down (point A in Figure 11-6(a)). In that case the firm's loss from producing would be more than $169, and it would do better to simply stop producing temporarily and avoid paying the variable cost. Thus, the point at which price equals AVC is the **shutdown point** (*that point at which the firm will be better off if it temporarily shuts down than it will if it stays in business*). When price falls below the shutdown point, the average variable costs the firm can avoid paying by shutting down exceed the price it would get for selling the good. When price is above average variable cost, in the short run a firm should keep on producing even though it's making a loss. As long as a firm's total revenue is covering its total variable cost, temporarily producing at a loss is the firm's best strategy because it's making a smaller loss than it would make if it were to shut down.

Q-7 In the early 2000s, many airlines were making losses, yet they continued to operate. Why?

The shutdown point is the point at which the firm will be better off if it shuts down than it will if it stays in business.

If $P >$ minimum of AVC, the firm will continue to produce in the short run. If $P <$ minimum of AVC, the firm will shut down.

SHORT-RUN MARKET SUPPLY AND DEMAND

Most of the preceding discussion has focused on supply and demand analysis of a firm. Now let's consider supply and demand in an industry. We've already discussed industry

To find a competitive firm's price, level of output, and profit given a firm's marginal cost curve and average total cost curve, use the following three steps:

1. Determine the market price at which market supply and demand curves intersect. This is the price the competitive firm accepts for its products. Draw the horizontal marginal revenue (MR) curve at the market price.

2. Determine the profit-maximizing level of output by finding the level of output where the MR and MC curves intersect.

3. Determine profit by subtracting average total costs at the profit-maximizing level of output from the price and multiplying by the firm's output.

If you are demonstrating profit graphically, find the point at which MC = MR. Extend a line down to the ATC curve. Extend a line from this point to the vertical axis. To complete the box indicating profit, go up the vertical axis to the market price.

---

demand. Even though the demand curve faced by the firm is perfectly elastic, the industry demand curve is downward sloping.

How about the industry supply curve? We previously demonstrated that the supply curve for a competitive firm is that firm's marginal cost curve (above the average variable cost curve). To discuss the industry supply curve, we must use a market supply curve. In the short run when the number of firms in the market is fixed, the **market supply curve** is just the *horizontal sum of all the firms' marginal cost curves, taking account of any changes in input prices that might occur.* To move from individual firms' marginal cost curves or supply curves to the market supply curve we add the quantities all firms will supply at each possible price. Since all firms have identical marginal cost curves, a quick way of summing the quantities is to multiply the quantities from the marginal cost curve of a representative firm at each price by the number of firms in the market. As the short run evolves into the long run, the number of firms in the market can change. As more firms enter the market, the market supply curve shifts to the right because more firms are supplying the quantity indicated by the representative marginal cost curve. Likewise, as the number of firms in the market declines, the market supply curve shifts to the left. Knowing how the number of firms in the market affects the market supply curve is important to understanding long-run equilibrium in perfectly competitive markets.

> The market supply curve is the horizontal sum of all the firms' marginal cost curves, taking account of any changes in input prices that might occur.

LONG-RUN COMPETITIVE EQUILIBRIUM

The analysis of the competitive firm consists of two parts: the short-run analysis just presented and the long-run analysis. In the short run the number of firms is fixed and the firm can either earn economic profit or incur economic loss. In the long run, firms enter and exit the market and neither economic profits nor economic losses are possible. In the long run, firms make zero economic profit. Thus, in the long run, only the zero profit equilibrium shown in Figure 11-6(b) is possible. As you can see, at that long-run equilibrium, the firm is at the minimum of both the short-run and the long-run average total cost curves.

Why can't firms earn economic profit or make economic losses in the long run? Because of the entry and exit of firms: If there are economic profits, firms will enter the

Applying the Tools

Chapters 9 and 10 emphasized that it is vital to choose the relevant costs to the decision at hand. Discussing the shutdown decision gives us a chance to demonstrate the importance of those choices. Say the firm leases a large computer it needs to operate. The rental cost of that computer is a fixed cost for most decisions, if, as long as the firm keeps the computer, the rent must be paid whether or not the computer is used. However, if the firm can end the rental contract at any time, and thereby save the rental cost, the computer is not a fixed cost. But neither is it your normal variable cost. Since the firm can end the rental contract and save the cost only if it shuts down, that rental cost of the computer is an *indivisible setup cost*. For the shutdown decision, the computer cost is a variable cost. For other decisions about changing quantity, it's a fixed cost.

The moral: The relevant cost can change with the decision at hand, so when you apply the analysis to real-world situations, be sure to think carefully about what the *relevant cost* is.

---

market, shifting the market supply curve to the right. As market supply increases, the market price will decline and reduce profits for each firm. Firms will continue to enter the market and the market price will continue to decline until the incentive of economic profits is eliminated. At that price, all firms are earning zero profit. Similarly, if the price is lower than the price necessary to earn a profit, firms incurring losses will leave the market and the market supply curve will shift to the left. As market supply shifts to the left, market price will rise. Firms will continue to exit the market and market price will continue to rise until all remaining firms no longer incur losses and earn zero profit. Only at zero profit do entry and exit stop.

> Since profits create incentives for new firms to enter, output will increase, and the price will fall until zero profits are being made.

Zero profit does not mean that entrepreneurs don't get anything for their efforts. The entrepreneur is an input to production just like any other factor of production. In order to stay in the business the entrepreneur must receive the opportunity cost, or **normal profit** (*the amount the owners of business would have received in the next-best alternative*). That normal profit is built into the costs of the firm; economic profits are profits above normal profits.

 Web Note 11.2
Barriers to Exit

Another aspect of the zero profit position deserves mentioning. What if one firm has superefficient workers or machinery? Won't the firm make a profit in the long run? The answer is, again, no. In a long-run competitive market, other firms will see the value of those workers and machines and will compete to get them for themselves. As firms compete for the superefficient factors of production, the price of those specialized inputs will rise until all profits are eliminated. Those factors will receive what are called rents to their specialized ability. For example, say the average worker receives $400 per week, but Sarah, because she's such a good worker, receives $600. So $200 of the $600 she receives is a rent to her specialized ability. Either her existing firm matches that $600 wage or she will change employment.

> Q.8 If a competitive firm makes zero profit, why does it stay in business?

The zero profit condition is enormously powerful; it makes the analysis of competitive markets far more applicable to the real world than can a strict application of the assumption of perfect competition. If economic profit is being made, firms will enter and compete that profit away. Price will be pushed down to the average total cost of production as long as there are no barriers to entry. As we'll see in later chapters, in their analysis of whether markets are competitive, many economists focus primarily on whether barriers to entry exist.

> The zero profit condition is enormously powerful; it makes the analysis of competitive markets far more applicable to the real world than would otherwise be the case.

Figure 11-7 (a and b)   Market Response to an Increase in Demand
Faced with an increase in demand, which it sees as an increase in price and hence profits, a competitive firm will respond by increasing output (from A to B) in order to maximize profit. The market response is shown in (a); the firm's response is shown in (b). As all firms increase output and as new firms enter, price will fall until all profit is competed away. Thus the long-run market supply curve will be perfectly elastic, as is S_{LR} in (a). The final equilibrium will be the original price but a higher output. The original firms return to their original output (A), but since there are more firms in the market, the market output increases to C.

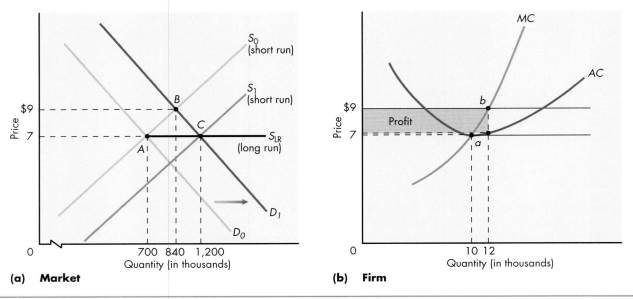

(a)   **Market**   (b)   **Firm**

ADJUSTMENT FROM THE SHORT RUN TO THE LONG RUN

Now that we've been through the basics of the perfectly competitive supply and demand curves, we're ready to consider the two together and to see how the adjustment to long-run equilibrium will likely take place in the firm and in the market.

AN INCREASE IN DEMAND

Q-9 If berets suddenly became the "in" thing to wear, what would you expect to happen to the price in the short run? In the long run?

First, in Figure 11-7(a and b), let's consider a market that's in equilibrium but that suddenly experiences an increase in demand. Figure 11-7(a) shows the market reaction. Figure 11-7(b) shows a representative firm's reaction. Originally market equilibrium occurs at a price of $7 and market quantity supplied of 700 thousand units (point A in (a)), with each of 70 firms producing 10 thousand units (point a in (b)). Firms are making zero profit because they're in long-run equilibrium. If demand increases from D_0 to D_1, the firms will see the market price increasing and will increase their output until they're once again at a position where MC = P. This occurs at point B at a market output of 840 thousand units in (a) and at point b at a firm output of 12 in (b). In the short run the 70 existing firms each make an economic profit (the shaded area in Figure 11-7(b)). Price has risen to $9, but average cost is only $7.10, so if the price remains $9 each firm is making a profit of $1.90 per unit. But price cannot remain at $9 since each firm will have an incentive to expand output and new firms will have an incentive to enter the market.

As existing firms expand and new firms enter, if input prices remain constant, the short-run market supply curve shifts from S_0 to S_1 and the market price returns to $7.

Four things to remember when considering a perfectly competitive industry are

1. The profit-maximizing condition for perfectly competitive firms is $MC = MR = P$.

2. To determine profit or loss at the profit-maximizing level of output, subtract the average total cost at that level of output from the price and multiply the result by the output level.

3. Firms will shut down production if price is equal to or falls below the minimum of their average variable costs.

4. A perfectly competitive firm is in long-run equilibrium only when it is earning zero economic profit, or when price equals the minimum of long-run average total costs.

The entry of 50 new firms provides the additional output in this example, bringing market output to 1.2 million units sold for $7 apiece. The final equilibrium will be at a higher market output but the same price.

LONG-RUN MARKET SUPPLY

The long-run market supply curve is a schedule of quantities supplied when firms are no longer entering or exiting the market. This occurs when firms are earning zero profit. In this case, the long-run supply curve is created by extending to the right the line connecting points A and C. Since equilibrium price remains at $7, the long-run supply curve is perfectly elastic. The long-run supply curve is horizontal because factor prices are constant. That is, factor prices do not increase as industry output increases. Economists call this market a *constant-cost industry*. Two other possibilities exist: an *increasing-cost industry* (in which factor prices rise as more firms enter the market and existing firms expand production) and a *decreasing-cost industry* (in which factor prices fall as industry output expands).

Factor prices are likely to rise when industry output increases if the factors of production are specialized. An increase in the demand for the factors of production that accompanies an increase in output, in this case, will bid up factor prices. The effect on long-run supply is the following: The rise in factor prices forces costs up for each individual firm and increases the price at which firms earn zero profit. Firms will stop entering the market and expanding production at a higher equilibrium price since the price at which zero profit is made has risen. Therefore, in increasing-cost industries, the long-run supply curve is upward sloping. In the extreme case, in which all firms in an industry are competitively supplying a perfectly inelastic resource or factor input, the long-run market supply curve is perfectly inelastic (vertical). Any increase in demand would increase the price of that factor. Costs would rise in response to the increase in demand; output would not. Input costs would also rise if there are diseconomies of scale. In both cases, the long-run equilibrium price would have been higher and output would have been lower than if input prices remained constant.[3]

In the long run firms earn zero profits.

Q.10 In 2001, demand for burkhas (the garment the Taliban required all Afghani women to wear) declined when the Taliban was ousted. In the short run, what would you expect to happen to the price of burkhas? How about in the long run?

---

[3]To check your understanding, ask yourself the following question: What if there had been economies of scale? If you answered, "There couldn't have been," you're really into economic thinking. (For those of you who aren't all that heavily into economic thinking, the reason is that if there had been economies of scale, the market structure would not have been perfectly competitive. One firm would have kept expanding and expanding and, as it did, its costs would have kept falling.)

The other possibility is a decreasing-cost industry. If factor prices decline when industry output expands, individual firms' cost curves shift down. As they do, the price at which the zero profit condition falls and the price at which firms cease to enter the market also falls. In this case, the long-run market supply curve is downward sloping. Factor prices may decline as output rises when new entrants make it more cost-effective for other firms to provide services to all firms in the area. The supply of factors of production expands and reduces the price of inputs to production.

Notice that in the long-run equilibrium, once again zero profit is being made. Long-run equilibrium is defined by zero economic profit. Notice also that the long-run supply curve is more elastic than the short-run supply curve. That's because output changes are much less costly in the long run than in the short run. *In the short run, the price does more of the adjusting. In the long run, more of the adjustment is done by quantity.*

In the short run, the price does more of the adjusting. In the long run, more of the adjustment is done by quantity.

AN EXAMPLE IN THE REAL WORLD

The perfectly competitive model and the reasoning underlying it are extremely powerful. With them you have a simple model to use as a first approach to predict the effect of an event, or to explain why an event occurred. For example, consider the decision of the owners of the Kmart chain of department stores to close nearly 300 stores after experiencing two years of losses.

Figure 11-8 shows what happened. Initially, Kmart saw the losses it was suffering as temporary. In the two years prior to the shutdown decision, Kmart's cost curves looked like those in Figure 11-8. Since price exceeded average variable cost, Kmart continued to produce even though it was making a loss.

But after two years of losses Kmart's perspective changed. The company moved from the short run to the long run. Kmart began to believe that the demand wasn't temporarily low but rather permanently low. It began to ask: What costs are truly fixed and what costs are simply indivisible costs that we can save if we close down completely, selling our buildings and reducing our overhead? Since in the long run all costs are variable, the ATC became its relevant AVC. Kmart recognized that demand had fallen below these long-run average costs. At that point, it shut down those stores for which $P < AVC$.

There are hundreds of other real-world examples to which the perfectly competitive model adds insight. That's one reason why it's important to keep it in the back of your mind.

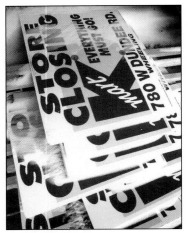

Tim Boyle/Getty Images.

Figure 11-8   A Real-World Example: A Shutdown Decision
Supply/demand analysis can be applied to a wide variety of real-world examples. This exhibit shows one, but there are many more. As you experience life today, a good exercise is to put on your supply/demand glasses and interpret everything you see in a supply/demand framework.

CONCLUSION

We've come to the end of the presentation of perfect competition. It was tough going, but if you went through it carefully, it will serve you well, both as a basis for later chapters and as a reference point for how real-world economies work. But like many good things, a complete understanding of the chapter doesn't come easy.

SUMMARY

- The necessary conditions for perfect competition are that buyers and sellers be price takers, the number of firms be large, there be no barriers to entry, firms' products be identical, there be complete information, and sellers be profit-maximizing entrepreneurial firms.

- The profit-maximizing position of a competitive firm is where marginal revenue equals marginal cost.

- The supply curve of a competitive firm is its marginal cost curve. Only competitive firms have supply curves.

- To find the profit-maximizing level of output for a perfect competitor, find that level of output where $MC = MR$. Profit is price less average total cost times output at the profit-maximizing level of output.

- In the short run, competitive firms can make a profit or loss. In the long run, they make zero profits.

- The shutdown price for a perfectly competitive firm is a price below the minimum point of the average variable cost curve.

- The short-run market supply curve is the horizontal summation of the marginal cost curves for all firms in the market. An increase in the number of firms in the market shifts the market supply curve to the right, while a decrease shifts it to the left.

- Perfectly competitive firms make zero profit in the long run because if profit were being made, new firms would enter and the market price would decline, eliminating the profit. If losses were being made, firms would exit and the market price would rise, eliminating the loss.

- The long-run supply curve is a schedule of quantities supplied where firms are making zero profit. The slope of the long-run supply curve depends on what happens to factor prices when output increases. Constant-cost industries have horizontal long-run supply curves. Increasing-cost industries have upward-sloping long-run supply curves, and decreasing-cost industries have downward-sloping long-run supply curves.

KEY TERMS

barriers to entry (242)
marginal cost (MC) (245)

marginal revenue (MR) (245)
market supply curve (254)

normal profit (255)
perfectly competitive market (241)
price taker (242)

profit-maximizing condition (247)
shutdown point (253)

QUESTIONS FOR THOUGHT AND REVIEW

1. Why must buyers and sellers be price takers for a market to be perfectly competitive?

2. Draw marginal cost, marginal revenue, and average total cost curves for a typical perfectly competitive firm and indicate the profit-maximizing level of output and total profit for that firm. Is the firm in long-run equilibrium? Why or why not?

3. Draw marginal cost, marginal revenue, and average total cost curves for a typical perfectly competitive firm in long-run equilibrium and indicate the profit-maximizing level of output and total profit for that firm.

4. What portion of the marginal cost curve is the firm's supply curve? How is a firm's marginal cost curve related to the market supply curve?

5. Draw the ATC, AVC, and MC curves for a typical firm. Label the price at which the firm would shut down temporarily and the price at which the firm would exit the market in the long run.

6. Under what cost condition is the shutdown point the same as the point at which a firm exits the market?

7. Why is long-run market supply curve upward-sloping in an increasing-cost industry, downward-sloping in a decreasing-cost industry, and horizontal in a constant-cost industry?

8. What will be the effect of a technological development that reduces marginal costs in a competitive market on short-run price, quantity, and profit?

9. If a firm is owned by its workers but otherwise meets all the qualifications for a perfectly competitive firm, will its price and output decisions differ from the price and output decisions of a perfectly competitive firm? Why?

10. You're thinking of buying one of two firms. One has a profit margin of $8 per unit; the other has a profit margin of $4 per unit. Which should you buy? Why?

11. If marginal cost is four times the quantity produced and the price is $20, how much should the firm produce? Why?

12. Find three events in the newspaper that can be explained or interpreted with supply/demand analysis.

13. State what is *wrong* with each of the graphs.

(a)   (b)

(c)   (d)

14. In the late 1990s and early 2000s, hundreds of music stores closed in the face of stagnant demand for CDs and new competitors—online music vendors and discount retailers. Explain how price competition from these new sources would cause a retail store to close. In the long run, what effect will new entrants have on the price of CDs?

PROBLEMS AND EXERCISES

1. a. Based on the following table, what is the profit-maximizing output?

Output	Price	Total Costs
0	$10	$ 31
1	10	40
2	10	45
3	10	48
4	10	55
5	10	65
6	10	80
7	10	100
8	10	140
9	10	220
10	10	340

b. How would your answer change if, in response to an increase in demand, the price of the good increased to $15?

2. A profit-maximizing firm has an average total cost of $4, but it gets a price of $3 for each good it sells.
   a. What would you advise the firm to do?
   b. What would you advise the firm to do if you knew average variable costs were $3.50?

3. Say that half of the cost of producing wheat is the rental cost of land (a fixed cost) and half is the cost of labor and machines (a variable cost). If the average total cost of producing wheat is $8 and the price of wheat is $6, what would you advise the farmer to do? ("Grow something else" is not allowed.)

4. Use the accompanying graph, which shows the marginal cost and average total cost curves for the shoe store Zapateria, a perfectly competitive firm.
   a. How many pairs of shoes will Zapateria produce if the market price of shoes is $70 a pair?
   b. What is the total profit Zapateria will earn if the market price of shoes is $70 a pair?
   c. Should Zapateria expect more shoe stores to enter this market? Why or why not?

   d. What is the long-run equilibrium price in the shoe market assuming it is a constant-cost industry?

5. Each of 10 firms in a given industry has the costs given in the left-hand table. The market demand schedule is given in the right-hand table.

Quantity	Total Cost
0	12
1	24
2	27
3	31
4	39
5	53
6	73
7	99

Price	Quantity Demanded
2	110
4	100
6	90
8	80
10	70
12	60
14	50
16	40

   a. What is the market equilibrium price and the price each firm gets for its product?
   b. What is the equilibrium market quantity and the quantity each firm produces?
   c. What profit is each firm making?
   d. Below what price will firms begin to exit the market?

6. Suppose an increasing-cost industry is in both long-run and short-run equilibrium. Explain what will happen to the following in the long run if the demand for that product declines:
   a. Price.
   b. Quantity.
   c. Number of firms in the market.
   d. Profit.

7. Graphically demonstrate the quantity and price of a perfectly competitive firm.
   a. Explain why a slightly larger quantity would not be preferred.
   b. Explain why a slightly lower quantity would not be preferred.
   c. Label the shutdown point in your diagram.
   d. You have just discovered that shutting down means that you would lose your land zoning permit which is required to start operating again. How does that change your answer to c?

8. A California biotechnology firm submitted a tomato that will not rot for weeks to the U.S. Food and Drug Administration. It designed such a fruit by changing the genetic structure of the tomato. What effect will this technological change have:
   a. On the price of tomatoes?
   b. On farmers who grow tomatoes?
   c. On the geographic areas where tomatoes are grown?
   d. On where tomatoes are generally placed on salad bars in winter?

9. Currently central banks (banks of governments) hold 35,000 tons of gold—one-third of the world's supply. This is the equivalent of 17 years' production. In the 1990s there was discussion about the central banks selling off their gold, since it is no longer tied to money supplies. Assuming they did sell it:
   a. Demonstrate, using supply/demand analysis, the effect on the price of gold in the long run and the short run.
   b. If you were an economist advising the central banks and you believed that selling off the gold made sense, would you advise them to do it quickly or slowly? Why?

10. The milk industry has a number of interesting aspects. Provide economic explanations for the following:
    a. Fluid milk is 87 percent water. It can be dried and reconstituted so that it is almost indistinguishable from fresh milk. What is a likely reason that such reconstituted milk is not produced?
    b. The United States has regional milk-marketing regulations whose goals are to make each of the regions self-sufficient in milk. What is a likely reason for this?
    c. A U.S. senator from a milk-producing state has been quoted as saying, "I am absolutely convinced . . . that simply bringing down dairy price supports is not a way to cut production." Is it likely that he is correct? What is a probable reason for his statement?

11. Subtle changes in the tax laws often mean enormous amounts of money to individuals and groups. Consider the case of whiskey, as did economists Jack High and Clayton Coppin. Whiskey is distilled grain. The distilling process produces poisonous impurities, called fusel oil, that must be removed before the whiskey is drinkable. One way to remove these impurities is by aging the whiskey in wooden barrels. Whiskey produced in this manner is "straight whiskey." The second method is distillation—removing the fusel oil through additional distilling. The latter method removes more impurities and is cheaper, but it results in a whiskey with little taste. However, taste can be added back through flavorings or blending with aged whiskey. Up until 1868 distilled or blended whiskey predominated, but in that year a law was passed that allowed straight-whiskey producers who stored their whiskey in government warehouses to defer their taxes on it until it was fully aged.

a. What advantage would this law have for straight-whiskey producers?

b. After the tax was paid the whiskey received a tax stamp, certifying that its producers had paid the tax and that their straight whiskey had been stored in a "bonded government warehouse." If you were a straight-whiskey producer, how might you try to use that tax stamp to your advantage in advertising?

c. How might competing producers of distilled whiskey certify the quality of their product?

WEB QUESTIONS

1. A number of markets are developing on the Internet. One of those markets is eBay. Check out eBay at www.ebay.com and explain whether you believe that the eBay Internet auction market is perfectly competitive. Be sure to explain which of the six conditions are met and how.

2. Find 60-month new auto loans in five different states using a loan information center on the Internet such as www.bankrate.com and answer the following questions:

a. By how much did the interest rates differ among those institutions you sampled?

b. Which of the six conditions for perfect competition does the auto loan market meet?

c. Is your answer to b consistent with your answer to a? Why or why not?

ANSWERS TO MARGIN QUESTIONS

1. Without the assumption of no barriers to entry, firms could make a profit by raising price; hence, their demand curve would not be perfectly elastic and, hence, perfect competition would not exist. (242)

2. The competitive firm is such a small portion of the total market that it can have no effect on price. Consequently it takes the price as given, and hence its perceived demand curve is perfectly elastic. (244)

3. To determine the profit-maximizing output of a competitive firm, you must know price and marginal cost. (246)

4. Firms are interested in getting as much for themselves as they possibly can. Maximizing total profit does this. Maximizing profit per unit might yield very small total profits. (248)

5. If the firm in Figure 11-5 were producing 4 units, I would explain to it that the marginal cost of increasing output is only $12 and the marginal revenue is $35, so it should significantly expand output until 8, where the marginal cost equals the marginal revenue, or price. (251)

6. The diagram is drawn with the wrong profit-maximizing output and hence the wrong profit. Output is determined where marginal cost equals price and profit is the difference between the average total cost and price at that output, not at the output where marginal cost equals average total cost. The correct diagram is shown here. (252)

7. The marginal cost for airlines is significantly below average total cost. Since they're recovering their average variable cost, they continue to operate. In the long run, if this continues, some airlines will be forced out of business. (253)

8. The costs for a firm include the normal costs, which in turn include a return for all factors. Thus it is worthwhile for a competitive firm to stay in business, since it is doing better, or at least as well, as it could in any other activity. *(255)*

9. Suddenly becoming the "in" thing to wear would cause the demand for berets to shift out to the right, pushing the price up in the short run. In the long run it would probably push the price down, as there probably are considerable economies of scale in the production of berets. *(256)*

10. A decline in demand pushed the short-run price of these burkhas down. In the long run, however, once a number of burkha makers go out of business, the price of burkhas should eventually move back to approximately where it was before the decline, assuming constant returns to scale. *(257)*

12 MONOPOLY

After reading this chapter, you should be able to:

- Summarize how and why the decisions facing a monopolist differ from the collective decisions of competing firms.

- Explain why *MC = MR* maximizes total profit for a monopolist.

- Determine a monopolist's price, output, and profit graphically and numerically.

- Show graphically the welfare loss from monopoly.

- Explain why a price-discriminating monopolist will earn more profit than a normal monopolist.

- Explain why there would be no monopoly without barriers to entry.

- List three normative arguments against monopoly.

> Monopoly is business at the end of its journey.
>
> —*Henry Demarest Lloyd*

In Chapter 11 we considered perfect competition. We now move to the other end of the spectrum: monopoly. **Monopoly** is *a market structure in which one firm makes up the entire market*. It is the polar opposite to competition. It is a market structure in which the firm faces no competitive pressure from other firms.

Monopolies exist because of barriers to entry into a market that prevent competition. These can be legal barriers (as in the case where a firm has a patent that prevents other firms from entering), sociological barriers where entry is prevented by custom or tradition, natural barriers where the firm has a unique ability to produce what other firms can't duplicate, or technological barriers where the size of the market can support only one firm.

THE KEY DIFFERENCE BETWEEN A MONOPOLIST AND A PERFECT COMPETITOR

A key question we want to answer in this chapter is: How does a monopolist's decision differ from the collective decision of competing firms (i.e., from the competitive solution)? Answering that question brings out a key difference between a competitive firm and a monopoly. Since a competitive firm is too small to affect the price, it does not take into account the effect of its output decision on the price it receives. A competitive firm's marginal revenue (the additional revenue it receives from selling an additional unit of output) is the given market price. A monopolistic firm takes into account that its output decision can affect price; its marginal revenue is not its price. A monopolistic firm will reason: "If I increase production, the price I can get for each unit sold will fall, so I had better be careful about how much I increase production."

Let's consider an example. Say your drawings in the margins of this book are seen by a traveling art critic who decides you're the greatest thing since Rembrandt, or at least since Andy Warhol. Carefully he tears each page out of the book, mounts them on special paper, and numbers them: Doodle Number 1 (Doodle While Contemplating Demand), Doodle Number 2 (Doodle While Contemplating Production), and so on.

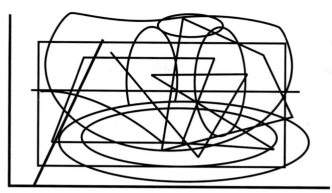

Doodle Number 27: Contemplating Costs

All told, he has 100. He figures, with the right advertising and if you're a hit on the art circuit, he'll have a monopoly in your doodles. He plans to sell them for $20,000 each: He gets 50 percent, you get 50 percent. That's $1 million for you. You tell him, "Hey, man! I can doodle my way through the entire book. I'll get you 500 doodles. Then I get $5 million and you get $5 million."

The art critic has a pained look on his face. He says, "You've been doodling when you should have been studying. Your doodles are worth $20,000 each only if they're rare. If there are 500, they're worth $1,000 each. And if it becomes known that you can turn them out that fast, they'll be worth nothing. I won't be able to limit quantity at all, and my monopoly will be lost. So obviously we must figure out some way that you won't doodle anymore—and study instead. Oh, by the way, did you know that the price of an artist's work goes up significantly when he or she dies? Hmm?" At that point you decide to forget doodling and to start studying, and to remember always that increasing production doesn't necessarily make suppliers better off.

As we saw in Chapter 11, competitive firms do not take advantage of that insight. Each individual competitive firm, responding to its self-interest, is not doing what is in the interest of the firms collectively. In competitive markets, as one supplier is pitted against another, consumers benefit. In monopolistic markets, the firm faces no competitors and does what is in its best interest. Monopolists can see to it that the monopolists, not the consumers, benefit; perfectly competitive firms cannot.

Q-1 Why should you study rather than doodle?

Monopolists see to it that monopolists, not consumers, benefit.

A MODEL OF MONOPOLY

How much should the monopolistic firm choose to produce if it wants to maximize profit? To answer that we have to consider more carefully the effect that changing output has on the total profit of the monopolist. That's what we do in this section. First, we consider a numerical example; then we consider that same example graphically. The relevant information for our example is presented in Table 12-1.

DETERMINING THE MONOPOLIST'S PRICE AND OUTPUT NUMERICALLY

Table 12-1 shows the price, total revenue, marginal revenue, total cost, marginal cost, average total cost, and profit at various levels of production. It's similar to the table in Chapter 11 where we determined a competitive firm's output. The big difference is that marginal revenue changes as output changes and is not equal to the price. Why?

First, let's remember the definition of marginal revenue: Marginal revenue is the change in total revenue associated with a change in quantity. In this example, if a

Table 12-1 Monopolistic Profit Maximization

1 Quantity	2 Price	3 Total Revenue	4 Marginal Revenue	5 Total Cost	6 Marginal Cost	7 Average Total Cost	8 Profit
0	$36	$ 0		$ 47			$−47
			$33		$ 1		
1	33	33		48		$48.00	−15
			27		2		
2	30	60		50		25.00	10
			21		4		
3	27	81		54		18.00	27
			15		8		
4	24	96		62		15.50	34
			9		16		
5	21	105		78		15.60	27
			3		24		
6	18	108		102		17.00	6
			−3		40		
7	15	105		142		20.29	−37
			−9		56		
8	12	96		198		24.75	−102
			−15		80		
9	9	81		278		30.89	−197

monopolist increases output from 4 to 5, the price it can charge falls from $24 to $21 and its revenue increases from $96 to $105, so marginal revenue is $9. Marginal revenue of increasing output from 4 to 5 for the monopolist reflects two changes: a $21 gain in revenue from selling the 5th unit and a $12 decline in revenue because the monopolist must lower the price on the previous 4 units it produces by $3 a unit, from $24 to $21. This highlights the key characteristic of a monopolist—its output decision affects its price. Because an increase in output lowers the price on all previous units, a monopolist's marginal revenue is always below its price. Comparing columns 2 and 4, you can confirm that this is true.

> A monopolist's marginal revenue is always below its price.

Now let's see if the monopolist will increase production from 4 to 5 units. The marginal revenue of increasing output from 4 to 5 is $9, and the marginal cost of doing so is $13. Since marginal cost exceeds marginal revenue, increasing production from 4 to 5 will reduce total profit and the monopolist will not increase production. If it decreases output from 4 to 3, where MC < MR, the revenue it loses ($15) exceeds the reduction in costs ($8). It will not reduce output from 4 to 3. Since it cannot increase total profit by increasing output to 5 or decreasing output to 3, it is maximizing output at 4 units.

> Q-2 In Table 12-1, explain why 4 is the profit-maximizing output.

As you can tell from the table, profits are highest ($34) at 4 units of output and a price of $24. At 3 units of output and a price of $27, the firm has total revenue of $81 and total cost of $54, yielding a profit of $27. At 5 units of output and a price of $21, the firm has a total revenue of $105 and a total cost of $78, also for a profit of $27. The highest profit it can make is $34, which the firm earns when it produces 4 units. This is its profit-maximizing level.

Here's a trick to help you graph the marginal revenue curve. The MR line starts at the same point on the price axis as does a linear demand curve, but it intersects the quantity axis at a point half the distance from where the demand curve intersects the quantity axis. (If the demand curve isn't linear, you can use the same trick if you use lines tangent to the curved demand curve.) So you can extend the demand curve to the two axes and measure halfway on the quantity axis (3 in the graph below). Then draw a line from where the demand curve intersects the price axis to that halfway mark. That line is the marginal revenue curve.

DETERMINING THE MONOPOLIST'S PRICE AND OUTPUT GRAPHICALLY

The monopolist's output decision can also be seen graphically. Figure 12-1 graphs the table's information into a demand curve, a marginal revenue curve, and a marginal cost curve. The marginal cost curve is a graph of the change in the firm's total cost as it changes output. It's the same curve as we saw in our discussion of perfect competition. The marginal revenue curve tells us the change in total revenue when quantity changes. It is graphed by plotting and connecting the points given by quantity and marginal revenue in Table 12-1.

The marginal revenue curve for a monopolist is new, so let's consider it a bit more carefully. It tells us the additional revenue the firm will get by expanding output. It is a downward-sloping curve that begins at the same point as the demand curve but has a steeper slope. In this example, marginal revenue is positive up until the firm produces 6 units. Then marginal revenue is negative; after 6 units the firm's total revenue decreases when it increases output.

Notice specifically the relationship between the demand curve (which is the average revenue curve) and the marginal revenue curve. Since the demand curve is downward-sloping, the marginal revenue curve is below the average revenue curve. (Remember, if the average curve is falling, the marginal curve must be below it.)

Having plotted these curves, let's ask the same questions as we did before: What output should the monopolist produce, and what price can it charge? In answering those questions, the key curves to look at are the marginal cost curve and the marginal revenue curve.

MR = MC *Determines the Profit-Maximizing Output*   The monopolist uses the general rule that any firm must follow to maximize profit: Produce the quantity at which MC = MR. If you think about it, it makes sense that the point where marginal revenue equals marginal cost determines the profit-maximizing output. If the marginal revenue is below the marginal cost, it makes sense to reduce production. Doing so decreases marginal cost and increases marginal revenue. When MR < MC, reducing output increases total profit. If marginal cost is below marginal revenue, you should

Q-3   In the graph below, indicate the monopolist's profit-maximizing level of output and the price it would charge.

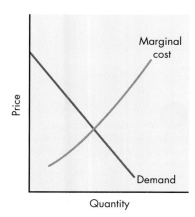

Figure 12-1   Determining the Monopolist's Price and Output Graphically

The profit-maximizing output is determined where the MC curve intersects the MR curve. To determine the price (at which MC = MR) that would be charged if this industry were a monopolist with the same cost structure, we first find that output and then extend a line to the demand curve, in this case finding a price of $24. This price is higher than the competitive price, $20.50, and the quantity, 4, is lower than the competitor's quantity, 5.17.

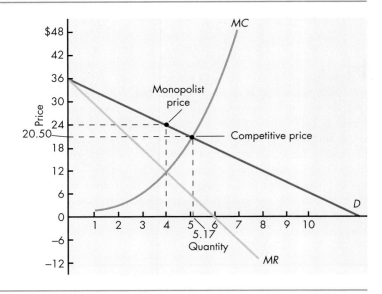

The general rule that any firm must follow to maximize profit is: Produce at an output level at which MC = MR.

increase production because total profit will rise. If the marginal revenue is equal to marginal cost, it does not make sense to increase or reduce production. So the monopolist should produce at the output level where MC = MR. As you can see, the output the monopolist chooses is 4 units, the same output that we determined numerically.[1] This leads to the following insights:

If MR > MC, the monopolist gains profit by increasing output.

If MR < MC, the monopolist gains profit by decreasing output.

If MC = MR, the monopolist is maximizing profit.

Thus, MR = MC is the profit-maximizing rule for a monopolist.

The Price a Monopolist Will Charge   The MR = MC condition determines the quantity a monopolist produces; in turn, that quantity determines the price the firm will charge. A monopolist will charge the maximum price consumers are willing to pay for that quantity. Since the demand curve tells us what consumers will pay for a given quantity, to find the price a monopolist will charge you must extend the quantity line up to the demand curve. We do so in Figure 12-1 and see that the profit-maximizing output level of 4 allows a monopolist to charge a price of $24.

COMPARING MONOPOLY AND PERFECT COMPETITION

For a competitive industry, the horizontal summation of firms' marginal cost curves is the market supply curve.[2] Output for a perfectly competitive industry would be 5.17, and price would be $20.50, as Figure 12-1 shows. The monopolist's output was 4 and its

Q-4   Why does a monopolist produce less output than would perfectly competitive firms in the same industry?

---

[1]This could not be seen precisely in Table 12-1 since the table is for discrete jumps and does not tell us the marginal cost and marginal revenue exactly at 4; it only tells us the marginal cost and marginal revenue ($8 and $15, respectively) of moving from 3 to 4 and the marginal cost and marginal revenue ($16 and $9, respectively) of moving from 4 to 5. If small adjustments (1/100 of a unit or so) were possible, the marginal cost and marginal revenue precisely at 4 would be $12. Because drawing the curve implicitly assumes we can make very small changes, the graphs of the marginal revenue curve and marginal cost curve will intersect at an output of 4 and a marginal cost and marginal revenue of $12.
[2]The above statement has some qualifications best left to intermediate classes.

Figure 12-2 (a, b, c, and d) Finding the Monopolist's Price and Output
Determining a monopolist's price and output can be tricky. The text discusses the steps shown in this exhibit. To make sure you understand, try to go through the steps on your own, and then check your work with the text.

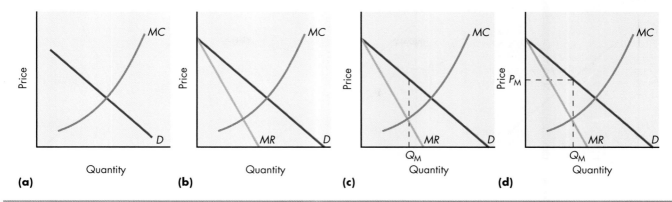

price was $24. So, if a competitive market is made into a monopoly, you can see that output would be lower and price would be higher. The reason is that the monopolist takes into account the effect that restricting output has on price.

Equilibrium output for the monopolist, like equilibrium output for the competitor, is determined by the MC = MR condition, but because the monopolist's marginal revenue is below its price, its equilibrium output is different from a competitive market.

AN EXAMPLE OF FINDING OUTPUT AND PRICE

We've covered a lot of material quickly, so it's probably helpful to go through an example slowly and carefully review the reasoning process. Here's the problem:

Say that a monopolist with marginal cost curve MC faces a demand curve D in Figure 12-2(a). Determine the price and output the monopolist would choose.

The first step is to draw the marginal revenue curve, since we know that a monopolist's profit-maximizing output level is determined where MC = MR. We do that in Figure 12-2(b), remembering the trick in the box on page 267 of extending our demand curve back to the vertical and horizontal axes and then bisecting the horizontal axis.

The second step is to determine where MC = MR. Having found that point, we extend a line up to the demand curve and down to the quantity axis to determine the output the monopolist chooses, Q_M. We do this in Figure 12-2(c).

Finally we see where the quantity line intersects the demand curve. Then we extend a horizontal line from that point to the price axis, as in Figure 12-2(d). This determines the price the monopolist will charge, P_M.

PROFITS AND MONOPOLY

The monopolist's profit can be determined only by comparing average total cost to price. So before we can determine profit, we need to add another curve: the average total cost curve. As we saw with a perfect competitor, it's important to follow the correct sequence when finding profit:

- First, draw the firm's marginal revenue curve.
- Second, determine the output the monopolist will produce by the intersection of the marginal cost and marginal revenue curves.

Figure 12-3 (a, b, and c)   The Monopolist Makes a Profit

(a)   (b)   (c)

- Third, determine the price the monopolist will charge for that output. (Remember, the price it will charge depends on the demand curve.)
- Fourth, determine the monopolist's profit (loss) by subtracting average total cost from average revenue (P) at that level of output and multiplying by the chosen output.

If price exceeds average total cost at the output it chooses, the monopolist will make a profit. If price equals average total cost, the monopolist will make no profit (but it will make a normal return). If price is less than average cost, the monopolist will incur a loss: Total cost exceeds total revenue.

A MONOPOLIST MAKING A PROFIT

I consider the case of a profit in Figure 12-3, going through the steps slowly. The monopolist's demand, marginal cost, and average total cost curves are presented in Figure 12-3(a). Our first step is to draw the marginal revenue curve, which has been added in Figure 12-3(b). The second step is to find the output level at which marginal cost equals marginal revenue. From that point draw a vertical line to the horizontal (quantity) axis. That intersection tells us the monopolist's output, Q_M in Figure 12-3(b). The third step is to find what price the monopolist will charge at that output. We do so by extending the vertical line to the demand curve (point A) and then extending a horizontal line over to the price axis. Doing so gives price, P_M. Our fourth step is to determine the average total cost at that quantity. We do so by seeing where our vertical line at the chosen output intersects the average total cost curve (point B). That tells us the monopolist's average cost at its chosen output.

To determine profit, we extend lines from where the quantity line intersects the demand curve (point A) and the average total cost curve (point B) to the price axis in Figure 12-3(c). The resulting shaded rectangle in Figure 12-3(c) represents the monopolist's profit.

A MONOPOLIST BREAKING EVEN AND MAKING A LOSS

In Figure 12-4 we consider two other average total cost curves to show you that a monopolist may make a loss or no profit as well as an economic profit. In Figure 12-4(a)

Q-5 Indicate the profit that the monopolist shown in the graph below earns.

FINDING A MONOPOLIST'S OUTPUT, PRICE, AND PROFIT

To find a monopolist's level of output, price, and profit, follow these four steps:

1. Draw the marginal revenue curve.

2. Determine the output the monopolist will produce: The profit-maximizing level of output is where MR and MC curves intersect.

3. Determine the price the monopolist will charge: Extend a line from where MR = MC up to the

demand curve. Where this line intersects the demand curve is the monopolist's price.

4. Determine the profit the monopolist will earn: Subtract the ATC from price at the profit-maximizing level of output to get profit per unit. Multiply profit per unit by quantity of output to get total profit.

(a)   Zero profit   **(b)   Loss**

Figure 12-4 (a and b)   Other Monopoly Cases
Depending on where the ATC curve falls, a monopolist can make a profit, break even (as in (a)), or make a loss (as in (b)) in the short run. In the long run, a monopolist who is making a loss will get out of business.

the monopolist is making zero profit; in Figure 12-4(b) it's making a loss. Whether a firm is making a profit, zero profit, or a loss depends on average total costs relative to price. So clearly in the short run a monopolist can be making either a profit or a loss, or it can be breaking even.

Most of you, if you've been paying attention, will say, "Sure, in the model monopolists might not make a profit, but in the real world monopolists are making a killing." And it is true that numerous monopolists make a killing. But many more monopolists just break even or lose money. Each year the U.S. Patent Office issues about 175,000 patents. A **patent** is *legal protection of a technical innovation that gives the person holding it sole right to use that innovation*—in other words, it gives the holder a monopoly to produce a good. Most patented goods make a loss; in fact, the cost of getting the patent often exceeds the revenues from selling the product.

Each year the Home Shopping Network (HSN) considers thousands of products, and only a very few actually make it onto the network. Let's consider an example—the self-stirring pot. It was a pot with a battery-operated stirrer attached to its lid. The stirrer was designed to prevent the bottom of the pot from burning. Unfortunately for the inventor, HSN considered the cost (even after economies of scale were taken into account) far more than what people would be willing to pay and therefore decided not to

Figure 12-5   The Welfare Loss from Monopoly
The welfare loss from a monopoly is represented by the triangles B and D. The rectangle C is a transfer from consumer surplus to the monopolist. The area A represents the opportunity cost of diverted resources. This is not a loss to society since the resources will be used in producing other goods.

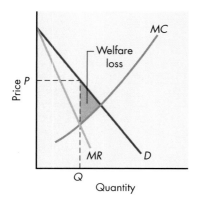

Q-6 Why is area C in Figure 12-5 not considered a loss from monopoly?

The welfare loss from monopoly is a triangle, as in the graph below. It is not the loss that most people consider. They are often interested in normative losses that the graph does not capture.

include the pot in its offerings. The inventor had a monopoly on the production and sale of the self-stirring pot, but only a loss to show. Examples like this can be multiplied by the thousands. The reality for many monopolies is that their costs exceed their revenues, so they make a loss.

THE WELFARE LOSS FROM MONOPOLY

As we saw above, there is no necessary reason to believe that a monopolist is guaranteed a profit. Thus, profits can't be the primary reason that the economic model we're using sees monopoly as bad. If not because of profits, then what standard is the economic model using to conclude that monopoly is undesirable?

One reason can be seen by reconsidering graphically the normal monopolist equilibrium and perfectly competitive equilibrium in reference to producer and consumer surplus. This we do in Figure 12-5. In a competitive equilibrium, the total consumer and producer surplus is the area between the demand curve and the marginal cost curve up to market equilibrium quantity Q_C. The monopolist reduces output to Q_M and raises price to P_M. The benefit lost to society from reducing output from Q_C to Q_M is measured by the area under the demand curve between output levels Q_C and Q_M. That area is represented by the shaded areas labeled A, B, and D. Some of that loss is regained. Society gains the opportunity cost of the resources that are freed up from reducing production—the value of the resources in their next-best use indicated by the shaded area A. So the net cost to society of decreasing output from Q_C to Q_M is represented by areas B and D. (Area C is the monopolist's profit. It is neither a gain nor a loss to society. It represents a transfer of income from the consumer to the monopolist that would occur with a rise in price. Since both monopolist and consumer are members of society, the gain and loss net out.) The triangular areas B and D are the net cost to society from the existence of monopoly.

As discussed in Chapter 7, this area designated by B and D is often called the *deadweight loss* or *welfare loss triangle*. That welfare cost of monopoly is one of the reasons economists oppose monopoly. That cost can be summarized as follows: Because monopolies charge a price higher than marginal cost, people's decisions don't reflect the true cost to society. Price exceeds marginal cost. Because price exceeds marginal cost, people's choices are distorted; they choose to consume less of the monopolist's output and more of some other output than they would if markets were competitive. That

Monopoly occurs when there is a single seller; there are also markets in which there is a single buyer. Such markets are called monopsonies. An example of a monopsony is a "company town" in which a single firm is the only employer. Whereas a monopolist takes into account the fact that if it sells more it will lower the market price, a monopsonist takes into account the fact that it will raise the market prices if it buys more. Thus, it buys less and pays less than would a market with an equivalent number of competitive buyers.

---

distinction means that the marginal cost of increasing output is lower than the marginal benefit of increasing output, so there's a welfare loss.

THE PRICE-DISCRIMINATING MONOPOLIST

So far we've considered monopolists that charge the same price to all consumers. Let's consider what would happen if our monopolist suddenly gained the ability to **price-discriminate**—*to charge different prices to different individuals or groups of individuals* (for example, students as compared to businesspeople). If a monopolist can identify groups of customers who have different elasticities of demand, separate them in some way, and limit their ability to resell its product between groups, it can charge each group a different price. Specifically, it could charge consumers with less elastic demands a higher price and individuals with more elastic demands a lower price. By doing so, it will increase total profit. Suppose, for instance, Megamovie knew that at $6 it would sell 1,000 movie tickets and at $3 a ticket it would sell 1,500 tickets. Assuming Megamovie could show the film without cost, it would maximize profits by charging $6 to 1,000 moviegoers, earning a total profit of $6,000. If, however, it could somehow attract the additional 500 viewers at $3 a ticket without reducing the price to the first 1,000 moviegoers, it could raise its profit by $1,500, to $7,500. As you can see, a price-discriminating monopolist increases its profit.

We see many examples of price discrimination in the real world:

1. *Movie theaters give discounts to senior citizens and children.* Movie theaters charge senior citizens and children a lower price because they have a more elastic demand for movies.

2. *Airline Super Saver fares include Saturday-night stayovers.* This is a method of price discrimination. Businesspeople who have highly inelastic demands generally aren't willing to stay over a Saturday night, so they're charged a high price while tourists and leisure travelers who have a far more elastic demands and who are willing to stay over a Saturday night are charged a lower price.

3. *Automobiles are seldom sold at list price.* Once again we have an example of price discrimination. Salespeople can size up the customer and determine the customer's elasticity. People who haven't done the research and don't know that selling at 10 percent off list is normal (i.e., people with inelastic demands) pay higher prices than people who search out all the alternatives (people with elastic demand).

To see whether you are following the reasoning, try to provide a price discrimination explanation for the following:

When a monopolist price-discriminates, it charges individuals high up on the demand curve higher prices and those low on the demand curve lower prices.

Web Note 12.1
Divide and Conquer

Automobiles are seldom sold at list price.
Vincent Hobbs/Superstock.

Q.7 Why does a price-discriminating monopolist make a higher profit than a normal monopolist?

1. Theaters have special rates on Monday and Tuesday nights.
2. Retail tire companies run special sales about half the time.
3. Restaurants generally make most of their profit on alcoholic drinks and just break even on food.
4. College-town stores often give students discounts.

Now that you've answered those, see if you can extend your understanding by listing the central characteristics of markets that make them highly susceptible to price discrimination.

If you answered, "The market demand is made up of distinguishable individuals who have different demand elasticities," you've got it.

BARRIERS TO ENTRY AND MONOPOLY

The standard model of monopoly just presented is simple, but, like many things simple, it hides some issues. One issue the standard model of monopoly hides is in this question: What prevents other firms from entering the monopolist's market? You should be able to answer that question relatively quickly. If a monopolist exists, it must exist due to some type of barrier to entry (a social, political, or economic impediment that prevents firms from entering the market). Three important barriers to entry are natural ability, economies of scale, and government restrictions. In the absence of barriers to entry, the monopoly would face competition from other firms, which would erode its monopoly.

If there were no barriers to entry, profit-maximizing firms would always compete away monopoly profits.

This recognition is one of the main reasons why economists generally support free international trade and oppose tariffs. Tariffs are a barrier to entry to foreign firms and thus provide monopoly power to U.S. firms, allowing them to charge the consumer more than they otherwise could.

Studying how these barriers to entry are established enriches the standard model and lets us distinguish different types of monopoly.

Web Note 12.2
Diamonds are Forever

NATURAL ABILITY

A barrier to entry that might exist is that a firm is better at producing a good than anyone else. It has unique abilities that make it more efficient than all other firms. The barrier to entry in such a case is the firm's natural ability. The defense attorneys in the Microsoft antitrust case argued that it was Microsoft's superior products that led to its capture of 90 percent of the market.

Monopolies based on ability usually don't provoke the public's ire. Often in the public's mind such monopolies are "just monopolies." The standard economic model doesn't distinguish between a "just" and an "unjust" monopoly. The just/unjust distinction raises the question of whether a firm has acquired a monopoly based on its ability or on certain unfair tactics such as initially pricing low to force competitive companies out of business but then pricing high. Many public debates over monopoly focus on such normative issues, about which the economists' standard model has nothing to say.

ECONOMIES OF SCALE

An alternative reason why a barrier to entry might exist is that there are significant economies of scale. If sufficiently large economies of scale exist, it would be inefficient to have two producers since if each produced half of the output, neither could take advantage of the economies of scale. Such industries are called natural monopolies. A **natural monopoly** is *an industry in which a single firm can produce at a lower cost than*

In a natural monopoly a single firm can produce at a lower cost than can two or more firms.

In Chapter 7 you learned how effective price ceilings increase market price, reduce output, and reduce the welfare of society. With any type of price control in a competitive market, some trades that individuals would like to have made are prevented. Thus, with competitive markets, price controls of any type are seen as generally bad (though they might have some desirable income distribution effects).

When there is monopoly the argument is not so simple. The monopoly price is higher than the marginal cost and society loses out; monopolies create their own deadweight loss. In the monopoly case price controls can actually lower price, increase output, and reduce deadweight loss. Going through the reasoning why provides a good review of the tools.

The exhibit below shows you the argument.

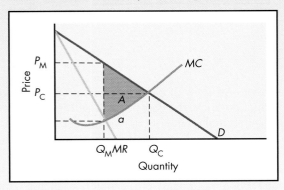

The monopoly sets its quantity where $MR = MC$. Output is Q_M and price is P_M; the welfare loss is the blue shaded triangle A. Now say that the government comes in and places a price ceiling on the monopolist at the competitive price, P_C. Since the monopolist is compelled by law to charge price P_C, it no longer has an incentive to restrict output. Put another way, the price ceiling—the dashed line P_C—becomes the monopolist's demand curve and marginal revenue curve. (Remember, when the demand curve is horizontal, the marginal revenue curve is identical to the demand curve.) Given the law, the monopolist's best option still is to produce where $MC = MR$, but that means charging price P_C and increasing output to Q_C. As you can see

from the exhibit, the price ceiling causes output to rise and price to fall.

If, when there is monopoly, price controls can increase efficiency, why don't economists advocate price controls more than they do? Let's review four reasons why.

1. For price controls to increase output and lower price, the price has to be set within the right price range—below the monopolist's price and above the price where the monopolist's marginal cost and marginal revenue curves intersect. It is unclear politically that such a price will be chosen. Even if regulators could pick the right price initially, markets may change. Demand may increase or decrease, putting the controlled price outside the desired range.

2. All markets are dynamic. The very existence of monopoly profits will encourage other firms in other industries to try to break into that market, keeping the existing monopolist on its toes. Because of this dynamic element, in some sense no market is ever a pure textbook monopoly.

3. Price controls create their own deadweight loss in the form of rent seeking. Price controls do not eliminate monopoly pressures. The monopolist has a big incentive to regain its ability to set its own price and will lobby hard to remove price controls. Economists see resources spent to regain their monopoly price as socially wasteful.

4. Economists distrust government. Governments have their own political agendas—there is no general belief among economists that governments will try to set the price at the competitive level. Once one opens up the price control gates in cases of monopoly, it will be difficult to stop government from using price controls in competitive markets.

The arguments are, of course, more complicated, and will be discussed in more detail, but this should give you a good preview of some of the policy arguments to come in later chapters.

can two or more firms. A natural monopoly will occur when the technology is such that indivisible setup costs are so large that average total costs fall within the range of possible outputs. I demonstrate that case in Figure 12-6(a).

Figure 12-6 (a and b)   A Natural Monopolist

This graph in (**a**) shows the average cost curve for a natural monopoly. One firm producing Q_1 would have average cost of C_1. If total production remains at Q_1 and another firm enters the market, sharing quantity produced, each firm would produce $Q_{1/2}$ goods at average cost C_2. If three firms each produced $Q_{1/3}$, the average cost for each would be C_3. In a case of a natural monopoly, as the number of firms in the industry increases, the average cost of producing a fixed number of units increases.

The graph in (**b**) shows that a natural monopolist would produce Q_M and charge a price P_M. It will earn a profit shown by the orange shaded box. If the monopolist were required to charge a price equal to marginal cost, P_C, it would incur a loss shown by the blue shaded box.

(a)

(b)

Q.8 Why is the competitive price impossible for an industry that exhibits strong economies of scale?

If one firm produces Q_1, its cost per unit is C_1. If two firms each produce half that amount, $Q_{1/2}$, so that their total production is Q_1, the cost per unit will be C_2, which is significantly higher than C_1. In cases of natural monopoly, as the number of firms in the industry increases, the average total cost of producing a fixed number of units increases. For example, if there were three firms in the industry and they each had a third of the market, each firm would have an average cost of C_3.

Until the 1990s local telephone service was a real-world example of such a natural monopoly. It made little sense to have two sets of telephone lines going into people's houses. I say "until recently" because technology changes and now, with wireless communications and cable connections, the technical conditions that made local telephone service a natural monopoly are changing. Such change is typical; natural monopolies are only natural given a technology.

A natural monopoly can also occur when a single industry standard is more efficient than multiple standards, even when that standard is owned by one firm. An example is the operating system for computers. It is much more efficient (because the communication among users is easier) for there to be a single standard rather than multiple standards.

From a welfare standpoint natural monopolies are different from other types of monopolies. In the case of a natural monopoly, even if a single firm makes some monopoly profit, the price it charges may still be lower than the price two firms making normal profit would charge because its average total costs will be lower. In the case of a natural monopoly not only is there no welfare loss from monopoly but there can actually be a welfare gain since a single firm producing is so much more efficient than many firms producing. Such natural monopolies are often organized as public utilities. For example, most towns have a single water department supplying water to residents.

Figure 12-6(b) shows the profit-maximizing level of output and price that a natural monopolist would choose. To show the profit-maximizing level of output, I've added a marginal cost curve that is below the average total cost curve and also falling. (If you don't know why this must be the case, a review of costs is in order.) A natural monopolist uses the same $MC = MR$ rule that a monopolist uses to determine output. The monopolist will produce Q_M and charge a price P_M. Average total costs are C_M and the natural monopolist earns a profit shown by the orange shaded box.

Where natural monopoly exists, the perfectly competitive solution is impossible, since average total costs are not covered where $MC = P$. A monopolist required by government to charge the competitive price P_C, where $P = MC$, will incur a loss shown by the blue shaded box because marginal cost is always below average total cost. Some output restriction is necessary in order for production to be feasible. In such cases monopolies are often preferred by the public as long as they are regulated by government. I will discuss the issues of regulating natural monopolies in Chapter 14.

GOVERNMENT-CREATED MONOPOLIES

A third reason monopolies can exist is that they're created by government. The support of laissez-faire by Classical economists such as Adam Smith and their opposition to monopoly arose in large part in reaction to those government-created monopolies, not in reaction to any formal analysis of welfare loss from monopoly.

NORMATIVE VIEWS OF MONOPOLY

Many laypeople's views of government-created monopoly reflect the same normative judgments that Classical economists made. Classical economists considered, and much of the lay public considers, such monopolies unfair and inconsistent with liberty. Monopolies prevent people from being free to enter whatever business they want and are undesirable on normative grounds. In this view, government-created monopolies are simply wrong.

This normative argument against government-created monopoly doesn't extend to all types of government-created monopolies. The public accepts certain types of government-created monopoly that it believes have overriding social value. An example is patents. To encourage research and development of new products, government gives out patents for a wide variety of innovations, such as genetic engineering, Xerox machines, and cans that can be opened without a can opener.

Q.9 If a patent is a monopoly, why does the government give out patents?

A second normative argument against monopoly is that the public doesn't like the income distributional effects of monopoly. Although, as we saw in our discussion of monopoly, monopolists do not always earn an economic profit, they often do, which means that the monopoly might transfer income in a way that the public (whose normative views help determine society's policy toward monopoly) doesn't like. This distributional effect of monopoly based on normative views of who deserves income is another reason many laypeople oppose monopoly: They believe it transfers income from "deserving" consumers to "undeserving" monopolists.

A third normative reason people oppose government-created monopoly that isn't captured by the standard model of monopoly is that the possibility of government-created monopoly encourages people to spend a lot of their time in political pursuits trying to get the government to favor them with a monopoly, and less time doing "productive" things. It causes *rent-seeking* activities in which people spend resources to gain monopolies for themselves.

Possible economic profits from monopoly lead potential monopolists to spend money to get government to give them a monopoly.

Each of these arguments probably plays a role in the public's dislike of monopoly. As you can see, these real-world arguments blend normative judgments with objective analysis, making it difficult to arrive at definite conclusions. Most real-world problems require this blending, making applied economic analysis difficult. The economist must interpret the normative judgments about what people want to achieve and explain how public policy can be designed to achieve those desired ends.

Let's now consider how economic theory might be used to analyze monopoly and to suggest how government might deal with that monopoly.

GOVERNMENT POLICY AND MONOPOLY: AIDS DRUGS

Let's consider the problem of acquired immune deficiency syndrome (AIDS) and the combination of medicinal drugs, including azidothymidine (AZT), used to treat it. AZT, used in combination with other drugs in mixtures called cocktails, is believed to arrest AIDS completely. These drugs were developed by a small group of pharmaceutical companies, which own patents on them, giving them a monopoly. Patents are given on medicine to encourage firms to find cures for various diseases. The monopoly the patent gives them lets them charge a high price so that the firms can expect to make a profit from their research. Whether such patents are in the public interest isn't an issue, since the patent has already been granted.

What is an issue is what to do about these drugs. Currently demand for them is highly inelastic, so the price pharmaceutical companies can charge is high even though their marginal cost of producing them is low. Whether they are making a profit depends on their cost of development. But since that cost is already spent, that's irrelevant to the current marginal cost; development cost affects their *ATC* curve, not their marginal cost curve. Thus, the pharmaceutical companies are charging an enormously high price for drugs that may help save people's lives and that cost them a very small amount to produce.

What, if anything, should the government do? Some people have suggested that the government regulate the price of the drugs, requiring the firms to charge only their marginal cost. This would make society better off. But most economists have a problem with that policy. They point out that doing so will significantly reduce the incentives for drug companies to research new drugs. One reason drug companies spend billions of dollars for drug research is their expectation that they'll be able to make large profits if they're successful. If drug companies expect the government to come in and take away their monopoly when they're successful, they won't search for cures. So forcing these pharmaceuticals to charge a low price for their drugs would help AIDS victims, but it would hurt people suffering from diseases that are currently being researched and that might be researched in the future. So there's a strong argument not to regulate.

But the thought of people dying when a cheap cure—or at least a partially effective treatment—is available is repulsive to me and to many others. African countries, where 70 percent of all people infected with the virus that causes AIDS live, have threatened to license production of these drugs to local manufacturers and make them available at cost. U.S. pharmaceutical companies pressured the United States to cut off foreign aid if the African countries carried out their threat. That did not provide them with good public relations and the major drug companies felt the pressure, leading them to make drugs for AIDS available to AIDS patients in poor nations at a much lower price than they do to others (an example of price discrimination).

An alternative policy suggested by economic theory is for the government to buy the patents and allow anyone to make the drugs so their price would approach their marginal cost. Admittedly, this would be expensive. It would cause negative incentive effects, as the government would have to increase taxes to cover the buyout's costs. But this approach would avoid the problem of the regulatory approach and achieve the same ends. However, it would also introduce new problems, such as determining which patents the government should buy.

Q-10 The medicinal drug tetracycline sold for animals costs about ½₀ as much as the same drug sold for human beings. What is the likely explanation?

Whether such a buyout policy makes sense remains to be seen, but in debating such issues the power of the simple monopoly model becomes apparent.

CONCLUSION

We've come to the end of the presentation of the formal models of perfect competition and monopoly. Working through the models takes a lot of effort, but it's effort well spent. In Chapter 1, I quoted Einstein: "A theory should be as simple as possible, but not more so." This chapter's analysis isn't simple; it takes repetition, working through models, and doing thought experiments to get it down pat. But it's as simple as possible. Even so, it's extremely easy to make a foolish mistake, as I did in my Ph.D. oral examination when I was outlining an argument on the blackboard. ["*What* did you say the output would be for this monopolist, Mr. Colander?"] As I learned then, it takes long hours of working through the models again and again to get them right.

SUMMARY

- The price a monopolist charges is higher than that of a competitive market due to the restriction of output; a monopolist can make a profit in the long run.

- A monopolist's profit-maximizing output is where marginal revenue equals marginal cost.

- A monopolist can charge the maximum price consumers are willing to pay for the quantity the monopolist produces.

- To determine a monopolist's profit, first determine its output (where $MC = MR$). Then determine its price and average total cost at that output level. The difference between price and average total cost at the profit-maximizing level of output is profit per unit. Multiply this by output to find total profit.

- Because monopolists reduce output and charge a price that is higher than marginal cost, monopolies create a welfare loss to society.

- If a monopolist can (1) identify groups of customers who have different elasticities of demand, (2) separate them in some way, and (3) limit their ability to resell its product between groups, it can price discriminate.

- A price-discriminating monopolist earns more profit than a normal monopolist because it can charge a higher price to those with less elastic demands and a lower price to those with more elastic demands.

- Three important barriers to entry are natural ability, increasing returns to scale, and government restrictions.

- Natural monopolies exist in industries with strong economies of scale. Because their average total costs are always falling, it is more efficient for one firm to produce all the output.

- The competitive price is impossible in a natural monopoly because marginal cost is always below average total cost. No firm would enter an industry where not even normal (zero economic) profit can be made.

- Normative arguments against monopoly include the following: (1) monopolies are inconsistent with freedom, (2) the distributional effects of monopoly are unfair, and (3) monopolies encourage people to waste time and money trying to get monopolies.

KEY TERMS

monopoly (264)   natural monopoly (274)   patent (271)   price-discriminate (273)

QUESTIONS FOR THOUGHT AND REVIEW

1. Demonstrate graphically the profit-maximizing positions for a perfect competitor and a monopolist. How do they differ?

2. Monopolists differ from perfect competitors because monopolists make a profit. True or false? Why?

3. Why is marginal revenue below average revenue for a monopolist?

4. Explain the effects on college education of the development of a teaching machine that you plug into a student's brain and that makes the student understand everything. How would your answer differ if a college could monopolize production of this machine?

5. Say you place a lump sum tax (a tax that is treated as a fixed cost) on a monopolist. How will that affect her output and pricing decisions?

6. A monopolist is selling fish. But if the fish don't sell, they rot. What will be the likely elasticity at the point on the demand curve at which the monopolist sets the price?

7. When you buy a cheap computer printer or home fax you can sometimes get it for free after the rebate. Why would a firm sell you something for a zero price? (The answer isn't that it wants to be nice.)

8. In late 2001, the U.S. government threatened to disregard Bayer's patent of ciprofloxacin, the most effective drug to fight anthrax, and license the production of the drug to American drug companies to stockpile the drug in case of an anthrax epidemic. While the policy

would lower costs to the U.S. government of stockpiling the drug, it also would have other costs. What are those costs?

9. Provide a price discrimination argument for the existence of the four unexplained examples of price discrimination in the text.

10. Airlines are always running sales. On closer look, however, existing fares can be cheaper than restricted flights. What accounts for the practice of advertising "bargain" fares that may not be the lowest fare available? What conditions in the airline market make this practice possible?

11. Demonstrate the welfare loss created by a monopoly.

12. Will the welfare loss from a monopolist with a perfectly elastic marginal cost curve be greater or less than the welfare loss from a monopolist with an upward-sloping marginal cost curve?

13. In the late 1990s, the Government Accounting Office reported that airlines block new carriers at major airports. What effect does this have on fares and the number of flights at those airports? How much are airlines willing to spend to control the use of gates to block new carriers?

14. Copyrights provide authors with a monopoly. What effect would eliminating copyrights have on the price and output of textbooks? Should copyrights be eliminated?

15. How is efficiency related to the number of firms in an industry characterized by strong economies of scale?

PROBLEMS AND EXERCISES

1. A monopolist with a straight-line demand curve finds that it can sell two units at $12 each or 12 units at $2 each. Its fixed cost is $20 and its marginal cost is constant at $3 per unit.
   a. Draw the MC, ATC, MR, and demand curves for this monopolist.
   b. At what output level would the monopolist produce?
   c. At what output level would a perfectly competitive firm produce?

2. State what's wrong with the following graphs:

(c)   (d)

(a)   (b)

3. Wyeth-Ayerst Laboratories developed Norplant, a long-acting contraceptive, in the early 1990s. In the United States, the firm priced the contraceptive at $350, and in other countries, the firm priced it at $23.
   a. Why would the firm price it differently in different countries?
   b. Was the pricing fair?
   c. What do you think will happen to the price over time? Why?

4. Assume your city government has been contracting with a single garbage collection firm that has been granted an exclusive franchise, or sole right to pick up trash within the entire city limits. However, it has been proposed that the companies be allowed to compete for business with residents on an individual basis. The city government has estimated the price residents are willing to pay for various numbers of garbage collections per month and the total costs per resident as shown in the following table.

Pickup (Q)	Price per Pickup (Demand)	Total Revenue (TR)	Marginal Revenue (MR)	Total Cost (TC)	Marginal Cost (MC)	Average Total Cost (ATC)
0	$4.20	0	—	$ 3.20	—	—
1	3.80	____	____	4.20	____	____
2	3.40	____	____	5.60	____	____
3	3.00	____	____	7.80	____	____
4	2.60	____	____	10.40	____	____
5	2.20	____	____	13.40	____	____
6	1.90	____	____	16.80	____	____

a. What are the fixed costs per month of garbage collection per resident?

b. Considering that the current garbage collection firm the city has contracted with has a monopoly in garbage collection services, what is the current number of collections residents receive per month and the price charged residents for each collection? What is the economic profit received from each resident by the monopoly firm?

c. If competitive bidding were allowed and therefore a competitive market for garbage collection services developed, what would be the number of collections per month and the price charged residents per collection? What is the economic profit received from each resident by the competitive firms?

d. Based on the above analysis, should the city government allow competitive bidding? Why? Would you expect there to be any quality differences between the monopolistic and competitive trash collection firms?

5. Econocompany is under investigation by the U.S. Department of Justice for violating antitrust laws. The government decides that Econocompany has a natural monopoly and that, if it is to keep its business, it must sell at a price equal to marginal cost. Econocompany says that it can't do that and hires you to explain to the government why it can't.

a. You do so in reference to the following graph.

b. What price would it charge if it were unregulated?

c. What price would you advise that it should be allowed to charge?

6. New York City has issued 12,000 taxi licenses, called *medallions*, and has not changed that number since 1937.

a. What does that limitation likely do to the price of taxi medallions?

b. In the early 1990s, the New York City Taxi Commission promulgated a rule that required single-cab medallion owners to drive their cabs full-time. What will that rule do to the price of the medallion?

c. If New York City increased the number of medallions by 1,000, selling the additional 1,000 at the market rate, and gave half the proceeds to owners of existing medallions, what would happen to the price of medallions?

d. What would happen to the wealth of existing medallion owners?

WEB QUESTIONS

1. The Federal Communications Commission regulates interstate and international communications, including merger activity within industry. Go to the FCC website at www.fcc.gov and search for "monopoly." Select one document in support of and another opposed to a proposed merger between communication companies.

a. What reasons do consumers have for opposing the merger?

b. What reasons do consumers have for supporting the merger?

c. Does the theory of a monopolist found in the chapter support the reasons stated in your answers to a and b. Explain.

2. Go to the U.S. Patent and Trademark Office's homepage at www.ustpo.gov to answer the following questions:

a. What right does a patent give the holder of a patent? Can inventors produce and sell their inventions without patents?

b. What can a patent-holder expect to pay the Patent and Trademark office over the lifetime of the patent?

c. What is the length of a patent? Why do you believe government sets expiration dates for patents?

ANSWERS TO MARGIN QUESTIONS

1. If you doodle too much, your doodles will become worthless. Besides, if you want to pass the next test you have to study. (265)

2. At output 4, the marginal cost of $12 (between $8 and $16) equals the marginal revenue of $12 (between $15 and $9), making it the profit-maximizing output. It has the highest total profit, $34. (266)

3. To determine the profit-maximizing price and output, one must determine where the marginal revenue curve equals marginal cost. So one must first draw the marginal revenue curve and see where it intersects marginal cost. That intersection determines the quantity, as in the graph below. Carrying the line up to the demand curve determines the price. (267)

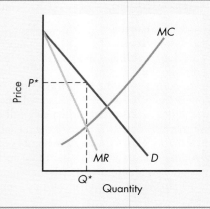

4. A monopolist produces less output than a perfectly competitive firm because it takes into account the fact that increasing output will lower the price of all previous units. (268)

5. To determine profit, follow the following four steps: (1) draw the marginal revenue curve, (2) find the level of output where MC = MR indicated in the graph in the next column by Q*, (3) find the price the monopolist would charge indicated by P* and extend a horizontal line from the demand curve at that price to the price axis, (4) determine the average total cost at Q* shown by C* and extend a horizontal line from the ATC curve at that cost to the price axis. The box created is the monopolist's profit. The profit is the shaded box shown in the graph below. (270)

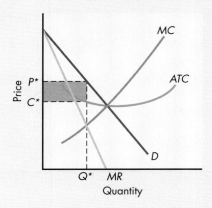

6. Area C represents the profit going to a monopolist. It is not considered a loss since, while consumers lose it, monopolists gain it. It is a redistribution of resources rather than an efficiency loss. (272)

7. A price-discriminating monopolist makes a greater profit than a normal monopolist because a price-discriminating monopolist is able to charge a higher price to those consumers who have less elastic demands. (274)

8. The marginal cost curve for an industry that exhibits strong economies of scale is always below average total costs. Therefore, the competitive price, where P = MC, will always result in losses for firms. Firms would not enter into such an industry and there would be no supply. (276)

9. The government gives out patents to encourage research and development of new products. This suggests that the public and government believe that certain monopolies have overriding social value. (277)

10. A likely explanation for medicinal drugs being sold at a much lower cost for animals than for human beings is differing elasticities of demand. The demand for drugs for human beings is highly inelastic, whereas the demand for medicinal drugs for animals is elastic. When there is a price-discriminating monopolist for these drugs, those with more inelastic demands are charged higher prices. (278)

The Algebra of Competitive and Monopolistic Firms

In the Appendix to Chapter 5, I presented the algebra relevant to supply and demand. To relate that algebra to competitive firms, all you must remember is that the market supply curve equals the marginal cost curve for the competitive industry. Let's review it briefly.

Say that marginal costs, and thus market supply, for the industry is given by

$$P = 2Q_S + 4$$

Let's also say that the market demand curve is

$$Q_D = 28 - \frac{1}{4}P$$

To determine equilibrium price and quantity in a competitive market, you must equate quantity supplied and quantity demanded and solve for price. First, rewrite the marginal cost equation with quantity supplied on the left:

$$Q_S = \frac{1}{2}MC - 2$$

Then set quantity demanded equal to quantity supplied and $MC = P$. Then solve for equilibrium price:

$$Q_S = Q_D \Rightarrow 28 - \frac{1}{4}P = \frac{1}{2}P - 2$$
$$112 - P = 2P - 8$$
$$3P = 120$$
$$P = 40$$

Thus, the equilibrium price is \$40. Competitive firms take this price as given and produce up until their marginal cost equals price. The industry as a whole produces 18 units.

Now let's consider the algebra relevant for a monopolistic firm. In the monopolistic case, supply and demand are not enough to determine where the monopolist will produce. The monopolist will produce where marginal revenue equals marginal cost. But, for the monopolist, the industry demand curve is the demand curve, which means that in order to determine where the monopolist will produce, we must determine the marginal revenue curve that goes along with the above demand curve. There are two ways to do that.

First, if you know calculus you can determine the marginal revenue curve in the following manner: Since marginal revenue tells us how much total revenue will change with each additional unit produced, you first specify the demand curve in terms of quantity produced.

$$P = 112 - 4Q$$

Since $TR = PQ$ we can multiply this by Q to get total revenue. Doing so gives us:

$$TR = PQ = 112Q - 4Q^2$$

To find marginal revenue, take the first derivative of total revenue with respect to Q.

$$P = 112 - 8Q$$

Second, if you don't know calculus, all you need to remember is the trick shown in a box in the chapter on how to graph the marginal revenue curve. Remember, the marginal revenue curve starts at the same price as the demand curve and bisects the quantity axis at one-half the value of the quantity axis intercept of the demand curve. The marginal revenue curve, because it bisects the quantity axis at one-half the value of the quantity axis intercept of the accompanying demand curve, must fall twice as fast as the market demand curve. That is, its slope is twice the slope of the market demand curve.

Knowing that its slope is twice the market demand curve slope, you can write the marginal revenue curve with the same price axis intercept as the demand curve and a slope of two times the slope of the demand curve. (Warning: this only works with linear demand curves.) The price-axis intercept of the demand curve is the value of P where Q equals 0: 112. The quantity-axis intercept of the demand curve is the value of Q where P equals 0: 28. So, the marginal revenue curve has a price-axis intercept at 112 and a quantity-axis intercept at 14. Mathematically, such a curve is represented by

$$P = 112 - (112/14)P$$

or

$$P = 112 - 8Q$$

Now that we've determined the monopolist's marginal revenue curve, we can determine its equilibrium quantity by setting $MR = MC$ and solving for Q. Doing so gives us:

$$112 - 8Q = 2Q + 4$$
$$-10Q = -108$$
$$Q = 10.8$$

The monopolist then charges the price consumers are willing to pay for that quantity. Mathematically, substitute 10.8 into the demand equation and solve for price:

$P = 112 - 4(10.8)$

$P = \$68.80$

Comparing the price and quantity produced by a monopolist and those of a competitive industry shows that the monopolist charges a higher price and produces a lower output.

QUESTIONS FOR THOUGHT AND REVIEW

1. The market demand curve is $Q_D = 50 - P$. The marginal cost curve is $MC = 4Q + 6$.
   a. Assuming the marginal cost curve is for a competitive industry as a whole, find the profit-maximizing level of output and price.
   b. Assuming the marginal cost curve is for only one firm which comprises the entire market, find the profit-maximizing level of output and price.
   c. Compare the two results.

2. The market demand curve is $Q_D = 160 - 4P$. A monopolist's total cost curve is $TC = 6Q^2 + 15Q + 50$.
   a. Find the profit-maximizing level of output and price for a monopolist.
   b. Find its average cost at that level of output.
   c. Find its profit at that level of output.

3. Suppose fixed costs for the monopolist in question 2 increases by 52.
   a. Find the profit-maximizing level of output and price for a monopolist.
   b. Find its average cost at that level of output.
   c. Find its profit at that level of output.

4. The market demand curve is $Q_D = 12 - \frac{1}{3}P$. Costs do not vary with output.
   a. Find the profit-maximizing level of output and price for a monopolist.
   b. Find the profit-maximizing level of output and price for a competitive industry.

MONOPOLISTIC COMPETITION, OLIGOPOLY, AND STRATEGIC PRICING

> Competition, you know, is a lot like chastity.
> It is widely praised, but alas, too little practiced.
>
> —*Carol Tucker*

After reading this chapter, you should be able to:

- Describe two methods of determining market structure.

- List the four distinguishing characteristics of monopolistic competition.

- Demonstrate graphically the equilibrium of a monopolistic competitor.

- State the central element of oligopoly.

- Explain why decisions in the cartel model depend on market share and decisions in the contestable market model depend on barriers to entry.

- Illustrate a strategic decision facing a duopolist using the prisoner's dilemma.

As soon as economists start talking about real-world competition, market structure becomes a focus of the discussion. **Market structure** refers to *the physical characteristics of the market within which firms interact*. It involves the number of firms in the market and the barriers to entry. Monopoly and competition are the two polar cases of market structure. Real-world markets generally fall in between, and it is essential to introduce briefly two market structures between perfect competition and monopoly: monopolistic competition and oligopoly. They not only provide you with a sense of how the models can apply to the real world but also help cement in your mind the concepts introduced in Chapter 12.

Perfect competition has an almost infinite number of firms; monopoly has one firm. **Monopolistic competition** is *a market structure in which there are many firms selling differentiated products; there are few barriers to entry*. **Oligopoly** is *a market structure in which there are only a few firms; there are often significant barriers to entry*.

THE PROBLEMS OF DETERMINING MARKET STRUCTURE

Any estimate of the distribution of market structures must be treated with care. Defining an industry is a complicated task—inevitably, numerous arbitrary decisions must be made. Similarly, defining the relevant market of a given industry is complicated. For example, there are fewer than 10,000 banks in the United States, and banking is considered reasonably competitive. However, a particular small town may have only one or two banks, so there will be a monopoly or oligopoly with respect to banks in that town. Is the United States or the town the relevant market? The same argument exists when we think of international competition. Many firms sell in international markets and, while a group of firms may compose an oligopoly in the United States, the international market might be more accurately characterized by monopolistic competition.

Another dimension of the definitional problem concerns deciding what is to be included in an industry. If you define the industry as "the transportation industry," there are many firms. If you define it as "the urban transit industry," there are fewer firms; if you define it as "the commuter rail industry," there are still fewer firms. Similarly with the geographic dimension of industry. There's more competition in the global market than in the local market. The narrower the definition, the fewer the firms.

CLASSIFYING INDUSTRIES

One of the ways in which economists classify markets is by cross-price elasticities (the responsiveness of the change in the demand for a good to change in the price of a related good). Industrial organization economist F. M. Sherer has suggested the following rule of thumb: When two goods have a cross-price elasticity greater than or equal to 3, they can be regarded as belonging to the same market.

The **North American Industry Classification System (NAICS)** is *an industry classification that categorizes firms by type of economic activity and groups firms with like production processes.* It was adopted by the United States, Mexico, and Canada in 1997 and replaces the Standardized Industrial Classification (SIC) codes developed in the 1930s. All firms are placed into 20 broadly defined two-digit sectors. These two-digit sectors are further subdivided into three-digit subsectors, four-digit industry groupings, five-digit industries, and six-digit national industry groupings. Each subgrouping becomes more and more narrowly defined. Table 13-1 lists the 20 sectors and shows the subgroupings for one sector, Information, to give you an idea of what's included in each.

When economists talk about industry structure, they generally talk about industries in the four- to six-digit subsector groupings in the United States. This is a convention. Economists are often called on to give expert testimony in court cases, and if an

Q-1 Which would have more output: the two-digit industry 21 or the four-digit industry 2111? Explain your reasoning.

Table 13-1 Industry Groupings in the North American Industry Classification System

Two-Digit Sectors		Three- to Six-Digit Subsectors
11	Agriculture, forestry, fishing, and hunting	
21	Mining	
22	Utilities	
23	Construction	
31–33	Manufacturing	
42	Wholesale trade	
44–45	Retail trade	
48–49	Transportation and warehousing	
51	Information	513 Broadcasting and telecommunications
52	Finance and insurance	5133 Telecommunications
53	Real estate and rental and leasing	51332 Wireless telecommunications carriers, except satellite
54	Professional, scientific, and technical services	513321 Paging
55	Management of companies and enterprises	
56	Administrative and support, and waste management and remediation services	
61	Education services	
62	Health care and social assistance	
71	Arts, entertainment, and recreation	
72	Accommodation and food services	
81	Other services (except public administration)	
92	Public administration	

Source: U.S. Census Bureau (www.census.gov/epcd/www/naics.html).

economist wants to argue that an industry is more competitive than its opponents say it is, he or she challenges this convention of using a four- to six-digit classification of industry, asserting that the classification is arbitrary (which it is) and that the relevant market should be the two- to three-digit classification.

DETERMINING INDUSTRY STRUCTURE

To measure industry structure, economists use one of two methods: the concentration ratio or the Herfindahl index.

A **concentration ratio** is *the value of sales by the top firms of an industry stated as a percentage of total industry sales.* The most commonly used concentration ratio is the four-firm concentration ratio. For example, a four-firm concentration ratio of 60 tells you that the top four firms in the industry produce 60 percent of the industry's output. The higher the ratio, the closer the industry is to an oligopolistic or monopolistic type of market structure.

The **Herfindahl index** is *an index of market concentration calculated by adding the squared value of the individual market shares of all the firms in the industry.* For example, say that 10 firms in the industry each have 10 percent of the market:

$$\text{Herfindahl index} = 10^2+10^2+10^2+10^2+10^2+10^2+10^2+10^2+10^2+10^2 = 1{,}000$$

The Herfindahl index gives higher weights to the largest firms in the industry because it squares market shares.

The two measures can differ because of their construction, but generally if the concentration ratio is high, so is the Herfindahl index. Table 13-2 presents the four-firm concentration ratio and the Herfindahl index of selected industries.

The Herfindahl index plays an important role in government policy; it is used as a rule of thumb by the U.S. Department of Justice in determining whether an industry is sufficiently competitive to allow a merger between two large firms. If the Herfindahl index is less than 1,000, the Department of Justice generally assumes the industry is sufficiently competitive, and it doesn't look more closely at the merger. We'll discuss this in more detail in Chapter 15.

The Herfindahl index is a method used by economists to classify how competitive an industry is.

Because it squares market shares, the Herfindahl index gives more weight to firms with large market shares than does the concentration ratio measure.

Table 13-2 Concentration Ratios and the Herfindahl Index

Industry	Four-Firm Concentration Ratio	Herfindahl Index
Meat products	35	393
Fruit and vegetable canning	24	259
Breakfast cereal	82	2,445
Women's and misses' dresses	13	76
Book printing	32	364
Stationery	56	1,128
Soap and detergent	66	1,619
Men's footwear	50	857
Women's footwear	50	795
Bolts, nuts, rivets, and washers	9	40
Electronic computer	45	728
Radio, TV, wireless broadcasting	49	972
Burial caskets	74	2,965

Source: *Census of Manufacturers*, (factfinder.census.gov).

CONGLOMERATE FIRMS AND BIGNESS

Neither the four-firm concentration ratio nor the Herfindahl index gives us a picture of corporations' bigness. That's because many corporations are conglomerates—companies that span a variety of unrelated industries. For example, a conglomerate might produce both shoes and automobiles.

To see that concentration ratios are not an index of bigness, say there were only 11 firms in the entire United States, each with a 9 percent share of each industry. Both indexes would classify the U.S. economy as unconcentrated, but many people would seriously doubt whether that were the case. Little work has been done on classifying conglomerates or in determining whether they have any effect on an industry's performance.

THE IMPORTANCE OF CLASSIFYING INDUSTRY STRUCTURE

A basic rule of economics is that less concentrated industries are more likely to resemble perfectly competitive markets. In terms of formal modeling it's important to classify industries because the number of firms in an industry plays an important role in determining whether firms will tend to explicitly take other firms' actions into account. In monopolistic competition, there are so many firms that individual firms tend not to explicitly take into account rival firms' likely responses to their decisions. Collusion is difficult. In oligopoly there are fewer firms, and each firm is more likely to explicitly engage in **strategic decision making**—*taking explicit account of a rival's expected response to a decision you are making*. In oligopolies all decisions, including pricing decisions, are strategic decisions. Collusion is much easier. Thus, one distinguishes between monopolistic competition and oligopoly by whether or not firms explicitly take into account competitors' reactions to their decisions.

Why is the distinction important? Because it determines whether economists can model and predict the price and output of an industry. Nonstrategic decision making can be predicted relatively accurately if individuals behave rationally. Strategic decision making is much more difficult to predict, even if people behave rationally. What one person does depends on what he or she expects other people to do, which in turn depends on what others expect the one person to do. Consistent with this distinction, economists' model of monopolistic competition has a definite prediction. A model of monopolistic competition will tell us: Here's how much will be produced and here's how much will be charged. Economists' models of oligopoly don't have a definite prediction. There are no unique price and output decisions at which an oligopoly will rationally arrive; there are a variety of rational oligopoly decisions, and a variety of oligopoly models.

CHARACTERISTICS OF MONOPOLISTIC COMPETITION

The four distinguishing characteristics of monopolistic competition are:

1. Many sellers.
2. Differentiated products.
3. Multiple dimensions of competition.
4. Easy entry of new firms in the long run.

Let's consider each in turn.

Q-2 If the four-firm concentration ratio of an industry is 60 percent, what is the highest Herfindahl index that industry could have? What is the lowest?

Oligopolies take into account the reactions of other firms; monopolistic competitors do not.

Q-3 Your study partner, Jean, has just said that monopolistic competitors use strategic decision making. How would you respond?

Market structures change over time. Take, for instance, the automobile industry, which has always been used as the classic oligopoly model. Starting in the 1970s, however, foreign automakers have made large inroads into the U.S. market and have added new competition to it. Foreign companies such as Honda, Nissan, and Toyota have entered the U.S. market, as seen in the accompanying pie chart, which lists major automobile companies and their market shares.

The four-firm concentration ratio is over 75 percent, so the industry is still classified as an oligopoly. GM still considers what

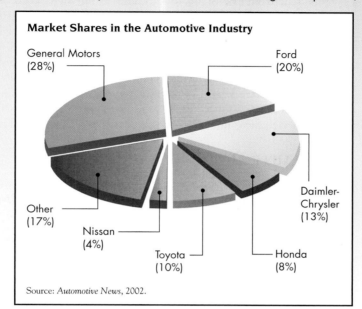

Market Shares in the Automotive Industry

General Motors (28%)
Ford (20%)
Other (17%)
Nissan (4%)
Toyota (10%)
Honda (8%)
Daimler-Chrysler (13%)

Source: *Automotive News*, 2002.

Ford's and Chrysler's reactions will be, but with the addition of foreign competition, there are getting to be too many firms for one firm to consider the reactions of all the other firms. The auto industry is becoming more monopolistically competitive.

Such change in industry structure is to be expected. Monopoly and oligopoly create the possibility that firms can make above-normal profits. Above-normal profits invite entry, and unless there are entry barriers, the result will likely be a breakdown in that monopoly or oligopoly.

MANY SELLERS

When there are only a few sellers, it's reasonable to explicitly take into account your competitors' reaction to the price you set. When there are many sellers, it isn't. In monopolistic competition firms don't take into account rivals' reactions. Here's an example. There are many types of soap: Ivory, Irish Spring, Yardley's Old English, and so on. So when Ivory decides to run a sale, it won't spend a lot of time thinking about Old English's reaction. There are so many firms that one firm can't concern itself with the reaction of any specific firm. The soap industry is characterized by monopolistic competition. In contrast, there are only a few major automobile firms, so when GM sets its price, it will explicitly consider what Ford's reaction may be. If GM raises its price, will Ford go along and also raise price? Or will it hold its price at its current level and try to sell its cars on the basis of lower prices? The automobile industry is an oligopoly.

The fact that there are many sellers in monopolistic competition also makes collusion difficult since, when there are many firms, getting all of them to act as one is difficult. In economists' models monopolistically competitive firms are assumed to act independently.

PRODUCT DIFFERENTIATION

The "many sellers" characteristic gives monopolistic competition its competitive aspect. Product differentiation gives it its monopolistic aspect. In a monopolistically competitive market, the goods that are sold aren't homogeneous, as in perfect competition; they

Web Note 13.1
Product Differentiation

are differentiated slightly. Irish Spring soap is slightly different from Ivory, which in turn is slightly different from Yardley's Old English.

So in one sense each firm has a monopoly in the good it sells. But that monopoly is fleeting; it is based on advertising to convince people that one firm's good is different from the goods of competitors. The good may or may not really be different. Bleach differs little from one brand to another, yet buying Clorox makes many people feel that they're getting pure bleach. I generally don't buy it; I generally buy generic bleach. Ketchup, however, while made from the same basic ingredients, differs among brands (in my view). For me, only Heinz ketchup is real ketchup.

Because a monopolistic competitor has some monopoly power, advertising to increase that monopoly power (and hence increase the firm's profits) makes sense as long as the marginal benefit of advertising exceeds the marginal cost. Despite the fact that their goods are similar but differentiated, to fit economists' monopolistically competitive model, firms must make their decisions as if they had no effect on other firms.

MULTIPLE DIMENSIONS OF COMPETITION

In the margin: *In monopolistic competition, competition takes many forms.*

In perfect competition, price is the only dimension on which firms compete; in monopolistic competition, competition takes many forms. Product differentiation reflects firms' attempt to compete on perceived attributes; advertising is another form competition takes. Other dimensions of competition include service and distribution outlets. These multiple dimensions of competition make it much harder to analyze a specific industry, but the alternative methods of competition follow the same two general decision rules as price competition:

- Compare marginal costs and marginal benefits; and
- Change that dimension of competition until marginal costs equal marginal benefits.

EASE OF ENTRY OF NEW FIRMS IN THE LONG RUN

The last condition a monopolistically competitive market must meet is that entry must be relatively easy; that is, there must be no significant entry barriers. Barriers to entry create the potential for long-run economic profit and prevent competitive pressures from pushing price down to average total cost. In monopolistic competition if there were long-run economic profits, other firms would enter until no economic profit existed.

OUTPUT, PRICE, AND PROFIT OF A MONOPOLISTIC COMPETITOR

Although a full analysis of the multiple dimensions of monopolistic competition cannot be compressed into two dimensions, a good introduction can be gained by considering it within the standard two-dimensional (price, quantity) graph.

To do so we simply consider the four characteristics of monopolistic competition and see what implication they have for the analysis. First, we recognize that the firm has some monopoly power; therefore, a monopolistic competitor faces a downward-sloping demand curve. The downward-sloping demand curve means that in making decisions about output, the monopolistic competitor will, as will a monopolist, use a marginal revenue curve that is below price. At its profit-maximizing output, marginal cost will be less than price (not equal to price as it would be for a perfect competitor). We consider that case in Figure 13-1(a).

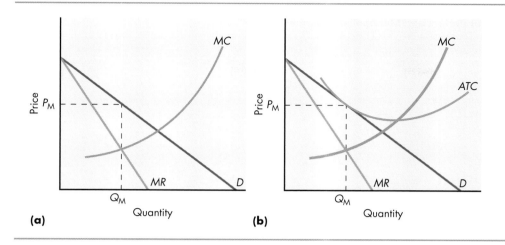

**Figure 13-1 (a and b)
Monopolistic Competition**
In (a) you can see that a monopolistically competitive firm prices in the same manner as a monopolist. It sets quantity where marginal revenue equals marginal cost. In (b) you can see that the monopolistic competitor is not only a monopolist but also a competitor. Competition implies zero economic profit in the long run.

The monopolistic competitor faces the demand curve D, marginal revenue curve MR, and marginal cost curve MC. This demand curve is its portion of the total market demand curve. Using the $MC = MR$ rule discussed in Chapter 12, you can see that the firm will choose output level Q_M (because that's the level of output at which marginal revenue intersects marginal cost). Having determined output, we extend a dotted line up to the demand curve and see that the firm will set a price equal to P_M. This price exceeds marginal cost. So far all we've done is reproduce the monopolist's decision.

Where does the competition come in? Competition implies zero economic profit in the long run. (If there's profit, a new competitor will enter the market, decreasing the existing firms' demand [shifting it to the left].) In long-run equilibrium a perfect competitor makes only a normal profit. Economic profits are determined by ATC, not by MC, so the competition part of monopolistic competition tells us where the average total cost curve must be at the long-run equilibrium output. It must be equal to price, and it will be equal to price only if the ATC curve is tangent to the demand curve at the output the firm chooses. We add that average total cost curve to the MC, MR, and demand curves in Figure 13-1(b). Profit or loss, I hope you remember, is determined by the difference between price and average total cost at the quantity the firm chooses.

To give this condition a little more intuitive meaning, let's say, for instance, that the monopolistically competitive firm is making a profit. This profit would set two adjustments in motion. First, it would attract new entrants. Some of the firm's customers would then defect, and its portion of the market demand curve would decrease. Second, to try to protect its profits the firm would likely increase expenditures on product differentiation and advertising to offset that entry. (There would be an All New, Really New, Widget campaign.) These expenditures would shift its average total cost curve up. These two adjustments would continue until the profits disappeared and the new demand curve is tangent to the new average total cost curve. A monopolistically competitive firm can make no long-run economic profit.

Q-4 How do the equilibrium for a monopoly and for a monopolistic competitor differ?

COMPARING MONOPOLISTIC COMPETITION WITH PERFECT COMPETITION

If both the monopolistic competitor and the perfect competitor make zero economic profit in the long run, it might seem that, in the long run at least, they're identical. They aren't, however. The perfect competitor perceives its demand curve as perfectly elastic, and the zero economic profit condition means that it produces at the minimum

The difference between a monopolist and a monopolistic competitor is in the position of the average total cost curve in long-run equilibrium.

Figure 13-2 (a and b)   A Comparison of Perfect and Monopolistic Competition
The perfect competitor perceives its demand curve as perfectly elastic, and zero economic profit means that it produces at the minimum of the ATC curve, as represented in (a). A monopolistic competitor, on the other hand, faces a downward-sloping demand curve and produces where marginal cost equals marginal revenue, as represented in (b). In long-run equilibrium the ATC curve is tangent to the demand curve at that level, which is *not* at the minimum point of the ATC curve. The monopolistic competitor produces Q_M at price P_M. A perfect competitor with the same marginal cost curve would produce Q_C at price P_C.

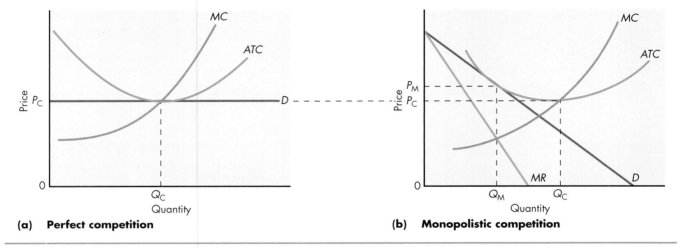

(a)   Perfect competition   **(b)   Monopolistic competition**

of the average total cost curve where the marginal cost curve equals price. We demonstrate that case in Figure 13-2(a).

The monopolistic competitor faces a downward-sloping demand curve for its differentiated product. It produces where the marginal cost curve equals the marginal revenue curve, and not where MC equals price. In equilibrium, price exceeds marginal cost. The average total cost curve of a monopolistic competitor is tangent to the demand curve at that output level, which cannot be at the minimum point of the average total cost curve since the demand curve is sloping downward. The minimum point of the average total cost curve (where a perfect competitor produces) is at a higher output (Q_C) than that of the monopolistic competitor (Q_M). I demonstrate the monopolistically competitive equilibrium in Figure 13-2(b) to allow you to compare monopolistic competition with perfect competition.

The perfect competitor in long-run equilibrium produces at a point where MC = P = ATC. At that point, ATC is at its minimum. A monopolistic competitor produces at a point where MC = MR. Price is higher than marginal cost. For a monopolistic competitor in long-run equilibrium:

$$(P = ATC) \geq (MC = MR)$$

At that point, ATC is *not* at its minimum.

What does this distinction between a monopolistically competitive industry and a perfectly competitive industry mean in practice? It means that for a monopolistic competitor, since increasing output lowers average cost, increasing market share is a relevant concern. If only the monopolistic competitor could expand its market, it could do better. For a perfect competitor, increasing output offers no benefit in the form of lower average cost. A perfect competitor would have no concern about market share (the firm's percentage of total sales in the market).

For a monopolistic competitor in long-run equilibrium, $(P = ATC) \geq (MC = MR)$.

COMPARING MONOPOLISTIC COMPETITION WITH MONOPOLY

An important difference between a monopolist and a monopolistic competitor is in the position of the average total cost curve in long-run equilibrium. For a monopolist, the average total cost curve can be, but need not be, at a position below price so that the monopolist makes a long-run economic profit. The average total cost curve of a monopolistic competitor must be tangent to the demand curve at the price and output chosen by the monopolistic competitor. No long-run economic profit is possible.

ADVERTISING AND MONOPOLISTIC COMPETITION

While firms in a perfectly competitive market have no incentive to advertise (since they can sell all they want at the market price), monopolistic competitors have a strong incentive. That's because their products are differentiated from the others; advertising plays an important role in providing that differentiation.

Goals of Advertising   Goals of advertising include shifting the firm's demand curve to the right and making it more inelastic. Advertising works by providing consumers with information about the firm's product and by making people want only a specific brand. That allows the firm to sell more, to charge a higher price, or to enjoy a combination of the two. It is advantageous to the firm if the marginal revenue of advertising exceeds the marginal cost of advertising. Advertising has two effects: It shifts the demand curve to the right, and it shifts the average total cost curve up.

When many firms are advertising, the advertising might be done less to shift the demand curve out than to keep the demand curve where it is—to stop consumers from shifting to a competitor's product. In either case, firms advertise to move the demand curve further out and to make it more inelastic than it would be if the firms weren't advertising.

Does Advertising Help or Hurt Society?   Our perception of products (the degree of trust we put in them) is significantly influenced by advertising. Think of the following pairs of goods:

Rolex	Cheerios	Clorox bleach	Bayer
Timex	Oat Circles	generic bleach	generic aspirin

Each of these names conveys a sense of what it is and how much trust we put in the product, and that determines how much we're willing to pay for it. For example, most people would pay more for Cheerios than for Oat Circles. Each year firms in the United States spend more than $150 billion on advertising. A 30-second commercial during the Super Bowl can cost as much as $3 million. That advertising increases firms' costs but also differentiates their products.

Are we as consumers better off or worse off with differentiated products? That's difficult to say. There's a certain waste in much of the differentiation that occurs. It shows up in the graph by the fact that monopolistic competitors don't produce at the minimum point of their average total cost curve. But there's also a sense of trust that we get from buying names we know and in having goods that are slightly different from one another. I'm a sophisticated consumer who knows that there's little difference between generic aspirin and Bayer aspirin. Yet sometimes I buy Bayer aspirin even though it costs more.

Edward Chamberlin, who, together with Joan Robinson, was the originator of the description of monopolistic competition, believed that the difference between the cost of a perfect competitor and the cost of a monopolistic competitor was the cost of what

Goals of advertising include shifting the firm's demand curve to the right and making it more inelastic.

Q₅ Why do monopolistically competitive firms advertise and perfect competitors do not?

Web Note 13.2
Brand Names

he called "differentness."[1] If consumers are willing to pay that cost, then it's not a waste but, rather, it's a benefit to them.

We must be careful about drawing any implications from this analysis. Average total cost for a monopolistically competitive firm includes advertising and costs of differentiating a product. It's debatable whether we as consumers are better off with as much differentiation as we have, or whether we'd all be better off if all firms produced a generic product at a lower cost.

CHARACTERISTICS OF OLIGOPOLY

The central element of oligopoly is that there are a small number of firms in an industry so that, in any decision it makes, each firm must take into account the expected reaction of other firms. Oligopolistic firms are mutually interdependent and can be collusive or noncollusive.

Most industries in the United States have some oligopolistic elements. If you ask almost any businessperson whether he or she directly takes into account rivals' likely response, the answer you'll get is "In certain cases, yes; in others, no."

Most retail stores that you deal with are oligopolistic in your neighborhood or town, although by national standards they may be quite competitive. For example, how many grocery stores do you shop at? Do you think they keep track of what their competitors are doing? You bet. They keep a close eye on their competitors' prices and set their own accordingly.

MODELS OF OLIGOPOLY BEHAVIOR

No single general model of oligopoly behavior exists. The reason is that an oligopolist can decide on pricing and output strategy in many possible ways, and there are no compelling grounds to characterize any of them as *the* oligopoly strategy. Although there are five or six formal models, I'll focus on two informal models of oligopoly behavior that give you insight into real-world problems rather than exercise your reasoning and modeling abilities as my earlier discussion did. The two models we'll consider are the cartel model and the contestable market model. These should give you a sense of how real-world oligopolistic pricing takes place.

Why, you ask, can't economists develop a simple formal model of oligopoly? The reason lies in the interdependence of oligopolists. Since there are few competitors, what one firm does specifically influences what other firms do, so an oligopolist's plan must always be a contingency or strategic plan. If my competitors act one way, I'll do X, but if they act another way, I'll do Y. Strategic interactions have a variety of potential outcomes rather than a single outcome such as shown in the formal models we discussed. An oligopolist spends enormous amounts of time guessing what its competitors will do, and it develops a strategy of how it will act accordingly.

THE CARTEL MODEL

A **cartel** is *a combination of firms that acts as if it were a single firm;* a cartel is a shared monopoly. If oligopolies can limit entry by other firms, they have a strong incentive to cartelize the industry and to act as a monopolist would, restricting output to a level that maximizes profit to the combination of firms. Thus, the **cartel model of oligopoly** is *a model that assumes that oligopolies act as if they were monopolists that have assigned output*

Oligopolistic firms are mutually interdependent.

If oligopolies can limit the entry of other firms and form a cartel, they increase the profits going to the combination of firms in the cartel.

---

[1]Joan Robinson, a Cambridge, England, economist, called this the theory of imperfect competition, rather than the theory of monopolistic competition.

quotas to individual member firms of the oligopoly so that total output is consistent with joint profit maximization. All firms follow a uniform pricing policy that serves their collective interest.

Since a monopolist makes the most profit that can be squeezed from a market, cartelization is the best strategy for an oligopoly. It requires each oligopolist to hold its production below what would be in its own interest were it not to collude with the others. Such explicit formal collusion is against the law in the United States, but informal collusion is allowed and oligopolies have developed a variety of methods to collude implicitly. Thus, the cartel model has some relevance.

The model has some problems, however. For example, various firms' interests often differ, so it isn't clear what the collective interest of the firms in the industry is. In many cases a single firm, often the largest or dominant firm, takes the lead in pricing and output decisions, and the other firms (which are often called *fringe firms*) follow suit, even though they might have preferred to adopt a different strategy.

This dominant-firm cartel model works only if the smaller firms face barriers to entry, or the dominant firm has significantly lower cost conditions. If that were not the case, the smaller firms would pick up an increasing share of the market, eliminating the dominant firm's monopoly. An example of such a dominant-firm market was the copier market in the 1960s and 1970s, in which Xerox set the price and other firms followed. That copier market also shows the temporary nature of such a market. As the firms became more competitive on cost and quality, Xerox's market share fell and the company lost its dominant position. The copier market is far more competitive today than it used to be.

In other cases the various firms meet—sometimes only by happenstance, at the golf course or at a trade association gathering—and arrive at a collective decision. In the United States meetings for this purpose are illegal, but they do occur. In yet other cases the firms engage in **implicit collusion**—*multiple firms make the same pricing decisions even though they have not explicitly consulted with one another.* They "just happen" to come to a collective decision.

Implicit Price Collusion

Implicit price collusion, in which firms just happen to charge the same price but didn't meet to discuss price strategy, isn't against the law. Oligopolies often operate as close to the fine edge of the law as they can. For example, many oligopolistic industries allow a price leader to set the price, and then the others follow suit. The airline and steel industries take that route. Firms just happen to charge the same price or very close to the same price.

It isn't only in major industries that you see such implicit collusion. In small towns, you'll notice that most independent carpenters charge the same price. There's no explicit collusion, but were a carpenter to offer to work for less than the others, he or she would feel unwelcome at the local breakfast restaurant.

Or let's take another example: the Miami fish market where sport fishermen sell their catch at the dock. When I lived in Miami I often went to the docks to buy fresh fish. There were about 20 stands, all charging the same price. Price fluctuated, but it was by subtle agreement, and close to the end of the day the word would go out that the price could be reduced.

I got to know some of the sellers and asked them why they priced like that when it would be in their individual interest to set their own price. Their answer: "We like our boat and don't want it burned." They may have been talking in hyperbole, but social pressures play an important role in stabilizing prices in an oligopoly.

Cartels and Technological Change

Even if all firms in the industry cooperate, other firms, unless they are prevented from doing so, can always enter the market with

Web Note 13.3
Price-Fixing

Q.6 Why is it difficult for firms in an industry to maintain a cartel?

In some cases firms collude implicitly—they just happen to make the same pricing decisions. This is not illegal.

a technologically superior new product at the same price or with the same good at a lower price. It is important to remember that technological changes are constantly occurring, and that a successful cartel with high profits will provide incentives for significant technological change, which can eliminate demand for its monopolized product.

Why Are Prices Sticky?   Informal collusion happens all the time in U.S. businesses. One characteristic of informal collusive behavior is that prices tend to be sticky. They don't change frequently, so the existence of informal collusion is an important reason why prices are sticky. But it's not the only reason.

Another reason is that firms don't explicitly collude, but they have certain expectations of other firms' reactions, which changes their perceived demand curves. Specifically, they perceive a kinked demand curve facing them. This kinked demand curve is used especially to explain why firms often do not use lower-price strategies to increase sales.

Let's go through the reasoning behind the kinked demand curve. If a firm increases its price, and the firm believes that other firms won't go along, its perceived demand curve for increasing price will be very elastic (D_1 in Figure 13-3). It will lose lots of business to the other firms that haven't raised their price. The relevant portions of its demand curve and its marginal revenue curve are shown in blue in Figure 13-3.

If it decreased its price, however, the firm assumes that all other firms would immediately match that decrease, so it would gain very few, if any, additional sales. A large fall in price would result in only a small increase in sales, so its demand is very inelastic (D_2 in Figure 13-3). This less elastic portion of the demand curve and the corresponding marginal revenue curve are shown in orange in Figure 13-3.

Notice that when you put these two curves together you get a rather strange demand curve (it's kinked) and an even stranger marginal revenue curve (one with a gap). I didn't make a mistake in drawing the curves; that's the way they come out given the assumptions. When the demand curve has a kink, the marginal revenue curve must have a gap.

If firms do indeed perceive their demand curves to be kinked at the market price, we have another explanation of why prices tend to be sticky. Shifts in marginal cost (such as MC_0 to MC_1) will not change the firm's profit maximization position. A large shift in marginal cost is required before firms will change their price. Why should this be the case? The intuitive answer lies in the reason behind the kink. If the firm raises its price, other firms won't go along, so it will lose lots of market share. However, when the firm

Q-7 Is the demand curve as perceived by an oligopolist likely to be more or less elastic for a price increase or a price decrease?

When the demand curve has a kink, the marginal revenue curve must have a gap.

Figure 13-3   The Kinked Demand Curve
One explanation of why prices are sticky is that firms face a kinked demand curve. When we draw the relevant marginal revenue curve for the kinked demand we see that the corresponding *MR* curve is discontinuous. It has a gap in it. Shifts in marginal costs between *c* and *d* will not change the price or the output that maximizes profits.

lowers price, other firms will go along and the firm won't gain market share. Thus, the firm has strong reasons not to change its price in either direction.

I should emphasize that the kinked demand curve is not a theory of oligopoly pricing. It does not say why the original price is what it is; the kinked demand curve is simply a theory of sticky prices.

THE CONTESTABLE MARKET MODEL

A second model of oligopoly is the *contestable market model*. The **contestable market model** is *a model of oligopoly in which barriers to entry and barriers to exit, not the structure of the market, determine a firm's price and output decisions*. Thus, it emphasizes entry and exit conditions, and says that the price that an oligopoly will charge will exceed the cost of production only if new firms cannot exit and enter the market. The higher the barriers, the more the price exceeds cost. Without barriers to entry or exit, the price an oligopolist sets will be equivalent to the competitive price. Thus, an industry that structurally looks like an oligopoly could set competitive prices and output levels.

> In the contestable market model of oligopoly, pricing and entry decisions are based only on barriers to entry and exit, not on market structure. Thus, even if the industry contains only one firm, it could still be a competitive market if entry is open.

COMPARISON OF THE CONTESTABLE MARKET MODEL AND THE CARTEL MODEL

Because of the importance of social pressures in determining strategies of oligopolies, no one "oligopolistic model" exists. Oligopolies with a stronger ability to collude (i.e., more social pressures to prevent entry) are able to get closer to a monopolist solution. Equilibrium of oligopolies with weaker social pressures and less ability to prevent new entry is closer to the perfectly competitive solution. That's as explicit as we can be.

An oligopoly model can take two extremes: (1) the cartel model, in which an oligopoly sets a monopoly price; and (2) the contestable market model, in which an oligopoly with no barriers to entry sets a competitive price. Thus, we can say that an oligopoly's price will be somewhere between the competitive price and the monopolistic price. Other models of oligopolies give results in between these two.

> **Q-8** What are the two extremes an oligopoly model can take?

Much of what happens in oligopoly pricing is highly dependent on the specific legal structure within which firms interact. In Japan, where large firms are specifically allowed to collude, we see Japanese goods selling for a much higher price than those same Japanese goods sell for in the United States. For example, you may well pay twice as much for a Japanese television in Japan as you would in the United States. From the behavior of Japanese firms, we get a sense of what pricing strategy U.S. oligopolists would follow in the absence of the restrictions placed on them by law.

STRATEGIC PRICING AND OLIGOPOLY

Notice that both the cartel model and the contestable market model use **strategic pricing** decisions—*firms set their price based on the expected reactions of other firms*. Strategic pricing and interdependence are central characteristics of oligopoly.

> Strategic pricing and interdependence are central characteristics of an oligopoly.

One can see the results of strategic decision making all the time. For example, consider a firm that announces that it will not be undersold—that it will match any competitor's lower price and will even go under it. Is that a pro-competitive strategy, leading to a low price? Or is it a strategy to increase collusive information and thereby prevent other firms from breaking implicit pricing agreements? Recent work in economics suggests that it is the latter.

Let's now see how a specific consideration of strategic pricing decisions shows that the cartel model and the contestable market model are related.

New Entry as a Limit on the Cartelization Strategy   One of the things that limits oligopolies from acting as a cartel is the threat from outside competition. The

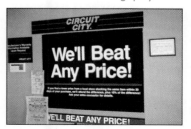

Guaranteed price matches are a way for firms to implicitly collude on prices. Tony Freeman/Photoedit.

threat will tend to be more effective if this outside competitor is much larger than the firms in the oligopoly.

For example, small-town banks have a tendency to collude (implicitly, of course), offering lower interest to savers and charging higher interest to borrowers than big banks charge, even though their average costs aren't significantly higher. When I ask small-town banks why this is, they tell me that my perceptions are faulty and that I should mind my own business. But if a big bank, which couldn't care less about increasing the wealth of a small-town banker, enters the town and establishes a branch office, interest rates to savers seem to go up and interest rates to borrowers seem to go down. The big bank can add significant competition—competition that couldn't come from within the town.

On a national scale, the outside competition often comes from international firms. For example, implicit collusion among U.S. automobile firms led to foreign firms' entry into the U.S. automobile market. There are many such examples of this outside competition breaking down cartels with no barriers to entry. Thus, a cartel with no barriers to entry faces a long-run demand curve that's very elastic. This means that its price will be very close to its marginal cost and average cost. This is the same prediction that came from the contestable market theory.

Price Wars   Whenever there's strategic decision making there's the possibility of a price war. Price wars are the result of strategic pricing decisions gone wild. Thus, in any oligopoly it's possible that firms can enter into a price war where prices fall below average total cost.

The reasons for such wars are varied. Since oligopolistic firms know their competitors, they can personally dislike them; sometimes a firm's goal can be simply to drive a disliked competitor out of business, even if that process hurts the firm itself. Passion and anger play roles in oligopoly pricing because interpersonal and interfirm relations are important.

Alternatively, a firm might follow a predatory pricing strategy—a strategy of pushing the price down temporarily to drive the other firm out of business to increase long-term profits. Some argue that Microsoft followed a predatory pricing strategy by virtually giving away its Office Suite on new computer systems to make its software the industry standard. If the predatory pricing strategy is successful, the firm can charge an even higher price because potential entrants know that the existing firm will drive them out if they try to enter. It's this continual possibility that strategies can change that makes oligopoly prices so hard to predict.

GAME THEORY, OLIGOPOLY, AND STRATEGIC DECISION MAKING

The inability to come to an explicit conclusion about what price and quantity an oligopoly will choose doesn't mean that economic reasoning and principles don't apply to oligopoly. They do. Most oligopolistic strategic decision making is carried out with the implicit or explicit use of **game theory** *(an application of economic principles in which players make interdependent choices)*. Game theory is economic reasoning applied to decision making.

To give you a sense of game theory, I'll present the **prisoner's dilemma**, *a well-known game that demonstrates the difficulty of cooperative behavior in certain circumstances.* The standard prisoner's dilemma can be seen in the following example: Two suspects are caught and are interrogated separately. Each prisoner is offered the following options:

Despite the fact that almost all economists are suave, debonair, exciting people, it isn't often that one is the main character in an Oscar-winning movie, but John Nash was. The movie is *A Beautiful Mind*. It tells the story of John Nash, a mathematician who won the Nobel Prize in economics for his work in game theory. Nash's contribution was the development of an equilibrium concept in non-cooperative games (games in which individuals do not collude), which goes by the name Nash equilibrium. A Nash equilibrium is one in which individuals follow their best strategy, assuming that all other people in the game will do the same. You already know one Nash equilibrium: the prisoner's dilemma game presented in the text. (Al Tucker, who was Nash's mentor at Princeton, invented the prisoner's dilemma.)

Now, many economists make similar important contributions to economic thinking, and the Nobel Prize for game theory could have been given to a number of different economists, and in fact was shared by two other economists (John Harsanyi and Reinhard Selten). What made Nash's story compelling enough for a movie was his fight with schizophrenia, which after his initial professional success caused him to resign his position at the Massachusetts Institute of Technology and be placed in a mental institution by his wife. After being released, he walked the Princeton campus, where he'd been a graduate student, and was helped by his former colleagues. The story became perfect for Hollywood when in the 1990s Nash gained control over the disease and was able to get back to work and accept the prize.

The movie gives you a sense of John Nash's life and work, but Sylvia Nasar's book, *A Beautiful Mind*, upon which the movie is based, provides a much more accurate depiction of his life. Actually, both the book and the movie employ a certain amount of artistic discretion in presenting the story, but both not only show how much of the work in economic theory today is mathematical and technical but also provide a fun introduction to game theory.

- If neither prisoner confesses, each will be given a 6-month sentence on a minor charge.
- If one prisoner confesses and the other does not, the one who confesses will go free and the other will be given a 10-year sentence.
- If they both confess, they'll each get a 5-year sentence.

What strategy will each choose? If neither can count on the other not to confess, the optimal strategy (the one that maximizes expected benefits) will be for each to confess, because each must assume the other will do the same. Confessing is the rational thing for each prisoner to do. That's why it's called the *prisoner's dilemma*. Trust gets one out of the prisoner's dilemma. If the prisoners can trust each other, the optimal strategy is not to confess, and they both get only a light sentence. But trust is a hard commodity to come by without an explicit enforcement mechanism.

In the prisoner's dilemma, where mutual trust gets each one out of the dilemma, confessing is the rational choice.

PRISONER'S DILEMMA AND A DUOPOLY EXAMPLE

The prisoner's dilemma has its simplest application to oligopoly when the oligopoly consists of only two firms. So let us consider the strategic decisions facing a "foam peanut" (packing material) **duopoly**—*an oligopoly with only two firms*. Let us assume that the average total cost and marginal cost of producing foam peanuts are the same for both firms, and are such that only two firms can exist in the industry. These costs are shown in Figure 13-4(a).

Assume that a production facility with a minimum efficient scale of 4,000 tons is the smallest that can be built. In Figure 13-4(b), the marginal costs are summed and the industry demand curve is drawn in a way that the competitive price is $500 per ton and

Web Note 13.4
The Prisoner's Dilemma

Figure 13-4 (a and b) Firm and Industry Duopoly Cooperative Equilibrium
In (a) I show the marginal and average total cost curve for either firm in the duopoly. Thus to get the average and marginal cost for the industry, you double each. In (b) the industry marginal cost curve (the horizontal sum of the individual firms' marginal cost curves) is combined with the industry demand and marginal revenue curves. At the competitive solution for the industry, output is 8,000 and price is $500. As you can see in (a), at that price economic profits are zero. At the monopolistic solution, output is 6,000 and price is $600. As you can see in (a), ATC is $575 at an industry output of 6,000 (firm output of 3,000), so each firm's profit is 25 × $3,000 = $75,000 (the shaded area in (a)).

(a) Firm's cost curves

(b) Industry: Competitive and monopolist solution

the competitive output is 8,000 tons. The relevant industry marginal revenue curve is also drawn.

If the firms collude fully, they will act as a joint monopolist setting total output at 6,000 tons where MR = MC (3,000 tons each). This gives them a price of $600 with a cost of $575 per ton, for a joint economic profit of $150,000, or $75,000 each. The firms prefer this equilibrium to the competitive equilibrium where they earn zero economic profit.

If they can ensure that they will both abide by the agreement, the monopolist output will be the joint profit-maximizing output. But what if one firm cheats? What if one firm produces 4,000 tons (1,000 tons under the counter)? The additional 1,000 tons in output will cause the price to fall to $550 per ton. The cheating firm's average total costs fall to $500 as its output rises to 4,000, so its profit rises to $200,000. The noncheating firm's profit moves in the opposite direction. Its average total costs remain $575, but the price it receives falls to $550, so it loses $75,000 instead of making $75,000. This gives it a large incentive to cheat also. The division of profits and output split is shown in Figure 13-5. If the noncheating firm decides to become a cheating firm, it eliminates its loss and the other firm's profit, and the duopoly moves to a zero profit position.

In Figure 13-5(a), you can see that the firm that abides by the agreement and produces 3,000 units makes a loss of $75,000; its average total costs are $575 and the price it receives is $550. In Figure 13-5(b) you can see that the cheating firm makes a profit of $200,000; its average costs are $500, so it is doing much better than when it did not cheat. The combined profit of the cheating and the noncheating firms is $200,000 − $75,000 = $125,000, which is lower than if they cooperated. By cheating, the firm has essentially transferred $125,000 of the other firm's profit to itself and has reduced their combined profit by $25,000. Figure 13-5(c) shows how output is split between the two firms. If both firms cheat, the equilibrium output moves to the competitive output, 8,000, and both of the firms make zero profit.

Figure 13-5 (a, b, and c)   Firm and Industry Duopoly Equilibrium When One Firm Cheats

In this figure I demonstrate the three different outcomes. Figures (a) and (b) show the noncheating and the cheating firms' output and profit, respectively, while (c) shows the industry output and price.

Say they both cheat. The price is $500 and output is 8,000 (4,000 per firm) (point A in (c)). Both firms make zero profit since their average total costs of $500 equal the price they receive.

If neither cheats, the industry output is 6,000, the price is $600, and their ATC is $575. This outcome gives them a profit of $75,000 each and would place them at point C in (c). This outcome was considered in Figure 13-4.

If one firm cheats and the other does not, the output is 7,000 and the industry price is $550 (point B in (c)). The noncheating firm's loss is shown by the shaded area in (a); its costs are $575, its output is 3,000, the price it receives is $550, and its loss is $75,000. The cheating firm's profit is shown by the shaded area in (b). Its average total costs are $500, the price it receives is $550, and its output is 4,000, so its profit is $200,000. So if one firm is cheating, it pays to be that firm; it doesn't pay to be honest when the other firm cheats.

(a) Noncheating firm's loss   **(b) Cheating firm's profit**   **(c) Cheating solution**

It is precisely to provide insight into this type of strategic situation that game theory was developed. It does so by analyzing the strategies of both firms under all circumstances and placing the combination in a payoff matrix—a box that contains the outcomes of a strategic game under various circumstances.

DUOPOLY AND A PAYOFF MATRIX

The duopoly presented above is a variation of the prisoner's dilemma game. The results can also be presented in a payoff matrix that captures the essence of the prisoner's dilemma. In Figure 13-6, each square shows the payoff from a pair of decisions listed in the columns and rows. The blue triangles show A's profit; the gold triangles show B's profit. For example, if neither cheats, the result for both is shown in the upper left-hand square, and if they both cheat, the result is shown in the lower right-hand square.

Notice the dilemma they are in if detecting cheating is impossible. If they can't detect whether the other one cheated and each believes the other is maximizing profit, each must expect the other one to cheat. But if firm A expects firm B to cheat, the relevant payoffs are in the second row. Given this expectation, if firm A doesn't cheat, it loses $75,000. So firm A's optimal strategy is to cheat. Similarly for firm B. If it expects firm A to cheat, its relevant payoffs are in the second column. Firm B's optimal strategy is to cheat. But if they both cheat, they end up in the lower right-hand square with zero profit.

In reality, of course, cheating is partially detectable, and even though explicit collusion and enforceable contracts are illegal in the United States, implicit collusive contracts are not. Moreover, in markets where similar conditions hold time after time, the cooperative solution is more likely since each firm will acquire a reputation based on its

Game theory has offered significant insight into the structure of economic problems but arrives at the conclusion that a number of alternative solutions are possible. A new branch of economics—*experimental economics*—has developed that offers insight into which outcome will be forthcoming. Let's consider an example.

When game theorists have done experiments, they have found that people believe that the others in the game will work toward a cooperative solution. Thus, when the gains from cheating are not too great, often people do not choose the individual profit-maximizing position but instead choose a more cooperative strategy, at least initially. Such cooperative solutions tend to break down, however,

as the benefits of cheating become larger. Additionally, as the number of participants gets larger, the less likely it is that the cooperative solution will be chosen and the more likely it is that competitive solutions will be chosen.

Experimental economists have also found that the structure of the game plays an important role in deciding the solution. For example, posted-price markets, in which the prices are explicitly announced, are more likely to reach a collusive result than are nonposted or uncertain-price markets, where actual sale prices are not known. Experiments in game theory are used extensively in designing auctions for allocating such things as telecom licenses.

Figure 13-6   The Payoff Matrix of Strategic Pricing Duopoly

The strategic dilemma facing each firm in a duopoly can be shown in a payoff matrix that captures the four possible outcomes. **A**'s strategies are listed horizontally; **B**'s strategies are listed vertically. The payoffs of the combined strategies for both firms are shown in the four boxes of the matrix, with **B**'s payoff shown in the gold shaded triangles and **A**'s payoff shown in the blue shaded triangles. For example, if **A** cheats but **B** doesn't, **A** makes a profit of $200,000 but **B** loses $75,000.

Their combined optimal strategy is to cartelize and achieve the monopoly payoff, with both firms receiving a profit of $75,000. However, each must expect that if it doesn't cheat and the other does cheat, it will lose $75,000. To avoid losing that $75,000, both firms will cheat, which leads them to the payoff in the lower right-hand corner—the competitive solution with zero profit for each firm.

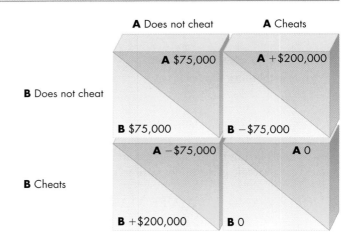

past actions, and firms can retaliate against other firms that cheat. But the basic dilemma remains for firms and tends to push oligopolies toward a zero profit competitive solution.

The push toward a zero profit equilibrium can be seen in the price war between Amazon.com and Buy.com in 2002. When Amazon.com lowered its threshold for free shipping from $99 to $49, Buy.com responded by offering free shipping on all sales the very next day and then added to that an offer to beat Amazon.com prices by 10 percent.

OLIGOPOLY MODELS, STRUCTURE, AND PERFORMANCE

The fourfold division of markets that I've considered so far has all been based on the structure of the markets. By *structure* I mean the number, size, and interrelationship of firms in an industry. A monopoly (one firm) is the least competitive; perfectly competitive industries (an almost infinite number of firms) are the most competitive.

Structure / Characteristics	Monopoly	Oligopoly	Monopolistic Competition	Perfect Competition
Number of Firms	One	Few	Many	Almost infinite
Barriers to Entry	Significant	Significant	Few	None
Pricing Decisions	$MC = MR$	Strategic pricing, between monopoly and perfect competition	$MC = MR$	$MC = MR = P$
Output Decisions	Most output restriction	Output somewhat restricted	Output restricted somewhat by product differentiation	No output restriction
Interdependence	Only firm in market, not concerned about competitors	Interdependent strategic pricing and output decision	Each firm acts independently	Each firm acts independently
Profit	Possibility of long-run economic profit	Some long-run economic profit possible	No long-run economic profit possible	No long-run economic profit possible
P and MC	$P > MC$	$P > MC$	$P > MC$	$P = MC$

Classification by structure is easy for students to learn and accords nicely with intuition. The cartelization model fits best with this classification system because it assumes the structure of the market (the number of firms) is directly related to the price a firm charges. It predicts that oligopolies charge higher prices than do monopolistic competitors.

The contestable market model gives far less weight to market structure. According to it, markets that structurally look highly oligopolistic could actually be highly competitive—much more so than markets that structurally look less competitive. This contestable market model view of judging markets by performance, not structure, has had many reincarnations. Close relatives of it have previously been called the *barriers-to-entry* model, the *stay-out pricing* model, and the *limit-pricing* model. These models provide a view of competition that doesn't depend on market structure.

Q-9 The Herfindahl index is 1,500. Using a contestable market approach, what would you conclude about this industry?

Q-10 The Herfindahl index is 1,500. Using a structural analysis of markets approach, what would you conclude about this industry?

To see the implications of the contestable market approach, let's consider an oligopoly with a four-firm concentration ratio of 60 percent and a Herfindahl index of 1,500. Using the structural approach we would say that, because of the multiplicity of oligopoly models, we're not quite sure what price firms in this industry would charge, but that it seems reasonable to assume that there would be some implicit collusion and that the price would be closer to a monopolist price than to a competitive price. If that same market had a four-firm concentration ratio of 30 percent and a Herfindahl index of 700, the industry would be more likely to have a competitive price.

A contestable market model advocate would disagree, arguing that barriers to entry and exit are what's important. If no significant barriers to entry exist in the first case but significant barriers to entry exist in the second case, the second case would be more monopolistic than the first. An example is the Miami fish market mentioned earlier, where there were 20 sellers (none with a large percentage of the market) and significant barriers to entry (only fishers from the pier were allowed to sell fish there and the slots at the pier were limited). Because of those entry limitations, the pricing and output decisions would be close to the monopolistic price. If you took that same structure but had free entry, you'd get much closer to competitive decisions.

As I presented the two views, I emphasized the differences in order to make the distinction clear. However, I must also point out that there's a similarity in the two views. Often barriers to entry are the reason there are only a few firms in an industry. And when there are many firms, that suggests that there are few barriers to entry. In such situations, which make up the majority of cases, the two approaches come to the same conclusion.

CONCLUSION

As you can see, the real world gets very complicated very quickly. I'll show you just how complicated in Chapter 14. But don't let the complicated real world get you down on the theories presented here. It's precisely because the real world is so complicated that we need some framework, like the one presented in this chapter. That framework lets us focus on specific issues—and hopefully the most important. Because the framework is so important, as a conclusion to this chapter I have summarized the primary market structures in the box "A Comparison of Various Market Structures" on page 303.

SUMMARY

- Industries are classified by economic activity in the North American Industry Classification System (NAICS). Industry structures are measured by concentration ratios and Herfindahl indexes.

- A concentration ratio is the sum of the market shares of individual firms with the largest shares in an industry.

- A Herfindahl index is the sum of the squares of the individual market shares of all firms in an industry.

- Conglomerates operate in a variety of different industries. Industry concentration measures do not assess the bigness of these conglomerates.

- Monopolistic competition is characterized by (1) many sellers, (2) differentiated products, (3) multiple dimensions of competition, and (4) ease of entry for new firms.

- The central characteristic of oligopoly is that there are a small number of interdependent firms.

- In monopolistic competition firms act independently; in an oligopoly they take account of each other's actions.

- Monopolistic competitors differ from perfect competitors in that the former face a downward-sloping demand curve.

- A monopolistic competitor differs from a monopolist in that a monopolistic competitor makes zero economic profit in long-run equilibrium.

- An oligopolist's price will be somewhere between the competitive price and the monopolistic price.

- Game theory and the prisoner's dilemma can shed light on strategic pricing decisions.

- A contestable market theory of oligopoly judges an industry's competitiveness more by performance and barriers to entry than by structure. Cartel models of oligopoly concentrate on market structure.

KEY TERMS

cartel (294)
cartel model of
   oligopoly (294)
concentration ratio (287)
contestable market
   model (297)

duopoly (299)
game theory (298)
Herfindahl index (287)
implicit collusion (295)
market structure (285)

monopolistic
   competition (285)
North American Industry
   Classification System
   (NAICS) (286)
oligopoly (285)

prisoner's dilemma (298)
strategic decision
   making (288)
strategic pricing (297)

QUESTIONS FOR THOUGHT AND REVIEW

1. Which industry is more highly concentrated: one with a Herfindahl index of 1,200 or one with a four-firm concentration ratio of 55 percent?

2. What are the ways in which a firm can differentiate its product from that of its competitors? What is the overriding objective of product differentiation?

3. What are the "monopolistic" and the "competitive" elements of monopolistic competition?

4. Does the product differentiation in monopolistic competition make us better or worse off? Why?

5. Both a perfect competitor and a monopolistic competitor choose output where MC = MR, and neither makes a profit in the long run. How is it, then, that the monopolistic competitor produces less than a perfect competitor?

6. If a monopolistic competitor is able to restrict output, why doesn't it earn economic profits?

7. What are some of the barriers to entry in the restaurant industry? In the automobile industry?

8. Is an oligopolist more or less likely to engage in strategic pricing compared to a monopolistic competitor?

9. What is the difference between the contestable market model and the cartel model of oligopoly? How are they related?

10. Is a contestable model or cartel model more likely to judge an industry by performance? Explain your answer.

11. What did Adam Smith mean when he wrote, "Seldom do businessmen of the same trade get together but that it results in some detriment to the general public"?

12. Private colleges of the same caliber generally charge roughly the same tuition. Would you characterize these colleges as a cartel type of oligopoly?

13. Describe a situation you have faced in your lifetime that can be characterized as a prisoner's dilemma.

14. In the late 1990s, Kellogg's, which controlled 32 percent of the breakfast cereal market, cut the prices of some of its best-selling brands of cereal to regain market share lost to Post, which controlled 20 percent of the market. General Mills had 24 percent of the market. The price cuts were expected to trigger a price war. Based on this information, what market structure best characterizes the market for breakfast cereal?

PROBLEMS AND EXERCISES

1. Suppose a monopolistic competitor in long-run equilibrium has a constant marginal cost of $6 and faces the demand curve given in the following table:

Q	20	18	16	14	12	10	8	6
P	$ 2	4	6	8	10	12	14	16

   a. What output will the firm choose?
   b. What will be the monopolistic competitor's average fixed cost at the output it chooses?

2. A firm is convinced that if it lowers its price, no other firm in the industry will change price; however, it believes that if it raises its price, some other firms will match its increase, making its demand curve more inelastic. The current price is $8 and its marginal cost is constant at $4.
   a. Sketch the general shape of the firm's MR, MC, and demand curves and show why there are two possible equilibria.
   b. If there are two equilibria, which of the two do you think the firms will arrive at? Why?
   c. If the marginal cost falls to $3, what would you predict would happen to price?
   d. If the marginal cost rises to $5, what would you predict would happen to price?
   e. Do a survey of five or six firms in your area. Ask them how they believe other firms would respond to their increasing or decreasing price. Based on that survey, discuss the relevance of this kinked demand model compared to the one presented in the book.

3. You're the manager of a firm that has constant marginal cost of $6. Fixed cost is zero. The market structure is monopolistically competitive. You're faced with the following demand curve:

   a. Determine graphically the profit-maximizing price and output for your firm in the short run. Demonstrate what profit or loss you'll be making.

   b. Do the same for the long run.
   c. Thanks to a technological innovation, you have zero marginal cost. Demonstrate the new profit-maximizing price and output in the short run. Demonstrate graphically the short-run profit at that new profit-maximizing output.

4. The pizza market is divided as follows:

Pizza Hut	20.7%
Domino's	17.0
Little Caesars	6.7
Pizza Inn/Pantera's	2.2
Round Table	2.0
All others	51.4

   a. How would you describe its market structure?
   b. What is the approximate Herfindahl index?
   c. What is the four-firm concentration ratio?

5. In 1982 Robert Crandell, CEO of American Airlines, phoned the Braniff Airways CEO and said, "Raise your fares 20 percent and I'll raise mine the next morning."
   a. Why would he do this?
   b. If you were the Braniff Airways CEO, would you have gone along?
   c. Why should Crandell not have done this?

6. Two firms, TwiddleDee and TwiddleDum, make up the entire market for wodgets. They have identical costs. They are currently colluding explicitly and are making $2 million each. TwiddleDee has a new CEO, Mr. Notsonice, who is considering cheating. He has been informed by his able assistant that if he cheats he can increase the firm's profit to $3 million, but that cheating will reduce TwiddleDum's profit to $1 million. You have been hired to advise Mr. Notsonice.
   a. Construct a payoff matrix for him that captures the essence of the decision.
   b. If the game is only played once, what strategy would you advise?
   c. How would your answer to b change if the game were to be played many times?
   d. What change in the profit made when colluding (currently $2 million) would be needed to change your advice in b?

7. In 1993, the infant/preschool toy market four-firm concentration ratio was 72 percent. With 8 percent of the market, Mattel was the fourth largest firm in that market. Mattel proposed to buy Fisher-Price, the market leader with 27 percent. At this time the new Clinton administration was trying to develop a set of rules dealing with such mergers. Your assignment is to help it decide by answering questions a through d.

a. Why would Mattel want to buy Fisher-Price?

b. What arguments can you think of in favor of allowing this acquisition?

c. What arguments can you think of against allowing this acquisition?

d. How do you think the four-firm concentration ratio for the entire toy industry would compare to this infant/preschool toy market concentration ratio?

e. What did the Clinton administration decide? (Requires library or online research.)

8. The text recounts how Amazon.com cut its free-shipping threshold from $99 to $49 and how, the very next day,

Buy.com offered free shipping on everything and promised to beat any Amazon.com price by 10 percent.

a. Construct a hypothetical payoff matrix for the decision of whether to offer free shipping or not.

b. In what solution is Buy.com better off?

c. In what solution is Amazon.com better off?

d. In what solution are joint profits maximized?

e. What are Amazon's and Buy.com's current rates for shipping?

WEB QUESTIONS

1. Go to the electronic reading room of the U.S. Department of Justice (DOJ) at www.usdoj.gov and search to find the document "Horizontal Merger Guidelines." Use the table of contents to find the sections "Product Market Definition" and "Concentration and Market Shares."

a. How does the DOJ determine the relevant product market?

b. Explain how the definition of market depends on cross-price elasticity of demand.

c. What measure of market concentration does the DOJ use?

d. Above what level for the market concentration measure does the DOJ believe the market to be highly concentrated?

2. Go to the U.S. Census Bureau's home page at www.census.gov and "Business" click on NAICS to answer the following questions:

a. What are the industry codes for potato farming, tire manufacturing, and family clothing stores?

b. The NAICS replaced the Standard Industrial Classification (SIC). How did the SIC classify industries? How does the NAICS classify industries?

c. Why did the Census Bureau change its method of classification? Will the new classification be more or less helpful than the SIC when classifying firms to determine market structure? Explain.

3. The Organization of Petroleum Exporting Countries (OPEC) is an international cartel. Go to its home page at www.opec.org to answer the following questions:

a. What are OPEC's objectives? How does it meet those objectives?

b. What countries are members of OPEC? What percentage of world oil production comes from these nations? In what way is OPEC a cartel?

c. What significant oil-exporting countries are not members? What has OPEC done to limit the effect of nonmember production on its pricing decisions?

ANSWERS TO MARGIN QUESTIONS

1. The smaller the number of digits, the more inclusive the classification. Therefore, the two-digit industry would have significantly more output. (286)

2. The highest Herfindahl index for this industry would occur if one firm had the entire 60 percent, and all other firms had an infinitesimal amount, making the Herfindahl index slightly over 3,600. The lowest Herfindahl index this industry could have would occur if each of the top four firms had 15 percent of the market, yielding a Herfindahl index of 900. (288)

3. I would respond that monopolistic competitors, by definition, do not take into account the expected reactions of competitors to their decisions; therefore, they cannot use strategic decision making. I would tell Jean she probably meant, "*Oligopolies* use strategic decision making." (288)

4. Both a monopoly and a monopolistic competitor produce where marginal cost equals marginal revenue. The difference is in the positioning of the average total cost curve. For a monopolistic competitor, that average total cost curve must be tangent to the demand curve because a monopolistic competitor makes no profits in the long run. A monopoly can make profits in the long run, so its average total cost can be below the price. (291)

5. Monopolistically competitive firms advertise because their products are differentiated from others. Advertising can convince people that a firm's product is better than that of other firms and increase the demand curve it faces. Perfect competitors, in contrast, have no incentive to advertise since their products are the same as every other firm's product and they can sell all they want at the market price. (293)

6. Maintaining a cartel requires firms to make decisions that are not in their individual best interests. Such decisions are hard to enforce unless there is an explicit enforcement mechanism, which is difficult in a cartel. *(295)*

7. The demand curve perceived by an oligopolist is more elastic above the current price because it believes that others will not follow price increases. If it increased price, it would see quantity demanded fall by a lot. The opposite is true below the current price. The demand curve below current price is less elastic. Price declines would be matched by competitors and the oligopolist would see little change in quantity demanded with a price decline. *(296)*

8. The two extremes an oligopoly model can take are: (1) a cartel model, which is the equivalent of a monopoly; and (2) a contestable market model, which, if there are no barriers to entry, is the equivalent of a competitive industry. *(297)*

9. The contestable markets approach looks at barriers to entry, not structure. Therefore, we can conclude nothing about the industry from the Herfindahl index. *(303)*

10. In a market with a Herfindahl index of 1,500, the largest firm would have, at most, slightly under 38 percent of the market. The least concentrated such an industry could be would be if seven firms each had between 14 and 15 percent of the market. In either of these two cases, the industry would probably be an oligopolistic industry and could border on monopoly. *(304)*

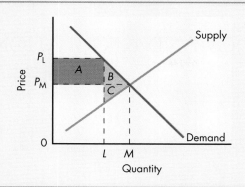

If suppliers producing $0L$ got together and limited supply to L, they could push the price up to P_L and could gain the rectangle A for themselves. Consumers and suppliers who are kept out of the market lose triangles B and C respectively, which, in the diagram, are not only each smaller than A, but also B and C combined are smaller than A. Of course, the area A is lost to the consumers, but the costs of organizing those consumers to fight and protect competition are often prohibitively large. *(314)*

6. It is almost impossible for perfect monopoly to exist because preventing entry is nearly impossible. Monopoly rents are a signal to potential entrants to get the barriers of entry removed. *(315)*

7. The problem with cost-based regulation that sets prices relative to costs is that this removes the incentive for firms to hold down costs and can lead to X-inefficiency. While, in theory, regulators could scrutinize every cost, in practice that is impossible—there would have to be a regulatory board duplicating the work that a firm facing direct market pressure undertakes in its normal activities. *(317)*

8. If the additional benefits of creating or maintaining a monopoly exceed the cost of doing so, do it. If it doesn't, don't. *(318)*

9. Perfect competition is not conducive to technological advance because firms don't earn the profits needed to invest in research and development. It also doesn't have the promise of future above-normal profits needed to motivate researchers to innovate. *(320)*

10. Oligopoly is the best market structure for technological advance because oligopolists have the profits to devote to research and development and have the incentive to innovate. Innovation may provide the oligopolist with a way to increase market share. *(321)*

15

ANTITRUST POLICY AND REGULATION

We have always known that heedless self-interest was bad morals;
we now know that it is bad economics.

—Franklin Delano Roosevelt

After reading this chapter, you should be able to:

- Explain the difference between the structure and the performance methods of judging competition.

- Give a brief history of U.S. antitrust policy.

- State the resolution of the IBM, AT&T, and Microsoft antitrust cases.

- Differentiate among horizontal, vertical, and conglomerate mergers.

- List five reasons why unrelated firms would want to merge.

- Compare U.S. antitrust policy with antitrust policy of other countries.

- List three alternatives to antitrust policy that government can use to affect the competitive process.

In the courtroom everyone waits for the Microsoft star witness, an economist who is arguing that Microsoft does not have a monopoly. On the stand he testifies, "The market is too dynamic, too much in flux for a monopoly to exist."

"But how about the fact that Microsoft intentionally tied its Web browser to its Windows operating system in order to harm Netscape's ability to compete?" the government lawyer asks.

"Those were technical decisions," the economist answers, "necessary to make the Web browser operate efficiently."

"Yeah, right," replies the government lawyer.

The above is a paraphrase of what was said in a federal court in an antitrust case the government brought against Microsoft. It captures a very real aspect of all theoretical discussions of market structure and policy. Once theory is translated into policy, market structure and behavior play an important role in how the economy functions. One way in which theory is translated into policy is through antitrust policy and regulation. In this chapter we consider both.

ANTITRUST POLICY: JUDGMENT BY PERFORMANCE OR STRUCTURE?

Antitrust policy is *the government's policy toward the competitive process*. It's the government's rulebook for carrying out its role as referee. In volleyball, for instance, the rulebook would answer such questions as: When should a foul be called? When has a person caught and thrown rather than hit the ball over the net? In business a referee is needed for such questions as: When can two companies merge? What competitive practices are legal? When is a company too big? To what extent is it fair for two companies to coordinate their pricing policies? When is a market sufficiently competitive or too monopolistic?

The United States has seen wide swings in economists' prescriptions concerning such questions, depending on which of the two views of competition has held sway. The two competing views are:

1. **Judgment by performance:** *We should judge the competitiveness of markets by the performance (behavior) of firms in that market.*
2. **Judgment by structure:** *We should judge the competitiveness of markets by the structure of the industry.*

To show how the U.S. government has applied these two views of competition in promoting workable and effective competition, this chapter considers government's application of antitrust laws to regulate business. It then considers how recent structural changes in the economy are altering the government's role in refereeing the market.

Judgment by performance is the view that competitiveness of a market should be judged by the behavior of firms in that market.

Judgment by structure is the view that competitiveness of a market should be judged by the structure of that market.

HISTORY OF U.S. ANTITRUST LAWS

Although U.S. ideology has always been strongly in favor of laissez-faire and government noninvolvement in business, there has simultaneously been a populist (pro-people) sensibility that fears bigness and monopoly. These fears of bigness and monopoly burst forth in the late 1800s as many firms were merging or organizing together to form trusts or cartels. As stated in Chapter 13, a *cartel*—or, as we'll use the term in this chapter, a *trust*—is a combination of firms in which the firms haven't actually merged but nonetheless act essentially as a single entity. A trust sets common prices and governs the output of individual member firms. A trust can, and often does, act like a monopolist.

In the 1870s and 1880s, trusts were forming in a number of industries, including railroads, steel, tobacco, and oil. Some of these trusts' actions are typified by John D. Rockefeller's Standard Oil. Standard Oil demanded that railroads pay it kickbacks on freight rates. These payments allowed Standard Oil to set lower prices for its products than other companies, which had to pay the railroads full price on freight. Standard Oil thus could sell at lower prices than its competitors.

If prices had remained low, this would have had a positive effect on consumers and a negative effect on Standard Oil's competitors. But prices didn't remain low. By 1882, Standard Oil had driven many of its competitors out of business, and the writing was on the wall for those competitors that remained. At that time, Standard Oil created a trust and "invited" its few surviving competitors to join. Then Standard Oil Trust used the monopoly power it had gained to close down refineries, raise prices, and limit the production of oil. The price of oil rose from a competitive level to a monopolistic level, and the consumer, as well as Standard Oil's competitors, ended up suffering.

Bettmann/Corbis.

THE SHERMAN ANTITRUST ACT

Public outrage against trusts like Standard Oil's was high. The organizers of the trusts were widely known as *robber barons* because of their exploitation of natural resources and their other unethical behavior. The trusts were seen as making enormous profits, preventing competition, and in general bullying everyone in sight. In response the U.S. Congress passed the **Sherman Antitrust Act** of 1890—*a law designed to regulate the competitive process.*

The Sherman Act contained two main sections:

Section 1: Every contract, combination in the form of trust or otherwise, or conspiracy in restraint of trade or commerce among the several States, or with foreign nations, is hereby declared to be illegal.

Public outrage at the formation and activities of trusts such as Standard Oil led to the passage of the Sherman Act, the Clayton Act, and the Federal Trade Commission Act.

Section 2: Every person who shall monopolize, or attempt to monopolize, or combine or conspire with any other person or persons, to monopolize any part of the trade or commerce among the several States, or with foreign nations, shall be deemed guilty of a misdemeanor, and, on conviction thereof, shall be punished by a

Q-1 What were the two provisions of the Sherman Antitrust Act?

fine not exceeding five thousand dollars, or by imprisonment not exceeding one year, or by both said punishments, in the discretion of the court.

The Sherman Act was broad and sweeping, but vague.

The Sherman Act was meant to be as sweeping and broad as its language sounds. After all, it was passed in response to a public outcry against trusts. But if you look at it carefully, in some respects it is vague and weak. For example, offenses under Section 2 were initially only misdemeanors, not felonies.[1] It's unclear what constitutes "restraint of trade." Moreover, although the act prohibits monopolization, it does not explicitly prohibit monopolies. In short, with the Sherman Act, Congress passed the buck to the courts, letting them decide U.S. antitrust policy.[2]

The following story summarizes the courts' role in antitrust policy. Three umpires are describing their job. The youngest of the three says, "I call them as I see them." The middle-aged umpire says, "No, that's not what an umpire does. An umpire calls them the way they are." The senior umpire says, "You're both wrong. They're nothing until I call them." And that's how it is with the courts and monopoly. Whether a firm is behaving monopolistically isn't known until the court makes its decision.

As Congress was passing the Sherman Act, economists too were debating the implications of trusts and whether it was in the public interest to restrict them. Part of the debate concerned whether the mergers reflected technological changes in production and expanding transportation systems that made increased economies of scale more important (in which case restricting trusts might not be in the public interest since doing so might prevent firms from taking advantage of economies of scale), or whether trusts simply represented attempts at monopolization to restrict output and generate monopoly profits (in which case restricting trusts would more likely be in the public interest since doing so would reduce monopoly).

Economists reflecting the performance viewpoint argued that competition was strong and would ultimately limit monopolies.

A second part of the debate concerned how fast economic forces would operate and how fragile competition was. Some economists argued that competition was strong and that it would limit the profit trusts and monopolies made and force them to charge the competitive price (in which case restricting trusts might not be in the public interest). These economists were reflecting the performance viewpoint—that competition should be relied on to break down the monopolies. They argued that bigness doesn't imply the absence of market competition and that the government's role should merely be to make sure that no significant barriers to entry are created.

Economists reflecting the structure viewpoint argued that trusts should be broken up by government.

Other economists, reflecting the structure viewpoint, argued that competition was fragile and that it wouldn't operate unless there were a large number of small firms. They argued that trusts and monopolies (even if they don't charge monopolistic prices) are bad, that the trusts should be broken up by government, and that laws should not allow new monopolies or trusts to be formed. However, the debate was for the courts, not economists, to settle.

THE STANDARD OIL AND AMERICAN TOBACCO CASES: JUDGING MARKET COMPETITIVENESS BY PERFORMANCE

Web Note 15.1
The Trusts

In 1911, the U.S. Supreme Court established its interpretation of the Sherman Act by handing down its opinions in cases involving Standard Oil and the American Tobacco Company. The Court determined that both companies were structural monopolies; each company controlled 90 percent of its market. However, the Court decided that the monopolistic structure of the markets did not violate the Sherman Antitrust Act. A

[1]Under federal law, a misdemeanor is any misconduct punishable by only a fine or by a jail sentence of a year or less. A felony requires a sentence of more than a year.
[2]Subsequent amendments to the Sherman Act have strengthened it. For example, offenses under Section 2 are now felonies, not misdemeanors.

company's violation of the act was determined not by the structure of the industry but by the particular firm's performance—that is, by whether or not the firm engaged in "unfair business practices." This judgment by performance, not judgment by structure, is often called the *abuse theory* because a firm is legally considered a monopoly only if it commits monopolistic abuses.

In these two cases the distinction was academic. Both Standard Oil and American Tobacco were judged guilty (very guilty) of unfair business practices and were broken up. But the academic distinction played an important role in determining the industrial structure of the United States. It allowed structural monopolies to continue to exist, but it prohibited them from using certain monopolistic practices, such as demanding kickbacks.

In 1920, this structure/performance distinction was important in a case involving U.S. Steel. Here the Supreme Court ruled that, while U.S. Steel was a structural monopoly, it was not a monopoly in performance. That is, the firm had not used unfair business practices to become a monopolist and thus was not in violation of antitrust law. Unlike Standard Oil, U.S. Steel was not required to break up into a group of smaller companies.

> Standard Oil and the American Tobacco Company were judged guilty, not because of their structure, but because of their performance.
>
> **Q-2** What was the resolution of the Standard Oil case?

THE CLAYTON ACT AND THE FEDERAL TRADE COMMISSION ACT

In an attempt to give more guidance to the courts and to provide for more vigorous enforcement of the antitrust provisions, in 1914 Congress passed the Clayton Antitrust Act and the Federal Trade Commission Act.

The **Clayton Antitrust Act** is *a law that made four specific monopolistic practices illegal* when their effect was to lessen competition:

1. Price discrimination, that is, selling identical goods to different customers at different prices.
2. Tie-in contracts, in which the buyer must agree to deal exclusively with one seller and not to purchase goods from competing sellers.
3. Interlocking directorships, in which memberships of boards of directors of two or more firms are almost identical.
4. Buying stock in a competitor's company when the purpose of buying that stock is to reduce competition.

> The Clayton Antitrust Act made four specific monopolistic practices illegal:
> 1. Price discrimination.
> 2. Tie-in contracts.
> 3. Interlocking directorships.
> 4. Purchase of a competitor's stock.

In establishing the Federal Trade Commission (FTC) in 1914, Congress gave it the power to regulate competition and police markets. The **Federal Trade Commission Act** is *a law that made it illegal for firms to use "unfair methods of competition" and to engage in "unfair or deceptive acts or practices,"* whether or not those actions had any impact on competition. Other than that broad mandate, Congress gave the FTC little direction as to what rules it was to use to regulate trade and police markets. As a result, for more than 20 years the commission was rather ineffective. In 1938, however, it was given the job of preventing false and deceptive advertising, which remains one of its primary roles.

THE ALCOA CASE: JUDGING MARKET COMPETITIVENESS BY STRUCTURE

Judgment by performance was the primary criterion governing U.S. antitrust policy until 1945. In 1945 the U.S. courts changed their interpretation of the law with the Aluminum Company of America (ALCOA) case. In the ALCOA case, the company was found guilty of violating the antitrust statutes even though the court did not rule that

> **Q-3** What was the resolution of the ALCOA case?

Web Note 15.2
Predatory Pricing

ALCOA had been guilty of unfair practices. What ALCOA had done was to use its knowledge of the market to expand its capacity before any competitors had a chance to enter the market. In addition, it had kept its prices low to prevent potential entry by competitors, an activity known as *predatory pricing*. It showed no signs of exploiting its monopoly power to charge high prices or to force competing firms out of business. Thus, on performance standards, it was not violating the law. But in the ALCOA case, the structure of the market, not the company's performance, was used to determine whether ALCOA was in violation of antitrust law.

JUDGING MARKETS BY STRUCTURE AND PERFORMANCE: THE REALITY

Judgment by structure seems unfair on a gut level. After all, in economics the purpose of competition is to motivate firms to produce better goods than their competitors are producing, and to do so at lower cost. If a firm is competing so successfully that all the other firms leave the industry, the successful firm will be a monopolist, and on the basis of judgment by structure will be guilty of antitrust violations. Under the judgment-by-structure criterion, a firm is breaking the law if it does what it's supposed to be doing: producing the best product it can at the lowest possible cost.

Supporters of the judgment-by-structure criterion recognize this problem but nonetheless favor the structure criterion. An important reason for this is practicality.

An important reason supporting the structure criterion is practicality.

Contextual Judgments and the Capabilities of the Courts   Judgment by performance requires that each action of a firm be analyzed on a case-by-case basis. Doing that is enormously time-consuming and expensive. In some interpretations, actions of a firm might be considered appropriate competitive behavior; in other interpretations, the same actions might be considered inappropriate. For example, say that an automobile company requires that in order for its warranty to hold, owners of its warranted vehicles must use only the company's parts and service centers. Is this requirement of the automobile company intended to create a monopoly position for its parts and service center divisions or to ensure proper maintenance? The answer depends on the context of the action.

But judging each case contextually is beyond the courts' capabilities. There are so many firms and so many actions that the courts can't judge all industries on their performance. They must devise a way to limit the issues they look at. In order to apply the performance criterion reasonably, the Supreme Court must set out certain guidelines to tell firms in what situations the Court will take a closer look at their performance. Because the available information concerns structure, those guidelines inevitably refer to market structure, even though it is firms' performance that will ultimately be judged. So even though judging by structure may have problems, it is necessary.

It's very much like the procedure college admissions offices use in deciding which applicants to accept. They judge applicants on their "total performance," not just on their quantitative scores on standardized tests. However, they often use a certain quantitative score as a cutoff point in order to reduce applications to a manageable number. Applicants below the cutoff point are automatically rejected; applicants above it are considered one by one.

Another argument in favor of judging competitiveness by structure is that structure can be a predictor of future performance. Advocates of the structure criterion argue that a monopolist may be pricing low now, but it is, after all, a monopolist, and it won't price low in the future. The low price will eliminate competition now, and, once the

WAL-MART, STATE LAWS, AND COMPETITION

It isn't only the federal government that has laws on competition. States have a variety of laws that govern competitive practices. One such state law is Arkansas's Unfair Practices Act, which prohibits selling, or advertising for sale, items below cost "for the purpose of injuring competitors and destroying competition." In the early 1990s, three Arkansas pharmacies sued Wal-Mart for violating this law by selling its goods at "too low" a price. The background of the case is the following.

Wal-Mart had been expanding aggressively throughout the United States reaching a total of about 3,000 stores in the mid 1990s. It does not deny that it, like many other stores, sells some goods below cost. But it argues that when it sells below cost it does not do so to "destroy competition" or "injure competitors," but rather to maintain low prices for consumers. It claims that its pricing policies promote, not destroy, competition.

In principle, most economists agree with Wal-Mart; new competition, by its very nature, hurts existing businesses—

that's the way the market competitive process works. Those who don't sell for the lowest price lose, and those who sell for the lowest price gain. But most economists also recognize that Wal-Mart's brand of competition can have externalities affecting the social fabric of small-town economies. A new Wal-Mart store can undermine the town centers and replace them with commercial sprawl on the outskirts of these towns. Whether these externalities are a reason to limit Wal-Mart's aggressive pricing policies is a debatable question.

Wal-Mart initially lost its suit in Arkansas; however, in 1995 the Arkansas Supreme Court overturned the lower court decision and held that Wal-Mart's pricing was not part of a strategy to price below cost over a prolonged period. While Wal-Mart won this suit, the threat of other suits discouraged the company from following quite as aggressive a pricing policy as it otherwise would have.

---

competition is gone, the firm will not be able to resist the temptation to use its monopoly power.

Determining the Relevant Market and Industry   Supporters of the performance criterion admit that this standard has problems, but they point out that the structure criterion also has problems. As you saw in Chapter 13, it's difficult to determine the relevant market (local, national, or international) and the relevant industry (three-digit or five-digit NAICS code) necessary to identify the structural competitiveness of any industry.

Such questions have been the center of many antitrust court cases. For example, in the ALCOA case, the company argued that metals such as copper and steel were interchangeable with aluminum, and that therefore the relevant industry to consider was the metals industry. If the Court had chosen metals, not aluminum, as the relevant industry, ALCOA wouldn't have been found to have a monopoly. The Court decided, however, that aluminum had sufficiently unique properties to constitute its own market. Since it determined that ALCOA had 90 percent of the aluminum market, ALCOA was declared a monopoly and was broken up.

The arguments in the Du Pont case (1956) again centered on the definition of *industry*. The Supreme Court found that Du Pont was innocent of monopolizing the production of cellophane even though Du Pont was the only producer of cellophane. The Court reasoned that the relevant industry was not the cellophane industry but rather the flexible wrap industry, which also included aluminum foil and wax paper. Du Pont did not have a monopoly of the flexible wrap industry and thus, the Court said, was not in violation of the antitrust laws.

Choosing the relevant market when evaluating competitiveness is difficult to do.

Q-4   What was the resolution of the Du Pont case?

More recently, in 1993, the Department of Justice opposed a merger between Gillette and Parker Pens, arguing that the combined firm would control about 40 percent of the premium-fountain-pen market. The Court, however, allowed the merger, arguing that the relevant market was much larger—the market for premium writing instruments, which also included mechanical pencils, ballpoint pens, rollerballs, and fountain pens. The premium-writing-instruments market had many more competitors than the premium-fountain-pen market.

Similar ambiguities exist with the decision about the relevant geographic market. In the Pabst Brewing case (1966), the definition of the market played a key role. Pabst wanted to merge with the Blatz Brewing Company. On a national scale, both companies were relatively small, accounting together for about 4.5 percent of beer sales in the United States as a whole. Pabst argued that the United States was the relevant market. The Court, however, decided that Wisconsin, where Pabst had its headquarters, was the relevant market, and since the two firms held a 24 percent share of that market, the merger was not allowed.

What should one make of debates regarding relevant markets? The bottom line is that both structure and performance criteria have ambiguities, and in the real world there are no definitive criteria for judging whether a firm has violated the antitrust statutes. A firm isn't at fault or in the clear until the courts make the call.

> Both structure and performance criteria have ambiguities, and in the real world there are no definitive criteria for judging whether a firm has violated the antitrust statutes.

RECENT ANTITRUST ENFORCEMENT

In recent years, few mergers have been challenged by the government. In 2000, for example, the Department of Justice challenged only 48 of the more than 9,500 mergers that took place among U.S. companies. Most of the mergers that were challenged were settled, abandoned, or restructured. Only one went to court. Despite the fact that few recent mergers have been challenged, antitrust law still works mainly through its deterrent effect. Many potential mergers are never even proposed because firms know they would not be allowed. Few major antitrust cases have been brought, in part because a century of experience has taught business what the law allows, and in part because the government has been lenient in its interpretation of the antitrust laws. That leniency has three interrelated causes. The first is a change in the American ideology. Whereas in the 1950s and 1960s the prevailing ideology saw big business as "bad," by the 1980s the view became more complex—big business was seen as a combination of good and bad. In this new ideological framework, the political pressure to push antitrust enforcement waned.

> Since the 1980s the United States has been more lenient in antitrust cases because of a change in ideology, the globalization of the U.S. economy, and the increasing complexity of technology.

Second, as the United States became more integrated into the global economy, big business faced significant international competition and hence competition created by U.S. market structure became less important.

Third, as technologies became more complicated, the issues in antitrust enforcement also became more complicated for the courts to handle. By the time the legal system had resolved a case, the technology would have changed so much that the issues in that case were no longer relevant.

THREE MODERN ANTITRUST CASES

The modern era of antitrust policy has been marked by important cases in the computer and telecommunications markets. One such case was against IBM.

THE IBM CASE

In 1967 the U.S. Department of Justice sued IBM for violating the antitrust laws. The department argued that the company had a 72 percent share of the general-purpose

In a secretly recorded comment during a price-fixing meeting, the former president of ADM stated, "Our competitors are our friends and our customers are our enemies."

The U.S. antitrust laws concern far more than mergers and market structure; they also place legal restrictions on certain practices of businesses such as price-fixing. By law, firms are not allowed to *explicitly* collude in order to fix prices above the competitive level. A key aspect of the law is the explicit nature of the collusion that is disallowed. Airlines, gas stations, and firms in many other industries have prices that generally move in tandem—when one firm changes its price, others seem to follow. Such practices would suggest that these firms are implicitly colluding, but they are not violating the law unless there is explicit collusion.

To prove explicit collusion is difficult—there must be a smoking gun, and there is seldom sufficient evidence of explicit collusion to prosecute businesses. There are exceptions, however. In 1996, Archer Daniels Midland (ADM), a major supplier of food and grains, was caught red-handed when one of its former officials gave prosecutors tapes of meetings in which price-fixing occurred. Meeting secretly around the world, in countries like Mexico, France, Canada, and Japan, ADM executives tried to set prices of Lysine, a feed additive, and citric acid. One of ADM's officials, working undercover for the FBI, secretly recorded these meetings. Faced with the taped evidence against them, ADM agreed to pay $100 million in fines—the largest criminal antitrust fine in history up to that year. Since 1996 four other companies have been fined even greater sums, with Roche Holding paying a fine of $500 million.

Company	Fine (in millions)
Roche Holding	$500
BASF	225
SGL Carbon	135
Ucar International	110
ADM	100

electronic digital computing industry, and that it had acquired that market share because of unfair business practices such as bundling of hardware, software, and maintenance services at a single price (that is, requiring customers to buy all three together). If you wanted IBM equipment (hardware), you also had to take IBM service and software whether you wanted them or not. When you bought an IBM machine you bought everything, so other companies had little chance to compete. Moreover, the department argued that IBM constantly redesigned its computers, making it impossible for other companies to keep up and compete fairly on the sale of any IBM mainframe-compatible item.

In technology industries the market is continually changing.

IBM argued that the relevant market was broader, that it included all types of computers such as military computers, programmable calculators, and other information-processing products. It further claimed that its so-called unfair practices were simply a reflection of efficient computer technology. Fast-moving technological developments required it to continually redesign its products merely to provide its customers with the latest, best equipment. And, it said, the only way to provide the best level of service to its customers was to include its maintenance services in the price of its products. The case dragged on for years until finally, in 1982, the government withdrew its case.

The reason it did so was that the market had changed. Many of the government's objections had become moot; mainframe computers were being replaced with personal computers, a market in which Apple and DEC had become serious competitors, and the globalization of the computer industry made IBM's dominance in the United States far less important.

IBM may have triumphed in the antitrust case against it, but in doing so it may have lost the war. Here's why.

Q.5 What was the resolution of the IBM case?

About the same time as the case was at its height, IBM was negotiating with an up-start company about an operating system for a small part of its market—the personal computer (PC) market, which was just developing. Bill Gates, the president of the young company, offered to sell its disk operating system (DOS) to IBM for $75,000. IBM refused to buy it; to have bought DOS would have given IBM greater control over the PC market, and would have made a court-ordered breakup of IBM more likely. Instead, IBM left Bill Gates to license DOS to IBM and everyone else, while IBM concentrated on mainframe computers and the production of PCs.

By the early 1990s, the cost of that decision was clear. The mainframe market was dying, and IBM was hemorrhaging losses. Meanwhile, Bill Gates had become a multi-billionaire, and his company—Microsoft—had become a controlling force in the PC market. Now the tables were turned and in 1994 it was Microsoft that was being pursued by the U.S. government for violating antitrust laws.

The losses at IBM ended in the mid-1990s and its competitive position improved. Thus, ultimately it weathered the antitrust case, but its history was forever changed by it.

The IBM case was dropped by the United States, but the prosecution likely led to IBM's problems in the 1990s. It won but it also lost.

THE AT&T CASE

The other major antitrust case of the 1980s, the AT&T case, demonstrates another aspect of U.S. antitrust policy and shows how technological change plays an important role in competition and questions of industrial market structure.

AT&T as a Regulated Monopoly   Up until 1982, AT&T was what was called a *regulated monopoly*. It had the exclusive right to provide telephone service in the United States. AT&T controlled 90 percent of the telecommunications market: long-distance and local telephone service, and the production of telephones themselves as well as other communications equipment.

Why was it given that right? Because it was felt that economies of scale and network externalities made supplying telephone service a **natural monopoly** (*an industry in which significant economies of scale make the existence of more than one firm inefficient*). Telephone service required every house to be connected with lines, which had to be buried under-ground or strung overhead on poles. It made little sense to have more than one company stringing competing lines. Moreover, the government decided that universal telephone service was socially desirable, and AT&T was required to provide universal service. Unregulated companies likely would have practiced *cream skimming* (providing service to low-cost areas and avoiding high-cost areas).

A natural monopoly is an industry in which significant economies of scale make the existence of more than one firm inefficient.

In return for its monopoly, AT&T was subjected to regulatory control by the Federal Communications Commission and state utility commissions. This government regulation was designed to limit the company's profit to a fair level and prevent it from abusing its monopoly.

Under AT&T's monopoly, phone service in the United States was the best and cheapest in the world, although some believed it could and should have been even cheaper. Some economists argued that AT&T's guarantee of a "fair" return on its investment gave it a strong incentive to act as a lazy monopolist and to invest heavily, thereby increasing costs. If a company knows it can pass its costs on to customers (and add a profit margin as well), it has little incentive to hold down costs. But even if service was more expensive than it needed to be, on the whole most agreed that the system worked well.

Technological Change and Competition   In the 1970s technological changes fundamentally altered the nature of the long-distance telephone industry. The development of satellite transmission and fiber optics made physical line connections no longer the only option, so long-distance telephone service was no longer a natural monopoly. In fact, significant competition began to develop, and AT&T's new competitors claimed that they weren't being allowed reasonable access to the AT&T-controlled local telephone network. AT&T charged competing firms high fees for access to all their local lines—fees that competitors argued were unfair.

The issue was complicated by the fact that the regulatory commissions had set local charges low and long-distance rates high (implicitly subsidizing local service with AT&T's long-distance profits). As long as AT&T controlled both local and long-distance calling its revenues were unaffected by this rule. But when competitors began to undercharge AT&T on long-distance service, AT&T grew increasingly concerned. AT&T's high access charges were an attempt to see that the competitors used some of their own profits to help subsidize local rates.

As a result of these claims and counterclaims, the Department of Justice introduced an antitrust suit against AT&T in 1978, alleging that potential competitors were not being allowed reasonable access to AT&T's local telephone network. The case had merit, but so did AT&T's defense: How could a firm provide high-cost local service at a low price with no way to pay for it? As is now usual for any contested antitrust case, the case went on and on, and no conclusion was in sight.

Resolution of the AT&T Case   In January 1982, AT&T and the Department of Justice announced that they had settled the case and that AT&T had agreed to be broken up. Specifically, AT&T agreed that by January 1, 1984, it would divest itself of 22 local operating companies, which accounted for more than 75 percent of AT&T's assets. These companies quickly merged into seven local operating companies that became known as the *Baby Bells*. AT&T kept its long-distance telephone service, its manufacturing division, and its research facilities. In return, AT&T was subject to far less regulation. After the settlement, AT&T could enter any unregulated business it desired, such as data transmission and computers. The Baby Bells, alternatively, were restricted to the local telephone market.

The result of this settlement was an enormous upheaval in the telephone industry. Local rates for phone service went up twofold or even threefold, while long-distance rates fell substantially. Two major competitors, MCI and Sprint, emerged, and competition for long-distance business became fierce. (Now more than 800 firms offer long-distance service.)

Developments since the AT&T Case   The breakup of AT&T was not the end of the changes. The seven Baby Bells continued merging with one another, and in 2003 only four remained—SBC Communications, Verizon, Bell South, and Qwest. In 1995, AT&T had divided itself into three companies—AT&T, Lucent Technologies, and National Cash Register. Only AT&T remained in the market for communication services, expanding its offerings into wireless communications, digital cable, cable, and long distance.

Technological innovations continued to change the nature of the telecommunications industry. Advances in wireless technology provided competition for both local and long-distance carriers, while the Internet became a larger and larger market. Simultaneously, new high-speed fiber-optic networks turned telephone lines into a potential competitor for regulated cable TV monopolies. Data, voice, and video could be transmitted by copper wire (phone lines), cable, and wireless (satellite).

Because of these changes the market divisions established by the FCC no longer made sense, and in 1996 Congress passed the Telecommunications Act, which deregulated the telecommunications industry and allowed long-distance carriers, local phone

Q-6   What was the resolution of the AT&T case?

The AT&T case was settled by AT&T agreeing to be split up into regional companies handling local service, and AT&T itself competing in the long-distance market.

companies, and cable television companies to enter one another's markets. Cable, long-distance, local, cellular phone, and Internet were combined and seen as an "information flow" market. In exchange for being able to compete in the market for long-distance services, the Baby Bells were required to offer access to their local networks to their competitors for a fee.

The Baby Bells fought competition in the local phone market by setting difficult technical requirements for use of their lines and by taking advantage of every loophole in the 1996 act they could find. For instance, they fought pressure to open up local networks for high-speed Internet access, arguing that doing so meant sharing lines, which was not required by the 1996 act. Competing companies such as AT&T claimed that the Baby Bells' access fees were too high, precisely the charge that had been levied earlier against AT&T. The delaying tactics worked; in the early 2000s, the four Baby Bells still controlled 90 percent of the local telephone market. As they attempted to maintain control of the local market, they simultaneously expanded into long distance. Verizon, for example, won a 20 percent market share in those states where it had permission to offer long-distance service. This move by local phone companies into long-distance markets is expected to expand in the near future as the companies continue to open up their local markets to others.

The competition is not only between long-distance and local service providers. Competition has also come from wireless communication providers and international telecommunications companies. For example, wireless communications companies are attempting to be the sole providers of telephone service for households. By 2002, they had made some inroads; 3 percent of Americans relied entirely on wireless services. Similarly, international companies have entered the U.S. market just as U.S. companies have entered world markets.

The competition in telecommunications, as in most industries, takes place on both the regulatory front and the business front. On the regulatory front companies try to interpret any regulatory ruling in a manner that is most advantageous to them, and to force competitors to bring legal proceedings to achieve a different ruling. By doing so, they often win even when they lose because the delay of entry allows them to establish their position in the market and make it difficult for competitors to enter even when they are allowed to do so. With the ongoing technological developments, government antitrust policy regarding telecommunications firms is likely to stay in the news in the indefinite future.

Given the technological developments, government antitrust policy regarding telecommunications is likely to stay in the news.

THE MICROSOFT CASE

One of the most important antitrust cases brought in the 1990s was the Microsoft case. This is an extremely interesting case to consider both because of its similarities to the IBM case and because of the issues it raises about competition, the competitive process, and government's role in that competitive process.

Microsoft makes computer software. From the company's small start some 20 years ago, sales of Microsoft software have grown to account for about 50 percent of the world's software market. Its PC operating system, Windows, accounts for an even larger share—more than 90 percent—of the world's operating system software market.

Since all software must be compatible with an operating system, the widespread use of Windows gives Microsoft enormous power—power that competitors claim it has used to gain competitive advantage for its other divisions. Competitors' calls for action, and reports of monopolistically abusive acts by Microsoft, led the U.S. Department of Justice in 1998 to charge Microsoft with violating antitrust laws.

The government suit against Microsoft charged the company with being a monopoly and using that monopoly power in a predatory way. Specifically, it charged Microsoft with:

1. Possessing monopoly power in the market for personal computer operating systems.

2. Tying other Microsoft software products to its Windows operating system.

3. Entering into agreements that keep computer manufacturers that install Windows from offering competing software.

Microsoft had dominated the market for PC operating systems for about a decade. The U.S. Department of Justice argued that this long-standing monopoly position was the result of unfair business practices. Microsoft argued that Windows sold so well because it was a superior product. Microsoft further argued that, because it faced competition from technological change, it was not a monopolist.

Because of their experience with the AT&T and IBM cases, prosecutors were initially hesitant to bring charges against Microsoft. They knew that the case would be extremely complicated, contentious, and long. And they fully expected that the competitive issues would change significantly in the interim. They eventually decided to bring the case, however, because the judge granted them an expedited process—meaning that the case would be resolved much faster than previous cases—and because they felt that Microsoft had violated a 1994 consent that it had entered into following an earlier antitrust investigation.

Is Microsoft a Monopolist?   The computer software industry is a market with barriers to entry that originate from two sources—network externalities and economies of scale. Network externalities exist because as the number of applications supported by a single platform increase, the value of the platform also increases. Economies of scale exist because the cost of developing a new platform and new software is significant, while the cost of producing it is minimal. It is a potential candidate for monopoly.

Is Microsoft a monopoly in the market for operating systems? Looking only at the market within a static framework, Microsoft, given its stable 90 percent share, almost definitely has a monopoly. Looking at the market from a dynamic perspective, the issue is much more complicated. Competing operating systems exist; Jaguar (developed by Apple), and Linux are both competitors to Windows.

The Linux operating system is a particularly strong potential competitor because it is an "open-source" operating system. All programmers can get the code and modify it, allowing them to tailor it for their software and streamline the structure of their programs. Linux reduces the costs of software development and leads to more efficient programs.

Another potential competitive force is the merging of software and hardware. As the power of computers increases according to Moore's law, it is becoming more and more feasible to design specific chips to do specific jobs, incorporating into a single chip aspects that were previously separated into hardware and software. Within 10 years the entire PC structure—a machine to handle a multitude of tasks—could become obsolete, and instead the market may consist of $10 or $15 machines that will perform specific tasks more efficiently than can a multipurpose machine like the PC. Each of these changes could eliminate Microsoft's monopoly advantage. In this dynamic view of the market, Microsoft's monopoly is at best temporary, and will survive only if it outcompetes the other technologies.

Is Microsoft a Predatory Monopolist?   The U.S. Department of Justice argued that Microsoft used its monopoly in the operating systems market to gain a larger share of the software market and engaged in unfair practices against its competitors to maintain the barriers to entry in the operating systems market. Let's first look at its actions to gain market share in the software market.

Whether one sees Microsoft as a monopolist depends in part on whether one views it in a static or dynamic framework.

Courtesy Microsoft Corporation.

Competing software companies alleged that companies like Novell (now Corel), which had the leading word-processing software, WordPerfect, were put at a significant disadvantage because Microsoft combined its software with the Windows operating system. Not surprisingly, Microsoft's Word has become the dominant word-processing system. By directing the development of new software to favor Windows, Microsoft strengthened the barrier to entry created by network externalities. Microsoft also penalized computer manufacturers that installed Windows if they installed competing software. IBM, for example, was denied Windows 95 when it decided to pre-install its PCs with Lotus, a direct competitor to Microsoft's Excel.

Microsoft was also alleged to have engaged in unfair practices in how it addressed the threat of competition in the operating system market. Direct competitive threats came mainly from two firms—Netscape and Sun Microsystems. Netscape and Sun were developing programs that operated across multiple platforms and were developing potential rival operating systems.

Netscape designed and marketed a very popular Web browser called Netscape Navigator. Navigator posed a threat to Microsoft not only because it could serve as a platform for other software applications and circumvent the need for Windows but also because Navigator could work on many operating systems, increasing the ability of software to work on systems other than Windows. In response to that threat, Microsoft attempted to get Netscape to agree to stop developing Navigator as a competing platform in exchange for a "special relationship" with Microsoft. Netscape wouldn't agree. In response, Microsoft withheld the source code Netscape needed to provide its browser on the Windows platform for three months. This gave Microsoft an advantage to offer its own Web browser, Internet Explorer, with Windows starting in 1995. Microsoft then bundled its browser to Windows (essentially offering it at no cost) and made it virtually impossible for consumers to remove the Internet Explorer icon from the PC screen. Installing Windows actually disabled competing Internet browsers. Microsoft also prohibited computer manufacturers such as Compaq from offering Netscape as an alternative browser when they sold PCs with Windows.

The government argued that this competition was unfair and predatory. Microsoft argued that Internet Explorer was a Windows program improvement; it was part of Windows. Netscape Navigator, which had been more popular than Internet Explorer and had seen its sales climbing rapidly, was in a matter of a few years nearly replaced by the Microsoft browser.

Another potential competitor was Sun Microsystems, which was developing Java, a programming language designed to create software applications on a variety of platforms, not just Windows. Sun Microsystems had entered into an agreement with Microsoft that allowed Microsoft to distribute the Java code under explicit instructions not to change it. But Microsoft created a version of Java that kept it tied to Windows and changed the platform-neutral characteristics of Java. Microsoft also instructed other companies not to cooperate with Sun. These actions stunted the development of a program that would allow software to run across multiple platforms, which would have reduced the network externality barriers to trade enjoyed by Microsoft.

Resolution of the Microsoft Case   So is Microsoft a monopoly? And has it been involved in anticompetitive practices? The answer the court gave was yes. In 2000 the judge concluded that Microsoft violated Section 2 of the Sherman Act by attempting to maintain its monopoly power by anticompetitive means. He also ruled that Microsoft violated Section 1 of the Sherman Act by unlawfully tying its Web browser to its operating system. In a strongly worded decision he stated that "Microsoft mounted a deliberate assault upon entrepreneurial efforts that, left to rise or fall on their own merits, could well have enabled the introduction of competition into the market." As a remedy

Microsoft used its power in one market to give it advantages in other markets.

Web Note 15.3
More on Microsoft

the government proposed breaking up Microsoft into two companies. Microsoft quickly appealed, and in mid-2001 the appeals court ruled that, while Microsoft was indeed a monopoly, a breakup was not necessary—instead, the case should be resolved by mediation. A few months later the federal government, nine states, and Microsoft agreed to a settlement. Microsoft agreed not to engage in contracts that prohibited PC makers from using competing products or in practices that favored PC makers that offered only Microsoft products. It also agreed to release technical information about Windows improvements to software developers. Microsoft maintained its right to keep e-mail systems and software programs such as media players bundled with Windows. Nine other states (co-plaintiffs) objected to the settlement because they believed the restrictions on Microsoft were too mild.

The nine states continued suing Microsoft, contending that software developers in applications such as media players could compete only if Microsoft made its operating system modular and provided the relevant code to competitors so they could integrate their software into the Windows operating system as seamlessly as they could integrate Microsoft products. Both sides brought in experts on whether this was easy to do or not.

In November 2002 the Court decided against the dissenting states. Thus, the agreement that Microsoft had entered into with the federal government stood. However, the judge stated that she would be following Microsoft's actions carefully to see that it abided by the agreement. (Two states appealed.) So the end result of the Microsoft case was that even though Microsoft had been declared a monopoly, it was not broken up. Instead it agreed to a set of rules of competition that required it to provide technical information to competitors and to allow firms to use software from Microsoft competitors.

Most observers believe that these limitations do not place a serious constraint on Microsoft's domination of the software industry since, for a number of its competitors, that technical information will be too late, because in the four years that had passed since the beginning of the case, Microsoft had already integrated its Windows operating system with Microsoft media players, and had developed a head start in integrating a number of other new technologies into its Windows operating system. So even if it lives up to the spirit of the agreement, it will retain a lead for years to come. And if it doesn't live up to its agreement, since any legal action against Microsoft will take additional years to litigate, the same process can be expected to continue and Microsoft will have likely established its position in even newer technologies before any limitations can be imposed on it by the government.

ASSESSMENT OF ANTITRUST POLICY

Economic scholars' overall assessment of antitrust policy is mixed. In certain cases, such as the IBM case, most agree that antitrust prosecution went too far. But most believe that other decisions (as in the 1911 Standard Oil and American Tobacco cases) set a healthy precedent by encouraging a more competitive U.S. business environment. Almost all agree that antitrust enforcement has not reduced the size of firms below the minimally efficient level, the level at which a firm can take full advantage of economies of scale. But they are mixed in their judgments as to whether the enforcement was needed. Performance advocates generally believe that it was not, while structural advocates generally believe that it was. They are also mixed in their judgment about whether any type of antitrust action is feasible in a technologically dynamic industry such as computers or telecommunications.

Economists' judgment on antitrust is mixed.

MERGERS, ACQUISITIONS, AND TAKEOVERS

Other than the Microsoft case, antitrust activity was minimal in the 1990s and early 2000s. But industrial structure has changed significantly. The nature of those changes was treated in Chapter 10, where I discussed how firms are increasingly looking for alternative ways of structuring themselves so that they can achieve economies of scope and economies of scale that go along with specialization. To do this, firms are simultaneously merging and breaking up. Firms are allowed to break up as much as they want; when they merge, however, they must see that any merger falls within the antitrust guidelines. In order to put recent merger activity into perspective, let's consider the various subcategories and types of mergers that are possible.

ACQUISITIONS AND TAKEOVERS

Merger is *a general term meaning the act of combining two firms*. The picture it conveys is of two firms combining to form one firm. That picture isn't always appropriate, however. For example, often the firm buying another company is essentially what's called a *shell corporation*, which exists primarily to buy up other firms. A combination that is technically a merger but has distinguishing characteristics all its own is the **takeover**—*the purchase of one firm by a shell firm that then takes direct control of all the purchased firm's operations*. The term *takeover* is used to emphasize that little true merging is taking place. Takeovers change the control over the firm, but do not affect market concentration.

Another kind of merger is an **acquisition**—*a merger in which a company buys another company and the purchaser has the right of direct control over the resulting operation (but does not always exercise that right)*. It is a merger, but it is not a merger of equals, and the acquiring firm does not necessarily take over direct control of the acquired firm's operations. In a merger of equals, neither firm takes over the other, and it's not clear who'll be in charge after the merger.

Takeovers and acquisitions are said to be *friendly* or *hostile*. In a friendly takeover, one corporation is willing to be acquired by the other. A **hostile takeover** is *a merger in which the firm being taken over doesn't want to be taken over*. How can that happen?

Remember the discussion of corporations from Chapter 3. Corporations are owned by stockholders, but are managed by a different group of individuals. The two groups' interests do not necessarily coincide. When it is said that a corporation doesn't want to be taken over, that means that the corporation's managers don't want the company to be taken over. In a hostile takeover, the management of each corporation presents its side to the shareholders of both corporations. The shareholders of the corporation that is the takeover target ultimately decide whether or not to sell their shares. If enough shareholders sell, the takeover succeeds.

In a hostile takeover, the shareholders ultimately decide whether to sell their shares.

MERGERS

Mergers are also classified by the types of businesses that are merging.

Horizontal Mergers   Most U.S. antitrust policy has concerned **horizontal mergers**—*the combining of two companies in the same industry*. The creation of Standard Oil is an example of a horizontal merger. The 2000 merger between pharmaceutical companies Glaxo Wellcome and SmithKline, GlaxoSmithKline, is another. Since the passage of the Cellar-Kefauver Act of 1950, almost all mergers of companies with substantial market shares in the same industry have been prohibited, even though enforcement was loosened in the 1980s. For example, in 2000 the FTC blocked a proposed merger between WorldCom and Sprint because the combined firm would have controlled 30 to 50 percent of telecommunications markets in several locations.

Horizontal mergers are companies in the same industry merging together.

Exactly what is considered substantial market share has changed over time. The general guideline government used in the 1970s and early 1980s was that, in highly concentrated industries, the government would challenge all mergers involving the following combinations of market share:

Acquiring Firm	Acquired Firm
4%	4% or more
10%	2% or more
15%	1% or more

For less-concentrated industries, the guidelines used slightly different percentages. In 1982, the Department of Justice changed the guidelines and began looking at all mergers in which the Herfindahl index, after the merger, would be above 1,000. Special highly restrictive rules regarding mergers existed for industries with Herfindahl indexes above 1,800. Since then the rules have evolved and have become more flexible; for example, in 1997 the government issued new rules that allow some mergers if the companies can show that the merger will lower price, or will improve a product or service, even if the merger doesn't meet the guidelines.

Vertical Mergers

A **vertical merger** is *a combination of two companies that are involved in different phases of producing a product*, one company being a buyer of products the other company supplies. For example, if a computer company merges with an electronic chip company, a vertical merger has taken place. Similarly, if a clothes manufacturer buys a retail boutique, that's a vertical merger. If either of the merged firms is able to limit access of other buyers or sellers to the market, such a merger is in violation of the Clayton Act.

A famous vertical merger case is the Du Pont/General Motors case (1961), in which Du Pont was required to sell its 23 percent share of General Motors because Du Pont was a major supplier to the automobile industry. The Supreme Court felt Du Pont's ownership share of GM was restricting competition. Similarly in the Brown Shoe/Kinney Shoe case (1962), Brown Shoe, primarily a wholesaler, was forbidden to buy Kinney Shoe, which was a chain of shoe retailers.

In most of the 1980s, the U.S. government challenged any vertical merger in which the supplying firm had a 10 percent or more market share and the buyer company purchased 6 percent or more of the market. This rule was loosened some as the 1980s progressed, but specific new guidelines were not developed. Although today few vertical mergers are challenged, in 1994, Silicon Graphics, a producer of computer workstations, was not allowed to purchase Alias Research or Wavefront Technologies, which produced three-dimensional graphics software that ran on their workstations, because Silicon Graphics controlled 90 percent of the workstation market. The FTC believed that after the purchase Silicon Graphics could potentially limit the software's compatibility on rival stations, reducing competition in the workstation market even further.

Vertical mergers are combinations of two companies, one of which supplied inputs to the other's production.

 If Ben & Jerry's, a maker of ice cream, bought a dairy farm, what type of merger would it be?

 Web Note 15.4
Vertical Power

Conglomerate Mergers

A third type of merger is a conglomerate merger. **Conglomerate mergers** involve *the merging of relatively unrelated businesses*. Conglomerate mergers are generally approved by the U.S. antitrust laws under the assumption that they do not significantly restrict competition. Thus, when Tyco acquired nine firms in 2001 in the health care, finance, personal care, and security industries, no antitrust action was taken to prevent the mergers because the firms were unrelated.

Why would unrelated firms want to merge? Or why would one firm want to be bought out by another? There are five general reasons:

1. *To achieve economies of scope*. Although the businesses are unrelated, some overlap is almost inevitable, so economies of scope are likely. For example, one firm's technical or marketing expertise may be helpful to the other firm, or the conglomerate's increased size may give it better bargaining power with its suppliers.

Conglomerate mergers are combinations of unrelated businesses. Five reasons why unrelated firms merge are:

1. To achieve economies of scope.
2. To get a good buy.
3. To diversify.
4. To ward off a takeover bid.
5. To strengthen their political-economic influence.

Q-8 When the long-distance phone company AT&T merged with the cellular phone company McCaw to create AT&T Wireless Services, what type of merger was it?

2. *To get a good buy.* Firms are always on the lookout for good buys. If a firm believes that another firm's stock is significantly undervalued, it can buy that stock at its low price and then sell it at a profit later when the stock is no longer undervalued.

3. *To diversify.* Many industries have a cyclical nature. In some parts of the business cycle they do poorly; in other parts of the business cycle they do just fine. Buying an unrelated company allows a firm to diversify and thereby to even out the cyclical fluctuation in its profits.

4. *To ward off a takeover bid.* Firms are always susceptible to being bought out by someone else. Sometimes they prevent an unwanted buyout by merging with another firm in order to become so large that they're indigestible. For example, in 1989 Time, Inc., merged with Warner Communications to reduce the likelihood that Time would be taken over by a third firm, Paramount. (Since then Time Warner has merged with America Online for other reasons.)

5. *To strengthen their political-economic influence.* The bigger you are, the more influence you have. Individuals who run companies like to have and use influence. Merging can increase their net influence considerably.

RECENT MERGER ACTIVITY AND DEACQUISITIONS

Figure 15-1 presents the number of mergers in the United States each year since 1892. As you can see mergers rose significantly in the late 1990s and into the early 2000s. The primary reasons for the increase in the number of mergers are globalization, deregulation, and technological change. Globalization leads to mergers because firms can gain instant foreign distribution networks and knowledge of local markets from mergers. They can also lower costs by restructuring production to low-cost areas. Deregulation of the telecommunications, electricity, and financial industries has encouraged mergers that take advantage of economies of scale and scope. Bank mergers and phone company mergers are examples.

The acceleration of technological change in recent years is another contributor to merger activity. Firms are looking for ways to develop new technologies or take advantage of new technologies, and merging with another company is one way to acquire a

Figure 15-1   Mergers in the United States since 1892

The number of mergers in the United States has fluctuated substantially in the last 100 years. Source of data changed in 1962, accounting for the break in the series.

Source: Federal Trade Commission, national press, Mergerstat.com, and author extrapolations.

new technology. The merger of America Online and Time Warner is an example of an Internet (technology) company combining with a "content" company.

At the same time that these mergers are taking place, firms are also engaging in **deacquisitions**—*one company's sale of parts of either another company it has bought, or parts of itself.* Sometimes regulators require such deacquisitions as a condition of a merger. Deacquisition also occurs as firms focus on those areas where they have comparative advantage and where growth is highest, and sell off aspects of their firms that are not part of their core business. Automobile firms are breaking off their component manufacturing operations. In the late 1990s Hewlett-Packard voluntarily split into two companies—Hewlett-Packard, which focuses on computers, and Agilent, which focuses on noncomputer aspects of the business. Then, in 2002 H-P combined with Compaq. The motto of the 2000s is that firms have to continually reinvent themselves.

As I mentioned at the beginning of this section, voluntarily breaking up companies is becoming much more prominent as firms try to find their niche in the global marketplace. Companies are continually spinning off portions of their business where they do not believe they have a comparative advantage, and buying businesses where they think they do have a comparative advantage. This process is likely to continue, making the U.S. market structure a continually changing landscape.

The U.S. market structure is a continually changing landscape.

ASSESSMENT OF MERGERS AND ACQUISITIONS

I've introduced a lot of terms in this section and, ideally, started you thinking about the issues involved in deciding on a merger and acquisition policy. This chapter does not arrive at definite conclusions, and in this it reflects the economics profession, which has no one position on what policy the United States should follow toward mergers.

But the economics profession's failure to come to an undivided view on mergers isn't necessarily a failing of economists. Mergers have both costs and benefits, and reasonable people will assess them differently.

INTERNATIONAL COMPETITION AND ANTITRUST POLICY IN OTHER COUNTRIES

As I discussed in Chapter 14, the nature of competition is changing in the United States. Ten or twenty years ago, when people talked about competition, they meant competition among U.S. firms. Now, however, they often mean international competition.

Because of this internationalization of competition, the political climate in the United States is changing. More and more, U.S. antitrust policymakers see the international market as the relevant market. The policy focus of government is shifting from "Is U.S. industry internally competitive so that it does not take advantage of the consumer?" to "Is U.S. industry internationally competitive so that it can compete effectively in the world economy?"

Other countries' approaches toward antitrust are a likely harbinger of future U.S. antitrust policy. The reason is that other countries, because most are smaller than the United States, have consistently seen the international market as the relevant market and have designed their antitrust laws accordingly. Their domestic markets were simply too small to take advantage of economies of scale.

What's interesting about other countries' antitrust laws is how lax they are when compared to U.S. laws. No other country forces companies to break up for antitrust violations, although some push for price rollbacks in cases of extreme monopolization. Even when, for example, the United States tried to export its stringent antitrust laws during its military occupation of Germany and Japan after World War II, those laws were repealed by those nations soon after the occupation ended.

Q-9 Does Japan have stricter or less strict antitrust laws than the United States has?

Britain: British Monopoly Commission

While it has the power to recommend structural reorganization, the British Monopoly Commission generally has not done so. Instead, it has pushed for price reductions in certain industries. After World War II, a number of major industries were nationalized, putting the government in direct control of prices, but many of these industries have been privatized in the past few years.

Japan: Fair Trade Commission

The Japanese Fair Trade Commission is weak and subordinated to the Ministry of International Trade and Industry and other government agencies. In retailing, small firms continue to dominate with the support of government. But the 1980s saw the beginnings of a retailing system with large stores, like the system in the United States. The Fair Trade Commission may take a role in suppressing that development.

Germany: Federal Cartel Office

The Federal Cartel Office is relatively small. Often it allows and even encourages cartels. It does have the authority to push for price reductions if it determines that the cartel has abused its power.

France: Commission on Competition

The Commission on Competition has been very weak and has often advocated mergers. In the 1960s, France actively promoted large-scale mergers, and during that period the government nationalized large industries without hearing objections from the Commission on Competition.

European Union: The European Commission

Starting in 1990, the EU's rules regarding mergers officially took precedence over member nations' local rules in those cases in which the merger involved significant activities in more than one member state. There were many such mergers; as expected, the expansion of the market that was made possible by the integration of the EU economies in 1992 generated significant merger activity as firms consolidated and tried to take advantage of new trading possibilities.

It wasn't only EU member firms that were merging. The largest percentage of growth in EU merger activity has been between EU firms and non-EU, especially U.S., firms. At times this has resulted in conflict between the European Commission (EC) and other countries' antitrust agencies. For instance, the EC had serious concerns regarding the 1997 merger between Boeing and McDonnell Douglas, but backed down after the United States pressured them to allow the merger. This case was unusual; for the most part the EC has been very lenient in allowing mergers and, from 1991 to 1998, the EC disallowed only 10 mergers. In the early 2000s, it has started to be less lenient to non-European firms.

In 2002, the EC started to actively promote mergers when the European Court ruled in favor of the EC's fight against "golden shares"—shares held by government with special voting rights. Specifically, these golden shares allowed governments that held these golden shares to block any mergers they wanted to. The courts ruled that mergers could be disallowed only for reasons of national security.

Other countries oppose antitrust laws because of economies of scale, lack of strong ideology supporting competition, and strong cultural ties between government and business.

One important reason other countries oppose antitrust regulation is that they recognize the importance of economies of scale. In many countries that have only small markets, the minimum efficient production level requires high concentration.

A second reason is their history. Most countries don't have the same populist worldview that exists in the United States. The ideological and cultural underpinning of strong antitrust laws (individualistic competition based on small producers) fits in nicely with the American populist worldview. In the United States, many people believe that bigness is bad. That belief is not as prevalent in other countries.

A third reason that other countries don't have strong antitrust laws is cultural. In the United States, government and business are often seen as enemies of each other. In cultures such as Japan's or Germany's, government and business are seen as allies, working together to increase exports and compete internationally.

In the early 2000s, serious accounting irregularities came to light in firms such as Enron and WorldCom. These firms, and many others, had used various accounting procedures—some legal, some not—to make their profits appear higher than they actually were. When the irregularities were revealed, these companies' stock values fell precipitously. In the case of Enron and WorldCom, the decline took the companies into bankruptcy.

Why would firms lie about profits? An important reason is that higher profits lead to higher stock prices—and top managers' pay (which includes stock options) depends on the price of the stock. *Options* are rights to buy a stock at a set price regardless of what happens to the price of the stock. If the stock price rises above the option price, those who exercise their options pocket the difference. Enough options and a high enough price can amount to tens or hundreds of millions of dollars. The high reported profits drive share prices high and, assuming the managers sell the stock before the accounting irregularity is discovered, they make a fortune even as the company is left in ruins.

In response to stories like these, the U.S. government increased regulation of company accounting rules, created a new board to oversee those rules, and required CEOs to sign off on the accuracy of the accounting figures provided to investors.

Will the new laws help? Perhaps somewhat, but problems remain. For example, despite most economists' suggestion that firms report stock options on the books as a cost, which would lessen the incentive of companies to give stock options to managers, the new government regulation does not require that. So there will remain an incentive on the part of managers to overstate profits and run. However, the New York Stock Exchange, a private company that oversees trading of many stocks, now requires including stock options as costs for companies listed on the exchange, so we will likely see this change taking place at many large companies.

Despite the fact that the antitrust laws are generally weaker abroad than in the United States sometimes they disallow mergers allowed in the United States and present another hurdle for global companies. For example, in the early 2000s General Electric attempted to merge with Honeywell. The merger was approved by U.S. authorities, and since both were U.S.-based companies, it seemed like the merger would go through. The European Commission, however, blocked the merger because the combined revenues were more than $4.2 billion, more than $212 million of which was from Europe, which meant they fell under EU as well as U.S. jurisdiction.

REGULATION, GOVERNMENT OWNERSHIP, AND INDUSTRIAL POLICIES

Antitrust policy is not the only way in which governments affect the competitive process. Other ways include (1) regulating the activities of firms, (2) government ownership—taking charge of the firms and operating them directly, and (3) industrial policy—influencing firms with laws and taxes. While I consider these issues in other parts of the book, here I want to briefly discuss some of the central elements of these three means of affecting the competitive process.

The government can also affect the competitive process by (1) regulation, (2) government ownership, and (3) industrial policy.

REGULATION

Regulation involves the setting of the rules that firms must follow if they are to conduct business. There are two types of regulation—price regulation and social regulation. *Price regulation* is regulation directed at industries that have natural monopoly elements. In order to allow them to take advantage of the economies of scale, firms are given an

Two types of regulation are price regulation and social regulation.

exclusive right to conduct business, but are subject to pricing controls. Examples include the Federal Energy Regulatory Commission (FERC), which regulates gas and oil pipelines and other energy-related areas; the Federal Communications Commission (FCC), which regulates cable television, telephones, television, and other communications areas; and the Securities and Exchange Commission (SEC), which regulates financial markets. *Social regulation* is concerned with the conditions under which goods and services are produced, the safety of those goods, and the side effects of production on society. Examples of social regulatory bodies include the Food and Drug Administration (FDA), the Environmental Protection Agency (EPA), and the Equal Employment Opportunity Commission (EEOC).

Price Regulation　　Price regulation is usually imposed in those industries where there seems to be a natural monopoly, as discussed in Chapter 12. In such cases, a single producer is most efficient because two firms could not take advantage of the economies of scale. But if the firm is to have the monopoly, it will be able to charge high prices to consumers and transfer the consumer surplus into its profit. Thus, when government grants such monopolies, it must also regulate the price they charge. Usually this has taken the form of requiring the firm to charge its average total cost plus a profit margin.

That sounds reasonable in theory, but the practice has problems. The first is that the regulated firm does not have an incentive to hold down costs. Cost increases lead directly to price increases. X-inefficiency will exist. Regulatory boards have tried to counteract that tendency of rising costs by permitting firms to pass on only "legitimate" costs, but generally the people on the regulatory boards do not have the accounting expertise to review costs and determine whether they are legitimate or not, especially when the companies have a strong incentive to make all costs look legitimate.

The problem is worsened by the fact that the boards are often made up of individuals from the industry that is being regulated. This gives the commission necessary expertise, but it also creates a potentially unhealthy connection between the regulatory commission and the firms being regulated. Some economists have argued that the connection is so close that the regulatory board simply reflects the regulated firms' interests, and that it protects them from competition arising from technological change.

Another problem raised by critics is that, once established, regulation may tend to extend far beyond natural monopolies and be introduced into industries where competition could work. Still another problem is that regulation continues even after technological change has created competitive market conditions. For example, the trucking and airline industries remained regulated industries for years after they became industries with significant competition. Often the regulatory boards simply function as a way of allowing an industry to operate as a legal cartel, holding prices up rather than keeping them down.

The above criticisms have led to significant deregulation over the last 20 years. Trucking, airlines, and aspects of phone service have all been deregulated, and electric power generation is currently being deregulated, as discussed in Chapter 14. In general, most economists' assessments of the results of this deregulation have been positive and some economists have estimated that deregulation saves consumers approximately $50 billion annually.

Social Regulation[3]　　Whereas most economists are skeptical of pricing regulation, they are far more divided on social regulation. Social regulation differs from pricing regulation in that:

---

[3]Social regulation is discussed more fully in Chapter 20.

Margin notes:

Price regulated firms often do not have an incentive to hold down costs.

Problems with price regulation have led to deregulation in recent years.

1. Social regulation applies to most firms and is not designed specifically for a natural monopoly. For example, when the Occupational Safety and Health Administration (OSHA) issues a requirement that all workers have a periodic break from work, it applies to all firms in the United States that fall under OSHA's control.

2. Social regulation affects large aspects of business: working conditions, the quality of the products, and the production processes firms are allowed to use.

Whereas pricing regulation has declined in the last 20 years, social regulation has increased substantially. Economists debate whether this is good or bad. Critics of social regulation point out that regulation has high administrative and compliance costs and that those costs hurt consumers more than the regulation benefits them. They believe that this occurs because the social regulation laws are too often poorly written and ambiguous, and put into law without information on what is reasonable and feasible. The result is higher prices, far less technical progress than there otherwise would have been, and fewer new entrants into a field as the regulatory burdens become unbearable for small firms.

Advocates of social regulation agree with some of the above but argue that the benefits of social regulation are worth the costs, and that the objections are simply a call for better regulation. They argue that social regulation has made manufacturing much safer in the United States, has improved the quality of life and the environment enormously, introduced far more justice into the economy, and reduced discrimination against minorities.

Judging between these two views is difficult because measurement of both the costs and benefits is difficult or impossible. In such cases, the economic cost/benefit framework cannot provide a definitive answer.

GOVERNMENT OWNERSHIP

Instead of regulation, an alternative way of dealing with the problems of natural monopolies is for the government to own the firms itself. European countries have used this approach much more often than has the United States. Instead of regulating the telephone (or other natural monopoly) industry, governments took it over and ran it with state employees. Since the 1980s most countries have been selling off government-owned businesses to private owners. Why? Most governments have found that government-owned firms did not have an incentive to hold costs down or to introduce new technology. Workers in government-owned firms, who were guaranteed jobs, used political threats to hold their wages high. Since the government firms faced little competition, they could raise prices and pass on the higher costs to consumers. The result was that European prices for telephone service, airline travel, and electricity were much higher than in the United States. Economic integration in Europe has been accompanied by privatization of many of the formerly government-owned industries, and a fall in prices in many of these industries.

Government-owned firms tend not to have an incentive to hold costs down.

Q-10 Why have European countries recently privatized many government-owned firms in the telecommunications, electricity, and airline industries?

INDUSTRIAL POLICIES

In the 1980s and 1990s, a rallying cry for many politicians was that the U.S. economy needed an industrial policy. An **industrial policy** is *a formal policy that government takes toward business*. These politicians wanted the United States to follow a policy like Japan's, where a branch of government—the Ministry of International Trade and Industry (MITI)—played an active role in guiding business decisions. Economists generally opposed such a policy, and when the Japanese economy faltered in the 1990s, the calls went away.

An industrial policy is a formal policy that government takes toward business.

Web Note 15.5
Military-Industrial
Policy

In thinking about government's relation with business, it is important to remember that, in actual fact, the United States has always had, and always will have, a type of industrial policy. That policy is embodied in its tax code, its laws, and its regulatory structure, and in the positions the government takes in international negotiations about tariffs and trade. An example is the U.S. government's strong support of international copyrights and patents, which prevent foreign firms from making "knockoffs" without paying a royalty to the U.S. firm. The policy is, however, an implicit policy of working with business, not an explicit policy of directing business.

Many close connections between government and business have developed. For example, the military works closely with its suppliers, and the relationship between them has been called a *military-industrial complex*. This combination of business and government plays important roles in making decisions about what is produced. For example, when Congress seemed about to cut production of the B-2 Stealth bomber, Northrup, the plane's manufacturer, took out full-page newspaper ads, pointing out that parts of the B-2 were produced in 48 states and that thousands of jobs would be lost if the government canceled the contract. Congress gave in, as it has done on many other defense items that are widely regarded as nonessential to national security. Many other business–government alliances exist in the United States, and there are similar government-drug complexes, government–higher-education complexes and government–high-tech complexes. In a democracy where politicians are dependent on business for funding their campaigns, such complexes are inevitable.

CONCLUSION

We've come to the end of our discussion of market structure and government policy toward the competitive process. What conclusion should we come to? That's a tough question because the problem has so many dimensions. What we can say is that market structure is important, and generally more competition is preferred to less competition. We can also say that, based on experience, government-created and protected monopolies have not been the optimal solution, especially when industries are experiencing technological change. But how government should deal with monopolies that develop as part of the competitive process is less clear. Competition has both dynamic elements and market structure elements, and often monopolies that develop as part of the competitive process are temporary—and they will be overwhelmed by other monopolies. Thus the debate about government entering into the market to protect competition has no single answer, which makes cases like the Microsoft antitrust case difficult to resolve.

SUMMARY

- Antitrust policy is the government's policy toward the competitive process.

- Judgment by performance means judging the competitiveness of markets by the behavior of firms in that market. Judgment by structure means judging the competitiveness of markets by how many firms operate in the industry and their market shares.

- There is a debate on whether markets should be judged on the basis of structure or on the basis of performance.

- Important antitrust laws include the Sherman Antitrust Act, the Clayton Act, and the Federal Trade Commission Act.

- The antitrust suit against IBM filed in 1967 was withdrawn in 1982 because the computer market had changed, making the charges against IBM moot.

- The antitrust suit against AT&T ended in a settlement that required AT&T to be broken up. AT&T has both divided itself and merged with other companies.

- In 2000 the courts found that Microsoft had a monopoly that was protected by barriers to entry and that Microsoft engaged in practices to maintain that monopoly power. Microsoft agreed to stop some practices.

- Three types of mergers are horizontal, vertical, and conglomerate.

- A horizontal merger is the combination of two companies in the same industry, a vertical merger is the

- combination of two companies in different industries, and a conglomerate merger is the combination of two companies in relatively unrelated industries.

- Five reasons that two unrelated firms would want to merge are economies of scope, a good buy, diversification, warding off a takeover bid, and strengthening political-economic influence.

- The increasing internationalization of the U.S. market has changed U.S. antitrust policy from looking at just domestic competition to considering international competition.

- Antitrust laws in other countries are generally more lenient than in the United Sates.

- Three ways other than antitrust policy that government affects the competitive process are regulation, government ownership, and industrial policy.

KEY TERMS

acquisition (342)
antitrust policy (328)
Clayton Antitrust Act (331)
conglomerate merger (343)
deacquisition (345)
Federal Trade Commission Act (331)
horizontal merger (342)
hostile takeover (342)
industrial policy (349)
judgment by performance (329)
judgment by structure (329)
merger (342)
natural monopoly (336)
Sherman Antitrust Act (329)
takeover (342)
vertical merger (343)

QUESTIONS FOR THOUGHT AND REVIEW

1. What is the difference between judgment by performance and judgment by structure?

2. Distinguish the basis of judgment for the Standard Oil and the ALCOA cases.

3. How would the U.S. economy likely differ today if Standard Oil had not been broken up?

4. How did the Clayton Antitrust Act clarify the Sherman Antitrust Act?

5. Colleges require that students take certain courses at that college in order to get a degree. Is that an example of a tie-in contract that limits consumers' choices? If so, should it be against the law?

6. Colleges give financial aid to certain students. Is this price discrimination? If so, should it be against the law?

7. Should interlocking directorships be against the law? Why or why not?

8. If you were an economist for a firm that wanted to merge, would you argue that the three-digit or five-digit NAICS industry is the relevant market? Why?

9. If you were an economist for Mattel, manufacturer of the doll Barbie, which was making an unsolicited bid to take over Hasbro, manufacturer of G.I. Joe, would you argue that the relevant market is dolls, preschool toys, or all toys including video games? Why? Would your answer change if you were working for Hasbro?

10. Has telephone service improved since AT&T was broken up? What does this imply about antitrust laws?

11. How did the antitrust suit against IBM affect IBM's future business?

12. In what market did Microsoft have a monopoly in the late 1990s? What technological advances threatened that monopoly?

13. Under the 1997 Department of Justice guidelines, would a merger be allowed between the number three firm in an industry and a firm with 2 percent of the market? The number four firm in the industry has 11 percent of the market.

14. Should the United States have a policy against conglomerate mergers? Why or why not?

15. How has the globalization of the U.S. economy changed U.S. antitrust policy?

16. What two methods does government have for dealing with natural monopolies? What problems are associated with each?

17. How would you design an industrial policy to avoid the problems inherent in industrial policies?

PROBLEMS AND EXERCISES

1. You're working at the Department of Justice. Ms. Eco-fame has just brought in a new index, the Ecofame index, which she argues is preferable to the Herfindahl index. The Ecofame index is calculated by cubing the market share of the top 10 firms in the industry.
   a. Calculate an Ecofame guideline that would correspond to the 1997 Department of Justice guidelines.
   b. State the advantages and disadvantages of the Ecofame index as compared to the Herfindahl index.

2. Using a monopolistic competition model, a cartel model of oligopoly, and a contestable market of oligopoly, discuss and demonstrate graphically, where possible, the effect of antitrust policy.

3. In 1993 Mattel proposed acquiring Fisher-Price for $1.2 billion. In the toy industry, Mattel is a major player with 11 percent of the market. Fisher-Price has 4 percent. The other two large firms are Tyco, with a 5 percent share, and Hasbro, with a 15 percent share. In the infant/preschool toy market, Mattel has an 8 percent share and Fisher-Price has a 27 percent share, the largest. The other two large firms are Hasbro, with a 25 percent share, and Rubbermaid, with a 12 percent share.
   a. What are the approximate Herfindahl and four-firm concentration ratios for these firms in each industry?

   b. If you were Mattel's economist, which industry definition would you suggest using in court if you were challenged by the government?
   c. Give an argument why the merger might decrease competition.
   d. Give an argument why the merger might increase competition.

4. In 1992 American Airlines offered a 50-percent-off sale and cut fares. In 1993 Continental Airlines and Northwest Airlines sued American Airlines over this action.
   a. What was the likely basis of the suit?
   b. How does the knowledge that Continental and Northwest were in serious financial trouble play a role in the suit?

5. Demonstrate graphically how regulating the price of a monopolist can both increase quantity and decrease price.
   a. Why did the regulation have the effect it did?
   b. How relevant to the real world do you believe this result is in the "contestable markets" view of the competitive process?
   c. How relevant to the real world do you believe this result is in the "cartel" view of the competitive process?

WEB QUESTIONS

1. Go to AT&T's corporate website at www.att.com to find out recent corporate events.
   a. What companies has AT&T acquired recently?
   b. How do those acquisitions affect AT&T's business?
   c. What antitrust issues might the mergers present?
   d. Is the FCC contesting the acquisition? (Search the FCC website at www.fcc.gov to find out.)

2. The Antitrust Division of the U.S. Department of Justice maintains a summary of its antitrust activities at www.usdoj.gov/atr. Go to this site, click on "Overview" and "Brochure: Antitrust Enforcement and the Consumer" to answer the following questions.

   a. According to this brochure, how does collusion among firms harm consumers and the economy?
   b. What type of collaboration, if any, does the Department of Justice recognize as legal?
   c. What are the three ways antitrust laws are enforced?
   d. How did vitamin producers worldwide in the 1990s violate U.S. antitrust laws? Was the U.S. Department of Justice able to impose penalties on non-U.S. entities?

ANSWERS TO MARGIN QUESTIONS

1. The Sherman Antitrust Act contained two main sections. The first stated that every contract, combination, or conspiracy in restraint of trade was illegal. The second stated that every person who shall monopolize or attempt to monopolize shall be deemed guilty of a misdemeanor. These provisions, while sounding strong, were so broad that they were almost unenforceable, and the interpretation was left to the courts. *(329)*

2. In the Standard Oil case, the Court determined that Standard Oil controlled 90 percent of the market. It said that this monopolistic structure of the market did not necessarily violate the Sherman Antitrust Act. However, the Court also decided that Standard Oil had engaged in systematic abuse and unfair business practices, and therefore was guilty of antitrust violations and must be broken up. *(331)*

3. In the ALCOA case, the Supreme Court changed the interpretation of the law. Here it found ALCOA was not guilty of any unfair practices. It agreed that ALCOA had simply used its knowledge of the market to expand capacity before any competitors had a chance to enter, and had kept its price low to prevent other entry. Thus, on performance standards, it was not violating the law. But the Court decided the structure of the market, not the company's performance, was the appropriate standard by which to judge cases, and, therefore, ALCOA was in violation of the antitrust law. *(331)*

4. In the 1956 Du Pont case, the Supreme Court found that Du Pont was innocent of monopolizing the production of cellophane, even though it was the only producer. The Court's reasoning was that the relevant market was the entire flexible wrap industry, not just cellophane. Since Du Pont did not dominate the flexible wrap industry, it was not in violation of antitrust law. *(333)*

5. In the late 1960s, the Department of Justice filed suit against IBM for violating the antitrust laws. It alleged that IBM had a monopoly of the general-purpose electronic digital computing industry and that it had acquired its market share because of unfair business practices. The

case dragged on for 13 years but never went to court. In 1982, the government withdrew its lawsuit. The antitrust case, however, had significant effects on IBM. It is likely that the experience caused IBM to shy away from the then-small personal computer market. This decision by IBM very likely was the beginning of the serious problems that IBM faced in the 1990s. *(335)*

6. In 1978, the Department of Justice sued AT&T, alleging that its potential competitors were not being allowed reasonable access to AT&T's local telephone network. The case was resolved in January 1982, when AT&T agreed to let itself be broken up. Specifically, AT&T divested itself of 22 operating companies and focused thereafter only on long-distance telephone service, manufacturing, and research and development. This settlement left AT&T free to enter into any unregulated business it desired, and in the 1990s AT&T expanded with fiber-optic networks. Ironically, these expansions placed it in direct competition with the still-regulated Baby Bells, which had inherited AT&T's monopoly rights. *(337)*

7. If Ben & Jerry's bought a dairy farm, it would be a vertical merger because Ben & Jerry's would be buying one of its suppliers. *(343)*

8. AT&T's merger with McCaw was a mixture of a horizontal merger and a conglomerate merger. It is a horizontal merger to the degree that one interprets the industry broadly as a "communications industry." It is a conglomerate merger if one interprets the industry narrowly and distinguishes the wireless communications industry from the wire communications industry. *(344)*

9. Japan has antitrust laws that are significantly less strict than those of the United States. *(345)*

10. European countries have been privatizing firms in telecommunications, electricity, and airline industries because the government-owned firms were inefficient, resulting in higher costs for consumers and less innovation. *(349)*

16 WORK AND THE LABOR MARKET

After reading this chapter, you should be able to:

- Use the theory of rational choice to explain why an increase in the marginal tax rate is likely to reduce the quantity of labor supplied.

- List four factors that influence the elasticity of market labor supply.

- Explain how the demand for labor is a derived demand.

- List four factors that influence the elasticity of market labor demand.

- Define *monopsony* and *bilateral monopoly.*

- Discuss real-world characteristics of labor markets in terms of market, political, and social forces.

- List three types of discrimination.

Work banishes those three great evils:
boredom, vice, and poverty.

—*Voltaire*

Most of us earn our living by working. We supply labor (get a job) and get paid for doing things that other people tell us they want done. Even before we get a job, work is very much a part of our lives. We spend a large portion of our school years preparing for work. Probably many of you are taking this economics course because you've been told that it will help prepare you for a job—or that it will get you more pay than you're getting in your present job. For you, this course is investment in human capital (skills embodied in workers through experience, education, and on-the-job training). If work in the marketplace isn't already familiar to you, once you get out of school it will become so (unless you're sitting on a hefty trust fund or marry somebody who is).

Your job will occupy at least a third of your waking hours. To a great extent, it will define you. When someone asks, "What do you do?" you won't answer, "I clip coupons, go out on dates, visit my children . . ." Instead you'll answer, "I work for the Blank Company" or "I'm an economist" or "I'm a teacher." Defining ourselves by our work means that work is more than the way we get income. It's a part of our social and cultural makeup. If we lose our jobs, we lose part of our identity.

There's no way I can discuss all the social, political, cultural, and economic dimensions of work and labor in one chapter, but it's important to begin by at least pointing them out in order to put my discussion of labor markets in perspective. A **labor market** is *a factor market in which individuals supply labor services for wages to other individuals and to firms that need (demand) labor services.* Because social and political pressures are particularly strong in labor markets, we can understand the nature of such markets only by considering how social and political forces interact with economic forces to determine our economic situation.

If the invisible hand were the only force operating, wages would be determined entirely by supply and demand. There's more to it than that, as you'll see, but it shouldn't be surprising to you that my discussion of the invisible hand and the labor market is organized around the concepts of supply and demand.

THE SUPPLY OF LABOR

The labor supply choice facing an individual (that is, the decisions of whether, how, and how much to work) can be seen as a choice between nonmarket activities and legal market activities. Nonmarket activities include sleeping, dating, studying, playing, cooking, cleaning, gardening, and black market trading. Legal market activities include taking some type of paid job or working for oneself, directly supplying products or services to consumers.

Many considerations are involved in individuals' choices of whether and how much to work and what kind of job to work at. Social background and conditioning are especially important, but the factor economists focus on is the **incentive effect** (*how much a person will change his or her hours worked in response to a change in the wage rate*). The incentive effect is determined by the value of supplying one's time to legal market activities relative to the value of supplying one's time to nonmarket activities. The normal relationship is:

The higher the wage, the higher the quantity of labor supplied.

This relationship between the wage rate and the quantity of labor supplied is shown in Figure 16-1. The wage rate is measured on the vertical axis; the quantity of labor supplied is measured on the horizontal axis. As you can see, the supply curve's upward slope indicates that as the wage rate increases, the quantity of labor supplied increases. Why is that the normal relationship? Because work involves opportunity cost. By working one hour more, you have one hour less to devote to nonmarket activities. Alternatively, if you devote the hour to nonmarket activities, you lose one hour's worth of income from working.

Say, for example, that by working you would have made $10 per hour. If you decide to work two hours less, you'll have $20 less to spend but two hours more available for other activities (including spending the smaller amount of money). When the wage rises, say to $12 per hour, an hour of leisure has a higher opportunity cost. As the cost of leisure goes up, you buy less of it, meaning that you work more.

As I noted in my general discussions of supply and demand, the incentive effects represented by the market supply curve come from individuals' either/or decisions to enter, or leave, the labor market; and from individuals' decisions to work more, or fewer, hours. Given the institutional constraints in the labor market, which require many people to work a fixed set of hours if they work at all, much of the incentive effect of higher wages influences the either/or decisions of individuals. This affects the labor force participation rate (the number of people employed or looking for work as a percentage of

Economists focus on the incentive effect when considering an individual's choice of whether and how much to work.

Applying rational choice theory to the supply of labor tells us that the higher the wage, the higher the quantity of labor supplied.

Q-1 Under the usual conditions of supply, what would you expect would happen to the amount of time you study if the wage of your part-time job rises?

Figure 16-1 The Supply of Labor
The supply of labor is generally considered to be upward-sloping because the opportunity cost of not working increases as wages get higher.

Because labor income is such an important component of most people's total income, when wages change other things often do not stay equal, and at times the effect can seem strange. For example, say that you earn $10 an hour and you decide to work eight hours per day. Suddenly demand for your services goes up and you find that you can receive $40 an hour. Will you decide to work more hours? According to the rational choice rule, you will, but you might also decide that at $40 an hour you'll work only six hours a day—$240 a day is enough; the rest of the day you want leisure time to spend your money. In such a case a higher wage means working less.

Does this violate the rational choice rule? The answer is no, because other things—specifically your income—do not remain equal. The higher wage makes you decide to work more—as the rational choice rule says; but the effect of the higher wage is overwhelmed by the effect of the higher income that allows you to decide to work less.

To distinguish between these two effects, economists have given them names. The decision, based on the rational choice rule, to work more hours when your pay goes up is called the *substitution effect*. You substitute work for leisure because the price of leisure has risen. The decision to work fewer hours when your pay goes up, based on the fact that you're richer and therefore can live a better life, is called the *income effect*.

It's possible that the income effect can exceed the substitution effect, and a wage increase can cause a person to work less, but that possibility does not violate the rational choice rule, which refers to the substitution effect only. For those of you who didn't make a deal with me in Chapter 8, on individual choice, a good exercise is to show the income and substitution effects with indifference curves and to demonstrate how it might be possible for an increase in the wage to lead to a decline in hours of work.

---

people able to work) rather than adjusting the number of hours worked. For example, when wages rise, retired workers may find it worthwhile to go back to work, and many teenagers may choose to find part-time jobs.

REAL WAGES AND THE OPPORTUNITY COST OF WORK

The upward-sloping supply curve of labor tells you that, other things equal, as wages go up, the quantity of labor supplied goes up. But if you look at the historical record, you will see that over the last century real wages in the United States increased substantially but the average number of hours worked per person fell. This difference is partly explained by the income effect. (See the box "Income and Substitution Effects.") Higher incomes make people richer, and richer people choose more leisure.

Given that people are far richer today than they were 50 or 100 years ago, it isn't surprising that they work less. What's surprising is that they work as much as they do—eight hours a day rather than the four or so hours a day that would be enough to give people the same income they had a century ago.

The explanation of why people haven't reduced their hours of work more substantially can be found in how leisure has changed. A century ago, conversation was an art. People could use their time for long, leisurely conversations. Letter writing was a skill all educated people had, and cooking dinner was a three-hour event. If today people were satisfied with leisure consisting of long conversations, whittling, and spending quality time with their families rather than skiing, golfing, or traveling, they could get by with working perhaps only four or five hours per day instead of eight hours. But that isn't the case.

Today leisurely dinners, conversations about good books, and witty letters have been replaced by "efficient" leisure: a fast-food supper, a home video, and the instant analysis of current events. Microwave ovens, frozen dinners, Pop-Tarts, cellular telephones,

Modern gadgets increase the efficiency of leisure but cost money, which means people must work more to enjoy their leisure.

the Internet—the list of gadgets and products designed to save time is endless. All these gadgets that increase the "efficiency" of leisure (increase the marginal utility per hour of leisure spent) cost money, which means people today must work more to enjoy their leisure! In the United States, one reason people work hard is so that they can play hard (and expensively).

The fast pace of modern society has led a number of people to question whether we, as a society, are better off working hard to play hard. Are we better off or simply more harried? Most economists don't try to answer this normative question; but they do point out that people are choosing their harried lifestyle, so to argue that people are worse off, one must argue that people are choosing something they don't really want. That may be true, but it's a tough argument to prove.

Economists do not try to answer the normative question of whether people are better off today, working hard to play hard, or simply are more harried.

THE SUPPLY OF LABOR AND NONMARKET ACTIVITIES

In addition to leisure, labor supply issues and market incentives play an important role in other nonmarket activities. For example, there's a whole set of illegal activities, such as selling illegal drugs, that are alternatives to taking a legal job.

Let's say that an 18-year-old street kid figures he has only two options: Either he can work at a minimum wage job or he can deal drugs illegally. Dealing drugs involves enormous risks of getting arrested or shot, but it also means earning $50 or $75 an hour. Given that choice, many risk takers opt to sell drugs. When an emergency room doctor asked a shooting victim in New York City why he got involved in selling drugs, he responded, "I'm not going to work for chump change. I make $3,000 a week, tax-free. What do they pay you, sucker?" The doctor had to admit that even he wasn't making that kind of money.

For middle-class individuals who have prospects for good jobs, the cost of being arrested can be high—an arrest can destroy their future prospects. For poor street kids with little chance of getting a good job, an arrest makes little difference to their future. For them the choice is heavily weighted toward selling drugs. This is especially true for the entrepreneurial types—the risk takers—the movers and shakers who might have become the business leaders of the future. I've asked myself what decision I would have made had I been in their position. And I suspect I know the answer.

Prohibiting certain drugs leads to potentially high income from selling those drugs and has significant labor market effects. The incentive effects that prohibition has on the choices of jobs facing poor teenagers is a central reason why some economists support the legalization of currently illegal drugs.

Web Note 16.1
Who Works?

INCOME TAXATION, WORK, AND LEISURE

It is after-tax income, not before-tax income, that determines how much you work. Why? Because after-tax income is what you give up by not working. The government, not you, forgoes what you would have paid in taxes if you had worked. This means that when the government raises your marginal rate (the tax you pay on an additional dollar), it reduces your incentive to work. When the marginal tax rate gets really high—say 60 or 70 percent—it can significantly reduce individuals' incentive to work and earn income.

One main reason why the U.S. government reduced marginal income tax rates in the 1980s was to reduce the negative incentive effects of high taxes. Whereas in the 1950s and 1960s the highest U.S. marginal income tax rate was 70 percent, today the highest marginal income tax rate is about 40 percent. European countries, which have significantly higher marginal tax rates than the United States, are currently struggling with the problem of providing incentives for people to work.

Q-2 Why do income taxes reduce your incentive to work?

European countries, which have relatively high marginal tax rates, are struggling with the problem of providing incentives for people to work.

Reducing the marginal tax rate in the United States hasn't completely eliminated the problem of negative incentive effects on individuals' work effort. The reason is that the amounts people receive from many other government programs are tied to earned income. When your earned income goes up, your benefits from these other programs go down.

Say, for example, that you're getting welfare and you're deciding whether to take a $6-an-hour job. Income taxes and Social Security taxes reduce the amount you take home from the job by 20 percent, to $4.80 an hour. But you also know that the Welfare Department will reduce your welfare benefits by 50 cents for every dollar you take home. This means that you lose another $2.40 per hour, so the marginal tax rate on your $6-an-hour job isn't 20 percent; it's 60 percent. By working an hour, you've increased your net income by only $2.40. When you consider the transportation cost of getting to and from work, the expense of getting new clothes to wear to work, the cost of child care, and other job-associated expenses, the net gain in income is often minimal. Your implicit marginal tax rate is almost 100 percent! At such rates, there's an enormous incentive either not to work or to work off the books (get paid in cash so you have no recorded income that the tax agent can trace).

The negative incentive effect can sometimes be even more indirect. For example, college scholarships are generally given on the basis of need. A family that earns more gets less in scholarship aid; the amount by which the scholarship is reduced as a family's income increases acts as a marginal tax on individuals' income. Why work hard to provide for yourself if a program will take care of you if you don't work hard? Hence, the irony in any need-based assistance program is that it reduces the people's incentive to prevent themselves from being needy. These negative incentive effects on labor supply that accompany any need-based program present a public policy dilemma for which there is no easy answer.

THE ELASTICITY OF THE SUPPLY OF LABOR

Exactly how these various incentives affect the amount of labor an individual supplies is determined by the elasticity of the individual's labor supply curve.

The elasticity of the market supply curve is determined by the elasticity of individuals' supply curves and by individuals entering and leaving the labor force. Both of these, in turn, are determined by individuals' opportunity cost of working. If a large number of people are willing to enter the labor market when wages rise, then the market labor supply will be highly elastic even if individuals' supply curves are inelastic.

The elasticity of supply also depends on the type of market being discussed. For example, the elasticity of the labor supply facing one firm of many in a small town will likely be far greater than the elasticity of the labor supply facing all firms combined in that town. If only one firm raises its wage, it will attract workers away from other firms; if all the firms in town raise their wages, any increase in labor must come from increases in labor force participation, increases in hours worked per person, or in-migration (the movement of new workers into the town's labor market).

Existing workers prefer inelastic labor supplies because that means an increase in demand for labor will raise their wage by more. Employers prefer elastic supplies because that means an increase in demand for labor doesn't require large wage increases. These preferences can be seen in news reports about U.S. immigration laws, their effects, and their enforcement. Businesses such as hotels and restaurants often oppose strict immigration laws. Their reason is that jobs such as janitor, chambermaid, and busperson are frequently filled by new immigrants or illegal aliens who have comparatively low expectations.

Q-3 What is the irony of any need-based program?

Elasticity of market supply depends on:

1. Individuals' opportunity cost of working.
2. The type of market being discussed.
3. The elasticity of individuals' supply curves.
4. Individuals entering and leaving the labor market.

Because of the importance of the elasticity of labor supply, economists have spent a great deal of time and effort estimating it. Their best estimates of labor supply elasticities to market activities are about 0.1 for heads of households and 1.1 for secondary workers in households. These elasticity figures mean that a wage increase of 10 percent will increase the quantity of labor supplied by 1 percent for heads of households (an inelastic supply) and 11 percent for secondary workers in households (an elastic supply). Why the difference? Institutional factors. Hours of work are only slightly flexible. Since most heads of households are employed, they cannot significantly change their hours worked. Many secondary workers in households are not employed, and the higher elasticity reflects new secondary workers entering the labor market.

IMMIGRATION AND THE INTERNATIONAL SUPPLY OF LABOR

International limitations on the flow of people, and hence on the flow of labor, play an important role in elasticities of labor supply. In many industries, wages in developing countries are 1/10 or 1/20 the rate of wages in the United States. This large wage differential means that many people from those low-wage countries would like to move to the United States to earn the higher wages. Because they cannot always meet the legal immigration restrictions that limit the flow, many people come into the United States illegally. In addition to about 800,000 legal immigrants per year, more than 400,000 people per year come illegally. Illegal immigrants take a variety of jobs at lower wages and worse conditions than U.S. citizens and legal immigrants are willing to take. The result is that the actual supply of labor is more elastic than the measured supply, especially in those jobs that cannot be easily policed.

Web Note 16.2
Leaving Home

In the early 1990s, the European Union introduced open borders among member countries. That institutional change has brought about a more open flow of individuals into higher-wage EU countries from lower-wage EU countries, although other institutionalized restrictions on flows of people, such as language and culture barriers, prevented the EU from being a unified labor market through the early 2000s.

THE DERIVED DEMAND FOR LABOR

The demand for labor follows the basic law of demand:

The higher the wage, the lower the quantity of labor demanded.

This relationship between the wage rate and the quantity of labor demanded is shown by the blue line in Figure 16-2. Its downward slope states that as the wage rate falls the quantity of labor demanded rises. The reason for this relationship differs between the demand for labor by self-employed individuals and by firms.

When individuals are self-employed (work for themselves), the demand for their labor is the demand for the product or service they supply—be it cutting hair, shampooing rugs, or filling teeth. You have an ability to do something, you offer to do it at a certain price, and you see who calls. You determine how many hours you work, what price you charge, and what jobs you take. The income you receive depends on the demand for the good or service you supply and your decision about how much labor you want to supply. In analyzing self-employed individuals, we can move directly from demand for the product to demand for labor.

When a person is not self-employed, determining the demand for labor isn't as direct. It's a two-step process: Consumers demand products from firms; firms, in turn, demand labor and other factors of production. The demand for labor by firms is a **derived demand**—*the demand for factors of production by firms, which depends on consumers' demands*. In other words, it's derived from consumers' demand for the goods that the firm sells. Thus, you can't think of demand for a factor of production such as labor separately

Derived demand is the demand for factors of production by firms, which depends on consumers' demands.

Figure 16-2 Equilibrium in the Labor Market

When the supply and demand curves for labor are placed on the same graph, the equilibrium wage, W_e, is where the quantity supplied equals quantity demanded. At this wage, Q_e laborers are supplied.

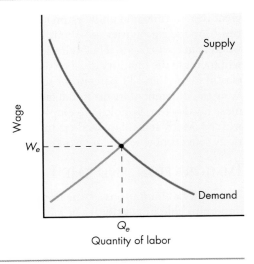

from demand for goods. Firms translate consumers' demands into a demand for factors of production.

FACTORS INFLUENCING THE ELASTICITY OF DEMAND FOR LABOR

The elasticity of the derived demand for labor, or for any other input, depends on a number of factors. One of the most important is (1) *the elasticity of demand for the firm's good*. The more elastic the final demand, the more elastic the derived demand. Other factors influencing the elasticity of derived demand include (2) *the relative importance of the factor in the production process* (the more important the factor, the less elastic is the derived demand); (3) *the possibility of, and cost of, substitution in production* (the easier substitution is, the more elastic is the derived demand); and (4) *the degree to which the marginal productivity falls with an increase in the factor* (the faster productivity falls, the less elastic is the derived demand).

Each of these relationships follows from the definition of *elasticity* (the percentage change in quantity divided by the percentage change in price) and a knowledge of production. To be sure you understand, ask yourself the following question: If all I knew about two firms was that one was a perfect competitor and the other was a monopolist, which firm would I say is likely to have the more elastic derived demand for labor? If your answer wasn't automatically "the competitive firm" (because its demand curve is perfectly elastic and hence more elastic than a monopolist's), I would suggest that at this point you review the discussion of factors influencing demand elasticity in Chapter 6 and relate that to this discussion. The two discussions are similar and serve as good reviews for each other.

LABOR AS A FACTOR OF PRODUCTION

The traditional factors of production are land, labor, capital, and entrepreneurship. When economists talk of the labor market, they're talking about two of these factors: labor and entrepreneurship. **Entrepreneurship** is *labor services that involve high degrees of organizational skills, concern, oversight responsibility, and creativity*. It is a type of creative labor.

The reason for distinguishing between labor and entrepreneurship is that an hour of work is not simply an hour of work. If high degrees of organizational skill, concern,

---

Q-4 Name at least two factors that influence the elasticity of a firm's derived demand for labor.

Four factors that influence the elasticity of demand for labor are:

1. The elasticity of demand for the firm's good.
2. The relative importance of labor in the production process.
3. The possibility of, and cost of, substitution in production.
4. The degree to which marginal productivity falls with an increase in labor.

Entrepreneurship is labor services that involve high degrees of organizational skills, concern, oversight responsibility, and creativity.

oversight responsibility, and creativity are exerted (which is what economists mean by *entrepreneurship*), one hour of such work can be the equivalent of days, weeks, or even years of simple labor. That's one reason that pay often differs between workers doing what seems to be the same job. It's also why one of the important decisions a firm makes is what type of labor to hire. Should the firm try to hire high-wage entrepreneurial labor or low-wage nonentrepreneurial labor?

In the appendix to this chapter, I formally develop the firm's derived demand. Here in the chapter itself I will simply point out that the demand for labor follows the basic law of demand—the lower the price, the higher the quantity demanded. Figure 16-2 shows a demand-for-labor curve combined with a supply-of-labor curve. As you would expect, equilibrium is at wage W_e and quantity supplied Q_e.

SHIFT FACTORS OF DEMAND

Factors that shift the demand curve for labor will put pressure on the equilibrium price to change. Let's consider some examples. Say the cost of a competing factor of supply, such as a machine that also could do the job, rises. That would shift the demand for this factor (labor) out, and in doing so put pressure on the wage to rise.

Alternatively, say a new technology develops that requires skills different from those currently being used—for instance, requiring knowing how to use a computer rather than knowing how to use a slide rule. The demand for individuals knowing how to use slide rules will decrease, and their wage will tend to fall.

Another example: Say an industry becomes more monopolistic. What will that do to the demand for labor in that industry? Since monopolies produce less output, the answer is that it would decrease the demand for workers, since the industry would hire fewer of them. The demand for workers would shift in and wages would tend to fall.

Finally, say the demand for the firm's good increases. Then it's clear that the firm's demand for labor will also increase. The way in which these shift factors work is developed in more detail in the appendix to this chapter.

Q.5 What would happen to the demand for labor if a firm's product became more popular?

Technology and the Demand for Labor   What effect will a change in technology have on the demand for labor? This question has often been debated, and it has no unambiguous answer. What economists do know is that the simple reasoning often used by laypeople when they argue that the development of new technology will decrease the demand for labor is wrong. That simple reasoning is as follows: "Technology makes it possible to replace workers with machines, so it will decrease the demand for labor." This is sometimes called *Luddite reasoning* because it's what drove the Luddites to go around smashing machines in early-19th-century England.

What's wrong with Luddite reasoning? First, look at history. Technology has increased enormously, yet the demand for labor has not decreased; instead it has increased as output has increased. In other words, Luddite reasoning doesn't take into account the fact that total output can change. A second problem with Luddite reasoning is that labor is necessary for building and maintaining the machines, so increased demand for machines increases the demand for labor.

Luddite reasoning isn't *all* wrong. Technology can sometimes decrease the demand for certain types of skills. The computer has decreased demand for calligraphers; the automobile reduced demand for carriage makers. New technology changes the types of labor demanded. If you have the type of labor that will be made technologically obsolete, you can be hurt by technological change. However, technological change hasn't reduced the overall demand for labor; it has instead led to an increase in total output and a need for even more laborers to produce that output.

Web Note 16.3
Productivity Studies

In the 21st century we're likely to see a continued increase in the use of robots to do many repetitive tasks that blue-collar workers formerly did. Thus, demand for manufacturing labor will likely continue to decline, but it will be accompanied by an increase in demand for service industry labor—designing and repairing robots and designing activities that will fill up people's free time.

International Competitiveness and a Country's Demand for Labor   Many of the issues in the demand for labor concern one firm's or industry's demand for labor relative to another firm's or industry's demand. When we're talking about the demand for labor by the country as a whole—an issue fundamentally important to many of the policy issues being discussed today—we have to consider the country's overall international competitiveness. A central determinant of a country's competitiveness is the relative wage of labor in that country compared to the relative wage of labor in other countries.

Wages vary considerably among countries. For example, in 2001 workers in the manufacturing industry earned an average $20.32 an hour in the United States, $22.86 an hour in Germany, and $2.34 an hour in Mexico. Multinational corporations are continually making decisions about where to place production facilities, and labor costs— wage rates—play an important role in these decisions. That means the country's exchange rate plays an important role in determining the demand for labor in a country. For example, in the early 1990s many Japanese automobile companies switched their production of cars to be sold in the United States from production facilities in Japan to facilities in the United States. Why? Because the rise in value of the yen, and fall in value of the dollar, meant that the hourly rate of labor in the United States was about $16 and the hourly rate in Japan was about $20.

But why produce in the United States when the hourly rate in Taiwan, for example, was only 1/4 that in the United States? Or in Mexico, where the hourly rate was only 1/10 that in the United States? The reasons are complicated, but include (1) differences in workers—U.S. workers may be more productive; (2) transportation costs—producing in the country to which you're selling keeps transportation costs down; (3) potential trade restrictions—Japan was under enormous pressure from the U.S. government to reduce its trade surplus with the United States, and producing in the United States helped it avoid future trade restrictions; and (4) compatibility of production techniques with social institutions—production techniques must fit with a society's social institutions. If they don't, production will fall significantly. Number (5) is the *focal point phenomenon*—a situation where a company chooses to move, or expand, production to another country because other companies have already moved or expanded there. A company can't consider all places, and it costs a lot of money to explore a country's potential as a possible host country. Japanese businesses know what to expect when they open a plant in the United States; they don't know in many other countries. So the United States and other countries that Japanese businesses have knowledge about become focal points. They are considered as potential sites for business, while other, possibly equally good, countries are not. Combined, these reasons lead to a "follow-the-leader" system in which countries fall in and out of global companies' production plans. The focal-point countries expand and develop; the others don't.

THE ROLE OF OTHER FORCES IN WAGE DETERMINATION

Supply and demand forces strongly influence wages, but they do not fully determine wages. Real-world labor markets are filled with examples of individuals or firms who resist these supply and demand pressures through organizations such as labor unions,

---

Wages aren't the only consideration when a firm decides where to locate production. Other factors include worker productivity, transportation costs, trade restrictions, and social institutions.

Q-6 Name two factors besides relative wages that determine the demand for labor in one country compared to another.

Supply and demand forces strongly influence wages, but they do not fully determine wages.

Figure 16-3   The Labor Market in Action

In (**a**) you can see the effect of an above-equilibrium wage: If workers force the firm to pay them a wage of W_1, more workers will be supplied (Q_S) than demanded (Q_D). With an excess supply of labor, jobs must be rationed. In (**b**) you can see the effect of an increase in the supply of labor. Assuming the demand for labor remains the same, the increase in the supply of labor will cause the wage level to drop from W_0 to W_1.

(a) Maintaining excess supply

(b) An increase in supply

professional associations, and agreements among employers. But, as I've emphasized throughout the book, supply/demand analysis is a useful framework for considering such resistance.

For example, say that you're advising a firm's workers on how to raise their wages. You point out that if workers want to increase their wages, they must figure out some way either to increase the demand for their services or to limit the labor supplied to the firm. One way to limit the number of workers the firm will hire (and thus keep existing workers' wages high) is to force the firm to pay an above-equilibrium wage, as in Figure 16-3(a). Say that in their contract negotiations the workers get the firm to agree to pay a wage of W_1. At wage W_1, the quantity of labor supplied is Q_S and the quantity of labor demanded is Q_D. The difference, $Q_S - Q_D$, represents the number of people who want jobs at wage W_1 compared to the number who have them. In such a case, jobs must be rationed. Whom you know, where you come from, or the color of your skin may play a role in whether you get a job with that firm.

As a second example, consider what would happen if U.S. immigration laws were liberalized. If you say the supply curve of labor would shift outward and the wage level would drop, you're right, as shown in Figure 16-3(b). In it the supply of labor increases from S_0 to S_1. In response, the wage falls from W_0 to W_1 and the quantity of labor demanded increases from Q_0 to Q_1.

In analyzing the effect of such a major change in the labor supply, however, remember that the supply and demand framework is relevant only if the change in the supply of labor doesn't also affect the demand for labor. In reality, a liberalization of U.S. immigration laws might increase the demand for products, thereby increasing the demand for labor and raising wages. When you look at the overall effect of a change, you will often find that the final result is less clear-cut. That's why it's important always to remember the assumptions behind the model you're using. Those assumptions often add qualifications to the simple "right" answer.

Q-7   How could an increase in the supply of labor lead to an increase in the demand for labor?

Looking at the overall effects of a change, rather than just the partial equilibrium effects, often makes the final result less clear-cut.

IMPERFECT COMPETITION AND THE LABOR MARKET

Just as product markets can be imperfectly competitive, so too can labor markets. For example, there might be a **monopsony** (*a market in which a single firm is the only buyer*).

A monopsony is a market in which a single firm is the only buyer.

Alternatively, laborers might have organized together in a union that allows workers to operate as if there were only a single seller. In effect, the union could operate as a monopoly. Alternatively again, there might be a **bilateral monopoly** (*a market with only a single seller and a single buyer*). Let's briefly consider these three types of market imperfections.

MONOPSONY

> A monopsonist takes into account the fact that hiring another worker will increase the wage rate it must pay all workers.

When there's only one buyer of labor services, it makes sense for that buyer to take into account the fact that if it hires another worker, the equilibrium wage will rise and it will have to pay more for all workers. The choice facing a monopsonist can be seen in Figure 16-4, in which the supply curve of labor is upward sloping so that the **marginal factor cost** (*the additional cost to a firm of hiring another worker*) is above the supply curve since the monopsonist takes into account the fact that hiring another worker will increase the wage rate it must pay to all workers.

Instead of hiring Q_c workers at a wage of W_c, as would happen in a competitive labor market, the monopsonist hires Q_m workers and pays them a wage of W_m. (A good exercise to see that you understand the argument is to show that where there's a monopsonist, a minimum wage simultaneously can increase employment and raise the wage.)

UNION MONOPOLY POWER

When a union exists, it will have an incentive to act as a monopolist, restricting supply to increase its members' wages. To do so it must have the power to restrict both supply and union membership. A union would have a strong tendency to act like a monopolist and to move to an equilibrium somewhat similar to the monopsonist case, except for one important difference. The wage the union would set wouldn't be set below the competitive wage; instead, the wage would be above the competitive wage at W_u, as in Figure 16-4. Faced with a wage of W_u, competitive firms will hire Q_u workers. Thus, with union monopoly power, the benefits of restricting supply accrue to the union members, not to the firm as in the monopsonist case.

Figure 16-4   Monopsony, Union Power, and the Labor Market
A monopsonist hires fewer workers and pays them less than would a set of competitive firms. The monopsonist determines the quantity of labor, Q_m, to hire at the point where the marginal factor cost curve intersects the demand curve. The monopsonist pays a wage of W_m. A union has a tendency to push for a higher wage, W_u, and a lower quantity of workers, Q_u.

BILATERAL MONOPOLY

As our final case, let's consider a bilateral monopoly in which a monopsonist faces a union with monopoly power. In this case, we can say that the equilibrium wage will be somewhere between the monopsonist wage W_m and the union monopoly power wage W_u. The equilibrium quantity will be somewhere between Q_u and Q_m in Figure 16-4. Where in that range the wage and equilibrium quantity will be depends on the two sides' negotiating skills and other noneconomic forces.

A bilateral monopoly is a market in which a single seller faces a single buyer.

DOWNSIZING, UPSIZING, AND X-INEFFICIENCY

From 1992 to 2003, employment rose in the United States by over 20 million jobs. At the same time there was much concern in the nation about **downsizing**—*a reduction in the workforce*—of major corporations, especially at the level of middle management. Considering these two issues—increased total employment and the downsizing at particular firms—gives us a good sense of how supply/demand analysis carries over into the real world.

First let's consider the increase in employment during this time period. What were the reasons total employment grew? First, the U.S. economy grew—that growth increased demand for goods and hence for labor. Second, the value of the dollar remained low relative to the value of the currencies of other major industrial countries. Demand for U.S. exports increased, and hence the demand for U.S. labor increased. Third, union power in the United States declined, lowering overall wages (adjusted for inflation) in unionized industries, thereby increasing the quantity of labor demanded. Combined, these three forces accounted for the rise in employment.

The downsizing was, in part, a way by which union power was reduced. Firms producing with a high-wage workforce had an incentive to shift their production to firms that had low-wage workforces—that is, to low-wage firms abroad and to low-wage U.S. firms. The term developed for this is **outsourcing**—*a firm shifting production from its own plant to other firms, either in the United States or abroad, where wages are lower.* Firms' outsourcing increased the demand for low-wage labor; they *upsized* as firms with high-wage labor downsized.

Why didn't high-wage firms simply cut wages? To some degree they did, but cutting wages often leads to bitter fights within a firm. Downsizing keeps the angry workers out of the production process and makes the workers who are not laid off feel lucky that they have kept their jobs.

Such outsourcing was only part of the cause of downsizing. A second part was a reduction in X-inefficiency. As discussed in Chapter 14, for a variety of reasons, such as the monitoring problem, managers have a tendency to become lazy and produce inefficiently. When faced with significant international and domestic competition, as firms have been in recent years, they must reduce that inefficiency or go out of business. Thus, downsizing is a normal part of the way the competitive process works. It results from a reduction in demand for labor from inefficient firms and a transfer of demand to more efficient firms, who, it might be said, are upsizing. In this period, upsizing significantly exceeded downsizing, but it was primarily the downsizing that was reported in the press.

Q-8 How is it that in the late 1990s and early 2000s total U.S. employment grew and companies downsized at the same time?

Some reasons employment grew in the 1990s and early 2000s include:

1. Economic growth.
2. Low value of the dollar.
3. Declining union power.

Downsizing is a normal part of the way the competitive process works.

POLITICAL AND SOCIAL FORCES AND THE LABOR MARKET

Let's now consider some real-world characteristics of U.S. labor markets. For example:

The four traditional categories of income are wages, rent, profits, and interest. Wages, discussed in the text, are determined by economic factors (the forces of supply and demand), with strong influences by political and social forces, which often restrict entry or hold wages at non-market-clearing levels. Supply and demand determine price and income, given an institutional structure that includes property rights and a contractual legal system.

The same holds true for nonwage income: rent, profits, and interest. The forces of supply and demand also determine these forms of income. But, as we have emphasized throughout the book, supply and demand are not necessarily the end of the story. Supply and demand determine price and income, given an institutional structure that includes property rights—the rights given to people to use specified property as they see fit—and the contractual legal system—the set of laws that govern economic behavior of the society. If you change property rights, you change the distribution of income. Thus, in a larger sense, supply and demand don't determine the distribution of income; the distribution of property rights does.

The system of property rights and the contractual legal system that underlie the U.S. economy evolved over many years. Many people believe that property rights were unfairly distributed to begin with; if you believe that, you'll also believe that the distribution of income and the returns to those property rights are unfair. In other words, you can favor markets but object to the underlying property rights. Many political fights about income ·distribution concern fights over property rights, not fights over the use of markets.

Such distributional fights have been going on for a long time. In feudal times much of the land was held communally; it belonged to everyone, or at least everyone used it. It was common land—a communally held resource. As the economy evolved into a market economy, that land was appropriated by individuals, and these individuals became landholders who could determine the use of the land and could receive rent for allowing other individuals to use that land. Supply and demand can explain how much rent will accrue to a landholder; it cannot explain the initial set of property rights.

The type of issues raised by looking at the underlying property rights are in large part academic for western societies. The property rights that exist, and the contractual legal system under which markets operate, are given. You're not going to see somebody going out and introducing a new alternative set of property rights in which the ownership of property is transferred to someone else. The government may impose shifts at the margin; for example, new zoning laws—laws that set limits on the use of one's property—will modify property rights and create fights about whether society has the right to impose such laws. But there will be no wholesale change in property rights. That's why most economic thinking simply takes property rights as given.

But taking property rights as given isn't a reasonable assumption for the developing countries or the formerly socialist countries now in the process of establishing markets. They must decide what structure of property rights they want. Who should be given what was previously government land and property? Who should own the factories? Do those societies want land to be given to individuals in perpetuity, or do they want it given to individuals for, say, 100 years? As these questions have been raised, economists have redirected their analysis to look more closely at the underlying legal and philosophical basis of supply and demand. As they do so they are extending and modifying the economic theory of income distribution.

1. English teachers are paid close to what economics teachers are paid even though the quantity of English teachers supplied significantly exceeds the quantity of English teachers demanded, while the quantity of economics teachers supplied is approximately equal to the quantity demanded.

2. On average, women earn about 85 cents for every $1 earned by men.

3. Certain types of jobs are undertaken primarily by members of a single ethnic group. For example, a large percentage of construction workers on high-rise buildings are Mohawk Indians. They have an uncanny knack for keeping their balance on high, open building frames.

4. Firms often pay higher than "market" wages.

5. Firms often don't lay off workers even when there is a decrease in the demand for their products.

6. It often seems that there are two categories of jobs: dead-end jobs and jobs with potential for career advancement. Once in a dead-end job, a person finds it almost impossible to switch to a job with potential.

7. The rate of unemployment among blacks is more than twice as high as the rate among whites.

Supply/demand analysis alone doesn't explain these phenomena. Each of them can, however, be explained as the result of market, political, and social forces. Thus, to understand real-world labor markets, it is necessary to broaden the analysis of labor markets to include other forces that limit the use of the market. These include legal and social limitations on the self-interest-seeking activities of firms and individuals. Let's consider a couple of the central issues of interaction among these forces and see how they affect the labor market.

To understand real-world labor markets, one must broaden the analysis.

FAIRNESS AND THE LABOR MARKET

People generally have an underlying view of what's fair. That view isn't always consistent among individuals, but it's often strongly held. The first lesson taught in a personnel or human resources course is that people aren't machines. They're human beings with feelings and emotions. If they feel good about a job, if they feel they're part of a team, then they will work hard; if they feel they're being taken advantage of, they can be highly disruptive.

On some assembly-line jobs, it is relatively easy to monitor effort, so individuals can be—and in the past often were—treated like machines. Their feelings and emotions were ignored. Productivity was determined by the speed of the assembly line; if workers couldn't or wouldn't keep up the pace, they were fired.

Efficiency Wages   Most modern jobs, however, require workers to make decisions and to determine how best to do a task. Today's managers are aware that workers' emotional state is important to whether they make sound decisions and do a good job. So most firms, even if they don't really care about anything but profit, will try to keep their workers happy. It's in their own interest to do so. That might mean paying workers more than the going market wage, not laying them off even if layoffs would make sense economically, providing day care so the workers aren't worried about their children, or keeping wage differentials among workers small to limit internal rivalry. Such actions can often make long-run economic sense, even though they might cost the firm in the short run. They are common enough that they have acquired a name—**efficiency wages** (*wages paid above the going market wage to keep workers happy and productive*).

Firms sometimes pay what's called efficiency wages to keep workers happy and productive.

Views of fairness also enter into wage determination through political channels. Social views of fairness influence government, which passes laws to implement those views. Minimum wage laws, comparable worth laws, and antidiscrimination laws are examples.

Comparable Worth Laws   Let's consider one of those, **comparable worth laws,** which are *laws mandating comparable pay for comparable work*—that is, mandatory "fairness." The problem in implementing these laws is in defining what is comparable. Do you define comparable work by the education it requires, by the effort the worker puts out, or by other characteristics? Similarly with pay: Compensation has many dimensions

Web Note 16.4
Comparable Worth

and it is not at all clear which are the relevant ones, or whether the political system will focus on the relevant ones.

Economists who favor comparable worth laws point out that social and intrafirm political issues are often the determining factors in setting pay. In fact, firms often have their own implicit or explicit comparable worth systems built into their structure. For example, seniority, not productivity, often determines pay. Bias against women and minorities and in favor of high-level management is sometimes built into firms' pay-setting institutions. In short, within firms, pay structure is influenced by, but is not determined by, supply and demand forces. Comparable worth laws are designed to affect those institutional biases and thus are not necessarily any less compatible with supply and demand forces than are current pay-setting institutions.

The Federal government is not the only government agency that establishes labor laws. State and local government also do. For example, recently a number of local governments have established "living wage" laws, which are a type of minimum wage laws that require specified employers to pay a "living wage." "Living wage" is most often defined as that wage that would allow a worker to support a family of four at the poverty level. The analysis of these laws is similar to that of the minimum wage.

JOB DISCRIMINATION AND THE LABOR MARKET

Discrimination exists in all walks of life: Women are paid less than men, and blacks are often directed into lower-paying jobs. Economists have done a lot of research to understand the facts regarding discrimination and what can be done about it. The first problem is to measure the amount of discrimination and get an idea of how much discrimination is caused by what. Let's consider discrimination against women.

On average, women receive somewhere around 85 percent of the pay that men receive. That has increased from about 60 percent in the 1970s. This pay gap suggests that discrimination is occurring. The economist's job is to figure out how much of this is statistically significant and, of the portion that is caused by discrimination, what the nature of that discrimination is.

Analyzing the data, economists have found that somewhat more than half of the pay difference can be explained by causes other than discrimination, such as length of time on the job. But that still leaves a relatively large difference that can be attributed to discrimination.

Three Types of Direct Demand-Side Discrimination   In analyzing discrimination, it's important to distinguish various types. The first is discrimination based on relevant individual characteristics. Firms commonly make decisions about employees based on individual characteristics that will affect job performance. For example, restaurants might discriminate against (avoid hiring) applicants with sourpuss personalities. Another example might be a firm hiring more young salespeople because its clients like to buy from younger rather than older employees. If that characteristic can be an identifying factor for a group of individuals, the discrimination becomes more visible.

A second type of discrimination is discrimination based on group characteristics. This occurs when firms make employment decisions about individuals because they are members of a group who on average have particular characteristics that affect job performance. A firm may correctly perceive that young people in general have a lower probability of staying on a job than do older people and therefore may discriminate against younger people.

A third type of discrimination is discrimination based on irrelevant individual characteristics. This discrimination is based either on individual characteristics that do not

Q-9 Economic theory argues that discrimination should be eliminated. True or false? Why?

Three types of discrimination are:
1. Discrimination based on individual characteristics that will affect job performance.
2. Discrimination based on correctly perceived statistical characteristics of the group.
3. Discrimination based on individual characteristics that don't affect job performance or are incorrectly perceived.

In the United States, slavery is illegal. You cannot sell yourself to someone else, even if you want to. It's an unenforceable contract. But work, which might be considered a form of partial slavery, is legal. You can sell your labor services for a specific, limited period of time.

Is there any inherent reason that such partial slavery should be seen as acceptable? The answer to that question is complicated. It deals with the rights of workers and is based on value judgments. You must answer it for yourself. I raise it because it's a good introduction to Karl Marx's analysis of the labor market (which deals with alienation) and to some recent arguments about democracy in the workplace.

Marx saw selling labor as immoral, just as slavery was immoral. He believed that capitalists exploited workers by alienating them from their labor. The best equivalent I can think of is the way most people today view the selling of sex. Most people see selling sex as wrong because it alienates a person from his or her own body. Marx saw all selling of labor that same way. A labor market makes workers see themselves as objects, not as human beings.

The underlying philosophical issues of Marx's concern are outside of economics. Most people in the United States don't agree with Marx's philosophical underpinnings. But it's nonetheless a useful exercise to think about this issue and ask yourself whether it helps explain why we somehow treat the labor market as different from other markets and limit by law the right of employers to discriminate in the labor market.

Some of Marx's philosophical tenets are shared by the modern democracy-in-the-workplace movement. In this view, a business isn't owned by a certain group; it is an association of individuals who have come together to produce a certain product. For one group—the owners of stock—to have all the say as to how the business is run, and for another group—the regular workers—to have no say, is immoral in the same way that not having a democratic government is immoral. According to this view, work is as large a part of people's lives as is national or local politics, and a country can call itself a democracy only if it has democracy in the workplace.

As with most grandiose ideas, this one is complicated, but it's worth considering because it's reflected in certain laws. Consider, for example, the 1989 federal law that limits firms' freedom to close plants without giving notice to their workers. The view that workers have certain inalienable rights played a role in passing that law.

For those of you who say "Right on!" to the idea of increasing workers' rights, let me add a word of caution. Increasing workers' rights has a cost. It makes it less likely that firms and individuals who can think up things that need doing will do so, and thus will decrease the number of jobs available. It will also increase firms' desire to discriminate. If you know you must let a person play a role in decisions once you hire that person, you're going to be much more careful about whom you hire.

None of these considerations mean that democracy in the workplace can't work. There are examples of somewhat democratic "firms." Universities are run as partial democracies, with the faculty deciding what policies should be set. (There is, however, serious debate about how well universities are run.) But as soon as you add worker democracy to production, more questions come up: What about consumers? Shouldn't they, too, have a voice in decisions? What about the community within which the firm is located?

Economics can't answer such questions. Economics can, however, be used to predict and analyze some of the difficulties such changes might bring about.

affect job performance or on incorrectly perceived statistical characteristics of groups. A firm might not hire people over 50 because the supervisor doesn't like working with older people, even though older people may be just as productive as, or even more productive than, younger people.

Of the three types, the third will be easiest to eliminate; it doesn't have an economic motivation. In fact, discrimination based on individual characteristics that don't affect job performance is costly to a firm. Competing firms will hire these people and be in a better competitive position because of it. Market forces will work toward eliminating this type of discrimination.

An example of the success of a firm's policy to reduce discrimination is the decision by McDonald's to create a special program to hire workers with learning disabilities. Individuals who are learning disabled often make good employees. They tend to have lower turnover rates and follow procedures better than do many of the more transient employees McDonald's hires. Moreover, through their advertising, McDonald's helped change some negative stereotypes about people with disabilities. So in this case market forces and political forces are working together.

If the discrimination is of either of the first two types (that is, based on characteristics that do affect job performance, either directly or statistically), the discrimination will be harder to eliminate. In these cases not discriminating can be costly to the firm, so political forces to eliminate discrimination will be working against market forces to keep discrimination.

Whenever discrimination saves the firm money, the firm will have an economic incentive to use subterfuges to get around an antidiscrimination law. These subterfuges will make the firm appear to be complying with the law, even when it isn't. For example, a firm will find some other reason besides age to explain why it isn't hiring an older person.

Institutional Discrimination   Institutional discrimination is discrimination in which the structure of the job makes it difficult or impossible for certain groups of individuals to succeed. Consider the policies of colleges and universities. To succeed as a professor, administrator, or other professional in the academic market, one must devote an enormous amount of effort during one's 20s and 30s. But these years are precisely the years when, given genetics and culture, many women have major family responsibilities. This makes it difficult for women to succeed in the academic market. Were academic institutions different—say, a number of positions at universities were designed for high-level, part-time work during this period—it would be easier for women to advance.

Requiring peak time commitment when women are also facing peak family responsibilities is the norm for many companies, too. Thus, women face significant institutional discrimination.

Whether this discrimination is embodied in the firm's structure or in the family is an open question. For example, sociologists have found that in personal relationships women tend to move to be with their partners more than men move to be with their partners. In addition, women in two-parent relationships do much more work around the house and take a greater responsibility for child rearing than men do even when both the man and the woman are employed.

How important are these sociological observations? In discussing discrimination I ask the members of my class if they expect their personal relationships with their partners to be fully equal. The usual result is the following: 80 percent of the women expect a fully equal relationship; 20 percent expect their partner's career to come first. Eighty percent of the men expect their own careers to come first; 20 percent expect an equal relationship. I then point out that somebody's expectations aren't going to be fulfilled. Put simply, most observers believe that the institutional discrimination that occurs in interpersonal relationships is significant.

Economists have made adjustments for these sociological factors, and have found that institutional factors explain a portion of the lower pay that women receive but that other forms of workplace discrimination also explain a portion.

Whether prejudice should be allowed to affect the hiring decision is a normative question for society to settle. In answering these normative questions, our society has passed laws making it illegal for employers to discriminate on the basis of race, religion, sex, age, disability, or national origin. The reason society has made it illegal is its

Discrimination based on characteristics that affect job performance is hard to eliminate.

Institutions can have built-in discrimination.

ethical belief in equal opportunity for all, or at least most, individuals. (Homosexuals still aren't protected by federal legislation assuring them equal opportunities.)

THE EVOLUTION OF LABOR MARKETS

Now that we've briefly considered how noneconomic forces can influence labor markets, let's turn our attention to how labor markets developed.

Labor markets as we now know them developed in the 1700s and 1800s. Given the political and social rules that operated at that time, the invisible hand was free to push wage rates down to subsistence level. Workweeks were long and working conditions were poor. Laborers began to turn to other ways—besides the market—of influencing their wage. One way was to use political power to place legal restrictions on employers in their relationship with workers. A second way was to organize together—to unionize. Let's consider each in turn.

Evolving Labor Laws   Over the years, government has responded to workers' political pressure with a large number of laws that limit what can and what cannot be done in the various labor markets. For example, in many areas of production, laws limit the number of normal hours a person can work in a day to eight. The laws also prescribe the amount of extra pay an employee must receive when working more than the normal number of hours. (Generally it's time-and-a-half.) Similarly, the number and length of workers' coffee breaks are defined by law (one coffee break every four hours).

Child labor laws mandate that a person must be at least 16 years old in order to be hired. The safety and health conditions under which a person can work are regulated by laws. (For example, on a construction site all workers are required to wear hard hats.) Workers can be fired only for cause, and employers must show that they had cause to fire a worker. (For example, a 55-year-old employee cannot be fired simply because he or she is getting old.) Employers must not allow sexual harassment in the workplace. (Bosses can't make sexual advances to employees and firms must make a good-faith attempt to see that employees don't sexually harass their co-workers.)

Combined, these laws play an enormously important role in the functioning of the labor market.

Unions and Collective Bargaining   Some of the most important labor laws concern workers' right to organize together in order to bargain collectively with employers. These laws also specify the tactics workers can use to achieve their ends. In the latter part of the 1800s, workers had few rights to organize themselves. The Knights of Labor was formed in 1869, and by 1886 it had approximately 800,000 members. But a labor riot in 1886 turned public opinion against these workers and led to the organization's breakup. In its place, the American Federation of Labor developed and began to organize strikes to achieve higher wages.

Web Note 16.5
Laws or Contracts?

Business opposed unions' right to strike, and initially the government supported business. Police and sometimes the army were sent in to break up strikes. Under the then-existing legal structure of the economy, unions were seen as monopolistic restraints on trade and an intrusion into management rights.

In the 1930s, society's view of unions changed (in part as a backlash to the strong-arm tactics used by firms to break up unions), and laws such as the National Labor Relations Act (also called the Wagner Act) were passed guaranteeing workers the right to form unions, to strike, and to engage in collective bargaining. As Figure 16-5 shows, from 1935 to 1980 unions grew significantly in size and importance.

Businesses weren't happy with unions' increasing strength, and in 1947 they managed to get the Taft-Hartley Act passed. That act placed limitations on union activities.

Figure 16-5   Change in Union Membership, 1895–2001

The graph shows union membership from 1895 to 2001. As can be seen, after the Depression in the 1930s, unions grew in importance. In the 1980s the importance of unions declined, even though the labor force was growing significantly.

Source: Bureau of Labor Statistics (http://stats.bls.gov).

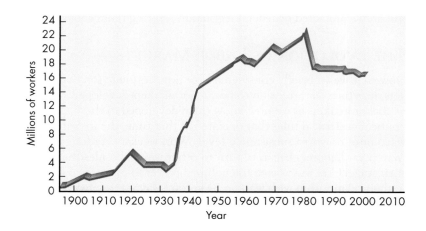

A closed shop is a firm in which the union controls hiring.

A union shop is a firm in which all workers must join the union.

It allowed states to pass "right-to-work" laws forbidding union membership to be made a requirement for continued employment. Moreover, it made **closed shops,** *firms where the union controls hiring,* illegal. Before anyone can be hired in a closed shop, he or she must be a member of the particular union. Federal law does permit **union shops**—*firms in which all workers must join the union.* Individuals are required to join a union after working for the firm for a period of time. The Taft-Hartley Act also outlawed *secondary boycotts.* In a secondary boycott, in order to strengthen its bargaining position, a union gets unions at other firms to force their firms to refuse to buy a firm's products, under threat of a strike.

Union power weakened further in 1981, when, in response to a strike by air traffic controllers, President Ronald Reagan fired all the controllers and refused to hire them back. Private firms similarly won the right to hire permanent replacements for striking workers.

Part of the reason labor union membership has declined in recent years is the unions' successes.

As Figure 16-5 shows, the number of workers in unions declined in the 1980s and has remained relatively constant since, even as the labor force has grown. Unions don't have the political or economic clout they once had. Part of the reason, ironically, is their success. By pressuring the government to pass laws that protected workers, unions made themselves less necessary. Another part of the reason is the changing nature of production in the United States. Labor unions were especially strong in manufacturing industries. As the relative number of manufacturing jobs has declined in the United States and the number of service jobs has increased, the base of union membership has been reduced. Unions have somewhat compensated for this change by pushing union-ization drives among public sector workers (that is, government employees), and this sector has seen the largest increase in union membership. Today, more than 40 percent of union members work in the public sector. These unions are becoming stronger and will likely be exerting their influence.

CONCLUSION: THE LABOR MARKET AND YOU

This chapter is meant to give you a sense of how the labor market works. But what does it all mean for those of you who'll soon be getting a job or are in the process of chang-ing jobs? I'll try to answer that question in this last section.

Table 16-1 shows a variety of potentially useful statistics about the labor market. Let's consider how some of them might affect you. For example, consider relative pay of jobs requiring a college degree compared to jobs requiring only a high school diploma.

Table 16-1 Some Typical Starting Salaries

Occupation	Private or State
Budget analyst	$32,000
Management analyst	34,000
Secretary	21,000
Physician assistant	47,000
Flight attendant	28,000
Secondary school teacher	28,000
Economist	34,000
Janitor	16,000
Retail sales (salary and commission)	17,000
Insurance sales	27,000

Sources: Author's estimates based on *Occupational Outlook Handbook 02/03* and U.S. Dept. of Labor Statistics (pay varies significantly by region) (http://stats.bls.gov).

(a) Some typical starting salaries of BAs: 2002

Degree	Annual Salary*
Law (3 years)	
Large firms	$105,000
Small firms	47,000
Engineering	
Bachelor's degree	47,000
Master's degree	60,000
Business	
Bachelor's degree	36,000
Master's (MBA) degree (2 years)	60,000
M.D. (4 years and 3-year internship)	115,000
Ph.D. (5 years)	
In economics	55,000
In humanities	50,000

*These figures are rough estimates based on data from the Department of Labor and informal surveys of author.

(b) Starting salaries for selected professional degrees, 2002

Jobs requiring a college degree pay significantly more, on average, than do jobs requiring only a high school diploma. In recent years the income gap between the two groups has noticeably increased. So the answer to the question of whether it's worthwhile to stick college out for another couple of years and get a degree is probably yes.

Next, consider the salaries of Ph.D.s compared to the salaries of MBAs. A Ph.D. is a person who has gone to graduate school after college, usually for a number of years, and earned an advanced degree called a **D**octorate of **Phi**losophy—even though there are many subjects besides philosophy (such as economics) in which one can earn a Ph.D. As you can see, Ph.D.s' starting salaries are lower than salaries of MBAs (masters of business administration) and professionals with other kinds of advanced degrees. Does this mean that Ph.D.s are discriminated against? Not necessarily. It's possible that Ph.D.s' lower pay suggests that Ph.D.s derive a "psychic income" from their work in addition to the amount of money they earn.

Since Ph.D.s are often quite smart, their willingness to accept psychic income as a substitute for higher pay suggests that there's much more to consider in a job than the salary. What's most important about a job isn't the wage, but whether you like what you're doing and the life that job is consistent with. (Of course, their lower salaries also could imply that Ph.D.s really aren't so smart.)

So my suggestion to you is definitely to finish college, especially if you enjoy it. (And with books like this, how could you help but enjoy it?) But go to graduate school only if you really enjoy learning. In picking your job, first and foremost pick a job that you enjoy (as long as it pays you enough to live on). Among jobs you like, choose a job in a field in which the supply of labor is limited, or the demand for labor is significantly increasing. Either of those trends is likely to lead to higher wages. After all, if you're doing something you like, you might as well get paid as much as possible for it.

Jobs in which the supply will likely be limited are those in which social or political forces have placed restrictions on entry or those requiring special abilities. If you have some special ability, try to find a job you enjoy in which you can use that ability. You might also look for a job in which entry is restricted, but beware: Jobs that are restricted

Q-10 Ph.D.s earn less than MBAs, so therefore one should get an MBA rather than a Ph.D. True or false? Why?

In the late 1800s, many workers worked in sweatshops; they often had quotas that required them to work 60 or more hours a week. Fines were imposed for such indiscretions as talking or smiling.
The Bettman Archive.

in supply must be rationed, so while such jobs pay higher wages, you may need personal connections to obtain one of them.

I'm sure most of you are aware that your choice of jobs is one of the most important choices you'll be making in your life. So I'm sure you feel the pressure. But you should also know that a job, unlike marriage, isn't necessarily supposed to be for life. There's enormous flexibility in the U.S. labor market. Many people change jobs six or seven times in their lifetimes. So while the choice is important, a poor choice can be remedied; don't despair if the first job you take isn't perfect. Good luck.

SUMMARY

- Incentive effects are important in labor supply decisions. The higher the wage, the higher the quantity supplied.

- Elasticity of market supply of labor depends on (1) individuals' opportunity cost of working, (2) the type of market being discussed, (3) the elasticity of individuals' supply curves, and (4) individuals entering and leaving the labor market.

- The demand for labor by firms is derived from the demand by consumers for goods and services. It

follows the basic law of demand—the higher the wage, the lower the quantity demanded.

- Elasticity of market demand for labor depends on (1) the elasticity of demand for the firm's good, (2) the relative importance of labor in production, (3) the possibility and cost of substitution in production, and (4) the degree to which marginal productivity falls with an increase in labor.

- Technological advances and changes in international competitiveness shift the demand for labor. Both have reduced demand for some types of labor and increased demand for other types. The net effect has been an increase in the demand for labor.

- A monopsony is a market in which a single firm is the only buyer. A monopsonist hires fewer workers at a lower wage compared to a competitive firm.

- A bilateral monopoly is a market in which there is a single seller and a single buyer. The wage and number of workers hired in a bilateral monopoly depend on the relative strength of the union and the monopsonist.

- Firms are aware of workers' well-being and will sometimes pay efficiency wages to keep workers happy and productive.

- Views of fairness in the labor market have led to laws that mandate comparable pay for comparable work.

- Discrimination may be based on (1) relevant individual characteristics, (2) group characteristics, and (3) irrelevant individual characteristics. The easiest to eliminate is discrimination based on irrelevant individual characteristics. The other two are motivated by market incentives.

- Labor laws have evolved and will continue to evolve. Since the 1980s, labor unions have been declining in importance.

KEY TERMS

bilateral monopoly (364)	derived demand (359)	incentive effect (355)	monopsony (363)
closed shops (372)	downsizing (365)	labor market (354)	outsourcing (365)
comparable worth laws (367)	efficiency wages (367)	marginal factor cost (364)	union shops (372)
	entrepreneurship (360)		

QUESTIONS FOR THOUGHT AND REVIEW

1. Why are social and political forces more active in the labor market than in most other markets?

2. "Welfare laws are bad, not for society, but for the people they are meant to help." Discuss.

3. Which would you choose: selling illegal drugs at $75 an hour (20 percent chance per year of being arrested) or a $6-an-hour factory job? Why?

4. If the wage goes up 20 percent and the quantity of labor supplied increases by 5 percent, what's the elasticity of labor supply?

5. My brother was choosing between being a carpenter and being a plumber. I advised him to take up plumbing. Why?

6. Why might it be inappropriate to discuss the effect of immigration policy using supply and demand analysis?

7. Demonstrate graphically the effect of a minimum wage law. Does economic theory tell us such a law would be a bad idea?

8. Show graphically how a minimum wage can simultaneously increase employment and raise the wage rate.

9. Comparable worth laws require employers to pay the same wage scale to workers who do comparable work or have comparable training. What likely effect would these laws have on the labor market?

10. Why is unemployment nearly twice as high among blacks as among whites? What should be done about the situation?

11. Give four reasons why women earn less than men. Which reasons do you believe are most responsible for the wage gap?

PROBLEMS AND EXERCISES

1. A study done by economists Daniel Hamermesh and Jeff Biddle found that people who are perceived as good-looking earn an average of 10 percent more than those who are perceived as homely and 5 percent more than people who are perceived as average-looking. The pay differential was found to be greater for men than for women.
   a. What conclusions can you draw from these findings?
   b. Do the findings necessarily mean that there is a "looks" discrimination?

c. What might explain the larger pay penalty for males for looks?

2. In the early 1990s a teen subminimum training wage law was passed by which employers were allowed to pay teenagers less than the minimum wage.
   a. What effect would you predict this law would have, based on standard economic theory?
   b. In analyzing the effects of the law, Professors Card and Kreuger of Princeton University found that few businesses used it and that it had little effect. Why might that have been the case?

3. Economists Mark Blaug and Ruth Towse did a study of the market for economists in Britain. They found that the quantity demanded was about 150–200 a year, and that the quantity supplied was about 300 a year.
   a. What did they predict would happen to economists' salaries?
   b. What likely happens to the excess economists?
   c. Why doesn't the price change immediately to bring the quantity supplied and the quantity demanded into equilibrium?

4. Some economists have argued against need-based scholarships because they work as an implicit tax on parents' salaries and hence discourage saving for college.
   a. If the marginal tax rate parents face is 20 percent, and 5 percent of parents' assets will be deducted from a student's financial aid each year for four years a child is in school, what is the implicit marginal tax on that portion of income that is saved? (For simplicity assume the interest rate is zero and that the parents' contribution is paid at the time the child enters college.)
   b. How would your answer differ if parents had two children with the second entering college right after the first one graduated? (How about three?) (Remember that the assets will likely decrease with each child graduating.)
   c. When parents are divorced, how should the contribution of each parent be determined? If your school has need-based scholarships, how does it determine the expected contributions of divorced parents?
   d. Given the above, would you suggest moving to an ability-based scholarship program? Why or why not?

5. Explain each of the following phenomena using the invisible hand or social or political forces:
   a. Firms often pay higher than market wages.
   b. Wages don't fluctuate much as unemployment rises.
   c. Pay among faculty in various disciplines at colleges does not vary much although market conditions among disciplines vary significantly.

6. A recent study by the International Labor Organization estimates that 250 million children in developing countries between the ages of 5 and 14 are working either full- or part-time. The estimates of the percentage of children working within countries is as high as 42 percent in Kenya. Among the reasons cited for the rise in child labor are population increases and poverty.
   a. Why do firms hire children as workers?
   b. Why do children work?
   c. What considerations should be taken into account by countries when deciding whether to implement an international ban on trade for products made with child labor?

7. Interview three married female and three married male professors at your college, asking them what percentage of work in the professor's household each adult household member does.
   a. Assuming your results can be extended to the population at large, what can you say about the existence of institutional discrimination?
   b. If gender-related salary data for individuals at your college are available, determine whether women or men of equal rank and experience receive higher average pay.
   c. Relate your findings in a and b.
   d. Does the existence of institutional discrimination suggest that no discrimination by employers exists? Why or why not?

Web Questions

1. The National Committee on Pay Equity (NCPE) is a central clearinghouse for information on pay equity. Go to its home page at www.feminist.com/fairpay to answer the following questions.
   a. What is pay equity?
   b. What two laws protect workers against wage discrimination?
   c. Does the NCPE believe that most of the pay gap is from women earning less in the same jobs or women working in lower-paying occupations? How does this affect the enforcement of antidiscrimination laws?

2. The Cato Institute is a public policy institute that favors a laissez-faire approach to the market. One of its commentaries, "Immigration Reform Means More High-Tech Jobs," argues that immigration creates jobs in the United States. Go to Cato's home page at www.cato.org, search for the commentary using keywords immigration and reform and read it to answer the following questions:
   a. For what type of workers is the author arguing immigration should be increased?
   b. How do highly skilled immigrants create jobs for Americans?

c. What was the state of the economy when the article was written? How does this affect the results of the study?

d. Do you believe the author would argue that the number of visas for unskilled laborers should be increased as well? Why or why not?

ANSWERS TO MARGIN QUESTIONS

1. Under usual conditions of supply, one would expect that if the wage of my part-time job rises, the quantity of labor I supply in that part-time job also rises. Institutional constraints such as tax considerations or company rules might mean that the quantity of labor I supply doesn't change. However, under the usual conditions of supply, I will study less if the wage of my part-time job rises. (355)

2. Taxes reduce the opportunity cost, or relative price, of nonwork activities. So you will substitute leisure for labor as marginal tax rates increase. (357)

3. The irony of any need-based program is that such a program reduces people's incentive to prevent themselves from becoming needy. (358)

4. Some factors that influence the elasticity of a firm's derived demand for labor include (1) the elasticity of demand for the firm's good; (2) the relative importance of labor in the production process; (3) the possibility, and cost, of substitution in production; and (4) the degree to which the marginal productivity falls with an increase in labor. (360)

5. The demand for laborers at that firm would shift out to the right. (361)

6. Differences among countries in productivity, transportation costs, trade restrictions, and social institutions all determine the relative demand for labor in one country compared to another country. (362)

7. If the increase in labor supply leads to an increase in the demand for products in general, the increase in labor supply will also lead to an increase in labor demand. (363)

8. General growth in the economy, the fall in the value of the dollar, and the decline in the power of unions all led to more employment in the late 1990s and early 2000s. Nonetheless, increasing competitive pressures caused many inefficient firms to downsize. The net effect, however, was a rise in total employment. (365)

9. Economic theory does not argue that discrimination should be eliminated. Economic theory tries to stay positive. Discrimination is a normative issue. If one's normative views say that discrimination should be eliminated, economic theory might be useful to help do that most efficiently. (368)

10. There is more to life than income, so it does not necessarily follow that one should take the job that pays the highest wage. (In the author's view, a Ph.D.'s life is far more fulfilling than an MBA's life, although some MBAs may disagree with that.) Each person must decide for him- or herself how to weigh the various dimensions of a job. (373)

APPENDIX A

Derived Demand

This appendix considers the issues of derived demand in more detail. Although it focuses on the derived demand for labor, you should note that the formal analysis of the firm's derived demand for labor presented in the chapter is quite general and carries over to the derived demand for capital and for land. Firms translate consumers' demands for goods into derived demands for any and all of the factors of production. Let's start our consideration by looking at the firm's decision to hire.

THE FIRM'S DECISION TO HIRE

What determines a firm's decision to hire someone? The answer is simple. A profit-maximizing firm hires someone if it thinks there's money to be made by doing so. Unless there is, the firm won't hire the person. So for a firm to decide whether to hire someone, it must compare the worker's **marginal revenue product (MRP)** (*the marginal revenue it expects to earn from selling the additional worker's*

Figure A16-1 (a and b)   Determining How Many Workers to Hire and the Firm's Derived Demand for Labor
The marginal revenue product is any firm's demand curve for labor. Since for a competitive firm $P = MR$, a competitive firm's derived demand curve is its value of the marginal product curve ($P \times MPP$). This curve tells us the additional revenue the firm gets from having an additional worker. From the chart in (**a**) we can see that when the firm increases from 27 to 28 workers, the marginal product per hour for each worker is 9. If the product sells for $2, then marginal revenue product is $18, which is one point on the demand curve for labor (point A in (**b**)). When the firm increases from 34 to 35 workers, the value of the marginal product decreases to $4. This is another point on the firm's derived demand curve (point B in (**b**)). By connecting the two points, as I have done in (**b**), you can see that the firm's derived demand curve for labor is downward-sloping.

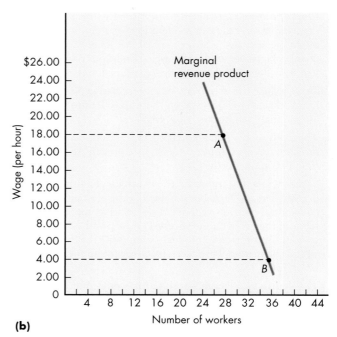

1	2	3	4	5
Number of Workers	Total Product per Hour	Marginal Physical Product per Hour	Average Product per Hour	Marginal Revenue Product (MRP)
27	270		10.00	
		9.00		$18
28	279		9.96	
		8.00		16
29	287		9.90	
		7.00		14
30	294		9.80	
		6.00		12
31	300		9.68	
		5.00		10
32	305		9.53	
		4.00		8
33	309		9.36	
		3.00		6
34	312		9.18	
		2.00		4
35	314		8.97	

(a)

(b)

output) with the wage that it expects to pay the additional worker. For a competitive firm (for which $P = MR$), that marginal revenue product equals the worker's **value of marginal product (VMP)**—the worker's **marginal physical product (MPP)** (*the additional units of output that hiring an additional worker will bring about*) times the price (P) at which the firm can sell the additional product.

Marginal revenue product = $MPP \times P$

Say, for example, that by hiring another worker a firm can produce an additional 6 widgets an hour, which it can sell at $2 each. That means the firm can pay up to $12 per hour and still expect to make a profit. Notice that a key question for the firm is: How much additional product will we get from hiring another worker? A competitive firm can increase its profit by hiring another worker as long as the value of the worker's marginal product (which also equals her marginal revenue product) ($MPP \times P$) is higher than her wage.

To see whether you understand the principle, consider the example in Figure A16-1(a). Column 1 shows the number of workers, all of whom are assumed to be identical. Column 2 shows the total output of those workers. Column 3 shows the marginal physical product of an additional worker. This number is determined by looking at the change in the total product due to this person's work. For example, if the firm is currently employing 30 workers and it hires one more, the firm's total product or output will rise from 294 to 300, so the marginal product of moving from 30 to 31 workers is 6.

Notice that workers' marginal product decreases as more workers are hired. Why is this? Remember the assumption of fixed capital: More and more workers are working with the same amount of capital and there is diminishing marginal productivity.

Column 4 shows **labor productivity**—*the average output per worker,* which is a statistic commonly referred to in economic reports. It's determined by dividing the total

The economic model of labor markets assumes that marginal productivities can be determined relatively easily. In reality they can't. They require guesses and estimates that are often influenced by a worker's interaction with the person doing the guessing and estimating. Thus, social interaction plays a role in determining wages. If you get along with the manager, his estimate of your marginal productivity is likely to be higher than if you don't. And for some reason, managers' estimates of their own marginal productivity tend to be high. In part because of difficulties in estimating marginal productivities, actual pay can often differ substantially from marginal productivities.

output by the number of workers. Column 5 shows the additional worker's marginal revenue product, which, since the firm is assumed to be competitive, is determined by multiplying the price the firm receives for the product it sells ($2) by the worker's marginal physical product.

Column 5, the marginal revenue product, is of central importance to the firm. It tells the firm how much additional money it will make from hiring an additional worker. That marginal revenue product represents a competitive firm's demand for labor.

Figure A16-1(b) graphs the firm's derived demand for labor, based on the data in column 5 of Figure A16-1(a). The resulting curve is the firm's **derived demand curve for labor,** which *shows the maximum amount of labor, measured in labor hours, that a firm will hire*. To see this, let's assume that the wage is $9 and that the firm is hiring 30 workers. If it hires another worker so it has 31 workers, workers' marginal revenue product of $12 exceeds their wage of $9, so the firm can increase profits by doing so. It increases output and profits since the additional revenue the firm gets from increasing workers from 30 to 31 is $12 and the additional cost the firm incurs is the wage of $9.

Now say the firm has hired 4 additional workers so it has 34 workers. As the firm hires more workers, the marginal product of workers declines. As you can see from the graph in Figure A16-1(b), the marginal revenue product of decreasing from 34 to 33 workers is $6. Since the workers' marginal revenue product of $6 is less than their wage of $9, now the firm can increase profits by laying off some workers. Doing so decreases output but increases profit, because it significantly increases the average product of the remaining workers.

Only when a worker's wage of $9 equals the marginal revenue product does the firm have no incentive to change the number of employees. In this example, the wage ($9) equals workers' marginal revenue product at 32 workers. When the firm is hiring 32 workers, either hiring another worker or laying off one worker will decrease prof-

its. Decreasing from 32 to 31 workers loses $10 in revenue, but increasing from 32 to 33 workers gains $8 in revenue, but costs $9 in wages. Since the marginal revenue product curve tells the firm, given a wage, how many workers it should hire, *the marginal revenue product curve is the firm's demand curve for labor*.

The fact that the demand curve for labor is downward sloping means that as more workers are hired, workers' marginal product falls. This might tempt you to think that the last worker hired is inherently less productive than the first worker hired. But that simply can't be because, by assumption, the workers are identical. Thus, the marginal product of any worker must be identical to the marginal product of any other worker, given that a specified number of workers are working. What the falling marginal product means is that *when 30 rather than 25 workers are working*, the marginal product of any one of those 30 workers is less than the marginal product of any one of 25 of those workers when only 25 are working. When the other inputs are constant, hiring an additional worker lowers the marginal product not only of the last worker but also of any of the other workers.

To understand what's going on here you must remember that when marginal product is calculated, all other inputs are held constant—so if a firm hires another worker, that worker will have to share machines or tools with other workers. When you share tools, you start running into significant bottlenecks, which cause production to fall. That's why the marginal product of workers goes down when a new worker is hired. This assumption that all other factors of production are held constant is an important one. If all other factors of production are increased, it is not at all clear that workers' productivity will fall as output increases.

Why does a firm hire another worker if doing so will lead to a fall in other workers' productivity and, possibly, a fall in the average productivity of all workers? Because the firm is interested in total profit, not productivity. As long as hiring an extra worker increases revenue by more than the worker costs, the firm's total profit increases. A profit-maximizing firm would be crazy not to hire another worker, even if by doing so it lowers the marginal product of the workers.

FACTORS AFFECTING THE DEMAND FOR LABOR

There are many technical issues that determine how the demand for products is translated through firms into a demand for labor (and other factors of production), but we need not go into them in detail. I will, however, state three general principles:

1. Changes in the demand for a firm's product will be reflected in changes in its demand for labor.

2. The structure of a firm plays an important role in determining its demand for labor.

3. A change in the other factors of production that a firm uses will change its demand for labor.

Let's consider each of these principles in turn.

CHANGES IN THE FIRM'S DEMAND

The first principle is almost self-evident. An increase in the demand for a product leads to an increase in demand for the laborers who produce that product. The increase in demand pushes the price up, raising the marginal revenue product of labor (which, you'll remember, for a competitive firm is the price of the firm's product times the marginal physical product of labor).

The implications of this first principle, however, are not so self-evident. Often people think of firms' interests and workers' interests as being counter to one another, but this principle tells us that in many ways they are not. What benefits the firm also benefits its workers. Their interests are in conflict only when it comes to deciding how to divide up the total revenues among the owners of the firm, the workers, and the other inputs. Thus, it's not uncommon to see a firm and its workers fighting each other at the bargaining table, but also working together to prevent imports that might compete with the firm's product or to support laws that may benefit the firm.

An example of such cooperation occurred when union workers at a solar energy firm helped fight for an extension of government subsidies for solar energy. Why? Because their contract included a clause that if the solar energy subsidy bill passed, the union workers' wages would be significantly higher than if it didn't. This cooperation between workers and firms has led some economists to treat firms and workers as a single entity, out to get as much as

they can as a group. These economists argue that it isn't helpful to separate out factor markets and goods markets. They argue that bargaining power models, which combine factor and goods markets, are the best way to analyze at what level wages will be set. In other words, the cost of labor to a firm should be modeled as if it is determined at the same time that its price and profitability are determined, not separately.

THE STRUCTURE OF THE FIRM AND ITS DEMAND FOR LABOR

The way in which the demand for products is translated into a demand for labor is determined by the structure of the firm. For example, let's consider the difference between a monopolistic industry and a competitive industry. For both, the decision about whether to hire is based on whether the wage is below or above the marginal revenue product. But the firms that make up the two industries calculate their marginal revenue products differently.

The price of a competitive firm's output remains constant regardless of how many units it sells. Thus, its marginal revenue product equals the value of the marginal product. To calculate its marginal revenue product we simply multiply the price of the firm's product by the worker's marginal physical product. For a competitive firm:

Marginal revenue product of a worker =

Value of the worker's marginal product =

$MPP \times$ Price of product

The price of a monopolist's product decreases as more units are sold since the monopolist faces a downward-sloping demand curve. The monopolist takes that into account. That's why it focuses on marginal revenue rather than price. As it hires more labor and produces more output, the price it charges for its product will fall. Thus, for a monopolist:

Marginal revenue product of a worker =

$MPP \times$ Marginal revenue

Since a monopolist's marginal revenue is always less than price, a monopolist industry will always hire fewer workers than a comparable competitive industry, which is consistent with the result we discussed in Chapter 12: that a monopolistic industry will always produce less than a competitive industry, other things equal.

To ensure that you understand the principle, let's consider the example in Table A16-1, a table of prices, wages, marginal revenues, marginal physical products, and marginal revenue products for a firm in a competitive industry and a monopolistic industry.

Table A16-1 The Effect of Monopoly and Firm Structure on the Demand for Labor

1	2	3	4	5	6	7
					Marginal Revenue Product	
Number of Workers	Wage	Price P	Marginal Revenue (Monopolist) MR	Marginal Physical Product MPP	Competitive ($MPP \times P$)	Monopolist ($MPP \times MR$)
5	$2.85	$1.00	$.75	5	$5.00	$3.75
6	2.85	.95	.65	3	2.85	1.95
7	2.85	.90	.55	1	.90	.55

A firm in a competitive industry will hire up to the point where the wage equals $MPP \times P$ (columns 5 × 3). This occurs at 6 workers. Hiring either fewer or more workers would mean a loss in profits for a firm in a competitive industry.

Now let's compare the competitive industry with an equivalent monopolistic industry. Whereas the firm in the competitive industry did not take into account the effect an increase in output would have on prices, the monopolist will do so. It takes into account the fact that in order to sell the additional output of an additional worker, it must lower the price of the good. The relevant marginal revenue product for the monopolist appears in column 7. At 6 workers, the worker's wage rate of $2.85 exceeds the worker's marginal revenue product of $1.95, which means that the monopolist would hire fewer than 6 workers—5 full-time workers and 1 part-time worker.

As a second example of how the nature of firms affects the translation of demand for products into demand for labor, consider what would happen if workers rather than independent profit-maximizing owners controlled the firms. You saw before that whenever another worker is hired, other inputs constant, the marginal physical product of all similar workers falls. That can contribute to a reduction in existing workers' wages. The profit-maximizing firm doesn't take into account that effect on existing workers' wages. It wants to hold its costs down. If existing workers are making the decisions about hiring, they'll take that wage decline into account. If they believe that hiring more workers will lower their own wage, they have an incentive to see that new workers aren't hired. Thus, like the monopolist, a worker-controlled firm will hire fewer workers than a competitive profit-maximizing firm.

There aren't many worker-controlled firms in the United States, but a number of firms include existing workers' welfare in their decision processes. Moreover, with the growth of the team concept, in which workers are seen as part of a team with managers, existing workers' input into managerial decision making is increasing. In many U.S. firms workers have some say in whether additional workers will be hired and at what wage they will be hired. Other firms have an implicit understanding or a written contract with existing workers that restricts hiring and firing decisions. Some firms, such as IBM, had never laid off a worker; if they had to reduce their workforce, they created early retirement incentives. Ultimately, however, if their business gets bad enough, the invisible hand wins out over the social forces, and they lay off workers. That happened for IBM, and many other large U.S. businesses, in the early 1990s.

Why do firms consider worker's welfare? They do so to be seen as a "good employer," which makes it easier for them to hire in the future. Given the strong social and legal limitations on firms' hiring and firing decisions, one cannot simply apply marginal productivity theory to the real world. One must first understand the institutional and legal structures of the labor market. However, the existence of these other forces doesn't mean that the economic forces represented by marginal productivity don't exist. Rather, it means that firms struggle to find a wage policy that accommodates both economic and social forces in their wage-setting process. For example, in the 1980s and 1990s, a number of firms (such as airline and automobile firms) negotiated two-tier wage contracts. They continued to pay their existing workers a higher wage, but paid new workers a lower wage, even though old and new workers were doing identical jobs. These two-tier wage contracts were the result of the interactions of the social and market forces.

CHANGES IN OTHER FACTORS OF PRODUCTION

A third principle determining the derived demand for labor is the amount of other factors of production that the firm has. Given a technology, an increase in other factors of production will increase the marginal physical product of existing workers. For example, let's say that a firm buys more machines so that each worker has more machines with which to work. The workers' marginal physical product increases, and the cost per unit of output for the firm decreases. The net effect on the demand for labor is unclear; it depends on how much the firm increases output, how much the firm's price is affected, and how easily one type of input can be substituted for another—or whether it must be used in conjunction with others.

While we can't say what the final effect on demand will be, we can determine the firm's **cost minimization condition**—where *the ratio of marginal product to the price of an input is equal for all inputs.*[1] When a firm is using resources as efficiently as possible, and hence is minimizing costs, the marginal product of each factor of production divided by the price of that factor must equal that of all the other factors. Specifically, the *cost minimization condition* is:

$$\frac{MP_l}{w} = \frac{MP_m}{P_m} = \frac{MP_x}{P_x}$$

where

w = Wage rate
l = Labor
m = Machines
x = Any other input

---

[1]This condition was explicitly discussed in terms of isocost/isoquant analysis in the appendix to Chapter 10.

If this cost minimization condition is not met, the firm could hire more of the input with the higher marginal product relative to price, and less of other inputs, and produce the same amount of output at a lower cost.

Let's consider a numerical example. Say the marginal product of labor is 20 and the wage is $4, while the marginal product of machines is 30 and the rental price of machines is $4. You're called in to advise the firm. You say, "Fire one worker, which will decrease output by 20 and save $4; spend that $4 on machines, which will increase output by 30." Output has increased by 10 while costs have remained constant. As long as the marginal products divided by the prices of the various inputs are unequal, you can make such recommendations to lower cost.

CONCLUSION

Changes in these factors make demand for labor shift around a lot. This shifting introduces uncertainty into people's lives and into the economic system. Often people attempt to build up institutional barriers to reduce uncertainty—either through social or political forces. Thus, labor markets function under an enormous volume of regulations and rules. We need to remember that while economic factors often lurk behind the scenes to determine pay and hiring decisions, these are often only part of the picture.

KEY TERMS

cost minimization condition (382)
derived demand curve for labor (379)

labor productivity (378)
marginal physical product (MPP) (378)

marginal revenue product (MRP) (377)

value of marginal product (VMP) (378)

QUESTIONS FOR THOUGHT AND REVIEW

1. Using the information in Figure A16-1, answer the following questions:
   a. If the market wage were $7 an hour, how many workers would the firm hire?
   b. If the price of the firm's product fell to $1, how would your answer to a change?

2. If firms were controlled by workers, would they likely hire more or fewer workers? Why?

3. In the 1980s and the 1990s farmers switched from small square bales, which they hired students on summer break to stack for them, to large round bales, which can be handled almost entirely by machines. What is the likely reason for the switch?

4. Should teachers be worried about the introduction of computer- and video-based teaching systems? Why or why not?

5. A competitive firm gets $3 per widget. A worker's average product is 4 and marginal product is 3. What is the maximum the firm should pay the worker?

6. How would your answer to question 5 change if the firm were a monopolist?

7. Fill in the following table for a competitive firm that has a $2 price for its goods.

Number of Workers	TP	MPP	AP	MRP
1	10		_____	
		_____		_____
2	19			
		8		_____
3	_____		_____	
				_____
4	_____		8.5	
		_____		$12
5	_____		_____	

8. Your manager comes in with three sets of proposals for a new production process. Each process uses three inputs: land, labor, and capital. Under proposal A, the firm would be producing an output where the MPP of land is 30, labor is 42, and capital is 36. Under proposal B, at the output produced the MPP would be 20 for land, 35 for labor, and 96 for capital. Under proposal C, the MPP would be 40 for land, 56 for labor, and 36 for capital. Inputs' cost per hour is $5 for land, $7 for labor, and $6 for capital.

a. Which proposal would you adopt?

b. If the price of labor rises to $14, how will your answer change?

17

WHO GETS WHAT?
THE DISTRIBUTION OF INCOME

After reading this chapter, you should be able to:

- State what a Lorenz curve is.

- Explain how the poverty definition is both an absolute and a relative measure.

- Discuss U.S. income inequality in a global context.

- Summarize the statistical findings on income and wealth distribution.

- State two alternative ways to describe income distribution.

- Explain three problems in determining whether an equal income distribution is fair.

- List three side effects of redistributing income.

- Summarize the U.S. tax and expenditure programs to redistribute income.

> "God must love the poor," said Lincoln, "or he wouldn't have made so many of them." He must love the rich, or he wouldn't divide so much mazuma among so few of them.
>
> —*H. L. Mencken*

In 2001, Lawrence Ellison, CEO of Oracle, earned $706 million (base pay plus stock options); that's more than $13 million per week. Assuming he worked 70 hours per week (you have to work hard to earn that kind of money), that's more than $193,000 per hour.

Today, the average doctor earns $180,000 per year; that's $3,462 per week. Assuming she works 70 hours per week (she's conscientious, makes house calls, and spends time with her hospitalized patients), that's $49 per hour.

Joe Smith, a cashier in a fast-food restaurant, earns $6.35 per hour. But to earn enough for his family to be able to eat, he works a lot of overtime, for which he is paid time-and-a-half, or $9.53 per hour. So he makes $28,079 per year, or $539 per week, by working 70 hours per week.

Nguyen, a peasant in Vietnam, earns $250 a year; that's $4.80 per week. Assuming he works 70 hours per week (you have to work hard at that rate of pay just to keep from starving), that's 7 cents per hour.

Are such major differences typical of how income is distributed among people in general? Are such differences fair? And if they're unfair, what can be done about them? This chapter addresses such issues. (I should warn you, however: If you're looking for answers, this chapter won't provide them; it will simply make the assumptions on both sides clear.)

The issues addressed in these questions play a fundamentally important role in policy debates today. The reason why is that in the last 20 years the income distribution in the United States has changed considerably. Many formerly middle-income people have moved into the upper-income levels; their wealth and their control of real assets have grown considerably. But simultaneously, lower-income people's income has stagnated or fallen. This change is bringing income distribution issues to center stage in modern policy debates.

WAYS OF CONSIDERING THE DISTRIBUTION OF INCOME

There are several different ways to look at income distribution. In the 1800s, economists were concerned with how income was divided among the owners of businesses (for whom profits were the source of income), the owners of land (who received rent), and workers (who earned wages). That concern reflected the relatively sharp distinctions among social classes that existed in capitalist societies at that time. Landowners, workers, and owners of businesses were separate groups, and few individuals moved from one group to another.

Time has changed that. Today workers, through their pension plans and investments in financial institutions, are owners of over 50 percent of all the shares issued on the New York Stock Exchange. Landowners as a group receive a relatively small portion of total income. Companies are run not by capitalists, but by managers who are, in a sense, workers. In short, the social lines have blurred.

This blurring of the lines between social classes doesn't mean that we can forget the question "Who gets what?" It simply means that our interest in who gets what has a different focus. We no longer focus on classification of income by source. Instead we look at the relative distribution of total income. How much income do the top 5 percent get? How much do the top 15 percent get? How much do the bottom 10 percent get? **Share distribution of income** is the name given to *the relative division of total income among income groups*.

A second distributional issue economists are concerned with is the **socioeconomic distribution of income** (*the allocation of income among relevant socioeconomic groupings*). How much do blacks get relative to whites? How much do the old get compared to the young? How much do women get compared to men?

Web Note 17.1
Rent, Profit, and Wages

The share distribution of income is the relative division of total income among income groups.

The socioeconomic distribution of income is the relative division or allocation of total income among relevant socioeconomic groups.

THE SHARE DISTRIBUTION OF INCOME

The U.S. share distribution of income measures aggregate family income, from the poorest segment of society to the richest. It ranks people by their income and tells how much the richest 20 percent (a quintile) and the poorest 20 percent receive. For example, the poorest 20 percent might get 5 percent of the income and the richest 20 percent might get 40 percent.

THE LORENZ CURVE

Figure 17-1(a) presents the share distribution of income for the United States in 2001. In it you can see that the 20 percent of Americans receiving the lowest level of income got 3.5 percent of the total income. The top 20 percent of Americans received 51.1 percent of the total income. The ratio of the income of the top 20 percent compared to the income of the bottom 20 percent was about 15:1.

A **Lorenz curve** is *a geometric representation of the share distribution of income among families in a given country at a given time*. It measures the cumulative percentage of *families* on the horizontal axis, arranged from poorest to richest, and the cumulative percentage of *family income* on the vertical axis. Since the figure presents cumulative percentages (all of the families with income below a certain level), both axes start at zero and end at 100 percent.

A perfectly equal distribution of income would be represented by a diagonal line like the one in Figure 17-1(b). That is, the poorest 20 percent of the families would have 20 percent of the total income (point A); the poorest 40 percent of the families would

A Lorenz curve is a geometric representation of the share distribution of income among families in a given country at a given time.

Q-1 When drawing a Lorenz curve, what do you put on the two axes?

Figure 17-1 (a and b)　A Lorenz Curve of U.S. Income, 2001
If income were perfectly equally distributed, the Lorenz curve would be a diagonal line. In (**b**) we see the U.S. Lorenz curve based on the numbers in (**a**) compared to a Lorenz curve reflecting a perfectly equal distribution of income.

Income Quintile	Percentage of Total Family Income	Cumulative Percentage of Total Family Income
Lowest fifth	3.5%	3.5%
Second fifth	8.8	12.3
Third fifth	14.5	26.8
Fourth fifth	23.1	49.9
Highest fifth	50.1	100.0

(a)

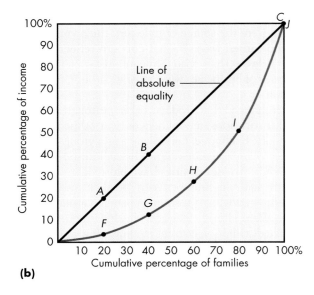

(b)

Source: *Current Population Reports*, U.S. Bureau of the Census, *2002* (www.census.gov).

have 40 percent of the income (point *B*); and 100 percent of the families would have 100 percent of the income (point *C*). An unequal distribution of income is represented by a Lorenz curve that's below the diagonal line. All real-world Lorenz curves are below the diagonal because income is always distributed unequally in the real world.

The green line in Figure 17-1(b) represents a Lorenz curve of the U.S. income distribution presented in Figure 17-1(a)'s table. From Figure 17-1(a) you know that, in 2001, the bottom 20 percent of the families in the United States received 3.5 percent of the income. Point *F* in Figure 17-1(b) represents that combination of percentages (20 percent and 3.5 percent). To find what the bottom 40 percent received, we must add the income percentage of the bottom 20 percent and the income percentage of the next 20 percent. Doing so gives us 12.3 percent (3.5 plus 8.8 percent from column 2 of Figure 17-1(a)). Point *G* in Figure 17-1(b) represents the combination of percentages (40 percent and 12.3 percent). Continuing this process for points *H*, *I*, and *C*, you get a Lorenz curve that shows the share distribution of income in the United States in 2001.

U.S. INCOME DISTRIBUTION OVER TIME

From 1929 to 1970, income inequality in the United States decreased. From 1970 to 2001, it increased.

Lorenz curves are most useful in visual comparisons of income distribution over time and between countries. Figure 17-2 presents Lorenz curves for the United States in 1929, 1970, and 2001. They show that from 1929 to 1970 the share distribution of income became more equal. (The curve for 1970 is closer to being a diagonal than the curve for 1929.) Income of the bottom fifth of families rose by a much higher proportion than did income of the top fifth. That was a continuation of a trend that had begun in the 1920s. In the 1970s that trend stopped and began to reverse. As you can see, from 1970 to 2001 income distribution became less equal. (The curve for 2001 is further from being diagonal than is the curve for 1970.) The income of the bottom fifth of families fell by over 10 percent, while the income of the top fifth rose significantly.

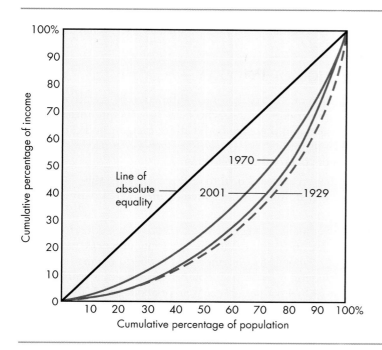

Figure 17-2   Lorenz Curves for the United States: 1929, 1970, and 2001
The amount of inequality of income distribution has fluctuated in the United States. Until about 1970, it decreased; since then it has increased.

Important reasons for the initial increase in equality are the redistribution measures instituted by the U.S. government between the 1930s and the 1970s, including welfare programs, unemployment insurance, Social Security, progressive taxation (taxation of higher income at higher rates, lower income at lower rates), and improved macroeconomic performance of the economy.

The trend back toward greater inequality starting in the 1970s was caused by a fall in the real income of the poor. This was due to wage increases that didn't keep up with price increases during that period, a movement away from progressive taxation, and a reduction in government funding for some social programs; this trend toward inequality will likely become a hot political topic in upcoming years.

The distribution of income over time is also affected by demographic factors. Many families have relatively low income in their early years, relatively higher income in their middle years, and then relatively low income again in their retirement years. The Lorenz curve reflects these differences, so even if lifetime income were equally distributed, income in any one year would not be. Moreover, when the percentages of these groups change, the Lorenz curve will change. For example, when the baby-boom generation's members retire and are no longer working, their collective income will fall. That decline in income relative to the income of the smaller number of working families will affect the Lorenz curve.

DEFINING POVERTY

Much of the government's concern with income distribution has centered on the poorest group—those in poverty. Defining poverty is not easy. Do we want to define it as an absolute amount of real income that does not change over time? If poverty were defined as an *absolute* amount of real income, few in the United States would be in poverty today; most of today's poor have higher real incomes than did the middle class 50 or 60 years ago. Or do we want to define it as a *relative* concept that rises as the average income in the society rises? For example, anyone with an income of less than one-fifth of the average income could be defined as being in poverty. If that relative concept of poverty were chosen, then the proportion of people classified as poor would always be the same.

THE OFFICIAL DEFINITION OF POVERTY

The United States uses a definition of poverty that is a combination of a relative and an absolute measure. Thus, it satisfies neither those who favor an absolute measure nor those who favor a relative measure, and there are both calls to increase and calls to decrease the **poverty threshold**—*the income below which a family is considered to live in poverty.* The official definition of poverty is the following:

> A family is in poverty if it has an income equal to or less than three times an average family's minimum food expenditures as calculated by the U.S. Department of Agriculture.

The minimum weekly food budget includes 4 eggs, 1½ pounds of meat, 3 pounds of potatoes, about 4 pounds of vegetables, and other foods; the cost is about $29.00 per person per week. Tripling that amount to about $87.00 (since food is said to require one-third of a family's income) and multiplying it by 52 (the number of weeks in a year), we arrive at a poverty level of about $4,524 per person per year, or about $18,100 for a family of four.

As Table 17-1 shows, using the official poverty measure, the number of people in poverty decreased in the 1960s and then began increasing in the 1970s. The number of poor rose to over 30 million in the 1980s. Then, due to a recession in the early 1990s, it rose even more. It declined throughout the remainder of the 1990s as the U.S. economy continued to grow but rose slightly in the early 2000s as the economy slowed. In 2001, 32.9 million Americans lived below the poverty threshold.

DEBATES ABOUT THE DEFINITION OF POVERTY

The minimum food budget used to determine the poverty line was determined in the 1960s and has not been recalculated to account for rising standards of living. Thus, it is in principle an absolute measure. However, it is adjusted by the rate of inflation rather than by the rise in the price of the originally selected foods. Since food prices have risen

---

Q-2 Is the U.S. definition of poverty an absolute or a relative definition?

Poverty is defined by the U.S. government as having an income being equal to or less than three times an average family's minimum food expenditures as calculated by the U.S. Department of Agriculture.

Table 17-1 Number and Percentage of Persons in Poverty, 1960–2001

	Number of People (in millions)	Percentage of Population	Poverty Income of Family of 4 (in current dollars)
1960	39.9	22.2%	$ 3,022
1970	24.4	12.6	3,986
1980	29.3	13.0	8,414
1990	33.6	13.5	13,359
1995	36.4	13.8	15,569
1996	36.5	13.8	16,036
1997	35.6	13.3	16,400
1998	34.5	12.7	16,660
1999	32.3	11.8	17,029
2000	31.6	11.3	17,603
2001	32.9	11.7	18,100

Source: *Current Population Reports,* U.S. Bureau of the Census, 2002 (www.census.gov).

by less than the rise in the general price level, the index of poverty has gone up by more than it would have had the fixed ratio of food to income remained constant. That means the definition includes significant aspects of relativity.

Those who favor a relative measure of poverty argue that our current poverty measure is too low. They point out that since food is now closer to a fourth of a family's total budget, it would make sense to increase the poverty threshold by multiplying food expenditures by a number a bit less than four rather than by three. Doing so would raise the poverty threshold to $21,500, and would add about 12 million people to the poverty roll.

Those who favor an absolute measure of poverty argue that the current measure is too high. They point out that U.S. poverty figures do not include in-kind (noncash) transfers, such as food stamps and housing assistance. Nor does the current poverty measure take into account underreporting of income, or the savings people have. (Many elderly people may have low incomes but significant wealth, which they could choose to spend.) If we make adjustments for in-kind transfers and underreporting of income, the official number of people in poverty decreases to about 60 percent of the official number. University of Texas economist Daniel Slesnick takes it further and points out that, since the price of food has increased at less than the rate of inflation, a much lower level of expenditures than the amount used to calculate the poverty threshold will provide a "nutritionally adequate diet." Slesnick calculated that when one takes the decrease in the relative price of food into account, the number of people in poverty would have fallen to one-seventh the official count.

The moral of this debate: Like most economic statistics, poverty statistics should be used with care.

THE COSTS OF POVERTY

People who favor policies aimed at achieving equality of income argue that poverty brings significant costs to society. One is that society suffers when some of its people are in poverty, just as the entire family suffers when one member doesn't have enough to eat. Most people derive pleasure from knowing that others are not in poverty.

Another cost of poverty is that it increases incentives for crime. In contrast, as people's incomes increase, they have more to lose by committing crimes, and therefore fewer crimes are committed. As the economy boomed in the 1990s, the crime rate decreased; it continued to decline in 2001.

Those who favor equality of income argue that the increased poverty in the late 1970s and 1980s represents a failure of the economic policies of that period. Others respond that the widening gap between rich and poor is not the result of government tax and spending policies. It has more to do with demographic changes. For example, the number of single-parent families increased dramatically during this period, while rapid growth of the labor force depressed wages for young unskilled workers.

Advocates of reducing poverty respond that this argument is unconvincing. They argue that the tax cuts of the 1980s favored the rich while decreased funding for government programs hurt the poor. To compensate, they argue, free day care should be provided for children so that single parents can work full-time, and government should supplement the low wages of the working poor. They argue that demographic changes are not a valid excuse for ducking a question of morality.

INTERNATIONAL DIMENSIONS OF INCOME INEQUALITY

When considering income distribution, we usually are looking at conditions within a single country. For example, the richest 5 percent of the U.S. population gets approximately 30 times what the poorest 5 percent of the American people get.

There are arguments both that the poverty line is too high and too low.

Web Note 17.2
Income Distribution
Data

THE GINI COEFFICIENT

A second measure economists use to talk about the degree of income inequality is the Gini coefficient of inequality. The Gini coefficient is derived from the Lorenz curve by comparing the area between the (1) Lorenz curve and the diagonal (area A) and (2) the total area of the triangle below the diagonal (areas A and B). That is:

Gini coefficient = Area A/(Areas A + B)

A Gini coefficient of zero would be perfect equality, since area A is 0 if income is perfectly equally distributed. The highest the Gini coefficient can go is 1. So all Gini coefficients must be between 0 and 1. The lower the Gini coefficient, the closer income distribution is to being equal. The Gini coefficient for the United States was 0.47 in 2001.

The following table gives Gini coefficients for a number of other countries. The Gini coefficients for transitional economies such as the Slovak Republic are most likely higher today because they are now market economies and their incomes are less equally distributed.

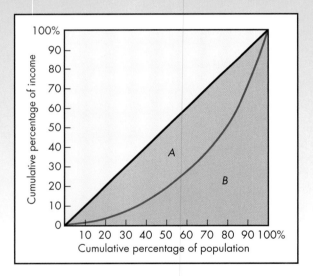

Gini Coefficients for Selected Countries	
Algeria	.353
Bangladesh	.336
Brazil	.591
Canada	.315
Czech Republic	.266
Denmark	.247
Germany	.300
Guatemala	.558
Hungary	.253
Indonesia	.317
Japan	.249
Latvia	.320
Netherlands	.326
Panama	.485
Philippines	.462
Romania	.305
Slovak Republic	.263
South Africa	.593
Thailand	.414
United Kingdom	.361
United States	.470

Source: *CIA World Factbook* 2002 (www.cia.gov)

There are other ways to look at income. We might judge income inequality in the United States relative to income inequality in other countries. Is the U.S. distribution of income more or less equal than another country's? We could also look at how income is distributed among countries. Even if income is relatively equally distributed within countries, it may be unequally distributed among countries.

COMPARING INCOME DISTRIBUTION ACROSS COUNTRIES

The United States has less income inequality than most developing countries but more income inequality than many developed countries.

Figure 17-3 gives us a sense of how the distribution of income in the United States compares to that in other countries. We see that the United States has significantly more income inequality than Sweden, but significantly less than Brazil (or most other developing and newly industrialized countries).

Figure 17-3 U.S. Income Distribution Compared to that of Other Countries

Among countries of the world, the United States has neither the most equal nor the most unequal distribution of income.

Source: *World Development Report*, The World Bank (www.worldbank.org).

An important reason why the United States has more income inequality than Sweden is that Sweden's tax system is more progressive. Until recently (when Sweden's socialist party lost power), the top marginal tax rate on the highest incomes in Sweden was 80 percent, compared to about 40 percent in the United States. Given this difference, it isn't surprising that Sweden has less income inequality. In a newly industrialized country like Brazil, where a few individuals earn most of the income and, to a large degree, control the government, the government is not likely to begin redistributing income to achieve equality.

Q.3 How does the income distribution in the United States compare with that in other countries?

INCOME DISTRIBUTION AMONG COUNTRIES

When we consider the distribution of world income, the picture becomes even more unequal than the picture we see within countries. The reason is clear: Income is highly unequally distributed among countries. The average per capita income of the richest countries in the world is approximately 100 times the average income of the poorest countries of the world. Thus, a Lorenz curve of world income would show much more inequality than the Lorenz curve for a particular country. Worldwide, income inequality is enormous. A minimum level of income in the United States would be a wealthy person's income in a poor country like Bangladesh.

THE TOTAL AMOUNT OF INCOME IN VARIOUS COUNTRIES

To gain a better picture of income distribution problems, you need to consider not only the division of income but also the total amounts of income in various countries. Figure 17-4 presents per capita income (gross domestic product) for various countries. Looking at the enormous differences of income among countries, we must ask which is more important: the distribution of income or the absolute level of income. Which would you rather be: one of four members in a family that has an income of $3,000 a

Figure 17-4   Per Capita Income (Gross Domestic Product) in Various Countries, 2001

Income is unequally distributed among the countries of the world. These relative comparisons change considerably over time as exchange rates fluctuate. These estimates are done using purchasing power parity, which eliminates much of the fluctuation due to exchange rate variation.

Source: *CIA World Factbook*, Central Intelligence Agency, 2002 (www.ocdi.gov) and various country home pages.

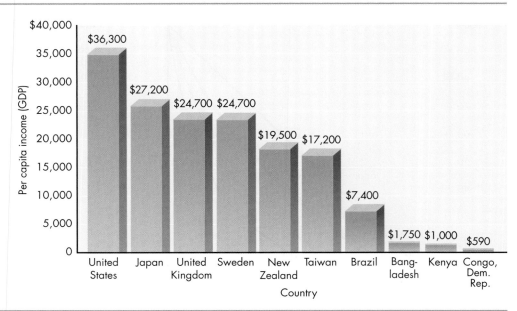

year, which places you in the top 10 percent of Bangladesh's income distribution, or one of four members of a family with an income of $12,000 (four times as much), which places you in the bottom 10 percent of the income earners in the United States?

THE DISTRIBUTION OF WEALTH

In considering equality, two measures are often used: *equality of wealth* and *equality of income*. Because of space limitations, my focus will be on income, but I want to mention wealth. **Wealth** is *the value of the things individuals own less the value of what they owe*. It is a *stock* concept representing the value of assets such as houses, buildings, and machines. For example, a farmer who owns a farm with a net worth of $1 million is wealthy compared to an investment banker with a net worth of $225,000.

Income is *payments received plus or minus changes in value in a person's assets in a specified time period*. In contrast to wealth, income is a *flow* concept. It's a stream through time. That farmer might have an income of $20,000 a year while the investment banker might have an income of $80,000 a year. The farmer, with $1 million worth of assets, is wealthier than the investment banker, but the investment banker has a higher income than the farmer.

A LORENZ CURVE OF THE DISTRIBUTION OF WEALTH

Figure 17-5 compares the Lorenz curve for wealth in the United States with the Lorenz curve for income in the United States. You can see that wealth in the United States is more unequally distributed than income and that the bottom 40 percent of the U.S. population has essentially zero wealth.

HOW MUCH WEALTH DO THE WEALTHY HAVE?

Relative comparisons such as those depicted by Lorenz curves don't give you a sense of how much wealth it takes to be "wealthy." The following numbers provide you with a better sense. Bill Gates, who founded Microsoft and became the richest person in the

Wealth is the value of assets individuals own less the value of what they owe.

Income is payments received plus or minus changes in value of a person's assets in a specified time period.

Wealth is significantly more unequally distributed in the United States than is income.

Billionaires often lose a billion here, gain a billion there; sometimes they even become multibillionaires. Seldom do they become poor.

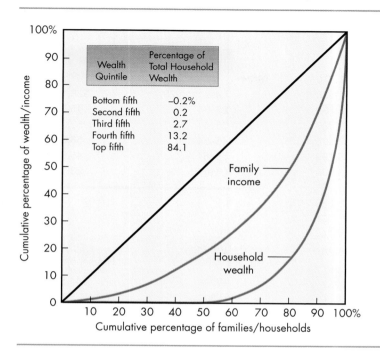

Wealth Quintile	Percentage of Total Household Wealth
Bottom fifth	–0.2%
Second fifth	0.2
Third fifth	2.7
Fourth fifth	13.2
Top fifth	84.1

Figure 17-5 Wealth Distribution in the United States and Wealth Compared to Income

Wealth is much more unequally distributed than income in the United States. In fact, the lowest 40 percent of the population has 0 percent of the wealth; these people have borrowed as much as they own.

Source: U.S. Bureau of the Census and Edward N. Wolf, New York University (with permission).

United States, had a net worth of about $54 billion in 2001. Five of the 10 wealthiest people in the United States were from the Walton family (whose father founded Wal-Mart), each with $17 billion. Most of us have little chance of joining that group; in fact, most of us have little possibility of becoming one of the top 5 percent of the wealth-holders in the United States, which would require total wealth of at least $4 million. Once there was a time when people's ultimate financial goal was to be a millionaire. In the 2000s, the ultimate financial goal for the wealthiest people is to be a billionaire. The millionaire's club is no longer highly exclusive.

Of course, people in the club don't always stay there; the club is constantly changing. For example, a number of families who were in the club earlier are no longer in it. Many of the Japanese billionaires lost billions in the fall of the Japanese stock market and fell off the top 10 in the world list of wealthiest people. Today, some of these people and families might only be multimillionaires.

SOCIOECONOMIC DIMENSIONS OF INCOME INEQUALITY

The size distribution of inequality is only one of the dimensions that inequality of income and wealth can take. As I mentioned before, the distribution of income according to source of income (wages, rents, and profits) was once considered important. Today's focus is on the distribution of income based on race, ethnic background, geographic region, and other socioeconomic factors such as gender and type of job.

INCOME DISTRIBUTION ACCORDING TO SOCIOECONOMIC CHARACTERISTICS

Table 17-2 gives an idea of the distribution of income according to socioeconomic characteristics.

You can see that income differs substantially by type of job, leading some economists to argue that a new professional/nonprofessional class distinction is arising in the

Table 17-2 Various Socioeconomic Income Distribution Designations

Median Income, 2001 By Occupational Category	Female	Male
Executive, administrators, and managerial	$39,217	$57,276
Professional specialists	40,930	57,628
Technical and related support	31,056	46,282
Sales	25,677	41,896
Administrative support, including clerical	26,355	32,995
Precision production, craft, and repair	26,031	35,199
Machine operators, assemblers, and inspectors	20,879	30,494
Transportation and material moving	25,095	31,908
Handlers, equipment cleaners, helpers, and lab	19,018	23,328
Service workers	17,763	25,004
Farming, forestry, and fishing	17,968	21,016

By Age, 2001	Median Household Income
Less than 25	$28,196
25–34	45,080
35–44	53,320
45–54	58,045
55–64	45,864
Over 65	23,118

Median Income By Sex	1970	1980	1990	2001
Male	$7,537	$15,340	$27,866	$38,215
Female	3,138	6,772	19,816	29,215

By Race, 2001	Median Household Income
White	$44,517
Black	29,470
Hispanic	33,565

Source: *Current Population Reports, Consumer Income,* U.S. Bureau of the Census, 2002 (www.census.gov).

United States. Substantial differences also exist between the incomes of women and men, and between whites and blacks.

INCOME DISTRIBUTION ACCORDING TO CLASS

As I stated above, early economists focused on the distribution of income by wages, profits, and rent because that division corresponded to their class analysis of society. Landowners received rent, capitalists received profit, and workers received wages. Tensions among these classes played an important part in economists' analyses of the economy and policy.

Even though class divisions by income source have become blurred, other types of socioeconomic classes have taken their place. The United States has a kind of upper class. In fact, a company in the United States publishes the *Social Register*, containing the names and pedigrees of about 35,000 socially prominent people who might be categorized "upper-class." Similarly, it is possible to further divide the U.S. population into a middle class and a lower class.

Class divisions are no longer determined solely by income source. For example, upper-class people do not necessarily receive their income from rent and profits. CEOs of major companies are generally considered upper-class, and they receive much of their income as payment for their services. Today we have "upper-class" people who derive their income from wages and "lower-class" people who derive their income from profits (usually in the form of pensions, which depend on profits from the investment of pension funds in stocks and bonds). Of course, once people become rich, they earn interest and profits on their wealth as well as income.

The United States has socioeconomic classes with some mobility among classes. This is not to say such classes should exist; it is only to say that they do exist.

The Importance of the Middle Class   What has made the most difference in today's class structure in the United States compared to its class structure in earlier

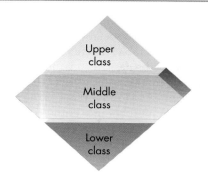

(a) Developing country's class system   **(b) U.S. class system**

Figure 17-6 (a and b)   The Class System as a Pyramid and as a Diamond
The class system in developing countries is a pyramid; in the United States the class system is more diamond-shaped.

periods and to the structure in today's developing countries is the tremendous growth in the relative size of the middle class. Economists used to see the class structure as a pyramid. From a base composed of a large lower class, the pyramid tapered upward through a medium-sized middle class to a peak occupied by the upper class (Figure 17-6(a)). The class structure is still pyramidal in developing countries. In the United States and other developed countries, the pyramid has bulged out into a diamond, as shown in Figure 17-6(b). The middle class has become the largest class, while the upper and lower classes are smaller in relative terms.

> In the United States the middle class is the largest class.

 How have distributional fights about income changed over time?

This enormous increase in the relative size of the middle class in developed countries has significantly blurred the distinction between capitalists and workers. In early capitalist society, the distributional fight (the fight over relative income shares) was largely between workers and capitalists. In modern market-based societies, the distributional fight is among various types of individuals. Union workers are pitted against nonunion workers; salaried workers are pitted against workers paid by the hour. The old are pitted against the young; women are pitted against men; blacks are pitted against Hispanics and Asians, and all three groups are pitted against whites.

Distributional Questions and Tensions in Society   While mainstream economists tend to focus on the size distribution of income, nonmainstream economists tend to emphasize class and group structures in their analysis. Radical economists emphasize the control that the upper class has over the decision process and the political process. Conservative economists emphasize the role of special interests of all types in shaping government policy. Both radical and conservative analyses bring out the tensions among classes in society much better than does the mainstream, classless analysis.

> Both radical and conservative analyses bring out the tensions among classes in society much better than does mainstream classless analysis.

When people feel they belong to a particular class or group, they will often work to further the interests of that class or group. They also generally have stronger feelings about inequalities among classes or groups than when they lack that sense of class or group identity. Using a classless analysis means overlooking the implications of class and group solidarity in affecting the tensions in society.

Those tensions show up every day in political disputes over the tax system, in the quiet fuming of individuals as they see someone else earning more for doing the same job, and in strikes and even riots. Such tensions exist in all countries. In some transitional and developing countries they break out into the open as armed insurrections or riots over food shortages.

Those tensions have been kept to a minimum in American society. A majority of Americans believe that income distribution is sufficiently fair for them to accept their share more or less contentedly. To remedy the unfairness that does exist, they don't demand that the entire system be replaced. Instead they work for change within the present system. They look to affirmative action laws, comparable worth laws, minimum wage laws, and social welfare programs for any improvement they perceive to be necessary or desirable. There's much debate about whether these government actions have achieved the desired ends, but the process itself reduces tensions and has worked toward the maintenance of the entire system.

People's acceptance of the U.S. economic system is based not only on what the distribution of income is but also on what people think it should be, what they consider fair. It is to that question that we now turn.

INCOME DISTRIBUTION AND FAIRNESS

Judgments about whether the distribution of income is fair or should be changed are normative ones, based on the values the analyst applies to the situation. Value judgments necessarily underlie all policy prescriptions.

PHILOSOPHICAL DEBATES ABOUT EQUALITY AND FAIRNESS

Depending on one's values, any income distribution can be justified. For example, Friedrich Nietzsche, the 19th-century Germany philosopher, argued that society's goal should be to support its supermen—its best and brightest. Lesser individuals' duty should be to work for the well-being of these supermen. Bertram de Juvenal, a 20th-century philosopher, has argued that a high level of income inequality is necessary to sustain the arts, beauty, education, and civilization. He and others say that a world of equally distributed income would be a world without beauty. Even if we don't personally own beautiful, expensive homes or aren't devoted opera fans, these philosophers argue, our lives are improved because some people do own such homes and because opera performances exist. Inequality creates diversity in our lives, and that diversity enriches the lives of everyone.

Other philosophers disagree strongly. They argue that equality itself is the overriding goal. That view is embodied in the Declaration of Independence: "We hold these truths to be self-evident, that all men are created equal." And for many people the inherent value of equality is not open to question—it is simply self-evident.

Believing that equality is an overriding goal does not necessarily imply that income should be equally distributed. For example, John Rawls (a Harvard University professor who believed that equality is highly desirable and that society's goal should be to maximize the welfare of the least well-off) agreed that to meet that goal some inequality is necessary. Rawls argued that if, in pursuing equality, you actually make the least well-off worse off than they otherwise would have been, then you should not pursue equality any further. For example, say under one policy there would be perfect equality and everyone would receive $10,000 per year. Under another policy, the least well-off person receives $12,000 per year and all others receive $40,000. Rawls argued that the second policy is preferable to the first even though it involves more inequality.

Economists, unlike philosophers, are not concerned about justifying any particular distribution of income. In their objective role, economists limit themselves to explaining the effects that various policies will have on the distribution of income; they let the policymakers judge whether those effects are desirable.

However, in order to judge economic policies, you, in your role as a citizen who elects policymakers, must make certain judgments about income distribution because all real-world economic policies have distribution effects. Accordingly, a brief discussion of income distribution and fairness is in order.

Q₅ Is it self-evident that greater equality of income would make the society a better place to live? Why?

WHAT SHOULD BE THE GOAL OF ECONOMIC POLICY?

Today, most discussions of economic policy focus on a goal of increasing income: Policies that achieve higher income are good policies; policies that do not are bad policies. Historically, that has not always been the goal. In the 1800s the economic policy focused on basic goods—distinguishing necessities from luxuries. Only policies that increased basic goods were good; the welfare implications of policies that increased luxuries were much more problematic.

The 1930s marked a major change in how economic policy was conceived. Economics began focusing much more on utility, downplaying the distinction between luxuries and basic goods. With this change the goal of economic policy became much more focused on total income, regardless of how that income was divided. The division of goods into necessities and luxuries was seen as adding a normative element to policy that was outside the purview of positive economics.

Recently, Nobel prize–winning economist Amartya Sen has argued against that utilitarian approach, pointing out that normative elements are unavoidable in policy analysis. He argues that using income as a measure of welfare is not the best approach and has suggested replacing it with a "capabilities" measure. For Sen, the goal of economic policy should be to increase a society's capabilities, which he defines as an individual's freedom within that society to achieve a particular life. For Sen, capabilities are best measured by basic indicators—such as life expectancy, literacy, and infant mortality rates—not by income. Poor ratings on such indicators impede people from leading good and happy lives. Sen's work is controversial, but it is important in reminding us that the goals of economic policy should always be kept in mind and that we should not simply accept the goal as being an increase in total income.

FAIRNESS AND EQUALITY

The U.S. population has a strong general tendency to favor equality—equality is generally seen as fair. Most people, including me, share that view. However, in some instances equality of income is not directly related to people's view of fairness. For example, consider this distribution of income between John and Fred:

John gets $50,000 a year.

Fred gets $12,000 a year.

Think a minute. Is that fair?

The answer I'm hoping for is that you don't yet have enough information to make the decision.

Here's some more information. Say that John gets that $50,000 for holding down three jobs at a time, while Fred gets his $12,000 for sitting around doing nothing. At this point, many of us would argue that it's possible John should be getting even more than $50,000 and Fred should be getting less than $12,000.

But wait! What if we discover that Fred is an invalid and unless his income increases to $15,000 a year he will die? Most of us would change our minds again and argue that Fred deserves more, regardless of how much John works.

But wait! How about if, after further digging, we discover that Fred is an invalid because he squandered his health on alcohol, drugs, and fried foods? In that case some people would likely change their minds again as to whether Fred deserves more.

By now you should have gotten my point. Looking only at a person's income masks many dimensions that most people consider important in making value judgments about fairness.

Q-6 You are dividing a pie among five individuals. What would be a fair distribution of that pie?

Fairness has many dimensions and it is often difficult to say what is fair and what isn't.

Three problems in determining whether an equal income distribution is fair are:

1. People don't start from equivalent positions.
2. People's needs differ.
3. People's efforts differ.

The concept of fairness is crucial and complicated, and it deserves deeper consideration than just a gut reaction.

FAIRNESS AS EQUALITY OF OPPORTUNITY

When most people talk about believing in equality in income, they mean they believe in equality of opportunity for comparably endowed individuals to earn income. If equal opportunity of equals leads to inequality of income, then the inequality in income is fair. Unfortunately, there's enormous latitude for debate on what constitutes equal opportunity of equals.

In the real world, needs differ, desires differ, and abilities differ. Should these differences be considered relevant differences in equality? You must answer that question before you can judge any economic policy, because to make a judgment on whether an economic policy should or should not be adopted, you must make a judgment about whether a policy's effect on income is fair. In making those judgments, most people rely on their immediate gut reaction. I hope what you have gotten out of the discussion about John and Fred and equality of opportunity is the resolve to be cautious about trusting your gut reactions. The concept of fairness is crucial and complicated, and it deserves deeper consideration than just a gut reaction.

THE PROBLEMS OF REDISTRIBUTING INCOME

Let's now say that we have considered all the issues discussed so far in this chapter and have concluded that some redistribution of income from the rich to the poor is necessary if society is to meet our ideal of fairness. How do we go about redistributing income?

First, we must consider what programs exist and what their negative side effects might be. The side effects can be substantial and can subvert the intention of the program so that far less money is available overall for redistribution and inequality is reduced less than we might expect.

THREE IMPORTANT SIDE EFFECTS OF REDISTRIBUTIVE PROGRAMS

Three side effects of redistribution of income are:

1. The labor/leisure incentive effect.
2. The avoidance and evasion incentive effect.
3. The incentive effect to look more needy than you are.

Three important side effects that economists have found in programs to redistribute income are:

1. A tax may result in a switch from labor to leisure.

2. People may attempt to avoid or evade taxes, leading to a decrease in measured income.

3. Redistributing money may cause people to make themselves look as if they're more needy than they really are.

All economists believe that people will change their behavior in response to changes in taxation and income redistribution programs. These responses, called *incentive effects of taxation*, are important and must be taken into account in policymaking. But economists differ significantly in the importance they assign to incentive effects, and empirical evidence doesn't resolve the question. Some economists believe that incentive effects are so important that little taxation for redistribution should take place. They argue that when the rich do well, the total pie is increased so much that the spillover benefits to the poor are greater than the proceeds the poor would get from redistribution. For example, supporters of this view argue that the growth in capitalist economies was made possible by entrepreneurs. Because those entrepreneurs invested in new technology, income in society grew. Moreover, those entrepreneurs paid taxes. The benefits resulting from entrepreneurial action spilled over to the poor, making the poor

Q-7 When determining the effects of programs that redistribute income, can one reasonably assume that other things will remain equal?

far better off than any redistribution would. The fact that some of those entrepreneurs became rich is irrelevant because all society was better off due to their actions.

Other economists believe that there should be significant taxation for redistribution. While they agree that sometimes the incentive effects are substantial, they see the goal of equality overriding these effects.

POLITICS, INCOME REDISTRIBUTION, AND FAIRNESS

We began this discussion of income distribution and fairness by making the assumption that our value judgments determine the taxes we pay—that if our values led us to the conclusion that the poor deserved more income, we could institute policies that would get more to the poor. Reality doesn't necessarily work that way. Often politics, not value judgments, plays a central role in determining what taxes individuals will pay. The group that can deliver the most votes will elect lawmakers who will enact tax policies that benefit that group at the expense of groups with fewer votes.

On the surface, the democratic system of one person/one vote would seem to suggest that the politics of redistribution would favor the poor, but it doesn't. One would expect that the poor would use their votes to make sure income was redistributed to them from the rich. Why don't they? The answer is complicated.

One reason is that many of the poor don't vote because they assume that one vote won't make much difference. As a result, poor people's total voting strength is reduced. A second reason is that the poor aren't seen by most politicians as a solid voting bloc. There's no organization of the poor that can deliver votes to politicians. A third reason is that those poor people who do vote often cast their votes with other issues in mind. An anti-income-redistribution candidate might have a strong view on abortion as well, and for many the abortion view is the one that decides their vote.

A fourth reason is that elections require financing. Much of that financing comes from the rich. The money is used for advertising and publicity aimed at convincing the poor that it's actually in their best interests to vote for a person who supports the rich. People are often misled by that kind of biased publicity.

Reasonable-sounding arguments can be made to support just about any position, and the rich have the means to see that the arguments supporting their positions get the publicity. Of course, some of their arguments are also correct. The issues are usually sufficiently complicated that a trained economist must study them for a long time to determine which arguments make sense.

> Often politics, not value judgments, plays a central role in determining what taxes an individual will pay.

Web Note 17.3
Macroeconomic Issues

INCOME REDISTRIBUTION POLICIES

The preceding discussion should have provided you with a general sense of the difficulty of redistributing income. Let's now consider briefly how income redistribution policies and programs have worked in the real world. In considering this, it is helpful to keep in mind that there are two direct methods and one indirect method through which government redistributes income. The direct methods are (1) *taxation* (policies that tax the rich more than the poor) and (2) *expenditures* (programs that help the poor more than the rich). The indirect method involves the establishment and protection of property rights. Let's first consider direct methods.

> Direct methods of redistribution are taxation and expenditures programs.

TAXATION TO REDISTRIBUTE INCOME

The U.S. federal government gets its revenue from a variety of taxes. The three largest sources of revenue are the personal income tax, the corporate income tax, and the Social Security tax.

Q.8 A progressive tax is preferable to a proportional tax. True or
false? Why?

State and local governments get their revenue from income taxes, sales taxes, and property taxes. The rates vary among states.

As I stated in Chapter 2, tax systems can be progressive, proportional (sometimes called *flat rate*), or regressive. A **progressive tax** is one in which *the average tax rate increases with income*. It redistributes income from the rich to the poor. A **proportional tax** is one in which *the average rate of tax is constant regardless of income level*. It is neutral in regard to income distribution. A **regressive tax** is one in which *the average tax rate decreases as income increases*. It redistributes income from poor to rich.

Federal Income Taxes   In the early 1940s, the federal personal income tax was made highly progressive, with a top tax rate of 90 percent on the highest incomes. The degree of progressivity went down significantly through various pieces of legislation after World War II until 1986, when the income tax system was amended to provide for an initial rate of 15 percent and a top rate of 28 percent. The changes did not reduce the actual progressivity of the personal income tax as much as they seemed to, because the 1986 reforms eliminated many of the loopholes in the U.S. Tax Code. Some loopholes had allowed rich people to legally reduce their reported incomes and to pay taxes on those lower incomes at lower rates. The top personal income tax rate on high-income individuals today is almost 40 percent.

Whereas the personal income tax is progressive, the Society Security tax is initially proportional. All individuals pay the same tax rate on wage income (7.65 percent for employer and 7.65 percent for employee; 15.3 percent for self-employed) up to a cap of about $85,000. Above that income cap, no Social Security tax is due (except for 1.45 percent for medical insurance, which has no cap on the amount to which it is applied). At this income cap the Social Security tax becomes regressive: Higher-income individuals pay a lower percentage of their total income in Social Security taxes than do lower-income individuals. (They also receive relatively less in Social Security benefits, compared to what they put in. So, while the Social Security tax is regressive, taken as a whole the Social Security system is progressive.)

Web Note 17.4
State Lotteries

State and Local Taxes   State and local governments get most of their income from the following sources:

1. Income taxes, which are generally somewhat progressive.

2. Sales taxes, which tend to be proportional (all people pay the same tax rate on what they spend) or slightly regressive. (Since poor people often spend a higher percentage of their incomes than rich people, poor people pay higher average sales taxes as a percentage of their incomes than rich people.)

3. Property taxes, which are taxes paid on the value of people's property (usually real estate, but sometimes also personal property like cars). Since the value of people's property is related (although imperfectly related) to income, the property tax is considered to be roughly proportional.

When all the taxes paid by individuals to all levels of governments are combined, the conclusion that most researchers come to is that little income redistribution takes place on the tax side. The progressive taxes are offset by the regressive taxes, so the overall tax system is roughly proportional. That is, on average the tax rates individuals pay are roughly equal. Recent changes in the tax laws have increased the rate that high-income people pay and lowered the rate that lower-income people pay. These changes may make the effective tax structure slightly more progressive, but meaningful statistics won't be available for a few years.

EXPENDITURE PROGRAMS TO REDISTRIBUTE INCOME

Taxation has not proved to be an effective means of redistributing income. However, the government expenditure system has been quite effective. The federal government's expenditures that contribute to redistribution include the following.

Expenditure programs have been more successful than taxation for redistributing income.

Social Security The program that redistributes the most money is the **Social Security** system, *a social insurance program that provides financial benefits to the elderly and disabled and to their eligible dependents and/or survivors.* Social Security also has a component called **Medicare,** which is a *multibillion-dollar medical insurance system.*

The amount of an individual's Social Security retirement, disability, or survivors' monthly cash benefits depends on a very complex formula, which is skewed in favor of lower-income workers. The program is not a pension program that pegs benefits to the amount paid in. Many people will get much more than they paid in; some who never paid anything in will get a great deal; and others who paid in for years will get nothing. (No benefits are payable if you die before you retire and leave no survivors eligible for benefits due to your work.) On the whole, the program has been successful in keeping the elderly out of poverty. In addition, Social Security benefits have helped workers' survivors and the disabled.

Q.9 The U.S. Social Security system is only a retirement system. True or false?

In the early 2000s, there were more than 45 million recipients of cash Social Security benefits, many of whom also received Medicare health insurance payments. Total benefits paid in the early 2000s, including Medicare, came to over $600 billion each year.

Public Assistance **Public assistance** programs are *means-tested social programs targeted to the poor and providing financial, nutritional, medical, and housing assistance.* (These programs are more familiarly known as *welfare payments.*) Public assistance programs exist in every state of the union, although the amount paid varies greatly from state to state. The main kinds of public assistance are:

Temporary Assistance for Needy Families (TANF). Provides temporary financial assistance to needy families with children under age 19.

Food stamps. Provide nutritional assistance in the form of coupons redeemable at most food stores.

Medicaid. Medical assistance for the poor, paid for by the individual states. It's different from, and usually more generous than, Medicare.

General assistance. State assistance to poor people when emergencies arise that aren't taken care of by any of the other programs.

By far the largest proportion of payments goes to needy families with dependent children, especially since these families are usually so poor that, in addition to qualifying for TANF, they meet the eligibility requirements for food stamps and Medicaid.

TANF was instituted by the Personal Responsibility and Work Opportunity Reconciliation Act of 1996 to replace Aid to Families with Dependent Children (AFDC). It has a number of provisions that distinguish it from earlier programs. One important provision is that it establishes a lifetime limit of 60 months (not necessarily consecutive) of benefits. The purpose of the law is to direct welfare recipients to work, and another provision in the law requires welfare recipients to take a job within two years. The law also gives states significant latitude in determining benefits and eligibility criteria. These changes are major ones; they raise many questions about job training and child care. The effects of this law are discussed in the box, "From Welfare to Work."

In an effort to reduce the negative incentive effects of welfare, in 1996 Congress passed the Personal Responsibility and Work Opportunity Reconciliation Act. The new law requires recipients of welfare assistance to work after two years on assistance and limits welfare assistance to a total of five years over a lifetime. Part of the act was also designed to offset the taxation implicit in moving from welfare to work, which could be as high as 90 percent or more, since under the old law welfare recipients who earned income above a certain level often lost almost all their welfare benefits. The new law extended funding to the working poor; for example, it provided funding for child care to help mothers move into the workforce and extended Medicaid to include the first year of work. With the changes, the implicit tax on income was reduced to about 40 percent: For every dollar of additional income, people lost 40 cents of benefits. Congress also promised monetary rewards to states that were successful in moving people off the welfare rolls.

This new law has played an important role in reducing the number of people on welfare from 14 million in 1994 to 5 million in 2002, in reducing the average stay on welfare from over 8 to under 4 years, and in reducing the unemployment rate among single mothers from over 40 percent in the early 1990s to under 30 percent in 2002.

Critics of the law have pointed out that much of the reduction occurred in the late 1990s and early 2000, when the economy was booming and one could expect the number of welfare recipients to fall anyway. But early figures suggested that the reductions continued into the recession in 2001–2002.

Of course, the law has negative effects. Some people run out of benefits and are forced into deeper poverty. Observers are keeping a close eye on the figures and on the overall effect of the law, but the general feeling is that the law has significantly increased the incentives to get off, and stay off, welfare.

Supplemental Security Income   Hundreds of thousands more people would be receiving public assistance if it weren't for **Supplemental Security Income (SSI),** *a federal program that pays benefits, based on need, to the elderly, blind, and disabled.* Although SSI is administered through the Social Security offices, it is unlike Social Security benefits because eligibility for SSI payments is based solely on the basis of need. Again unlike Social Security, the recipients pay nothing toward the cost of the program. To be eligible, though, people must have very low incomes and almost no resources except a home, if they are fortunate enough to own one, a wedding ring and engagement ring, and an automobile. In the early 2000s, over $30 billion was paid in SSI benefits each year.

Unemployment Compensation   **Unemployment compensation** is *short-term financial assistance, regardless of need, to eligible individuals who are temporarily out of work.* It is limited financial assistance to people who are out of work through no fault of their own and have worked in a covered occupation for a substantial number of weeks in the period just before they became unemployed.

Normally a person can receive unemployment benefits for only about six months in any given year, and the amount of the benefit is always considerably less than the amount the person earned when working.

A person can't just quit a job and live on unemployment benefits. While receiving unemployment benefits, people are expected to actively search for work. Lower-income workers receive unemployment payments that are more nearly equal to their working wage than do higher-income workers, but there is no income eligibility test. In the early 2000s about $20 billion was paid in unemployment benefits each year.

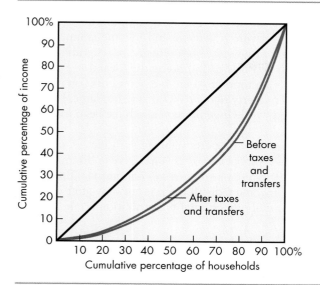

Figure 17-7   Distribution of Income before and after Taxes and Transfers, 2001

Although little redistribution takes place through the tax system, significant redistribution occurs through the transfer system, making the after-tax and transfer distribution of income more equal than the before-tax distribution of income.

Source: *Current Population Reports*, U.S. Bureau of the Census, 2002 (www.census.gov).

Housing Programs   Federal and state governments have many different programs to improve housing or to provide affordable housing. While many of these programs are designed to benefit low-income persons, there are also programs for moderate-income persons and lower-income persons (people whose incomes are lower than moderate but higher than low).

The federal agency overseeing most of these programs, the Department of Housing and Urban Development (HUD), has been criticized for abuse and mismanagement. Hundreds of millions of dollars that could have benefited the poor went instead to developers of housing and other projects, to consultants, and to others who skimmed off money before—or instead of—building or rehabilitating housing. In part because of these problems, federal funding for housing was steadily reduced during the 1980s. In the early 2000s, about $30 billion was allocated to housing programs each year.

HOW SUCCESSFUL HAVE INCOME REDISTRIBUTION PROGRAMS BEEN?

Figure 17-7 shows approximate Lorenz curves before and after analyzing the effect of both taxes and government programs on the redistribution of income. As you can see, the after-transfer income is significantly closer to being equally distributed. But because of the incentive effects of collecting and distributing the money, that redistribution has come at the cost of a reduction in the total amount of income earned by the society. The debate about whether the gain in equality of income is worth the cost in reduction of total income is likely to continue indefinitely.

While the direct methods of redistributing income get the most press and discussion, perhaps the most important redistribution decisions that the government makes involve an indirect method, the establishment and protection of property rights. Let's take an example: intellectual property rights. Intellectual property consists of things like a book you've written, a song you've composed, or a picture you've drawn. How these property rights are structured plays a fundamental role in determining the distribution of income.

For example, if strict private property rights are given for, say, a design for a computer screen (e.g., a neat little trash can in the corners and windows of various files) any

Most government redistribution works through its expenditure programs, not through taxes.

Q-10   Why are property rights important in the determination of whether any particular income distribution is fair?

user other than the designer herself will have to pay for the right to use it. The designer (or the person who gets the legal right to the design) becomes very rich. If no property rights are given for the design, then no payment is made and income is much more equally distributed. Of course, without a promise of high returns to designing a computer screen device, fewer resources will be invested in finding the ideal design. While most people agree that some incentive is appropriate, there is no consensus on whether the incentives embodied in our current property rights structure are too large. I suspect that the trash can (recycling bin) design, while ingenious, would have been arrived at with a much smaller incentive.

The point of the above example is not that property rights in such ideas should not be given out. The point is that decisions on property rights issues have enormous distributional consequences that are often little discussed, even by economists. Ultimately, we can answer the question of whether income redistribution is fair only after we have answered the question of whether the initial property rights distribution is fair.

CONCLUSION

Much more could be said about the issues involved in income redistribution. But limitations of time and space pressure us to move on. I hope this chapter has convinced you that income redistribution is an important but difficult question. Specifically, I hope I have given you the sense that income distribution questions are integrally related to questions about the entire economic system. Supply and demand play a central role in the determination of the distribution of income, but they do so in an institutional and historical context. Thus, the analysis of income distribution must include that context as well as the analyst's ethical judgments about what is fair.

SUMMARY

- The Lorenz curve is a measure of the distribution of income among families in a country. The farther the Lorenz curve is from the diagonal, the more unequally income is distributed.

- The official poverty measure is an absolute measure because it is based on the minimum food budget for a family. It is a relative measure because it is adjusted for average inflation.

- Income is less equally distributed in the United States than in some countries such as Sweden, but more equally distributed than in other countries such as Brazil. There is more income inequality among countries than income inequality within a country.

- Wealth is distributed less equally than income.

- Income differs substantially by class and by other socioeconomic characteristics such as age, race, and gender.

- Fairness is a philosophical question. People must judge a program's fairness for themselves.

- Income is difficult to redistribute because of incentive effects of taxes, avoidance and evasion effects of taxes, and incentive effects of redistribution programs.

- On the whole, the U.S. tax system is roughly proportional, so it is not very effective as a means of redistributing income.

- Government spending programs are more effective than tax policy in reducing income inequality in the United States.

KEY TERMS

income (392)
Lorenz curve (385)
Medicare (401)
poverty threshold (388)
progressive tax (400)

proportional tax (400)
public assistance (401)
regressive tax (400)
share distribution of
   income (385)

Social Security (401)
socioeconomic
   distribution of
   income (385)

Supplemental Security
   Income (SSI) (402)
unemployment
   compensation (402)
wealth (392)

QUESTIONS FOR THOUGHT AND REVIEW

1. Why are we concerned with the distribution of income between whites and blacks, but not between redheads and blonds?

2. The Lorenz curve for Bangladesh looks like this:

How much income do individuals in the top income quintile in Bangladesh receive?

3. If we were to draw a Lorenz curve for lawyers, what would it represent?

4. Should poverty be defined absolutely or relatively? Why?

5. Some economists argue that a class distinction should be made between managerial decision makers and other workers. Do you agree? Why or why not?

6. If a garbage collector earns more than an English teacher, does that mean something is wrong with the economy? Why or why not?

7. Is it ever appropriate for society to:
   Let someone starve?
   Let someone be homeless?
   Forbid someone to eat chocolate?

8. If you receive a paycheck, what percentage of it is withheld for taxes? What incentive effect does that have on your decision to work?

9. Which have been more successful in redistributing income—tax or expenditure programs?

10. "There are many more poor people in the United States than there are rich people. If the poor wanted to, they could exercise their power to redistribute as much money as they please to themselves. They don't do that, so they must see the income distribution system as fair." Discuss.

PROBLEMS AND EXERCISES

1. The accompanying table shows income distribution data for three countries.

Percentage of Total Income			
Income Quintile	India	Czech Republic	Mexico
Lowest 20%	8.5%	10.5%	4.1%
Second quintile	12.1	13.9	7.8
Third quintile	15.8	16.9	12.5
Fourth quintile	21.1	21.3	20.2
Highest 20%	42.5	37.4	55.4

a. Using this information, draw a Lorenz curve for each country.

b. Which country has the most equal distribution of income?

c. Which country has the least equal?

d. By looking at the three Lorenz curves, can you tell which country has the most progressive tax system? Why or why not?

2. "There are lies, damned lies, and statistics. Then, there are annual poverty figures." Both liberal and conservative economists believe U.S. poverty statistics are suspect. Here are some reasons:
   (1) They do not take into account in-kind benefits such as food stamps and tax credits.
   (2) They do not consider regional cost-of-living differences.
   (3) They do not take into account unreported income.

(4) Food accounts for one-fourth of a family's budget, not one-third.

(5) Ownership of assets such as homes, cars, and appliances is not taken into account.

a. What would the effect of correcting each of these be on measured poverty?

b. Would making these changes be fair?

3. The dissident Russian writer A. Amalrik has written:

> The Russian people . . . have . . . one idea that appears positive: the idea of *justice* . . . In practice, "justice" involves the desire that "nobody should live better than I do" . . . The idea of justice is motivated by hatred of everything that is outstanding, which we make no effort to imitate but, on the contrary, try to bring down to our level, by hatred of any sense of initiative, of any higher or more dynamic way of life than the life we live ourselves.

What implications would such a worldview have for the economy?

4. List four conditions you believe should hold before you would argue that two individuals should get the same amount of income.

a. How would you apply the conditions to your views on welfare?

b. How would you apply the conditions to your views on how progressive the income tax should be?

c. If the income tax were made progressive in wage rates (tax rates increase as wage rates increase) rather than progressive in income, would your conditions be better met? Why?

5. In Taxland, the first $10,000 earned per year is exempt from taxation. Between $10,000.01 and $30,000, the tax rate is 25 percent. Between $30,000.01 and $50,000, it's 30 percent. Above $50,000, it's 35 percent. You're earning $75,000 a year.

a. How much in taxes will you have to pay?

b. What is your average tax rate? Your marginal tax rate?

c. Taxland has just changed to a tax credit system in which, in lieu of any exemption, eligible individuals are given a check for $4,000. The two systems are designed to bring in the same amount of revenue. Would you favor or oppose the change? Why?

6. Some economists have proposed making the tax rate progressivity depend on the wage rate rather than the income level. Thus, an individual who works twice as long as another but who receives a lower wage would face a lower marginal tax rate.

a. What effect would this change have on incentives to work?

b. Would this system be fairer than our current system? Why or why not?

c. If, simultaneously, the tax system were made regressive in hours worked so that individuals who work longer hours faced lower marginal tax rates, what effect would this change have on hours worked?

d. What would be some of the administrative difficulties of instituting the above changes to our income tax code?

WEB QUESTIONS

1. About.com has information about a variety of economic topics. Go to www.taxes.about.com to answer the following questions:

a. At what rate are capital gains income taxed?

b. What is the alternative minimum tax?

c. What are education credits?

2. The federal government is a great source for information on the Web. Go to www.ssa.gov/pubs/10072.html. Answer the following questions:

a. What is a Social Security credit, and how much earnings does it take to get a credit?

b. How many credits do you need to collect benefits?

c. What is the charge for a Social Security number?

d. What are the eligibility requirements for Medicare?

e. What is the difference between Part A and Part B Medicare?

ANSWERS TO MARGIN QUESTIONS

1. When drawing a Lorenz curve, you put the cumulative percentage of income on the vertical axis and the cumulative percentage of families (or population) on the horizontal axis. (385)

2. The U.S. definition of poverty is an absolute measure, but the way poverty is calculated means that some relativity is included in the definition. (388)

3. The United States has significantly more income inequality than Sweden and Japan, but significantly less than Brazil. (391)

4. In early capitalist society, the distributional fight was between workers and capitalists. In modern capitalist society, the distributional fight is more varied. For example, in the United States minorities are pitted against whites and males against females. (395)

5. No, it is not self-evident that greater equality of income would make society a better place to live. Unequal income distribution has its benefits. Still, most people would prefer a somewhat more equal distribution of income than currently exists. *(396)*

6. What is fair is a very difficult concept. It depends on people's needs, people's wants, to what degree people are deserving, and other factors. Still, in the absence of any more information than is given in the question, I would divide the pie equally. *(397)*

7. No, one cannot reasonably assume other things remain constant. Redistributive programs have important side effects that can change the behavior of individuals and subvert the intent of the program. Three important side effects include substituting leisure for labor, a decrease in measured income, and attempts to appear more needy. *(398)*

8. As a general statement, "A progressive tax is preferable to a proportional tax" is false. A progressive tax may well be preferable, but that is a normative judgment (just as its opposite would be). Moreover, taxes have incentive effects that must be considered. *(400)*

9. False. The U.S. Social Security system includes many other aspects, such as disability benefits and survivors' benefits. *(401)*

10. The distribution of initial property rights underlies the initial distribution of income. Those with the property rights will reap the returns from those rights. Ultimately, we can answer the question whether income distribution is fair only after we have answered whether the initial property rights distribution is fair. *(403)*

18

GOVERNMENT POLICY AND MARKET FAILURES

After reading this chapter, you should be able to:

- Explain what an externality is and show how it affects the market outcome.

- Describe three methods of dealing with externalities.

- Define *public good* and explain the problem with determining the value of a public good to society.

- Explain how informational problems can lead to market failure.

- List five reasons why government's solution to a market failure could worsen the market failure.

Web Note 18.1
The Invisible Hand

The business of government is to keep the government out of business—that is unless business needs government aid.

—*Will Rogers*

There is an ongoing (indeed unending) debate: Should the government intervene in markets such as health care or agriculture? The supply/demand framework you learned in the previous chapters was created to provide some insight into answering that question, and those chapters began exploring the issues. In this chapter we explore economic policy questions more deeply and develop a fuller understanding of some of the roles of government first presented in Chapter 2.

The economic analysis of policy is set in the economic framework, which can also be called the *invisible hand framework*. It says that if markets are perfectly competitive they will lead individuals to make voluntary choices that are in the society's interest. It is as if individuals are guided by an invisible hand to do what society wants them to do.

MARKET FAILURES

For the invisible hand to guide private actions toward the social good, a number of conditions must be met. When those conditions are not met, economists say that there is a **market failure**—*a situation in which the invisible hand pushes in such a way that individual decisions do not lead to socially desirable outcomes.* In this chapter we consider three sources of market failures: externalities, public goods, and imperfect information.

Anytime a market failure exists, there is a reason for possible government intervention to improve the outcome. But it is important to remember that even if a market failure exists, it is not clear that government action will improve the result, since the politics of implementing the solution often lead to further problems. These problems of government intervention are often called *government failures*, so after discussing the three sources of market failures, we will discuss government failures. The economic policy debate will then be framed as a matter of choosing which failure is likely to be the lesser of two evils.

Perfect competition serves as a benchmark for judging policies. A foundation for this benchmark is in the work of Stanford economist Kenneth Arrow, who showed that the market translates self-interest into society's interest. (Arrow was given a Nobel Prize in 1972 for this work.) Arrow's ideas are based on many assumptions that can only be touched on in an introductory book. I will, however, discuss one here—the interpretation of the term *society's welfare*. In the economic framework society's welfare is interpreted as coming as close as one can to a *Pareto optimal position*—a position from which no person can be made better off without another being made worse off. (Pareto optimal policies will be discussed more in Chapter 20.)

Let's briefly consider what Arrow proved. He showed that if the market was perfectly competitive, and if there was a complete set of markets (a market for every possible good) now and in the future, the invisible hand would guide the economy to a Pareto optimal position. If these assumptions hold true, the supply curve (which represents the marginal cost to the suppliers) would represent the marginal cost to society. Similarly, the demand curve (which represents the marginal benefit to consumers) would represent the marginal benefit to society. In a supply/demand equilibrium, not only would an individual be as well off as he or she possibly could be, given where he or she started from, but so too would society. A perfectly competitive market equilibrium would be in a Pareto optimal position.

A number of criticisms exist to using perfect competition as a benchmark:

1. *The Nirvana criticism:* A perfectly competitive equilibrium is highly unstable. It's usually in some person's interest to restrict entry by others, and, when a market is close to a competitive equilibrium, it is in few people's interest to stop such restrictions. Thus, perfect competition will never exist in the real world. Comparing reality to a situation that cannot occur (i.e., to Nirvana) is unfair and unhelpful because it leads to attempts to achieve the unachievable. A better benchmark would be a comparison with workable competition—a state of competition that one might reasonably hope could exist.

2. *The second-best criticism:* The conditions that allow the conclusion that perfect competition leads to a Pareto optimal position are so restrictive that they are never even approached in reality. If the economy deviates in hundreds of ways from perfect competition, how are we to know whether a movement toward a competitive equilibrium in one of those ways will move the economy closer to perfect competition?

3. *The normative criticism:* Even if the previous two criticisms didn't exist, the perfect competition benchmark still isn't appropriate because there is nothing necessarily wonderful about Pareto optimality. A Pareto optimal position could be a horrendous position, depending on the starting position. For example, say the starting position is the following: One person has all the world's revenues and all the other people are starving. If that rich person would be made worse off by having some money taken from him and given to the starving poor, that starting position would be Pareto optimal. By most people's normative criteria, it would also be a lousy position.

Critics of the use of the perfect competition benchmark argue that society has a variety of goals. Pareto optimality may be one of them, but it's only one. They argue that economists should take into account all of society's goals—not just Pareto optimality—when determining a benchmark for judging policies.

EXTERNALITIES

An important requirement for the invisible hand to guide markets in society's interest is that market transactions have no side effects on anyone not involved in them. As I discussed in Chapter 2, such side effects are called **externalities**—*the effects of a decision on a third party that are not taken into account by the decision maker.* Externalities can be either positive or negative. Secondhand smoke and carbon monoxide emissions are examples of **negative externalities**, which occur *when the effects of a decision not taken into account by the decision maker are detrimental to others.* **Positive externalities** occur *when*

An externality is an effect of a decision on a third party not taken into account by the decision maker.

Figure 18-1   A Negative Externality
When there is a negative externality, the marginal private cost will be
below the marginal social cost and the competitive price will be too low to
maximize social welfare.

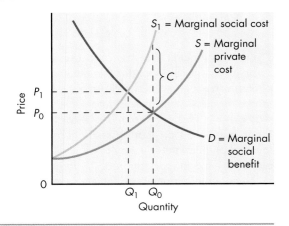

the effects of a decision not taken into account by the decision maker are beneficial to others.
An example is education. When you purchase a college education, it affects not only
you but others as well. Innovation is another example. The invention of the personal
computer has had significant beneficial effects on society, which were not taken into account by the inventors. When there are externalities, the supply and/or demand curves
no longer represent the marginal cost and marginal benefit curves to society.

A NEGATIVE EXTERNALITY EXAMPLE

Say that you and I agree that I'll produce steel for you. I'll build my steel plant on land
I own, and start producing. We both believe our welfare will improve. But what about
my plant's neighbors? The resulting smoke will pollute the air they breathe. The people
involved in the market trade (you and I) are made better off, but people external to the
trade are made worse off. Thus, there is a negative externality. My production of steel
has a cost to society that neither you nor I take into account.

The effect of a negative externality is shown in Figure 18-1. The supply curve S represents the marginal private cost to society of producing steel. The demand curve
D represents the marginal social benefit of consuming the steel. When there are no externalities, the marginal private costs and benefits represent the marginal social costs
and benefits, so the supply/demand equilibrium (P_0, Q_0) represents the point where the
marginal social benefit equals the marginal social cost. At that point society is as well
off as possible.

But now consider what happens when production results in negative externalities.
In that case people not involved in production also incur costs. This means that the
supply curve no longer represents both the marginal private and marginal social costs of
supplying the good. Marginal social cost is greater than the marginal private cost. This
case can be represented by adding a curve in Figure 18-1 called the *marginal social cost
curve*. The **marginal social cost** includes all the marginal costs that society bears—or *the
marginal private costs of production plus the cost of the negative externalities associated with
that production.*

Since in this case the externality represents an additional cost to society, the marginal social cost curve lies above the marginal private cost curve. The distance between
the two curves represents the additional marginal cost of the externality. For example,
at quantity Q_0, the private marginal cost faced by the firm is P_0. The marginal cost from
the externality at quantity Q_0 is shown by distance C. The externality cost is not taken

When there are externalities the
marginal social cost differs from
the marginal private cost.

Q-1 Why does the existence of
an externality prevent the market
from working properly?

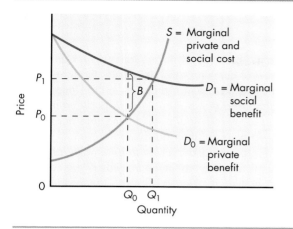

Figure 18-2   A Positive Externality
When there is a positive externality, the marginal social benefit will be above the marginal private benefit and the market price will be too low to maximize social welfare.

into account, and the supply/demand equilibrium is at too high a quantity, Q_0, and at too low a price, P_0.

Notice that the market solution results in a level of steel production that exceeds the level that equates the marginal social costs with the marginal social benefits. If the market is to maximize welfare, some type of government intervention may be needed to reduce production from Q_0 to Q_1 and raise price from P_0 to P_1.

A POSITIVE EXTERNALITY EXAMPLE

Private trades can also benefit third parties not involved in the trade. These are positive externalities. Again, an example is education. Consider a person who is working and takes a class at night. He or she will bring the knowledge from class back to co-workers through day-to-day interaction on projects. The co-workers will be learning the material from the class indirectly. They are outside the initial decision to take the class, but they benefit nonetheless.

In the case of positive externalities, the market will not provide enough of the good. Let's see how. In Figure 18-2, we start again with the standard demand and supply curves. The supply curve S represents the marginal private cost of the course. The demand curve D_0 is the marginal private benefit to those who take the course. Since others not taking the course also benefit, the marginal social benefit, shown by D_1, is above the marginal private benefit. The **marginal social benefit** equals *the marginal private benefit of consuming a good plus the benefits of the positive externalities resulting from consuming that good.* The vertical distance between D_0 and D_1 is the additional benefit that others receive at each quantity. At quantity Q_0, the market equilibrium, the marginal benefit of the externality is shown by distance B. At this quantity, the marginal social benefit exceeds the marginal social cost. The market provides too little of the good. The optimal price and quantity for society are P_1 and Q_1, respectively. Again, some type of intervention to increase quantity and lower price may be warranted.

ALTERNATIVE METHODS OF DEALING WITH EXTERNALITIES

Ways to deal with externalities include (1) direct regulation, (2) incentive policies (tax incentive policies and market incentive policies), and (3) voluntary solutions.

Q-2 If a positive externality exists, does that mean that the market works better than if no externality exists?

Positive externalities make the marginal private benefit below the marginal social benefit.

Externalities can be dealt with via:
1. Direct regulation.
2. Incentive policies.
3. Voluntary solutions.

Individuals tend to overuse commonly owned goods. Let's consider an example—say that grazing land is held in common. Individuals are free to bring their sheep to graze on the land. What is likely to happen? Each grazing sheep will reduce the amount of grass for other sheep. If individuals don't have to pay for grazing, when deciding how much to graze their sheep they will not take into account the cost to others of their sheep's grazing. The result may be overgrazing—killing the grass and destroying the grazing land. This is known as the *tragedy of the commons*. A more contemporary example of the tragedy of the commons is fishing. The sea is a common resource; no one owns it, and whenever people catch fish, they reduce the number of fish that others can catch. The result will likely be overfishing.

The tragedy of the commons is an example of the problems posed by externalities. Catching fish imposes a negative externality. Because of the negative effect on others, the social cost of catching a fish is greater than the private cost. Overfishing has been a problem in the United States and throughout the world. Thus, the tragedy of the commons is caused by individuals not taking into account the negative externalities of their actions.

Why doesn't the market solve the externality problem? Some economists argue that in the tragedy of the commons examples it would, if given a chance. The problem is a lack of property rights (lack of ownership). If rights to all goods were defined, the tragedy of the commons would disappear. In the fishing example, if someone owned the sea, he or she would charge individuals to fish. By charging for fishing rights the owner would internalize the externality and thus avoid the tragedy of the commons.

DIRECT REGULATION

In a program of **direct regulation,** *the amount of a good people are allowed to use is directly limited by the government.* Let's consider an example. Say we have two individuals, Ms. Thrifty, who uses 10 gallons of gasoline a day, and Mr. Big, who uses 20 gallons of gas a day. Say we have decided that we want to reduce total daily gas consumption by 10 percent, or 3 gallons. The regulatory solution might require both individuals to reduce consumption by some specified amount. Likely direct regulatory reduction strategies would be to require an equal quantity reduction (each consumer reducing consumption by 1.5 gallons) or an equal percentage reduction (each consumer reducing consumption by 10 percent).

Both of those strategies would work, but neither would be **efficient** *(achieving a goal at the lowest cost in total resources without consideration as to who pays those costs)*. This is because direct regulation does not take into account that the costs of reducing consumption may differ among individuals. Say, for example, that Ms. Thrifty could easily (i.e., almost costlessly) reduce consumption by 3 gallons while Mr. Big would find it very costly to reduce consumption by even 0.5 gallon. In that case, either regulatory solution would be **inefficient** *(achieving a goal in a more costly manner than necessary)*. It would be less costly (more efficient) to have Ms. Thrifty undertake most of the reduction. A policy that would automatically make the person who has the lower cost of reduction *choose* (as opposed to being *required*) to undertake the most reduction would achieve the same level of reduction at a lower cost. In this case the efficient policy would get Ms. Thrifty to choose to undertake the majority of the reduction.

INCENTIVE POLICIES

Two types of incentive policies would each get Ms. Thrifty to undertake the larger share of reduction. One is to create a tax incentive to achieve the desired reduction; the other

Q-3 It is sometimes said that there is a trade-off between fairness and efficiency. Explain one way in which that is true and one way in which that is false.

Economists tend to like incentive policies to deal with externalities.

Figure 18-3   Regulation through Taxation
If the government sets a tax sufficient to take into account a negative externality, individuals will respond by reducing the quantity of the pollution-causing activity supplied to a level that individuals would have supplied had they included the negative externality in their decision.

is to create a type of property right embodied in a permit or certificate, and to allow individuals to trade those property rights freely.

Tax Incentive Policies   Let's say that the government imposes a tax on gasoline consumption of 50 cents per gallon. This would be an example of a **tax incentive program** (*a program using a tax to create incentives for individuals to structure their activities in a way that is consistent with the desired ends*). Since Ms. Thrifty can almost costlessly reduce her gasoline consumption, she will likely respond to the tax by reducing gasoline consumption, say, by 2.75 gallons. She pays only $3.63 in tax but undertakes most of the conservation. Since Mr. Big finds it very costly to reduce his consumption of gasoline, he will likely respond by reducing gasoline consumption by very little, say by 0.25 gallon. He pays $9.88 in tax but does little of the conservation.

In this example, the tax has achieved the desired end in a more efficient manner than would the regulatory solution—the person for whom the reduction is least costly cuts consumption the most. Why? Because the incentive to reduce is embodied in the price, and individuals are forced to choose how much to change their consumption. The tax has made them internalize the externality. The solution also has a significant element of fairness about it. The person who conserves the most pays the least tax.

Let's now consider how the tax incentive solution will solve the problem in our earlier example of steel production creating an externality. Figure 18-3 shows the situation. Say the government determines that the additional marginal social cost of producing steel equals C. If the government sets the pollution tax on steel production at C, the firm will reduce its output to Q_1 on its own. Such taxes on externalities are often called **effluent fees**—*charges imposed by government on the level of pollution created*. The efficient tax equals the additional cost imposed on society but not taken into account by the decision maker. With such a tax, the cost the suppliers face is the social cost of supplying the good. With the tax, the invisible hand guides the traders to equate the marginal social cost to the marginal social benefit and the equilibrium is socially optimal.

Q-4   In what sense is the tax incentive approach fair?

Market Incentive Policies   A second incentive policy that gets individuals to internalize an externality is a **market incentive plan** (*a plan requiring market participants to certify that they have reduced total consumption—not necessarily their own individual consumption—by a specified amount*). Such a program would be close to the regulatory solution but involves a major difference. If individuals choose to reduce consumption by more than the required amount, they will be given a marketable certificate that they can sell to someone who has chosen to reduce consumption by less than the required amount. By buying that certificate, the person who has not personally reduced consumption by the requisite amount will have met the program's requirements. Let's see how the program would work with Mr. Big and Ms. Thrifty.

In our example, Mr. Big finds it very costly to reduce consumption while Ms. Thrifty finds it easy. So we can expect that Mr. Big won't reduce consumption much and will instead buy certificates from Ms. Thrifty, who will choose to undertake significant reduction in her consumption to generate the certificates, assuming she can sell them to Mr. Big for a high enough price to make that reduction worth her while. So, as was the case in the tax incentive program, Ms. Thrifty undertakes most of the conservation—but she reaps a financial benefit for it.

Obviously there are enormous questions about the administrative feasibility of these types of proposals, but what's important to understand here is not the specifics of the proposals but the way in which incentive policies are *more efficient* than the regulatory policy. As I stated before, *more efficient* means *less costly* in terms of resources, with no consideration paid to who is bearing those costs. Incorporating the incentive into a price and then letting individuals choose how to respond to that incentive lets those who find it least costly undertake most of the adjustment.

More and more, governments are exploring incentive policies for solving problems. Sin taxes (taxes on goods government believes to be harmful) are an example of the tax incentive approach. (These will be discussed further in Chapter 20.) Marketable permits for pollution are an example of the marketable certificate approach. You can probably see more examples discussed in the news.

VOLUNTARY REDUCTIONS

A third alternative method of dealing with externalities is to make the reduction voluntary, leaving individuals free to choose whether to follow what is socially optimal or what is privately optimal. Let's consider how a voluntary program might work in our Mr. Big and Ms. Thrifty example. Let's say that Ms. Thrifty has a social conscience and undertakes most of the reduction while Mr. Big has no social conscience and does not reduce consumption significantly. It seems that this is a reasonably efficient solution. But what if the costs were reversed and Mr. Big had the low cost of reduction and Ms. Thrifty had the high cost? Then the voluntary solution would not be so efficient. Of course, it could be argued that when people choose to do something voluntarily it makes them better off. So one could argue that even in the case where Ms. Thrifty has a high cost of reduction and voluntarily undertakes most of the reduction, she also has a high benefit from reducing her consumption.

The largest problem with voluntary solutions is that a person's willingness to do things for the good of society generally depends on that person's belief that others will also be helping.

If a socially conscious person comes to believe that a large number of other people won't contribute, he or she will often lose that social conscience: Why should I do what's good for society if others won't? This is an example of the **free rider problem** (*individuals' unwillingness to share in the cost of a public good*), which economists believe will often limit, and eventually undermine, social actions based on voluntary contributions. A small number of free riders will undermine the social consciousness of many in the society and eventually the voluntary policy will fail.

There are exceptions. During times of war and extreme crisis, voluntary programs are often successful. For example, during World War II the war effort was financed in part through successful voluntary programs. But for other long-term social problems that

Web Note 18.2
Union Shops

Q-5 What are two reasons to be dubious of solutions based on voluntary action that is not in people's self-interest?

Economists believe that a small number of free riders will undermine the social consciousness of many in the society and that eventually a voluntary policy will fail.

Incentive policies are more efficient than direct regulatory policies.

involve individuals accepting significant changes in their actions, generally the results of voluntary programs haven't been positive.

THE OPTIMAL POLICY

An **optimal policy** is *one in which the marginal cost of undertaking the policy equals the marginal benefit of that policy.* If a policy isn't optimal (that is, the marginal cost exceeds the marginal benefit or the marginal benefit exceeds the marginal cost), resources are being wasted because the savings from a reduction of expenditures on a program will be worth more than the gains that would be lost from reducing the program, or the benefit from spending more on a program will be worth more than the cost of expanding the program.

Let's consider an example of this latter case. Say the marginal benefit of a program significantly exceeds it marginal cost. That would seem good. But that would mean that we could expand the program by decreasing some other program or activity whose marginal benefit doesn't exceed its marginal cost, with a net gain in benefits to society. To spend too little on a beneficial program is as inefficient as spending too much on a non-beneficial program.

This concept of optimality carries over to economists' view of most problems. For example, some environmentalists would like to completely rid the economy of pollution. Most economists believe that doing so is costly and that since it's costly, one would want to take into account those costs. That means that society should reduce pollution only to the point where the marginal cost of reducing pollution equals the marginal benefit. That point is called the *optimal level of pollution*—the amount of pollution at which the marginal benefit of reducing pollution equals the marginal cost. To reduce pollution below that level would make society as a whole worse off.

> If a policy isn't optimal, resources are being wasted because the savings from reduction of expenditures on a program will be worth more than the gains that will be lost from reducing the program.

> Some environmentalists want to rid the world of all pollution, while most economists want to reduce pollution to the point where the marginal cost of reducing pollution equals the marginal benefit.

PUBLIC GOODS

A **public good** is *a good that is nonexclusive (no one can be excluded from its benefits) and nonrival (consumption by one does not preclude consumption by others).* As I discussed in Chapter 2, in reality there is no such thing as a pure public good, but many of the goods that government provides—education, defense, roads, and legal systems—have public-good aspects to them. Probably the closest example we have of a pure public good is national defense. A single individual cannot protect himself or herself from a foreign invasion without protecting his or her neighbors as well. Protection for one person means that many others are also protected. Governments generally provide goods with significant public aspects to them because private businesses will not supply them, unless they transform the good into a mostly private good.

What is and is not considered a public good depends on technology. Consider roads—at one point roads were often privately supplied, since with horses and buggies the road owners could charge tolls relatively easily. Then, with the increased speed of the automobile, collecting tolls on most roads became too time-consuming. At that point the nonexclusive public-good aspect of roads became dominant—once a road was built, it was most efficiently supplied to others at a zero cost—and government became the provider of most roads. Today, with modern computer technology, sensors that monitor road use can be placed on roads and in cars. Charging for roads has once again become more feasible. In the future we may again see more private provision of roads. Some economists have even called for privatization of existing roads, and private roads are being built in California and in Bangkok, Thailand.

One of the reasons that pure public goods are sufficiently interesting to warrant a separate discussion is that a modification of the supply/demand model can be used to

Web Note 18.3
Charging for Roads

neatly contrast the efficient supply of a private good with the efficient supply of a public good. The key to understanding the difference is to recognize that once a pure public good is supplied to one individual, it is simultaneously supplied to all, whereas a private good is supplied only to the individual who purchased it. For example, if the price of an apple is 50 cents, the efficient purchase rule is for individuals to buy apples until the marginal benefit of the last apple consumed is equal to 50 cents. The analysis focuses on the individual. If the equilibrium price is 50 cents, the marginal benefit of the last apple sold in the market is equal to 50 cents. That benefit is paid for by one individual and is enjoyed by one individual.

Now consider a public good. Say that the marginal benefit of an additional missile for national defense is 50 cents to one individual and 25 cents to another. In this case the value of providing one missile provides 75 cents (25 + 50) of total social benefit. With a public good the focus is on the group. The societal benefit in the case of a public good is the *sum* of the individual benefits (since each individual gets the benefit of the good). With private goods, we count only the benefit to the person buying the good, since only one person gets it.

The above reasoning can be translated into supply and demand curves. The market demand curve represents the marginal benefit of a good to society. As we saw in Chapter 4 in the case of a private good, the market demand curve is the *horizontal sum* of the individual demand curves. The total amount of a private good supplied is split up among many buyers. While the market demand curve for a private good is constructed by adding all the quantities demanded at every price, the market demand curve in the case of public goods is the *vertical sum* of the individual demand curves at every quantity. The quantity of the good supplied is not split up; the full benefit of the total output is received by everyone.

Figure 18-4 gives an example of a public good. In it we assume that society consists of only two households—A and B, with demand curves D_A and D_B. To arrive at the market demand curve for the public good, we vertically add the price that each individual is willing to pay for each unit since both receive a benefit when the good is supplied. Thus, at quantity 1 we add $0.60 to $0.50. We arrive at $1.10, the marginal benefit of providing the first missile. By adding together the willingness to pay by individuals A and B for quantities 2 and 3, we generate the market demand curve for missiles.

> With private goods you sum demand curves horizontally; with public goods you sum it vertically.

Figure 18-4   The Market Value of a Public Good
The market demand curve for a public good is constructed differently than for a private good. Since a public good is enjoyed by many people without diminishing its value to others, the market demand curve is constructed by adding the marginal benefit each individual receives from the public good at each quantity. For example, the value of the first unit to the market is $1.10, the sum of individual A's value ($0.50) and individual B's value ($0.60). In other words, vertically sum the individual demand curves to construct the market demand curve for a public good.

Extending this example from two individuals to the economy as a whole you can see that, even though the benefit of a public good is small to each person, the total benefit is large. With 290 million people in the United States, the benefit of that missile would be $145 million even if each person valued it on average at 50 cents.

Adding demand curves vertically is easy to do in textbooks, but not in practice. With private-good demand curves individuals reveal their demand when they buy a good. If they don't buy it, it wasn't worth the price. Since individuals do not purchase public goods, their demand is not revealed by their actions. Government must guess at it. If a public good is to be financed by a tax on the citizens who benefit from it, individuals have an incentive to conceal their willingness to pay for it. This is why in the supply of public goods we see the free rider problem. The self-interested citizen wants to benefit from the public good without bearing the cost of providing it. Similarly, if people think they will not be taxed, but will benefit from the public good, they have an incentive to exaggerate their willingness to pay.

> **Q-6** Why is it so difficult for government to decide the efficient quantity of a public good to provide?

INFORMATIONAL PROBLEMS

The final case of market failure I want to address is caused by imperfect information. The perfectly competitive model assumes that individuals have perfect information about what they are buying. So, if they voluntarily buy a good, it is a reasonable presumption that they expect that they are making themselves better off by doing so. But what happens if the buyer doesn't have perfect information? Say someone convinces you that he is selling an expensive diamond and you buy it, only to find out later that it is actually just glass. Or alternatively, say someone convinces you her used car is a cherry (in perfect condition). You buy it only to discover later that it is a lemon (faulty) and won't run no matter what you do to it.

Real-world markets often involve deception, cheating, and inaccurate information. For example, car dealers know about defects in the cars they sell but do not always reveal those defects to consumers. Another example is when consumers who want health insurance do not reveal their health problems to the insurance company. In both cases, it is in the interest of the knowledgeable person not to reveal information that the other person or firm would need to know to make an informed decision about the transaction. Hence, imperfect information can be a cause of market failure.

When there is a lack of information, or when buyers and sellers don't have equal information, markets in some goods may not work well. Let's consider the used-car example more carefully to make the point. Let's say that owners of used cars know everything about their cars, but buyers know nothing. If sellers are profit maximizers, they will reveal as little as possible about the cars' defects; they will reveal as much as they can about the cars' good qualities.

> Imperfect information can be a cause of market failure.

To make the example specific, let's say also that only two types of cars exist— "lemons" that are worth $4,000 and "cherries" that are worth $8,000. The market initially consists of equal quantities of lemons and cherries. Say also that the buyers cannot distinguish between lemons and cherries. What will happen? Individuals, knowing that they have a 50 percent chance of buying a lemon, may well offer around $6,000 (the average of $4,000 and $8,000). Given that price, individuals with cherries will be very hesitant to sell, and individuals with lemons will be anxious to sell. Eventually, buyers will recognize that the sellers of cherries have left the market. In the end only lemons will be offered for sale, and buyers will offer only $4,000 with the expectation that cars offered will be lemons. When the market for cherries—good used cars—has disappeared, the result is a market failure.

Such a market failure is called an **adverse selection problem**—*a problem that occurs when buyers and sellers have different amounts of information about the good for sale*. In the

> Adverse selection problems can occur when buyers and sellers have different amounts of information about the good for sale.

case of adverse selection, only lemons—those with the most problems—remain in the market. Take the example of medical insurance. Insurance providers need to make a profit. To do so, they set rates that reflect their estimate of the costs of providing health care. The problem is that individuals have better information about their health than do the insurance providers. Health insurers want a diverse group to spread out the costs, but they face a greater demand among those with the worst health problems. Seeing that their customers have more health problems than average, medical insurance providers raise the rates. Those who are in good health find those charges to be too high and reduce the quantity of health insurance they purchase. The providers are therefore left with a group with an even higher incidence of health problems and higher medical costs than the general population. Less than the desired amount of low-cost insurance exists for people in good health.

Workplace safety is another example of imperfect information causing market failure. Although businesses have an incentive to provide a safe working environment to limit costs, they may not choose a level of safety that would be preferred by employees. If the employer does not disclose unsafe working conditions, and those conditions cannot be easily identified by workers, there is again an informational problem. Employees may not be adequately compensated for the risks they face.

POLICIES TO DEAL WITH INFORMATIONAL PROBLEMS

What should society do about informational problems that lead to market failures? One answer is to regulate the market and see that individuals provide the right information. Another is for the government to license individuals in the market, requiring those with licenses to reveal full information about the good being sold. Government has set up numerous regulatory commissions and passed laws that require full disclosure of information. The Federal Trade Commission, the Consumer Product Safety Commission, the Occupational Safety and Health Administration, the Food and Drug Administration, and state licensing boards are all examples of regulatory solutions designed to partially offset informational market failures.

But these regulatory solutions have problems of their own. The commissions and their regulations introduce restrictions on individuals that can slow down the economic process and prevent trades that people want to make. Consider as an example the Food and Drug Administration (FDA). It restricts what drugs may be sold until sufficient information about the drugs' effects can be disclosed. The FDA testing and approval process can take 5 or 10 years, is extraordinarily costly, and raises the price of drugs. The delays have caused some people to break the law by taking the drugs before they are approved.

A MARKET IN INFORMATION

Economists who lean away from government regulation suggest that the problem presented by the information examples above are not really a problem of market failure but instead a problem of the lack of a market. Information is valuable and is an economic product in its own right. Left on their own, markets will develop to provide the information that people need and are willing to pay for. (For example, a large number of consumer magazines provide such information.) In the car example, the buyer can hire a mechanic who can test the car with sophisticated diagnostic techniques and determine whether it is likely a cherry or a lemon. Firms can offer guarantees that will provide buyers with assurance that they can either return the car or have it fixed if the car is a lemon. There are many variations of such market solutions. If the government regulates information, these markets may not develop; people might rely on government instead of markets. Thus, the informational problem is not a problem of the market; it is a problem of government regulation.

LICENSING OF DOCTORS

Let's consider another informational problem that contrasts the market approach with the regulatory approach: medical licensing.[1] Currently all doctors are required to be licensed in order to practice, but this was not always the case.

In the early 1800s, medical licenses were not required by law in the United States, so anyone who wanted to could set up shop as a physician. Today, however, it is illegal to practice medicine without a license. Licensing of doctors is justified by information problems. Since individuals often don't have an accurate way of deciding whether a doctor is good, government intervention is necessary. The information problem is solved because licensing requires that all doctors have at least a minimum competency. People have the *information* that a doctor must be competent because they see the license framed and hanging on the doctor's office wall.

A small number of economists, of whom Milton Friedman is the best known, have proposed that licensure laws be eliminated, leaving the medical field unlicensed. They argue that licensure was instituted as much, or more, to restrict supply as it was to help the consumer. Specifically, critics of medical licensure raise these questions:

Why, if licensed medical training is so great, do we even need formal restrictions to keep other types of medicine from being practiced?

Whom do these restrictions benefit: the general public or the doctors who practice mainstream medicine?

What have the long-run effects of licensure been?

Even the strongest critics of licensure agree that, in the case of doctors, the informational argument for government intervention is strong. But the question is whether licensure is the right form of government intervention. Why doesn't the government simply provide the public with information about doctors' training and about which treatments work and which don't? That would give the freest rein to *consumer sovereignty* (the right of the individual to make choices about what is consumed and produced). If people have the necessary information but still choose to treat cancer with laetrile or treat influenza with massive doses of vitamin C, why should the government tell them they can't?

If the informational alternative is preferable to licensure, why didn't the government choose it? Friedman argues that government didn't follow that path because the licensing was done as much for the doctors as for the general public. Licensure has led to a monopoly position for doctors. They can restrict supply and increase price and thereby significantly increase their incomes.

Let's now take a closer look at the informational alternative that critics say would be preferable.

Some economists argue that licensure laws were established to restrict supply, not to help the consumer.

THE INFORMATIONAL ALTERNATIVE TO LICENSURE

The informational alternative is to allow anyone to practice medicine, but to have the government certify doctors' backgrounds and qualifications. The government would require that doctors' backgrounds be made public knowledge. Each doctor would have to post the following information prominently in his or her office:

1. Grades in college.
2. Grades in medical school.

 Web Note 18.4
Medical Information

---

[1]The arguments presented here about licensing doctors also apply to dentists, lawyers, college professors, cosmetologists (in some states, cosmetologists must be licensed), and other professional groups.

Surgery should be the strongest case for licensure. Would you want an untrained butcher to operate on you? Of course not. But opponents of licensure point out that it's not at all clear how effectively licensure prevents butchery. Ask a doctor, "Would you send your child to any board-certified surgeon picked at random?" The honest answer you'd get is "No way. Some of them are butchers." How do they know that? Being around hospitals, they have access to information about various surgeons' success and failure rates; they've seen them operate and know whether or not they have manual dexterity.

Advocates of the informational alternative suggest that you ask yourself, "What skill would you want in a surgeon?" A likely answer would be "Manual dexterity. Her fingers should be magic fingers." Does the existing system of licensure ensure that everyone who becomes a surgeon has magic fingers? No. To become licensed as a surgeon requires a grueling seven-year residency after four years of medical school, but manual dexterity, as such, is never explicitly tested or checked!

The informational alternative wouldn't necessarily eliminate the seven-year surgical residency. If the public believed that a seven-year residency was necessary to create skilled surgeons, many potential surgeons would choose that route. But there would be other ways to become a surgeon. For example, in high school, tests could be given for manual dexterity. Individuals with superb hand/eye coordination could go to a one-year technical college to train to be "heart technicians," who would work as part of a team doing heart surgery.

Clearly open-heart surgery is the extreme case, and most people will not be convinced that it can be performed by unlicensed medical personnel. But what about minor surgery? According to informational alternative advocates, many operations could be conducted more cheaply and better (since people with better manual dexterity would be doing the work) if restrictive licensing were ended. Or, if you don't accept the argument for human medical treatments, how about for veterinarians? For cosmetologists? For plumbers? Might the informational alternatives work in these professions?

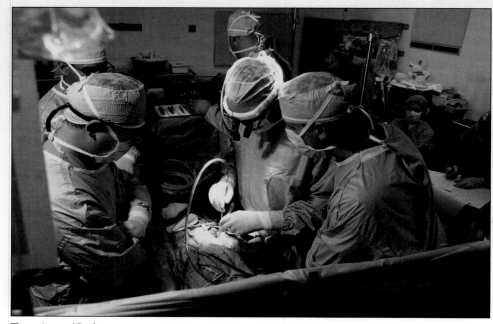

Tony Arruza/Corbis.

Q.8 Who would benefit and who would lose if an informational alternative to licensing doctors were used?

420

3. Success rate for various procedures.

4. References.

5. Medical philosophy.

6. Charges and fees.

According to supporters of the informational alternative, these data would allow individuals to make informed decisions about their medical care. Like all informed decisions, they would be complicated. For instance, doctors who take patients with minor problems only can show high "success rates," while doctors who are actually more skilled but who take on problem patients may have to provide more extensive information so people can see why their success rates shouldn't be compared to those of the doctors who take just easy patients. But despite the problems, supporters of the informational alternative argue that it's better than the current situation.

Current licensure laws don't provide any of this information to the public. All a patient knows is that a doctor has managed to get through medical school and has passed the medical board exams (which are, after all, only sets of multiple-choice questions). The doctor may have done all this 30 years ago, possibly by the skin of his or her teeth, but, once licensed, a doctor is a doctor for life. (A well-known doctor joke is the following: What do you call the person with the lowest passing grade point average in medical school? Answer: Doctor.) Thus, the informational alternative would provide much more useful data to the public than the current licensing procedure does.

The informational alternative relies on people having the ability to assess the information provided. Supporters of licensing argue that people do not have that ability; supporters of the informational alternative argue that they do.

GOVERNMENT FAILURE AND MARKET FAILURES

The above three types of market failure—externalities, public goods, and informational problems—give you a good sense of how markets can fail. They could be extended almost infinitely; all real-world markets in some way fail. But the point was to provide you not only with a sense of the way in which markets fail but also with a sense that economists know that markets fail and many of them support markets and oppose regulation anyway. Simply to point out a market failure is not necessarily to call for government to step in and try to rectify the situation. Why? The reason can be called **government failure**—when *the government intervention in the market to improve the market failure actually makes the situation worse*.

Why are there government failures? Let's briefly list some important reasons:

1. *Government doesn't have an incentive to correct the problem.* Government reflects politics, which reflects individuals' interests in trying to gain more for themselves. Political pressures to benefit some group or another will often dominate over doing the general good.

2. *Governments don't have enough information to deal with the problem.* Regulating is a difficult business. To intervene effectively, even if it wants to, government must have good information, but just as the market often lacks adequate information, so does the government. Individuals have the information and will be in a better position to decide the best plan of action.

3. *Intervention in markets is almost always more complicated than it initially seems.* Almost all actions have unintended consequences. Government attempts to offset market failures can prevent the market from dealing with the problem more effectively. The difficulty is that generally the market's ways of dealing with problems work only in the long run. As government deals with the short-run problems, it eliminates the incentives that would have brought about a long-run market solution.

4. *The bureaucratic nature of government intervention does not allow fine-tuning.* When the problems change, the government solution often responds far more slowly. An example is the Interstate Commerce Commission, which continued to exist years after its regulatory job had been eliminated.

Q.9 Would an economist necessarily believe that we should simply let the market deal with a pollution problem?

Q.10 If one accepts the three reasons for market failure, how might one still oppose government intervention?

5. *Government intervention leads to more government intervention.* Given the nature of the political process, opening the door in one area allows government to enter into other areas where intervention is harmful. Even in those cases where government action may seem to be likely to do some good, it might be best not to intervene, if that intervention will lead to additional government action in cases where it will not likely do good.

CONCLUSION

As a textbook writer, I wish I could say that some conclusions can be drawn about whether the government should, or should not, enter into the economy. I certainly have views about particular instances (in case you haven't guessed, I'm a highly opinionated individual), but to lay out arguments and information that would convince a reasonable person to agree with me would take an entire book for each area in which government might intervene.

What I can do in this textbook is to stimulate your interest in discovering for yourself the information and the subtleties of the debates for and against government intervention. Just about every time you read, hear, or are asked the question "Should the government intervene in a market?" the answer is "It depends." If your first impulse is to give any answer other than that one, you may have trouble maintaining the appropriate objectivity when you start considering the costs and benefits of government intervention.

Should the government intervene in the market? It depends.

SUMMARY

- Three sources of market failure are externalities, public goods, and imperfect information.

- An externality is the effect of a decision on a third party that is not taken into account by the decision maker. Positive externalities provide benefits to third parties. Negative externalities impose costs on third parties.

- The markets for goods with negative externalities produce too much of the good for too low of a price. The markets for goods with positive externalities produce too little of the good for too great a price.

- Economists generally prefer incentive-based programs to regulatory programs because incentive-based programs are more efficient. An example of an incentive-based program is to tax the producer of a good that results in a negative externality by the amount of the externality.

- Voluntary solutions are difficult to maintain for long periods of time because other people have an incentive to be free riders—to enjoy the benefits of others' volunteer efforts without putting forth effort themselves.

- An optimal policy is one in which the marginal cost of undertaking the policy equals its marginal benefit.

- Public goods are nonexclusive and nonrival. It is difficult to measure the benefits of public goods because people do not reveal their preferences by purchasing them in the marketplace.

- Theoretically, the market value of a public good can be calculated by summing the value that each individual places on every quantity. This is vertically summing individual demand curves.

- Individuals have an incentive to withhold information that will result in a lower price if one is a seller and a higher price if one is a consumer. Because of this incentive to withhold information, the markets for some goods disappear. Such market failures are known as adverse selection problems.

- Licensure and full disclosure are two solutions to the information problem.

- Government intervention may worsen the problem created by the market failure. Government failure occurs because (1) governments don't have an incentive to correct the problem, (2) governments don't have enough information to deal with the problem, (3) intervention is more complicated than it initially seems, (4) the bureaucratic nature of government precludes fine-tuning, and (5) government intervention often leads to more government intervention.

KEY TERMS

adverse selection problem (*417*)
direct regulation (*412*)
efficient (*412*)
effluent fees (*413*)
externality (*409*)

free rider problem (*414*)
government failure (*421*)
inefficient (*412*)
marginal social benefit (*411*)
marginal social cost (*410*)

market failure (*408*)
market incentive plan (*413*)
negative externality (*409*)
optimal policy (*415*)

positive externality (*409*)
public good (*415*)
tax incentive program (*413*)

QUESTIONS FOR THOUGHT AND REVIEW

1. State three reasons for a potentially beneficial role of government intervention.

2. Is the marginal social benefit of a good that exhibits positive externalities greater or less than the private social benefit of that good? Why?

3. Explain why a market incentive program is more efficient than a direct regulatory program.

4. How would an economist likely respond to the statement "There is no such thing as an acceptable level of pollution"?

5. Would a high tax on oil significantly reduce the amount of pollution coming from the use of oil? Why or why not?

6. Would a high tax on oil significantly reduce the total amount of pollution in the environment?

7. More than half of 30 economists polled recently stated that the federal gasoline tax should be $1 or higher. What do you suppose were their reasons?

8. List the public-good aspects (if any) of the following goods: safety, street names, a newspaper, a steak dinner, a lighthouse.

9. If you are willing to pay $1,000 for a used stereo that is a "cherry" and $200 for a used stereo that is a "lemon," how much will you be willing to offer to purchase a stereo if there is a 50 percent chance that the stereo is a lemon? If owners of cherry stereos want $700 for their cherries, how will your estimate of the chance of getting a cherry change?

10. Define the adverse selection problem. Does your understanding of adverse selection change your view of commercial dating services? If so, how?

11. If neither buyers nor sellers could distinguish between "lemons" and "cherries" in the used-car market, what would you expect to be the mix of lemons and cherries for sale?

12. Automobile insurance companies charge lower rates to married individuals than they do to unmarried individuals. What economic reason is there for such a practice? Is it fair?

13. Should government eliminate the Food and Drug Administration's role in restricting which drugs may be marketed? Why or why not?

14. List five ways you are affected on a daily basis by government intervention in the market. For what reason might government be involved? Is that reason justified?

15. Financial analysts are currently required to be licensed. Should they be licensed? Why or why not?

16. An advanced degree is required in order to teach at most colleges. In what sense is this a form of restricting entry through licensure?

17. Who would benefit and who would lose if an informational alternative to licensing doctors were introduced?

PROBLEMS AND EXERCISES

1. Using the table below, which shows the demand for a public good in an economy consisting of two households, A and B, answer the following questions:

Price		$0.00	$0.50	$1.00	$1.50	$2.00	$2.50	$3.00
Quantity	A	12	10	8	6	4	2	0
Demanded	B	4	3	2	1	0	0	0

a. Graph the individual demand curves and the market demand curve.
b. What would make you doubt that the table is an accurate reporting of the individual demand curves?
c. If the marginal cost of providing one unit of the good is $2.00, what is the socially optimal amount of the public good?
d. Given the free rider problem, is your answer to c most likely an underestimate or an overestimate?

2. There's a gas shortage in Gasland. You're presented with two proposals that will achieve the same level of reduction in the use of gas. Proposal A would force everybody to reduce their gas consumption by 5 percent. Proposal B would impose a 50-cent tax on the consumption of a gallon of gas, which would also achieve a 5 percent reduction. Demand curves for two groups are shown below.
a. Show the effect of both proposals on each group.
b. Which group would support a regulatory policy? Which would support a tax policy?

3. The marginal cost, marginal social cost, and demand for fish are represented by the curves in the graph in the following column. Suppose that there are no restrictions on fishing.
a. Assuming perfect competition, what is the catch going to be, and at what price will it be sold?

b. What are the socially efficient price and output?
c. Some sports fishers propose a ban on commercial fishing. As the community's economic adviser, you're asked to comment on it at a public forum. What do you say?

4. You are in Seattle, watching the Seattle Stomp—a dance home owners do in their trash cans.
a. What can you say about trash fees in Seattle? Be as specific as possible.
b. What change in fee structure might eliminate the Seattle Stomp?

5. In his book *At the Hand of Man*, Raymond Bonner argues that Africa should promote hunting, charging large fees for permits to kill animals (for example, $7,500 for a permit to shoot an elephant).
a. What are some arguments in favor of this proposal?
b. What are some arguments against?

6. California passed an air quality law that required 3.75 percent of all the cars sold in the state to emit zero pollution by 1998, and required 10 percent of all cars sold in the state to meet this standard by 2003.
a. What was the likely impact of this law?
b. Can you think of any way in which this law might actually increase pollution rather than decrease it?
c. How might an economist suggest modifying this law to better achieve economic efficiency?

7. Economics professors Thomas Hopkins and Arthur Gosnell of the Rochester Institute of Technology estimated that in the year 2000, regulations cost the United States $662 billion, or about $5,700 per family.
a. Do their findings mean that the United States has too many regulations?
b. How would an economist decide which regulations to keep and which to do away with?

8. A debate about dairy products concerns the labeling of milk produced from cows who have been injected with the hormone BST, which significantly increases milk

production. Since the FDA has determined that this syn-
thetically produced copy of a milk hormone is indistinguishable from the hormone produced naturally by the
cow, and has also determined that milk from cows treated
with BST is indistinguishable from milk from untreated
cows, some people have argued that no labeling requirement is necessary. Others argue that the consumer has a
right to know.

a. Where do you think most dairy farmers stand on this
   labeling issue?
b. If consumers have a right to know, should labels
   inform them of other drugs, such as antibiotics,
   normally given to cows?
c. Do you think dairy farmers who support BST labeling
   also support the broader labeling law that would be
   needed if other drugs were included? Why?

WEB QUESTIONS

1. The Emissions Trading Educational Initiative (ETEI) is a
   project of the Environmental Defense Fund and the
   Emissions Marketing Association to educate the public
   about emissions trading. Visit the ETEI website at
   www.etei.org. Answer the following questions:
   a. What is "cap and trade"?
   b. What type of market failure does cap and trade
      address in Case Study #1? Explain your answer.
   c. Is cap and trade efficient?
   d. What is the solution to the market failure in Case #1?
      Has the program been successful?

2. Visit the home page for Occupational Safety and Health
   Administration (OSHA) at www.osha.gov. Answer the
   following questions:
   a. When was OSHA established and what is its mission?
   b. What market failure is OSHA designed to address?
   c. Who is covered by OSHA? Who is not covered?
   d. How does OSHA enforce its workplace standards?

ANSWERS TO MARGIN QUESTIONS

1. An externality is an effect of a decision not taken into
   account by the decision maker. When there are externalities, the private price no longer necessarily reflects
   the social price, and therefore the market may not work
   properly. (410)

2. No. The existence of a positive externality does not
   mean that the market works better than if no externality
   existed. It means that the market is not supplying a sufficient amount of the resource or activity, and insufficient
   supply can be as inefficient as an oversupply. (411)

3. An example of the trade-off between fairness and efficiency is whether to allow nontaxpayers to enjoy the
   benefits of a public park maintained through local taxes.
   It would cost too much to exclude them from enjoying
   the park, so the exclusion is inefficient, but not to
   exclude that person is unfair to the taxpayers who pay
   to maintain the park. An example of a policy that might
   be seen as both fair and efficient is a gas tax designed to
   deter pollution. Consumers choose to reduce their gas
   use based on the new price, so the solution is efficient.
   The solution has an element of fairness in it since those
   causing the pollution are those paying more. (412)

4. The tax incentive approach to pollution is fair in the
   following sense: Individuals whose actions result in more
   pollution pay more. Individuals whose actions result in
   less pollution pay less. In some broader sense this may not
   be fair if one takes into account the initial positions of
   those polluting. For example, the poor may have older

cars that get fewer miles per gallon and have to pay a
higher cost of pollution resulting from gasoline use. (413)

5. Voluntary actions that are not in people's self-interest
   may not work in large groups because individuals will rely
   on others to volunteer. There is also a potential lack of
   efficiency in voluntary solutions since the person who
   voluntarily reduces consumption may not be the person
   who faces the least cost of doing so. (414)

6. It is difficult for government to decide the efficient
   quantity of a public good because public goods are not
   purchased by individuals in markets. Individuals do not
   reveal the value they place on public goods. Individuals
   also face incentives to overstate the value they place
   on public goods if they do not have to pay for them,
   and to understate the value if they do have to share the
   cost. (417)

7. Since adverse selection is a problem in the medical
   insurance industry, with fuller information, I would
   expect that average medical rates would decline since
   the adverse selection problem would disappear. Medical
   insurers would be able to offer lower-cost insurance to
   people who are less likely to get sick and who perhaps
   choose not to be covered at today's high rates. (418)

8. If an informational alternative to licensing were introduced, existing doctors would suffer a significant monetary loss, and students who would likely go on to medical
   school in existing institutions would face lower potential
   incomes when they entered practice. Gainers would

likely be (1) those who did not want to go through an entire medical school schedule but were willing to learn a specialty that required far less education and in which they had a particular proclivity to do good, and (2) consumers, who would get more for less. *(420)*

9. An economist would not necessarily believe that we should simply let the market deal with the pollution problem. Pollution clearly involves externalities. Where economists differ from many laypeople is how they would handle the problem. An economist is likely to look more carefully into the costs, try to build price incentives into whatever program is designed, and make the marginal private cost equal the marginal social cost. *(421)*

10. One can accept all three explanations for market failure and still oppose government intervention if one believes that government intervention will cause worse problems than the market failure. *(421)*

POLITICS AND ECONOMICS: THE CASE OF AGRICULTURAL MARKETS

American farmers have become welfare addicts, protected and assisted at every turn by a network of programs paid for by their fellow citizens. If Americans still believe in the virtue of self-reliance, they should tell Washington to get out of the way and let farmers practice it.

—*Stephen Chapman*

After reading this chapter, you should be able to:

- Describe the competitive nature of agricultural markets.

- Explain the good/bad paradox in farming.

- State the general rule of political economy in a democracy.

- Explain how a price support system works.

- Explain, using supply and demand curves, the distributional consequences of four alternative methods of price support.

- Discuss real-world pressures politicians face when designing agricultural policy.

In May 2002 the U.S. Congress passed an agricultural support bill that authorized approximately $180 billion in price supports and other aid to farmers between 2002 and 2010. This was an increase of $80 billion over already established programs, which had been reduced six years earlier, when Congress made large payments to farmers under a Freedom to Farm Act to try to wean them off government support systems. Why did it pass this bill? The answer is that a number of farm states would be swing votes in that year's upcoming election. Both parties wanted to please those states.

Agricultural markets provide good examples of the interaction between the invisible hand and political forces. Considering the economics of agricultural markets shows us how powerful a tool supply/demand analysis is in helping us understand not only the workings of perfectly competitive markets but also the effects of government intervention in a market.

While the chapter is about agricultural markets, bear in mind that the lessons of the analysis apply to a wide variety of markets in which the invisible hand and politics interact. As you read the chapter, applying the analysis to other markets will be a useful exercise.

THE NATURE OF AGRICULTURAL MARKETS

In many ways, agricultural markets fit the classic picture of perfect competition. First, there are many independent sellers who are generally *price takers*. Second, there are many buyers. Third, the products are interchangeable: Farm A's wheat can readily be substituted for farm B's wheat. And fourth, prices can, and do, vary considerably. On the basis of these inherent characteristics, it is reasonable to talk about agricultural markets as competitive markets.

In other ways, however, agricultural markets are far from perfectly competitive. The competitiveness of many agricultural markets is influenced by

When people think of agricultural products, they often think of the products they buy, like Wheaties. Doing so gives them the wrong impression of the cost of agricultural products. To see why, let's consider an 18-ounce box of Wheaties that costs you, say, $3.35.

If you look at the ingredients, you'll see that you're buying wheat, sugar, salt, malt syrup, and corn syrup. So you're buying agricultural products, right? Well, a little bit. Actually, the total cost of those agricultural ingredients is probably somewhere around 25 cents, less than 10 percent of the cost of the box of Wheaties. What are you

spending the other 90 percent on? Well, there's packaging, advertising, transporting the boxes, processing the ingredients, stocking the grocery store shelves, and profits. These are important components of Wheaties, but they aren't agricultural components.

The point of this example is simple: Much of our food expenditure isn't for agricultural goods; it's for the services that transform agricultural goods into processed foods, convince us we want to eat those foods, and get those foods to us.

---

government programs. In fact, neither the United States nor any other country allows the market, unhindered, to control agricultural prices and output. For example, the U.S. government sets a minimum price for milk; buys up large quantities of wheat and stockpiles it; and licenses tobacco growers, allowing only those with licenses to grow tobacco.

I could have made the list of government programs much longer, because the government has a program for just about every major agricultural market. The point is clear, however: The competitive market in agriculture is not a story of the invisible hand alone. It's the story of a constant struggle between political and economic forces. Whenever the invisible hand pushes prices down, various coalitions of political forces generally work to push them back up. Without continued political pressure and government programs, far fewer farms would exist. Farm states know this and are strongly encouraging their farmers to engage in *value-added farming*, in which farmers take over some of the other activities that give agricultural goods their value to the consumer.

> Agricultural markets involve a constant struggle between political and economic forces.

THE GOOD/BAD PARADOX IN AGRICULTURE

Agriculture is characterized by what might be called a **good/bad paradox** (*the phenomenon of doing poorly because you're doing well*). This good/bad paradox shows up in a variety of ways. Looking at the long run, we see that the enormous increase in agricultural productivity over the past few centuries has reduced agriculture's importance in U.S. society and has forced many farmers off the farm. Looking at the short run, we see that when harvests are good, farmers often fare badly financially; when harvests are poor, some farmers do very well financially. Let's consider these two cases in some detail.

> The good/bad paradox is the phenomenon of doing poorly because you're doing well.

THE LONG-RUN DECLINE OF FARMING

Most countries, the United States included, began as predominantly agricultural societies. When the United States was founded a little more than 200 years ago, 97 percent of the labor force was engaged in farming. Today just over 2 percent of the U.S. labor force works in agriculture.

The decline in the number of farmers isn't the result of the failure of U.S. agriculture. Rather, it's the result of its tremendous success—the enormous increase in its productivity. It used to take the majority of the population to provide food for the United

Figure 19-1 The Good/Bad Paradox
The good/bad paradox is demonstrated in this graph. At price P_0 the quantity of wheat produced is Q_0. Total income is P_0Q_0. But if the supply of wheat increases from S_0 to S_1 due to increased productivity, the price of wheat will fall from P_0 to P_1 and quantity demanded will increase from Q_0 to Q_1. The increase in farmers' income (area C) is small. The decrease in farmers' income (area A) is large. Overall, the increased productivity has led to a decrease in farmers' incomes.

States. Today it takes only a small proportion to produce more food than the U.S. population can consume.

Figure 19-1 shows how success, however, can lead to problems. In the long run the demand for wheat is inelastic (i.e., the percentage change in quantity demanded is small relative to the percentage change in price), as it is for most agricultural products, so the figure shows the equilibrium in the inelastic portion of the demand curve.

In this example, initially farmers are selling quantity Q_0 for price P_0. Their total income is P_0Q_0, shown by rectangles A and B. Now say that increases in productivity shift the supply curve out from S_0 to S_1. Output increases from Q_0 to Q_1, and price falls by a proportionately greater amount to P_1. Income falls to P_1Q_1, shown by the B and C rectangles. Farmers have gained the C rectangle but lost the A rectangle. The net effect is the difference in size between the two rectangles. So in this example, the net effect is negative.

In short, although productivity has increased, total revenue has fallen and many farmers have stopped farming altogether. They've done good by producing a lot, but the result for themselves is bad. This good/bad paradox will occur whenever the supply curve shifts outward in the inelastic range of the demand curve.

Due to competition among farmers, most benefits of productivity increases in agriculture have gone to consumers in the form of lower prices. As an example, consider chicken. In the early 1930s, when Herbert Hoover was president of the United States and running for reelection, he promised prosperity to the country by saying there would be "two chickens in every pot." That promise meant a lot because, in today's money, chicken then cost $8 a pound. In the early 2000s, the price of chicken has fallen to under $2 a pound, only about one-quarter of its price in 1930.

THE SHORT-RUN CYCLICAL PROBLEM FACING FARMERS

The long-run good/bad paradox for farmers is mirrored by a short-run good/bad paradox: Good harvests often mean bad times and a fall in income; poor harvests often mean a rise in income.

A fact of life that farmers must deal with is that agricultural production tends to be highly unstable because it depends on weather and luck. Crops can be affected by too little rain, too much rain, insects, frost, heat, wind, hail—none of which can be easily controlled. Say you're an apple grower and you're having a beautiful spring—until the

Q-1 What is the good/bad paradox?

Due to competition among farmers, most benefits of productivity increases in agriculture have gone to consumers in the form of lower prices.

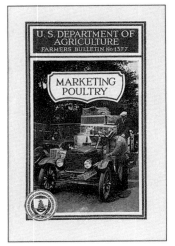

Marketing Poultry, a 1936 Department of Agriculture publication, is representative of the major role government has played in agriculture.

Q-2 How can it be in the interest of the agricultural industry to have a "bad year"?

Q-3 What are two ways around the good/bad paradox?

week that your trees are blossoming, when it rains continually. Bees don't fly when it rains, so they don't pollinate your trees. No pollination, no apple crop. There goes your apple crop for this year, and there goes your income.

The short-run demand for most agricultural goods is even more inelastic than the long-run demand. Because short-run demand is so inelastic, short-run changes in supply can have a significant effect on price. The result is that good harvests for farmers in general can lower prices significantly, while poor harvests can raise prices significantly. When the short-run price effect overwhelms the short-run quantity effect (as it does when demand is inelastic), farmers face the short-run good/bad paradox.

THE DIFFICULTY OF COORDINATING FARM PRODUCTION

This good/bad paradox caused by inelastic demand isn't lost on farmers. They, quite naturally, aren't wild about passing on the gains to consumers instead of keeping the gains themselves. However, because agriculture is competitive, it is not in any one farmer's interest to decrease his or her supply to avoid encountering the paradox. Competitive farmers take the market price as given. That's the definition of a competitive industry. While it is in the industry's interest to have a "bad year" (to reduce total supply), it is in each individual farmer's interest to have a good year (to increase output) even if the combination of *all* farmers having a good year would cause all farmers to have a bad year (revenues would fall).

It is, however, in farmers' joint interest to figure out ways to have continually "bad" years—which are, of course, actually "good" years for them. In other words, it's in their interest to figure out ways to limit the production of all farmers.

In a competitive industry, limiting production is easier said than done. It is difficult for farmers to limit production privately among themselves, because although they make up only a small percentage of the total U.S. population, there are still a lot of them—3.1 million. That's too many to coordinate easily.

WAYS AROUND THE GOOD/BAD PARADOX

The difficulty of organizing privately to limit supply can be avoided by organizing through government. The U.S. political structure provides an alternative way for farmers (and other suppliers) to coordinate their actions and limit supply. Suppliers can organize and get government to establish programs to limit production or hold price high, thereby avoiding the good/bad paradox. And that's what farmers did, which is why so many government agricultural programs exist today. (For a history of the U.S. government farm programs, go to the Colander website: www.mhhe.com/economics/colander.) These programs have been a combination of **price stabilization programs**—*programs designed to eliminate short-run fluctuations in prices, while allowing prices to follow their long-run trend line* and **price support programs**—*programs designed to maintain prices at levels higher than the market prices.*

THE GENERAL RULE OF POLITICAL ECONOMY

If farmers are helped by farm programs, who is hurt? The answer is taxpayers and consumers. One would expect that these broad groups would strongly oppose farm programs because farm programs cost them in two ways: (1) higher taxes that government requires in order to buy up surplus farm output, and (2) higher prices for food. It's not easy for a politician to tell nonfarm constituents, "I'm supporting a bill that means higher prices and higher taxes for you." Nevertheless, the farm lobby has been quite successful in seeing that these programs are retained.

Economists who specialize in the relationship between economics and politics (known as *public choice economists*) have suggested that the reasons for farm groups' success involve the nature of the benefits and costs. The groups that are hurt by agricultural subsidies are large, but the negative effect on each individual in that group is relatively small. Large groups that experience small costs per individual don't provide a strong political opposition to a small group that experiences large gains. This seems to reflect a **general rule of political economy** in a democracy: *When small groups are helped by a government action and large groups are hurt by that same action, the small group tends to lobby far more effectively than the large group; thus, policies tend to reflect the small group's interest, not the interest of the large group.*

> The general rule of political economy states that small groups that are significantly affected by a government policy will lobby more effectively than large groups that are equally affected by that same policy.

This bias in favor of farm programs is strengthened by the historical representation of farmers in Congress. Right from its beginnings in 1787, the U.S. political system has reflected the importance of agriculture. The Constitution gives representation in the Senate equally to all states. Only representation in the House of Representatives is based on a state's population. Since farm states have smaller populations than urban states, this arrangement gives farmers relatively more political power per capita than nonfarmers. This political structure played an important role in making the farm states the voter swing states in 2002 and, in part, explains why farmers can lobby effectively for strong support packages.

Farmers' strong political representation in Congress establishes a core of lawmakers who favor price supports. That core is supplemented with individuals who like the countryside filled with farms rather than with suburban sprawl. Consumers and taxpayers in general, who would be hurt by price supports, generally lack the political organization necessary to make their will known and counter the pressure for price controls.

> Farmers' strong political representation in Congress establishes a core of lawmakers who favor price supports.

FOUR PRICE SUPPORT OPTIONS

Let's now consider the theory underlying some alternative farm price support options. In doing so, we'll try to understand which options, given the political realities, would have the best chance of being implemented, and why.

In a price support system, the government maintains a higher-than-equilibrium price, as diagrammed in Figure 19-2. At support price P_1, the quantity people want to supply is Q_S, but the quantity demanded at that price is Q_D.

> In a price support system, the government maintains a higher-than-equilibrium price.

Figure 19-2   A Price Support System
In a price support system, the government maintains a higher-than-equilibrium price. At support price P_1, the quantity of product demanded is only Q_D, while the quantity supplied is Q_S. This causes downward pressures on the price, P_1, which must be offset by various government measures.

At price P_1, there's excess supply, which exerts a downward pressure on price (arrow A). To maintain price at P_1, some other force (arrow B) must be exerted; otherwise the invisible hand will force the price down.

The government has various options to offset the downward pressure on price. These include:

1. Using legal and regulatory force to prevent anyone from selling or buying at a lower price.
2. Providing economic incentives to reduce the supply enough to eliminate the downward pressure on price.
3. Subsidizing the sale of the good to consumers so that while suppliers get a high price, consumers have to pay only a low price.
4. Buying up and storing, giving away, or destroying enough of the good so that the total demand (including government's demand) increases enough to eliminate downward pressure on price.

These methods distribute the costs and benefits in slightly different ways. Let's consider each in detail.

SUPPORTING THE PRICE BY REGULATORY MEASURES

Suppose the government simply passes a law saying that, from now on, the price of wheat will be at least $5 per bushel. No one may sell wheat at a lower price. If the competitive equilibrium price is higher than $5, the law has no effect. When the competitive equilibrium is below the price floor (say the competitive equilibrium is $3.50 per bushel), the law limits suppliers from selling their wheat at that lower price.

The price floor helps some suppliers and hurts others. Those suppliers who are lucky enough to sell their wheat benefit. Those suppliers who aren't lucky and can't find buyers for their wheat are hurt. How many suppliers will be helped and how many will be hurt depends on the elasticities of supply and demand. When supply and demand are inelastic, a large change in price brings about a small change in quantity supplied, so the hurt group is relatively small. When the supply and demand are elastic, the hurt group is larger.

In Figure 19-3(a), at $5 suppliers would like to sell quantity Q_2 but they can sell only Q_1. They end up with a surplus of wheat, $Q_2 - Q_1$. Consumers, who must pay the higher price, $5, and receive only Q_1 rather than Q_e, are also hurt.

The Need for Rationing   The law may or may not specify who will, and who will not, be allowed to sell, but it must establish some noneconomic method of rationing the limited demand among the suppliers. If it doesn't, buyers are likely, for example, to buy from farmers who are their friends. If individual farmers have a surplus, they'll probably try to dispose of that surplus by selling it on the black market at a price below the legal price. To maintain the support price, the government will have to arrest farmers who sell below the legal price. If the number of producers is large, such a regulatory approach is likely to break down quickly, since individual incentives to sell illegally are great and the costs of enforcing the law are accordingly high.

In understanding who benefits and who's hurt by price floors, it's useful to distinguish between two groups of farmers: the farmers who were producing before the law went into effect, and the farmers who entered the market afterward. In Figure 19-3(a), the first group supplies Q_e; the second group, which would want to enter the market when the price went up, would supply $Q_2 - Q_e$. Why must these groups be clearly identified? Because one relatively easily enforceable way to limit the quantity supplied is to

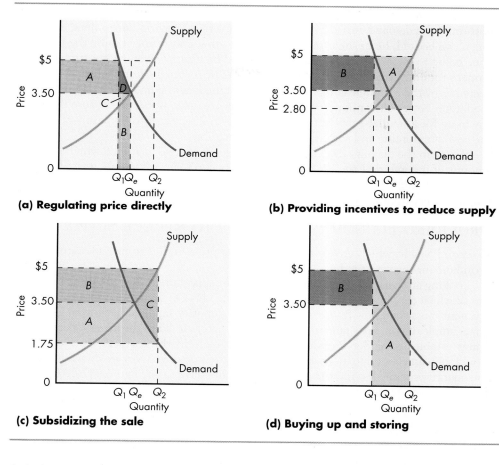

Figure 19-3 (a, b, c, and d) Alternative Methods of Government Price Supports

Alternative methods have different distributional consequences. The consequences of regulatory measures are shown in (**a**); the consequences of providing economic incentives to reduce supply in (**b**); the consequences of subsidizing the sale in (**c**); and the consequences of buying up and storing the good in (**d**).

(a) Regulating price directly

(b) Providing incentives to reduce supply

(c) Subsidizing the sale

(d) Buying up and storing

forbid any new farmers to enter the market. Only people who were producing at the beginning of the support program will be allowed to produce, and they will be allowed to produce only as much as they did before the program went into effect. Restricting production to the existing suppliers will reduce the quantity supplied to Q_e, leaving only $Q_e - Q_1$ to be rationed among suppliers.

To use this method of restriction is to **grandfather**—*to pass a law affecting a specific group but providing that those in the group before the law was passed are exempt from some provisions of the law.* To "grandfather in" existing suppliers is one of the easiest provisions to enact into law and one of the easiest to enforce; thus, it is one of the most widely used. For example, when supply limitations were placed on tobacco, existing growers were all allowed to grow tobacco on land they were currently using for tobacco production. They could not, however, devote any new land to growing tobacco. (Later, tobacco farmers were allowed to sell their acreage allocations so that if old land was taken out of tobacco production, new land could be added.)

When it comes to keeping groups out of production, foreign producers are perhaps the politically easiest targets. To keep the domestic price of a good up, foreign imports must be limited as well as domestic production. U.S. taxpayers might put up with subsidizing U.S. farmers, but they're likely to balk at subsidizing foreign farmers. So most farm subsidy programs are supplemented with tariffs and quotas on foreign imports of the same commodity. (See Chapter 21 for definitions and further discussion of tariffs and quotas.)

> Grandfathering is one of the politically easiest ways of restricting supply.

Distributional Consequences   Notice that with the equilibrium in the inelastic portion of the demand curve, even though the average farmer is constrained as to how much can be sold, he or she is made better off by that constraint because the total revenue going to all farmers is higher than it would be if supply weren't constrained. The farmer's total revenue from this market increases by rectangle A in Figure 19-3(a) and decreases by the rectangle composed of the combined areas B and C. Of course, making the farmer better off is not cost-free. Consumers are made worse off because they must pay more for a smaller supply of wheat. There's no direct cost to taxpayers other than the cost of enforcing and administering the regulations.

Notice in the diagram the little triangle made up of areas C and D, which shows an amount of income that society loses but farmers don't get. It's simply wasted. As discussed in Chapter 7, that little triangle is the welfare loss of producer and consumer surplus to society from the restriction.

PROVIDING ECONOMIC INCENTIVES TO REDUCE SUPPLY

A second way in which government can keep a price high is to provide farmers with economic incentives to reduce supply.

Looking at Figure 19-3(b), you see that at the support price, $5 per bushel, the quantity of wheat supplied is Q_2 and quantity demanded is Q_1. To avoid a surplus, the government must somehow find a way to shift the quantity supplied back from Q_2 to Q_1. For example, it could pay farmers not to grow wheat, as it did in the acreage control programs established under President John F. Kennedy in the early 1960s. How much would such an economic incentive cost? Given the way the curves are drawn, to reduce the quantity supplied to Q_1, the government would have to pay farmers $2.20 ($5.00 − $2.80) for each bushel of wheat they didn't grow. This payment of $2.20 would induce suppliers producing $Q_2 − Q_1$ not to produce, reducing the quantity supplied to Q_1. The payment is shown by the A rectangle.

The Need for Rationing   There is, however, a problem in identifying those individuals who would truly supply wheat at $5 a bushel. Knowing that the government is paying people not to grow wheat, people who otherwise had no interest in growing wheat will pretend that at $5 they would supply the wheat, simply to get the subsidy. To avoid this problem, often this incentive approach is combined with our first option, regulatory restrictions. Farmers who are already producing wheat at Q_e are grandfathered in; only they are given economic incentives not to produce. All others are forbidden to produce.

Distributional Consequences   When economic incentives are supplied, the existing farmers do very well for themselves. Their income goes up for two reasons. They get part of the A rectangle from the government in the form of payments not to grow wheat, and they get the B rectangle from consumers in the form of higher prices for the wheat they do grow. Farmers are also free to use their land for other purposes, so their income rises by the amount they can earn from using the land taken out of wheat production for something other than growing wheat. Consumers are still being hurt as before: They are paying a higher price and getting less. In addition, they're being hurt in their role as taxpayers because the lightly shaded area (rectangle A) represents the taxes they must pay to finance the government's economic incentive program. Thus, this option is much more costly to taxpayers than the regulatory option.

SUBSIDIZING THE SALE OF THE GOOD

A third option is for the government to subsidize the sale of the good to hold down the price consumers pay but keep the amount suppliers receive high. Figure 19-3(c) shows

Q-4   Which of the four methods of price support would farmers favor least? Why?

how this works. Suppliers supply quantity Q_2 and are paid $5 per bushel. The government then turns around and sells that quantity at whatever price it can get—in this case, $1.75. No direct transfer takes place from the consumer to the supplier. Both are made better off. Consumers get more goods at a lower price. They are benefited by area A. Suppliers get a higher price and can supply all they want. They are benefited by area B. What's the catch? The catch, of course, is that taxpayers foot the entire bill, paying the difference between the $5 and the $1.75 ($3.25) for each bushel sold. The cost to taxpayers is represented by areas A, B, and C. This option costs taxpayers the most of any of the four options.

Q.5 Which of the four methods of price support would taxpayers favor least? Why?

BUYING UP AND STORING, GIVING AWAY, OR DESTROYING THE GOOD

The final option is for the government to buy up all the quantity supplied that consumers don't buy at the support price. This option is shown in Figure 19-3(d). At the support price of $5 a bushel consumers buy Q_1 and the government buys $Q_2 - Q_1$ at a total cost represented by the A rectangle.

Distributional Consequences   In this case consumers transfer the B rectangle to suppliers when they pay $5 rather than $3.50, the competitive equilibrium price. The government (i.e., the taxpayers) pays farmers rectangle A. The situation is very similar to our second option, in which the government provides suppliers with economic incentives not to produce. However, this fourth option is more expensive for the government since it must pay $5 rather than providing a $2.20 per bushel incentive not to grow as it did in option (b). In return for this higher payment, the government is getting something in return: $Q_2 - Q_1$ of wheat.

Q.6 Which of the four methods of price support would consumers favor least? Why?

The Need to Dispose of Surplus   Of course, if the government buys the surplus wheat, it takes on the problem of what to do with this surplus. Say the government decides to give it to the poor. Since the poor were already buying food, in response to a free food program they will replace some of their purchases with the free food. This replacement brings about a drop in demand—which means that the government must buy even more surplus. Instead of giving it away, though, the government can burn the surplus or store it indefinitely in warehouses and grain elevators. Burning up the surplus or storing it, at least, doesn't increase the amount government must buy.

Web Note 19.1
Food for Peace

Why, you ask, doesn't the government give the surplus to foreign countries as a type of humanitarian aid? The reason is that just as giving the surplus to our own poor creates problems in the United States, giving the surplus to the foreign poor creates problems in the countries involved. To the degree that the foreign poor have any income, they're likely to spend most of it on food. Free food would supplant some of their demand, thus lowering the price for those who previously sold food to them. Giving anything away destroys somebody's market, and when markets are destroyed someone gets upset. So when the United States has tried to give away its surplus food, other foreign countries have put enormous pressure on the United States not to "spoil the world market."

WHICH GROUP PREFERS WHICH OPTION?

The four price support options I've just described can, of course, be used in various combinations. It's a useful exercise at this point to think through which of the options farmers, taxpayers, and consumers would likely favor and to relate current debates about farm programs to these options.

The U.S. House Committee on Agriculture posts information about current farm legislation at www.agriculture.house.gov.

The first option, regulation, costs the government the least, but it benefits farmers the least. Since existing farmers are likely to be the group directly pushing for price supports, government is least likely to choose this approach. If it is chosen, most of the required reduction in quantity supplied will probably come from people who might enter farming at some time in the future, not from existing farmers.

The second option, economic incentives, costs the government more than the first option but less than the third and fourth options. Farmers are benefited by economic incentive programs in two ways. They get paid not to grow a certain crop, and they can sometimes get additional income from using the land for other purposes. When farmers aren't allowed to use their land for other purposes, they usually oppose this option, preferring the third or fourth option.

The third option, subsidies on the sales to keep prices down, benefits both consumers (who get low prices) and farmers (who get high prices). Taxpayers are harmed the most by this option. They must finance the subsidy payments for all subsidized farm products.

The last option, buying up and storing or destroying the goods, costs taxpayers more than the first two options but less than the third, since consumers pay part of the cost. However, it leaves the government with a surplus to deal with. If there's a group who can take that surplus without significantly reducing their current demand, then that group is likely to support this option.

ECONOMICS, POLITICS, AND REAL-WORLD POLICIES

Q-7 What two farm programs have been the most prevalent in the United States?

The two farm programs most prevalent in the United States have been the **land bank program** (in which *government supports prices by giving farmers economic incentives to reduce supply*) and the **nonrecourse loan program** (in which *government "buys" goods in the form of collateral on defaulting loans*). Programs that support prices through regulation, our first option, generally haven't been applied to existing farmers. They have, however, often been used to prevent new farmers from entering the market—which isn't surprising since the political impetus for farm programs comes from existing farmers. The third option, to subsidize the sale of the good so the farmer gets a high price and the consumer pays a low price, hasn't been used because, as discussed previously, it would be the most costly to taxpayers.

INTEREST GROUPS

The actual political debate is, of course, much more complicated than presented here. For example, other pressure groups are involved. Recently, farm groups and environmental groups have combined forces and have become more effective in shaping and supporting farm policy. Thus, recent new restrictions on supply in farming often operate in ways that environmentalists would favor, such as regulating the types of fertilizer and chemicals farmers can use.

Q-8 Are taxpayers, farmers, and consumers separate groups that are independent of each other?

Moreover, the three interest groups discussed here—farmers, taxpayers, and consumers—aren't entirely distinct one from another. Their memberships overlap. All taxpayers are also consumers, farmers are both taxpayers and consumers, and so on. Thus, much of the political debate is simply about from whose pocket the government is going to get money to help farmers. Shall it be the consumer's pocket (through higher prices)? Or the taxpayer's (through higher taxes)? That said, the political reality is that consumer and taxpayer interests and the lobbying groups that represent them generally examine only part of the picture—the part that directly affects them. Accordingly, politicians often act as if these groups had separate memberships. Politicians weigh the

In 1996 the U.S. government voted for sweeping reforms designed to eliminate major aspects of the farm support programs by 2002. What made that politically possible was a combination of three forces: (1) the government deficit, which put pressure on government to eliminate costly programs; (2) the ability of U.S. farmers to sell abroad, which reduced the benefits of the existing farm support program to them; and (3) the general pro-market ideology that gained favor in the late 1990s and early 2000s.

When we look at the reforms more carefully, they look less sweeping than they initially appeared. There are three reasons why. First, three of the programs that most sharply limit production—peanut, sugar, and dairy programs—were left untouched because of strong lobbying efforts directed at members of Congress. Second, while in a number of areas direct price supports were eliminated, other indirect price support systems were not. The most important of these was the program that allows farmers to borrow money cheaply from the government, using the expected crop as collateral. This program allows the farmer to default on the loan, instead of paying it back, should the price of their crop be less than the prices set as collateral. This means that if agricultural prices fall significantly, the buy-up-and-store option discussed in the text will still exist and will hold prices up. This method of price support is extraordinarily costly to taxpayers.

Third, to "compensate" farmers for their elimination of direct price supports, the government gave direct grants to farmers. These grants started at $5.8 billion in 1998 and fell to $4 billion in 2002, when the law ended. With agricultural prices high, as they were at the time the law was passed, the net result of this "compensation" was that the total payments to farmers were initially higher than they were under the old price support system. As prices fell in 1999 large emergency grants were given to farmers, and as mentioned at the beginning of the chapter, in 2002 Congress passed a large farm bill that reintroduced and expanded subsidies to U.S. farmers. So the grand hopes of eliminating farm subsidies in 1996 were dashed.

---

options by attempting to balance their view of the general good with the power and preferences of the special interest groups that they represent or that contribute to their election campaigns.

INTERNATIONAL ISSUES

The final real-world complication that must be taken into account is the international dimension. If you think government is significantly involved in U.S. agriculture, you should see its role in other countries such as the members of the European Union (EU) and Japan. For example, more than half the EU's budget is devoted to farm subsidies, and most of its farms stay in business only because of protection. Our agricultural policy is, in part, determined by trade negotiations with these other countries. For example, a reduction in EU subsidies could bring about a reduction in our subsidies.

Web Note 19.2
EU Agricultural Policy

If you think government is significantly involved in U.S. agriculture, you should see its role in other countries, such as the members of the European Union and Japan.

CONCLUSION

This chapter has focused on agricultural markets, but it should be clear that the discussion is about much more than just agriculture; it's about the interrelationship between economics and politics. If individuals are self-interested maximizers, it's reasonable to assume that they're maximizers in all aspects of their lives. What they can't achieve in the economic sphere, they might be able to achieve in the political sphere.

To understand the economic policies that exist, we must consider how people act in both spheres. Consideration of the economics underlying government policies often leads to useful insights. For example, as discussed in Chapter 7, a military draft can be seen as a mechanism for shifting the costs of defense away from the taxpayer and onto

Q.9 Is the military draft a cheaper way of maintaining defense than a volunteer army?

Q-10 Economic theory tells us that a volunteer army is preferable to an army maintained by a draft. True or false? Why?

a specific group of individuals—young people. The government's support for the arts can be seen as a transfer from general taxpayers to a specific group of individuals who like the arts. Government support for education can be seen as a transfer from general taxpayers to a specific group of individuals: students and instructors. These groups maintain strong lobbies to achieve their political ends, and the interaction of the various lobbying groups typically strongly influences what policies government will follow.

Economics doesn't tell you whether government intervention or any particular policy is good or bad. That, you must decide for yourself. But what economics can do is pose the policy question in terms of gains and losses for particular groups. Posing the question in that framework often cuts through to the real reasons behind various groups' support for this or that policy. Often people support programs that transfer money from other taxpayers and consumers to themselves. They are, however, unlikely to say that is their motive. For example, I've seldom heard teachers say that the reason they favor government support for education is that those policies transfer money to them.

The economic framework directs you to look beyond the reasons people say they support policies; it directs you to look for the self-interest. The supply/demand framework provides a neat graphical way to picture the relative gains and losses resulting from various policies.

But as usual there's an *on the other hand*. Just because some groups may support policies for self-serving reasons, it is not necessarily the case that the policies are bad or shouldn't be adopted. Reality is complicated, with many more gray answers than black-and-white ones.

SUMMARY

- Agricultural markets have many qualities of perfectly competitive markets: sellers are price takers, there are many buyers, products are interchangeable, and prices vary considerably. The competitiveness of agricultural markets is affected by significant government intervention.

- The good/bad paradox is the result of the inelastic demand in most agricultural markets. Increases in productivity increase supply; but, because demand is inelastic, the percentage decline in price is greater than the percentage increase in equilibrium quantity. Total revenue declines.

- A general rule of political economy in a democracy is that policies tend to reflect small groups' interests, not the interests of large groups.

- Because farmers are a small, easily identifiable group, and because farm states get larger representation relative to population in the Senate, the farm lobby is very strong.

- A price support program works by government maintaining higher-than-equilibrium prices through regulations, economic incentives, subsidies, and buying up and storing or destroying.

- Regulatory price supports cost government the least, but benefit the farmers the least.

- Economic incentive price supports cost the government and taxpayers more than regulatory price supports, but less than subsidy price supports or buying up and storing the good.

- Subsidy price supports benefit consumers, who pay lower prices, and farmers, who receive higher prices. Subsidy price supports cost taxpayers the most.

- Buying up and storing the good gives government a surplus to deal with.

- Two prevalent farm programs in the United States are the land bank program, in which government gives farmers economic incentives to reduce supply, and the nonrecourse loan program, in which government "buys" goods in the form of collateral on defaulting loans.

- Agricultural policy is affected by interest groups (consumers, taxpayers, and farmers) and international issues (farm policies of our trading partners).

KEY TERMS

general rule of political economy *(431)*
good/bad paradox *(428)*

grandfather *(433)*
land bank program *(436)*
nonrecourse loan program *(436)*

price stabilization programs *(430)*

price support programs *(430)*

QUESTIONS FOR THOUGHT AND REVIEW

1. If the demand for farm products were elastic rather than inelastic, would the good/bad paradox still exist? Why or why not?

2. Demonstrate, using supply and demand curves, the distributional consequences of a price support system achieved through acreage restriction.

3. Which would a taxpayers' group prefer: price support achieved through buying up the surplus or through providing economic incentives for not producing? Why?

4. What is the most costly method of price support to the taxpayer? Demonstrate graphically.

5. What is the least costly method of price support to the taxpayer? Demonstrate graphically.

6. Why do tariffs and quotas generally accompany price support systems?

7. How does the elasticity of supply affect the cost of price supports in each of the four options?

8. Why is grandfathering an attractive option for governments when they institute price supports?

9. All government intervention in markets makes society worse off. True or false? Evaluate.

10. What type of price support program is the nonrecourse loan? the land bank program?

PROBLEMS AND EXERCISES

1. Show graphically how the effects of an increase in supply will differ according to the elasticities of supply and demand.
   a. Specifically, demonstrate the following combinations:
      (1) An inelastic supply and an inelastic demand.
      (2) An elastic supply and an inelastic demand.
      (3) An elastic supply and an elastic demand.
      (4) An inelastic supply and an inelastic demand.
   b. Demonstrate the effect of a government guarantee of the price in each of the four cases.
   c. If you were a farmer, which of the four combinations would you prefer?

2. Congratulations. You've been appointed finance minister of Farmingland. The president wants to protect her political popularity by increasing farmers' incomes. She's considering two alternatives: (a) bolstering agricultural prices by adding governmental demand to private demand; and (b) giving farmers financial incentives to restrict supply and thereby increase price. She wants to use the measure that's least costly to the government. The conditions of supply and demand are illustrated in

the accompanying diagram. (S_1 is what the restricted supply curve would look like. P_s is the price that the president wants to establish.) Which measure would you advise?

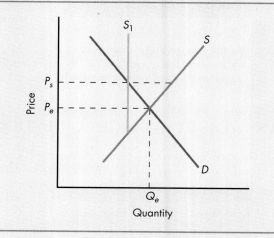

3. The Pure Food and Drug Act of 1906 is known as "Dr. Wiley's Law." It is generally regarded by non-economic historians as representing the triumph of consumer interests over producer interests.
   a. Why might an economist likely be somewhat wary of this interpretation?
   b. What evidence would a skeptical economist likely look for to determine the motives behind the passage of this law?
   c. What would be the significance of the fact that the Pure Food and Drug Act was passed in 1906, right when urbanization and technological change were fostering new products that competed significantly with existing producers' interests?

4. The U.S. government makes it against the law to grow peanuts unless the grower has been granted a government quota. It also essentially forbids peanut imports and sets a minimum U.S. price of peanuts at about 50 percent higher than the price of peanuts on the world market. This program costs the government $4 million a year in administrative costs.
   a. Are there likely any other costs associated with the program?
   b. Demonstrate graphically how to come up with about $250 million of additional costs.
   c. When "peanut land"—land with peanut quotas—is sold, what is the likely price of that land compared to equivalent land without a peanut quota?

   d. Say that, under the World Trade Organization, the United States agrees to allow open imports of peanuts into the United States and guarantees that all sellers receive the existing price. What will happen to the governmental costs of the program?
   e. Say the government limits the guaranteed high price to U.S. producers. What will it have to do to make that guarantee succeed?

5. Say that a law, if passed, will reduce Mr. A's wealth by $100,000 and increase Mr. B's wealth by $100,000.
   a. How much would Mr. A be willing to spend to stop passage of the law?
   b. How much would Mr. B be willing to spend to ensure passage of the law?
   c. What implications for social policy do your answers to *a* and *b* have?

6. The U.S. Bureau of Land Management sets a fee for ranchers who graze their animals on public land equal to $1.43 per animal unit per month—the amount of forage needed to feed one cow and its calf, or five sheep, for a month. The market rate for grazing on private land is about $14 per animal unit per month.
   a. Why do you think there is a difference?
   b. What are the advantages of setting the lower fee?
   c. Would you expect excess demand for government grazing land? Why? Demonstrate graphically.

WEB QUESTIONS

1. The U.S. Department of Agriculture provides a Foreign Agriculture Service that reports prices for agricultural goods. Go to its home page at www.fas.usda.gov, look up the commodity pages, and search for recent world and domestic sugar prices. Answer the following questions:
   a. What is the cost of raw sugar on world markets? What is the cost of domestic raw sugar?
   b. What accounts for the difference between domestic and world price for raw sugar?
   c. At the Foreign Agriculture Service home page, search for and read the report "Import Requirements for Sugar and Sugar Containing Articles." How does U.S.

   trade policy help maintain high U.S. domestic sugar prices?

2. Go to the Council on Biotechnology Information's home page at www.whybiotech.com to answer the following questions:
   a. What are genetically engineered crops and what are their benefits to farmers?
   b. What has been the effect on farm profits in the short run?
   c. What are the possible long-term effects of genetically engineered crops on farm production? On farm income?

ANSWERS TO MARGIN QUESTIONS

1. The good/bad paradox is the phenomenon of doing poorly because you're doing well. It exists when demand for your product is inelastic. Specifically, as it applies to agriculture, it means that when most farmers produce a lot, prices are low and their net income drops. (429)

2. Because demand is inelastic, it is in the interest of the agricultural industry for the supply of agricultural goods

   to decline from bad weather or other supply disruptions. The percentage rise in price will be greater than the percentage decline in quantity demanded, and total revenue for the industry will rise. (430)

3. There are two ways around the good/bad paradox. One is for suppliers to coordinate their activity and limit supply. The second way is for suppliers to lobby and get

government to establish programs to limit production, stabilizing the price and holding it high. Because of the difficulty of coordinating the large number of farmers, it is this second track that U.S. farmers have followed. *(430)*

4. Farmers are least likely to support the regulatory method of price support, in which regulatory force is used to prevent anyone from selling or buying at a lower price. Although such a policy benefits farmers, it benefits them far less than other price support policies. *(434)*

5. Taxpayers will likely least favor the price support method of subsidizing the sale of goods to consumers, because this method costs taxpayers the most. The low price paid by consumers and the high price received by farmers together necessitate large subsidies. *(435)*

6. Consumers would least favor the price support method of providing economic incentives to reduce supply and the price support method of regulatory force. Both these methods reduce the supply and push up the price. Some consumers would benefit from the buying up, giving away, or destroying method, which suggests that consumers on average would prefer this to the regulatory or the economic incentive method. *(435)*

7. The land bank program, which gives farmers incentives to reduce supply, and the nonrecourse loan program, which buys up goods, have been the two most prevalent U.S. farm programs. *(436)*

8. While this chapter discusses taxpayers, farmers, and consumers as separate groups independent of each other, in reality they are not. Each individual is, generally, both a taxpayer and a consumer, while farmers are generally members of all three groups. It is nonetheless useful to treat them as separate groups because specific interests predominate: for example, farmers' interests as farmers significantly outweigh their interests as taxpayers or as consumers. *(436)*

9. In terms of actual money payment by the government, having a military draft likely is a cheaper way of maintaining defense than is a volunteer army. However, a military draft can be seen as a type of hidden tax on a specific group of individuals—young people who are subject to the draft—to the degree that they are paid less than the going wage. If that hidden tax is also included in the cost, the military draft is not a cheaper way of maintaining defense. Because it involves inefficiencies in who participates, it can, indeed, be seen as more expensive than an all-volunteer army. *(437)*

10. False. Economic theory tells us nothing about what is preferable. Choices about what is preferable can only be made by specifying one's value judgments. Such choices belong in normative economics and in the art of economics, where distributional effects, broader sociological issues, and value judgments are included in the analysis. *(438)*

20

MICROECONOMIC POLICY, ECONOMIC REASONING, AND BEYOND

After reading this chapter, you should be able to:

- List three reasons why economists sometimes differ in their views on social policy.

- Explain why liberal and conservative economists often agree in their views on social policy.

- Explain the cost/benefit approach the typical economist takes to analyze regulations.

- Describe three types of failure of market outcomes.

- Explain why economists are doubtful government can correct failure of market outcomes.

> If an economist becomes certain of the solution of any problem, he can be equally certain that his solution is wrong.
>
> —H. A. Innis

One important job of economists is to give advice to politicians and other policymakers on a variety of questions relating to social policy: How should unemployment be dealt with? How can society distribute income fairly? Should the government redistribute income? Would a program of equal pay for jobs of comparable worth (a pay equity program) make economic sense? Should the minimum wage be increased? These are tough questions.

In Chapter 18 I discussed the supply/demand framework that economists use to think about such issues. In this chapter I consider economic reasoning in a broader context.

The reason for doing so is that economic reasoning, and the supply/demand model are tools, not rules. To draw policy implications from it, the supply/demand model has to be placed in context. Used in the proper context, the supply/demand model is enormously strong, something no one should be without. Used out of context, it can lead to conclusions that don't seem right, and that maybe are not right. Consider the assembly-line chicken-production example in Chapter 10. Some of you may have felt that the assembly-line production of chickens was somehow not right—that the efficiency of the production process somehow did not outweigh the chickens' suffering. Yet the economic model, which focuses on efficiency, directs production toward that assembly line. This chapter considers when you might want to use economic reasoning, and when you might not.

The chapter is divided into two parts. The first part of the chapter extends the supply/demand model to a broader cost/benefit framework, tying together the discussion we had about economic reasoning in the introductory chapters with the chapters that developed the foundations of the supply/demand model. It shows you how economic reasoning is used in practice. The second part of the chapter turns economic reasoning back upon itself, considering not only the benefits (which are considerable) but also the costs of using economic reasoning. In doing so I discuss how markets that are working perfectly may still lead to outcomes that are undesirable.

Answers to Even-Numbered End-of-Chapter Questions

A Note about the Answers

The following answers are meant as guides to answering the end-of-chapter questions, not as definitive answers. The same questions often have many answers; this is especially true of policy-oriented questions. Although we have tried hard to see that mistakes are eliminated, the reality is that, as in any human endeavor, mistakes are inevitable. If you have checked and double-checked your answer and it is substantially different from that found here, assume that our answer is wrong, not yours. If you do come to a different answer, or think an answer misses an important aspect of the question, please check for corrections at my website to see if the answer has changed. If you don't find it there, please e-mail me at Colander@ Middlebury.edu with your answer and an explanation of why you think it is better. I will get back to you and if I think you are right, I will post the change on the Web page marked "Corrections," together with your name and a thank-you.

Chapter 1: Economics and Economic Reasoning
Questions for Thought and Review

2. The responses will be varied since this question asks individual students about choices they have made. In these responses students should be encouraged to consider all the costs and benefits, and to be clear about the concept of the marginal costs and marginal benefits.

4. The opportunity cost of buying a $20,000 car is the benefit we would have gained by using that $20,000 for the next-best alternative, which could be spending or saving it.

6. I would spend the $5 million on those projects that provide the highest marginal benefit per dollar spent. The opportunity cost of spending the money on one project is the lost benefit that the college would have received by spending it on some other project. Thus, another way to restate the decision rule is to spend the money on the project that minimizes opportunity cost per dollar.

8. Two examples of social forces are our unwillingness to charge interest to friends, and our unwillingness to "buy" dates with other people. These issues are still subject to economic forces; however, there is no market in "dates" or in loans to friends, and hence the economic force does not become a market force.

10. An economic model is a framework that places the generalized insights of the theory in a more specific contextual setting. Policymakers need to understand the empirical evidence supporting the theory as well as real-world economic institutions to make policy recommendations.

12. Two microeconomic problems are the pricing policies of firms (price fixing in particular) and how wages are determined in labor markets. (Why do athletes and celebrities make so much money anyway?) Two macroeconomic problems are unemployment and inflation.

14. A good economist always tries to be objective. However, no one can ever be completely objective, even some of the time. Sometimes the best we can hope for is to be aware of the cultural norms and value judgments that influence our views and decisions.

Chapter 1: Problems and Exercises

2. a. The opportunity cost of attending college is the sacrifice one must make by attending college. It can be estimated by figuring out the benefit of the next-best alternative. If that alternative is working, one would guess the likely wage that could be earned at a job that does not require a college degree (minimum wage? more?) and then multiply by 40 hours for each week in college.

   b. The opportunity cost of taking this course could also be estimated using the same technique as in a if you otherwise would be working for these hours. If you had taken another course instead, the opportunity cost would be the benefit you would have received from taking that course.

c. The opportunity cost of attending yesterday's lecture again would depend on what you otherwise could have done with the time (sleep? eat lunch with an interesting person?). Although this is no longer a choice to you, past activities do have opportunity costs.

4. Assuming who pays for dates reflects supply and demand considerations, and assuming that the majority of the Chinese are heterosexual, this suggests there will be a shortage of women, and thus men will be paying a higher percentage of the cost of dates in the future.

6. a. In this exercise you are asked to obtain prices on a gallon of milk from a supermarket and a convenience store.

b. Most likely, the price in the convenience store is higher (unless they are being used as a loss-leader).

Someone will buy milk at a higher price because it is easier to purchase it at that store or the store may be the only source at a given time.

c. Unlike milk (which is a standardized product), clothes come in different brands, types, and perhaps quality. Saks clothes cost more, but one is also buying the Saks cachet.

8. *The Theory of Moral Sentiments* emphasizes the importance of morality. The invisible hand directs people's selfish desires (tempered by the social and political forces) to the common good but is based on certain presuppositions about the morality of individuals, which constrains individuals' selfish actions. What Smith is suggesting is that the marginal cost and marginal benefit used by individuals must be interpreted within a social context.

CHAPTER 2: TRADE, TRADE-OFFS, AND GOVERNMENT POLICY
QUESTIONS FOR THOUGHT AND REVIEW

2. If there were decreasing marginal opportunity costs, the production possibility curve would be convex with respect to the origin instead of concave. This means that (in terms of the example on page 24 of the text) we would gain more and more guns for every pound of butter we give up. An example of this is found in a situation in which a practice makes perfect; i.e., smaller and smaller numbers of hours devoted to a task, or sport, will result in bigger and bigger gains in performance.

4. If a society became equally more productive in the production of both widgets and wadgets, the production possibility curve would shift out to the right as shown in the following graph:

6. This statement is true or false depending on the implicit assumptions made in the analysis. It is true since individ-

uals will eliminate all inefficiencies they see through trading. It might be false if not everyone knows all the benefits and the inefficiencies, but do not have the opportunity to correct the inefficiencies.

8. The combined production possibility curve of two countries that have no comparative advantage in either of two goods will be a straight line with the same slope as the production possibility curve of each of the countries, just shifted out to the right, reflecting the fact that the production levels reflect that of both countries combined. There are no gains to trade.

10. If a particular distribution of income is one of society's goals, a particular production technique that leads to greater output but also an undesirable distribution of income might be considered an inefficient method of production. Remember, efficiency is achieving a goal as cheaply as possible. Maximizing output is not the only goal of a society.

12. The six roles of government in a market economy are (1) providing a stable set of institutions and rules, (2) promoting effective and workable competition, (3) correcting for externalities, (4) ensuring economic stability and growth, (5) providing public goods, and (6) adjusting for undesired market results. Which of the six is the most controversial is open to debate. One possibility is the sixth role, adjusting for undesired market results. The problem is determining what rules should guide government in deciding on the desired result. Intervening in the market might create more problems than it solves.

14. Pollution permits require firms pay the cost of pollution they create. By making these permits tradable, firms that face the lowest cost of reducing pollution will reduce pollution emissions the most. Permits assign rights, thereby correcting for the externality.

CHAPTER 2: PROBLEMS AND EXERCISES

2. a. See the graph below.
    b. The United States has a comparative advantage in the production of wheat because it can produce 200 additional tons of wheat for every 100 fewer bolts of cloth while Japan can produce 50 additional tons for every 100 fewer bolts of cloths. Japan has a comparative advantage in producing cloth.
    c. The joint production possibility curve without specialization or trade is shown in the graph below.
    d. The joint production possibility curve *with* specialization and trade is shown in the graph below. It is the outermost curve.

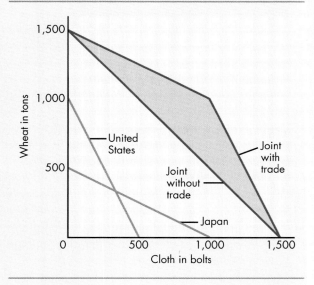

4. The fact that lawns occupy more land in the United States than any single crop does not mean that the United States is operating inefficiently. Although the cost of enjoying lawns is not included in GDP, lawns are nevertheless produced consumption goods and are included in the production possibility curve for the United States. The high proportion of land devoted to lawns implies that the United States has sufficient food that it can devote a fair amount of land to the production of goods for enjoyment such as lawns.

6. This exercise asks students to gather information about the limitations on businesses of different types in their communities. They are then asked to make judgments as to whether the limitations were necessary (are they clear about the goals involved?) and whether the number of limitations is correct. The information is linked to the text's material in part *d*. Part *e* asks students to learn about business taxes in their communities, and part *f* has them gather a sense of business satisfaction.

CHAPTER 2: APPENDIX A

2. See the graph at the top of the next page.
    a. The relationship is nonlinear because it is not straight. It is curved.
    b. From 0 to 5, cost declines as quantity rises (inverse). From 5 to 10, cost rises as quantity rises (direct).

    c. From 0 to 5, the slope is negative (slopes down). From 5 to 10, the slope is positive (slopes up).
    d. The slope between 1 and 2 units is the change in cost $(30 - 20)$ divided by the change in quantity $(1 - 2)$, or -10.

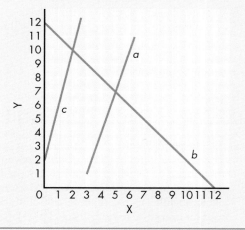

4. a. 1
   b. −3
   c. ⅓
   d. −¼
   e. 0

6. a. See line *a* in the graph in the next column.
   b. See line *b* in the graph in the next column.
   c. See line *c* in the graph in the next column.

8. a. line graph
   b. bar graph
   c. pie chart
   d. line graph

Chapter 3: The Evolving U.S. Economy in Perspective
Questions for Thought and Review

2. The central coordinating mechanism in Soviet-style socialism is the central planners.

4. Soviet-style socialism solves the three problems by using administrative control. Central planners decide what to produce according to what they believe is socially beneficial. Central planners decide how to produce guided by what they believe is good for the country. Central planners decide distribution based on their perception of individuals' needs.

6. Markets have little role in most families. In most families decisions about who gets what are usually made by benevolent parents. Because families are small and social bonds strong, this benevolence can work. Thus, a socialist organization seems more appropriate to a family and a market-based organization to a large economy where social bonds don't hold the social unit together.

8. An economy depends on coordination, and the mechanisms of coordination depend on people. What is considered a resource depends on technology, and people develop new technologies. It follows that the economy's ultimate strength resides in its people.

10. Business is dynamic; it involves meeting new problems constantly, recognizing needs, and meeting those needs in a timely fashion. These are precisely the skills of entrepreneurship.

12. The two largest categories of federal expenditures are income security and health and education.

14. The Internet has added competition by increasing the amount of information available to consumers and reducing the importance of geographic location to production and sales. Increasing the amount of information to consumers lowers the cost of comparison shopping, which gives consumers more negotiating power with sellers. Because location doesn't matter, the Internet broadens the potential marketplace for both inputs and outputs, increasing competitive pressures in both factor and goods markets.

CHAPTER 3: PROBLEMS AND EXERCISES

2. a. The fact that more money is spent on adults than on children in the family does not imply that the children are deprived or that the distribution is unfair. Children and adults have different needs. Moreover, it is the parents who earn the money, so it is only through their beneficence, and requirements of law, that they provide for their children at all.

   b. Yes, these percentages probably change with income. The lower the income, the larger the percent of total expenditures spent on children. The reason is that most families want to provide a basic level of needs for their children. Many families feel that luxuries should not be given to children until the children have learned how to work for them themselves.

   c. Our suspicion is that the allocation would not be significantly different in Soviet-style socialist countries as compared to capitalist countries. If, however, the average income in socialist countries were lower, the percentage of total expenditure spent on children might be higher, as described in *b*.

4. a. Innovation requires a certain level of freedom of thought and a possibility of profit-making from the innovation. Neither was the case with Soviet-style socialism. Government planners directed production with income based on need, so workers had neither the freedom nor the incentive to innovate.

   b. Both freedom and the possibility of making profits provide the means and incentives for innovation in capitalist countries.

   c. Schumpeter's argument was based on the idea that profit-making by innovators was necessary for innovation to occur. As firms become larger, however, the individual ceases to become the direct beneficiary of his or her innovations.

   d. Since his predictions did not materialize, one must believe either that firms have been able to create incentive structures to foster innovation or that some other venue for innovation has arisen. Firms have large research and development departments designed to promote innovation. In addition, individual innovators have been able to raise enough capital to start their own companies to profit directly from their innovations. In the United States there has been enormous growth in the number of such firms. The U.S. government has been a large motivator of innovation through subsidies to basic research at universities and through support of military innovations, both of which have large spillovers into private industry.

CHAPTER 4: SUPPLY AND DEMAND QUESTIONS FOR THOUGHT AND REVIEW

2. The law of supply states that quantity supplied rises as price increases or, alternatively, that quantity supplied falls as price decreases. Price is directly related to quantity supplied because, as price rises, people and firms rearrange their activities to supply more of that good.

4. A change in the price causes a movement along the demand curve, a movement to a new point on the same curve. A shift in the demand curve means that the quantities will be different at all prices; the entire curve shifts.

6. Shift factors of supply include the price of inputs, technological advances, changes in expectations, and taxes and subsidies. As the price of inputs increase, the supply curve shifts to the left. As technological advances are made that reduce the cost of production, the supply curve shifts to the right. If a supplier expects the price of her good to rise, she may decrease supply now to save and sell later. Other expectional effects are also possible. Taxes paid by suppliers shift the supply curve to the left. Subsidies given to producers shift the supply curve to the right.

8. In the graph in the next column, the demand curve has shifted to the left, causing a decrease in the market price and the market quantity.

10. Sales volume increases (equilibrium quantity rises) when the government suspends the tax on sales by retailers because the price to demanders falls and hence equilibrium quantity demanded rises. This occurs because the supply curve shifts to the right.

12. Customers will flock to stores demanding that funky "economics professor" look, creating excess demand. This

excess demand will soon catch the attention of suppliers, and prices will be pushed upward.

14. It suggests that the job is being rationed, which means that the wage is above the equilibrium wage.

16. The fallacy of composition is the false assumption that what is true for a part will also be true for the whole. It affects the supply/demand model by drawing our atten-

tion to the possibility that supply and demand are inter-dependent. Feedback effects must be taken into account to made the analysis complete.

18. The greatest feedback effects are likely to occur in the markets that are the largest. This is most likely to be true for housing and manufactured-goods markets.

Chapter 4: Problems and Exercises

2. a. The market demand and market supply curves are shown below.
   b. At a price of $37, quantity demanded is 32 and quantity supplied is 18. Excess demand is 14. At a price of $67, quantity demanded is 10 and quantity supplied is 46. Excess supply is 36.
   c. Equilibrium price is $47. Equilibrium quantity is 24.

4. a. I would expect wheat prices to decline since the supply of wheat is greater than expected. Wheat commodity markets are very competitive, so the initial 35 percent increase in output was already reflected in the current price of wheat. It is only the additional 9 percent increase that will push down the price of wheat.
   b. This is graphically represented by a shift to the right in the supply of wheat, as shown in the next column.

6. a. Because the market for pencils is relatively small, supply/demand analysis would be appropriate without modification.
   b. Because the labor market is very large, supply/demand analysis would not be appropriate without modification. For example, an increase in labor supply will likely lead to greater income and greater demand for goods, which will lead to an increase in quantity of goods produced and therefore an increase in the demand for labor. In this case there are significant feedback effects.
   c. Aggregate markets such as savings and expenditures include feedback effects, so supply/demand analysis would not be appropriate without modification.
   d. The CD market is relatively small. Supply/demand analysis would be appropriate without modification.

Chapter 5: Using Supply and Demand Questions for Thought and Review

2. If price fell and quantity remained constant, a possible cause would be a shift out of the supply curve and a shift of the demand curve in to the left. Another possibility would be a shift of the demand curve in to the left with a vertical supply curve.

4. As you can see in the graph on the next page the rent controls create a situation in which demanders are willing to pay much more than the controlled price and much more than the equilibrium price. These payments are sometimes known as *key money*. In this graph,

landlords are willing to supply Q_S at the current controlled rent, P_C. Consumers are willing to pay up to P_B for the quantity Q_S. Key money can be an amount up to the difference between P_B and P_C.

6. A minimum wage, W_{min}, above the equilibrium wage W_E will result in the quantity of laborers looking for work to increase to Q_S and the quantity of employers looking to hire to decrease to Q_D. The difference between the two is a measure of the number of unemployed.

8. Political turmoil in South Africa likely led both foreign and domestic investors to question the economic stability of the country. Foreign investors reduced their demand for South African investments, and therefore their demand for the rand. This shifted the demand for the rand to the left. Domestic investors did likewise, shifting their investments to those outside South Africa, shifting the supply of rand to the right. The combination led to a lower price for the rand in terms of other currencies.

10. Excess supply in U.S. agricultural markets is caused by the government's policy of agricultural price supports, or price floors on agricultural products. The political forces prevent the invisible hand from working.

12. Governments likely support third-party-payer markets for a variety of reasons. It could be that they believe the market does not distribute the good equitably (poorer people have less access to the good); there are positive externalities associated with the good (for example, public education); or that some other market failure exists.

CHAPTER 5: PROBLEMS AND EXERCISES

2. a. A weakly enforced antiscalping law would add an additional cost to those selling scalping tickets and push up the resale cost of tickets to include the expected cost of being caught. In the graph on the right, this shifts the supply curve from S_0 to S_1, raising equilibrium price from P_0 to P_1. (Note: This assumes that only selling, not buying, is illegal.)
   b. A strongly enforced antiscalping law (against suppliers) would push up prices far more. If enforcement were sufficiently strong, a two-tier price system would emerge with a low legal resale price at P_0 and another a very high price, P_2.

4. a. The government subsidy of mohair provided an enormous incentive for those who were allowed to sell mohair to sell large quantities at lower price than otherwise. The elimination of this subsidy shifted the supply curve to the left (shown below as a shift from S_0 to S_1, increasing the market price for mohair from P_0 to P_1 and decreasing the quantity demanded and supplied from Q_0 to Q_1.

   b. This program was likely kept in existence because not many people knew about it (mohair is a relatively small market), and ranchers had no incentive to broadcast the subsidy.

   c. If a law were passed so that suppliers would receive $3.60 more than the market price, the demand curve would shift to the left to include this tax. The quantity demanded would fall dramatically. Consumers would not support this law because they would have to pay an enormously high price. Suppliers would support this law only if they were guaranteed that they could sell at that high price.

6. a. Boards often exist to benefit the consumer, but also to benefit those who currently produce. Often those who are currently certified attempt to limit the number of new certifications to limit the supply and thus boost the price.

   b. Possible changes include eliminating the board of certification, limiting its regulation to only those skills that it addresses directly, or requiring continual recertification so that skills of those already certified reflect the current demand for skills in that market.

   c. A political difficulty with implementing these changes is that a relatively small group of those currently certified will be hurt and will lobby hard for the status quo. The benefits of the changes are also large, but they are spread out over large groups of consumers, with each consumer benefiting very little. Therefore, it will be easier for the small group, whose benefit per individual is large, to organize.

8. a. Frequent-flyer programs allow companies to lower their effective prices without lowering their reported prices. Companies also use them to get business travelers to choose their airline. Such programs are an example of a third-party-payer system: The business traveler gets the benefit (frequent-flyer miles), while the business pays for the current flight.

   b. Other examples include points that hotels give to travelers and bonus checks based on charges that *Discover* gives those who use its credit card.

   c. Firms likely do not monitor these programs because it would be too costly to do so.

CHAPTER 5: APPENDIX A

2. a. The following are the demand and supply tables after the hormone is introduced:

Price (dollars per gallon)	Quantity Demanded (gallons per year)	Quantity Supplied (gallons per year)
0.00	600	−25
1.00	500	125
2.00	400	275
2.50	350	350
3.00	300	425
4.00	200	575
5.00	100	725
6.00	0	875

b. The original supply curve is S_0. The growth hormone shifts the supply curve to S_1 (to the right by 125).

Equilibrium price falls to $2.50 a gallon, and equilibrium quantity rises to 350 million gallons (point B).

c. The demand curve remains the same at $Q_D = 600 - 100P$. The supply curve becomes $Q_S = -25 + 150P$. To solve the two equations, set them equal to one another: $600 - 100P = -25 + 150P$ and solve for P. Doing so, we get $P = 2.5$. Substituting this value for P into either the demand or supply equation gives us equilibrium quantity of 350.

d. Quantity supplied would be 425 ($-25 + 150 \times 3$) and quantity demanded would be 300 ($600 - 100 \times 3$). There would be excess supply of 125. The price floor is shown in the graph above.

4. a. A demand curve follows the formula $Q_D = a - bP$, where a is the price-axis intercept and b is the slope of the curve. A shift in demand is reflected in a change in a. An increase in demand increases a and a decrease in demand reduces a.

b. A supply curve follows the formula, $Q_S = a + bP$, where a is the price-axis intercept and b is the slope of the curve. A shift in supply is reflected in a change in a. An increase in supply reduces a and a decrease in supply increases a.

c. A movement in supply or demand is reflected in the effect of a change in P on either Q_S or Q_D.

6. a. The new supply equation is $Q_S = -150 + 150(P - 1)$ where P is the equilibrium price, or $Q_S = -300 + 150P$.

b. $P = 3.60; Q = 240$.

c. Farmers receive $2.60 per gallon.

8. a. The new supply equation is $Q_S = -150 + 150(P + 1)$ where P is the equilibrium price, or $Q_S = 150P$.

b. $P = 2.40; Q = 360$.

c. Farmers receive $3.40 per gallon.

CHAPTER 6: DESCRIBING SUPPLY AND DEMAND: ELASTICITIES
QUESTIONS FOR THOUGHT AND REVIEW

2. I would check to see if other things remained equal, suspecting that they did not. The reason why is that the rise in price did not have the expected effect. If all other things did indeed remain equal, the elasticity would be zero. Percent change in quantity divided by the percentage change in price.

4. Price elasticity of demand is equal to the percentage change in quantity divided by the percentage change in price. Pizzas went from $8 to $2 and quantity from 1 to 100. The price elasticity of demand is ($1.96/1.2) = 1.63$.

6. They are both the same. Any supply curve that goes through the origin has an elasticity of 1.

8. To the degree that colleges are trying to get as much revenue as possible, they will keep raising tuition until the demand is no longer inelastic. Colleges don't raise their tuition by more than what they currently do because they are not profit maximizers, and because social pressures such as student protests would result if they raised tuition too much.

10. More eager students will agree to go to a school even if they don't get much financial aid. That is, they have less elastic demands and thus will tend to get less financial aid. Whether this practice is justified is a difficult normative issue, with many alternative views.

12. a. Vodka: luxury (except in Russia). Individuals tend to drink more hard liquor as their income rises. (It depends on the type: Absolut vodka is more of a luxury than store brands.)

b. Table salt: necessity. It is a small portion of people's income, and its consumption doesn't increase with income.

c. Furniture: luxury (depends on the type). While we all need some furniture, the wealthy spend large sums on furniture. The rest of us get by with cheap stuff.

d. Perfume: luxury (depends on the type). The rich blow money on perfume; the rest of us get by with toilet water, or we smell a bit.

e. Beer: necessity (depends on the type). Beer tends to be the poor person's drink. However, new micro breweries are trying to change beer's image, and to make certain types of beer be seen as a luxury.

f. Sugar: necessity. It is not used significantly more by rich than by poor.

14. If there were only two (assuming no saving) the goods must be substitutes because if a person doesn't consume one, he or she would have to consume the other.

CHAPTER 6: PROBLEMS AND EXERCISES

2. a. Using standard reasoning, we would answer that firms decreased the size of the coffee cans to hide price increases from consumers. However, in reality people often react differently to changes in the size of packages compared to the equivalent change in price.

b. Examples include candy bars, soap, and canned tuna fish.

4. a. A price rise of 10 percent will reduce fuel consumption anywhere from 4 to 8.5 percent. This translates to 9.15 to 9.6 million gallons demanded.

b. This suggests that there are other forces besides price at work here; making adjustments to higher prices is much easier than making adjustments to lower prices. This may be due to learning the true cost of substitutes when those substitutes are consumed. One can imagine a scenario in which a price hike significantly changes driving behavior—commuters may switch to ride sharing or public transportation, to which there may be perceived social barriers (costs). Once those barriers are overcome and the perceived costs are lowered after those alternatives are used, a larger decline in the price of gasoline is required to induce those who switched to return to driving their own cars.

6. Point A: 3; point B: 1/3; point C: 3/2; point D: 7/6.

8. a. 0.5
   b. 0.60

10. a. The supply shifts in and price rises as in the graph below.
    b. Elasticity of demand is 1.

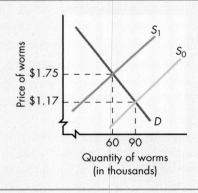

12. a. Peak hour travelers are likely to be commuters who have little choice but to go to work and therefore have lower demand elasticity than those who ride buses during off-peak hours. They could choose to stay at home instead.

b. Demand tends to be less elastic in the short run because there are fewer substitutes. If fares rose enough, in the long run people could find alternative modes of transportation—purchase a car, find someone to share rides with, etc.

c. Tolls are likely a much smaller portion of high-income commuter's total income, contributing to a less-elastic demand.

CHAPTER 7: TAXATION AND GOVERNMENT INTERVENTION
QUESTIONS FOR THOUGHT AND REVIEW

2. Decision making based on costs and benefits means you make purchases if the marginal benefits are greater than the price. The market price yields no benefits for the marginal producer or the marginal good. For all others the consumer gets the surplus.

4. If demand is inelastic, raising a tax increases revenue paid by consumers; similarly with supply. Thus, what happens to total tax revenue depends on the elasticity of both supply and demand.

6. I'd recommend goods with a price elasticity of demand or price elasticity of supply as close to zero as possible. Examples would be cigarettes, salt, required medications, a per capita tax, and land.

8. With a perfectly elastic demand, suppliers will pay the entire cost of the tax regardless of how elastic supply is—unless supply is also perfectly elastic, in which case no goods will be bought or sold after the tax, so no one will bear the burden.

10. If the economist wanted to get as much revenue as possible from as little output reduction as possible, he would suggest taxing inelastic supplies.

12. If the tax were based on street frontage rather than square feet of living space, individuals would have an incentive to build in this style.

14. Rent seeking is the restricting of supply in order to increase price. The firm would have a greater incentive to rent-seek when demand is inelastic.

CHAPTER 7: PROBLEMS AND EXERCISES

2. a. In the graph below, the government requirement has caused an increase in demand, which has raised the price. Consumers used to pay P_0 for Q_0, but now pay P_1 for Q_1. Welfare loss for society is the blue shaded triangle.

   b. If eating beets makes people healthy, their decisions ought to reflect that fact. One could argue that if the government knew better than consumers, this action would be justified if the marginal benefits exceeded the marginal costs. However, if people are choosing not to be healthy, and are rational, then any regulation making them eat beets would make them worse off.

4. a. A poll tax would have no incentive effect, as shown in the graph below. A tax on property, where supply is somewhat elastic, will reduce the quantity of property supplied (negative incentive effect), which may not be desirable.

   b. Margaret Thatcher was almost thrown out of office because of this tax, and her successor, John Major, returned to a property tax. Citizens were far more concerned with the distributional consequences associated with a poll tax than they were with the loss of efficiency associated with a property tax.

6. a. With time the job searchers will get discouraged and drop out of the labor force, disguising the unemployment. Another possibility is that firms invest in machinery to replace labor, increasing the productivity of labor and thereby increasing the demand for labor and reducing the shortage of jobs.

   b. It is likely to decrease.

8. a. Before the tax, equilibrium price is $6 and equilibrium quantity is 200. After the tax, equilibrium price is $8 and equilibrium quantity is 100.

   b. Producer surplus before the tax is the area above the supply curve and below price. This is a triangle with base 200 and height 4. So, producer surplus is $\frac{1}{2}(200)(4) = 400$. After the tax, the triangle representing producer surplus has a height of 2 and base of 100. So producer surplus is $\frac{1}{2}(100)(2) = 100$.

   c. Consumer surplus before the tax is the area below the demand curve and above price. This is a triangle with base 200 and height 4. So consumer surplus is $\frac{1}{2}(200)(4) = 400$. After the tax, the triangle representing consumer surplus has a height of 2 and base of 100. So consumer surplus is $\frac{1}{2}(100)(2) = 100$.

   d. Total tax revenue is $4 times equilibrium quantity, 100, or $400.

CHAPTER 8: THE LOGIC OF INDIVIDUAL CHOICE
QUESTIONS FOR THOUGHT AND REVIEW

2. According to the principle of diminishing marginal utility, marginal utility falls as one consumes more of a good. Marginal utility of the last unit consumed rises as one consumes less of the good.

4. Economists' theory of value depends on the underlying assumptions. Given those assumptions, price and value are related. If those assumptions (such as assumed rationality and freedom of choice) don't hold, the statement is true; if they do hold, the statement is false.

6. There are many psychological explanations for people's actions, but economists use an easy underlying psychological foundation: rational self-interest.

8. The law of demand states that quantity demanded falls as price rises and quantity demanded rises as price falls. If you are already in equilibrium and the price of a good rises, you will no longer be in equilibrium. The marginal

utility per dollar of the good whose price has risen is too low. To raise it, you must reduce your consumption of that good. Therefore, as the price of the good rises, you consume less of it—the law of demand.

10. If the supply curve is perfectly inelastic, the supplier has no alternative; thus, the opportunity cost is zero.

12. For Americans, a large part of utility (happiness) is relative to others. As everyone gets more, relative happiness does not increase.

14. Most people buy goods without a lot of thinking. An example of ours is when we buy meat at the store. We have a general idea of what the price should be, and if the price is lower than that (and a sign or sticker says *sale*) we buy it. It follows the principle of rational choice only if that principle takes into account the costs of deciding.

CHAPTER 8: PROBLEMS AND EXERCISES

2. Given the information in the table, the best combination to purchase will be where the (MU/P) is equal for all three goods. Doing the calculations, we have:

#	(MU/P) for A	(MU/P) for B	(MU/P) for C
1	20	10	8.33
2	18	7	1.67
3	15	6	1.67
4	10	5	1.67
5	5	4	1.67
6	2	4	1.67
7	−7	3	−1.67
8	−20	2	−1.67

(Note that marginal utility should be interpreted between units of consumption.) We start by buying that good with the highest util per dollar. With $20 to spend we would buy 1 of A, for 20 utils per dollar, leaving me with $10 to

spend. We would then buy 1 more of A, getting 18 utils to the dollar. This would exhaust our money.

4. You should continue your present pattern of consumption. One more widget will give you 2 more units of utility for $2, and one more wadget will give you 3 more units of utility for $3, and since ($MU_1/P_1$) = ($MU_2/P_2$), your present consumption pattern gives you as much total utility, considering your income and prices, as any variation.

6. a. If he or she is not a 100 percent rational economist, it is likely that you will lose your spouse or significant other—or at least lose his or her love or fondness.

   b. The utility gained from a diamond is not just its brilliance or perfection but also the knowledge that it is real (and thus expensive) and that some sacrifice (driven by affection) was made for its purchase. A fake diamond suggests that there was little sacrifice and thus the giver's love was cheap as well.

   c. Who is to say that the utility from the consumption of a product is not just?

CHAPTER 8: APPENDIX A

2. With budget constraint in *a*, Zach will be on utility curve II. With budget constraint in *b*, Zach will be on utility curve III. With budget constraint in *c*, Zach will be on a utility curve that is to the right of III.

   a. Zachary prefers the budget constraint that is the furthest to the right, *c*.

   b. The marginal rate of substitution for *a* is −2, for *b* is −1 and for *c* is −1. The marginal rate of substitution

equals the slope of the budget constraint at the optimal combination of goods. Even though we do not know the optimal combination with budget constraint *c*, we can still figure out the marginal rate of substitution for that combination.

4. It would be bowed away from the origin if there were increasing marginal utility.

CHAPTER 9: PRODUCTION AND COST ANALYSIS I
QUESTIONS FOR THOUGHT AND REVIEW

2. The terms *long run* and *short run* do not necessarily refer to specific periods of time independent of the production process. The long run, by definition, is a period in which the firm can vary the inputs as much as it wants; in the long run, all inputs are variable. The question is whether a firm ever really gets to this degree of flexibility. It may be true that firms are always constrained in regard to what production decisions they can make, so in reality this statement is probably true.

4. If average productivity is falling, short-run average variable cost is rising; to say that productivity falls is equivalent to saying that cost rises.

6. If average productivity is falling, average costs must be rising; if marginal productivity is falling, marginal cost must be rising. But there is no necessary relationship between average productivity and marginal costs.

8. The shapes of the short-run average cost curve and marginal cost curve would be the same as in the more usual case where machines are the fixed factor. Either way you are still adding more and more of a variable factor to a

fixed factor and encountering diminishing marginal productivity as a result. The marginal cost and average cost curves would be U-shaped.

10. Labor does not need to be produced (at least in the time periods that microeconomic analysis usually considers) and hence the choice for individuals is how to divide up that labor among various activities such as work, play, and studying (opportunity costs). Goods that need to be produced ultimately depend on the opportunity costs of the factors producing them, but in the standard economic model, those costs are assumed fixed; thus, the opportunity costs are assumed fixed. This leaves the analysis of production free to focus on technical aspects of production such as diminishing marginal productivity as the determinant of costs, and hence supply.

12. Productivity gains can reduce the percentage of labor costs per vehicle, allowing GM either to lower its price (thereby increasing the quantity of its cars sold) or to increase its profits (making its shareholders happy).

CHAPTER 9: PROBLEMS AND EXERCISES

2. Rent is $4,000; labor is $40,000; utilities are $5,000; total revenue is $100,000; the opportunity cost of the entrepreneur is $50,000; and that of the funds invested is $4,000. By the accounting definition of cost and profit, Economan is making a profit equal to $100,000 − ($4,000 + $40,000 + $5,000) = $51,000. From an economist's point of view, where explicit and implicit costs are considered, Economan now has a loss of $100,000 − ($4,000 + $40,000 + $5,000 + $50,000 + $4,000) = −$3,000.

4. a. Given the price of labor at $15 per hour, and the data in the total product table; the following table represents the average variable costs:

Labor	TP	VC	AVC	AP	MP	MC
1	5	15	3.00	5.0	5	3.00
2	15	30	2.00	7.5	10	1.50
3	30	45	1.50	10.0	15	1.00
4	36	60	1.67	9.0	6	2.50
5	40	75	1.88	8.0	4	3.75

b. This is done in the next column. The AVC curve is shown on the left, and the AP curve is shown on the right. You can see that the AVC curve and AP curve are mirror images of each other.

c. The MP curve is shown below on the right.
d. As you can see from the graph below, the MC curve and the MP curve are approximate mirror images of each other.

6. a. The AFC, ATC, AVC, and MC curves are shown at the top of the next page on the left.
   b. The AFC curve has its normal shape. Because average variable costs do not change, the marginal cost curve is coincident with the average variable cost as shown. The ATC curve is always falling since the costs are always above the MC curve. They asymptotically approach $25.
   c. The law of diminishing marginal productivity is not operative.

d. The new AFC, ATC, AVC, and MC curves are shown in the second graph on the right. The AFC curve remains the same. The MC curve is now upward-sloping, with a slope of 10. The AVC curve is also upward-sloping, with a slope of 5. The ATC curve now has a more normal shape, with a minimum where it intersects the MC curve.

e. Marginal costs would have to decline at first and then rise for the curves to have their "normal" shapes.

CHAPTER 10: PRODUCTION AND COST ANALYSIS II
QUESTIONS FOR THOUGHT AND REVIEW

2. It is incorrect because in the long run firms can change any input they want. In the long run there would be no fixed cost—all costs would be variable. The shape of the long-run average total cost curve is determined by economies of scale.

4. If production relationships were only technical relationships, diseconomies of scale would never occur because the same technical process could be used over and over again at the same cost. In reality, however, the social dimensions of production relationships introduce the potential for diseconomies of scale because, as the firm size increases, monitoring costs increase and team spirit or morale generally decreases.

6. An entrepreneur is an individual who sees an opportunity to sell an item at a price higher than the average cost of producing it. The entrepreneur then looks at the cost of production to see if a profit can be made. If so, he or she will create supply by organizing production.

8. Cost curves are defined within a period of time. In the short run, technology is assumed constant. In the long run, technological change shifts the cost curves down. It does not explain the downward-sloping portion of cost curves.

10. Producing steel in this fashion involves an enormous fixed cost. These fixed costs must be spread out over sufficient production to lower average total costs and make the average total production costs (which includes fixed costs) less than the price.

CHAPTER 10: PROBLEMS AND EXERCISES

2. a. Variable costs would likely include manufacturing labor and materials and possibly sales costs to the extent that they are for the sale of additional production. Certain other costs have a variable component to them, but they will unlikely vary directly with production.

b. Fixed costs would likely include factor overhead, operating expenses and profit, R&D, interest, and to some extent advertising. In the real world, the division between fixed and variable costs is not as clear-cut as in the texts.

c. If output were to rise, average total cost would likely fall because fixed costs seem relatively important. This is the case for many real-world firms.

4. a. The long-run cost curve is shown on the right. Initially it will fall because of economies of scale.

b. It will later rise due to diseconomies of scale.

c. The average cost curves in the short run are also U-shaped. Their shape is due initially to increasing marginal productivity and eventually decreasing marginal productivity.

d. There is no fixed component.

e. A straight line.

6. a. It is possible that both methods are technically efficient because neither dressmaker is using more of both inputs to produce the same number of garments.

   b. The economically efficient method is the least-cost method. The cost of 800 garments for the first dress-maker is $46,000 (160 × $100 + 3,000 × $10). The cost of the same number of garments for the second dressmaker is $40,000 (200 × $100 + 2,000 × $10). Therefore, the second method is economically efficient. The first method is not.

CHAPTER 10: APPENDIX A

2. See the graph below. The black line is the original isocost curve. Each of the following is shown with respect to the dotted line.

   a. This is line *a* in the graph below.

   b. The isocost curve rotates in along the machinery axis as shown in the graph below to line *b*.

   c. The isocost curve shifts in along both axes as shown below to line *c*.

4. Technical efficiency in production means that as few inputs as possible are used to produce a given output. On the graph in the next column, this would be anywhere on the isoquant curve, including points *A* and *B*. Economic efficiency means using that method that produces a given level of output at the lowest possible cost. Given the cost of inputs, the efficient point to produce that level of output corresponding to the isoquant curve is point *B*.

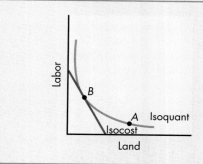

6. If the price of labor falls to $3, the isocost curve shifts out along the labor axis, intersecting at 20 units of labor. Producing 60 earrings with the new labor costs is now inefficient. The firm can produce more than 60 earrings, shown by point *D* and the new isoquant curve, I_2, to the right of the one corresponding to 60 earrings, I_1.

CHAPTER 11: PERFECT COMPETITION
QUESTIONS FOR THOUGHT AND REVIEW

2. Typical marginal cost, marginal revenue, and average total cost curves are shown on the next page. The profit-maximizing level of output is Q^*. The total profit is shown by the blue shaded rectangle. As we have drawn it, the firm is not in long-run equilibrium since it is earning a profit.

4. The firm's supply curve is that portion of the firm's marginal cost curve that lies above the minimum of the average variable cost curve curve. The sum of all individual firms' marginal cost curves (above the minimum AVC curve) is the market supply curve.

6. The shutdown point is the same as the point at which a firm exits a market in the long run when there are no fixed costs. That is, when AVC is the same as ATC.

CHAPTER 11: PROBLEMS AND EXERCISES

2. a. With the information given, the clear answer is to change output in an attempt to lower costs and achieve an economic profit. We are not told whether MR = MC at the level of output at which ATC = $4. If it is, then it is maximizing profit, even though at a loss. If the firm is perfectly competitive, in the long run it should close.

   b. If we now know that AVC = $3.50, we know that price is less than the average variable cost but not whether we are at the quantity where MR = MC. If AVC cannot be reduced, the firm should stop producing since it loses more by producing than it would if it shut down.

4. a. Zapateria will produce 500 pairs of shoes if the market price is $70 because at 500 pairs, the market price $70 equals marginal costs of $70.

   b. The total profit that Zapateria will earn is $20 times 500 pairs of shoes, or $10,000.

   c. Since Zapateria is making an economic profit, it should expect other shoe stores to enter the market.

   d. The long-run equilibrium price is $40 a pair because at $40 a pair, zero profit is made.

6. a. As demand decreases, price will decrease in the short run. As price declines, some firms will exit the market. As firms exit, marginal costs will decrease. The price at which zero profit is made falls. Market equilibrium price falls in the long run.

   b. The market equilibrium quantity falls.

   c. The number of firms also falls because the decrease in demand decreased economic profits, making firms exit the market.

8. A technological development that shifts the MC curve down will shift the market supply curve to the right. Market price will fall and output will rise. Profit for each firm will still be zero because the price will decline sufficiently so that each firm earns zero profit.

10. If both firms are producing where MR = MC and we could buy either for the same amount, I'd buy the one with the highest total profit. Remember, it is total profit, not profit per unit that is maximized by a firm. If there are perfectly competitive firms, however, eventually both will earn 0 economic profits regardless of which we bought.

12. This question requires students to find current articles in newspapers and apply supply/demand analysis to them.

14. If the older retail stores had higher costs than the new stores, they would be forced to cut prices below their costs. If that happened, they might stay in business in the short run, assuming they were covering their average variable costs, but they wouldn't stay in business in the long run. If the market remains perfectly competitive, equilibrium price will fall.

   d. Profit per firm returns to zero for all firms, and for the industry in the long run.

8. a. Once the new tomato is generally available, it will likely reduce the price of equal-quality tomatoes in the off-season. However, the new, higher-quality tomato may well sell for more than the cardboard-tasting ones normally bought in winter.

   b. Its effects on farmers depends on what the biotechnology firm charges for its seeds. Further, since the demand for tomatoes is fairly inelastic, the increased supply of good tomatoes (reducing their price) in the off-season will reduce revenues of farmers.

   c. Tomatoes will be grown in areas much farther from their point of sale.

   d. To the degree that the price of tomatoes falls, tomatoes in the winter will more likely be moved from the rear to the front of the salad bar.

10. a. Reconstituted milk can be shipped from low-cost production areas to high-cost production areas, threatening local dairy monopolies with competition.

   b. This probably resulted in strong regional lobbies to protect regional markets.

   c. He is most likely incorrect economically, but correct politically. Price supports cause overproduction of milk and its elimination most likely will cut production. He made this statement because he wanted to get reelected and his supporters are dairy farmers who benefit from the price supports.

CHAPTER 12: MONOPOLY
QUESTIONS FOR THOUGHT AND REVIEW

2. Monopolists may or may not make pure economic profit. In long-run equilibrium perfectly competitive firms tend to break even, which means they make only a normal profit. So profit is not the distinguishing factor. Instead, the distinguishing characteristic is that the monopolist will restrict output to hold up price; a perfect competitor will not.

4. The development of such a machine would probably reduce the demand for college education to the extent that it would be a lower-priced substitute. (But remember, gaining knowledge is not the only aspect of college—what about the social experiences, the sports, etc.?) If one college could monopolize the production of this machine, it could probably charge close to the current price of college and hire professors to do pure research with the proceeds.

6. A monopolist will tend to sell at a point on the demand curve where demand is elastic, but as the fish gets older (and smelly) the monopolist will wish to lower its price. The price will not be likely to be in the inelastic range, but it may if disposing of the fish is costly.

8. The additional costs are the lost profit by Bayer. If drug makers believe that government will ignore patents on future drugs, thereby lowering future profits, they will spend less on developing new drugs. So the cost to society of a policy of disregarding a patent is having fewer drugs to fight disease in the future.

10. The most likely information involves price discrimination. Existing low fares can be used to attract highly price-elastic customers who spend a lot of time searching for the lowest fare. The individuals who happen to see the advertisement for the special fare likely have a less elastic demand, allowing the airlines to price-discriminate against them.

12. A perfectly elastic marginal cost curve is shown below as the horizontal straight line MC_0. Because the opportunity cost of providing additional units does not increase, welfare loss is greatest with constant marginal costs—shown below as the blue shaded triangle. One can see that welfare loss falls with increasing marginal costs by rotating the marginal cost curve up. An example, MC_1, is shown below. Welfare loss is bounded by the MC curve, the demand curve, and the quantity line.

14. The argument for copyrights (and patents) is that without some guarantee of profits from their ideas, people would be unlikely to engage in the effort (and incur the costs) associated with generating new ideas, products, etc. If that is the case, then copyrights may be justified. If people would write good books anyway, then probably society would be better off without copyrights because more books would be sold at a lower price.

CHAPTER 12: PROBLEMS AND EXERCISES

2. This is what is wrong in the graphs shown:
   a. The marginal revenue curve is too steep. It should cut the x-axis at Q. In addition, quantity should be determined where $MR = MC$.
   b. The curve labeled ATC is really the MC curve. Correctly labeled, the profit-maximizing level of output is determined where $MC = MR$.
   c. Quantity should be determined $MR = MC$, not $MC = ATC$. Also, the MC curve should intersect the ATC curve at the minimum point of the ATC curve.
   d. Quantity should be determined where $MR = MC$.

4.

Q	P	TR	MR	TC	MC	ATC
0	4.20	0.00		3.20		
1	3.80	3.80	3.80	4.20	1.00	4.20
2	3.40	6.80	3.00	5.60	1.40	2.80
3	3.00	9.00	2.20	7.80	2.20	2.60
4	2.60	10.40	1.40	10.40	2.60	2.60
5	2.20	11.00	0.60	13.40	3.00	2.68
6	1.90	11.40	0.40	16.80	3.40	2.80

a. Fixed cost is $3.20 per month per resident.
b. MC = MR at 3 collections per month. The price charged is $3 per pickup. Profit is 40 cents per pickup per person.
c. P = MC at 4 collections per month. The price charged would be $2.60 per pickup. There would be only normal profits. Economic profit would be zero.
d. The city government should prefer competitive bidding unless there is a natural monopoly. The quality of the pickup would be expected to be greater for the competitive industry because monopolists do not face competitors.

6. a. The limitation of medallions likely increases the price of taxi medallions because it creates a monopoly position for medallion holders. There is no threat of new suppliers to compete away profits. Since the demand for taxis is always shifting to the right as the population grows, the relative monopoly position also grows.

b. Requiring single cab medallion owners to drive their cabs full-time would reduce cab drivers' ability to limit supply and thus would tend to reduce the value of the medallion. However, it would also limit the use of the taxis (since they now rent them out when they are not using them). This effect would be the equivalent to a decrease in the number of medallions and would slightly offset the first effect.
c. The price of medallions would decline as the supply increased. Before the sale, however, the windfall from the sale of new medallions would increase the value of existing medallions mitigating the fall in price from the lower expected revenue from existing medallions.
d. The wealth of existing medallion owners, if one includes the value of the existing medallions, will increase by the windfall but decrease by the reduced value of the medallion from the sale because the expected future stream of profits will have declined. It's unclear what the final result would be.

CHAPTER 12: APPENDIX A

2. a. $Q = 2, P = \$39.50$
   b. $ATC = \$52$
   c. Profit $= -\$25$

4. a. $Q = 6, P = \$18$
   b. $Q = 12, P = 0$

CHAPTER 13: MONOPOLISTIC COMPETITION, OLIGOPOLY, AND STRATEGIC PRICING
QUESTIONS FOR THOUGHT AND REVIEW

2. Firms differentiate products through advertising. The overriding objective of product differentiation is to maintain or increase market share by creating their own small monopolistic niche.

4. Product differentiation makes us better off to the degree that we prefer having choices of different varieties of the same product. However, in some cases, the differences may be imagined rather than real. Firms reinforce product differentiation with advertising, and so there is a question whether devoting resources to advertising is a benefit (due to increased information) or a waste.

6. The monopolistic competitor does not earn economic profits because of free entry into the market.

8. Strategic pricing is the central characteristic of oligopoly. Monopolistic competitors face too many competitors to price strategically.

10. The contestable market is more interested in the pricing structure and firm behavior arising from free entry into the market. Therefore, the contestable market is more likely to judge by performance.

12. (In answering this question students may be aware of media coverage in the 1990s that suggested colleges colluded in establishing financial aid packages for students and in setting tuition.) Since colleges are not profit maximizers, it is difficult to characterize them as a cartel type of oligopoly. There certainly has been implicit and even explicit collusion; the goals of that collusion are complicated and not simply profit maximization.

14. The breakfast cereal market is definitely oligopolistic; the firms made interdependent decisions.

CHAPTER 13: PROBLEMS AND EXERCISES

2. a. The demand curve is kinked at $8 and the MR curve is discontinuous at $4. The kink for the demand curve

is the opposite to that in the text. There are two places where MC = MR, at quantities 4 and 8, as shown.

b. The firm would prefer the equilibrium with the lower output, higher price, and higher profit. This is where output is 4 and price is about $7 a unit.

c. If marginal cost falls, the level of output rises by a lot while the price decline falls by just a little.

d. If marginal cost rises, the level of output falls by a little while the price rises by a lot.

e. This part asks students to survey firms in their area about pricing strategies. The kinked demand model presented in the book is more likely.

4. a. This market is most likely characterized by oligopoly or possibly monopolistic competition. We say oligopoly because the largest firm will consider the response of its rivals in its decisions. We say monopolistic competition because there are many firms but their products are differentiated. There is some label recognition and loyalty.

b. The Herfindahl index is $428.49 + 289 + 44.9 + 4.84 + 4 + 51.4 = 822.63$.

c. The four-firm concentration ratio is $46.6\% = 20.7 + 17 + 6.7 + 2.2$.

6. a. See the table below.

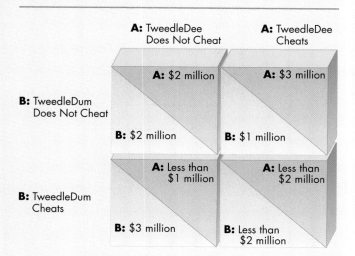

b. If the game is played only once, we would advise that Mr. Notsonice's profit-maximizing strategy is to cheat to maximize expected profit. What his "best" strategy is depends on how much he values being honest.

c. If the game were played over and over, we would advise that his profit-maximizing policy would be to develop some level of trust between the two players and agree not to cheat, avoiding the prisoner's dilemma.

d. The benefit of colluding compared to expected benefit of cheating would have to be greater. It would have to be greater by $2 million.

8. a. The hypothetical payoff matrix is shown below. If neither offers free shipping each earns $1,000 profit. If only Amazon.com offers free shipping its profits are $2,000 while Buy.com loses $300. If both offer free shipping each earns profit of $200.

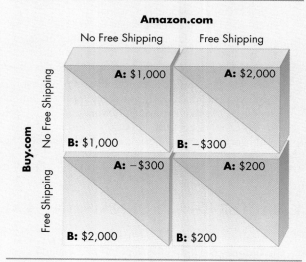

b. Amazon.com is best off when it offers free shipping and Buy.com does not. It makes a profit of $2,000.

c. Buy.com is best off when it offers free shipping and Amazon.com does not. It makes a profit of $2,000.

d. Joint profits are maximized when neither offers free shipping. Combined profits are $2,000, instead of $1,700 in the case when one offers free shipping and the other does not.

e. Answers to this question will vary. At the time we answered the question, Amazon.com offered free shipping on purchases of $25 or more and Buy.com offered free shipping with no minimum purchase.

CHAPTER 14: REAL-WORLD COMPETITION AND TECHNOLOGY QUESTIONS FOR THOUGHT AND REVIEW

2. False. While profits are important to business, because of internal monitoring problems it is not clear that managers maximize profit. They may waste profit potential in high-priced benefits for themselves and in inefficiency generally. The market, however, provides a limit on inefficiency, and firms that exceed the limit and have losses go out of business.

4. X-inefficiency is the result of firms operating far less efficiently than they could technically. The economic forces of a market would knock a firm out of business if it operates less efficiently than the rest of the market. Only a monopolist can produce inefficiently and remain in the game.

6. Even if existing colleges are inefficient, competition from for-profit colleges would not necessarily force them out of business. The political and social forces can keep such colleges from developing. Moreover, some colleges receive state assistance or have endowments that allow them to hold their costs down even if they are inefficient.

8. By the same reasoning used in the answer to question 7, the price could decrease below the competitive equilibrium level. At that below-equilibrium price, some consumers could not get goods, but the consumers who could get goods would be able to hold the prices low nonetheless; it would be in their interest to do so.

10. Natural monopolies, by definition, are the result of a process in which market conditions dictate that monopoly is the most efficient way to produce in that industry. To break up such firms would likely result in higher costs, and thus while there could be more competitors, the benefits associated with more competition (principally, lower prices) would not be achieved.

12. It launched a marketing campaign to retain brand recognition and loyalty to round up before the year 2000. In the year 2000 it also began to lower price to further cement its position in the market and discourage entry.

14. It needs funds to carry on research or new technologies and an ability to earn profits from that research. Oligopoly best meets these criteria.

16. Network externalities lower costs as more people use a product. As network externalities broaden the use of a product, the need for a single standard becomes more important and eventually wins out. The firm with the standard is the big winner and will dominate the market. Even better technology will have a hard time competing with the standard.

CHAPTER 14: PROBLEMS AND EXERCISES

2. If suppliers were able to restrict their output to Q_r, price would rise to P_r. Suppliers kept out of the market lose area E in producer surplus. The consumers, on the other hand, lose both areas D and B. Area B is transferred to suppliers as additional revenue leaving D and E as deadweight loss.

4. See the graph below. The monopolist would be willing to spend any of its profit. This is depicted as the shaded rectangle.

CHAPTER 15: ANTITRUST POLICY AND REGULATION
QUESTIONS FOR THOUGHT AND REVIEW

2. In the Standard Oil case the Court determined that the company was a structural monopoly (it controlled 90 percent of its market), but that alone was not a violation of the Sherman Act. Rather, it was the firm's behavior that brought it into violation. Thus, the firm was found guilty of unfair business practices. In the ALCOA case the key issue was the determination of the firm's market, and hence its share of that market. Determining that ALCOA had 90 percent of the aluminum market, the Court declared it a monopoly, and ALCOA was broken up.

4. The Clayton Antitrust Act gave more guidance and provided for more vigorous enforcement. It is a law that made four specific monopolistic practices illegal when their effect was to lessen competition.

6. Financial aid is often need-based, and so in some sense is an attempt to equalize the price as a proportion of income for students. Again, the test is the impact, and for many students financial aid is the key to access to the college of their choice. It may be more discriminatory in another sense not to have it. Moreover, the fact that something is discriminatory does not necessarily make it bad.

8. As an economist for the firm, I would want the broader definition of the market to make the firm's share a smaller proportion. Thus, I would argue for the three-digit industry as the definition of the market.

10. In some ways the service has improved, but in other ways it has worsened. What would have happened in the absence of the breakup is difficult to say. What this tells us is that making judgments about policy is enormously

difficult and requires intricate knowledge of the industry affected.

12. Microsoft was charged with having a monopoly in the personal computer operating systems market. In a dynamic view of the market, technological advances, such as open-source operating systems and the merging of software and hardware, will see the market open to more competition in the future.

14. Conglomerate mergers occur when two relatively unrelated businesses merge. They tend to be approved under our antitrust laws on the assumption that they do not significantly restrict competition. These mergers should be considered like other mergers in terms of their effect, and approved or not on that basis. A blanket policy against such mergers might foreclose some opportunities that would benefit firms and the economy.

16. The two methods government may use to deal with natural monopolies are regulation and government ownership. Price regulation usually takes the form of requiring the firm to charge its average total cost plus a profit margin; this gives the firm no incentive to hold down costs, and cost increases lead directly to price increases. Another problem is that once regulation is established it may extend far beyond the natural monopolies and be introduced into industries where competition could work. Government ownership of natural monopolies is used most often in countries outside the United States, and also has the problem of no incentive to hold costs down or to introduce new technologies. Government-owned firms guarantee jobs and offer high wages, but they pass these higher costs on to the consumers.

CHAPTER 15: PROBLEMS AND EXERCISES

2. In a monopolistic competition model the firms have only a small share of the market and make no profit, so antitrust would have little effect. The graph of monopolistic competition is the relevant graph. In a cartel market, firms get together and allocate market share. Antitrust would prevent that, holding prices down and increasing quantity. The graph of monopoly is the relevant graph. In a contestable market model, potential competition, not market structure, determines equilibrium, so antitrust would have little effect unless it influenced potential competition.

4. a. The likely basis of this suit was predatory pricing to keep price so low that American Airlines' competitors would go out of business and so that the company would enjoy a monopoly position and raise prices.

   b. Knowledge of their financial instability only strengthens the argument. It suggests that American Airlines would not have to hold prices down for too long before its competitors folded.

CHAPTER 16: WORK AND THE LABOR MARKET
QUESTIONS FOR THOUGHT AND REVIEW

2. This chapter opens with a quotation from Voltaire: "Work banishes those three great evils: boredom, vice, and poverty." Welfare laws, to the degree that they discourage work, therefore can be said to harm the people they are meant to help. While they help people in the short run, they establish a dependency relationship, which can hurt people in the long run.

4. The elasticity of the labor supply is measured by the percent change in the quantity supplied divided by the percent change in the wage. In this case, 5 divided by 20 is less than 1 (it is 0.25), so the supply is said to be inelastic.

6. Supply/demand analysis is partial equilibrium analysis; immigration policy often affects the general economy and thus requires an analysis of spillover effects and changes that partial equilibrium analysis cannot capture.

8. If the labor market were monopsonistic, so that the pay were less than the competitive wage, the minimum wage could change the effective supply facing the monopsonist and could raise the wage and increase employment simultaneously, as in the graph on the right. In the graph, the monopsonist would hire Q_m workers, paying W_m. With a minimum wage W_e, higher than W_m, the monopsonist would hire Q_e workers, higher than Q_m.

10. The fact that unemployment among blacks is nearly twice as high as it is among whites can be explained by many factors, including discrimination. There are also differences in existing income levels, with the result that many blacks reside in poorer neighborhoods and thus do not have equal access to education and other services that would lead to higher employment. The choices available in terms of opportunities may also lead young people to choose nonmarket activities over participation in the labor force.

CHAPTER 16: PROBLEMS AND EXERCISES

2. a. Based on standard economic theory, one would expect the number of teens employed to rise and the employment of nonteens to decline as the relative wage of teens declines. This assumes that the minimum wage is above the market-clearing wage. Further, one would expect that a large number of employees would lose their jobs at the end of their training period (six months) for "just" reasons, such as not learning the job adequately.

   b. It is likely that the administrative costs of participating in the program were higher than the benefits of hiring teens at the lower training wage. It could also be that market clearing wage in teen labor market was already higher than the subminimum wage. A third possibility is the focal point phenomenon: teens may focus on the mandated minimum wage as their reservation wage and refuse to accept a job at the subminimum training wage.

4. a. Since they will have to pay 20 percent of what they save in added tuition in addition to the 20 percent income tax rate, the implicit marginal tax rate they face on income they save will be 36 percent. The tax on assets is a tax on savings after income taxes have

been subtracted, so the tuition tax has to be adjusted to make it a tax on pre-income-tax income. So the relevant tax on tuition as a percent of pretax income is $(1 - t_i) \times t_t = [(1 - 0.2) \times 0.2 = 0.16]$ where t_i is income tax and t_t is the tuition tax. Add this to the 20 percent income tax to get 36 percent.

   b. The second child will raise it to 48.8% = $[(1 - 0.36) \times 0.2 + 0.36] \times 100$. The third child will raise it to 59.04% = $[(1 - 0.488) \times 0.2 + 0.488] \times 100$.

   c. This is a complicated question, but one could argue that divorced parents share in the obligation to pay for college equally and therefore the relative incomes and asset shares of combined incomes and assets should be used to determine contributions. In reality one parent might alone bear the burden of the cost, having to shoulder contributions by both. The second part to this question is for the student to research.

   d. An ability-based scholarship program would attract students of significantly higher caliber if their elasticity of demand is high, but it would most likely compromise the diversity of the student body with respect to income. It would also promote retaliation by other schools, and the long-run benefit in having brighter students might be very small.

6. a. Firms hire children because children's marginal productivity relative to their wage is higher than it is for alternative workers. Children's marginal product/wage ratio could be higher because the child wage is lower or because the marginal product is higher. Children are often energetic, pliable, and dexterous. For certain jobs these traits could make the children's productivity high. Children may also be more trainable than older employees, and they may work for a lower wage.

   b. Children work for the same reasons that others work—they need money, work is what is expected of them, and so on.

   c. In deciding whether there should be an international ban on child labor, one must look at the effects of that ban. What are the children's opportunity costs of working? If the ban will lead to children starving, the ban does them no good; if it allows them to go to school while the firm hires their parents instead, the ban may help the children. One must also look at the ease with which some firms may get around the ban. If it can be easily avoided in some countries, then the ban will likely hurt children in those countries where it is effective. Also, one should consider whether the work gives children anything useful (such as education) besides pay.

CHAPTER 16: APPENDIX A

2. They would likely hire fewer workers since they would take into account the fall in the marginal revenue product that hiring more workers would cause.

4. Yes. Widespread introduction of such programs would likely reduce the demand for teachers and lower their pay.

6. If the firm were a monopolist, the marginal revenue would be less than $3.00, and thus the amount it would be willing to pay would fall.

8. a. The proposal that should be adopted is the one that minimizes costs. Using the cost minimization condition, proposal A is the one that minimizes costs ($30/5 = 42/7 = 36/6$).

   b. If the price of labor rises to $14, none of the proposals meets the cost minimization condition. There are other combinations that would meet the cost minimization condition.

CHAPTER 17: WHO GETS WHAT? THE DISTRIBUTION OF INCOME
QUESTIONS FOR THOUGHT AND REVIEW

2. The top 20 percent of individuals in Bangladesh earn 38 percent of the income.

4. Arguments could be made for both approaches. Poverty could be defined relatively since one of our concerns is the distribution of income and the gap between the rich and poor. Poverty could also be defined absolutely since another of our concerns is that people have enough to eat, which is an absolute concept.

6. The observed difference may be due to supply and demand factors. If many people wish to be English teachers and few wish to be garbage collectors, then market factors will result in a higher wage for the garbage collectors—and if one believes in the market mechanism, this is right. That question raises other, more complicated questions about fairness of compensation and the social value of different occupations; it has no right answers.

8. The answer to this question will depend in part on the individual student's circumstances. In general, the incentive effects of a tax may result in a switch from labor to leisure.

10. On the surface the democratic system of one person/one vote would seem to suggest that the politics of redistribution would favor the poor, but it doesn't. One would expect that the poor would use their power to make sure that income was redistributed to them from the rich, but they don't. The reasons for this include the fact that many of the poor don't vote, and so consequently they are not seen as a voting bloc by politicians. Another reason is that when poor people do vote, they vote with other issues in mind. Also, campaigns require financing, which is often supplied by the rich, and so their interests may be more represented than those of the poor.

CHAPTER 17: PROBLEMS AND EXERCISES

2. a. Taking into account in-kind benefits and nonreported income would reduce the number of people seen in poverty. Taking account of the fact that food makes up only a quarter of the family's benefits would suggest

that the inflation adjustment was probably too high in reference to what was defined as poverty in the past, and that the measure of poverty has increased. Taking into account unreported income would reduce the measure of poverty. Taking account of home owner-ship and cost-of-living differences would involve distributional consequences. It would raise the level of poverty for some and lower it for others.

b. What is fair involves normative judgments. Even if the adjustments were made, one could still argue that the current definition of poverty is too low and that benefits should be increased.

4. Four conditions that you might list before you would favor equality of income are (1) that individuals have essentially the same needs, (2) that they work the same amount, (3) that they have essentially the same health, and (4) that they have put in the same effort up to this point.

a. Depending on what conditions you listed, it could change your views on welfare in a number of different ways.

b. Again, it depends on what conditions you chose. If the condition does not include differences in ability, then you would likely favor a progressive income tax.

c. If the tax were progressive in wage rates, rather than income, hard work would be encouraged and raw ability would be taxed more. If you did not list ability, then you should say that the conditions would be better met.

6. a. This would increase the incentive to work since working longer hours will not push one up into the higher tax bracket.

b. To the extent that the wage rate measures taxability better than income does, this tax system is fair.

c. Making the tax system regressive in hours worked would further increase the incentive to work longer hours.

d. Instituting such a tax system faces enormous difficul-ties. Wage rates for each individual would have to be measured, and many positions have no explicit wage rate. Some method for calculating wage rates of salaried positions would have to be designed.

CHAPTER 18: GOVERNMENT POLICY AND MARKET FAILURES
QUESTIONS FOR THOUGHT AND REVIEW

2. The marginal social benefit of a good that exhibits posi-tive externalities is greater than the private social benefit because the trade results in a benefit to people outside the trade.

4. An economist might argue about the word *acceptable*. While not many people would argue that any pollution is good, an economist who realizes that eliminating pollu-tion completely is probably an impossible goal would find pollution acceptable if it could be reduced to a cost-efficient level.

6. The tax on oil will affect the pollution coming from oil, but it is possible that users could switch to other fuel sources that actually result in other and greater forms of pollution. Moreover, some types of pollution would be unaffected. Thus, the net impact on the environment is difficult to predict.

8. The public aspect of safety is that if safety provides a safe environment, it is provided for all people and one person enjoying safety does not preclude others from benefiting from that safety. Naming streets allows people to orient themselves in towns and facilitates communication. Once a street is named, it benefits all people. No one can be excluded from referring to that name. In addition, one person using that street name does not preclude others from referring to that street with its name. Before the street is named, however, if a particular name is used to refer to more than one street, the value of that name in providing geographic orientation will be diminished. The public good aspect of the lighthouse and newspaper is

that once it is produced it can be consumed over and over again. Though in the case of the newspaper, the owner can keep others from benefiting by keeping it to himself.

10. In a market, when buyers and sellers have different amounts of information about the good for sale, a problem occurs called the adverse selection problem. The problem is that the market for quality products disappears. In commercial dating services, the seller certainly has more information about the negative (and positive) aspects of the product than the buyer. We suspect that the market has fewer "acceptable" dates than the general population.

12. To keep rates to a minimum, insurance companies esti-mate information about individuals by categorizing them. If everyone paid the same amount, low-cost customers would be paying for high-cost customers and eventually change companies, leaving only high-cost customers. One would expect that, statistically, married drivers are safer drivers.

14. Many answers are possible, beginning with (1) the label on their breakfast cereal, (2) the roads they use to get to school, (3) either the school they go to (if it is public) or the federal funds their school receives (if it is private), (4) the tax they pay on the snack at the snack bar, and (5) the laws that are enforced on the roadways.

16. The advanced degree serves the same purpose as a license. It reduces the supply and increases the wage.

CHAPTER 18: PROBLEMS AND EXERCISES

2. a. Proposal A would force a downward shift in each demand curve, while Proposal B would raise the price at each quantity, also shifting the demand curves down.

   b. The consumers in group 1 have a more elastic demand, so a small increase in price results in a large decrease in quantity; these consumers can more easily adjust their usage and would therefore favor Proposal A. The members of group 2 would be more likely to favor the tax because changing their usage is more difficult. Their inelasticity can be interpreted to mean that they are more willing to pay a higher price than to use less.

4. a. One could explain the Seattle Stomp if there were a per can charge for garbage. To maximize the amount of waste per can (and thus per flat fee), Seattle citizens stomp their garbage.

   b. A fee structure based on weight would eliminate the Seattle Stomp.

6. a. Most likely the price of all cars in California rose, and air quality rose as well.

   b. This law could possibly have increased pollution if consumers held on to their older, less efficient but lower-cost, higher-performance gas cars and delayed purchase of an electric car. This would have increased the average age of cars on the road, increasing pollution. Furthermore, if electric cars (the most likely candidates) were designed to meet the no-pollution

requirement, it could be that the process of generating sufficient electricity to run the cars would produce even more pollution, at which point even more regulation might be imposed. (The law was modified and never went fully into effect.)

   c. Economists generally favor market incentive programs over direct regulation. A market incentive program to reduce pollution by a certain percent might be to tax drivers of older, high-pollution cars and use the tax revenue to subsidize those who purchase the new, no-pollution cars. This approach will more likely equate marginal cost with marginal benefit.

8. a. Some dairy farmers would probably argue that labeling is unnecessary since the drugs they administer have been certified by the FDA. Dairy farmers who do not use BST would support BST labeling.

   b. If BST were to be listed on milk containers, one could argue that all drugs and antibiotics should be listed. However, such listing (without more information) may cause consumer concern. To support BST labeling and not other labeling, one must argue that BST is different.

   c. One would suspect that dairy farmers who support BST labeling would not support the broader law that might include so many drugs that consumers become outraged at dairy farmers. Only those few farmers who use wholly organic farming would support full labeling.

CHAPTER 19: POLITICS AND ECONOMICS: THE CASE OF AGRICULTURAL MARKETS
QUESTIONS FOR THOUGHT AND REVIEW

2. A price support system achieved through acreage restriction is illustrated below. The graph shows that, under this system, the farmers gain rectangle A as income from the government in the form of payments not to grow wheat, and rectangle B from consumers who pay more for the wheat the farmers do grow.

4. As shown below, the method of price support that is most costly to the taxpayer is the subsidies on sales to keep prices down; taxpayers must finance the subsidy payments on all subsidized farm products, represented by areas A, B, and C.

6. Tariffs and quotas generally accompany price support systems in order to prevent lower-priced foreign products from competing in the domestic market.

8. Governments find grandfathering a good option when they institute price supports because it is the easiest way of restricting supply. Existing suppliers retain their level of output, added or new entry is denied or limited, and the policy is easy to enact and easy to enforce.

10. The nonrecourse loan is a price support system in which government buys goods in the form of collateral on defaulting loans. The land bank program is a price support in which the government supports prices by giving farmers economic incentives to reduce supply.

CHAPTER 19: PROBLEMS AND EXERCISES

2. The graph on the right shows an increase in demand sufficient to raise the market price to P_s. The market quantity is also increased to Q_s. The cost to the government is the shaded rectangle. If instead supply is restricted (shown in the far right graph), the government must pay the farmers $(P_s - P_1)$ for every unit not grown at price P_s, resulting in a cost equal to the area of the bolded rectangle. Therefore, assuming that you cannot use the corn, the second policy is preferred.

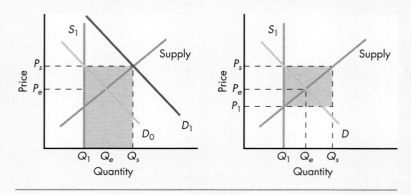

4. a. Consumers of peanuts pay more in higher prices—estimated at between $190 and $369 million a year—and suffer from reduced consumption.
   b. See the graph below. Area B represents additional costs to consumers, while areas D and E represent deadweight loss of the program.
   c. The land with peanut quotas is a government license to sell millions of pounds of peanuts and thus is priced higher to include the present value of the future returns to that license.
   d. The government's costs would likely rise enormously in the attempt to keep supply constrained to maintain the 50 percent above competitive equilibrium price.
   e. If the United States limited the guaranteed high price to U.S. producers only, administrative procedures would have to be set up to see that imported peanuts are not passed off as U.S.-produced peanuts.

6. a. The reason the difference exists is mostly political. A small group of ranchers benefits greatly from the reduced fee and is a strong lobby for the cause.
   b. The advantage could be that the U.S. government could require more from ranchers in their care of the land.
   c. One would expect excess demand because at the price below equilibrium, the quantity of land owners are willing to supply at $1.86 is lower than the quantity demanded.

CHAPTER 20: MICROECONOMIC POLICY, ECONOMIC REASONING, AND BEYOND
QUESTIONS FOR THOUGHT AND REVIEW

2. The problem with proposing only Pareto optimal policies would lie in developing them. As the text points out, there are no examples of real-world policies that benefit some people without hurting anyone. If economists seek to propose only Pareto optimal policies, they may end up proposing no policies. Focusing only on Pareto optimality condemns them to irrelevancy in real-world affairs, and to focusing on abstract models rather than on the real world.

4. The usual arguments against the buying and selling of body organs include the concern that people might seek to make such sales for the money involved and exploit the poor, and that those with the ability to pay would get needed organs sooner than those without means, again favoring the well-off over the poor. Some may believe that it is immoral to sell body parts. Arguments for selling body parts include that both parties freely enter the transaction, and that both sellers (since they decided they preferred the money to the body part) and buyers benefit. Economic theory provides no answers to such questions.

6. The textbook suggests a method for valuing one's life. Your answer should consider what you would pay to reduce their chance of dying by a certain amount. The value of life is that amount times the inverse of the reduced probability of dying.

8. An economist might propose a policy that has little chance of adoption because he or she might be removed from the concerns that make policies unadoptable (i.e., political concerns). In so doing, economists put ideas into the real world and may influence the way people think. The goal behind policy proposals is not always to get them implemented.

10. Most politicians say that they are out to do the public good, but in practice they often (in their quest to be reelected) do things that just sound good.

12. Any decision about prisons involves complicated ethical and moral as well as economic considerations. In reference to the economic issues alone, it would seem that it does make sense to build more prisons since, assuming prisons are currently full, the marginal benefits of additional prisons are greater than the marginal costs.

CHAPTER 20: PROBLEMS AND EXERCISES

2. a. A higher percentage of births by C-section are done at for-profit hospitals, most likely because the profit margin for C-sections is higher than that for vaginal births.
   b. The implication that can be drawn is that goodwill cannot be relied on to lead to low-cost health programs. Other mechanisms must be instituted to ensure efficiency.
   c. In the case of fixed payment, the for-profit hospital would probably do more vaginal births, which cost less than C-sections. The C-section rate would most likely rise at nonprofit institutions as necessary C-sections are limited at for-profit hospitals and shift toward nonprofit hospitals.

4. a. Since the supply of teenage baby-sitters shifted to the left just as the demand for them shifted to the right, the equilibrium wage probably rose dramatically, reducing the number of times parents go out without their children.
   b. The price of baby-sitters probably rose as described in a.
   c. The average age of baby-sitters probably fell as parents loosened their requirements of baby-sitters in an attempt to find substitutes for the reduced number of 14- to 17-year-olds.

6. a. According to standard economic reasoning, the value of an additional dollar spent in preventing death is (assuming the journal's figures are correct) more valuable in the United States than in Sweden and in Portugal, and thus more money should go to saving lives in the United States. However, there are moral issues that complicate matters and make the answer unclear.
   b. This is a complicated question. First, many Americans fly in Portugal and, second, it would be bad publicity for an airline to value lives of people differently by national origin or to even acknowledge making such a marginal cost/marginal benefit analysis with regard to safety precautions at all. Moreover, there are those sticky moral issues, which lead one to value all life equally.
   c. To the degree that the cost of the standard is the same, the standard economic answer is yes. If noneconomic factors are included, the answer is not so clear-cut.

8. a. The likely effect of that proposal would be a flood of criticism. Certain human rights such as the sanctity of the human body are held in high regard regardless of societal status.

A proposal that, on its face, seems economically sound is not acceptable if it does not include issues of human rights.

b. That was the effect because the economic model did not account for all issues. Morality issues provoke strong political reactions.

CHAPTER 21: INTERNATIONAL TRADE POLICY
QUESTIONS FOR THOUGHT AND REVIEW

2. The opportunity cost of producing 1 widget is 1 wadget in Wadgetland and 4 wadgets in Widgetland. Since the opportunity costs differ, there is a basis for trade. One possibility for trade is for Widgetland to produce 240 widgets, trading 60 widgets for 120 wadgets, and for Wadgetland to produce 720 wadgets, trading 120 wadgets for 60 widgets.

4. Smaller countries tend to get more of the gains from trade because more opportunities are opened up for them. This is true only under the condition that competition among traders prevails. International traders in small countries often have little competition and so keep large shares of the gains from trade for themselves; hence the small country may not get the gains from trade.

6. An equitable method might be to tax those who gain from the trade liberalization and give the proceeds to those who are hurt by it. Assuming the original distribution is equitable and the government is not trying to redistribute income, this method is equitable because the combined policies make everyone better off. The political problems with implementation include: (1) Everyone will try to exaggerate the amount they are hurt and minimize the amount they are helped. Thus actually finding a tax

that accomplishes the goal will be difficult. (2) Once the taxes and subsidies are in place, they may not be removed after the adjustment of displaced workers is complete. Losers will be overcompensated and gainers will be taxed too much.

8. When the United States economy fell into a recession in 1991 income and imports fell and the trade balance improved. This is consistent with predictions.

10. Economists support free trade because it forces domestic producers to operate efficiently and it increases consumer welfare.

12. Both increase the price of the import, helping the domestic producers. In the case of the voluntary restraint, increases in price result in increased revenue to foreign firms and increased demand is met entirely by the domestic market.

14. With a price floor, there is a loss of consumer surplus, higher prices, and lower quantities.

16. The WTO is the successor to GATT. Both work toward agreements to reduce trade. WTO includes enforcement mechanisms that GATT did not have.

CHAPTER 21: PROBLEMS AND EXERCISES

2. a. No. Both countries' opportunity cost of producing pickles is 2/1 (they must give up 2 olives to get 1 pickle). Neither has a comparative advantage, so there is no basis for trade.

b. If there are economies of scale, it definitely pays for both countries to specialize since doing so would lower total costs. Which one should specialize is an open question since neither has a comparative advantage.

4. a. Firms may produce in Germany, because (1) transportation costs in the other countries may be very high, so that if these costs are included, it would not be efficient to produce there; (2) there might be tariffs or quotas for imports into Germany that will prevent producing elsewhere; (3) the productivity of German labor may be so much higher that unit labor costs in Germany are the lowest; and (4) historical circumstances may have led to production in Germany and

the cost of moving production may exceed potential gains.

b. Yes, one would expect some movement from Greece and Italy into Germany, but this is limited by the minimum wage laws in Germany. Also, social restrictions such as language and culture will limit labor mobility. With such high unemployment in Germany already, one would not expect much short-run movement. Movement in the long run, however, may be substantial.

c. I would need to know how stable the political system is, what the worker productivity rates are, how sound the infrastructure (such as roads) is, and what the tax differences are between the two countries.

6. a. Three assumptions are that the good is tradable, that transportation costs are minimal, and that taxes between the two countries do not differ significantly.

b. To the degree that production facilities and labor can move easily, the law of one price should hold for labor, too. Given the wage differentials that exist among countries with seemingly equivalent productivities, it seems that these conditions do not hold for labor.

c. Since capital is more mobile than labor, the law of one price should have a greater tendency to hold for capital. Financial capital is a great example. Interest rates among countries tend to equate much faster than wages.

CHAPTER 21: APPENDIX A

2. a. The opportunity cost for Greece of making 1 million olives is 1,000 pounds of cheese. The opportunity cost for France of making 1 million olives is 250 pounds of cheese. The opportunity cost for Greece of making 1,000 pounds of cheese is 1 million olives. The opportunity cost for France of making 1,000 pounds of cheese is 4 million olives.

   b. They are worse off since France has a comparative advantage in producing olives and Greece has a comparative advantage in producing cheese. Under the new law France produces 50,000 pounds of cheese and Greece produces 500 million olives—point A. They could have had a greater combination: 100,000 pounds of cheese produced by Greece and 600 million olives (200 million by France and 400 million by Greece)—point B. Their *combined* possibility curve if

they were able to trade is the outermost production possibility curve shown.

Glossary

A

Ability-to-Pay Principle   The individuals who are most able to bear the burden of the tax should pay the tax.

Absolute Advantage   A country that can produce a good at a lower cost than another country is said to have an absolute advantage in the production of that good. When two countries have absolute advantages in different goods, there are gains of trade to be had.

Acquisition   A merger in which a company buys another company and the purchaser has the right of direct control over the resulting operation.

Adverse Selection Problem   Problem that occurs when buyers and sellers have different amounts of information about the good for sale.

Antitrust Policy   The government's policy toward the competitive process.

Art of Economics   The application of the knowledge learned in positive economics to the achievement of goals one has determined in normative economics.

Average Fixed Cost   Fixed cost divided by quantity produced.

Average Product   Output per worker.

Average Total Cost   Total cost divided by the quantity produced.

Average Variable Cost   Variable cost divided by quantity produced.

B

Balance of Trade   The difference between the value of the goods and services a country imports and the value of the goods and services it exports.

Bar Graph   Graph where the area under each point is filled in to look like a bar.

Barriers to Entry   Social, political, or economic impediments that prevent firms from entering a market.

Benefit Principle   Individuals who receive the benefit of a good or service should pay the tax necessary to supply that good.

Bilateral Monopoly   Market with only a single seller and a single buyer.

Budget Constraint   A curve that shows us the various combinations of goods an individual can buy with a given income.

Business   Private producing unit in our society.

C

Capitalism   An economic system based on the market in which the ownership of the means of production resides with a small group of individuals called capitalists.

Cartel   A combination of firms that acts as if it were a single firm.

Cartel Model of Oligopoly   A model that assumes that oligopolies act as if they were monopolists that have assigned output quotas to individual member firms of the oligopoly so that total output is consistent with joint profit maximization.

Clayton Antitrust Act   A U.S. law that outlawed four specific monopolistic practices: price discrimination, tie-in contracts, interlocking directorships, and buying stock in a competitor's company in order to reduce competition.

Closed Shop   Firm where unions control the hiring.

Comparable Worth Laws   Laws mandating comparable pay for comparable work.

Comparative Advantage   The ability to be better suited to the production of one good than to the production of another good. As long as the relative opportunity costs of producing goods (what must be given up in one good in order to get another good) differ among countries, there are potential gains from trade, even if one country has an absolute advantage in everything.

Complements   Goods that are used in conjunction with other goods.

Concentration Ratio   The percentage of the total industry that the top firms of the industry have.

Conglomerate Merger   The merging of two relatively unrelated businesses.

Conspicuous Consumption   The consumption of goods not for one's direct pleasure, but simply to show off to others.

Constant Returns to Scale   Situation in which long-run average total costs do not change with an increase in output. Also: Output will rise by the same proportionate increase as all inputs.

Consumer Sovereignty   Principle that the consumer's wishes rule what's produced.

Consumer Surplus   The value the consumer gets from buying a product less its price. Also: The difference between what consumers would have been willing to pay and what they actually pay.

Contestable Market Model   A model of oligopoly in which barriers to entry and barriers to exit, not the structure of the market, determine a firm's price and output decisions.

Coordinate System   Two-dimensional space in which one point represents two numbers.

Corporate Takeover   An action in which a firm or a group of individuals issues a tender offer for another company (that is, offers to buy up the stock of a company) to gain control and to install its own managers.

Corporation   Business that is treated as a person, legally owned by its stockholders. Its stockholders are not liable for the actions of the corporate "person."

Cost Minimization Condition Situation where the ratio of marginal product to the price of an input is equal for all inputs.

Cost/Benefit Approach Assigning costs and benefits, and making decisions on the basis of the relevant costs and benefits.

Cross-Price Elasticity of Demand The percentage change in demand divided by the percentage change in the price of another good.

D

Deadweight Loss The loss of consumer and producer surplus from a tax.

Deacquisition One company's sale of parts of either another company it has bought, or parts of itself.

Decision Tree A visual description of sequential choices.

Decreasing Returns to Scale Output rises by a smaller proportionate increase than all inputs.

Demand A schedule of quantities of a good that will be bought per unit of time at various prices, other things constant.

Demand Curve Graphic representation of the relationship between price and quantity demanded.

Demerit Goods or Activities Goods or activities the government deems bad for people even though they choose to use the goods or engage in the activities.

Derived Demand The demand for factors of production by firms, which depends on consumers' demands.

Derived Demand Curve for Labor Curve that shows the maximum amount of labor, measured in labor hours, that a firm will hire.

Diminishing Marginal Productivity Increasing one input, keeping all others constant, will lead to smaller and smaller gains in output.

Direct Regulation A program in which the amount of a good people are allowed to use is directly limited by the government.

Direct Relationship Relationship in which when one variable goes up, the other goes up too.

Diseconomies of Scale Situation when the long-run average total cost increases as output increases.

Division of Labor The splitting up of a task to allow for specialization of production.

Downsizing A reduction in the workforce.

Duopoly An oligopoly with only two firms.

Dynamic Efficiency A market's ability to promote cost-reducing or product-enhancing technological change.

E

E-commerce Buying and selling over the Internet.

Economic Decision Rule If the marginal benefits of doing something exceed the marginal costs, do it. If the marginal costs of doing something exceed the marginal benefits, don't do it.

Economic Efficiency Achieving a goal at the lowest possible cost.

Economic Forces The necessary reactions to scarcity.

Economic Model Framework that places the generalized insights of the theory in a more specific contextual setting.

Economic Policy An action (or inaction) taken by government, to influence economic events.

Economic Principle Commonly held economic insight stated as a law or general assumption.

Economic Profit Explicit and implicit revenue minus explicit and implicit cost.

Economically Efficient Describes a method of production that produces a given level of output at the lowest possible cost.

Economics The study of how human beings coordinate their wants and desires, given the decision-making mechanisms, social customs, and political realities of the society.

Economies of Scale Situation when long-run average total costs decrease as output increases. Also: Situation in which costs per unit of output fall as output increases.

Economies of Scope Situation when the costs of producing products are interdependent so that it's less costly for a firm to produce one good when it's already producing another.

Efficiency Achieving a goal as cheaply as possible (using as few inputs as possible).

Efficiency Wages Wages paid above the going-market wage in order to keep workers happy and productive.

Efficient Achieving a goal at the lowest cost in total resources without consideration as to who pays those costs.

Effluent Fees Charges imposed by government on the level of pollution created.

Elastic The percentage change in quantity is greater than the percentage change in price ($E > 1$).

Embargo A total restriction on the import or export of a good.

Entrepreneur An individual who sees an opportunity to sell an item at a price higher than the average cost of producing it.

Entrepreneurship The ability to organize and get something done. Also: Labor services that involve high degrees of organizational skills, concern, oversight responsibility, and creativity.

Equilibrium A concept in which opposing dynamic forces cancel each other out.

Equilibrium Price The price toward which the invisible hand drives the market.

Equilibrium Quantity The amount bought and sold at the equilibrium price.

Euro The currency used by 12 members of the European Union.

Excess Demand Quantity demanded is greater than quantity supplied.

Excess Supply Quantity supplied is greater than quantity demanded.

Exchange Rate The rate at which one country's currency can be traded for another country's currency.

Excise Tax A tax that is levied on a specific good.

Externality An effect of a decision on a third party not taken into account by the decision maker.

F

Failure of Market Outcomes   A situation in which, even though the market is functioning properly (there are no market failures), it is not achieving society's goals.

Fallacy of Composition   The false assumption that what is true for a part will also be true for the whole.

Federal Trade Commission Act   U.S. law that made it illegal for firms to use "unfair methods of competition" and to engage in "unfair or deceptive acts or practices."

Feudalism   Economic system in which traditions rule.

Firm   An economic institution that transforms factors of production into goods and services.

Fixed Costs   Costs that are spent and cannot be changed in the period of time under consideration.

Free Rider   Person who participates in something for free because others have paid for it.

Free Rider Problem   Individuals' unwillingness to share in the cost of a public good.

Free Trade Association   Group of countries that have reduced or eliminated trade barriers among themselves, and, as a group, puts up common barriers against all other countries' goods.

G

Game Theory   An application of economic principles in which players make interdependent choices.

General Agreement on Tariffs and Trade (GATT)   A regular international conference to reduce trade barriers held from 1947 to 1995. It has been replaced by the World Trade Organization (WTO).

General Rule of Political Economy   When small groups are helped by a government action and large groups are hurt by that same action, the small group tends to lobby far more effectively than the large group. Thus, policies tend to reflect the small group's interest, not the interest of the large group.

Global Corporations   Corporations with substantial operations on both the production and sales sides in more than one country.

Good/Bad Paradox   Phenomenon of doing poorly because you're doing well.

Government Failure   A situation where the government intervention the market to improve market failure actually makes the situation worse.

Grandfather   To pass a law affecting a specific group but providing that those in the group before the law was passed are exempt from some provision of the law.

Graph   Picture of points in a coordinate system in which points denote relationships between numbers.

H

Herfindahl Index   An index of market concentration calculated by adding the squared value of the individual market shares of all firms in the industry.

Horizontal Merger   The combining of two companies in the same industry.

Hostile Takeover   A merger in which the firm being taken over doesn't want to be taken over.

Households   Groups of individuals living together and making joint decisions.

I

Implicit Collusion   A type of collusion in which multiple firms make the same pricing decisions even though they have not explicitly consulted with one another.

Incentive Effect   How much a person will change his or her hours worked in response to a change in the wage rate.

Incentive-Compatible Contract   A contract in which the incentives of each of the two parties to the contract are made to correspond as closely as possible.

Income   Payments received plus or minus changes in value in one's assets in a specified time period.

Income Elasticity of Demand   The percentage change in demand divided by the percentage change in income.

Increasing Returns to Scale   Output rises by a greater proportionate increase than all inputs.

Indifference Curve   A curve that shows combinations of goods among which an individual is indifferent.

Indivisible Setup Cost   The cost of an indivisible input for which a certain minimum amount of production must be undertaken before the input becomes economically feasible to use.

Industrial Policy   Formal policy that government takes toward business.

Industrial Revolution   A time when technology and machines rapidly modernized industrial production and mass-produced goods replaced handmade goods.

Inefficiency   Getting less output from inputs which, if devoted to some other activity, would produce more output.

Inefficient   Achieving a goal in a more costly manner than necessary.

Inelastic   The percentage change in quantity is less than the percentage change in price ($E < 1$).

Infant Industry Argument   With initial protection, an industry will be able to become competitive.

Inferior Goods   Goods whose consumption decreases when income increases.

Input   What you put into a production process to achieve an output.

Interpolation Assumption   Assumption that the relationship between variables is the same between points as it is at the points.

Inverse Relationship   A relationship between two variables in which when one goes up the other goes down.

Invisible Hand   The price mechanism; the rise and fall of prices that guides our actions in a market.

Invisible Hand Theory   A market economy, through the price mechanism, will allocate resources efficiently.

Isocost Line   A line that represents alternative combinations of factors of production that have the same costs.

Isoquant Curve   A curve that represents combinations of factors of production that result in equal amounts of output.

Isoquant Map   A set of isoquant curves that show technically efficient combinations of inputs that can produce different levels of output.

J–K

Judgment by Performance   To judge the competitiveness of markets by the behavior (performance) of firms in that market.

Judgment by Structure   To judge the competitiveness of markets by the structure of the industry.

L

L   The broadest measure of money.

Labor Market   Factor market in which individuals supply labor services for wages to other individuals and to firms that need (demand) labor services.

Labor Productivity   The average output per worker.

Laissez-Faire   Economic policy of leaving individuals' wants to be controlled by the market.

Land Bank Program   Program in which government supports prices by giving farmers economic incentives to reduce supply.

Law of Demand   Quantity demanded rises as price falls, other things constant. Also can be stated as: Quantity demanded falls and price rises, other things constant.

Law of Diminishing Marginal Productivity   As more and more of a variable input is added to an existing fixed input, eventually the additional output one gets from that additional input is going to fall.

Law of Diminishing Marginal Rate of Substitution   As you get more and more of a good, if some of that good is taken away, then the marginal addition of another good you need to keep you on your indifference curve gets less and less.

Law of Supply   Quantity supplied rises as price rises, other things constant. Also can be stated as: Quantity supplied falls as price falls, other things constant.

Lazy Monopolist   Firm that does not push for efficiency, but merely enjoys the position it is already in.

Learning by Doing   As we do something, we learn what works and what doesn't, and over time we become more proficient at it. Also: To improve the methods of production through experience.

Limited Liability   The liability of a stockholder (owner) in a corporation; it is limited to the amount the stockholder has invested in the company.

Line Graph   Graph where the data are connected by a continuous line.

Linear Curve   A curve that is drawn as a straight line.

Long-Run Decision   Decision in which a firm chooses among all possible production techniques.

Lorenz Curve   A geometric representation of the share distribution of income among families in a given country at a given time.

Luxuries   Goods that have an income elasticity greater than 1.

M

Macroeconomic Externality   Externality that affects the levels of unemployment, inflation, or growth in the economy as a whole.

Macroeconomics   The study of the economy as a whole, which includes inflation, unemployment, business cycles, and growth.

Marginal Benefit   Additional benefit above what you've already derived.

Marginal Cost (MC)   Additional cost to you over and above the costs you have already incurred. Also: Increase (decrease) in total cost from increasing (or decreasing) the level of output by one unit. Also: The change in total cost associated with a change in quantity.

Marginal Factor Cost   The additional cost to a firm of hiring another worker.

Marginal Physical Product (MPP)   The additional units of output that hiring an additional worker will bring about.

Marginal Product   The additional output that will be forthcoming from an additional worker, other inputs constant.

Marginal Rate of Substitution   The rate at which one good must be added when the other is taken away in order to keep the individual indifferent between the two combinations.

Marginal Revenue (MR)   The change in total revenue associated with a change in quantity.

Marginal Revenue Product (MRP)   The marginal revenue a firm expects to earn from selling an additional worker's output.

Marginal Social Benefit   The marginal private benefit of consuming a good plus the benefits of the positive externalities resulting from consuming that good.

Marginal Social Cost   The marginal private costs of production plus the cost of the negative externalities associated with that production.

Marginal Utility   The satisfaction one gets from consuming one additional unit of a product above and beyond what one has consumed up to that point.

Market Demand Curve   The horizontal sum of all individual demand curves.

Market Economy   An economic system based on private property and the market in which, in principle, individuals decide how, what, and for whom to produce.

Market Failure   A situation where the market does not lead to a desired result. Also: Situation in which the invisible hand pushes in such a way that individual decisions do not lead to socially desirable outcomes.

Market Force   Economic force that is given relatively free rein by society to work through the market.

Market Incentive Plan   A plan requiring market participants to certify that they have reduced total consumption—not necessarily their own individual consumption—by a specified amount.

Market Structure   The physical characteristics of the market within which firms interact.

Market Supply Curve   Horizontal sum of all individual supply curves. Also: Horizontal sum of all the firms' marginal cost curves, taking account of any changes in input prices that might occur.

Marxian (Radical) Model   A model that focuses on equitable distribution of power, rights, and income among social classes.

Medicare   A multibillion-dollar medical insurance system.

Mercantilism   Economic system in which government determines the what, how, and for whom decisions by doling out the rights to undertake certain economic activities.

Merger   The act of combining two firms.

Merit Good or Activity   Good or activity that government believes is good for you, even though you may not choose to consume the good or engage in the activity.

Microeconomics   The study of individual choice, and how that choice is influenced by economic forces.

Minimum Efficient Level of Production   The amount of production that spreads setup costs out sufficiently for a firm to undertake production profitably.

Minimum Wage Law   Law specifying the lowest wage a firm can legally pay an employee.

Monitoring Costs   Costs incurred by the organizer of production in seeing to it that the employees do what they're supposed to do.

Monitoring Problem   The need to oversee employees to ensure that their actions are in the best interest of the firm.

Monopolistic Competition   A market structure in which there are many firms selling differentiated products; there are few barriers to entry.

Monopoly   A market structure in which one firm makes up the entire market.

Monopoly Power   The ability of individuals or firms currently in business to prevent other individuals or firms from entering the same kind of business.

Monopsony   Market in which a single firm is the only buyer.

Most-Favored Nation   A country that will be charged as low a tariff on its exports as any other country.

Movement along a Demand Curve   The graphic representation of the effect of a change in price on the quantity demanded.

Movement along a Supply Curve   The graphic representation of the effect of a change in price on the quantity supplied.

N

Natural Monopoly   An industry in which a single firm can produce at a lower cost than can two or more firms. Also: An industry in which significant economies of scale make the existence of more than one firm inefficient.

Necessity   A good that has an income elasticity less than 1.

Negative Externality   The effect of a decision that is not taken into account by the decision maker and is detrimental to others.

Network Externality   Phenomenon that greater use of a product increases the benefit of that product to everyone.

Nonlinear Curve   A curve that is drawn as a curved line.

Nonrecourse Loan Program   Program in which government "buys" goods in the form of collateral on defaulting loans.

Normal Goods   Goods whose consumption increases with an increase in income.

Normal Profit   The amount the owners of business would have received in the next-best alternative.

Normative Economics   The study of what the goals of the economy should be.

North American Industry Classification System (NAICS)   An industry classification that categorizes firms by type of economic activity and groups firms with like production processes.

O

Oligopoly   A market structure in which there are only a few firms; there are often significant barriers to entry.

Opportunity Cost   The benefit forgone by undertaking a particular activity.

Optimal Policy   Policy in which the marginal cost of undertaking the policy equals the marginal benefit of that policy.

Output   A result of a productive activity.

Outsourcing   A firm shifting production from its own plant to other firms, either in the United States or abroad, where wages are lower.

P

Pareto Optimal Policy   Policy that benefits some people and hurts no one.

Partnership   Business with two or more owners.

Patent   Legal protection of a technical innovation that gives the person holding it sole right to use that innovation. (Note: A patent is good for only a limited time.)

Perfectly Competitive Market   A market in which economic forces operate unimpeded.

Perfectly Elastic   Quantity responds enormously to changes in price ($E = \infty$).

Perfectly Inelastic   Quantity does not respond at all to changes in price ($E = 0$).

Pie Chart   A circle divided into "pie pieces," where the individual pie represents the total amount and the pie pieces reflect the percentage of the whole pie that the various components make up.

Positive Economics   The study of what is, and how the economy works.

Positive Externality   Positive effect on others not taken into account by the decision maker.

Poverty Threshold   The income below which a family is considered to live in poverty.

Present Value   A method of translating a flow of future income or saving into its current worth.

Price Ceiling   A government-imposed limit on how high a price can be charged. In other words, a government-set price below the market equilibrium price.

Price Discriminate   To charge different prices to different individuals or groups of individuals.

Price Elasticity of Demand The percentage change in quantity demanded divided by the percentage change in price.

Price Elasticity of Supply The percentage change in quantity divided by the percentage change in price.

Price Floor A government-imposed limit on how low a price can be charged. In other words, a government-set price above equilibrium price.

Price Stabilization Program Program designed to eliminate short-run fluctuations in prices, while allowing prices to follow their long-run trend line.

Price Support Program Program designed to maintain prices at higher levels than the market prices.

Price Taker Firm or individual who takes the market price determined by market supply and demand as given.

Principle of Diminishing Marginal Utility As you consume more of a good, after some point the marginal utility received from each additional unit of a good decreases with each additional unit consumed, other things equal.

Principle of Increasing Marginal Opportunity Cost In order to get more of something, one must give up ever-increasing quantities of something else.

Principle of Rational Choice Spend your money on those goods that give you the most marginal utility (*MU*) per dollar.

Prisoner's Dilemma Well-known game that demonstrates the difficulty of cooperative behavior in certain circumstances.

Private Good A good that, when consumed by one individual, cannot be consumed by other individuals.

Private Property Rights Control a private individual or firm has over an asset or a right.

Producer Surplus Price the producer sells a product for less the cost of producing it.

Production The transformation of factors into goods and services.

Production Function The relationship between the inputs (factors of production) and outputs.

Production Possibility Curve A curve measuring the maximum combination of outputs that can be obtained from a given number of inputs.

Production Possibility Table Table that lists a choice's opportunity costs by summarizing what alternative outputs you can achieve with your inputs.

Production Table A table showing the output resulting from various combinations of factors of production or inputs.

Productive Efficiency Achieving as much output as possible from a given amount of inputs or resources.

Productivity Output per unit of input.

Profit A return on entrepreneurial activity and risk taking. Alternatively, what's left over from total revenues after all the appropriate costs have been subtracted. Also: Total revenue minus total cost.

Profit-Maximizing Condition $MR = MC = P$.

Progressive Tax Tax whose rates increase as a person's income increases.

Proportional Tax Tax whose rates are constant at all income levels, no matter what a taxpayer's total annual income is.

Public Assistance Means-tested social programs targeted to the poor and providing financial, nutritional, medical, and housing assistance.

Public Choice (Conservative) Model A model that focuses on economic incentives as applied to politicians.

Public Choice Economists Economists who integrate an economic analysis of politics with their analysis of the economy.

Public Good A good that if supplied to one person must be supplied to all and whose consumption by one individual does not prevent its consumption by another individual.

Q

Quantity Demanded A specific amount that will be demanded per unit of time at a specific price, other things constant.

Quantity Supplied A specific amount that will be supplied at a specific price.

Quota Quantity limits on imports.

R

Rational Used to describe behavior individuals undertake in their own best interest.

Regressive Tax Tax whose rates decrease as income rises.

Regulatory Trade Restrictions Government-imposed procedural rules that limit imports.

Rent Control A price ceiling on rents, set by government.

Rent-Seeking Activities Activities designed to transfer surplus from one group to another.

Reverse Engineering The process of a firm buying other firms' products, disassembling them, figuring out what's special about them, and then copying them within the limits of the law.

S

Scarcity The goods available are too few to satisfy individuals' desires.

Share Distribution of Income The relative division of total income among income groups.

Sherman Antitrust Act A U.S. law designed to regulate the competitive process.

Shift in Demand The effect of anything other than price on demand.

Shift in Supply The graphic representation of the effect of a change in other than price on supply.

Short-Run Decision Decision in which the firm is constrained in regard to what production decisions it can make.

Shutdown Point Point at which the firm will be better off if it temporarily shuts down than it will if it stays in business.

Sin Tax A tax that discourages activities society believes are harmful (sinful).

Slope The change in the value on the vertical axis divided by the change in the value on the horizontal axis.

Social Security System A social insurance program that provides financial benefits to the elderly and disabled and to their eligible dependents and/or survivors.

Socialism   An economic system based on individuals' goodwill toward others, not on their own self-interest, and in which, in principle, society decides what, how, and for whom to produce.

Socioeconomic Distribution of Income   The allocation of income among relevant socioeconomic groupings.

Sole Proprietorship   Business that has only one owner.

Soviet-Style Socialist Economy   Economic system that uses administrative control or central planning to solve the coordination problems: what, how, and for whom.

Stock   Financial asset that conveys ownership rights in a corporation.

Strategic Bargaining   Demanding a larger share of the gains from trade than you can reasonably expect.

Strategic Decision Making   Taking explicit account of a rival's expected response to a decision you are making.

Strategic Pricing   A characteristic of oligopoly in which firms set their price based on the expected reactions of other firms.

Strategic Trade Policies   Threatening to implement tariffs to bring about a reduction in tariffs or some other concession from the other country.

Substitutes   Goods that can be used in place of one another.

Sunk Costs   Costs that have already been incurred and cannot be recovered.

Supplemental Security Income (SSI)   A federal program that pays benefits based on need to the elderly, blind, and disabled.

Supply   A schedule of quantities a seller is willing to sell per unit of time at various prices, other things constant. Put another way, a schedule of quantities of goods that will be offered to the market at various prices, other things constant.

Supply Curve   Graphical representation of the relationship between price and quantity supplied.

T

Takeover   The purchase of one firm by a shell firm that then takes direct control of all the purchased firm's operations.

Tariff   An excise tax on an imported (internationally traded) good.

Tax Incentive Program   A program of using a tax to create incentives for individuals to structure their activities in a way that is consistent with the desired ends.

Team Spirit   The feelings of friendship and being part of a team that bring out people's best efforts.

Technical Efficiency   Describes a situation in which as few inputs as possible are used to produce a given output.

Technological Change   An increase in the range of production techniques that leads to more efficient ways of producing goods, as well as the production of new and better goods.

Technological Development   The discovery of new or improved products or methods of production.

Technological Lock-In   The use of a technology makes the adoption of subsequent technology difficult.

Technology   The way we make goods and supply services.

Total Cost   Explicit payments to the factors of production plus the opportunity cost of the factors provided by the owners of the firm.

Total Revenue   The amount a firm receives for selling its product or service plus any increase in the value of the assets owned by the firm.

Total Utility   The total satisfaction one gets from consuming a product.

Trade Adjustment Assistance Programs   Programs designed to compensate people hurt by the removal of trade restrictions.

U

Unemployment Compensation   Short-term financial assistance, regardless of need, to eligible individuals who are temporarily out of work.

Union Shop   Firm in which all workers must join the union.

Unit Elastic   The percentage change in quantity is equal to the percentage change in price ($E = 1$).

Utility   The pleasure or satisfaction that one expects to get from consuming a good or service.

Utility-Maximizing Rule   Utility is maximized when the ratios of the marginal utility to price of two goods are equal.

V

Value of Marginal Product (VMP)   An additional worker's marginal physical product multiplied by the price at which the firm could sell that additional product.

Variable Costs   Costs that change as output changes.

Vertical Merger   A combination of two companies that are involved in different phases of producing a product.

W

Wealth   The value of the things individuals own less the value of what they owe.

Welfare Loss Triangle   A geometric representation of the welfare cost in terms of misallocated resources that are caused by a deviation from a supply/demand equilibrium.

World Trade Organization (WTO)   An organization whose functions are generally the same as GATT's were—to promote free and fair trade among countries. Also: Organization committed to getting countries to agree not to impose new tariffs or other trade restrictions except under certain limited conditions.

X–Z

X-inefficiency   The underperformance of a firm that has a monopoly position.

Colloquial Glossary

A

Ads (noun)   Short for "advertisements."

Ain't (verb)   An ungrammatical form of "isn't," sometimes used to emphasize a point although the speaker knows that "isn't" is the correct form.

All the Rage (descriptive phrase)   Extremely popular, but the popularity is likely to be transitory.

Andy Warhol (proper name)   American artist who flourished in the period 1960–1980. He was immensely popular and successful with art critics and the intelligentsia, but, above all, he gained worldwide recognition in the same way and of the same quality as movie stars and sports athletes do. His renown has continued even after his death.

Armada (proper noun)   Historic term for the Spanish navy. Now obsolete.

Automatic Pilot (noun)   To be on automatic pilot is to be acting without thinking.

B

Baby Boom (noun)   Any period when more than the statistically predicted number of babies is born. Originally referred to a specific group: those born in the years 1945–1964.

Baby Boomers (descriptive phrase)   Americans born in the years 1945 through 1964. An enormous and influential group of people whose large number is attributed to the "boom" in babies that occurred when military personnel, many of whom had been away from home for four or five years, were discharged from military service after the end of World War II.

Backfire (verb)   To injure a person or entity who intended to inflict injury.

Balloon (verb)   To expand enormously and suddenly.

Beluga Caviar (noun)   Best, most expensive, caviar.

Benchmark (noun)   A point of reference from which measurement of any sort may be made.

Better Mousetrap (noun)   Comes from the proverb, "Invent a better mousetrap and the world will beat a path to your door."

Bidding (or Bid) (verb sometimes used as a noun)   Has two different meanings. (1) Making an offer, or a series of offers, to compete with others who are making offers. Also the offer itself. (2) Ordering or asking a person to take a specified action.

Big Bucks (noun)   Really, really large sum of money.

Big Mac (proper noun)   Brand name of a kind of hamburger sold at McDonald's restaurants.

Blow It (verb; past tense: blew it)   To do a poor job, to miss an opportunity, to perform unsatisfactorily.

Boost (verb and noun)   To give a sudden impetus, or boost, to something or someone.

Botched Up (adjective)   Operated badly; spoiled.

Bring Home (verb)   To emphasize or convince.

Buffalo (adjective, as used in this book)   "Buffalo chicken wings" are a variety of tempting food developed in, and hence associated with, the city of Buffalo. (Not all chicken wings are Buffalo chicken wings.)

Bus Person (noun)   as no relation to transportation. It's a term for the person who clears the tables in a restaurant.

C

Call (verb)   In sports refereeing, one meaning of "to call" is for the referee to announce his or her decision on a specific point.

Calvin Coolidge (proper name)   President of the United States 1923–1928.

Carriage Maker (noun)   Person or firm that makes carriages, a type of horse-drawn conveyance almost never seen any more except in films. Members of the British royal family ride in carriages on important ceremonial occasions, such as weddings.

Cellophane (noun)   A transparent wrapping material. It differs from plastic wrap in that it is made of cellulose, not plastic.

Central Park West (proper noun)   A fashionable and expensive street in New York City.

CEO (noun)   Abbreviation of "chief executive officer."

Charade (noun)   A pretense, usually designed to convince someone that you are doing something that you are definitely not doing.

Chit (noun)   Type of IOU (which see) or coupon with a designated value that can be turned in toward the purchase or acquisition of some item.

Chump Change (noun)   Insignificant amount of money earned by or paid to a person who is not alert enough to realize that more money could rather easily be earned.

Clear-Cut (adjective)   Precisely defined.

Clip Coupons (verb)   To cut coupons out of newspapers and magazines. The coupons give you a discount on the price of the item when you present the item and the coupon at the cashier's counter in a store. Sometimes you are directed to buy the item and then send the coupon and an identifying code from the item's package to the manufacturer, who will mail you the discount.

Clout (noun)   Influence or power.

Coined (verb)   Invented or originated.

Coldhearted (adjective)   Without any sympathy; aloof; inhuman.

Co-opted (adjective)   Overwhelmed.

Cornrows (noun)   Hair style in which hair is braided in shallow, narrow rows over the entire head.

Corvette (noun)   A type of expensive sports car.

Couch (verb)   To construct and present an argument.

Crack (noun)   A strong form of cocaine.

Cry Over Spilt Milk (verb)   To indulge in useless complaint or regret. Note that there is a departure from standard English spelling in this phrase, which uses the spelling "spilt" instead of "spilled." Either is correct, but "spilt" is seldom used. (Another such variation is the rare "spelt" for usual "spelled.")

D

Deadbeat (noun)   Lazy person who has no ambition, no money, and no prospects.

Deadweight (noun)   Literally, the unrelieved weight of any inert mass (think of carrying a sack of bricks); hence, any oppressive burden.

Decent (adjective)   One of its specialized meanings is "of high quality."

Doodle (noun and verb)   Idle scribbles, usually nonrepresentational and usually made while actively thinking about something else, such as during a phone conversation or sitting in a class.

Drop in the Bucket (noun)   Insignificant quantity compared to the total amount available.

Dyed-in-the-Wool (adjective)   Irretrievably convinced of the value of a particular course of action or of the truth of an opinion. Literally, wool that is dyed after it is shorn from the sheep but before it is spun into thread.

E

'Em (pronoun)   Careless way of pronouncing "them." Written out, it reproduces the sound the speaker is making.

Establishment (noun and adjective)   As a noun, the prevailing theory or practice. As an adjective, something that is used by people whose views prevail over other people's views.

F

Fake (verb)   To fake is to pretend or deceive; to try to make people believe that you know what you're doing or talking about when you don't know or aren't sure.

Fire (verb)   To discharge an employee permanently. It's different from "laying off" an employee, an action taken when a temporary situation makes the employee superfluous but the employer expects to take the employee back when the temporary situation is over.

Fix (verb)   To prepare, as in "fixing a meal." This is only one of the multiplicity of meanings of this verb.

Fleeting (adverb)   This word's usage is elegant and correct, but rare. It means transitory or short-lived.

Flop (noun)   A dismal failure.

Follow Suit (verb)   To do the same thing you see others do. Comes from card games where if a card of a certain suit is played, the other players must play a card of that suit, if they have one.

Follow the Flag (verb)   To be committed to doing business only with firms that produce in your own country or in your "colonies"—that is, territories that belong to your country.

Follow the Leader (noun)   Name of a children's game. Metaphorically, it means to do what others are doing, usually without giving it much thought.

Funky (adjective)   Eccentric in style or manner.

G

G.I. Joe (noun)   A toy in the form of a boy (as "Barbie" is a girl). Original meaning was "government issue"—i.e., an item, such as a uniform, issued by the U.S. government to a member of the U.S. armed forces, and, by extension, the person to whom the item was issued.

GM (noun)   The General Motors automobile company.

Gadget (noun)   Generic term for any small, often novel, mechanical or electronic device or contrivance, usually designed for a specific purpose. For instance, the small wheel with serrated rim and an attached handle used to divide a pizza pie into slices is a gadget.

Gee (expletive)   Emphatic expression signaling surprise or enthusiasm.

Get Across (verb)   To convince.

Get You Down (descriptive phrase)   Make you depressed about something or make you dismiss something altogether. (Do not confuse with "get it down," which means to understand fully.)

Go-Cart (noun)   A small engine-powered vehicle that is used for racing and recreation.

Gold Mine (noun)   Metaphorically, any activity that results in making you a lot of money.

Good Offices (descriptive phrase)   An expression common in 18th-century England, meaning "services."

Got It Made (descriptive phrase)   Succeeded.

Grind (noun)   Slang for necessary intense effort that may be painful but will likely benefit your understanding.

Groucho Marx (proper name)   A famous U.S. comedian (1885–1977).

Gung-ho (adjective)   Full of energy and eager to take action.

Guns and Butter (descriptive phrase)   Metaphor describing the dilemma whether to devote resources to war or to peace.

H

Haggling (noun)   Bargaining, usually in a petty and confrontational manner.

Handy (adjective)   Convenient.

Hard Liquor (noun)   Alcoholic beverages with a high content of pure alcohol. Beer and wine are not "hard liquor" but most other alcoholic drinks are.

Hassle (noun)   Unreasonable obstacle. As a verb, *to hassle* means to place unreasonable obstacles or arguments in the way of someone.

Hawking (adjective)   Selling aggressively and widely.

Hefty (adjective)   Large; substantial.

Hero Sandwich (noun)   A type of very large sandwich.

Highfalutin (adjective)   American slang term, meaning pretentious, self-important, supercilious.

Hog Bellies (noun)   Commercial term for the part of a pig that becomes bacon and pork chops. (Also called *pork bellies*.)

Holds Its Own (descriptive phrase) Refuses to give up, even in the face of adversity or opposition.

Home Free (descriptive phrase) Safe and successful.

Hot Dog (noun) A type of sausage.

Hot Potatoes (noun) Slang term for anything that everyone wants to avoid confronting.

How Come (expression) Why? That is, "How has it come about that . . . ?"

I

"In" (preposition sometimes used as an adjective) Placed within quotation marks to show it is used with a special meaning. Here it is used as an adjective, to indicate: "fashionable or popular, usually just for a short period." Compare, in this glossary, *all the rage*.

Incidentals (noun) Blanket term covering the world of small items a person uses on a daily basis as the need happens to arise—that is, needed per incident occurring. Examples are aspirin, combs, and picture postcards.

Iron Curtain (noun) Imaginary but daunting line between Western Europe and adjacent communist countries. After the political abandonment of Communism in these countries, the Curtain no longer exists.

It'll (contraction) "It will."

J

Jolt (noun) A sudden blow.

Junk Food (noun) Food that tastes good but has little nutritional value and lots of calories. It is sometimes cheap, sometimes expensive, and it's quick and easy to buy and eat.

Just Say No (admonition) Flatly refuse. This phrase became common in the 1970s after Nancy Reagan, the wife of the then-president of the United States, popularized it in a campaign against the use of addictive drugs.

K

Ketchup (noun) Spicy, thick tomato sauce used on, among other foods, hot dogs.

Kick In (verb) To activate; to start or begin. (Can also mean "to contribute to.")

Kickback (noun) A firm's giving part of the price it has received for its product or service back to the firm or individual who authorized the purchase of that product or service. In effect it is a type of bribe or blackmail demanded or expected by a purchaser's agent.

Klutz (noun) Awkward, incompetent person.

Knockoff (noun) A cheap imitation.

L

Laetrile (noun) Substance derived from peach pits, thought by some people to be a cure for cancer.

Late Victorian (adjective or noun) Embodying some concept typical of the late period of Queen Victoria. Also, a person from that period or who acts like someone from that period. (Queen Victoria was queen of England from 1837 to 1901.)

Lay Off (verb) To discharge a worker temporarily.

Levi's (noun) Popular brand of jeans.

Lion's Share (noun) By far the best part of a bargain.

Lobby (verb and noun) To lobby is to attempt by organized effort to influence legislation. As a noun, a lobby is an organized group formed to influence legislation. A lobbyist is a member of a lobby.

Lousy (adjective) Incompetent or distasteful.

M

MBA (noun) An academic degree: master of business administration.

Mazuma (noun) U.S. slang term for money. It was used in the first half of the 20th century but is now rare, to say the least.

Medicaid (proper noun) Health insurance program for low-income people. It is administered jointly by the U.S. government and the individual states.

Medicare (proper noun) U.S. government health insurance program for people who are disabled or age 65 and over. There is no means test.

Messed Up (adjective) Damaged or badly managed.

Mind Your Own Business (admonition) Don't meddle in other people's affairs; don't ask intrusive questions.

Mind Your Ps and Qs (expression) Pay close attention to distinctions. It comes from the similarity of the small printed letters "p" and "q" where the only visual distinction is the location of the downstroke. Also, the letters are right next to each other in our alphabet.

Moot (adjective) Irrelevant because the issue in question has already been decided.

Mousetrap (noun) Producing a better mousetrap is part of the saying "Make a better mousetrap and the world will beat a path to your door." Metaphorically, producing a better mousetrap stands for doing anything better than it has previously been done.

N

NA (abbreviation) "Not available."

NASDAQ (also sometimes spelled "Nasdaq") (noun) Stock market operated by the National Association of Securities Dealers. The "AQ" stands for "Automated Quotations."

NATO (noun) North American Treaty Organization. Western alliance for joint economic and military cooperation. It includes the United States, Canada, and several European nations.

Nature of the Beast (descriptive phrase) Character of whatever you are describing (need not have anything to do with a "beast").

Nirvana (noun) This word is adopted from Buddhism. Its religious meaning is complicated, but it is used colloquially to mean salvation, paradise, harmony, perfection.

No Way (exclamation) Emphatic expression denoting refusal, denial, or extreme disapproval.

Nudge (noun and verb) A little push (noun); to give a little push (verb).

O

Off-the-cuff (adjective)   A quick, unthinking answer for which the speaker has no valid authority (comes from the alleged practice of writing an abbreviated answer on the cuff of your shirt, to be glanced at during an examination).

Oliver Wendell Holmes (proper name)   A justice of the U.S. Supreme Court, famous for his wit, his wisdom, his literary ability, his advocacy of civil rights, and his long life (1841–1935).

On Their Toes (descriptive phrase)   Alert; ready for any eventuality.

P–Q

Park Avenue (noun)   Expensive and fashionable street in New York City.

Pass the Buck (descriptive phrase)   Evade responsibility by forcing someone else to make the relevant decision.

Peanuts (noun)   Slang for a small amount, usually money but sometimes anything with a small value.

Pecking Order   Hierarchy.

Peer Pressure (descriptive phrase)   Push to do what everyone else in your particular group is doing.

Penny-Pincher (noun)   Person who is unusually careful with money, sometimes to the point of being stingy.

Perks (noun)   Short for "perquisites."

Philharmonic (adjective)   A philharmonic orchestra is an orchestra that specializes in classical music. Sometimes used as a noun, as in "I heard the Philharmonic."

Pie (noun)   Metaphor for the total amount of a specific item that exists.

Pop-Tart (noun)   Brand name of a type of junk food. It's a sweet filling enclosed in pastry that you pop into the toaster and when the pastry is hot, it pops out of the toaster.

Populist (noun and adjective)   As a noun, this means a member of a political party that purports to represent the rank and file of the people. As an adjective, it means a political party, a group, or an individual that purports to represent rank and file opinion.

Pound (noun)   Unit of British currency.

Practice Makes Perfect (expression)   The grammar of this phrase is illogical but the meaning is clear.

Premium Tires All Round (descriptive phrase)   Premium tires are tires of superior quality. When all the tires on your vehicle are premium tires, you have them "all round."

Proxy (noun)   A stockholder can give a "proxy" to the firm. It is an authorization that permits the firm's officials to vote for the proposition that the stockholder directs them to vote for. By extension, proxy means a substitute.

Ps and Qs   See under *Mind*.

Pub (noun)   Short for "public house," a commercial establishment where alcoholic drinks are served, usually with refreshments and occasionally with light meals.

R

Raise Your Eyebrows (verb)   To express surprise, usually by a facial expression rather than vocally.

Red Flag (noun)   A red flag warns you to be very alert to a danger or perceived danger. (Ships in port that are loading fuel or ammunition raise a red flag to signal danger.)

Red-Handed (adjective)   Indisputably guilty. Comes from being found at a murder or injury scene with the blood of the victim on one's hands.

Right On! (exclamation)   Expression of vigorous, often revolutionary, approval and encouragement.

Ritzy (adjective)   Very expensive, fashionable, and ostentatious. Comes from the entrepreneur Caesar Ritz, a Swiss developer of expensive hotels, active in the first quarter of the 20th century.

Rule of Thumb (descriptive phrase)   An estimate that is quick and easy to make and is reliable enough for rough calculations. Comes from using the space from the tip of your thumb to the thumb's first joint to represent an inch.

S

Sacred Cow (noun)   An institution or practice that social and/or political forces dictate is absolutely protected from change of any kind.

Saks (proper name)   A mid-size department store that sells expensive, fashionable items. There are very few stores in the Saks chain, and Saks stores are considered exclusive.

Savvy (adjective)   Slang term meaning very knowledgeable. Adaptation of the French verb *savoir*, meaning "to know."

Scab (noun)   Person who takes a job, or continues in a job, even though workers at that firm are on strike.

Scraps (noun)   Little pieces of leftover food. Also little pieces of anything that is left over: for example, steel that is salvaged from a wrecked car.

Sears Catalog (noun)   Sears, Roebuck and Co. is a large chain of stores that sells a wide variety of goods. Before shopping malls, interstate highways, and the Internet, Sears used to have a huge mailing list to which it sent enormous catalogs. A person receiving such a catalog would have information about, and access to, thousands of items, many of which the person might not have known existed before the catalog provided the prospect.

Set Up Shop (verb)   To go into business.

Shivering in Their Sandals (descriptive phrase)   Adaptation of standard English idiom *shivering in their shoes*, which means being afraid.

Shorthand (noun)   Any of several systems of abbreviated writing or writing that substitutes symbols for words and phrases. Shorthand was widely used in business until the introduction of mechanical and electronic devices for transmitting the human voice gradually made shorthand obsolete. Today it means to summarize very briefly or to substitute a short word or phrase for a long description.

Shy Away (verb)   To decisively refrain from something. (Comes from the world of horses, who are said to "shy at" things that startle them.)

Sixpence (noun)   A British coin that is no longer in use. It represented six British pennies and its U.S. equivalent in the 2000s would be about a nickel.

Skin of One's Teeth (descriptive phrase) To succeed by the skin of one's teeth means to just barely succeed. A micro-measure less and one would not have succeeded.

Smoke Screen (noun) Metaphorically, anything used intentionally to hide one's true intentions.

Smoking Gun (noun) This term has come to stand for any indisputable evidence of guilt or misdeeds.

Soft Drink (noun) Nonalcoholic beverage.

Sourpuss (noun) Dour; sulky; humorless. Derives from *sour*, which is self-explanatory, and *puss*, a slang word for "face."

Squash (verb) To crush or ruin.

Steady (noun) A person to whom you are romantically committed and with whom you spend a lot of time, especially in social activities.

Sticky (adjective) Resistant to change, as if glued on.

Strongarm (adjective) Repressive and violent.

Super Bowl (noun) Important football game played annually that attracts million of viewers (most of them see the game on TV).

Sucker (noun) A gullible person.

T

Tables Were Turned (descriptive phrase) The advantage of one side over the other reverses so that now the winner is the loser and the loser is the winner.

Tacky (adjective) In very poor taste.

Take the Heat (verb) To accept all criticism of one's action or inaction, whether or not one is actually the person that should be blamed.

Time-and-a-Half (noun) In labor law, 150 percent of the normal hourly wage.

Tombstone Ad (noun) Newspaper advertisement announcing the completion of a stock or bond offering.

Ton (noun) A ton weighs 2,000 pounds and an English ton (often spelled "tonne") weighs 2,240 pounds. In this book the term is used most frequently to mean simply "a large quantity."

Tough (adjective) Very difficult.

Trendy (adjective) A phenomenon that is slightly ahead of traditional ways and indicates a trend. Something trendy may turn into something traditional, or it may fade away without ever becoming mainstream.

Truck (verb) To exchange one thing for another. This was Adam Smith's definition in 1776 and it is still one of the meanings of the verb.

Turf (noun) Territory, especially the figurative territory of a firm.

Turn of the Century (expression) The few years at the end of an expiring century and the beginning of a new century. For example: 1998–2002.

Turn Up One's Nose (verb) To reject.

Twinkies (noun) Brand name of an inexpensive small cake.

U

Union Jack (noun) Nickname for the British flag.

Up in Arms (adjective) Furious and loudly protesting. Comes from the use of *arms* to stand for *firearms*.

V

Vanity License Plate (descriptive phrase) One-of-a-kind motor vehicle license plate issued to your individual specification. It might have your name, your profession, or any individual set of letters and numbers you choose that will fit on the plate.

W–X

Wadget (noun) Term used by economists to stand for any manufactured good except goods designated as widgets, which see.

Wal-Mart (proper name) A very large store that sells thousands of inexpensive items. There are hundreds of Wal-Marts in the United States and the company is beginning to expand into foreign markets.

Wheaties (proper noun) Name of a brand of dry breakfast cereal.

White knight (noun) A company that comes to the rescue of another company. The term comes from the game of chess—some chess sets have white pieces and black pieces—and from the children's book, *Alice Through the Looking Glass*, where the story is structured as a game of chess and a chess piece, the white knight, tries to rescue Alice.

Whiz (noun) An expert.

Whopper (proper noun) Brand name of a kind of hamburger sold at Burger King restaurants.

Widget (noun) The opposite of a wadget, which see.

Wild About (descriptive phrase) Extremely enthusiastic about undertaking a particular action or admiring a particular object or person.

Wind Up (descriptive phrase) To discover that you have reached a particular conclusion or destination.

With-It (adjective) Current in one's knowledge.

Wodget (noun) A made-up term for a produced good. Variation of *widget*, which see.

Wound Up (past tense of verb *wind up*) To have found oneself in a particular situation after having taken particular actions.

Writing on the Wall (descriptive phrase) To see the writing on the wall is to realize that a situation is inevitably going to end badly. It comes from the Biblical story that Nebuchadnezzar, king of Babylon, saw a fatal prediction written on a wall.

Y–Z

You Bet! (exclamation) Expression meaning "It certainly is!" or "Absolutely!"

Index